The RCP Bible

Reorganized Concise Paraphrased Bible

By: Obadiah Paulus

ISBN: 978-1-953162-23-6

Library of Congress Control Number: 2021912192

Tigard, OR

Copyright 2021 RCP Bible and Obadiah Paulus

All rights reserved

About the cover image:

The image on the cover is a triquetra, a representation of the Trinity.

Dedication:

This paraphrase of the Bible is dedicated to Jesus Christ and his glory. My prayer is that this book helps you in your faith journey to draw closer to God and make his kingdom great. I wrote this under a pseudonym so that it isn't about me. I want to thank my wife, my children, my mother, and all the other people who have helped make this work possible. I could not have done it without you. Until we all see each other together in heaven.

THE FIVE BOOKS OF THE RCP BIBLE

Book One: The First Five — Page 1

The first five books of the Bible set up God's story and covers Creation, the Fall, the Flood, and the story of Israel up to their entry into the Promised Land. It is the beginning of human history and sets up the rest of the Bible. It covers the first five books of the Old Testament: Genesis, Exodus, Leviticus, Numbers, and Deuteronomy.

Book Two: The Promised Land — Page 117

The Promised Land is a paraphrase and reorganization of the historical books of the Old Testament, Joshua through Esther. This harmonizes the material, updates the language, and adds explanatory boxes to make the material more accessible.

Book Three: The Poets and Prophets — Page 269

The Poets and Prophets of the Old Testament are the wisdom literature of the Bible. This book covers the books of Job - Malachi. They shave been reorganized and paraphrased to make them more understandable for the modern reader.

Book Four: The Life of Jesus — Page 485

Jesus of Nazareth is the most influential person in history. His birth divided our calendar, he is the central figure in the best-selling book of all time, and people even use his name as a curse word. This book is the story of his life and ministry. It is a harmonization of the books of Matthew, Mark, Luke, and John, the first four books of the New Testament. This book gives us a very accessible glimpse into his life and purpose for coming to earth.

Book Five: Spread of the Church — Page 641

The Spread of the Church is the rest of the gospel's spread from Jesus' ascension to the book of Revelation. This is the blueprint for our Christian lives and instruction for how we continue to participate in God's plan for the world. This book contains a paraphrase of the book of Acts and the letters to the churches that make up the rest of the New Testament.

parts and the explanations I've included. Not everyone will love what I've done, but my goal has always been to stay as close to orthodoxy as possible. I'm sure that I've made mistakes; I apologize in advance.

I've chosen to publish this book under the pseudonym Obadiah Paulus because I don't want this to be about me. I am nobody special. I am a teacher who lives in Oregon, and I'm putting this out there because it has blessed me, and I'm trusting that God will use it to bless you as well. It's probably not too difficult to figure out who I am, but I ask that you don't. I want this project to be about Jesus and his glory. I pray that you find this book useful in your pursuit of understanding God and Scripture.

courtroom trial. For example, at Jesus' Resurrection, one account says there were two angels, and others say there was one. It is possible to have one angel without mentioning the other, so I wrote that two angels were at the tomb.

I took out the genealogies and descriptions of worship implements that we no longer use. These still are useful for instruction, but they are not as relevant to the modern reader. I also did my best to condense longer narratives to make them easier to digest. For example, I condensed the account of Abraham bargaining over the number of righteous souls in Sodom.

I summarized the Law so that it makes more sense for us. I put events in chronological order and organized some of it thematically. I have also taken out portions that may not be relevant to the modern reader (mainly prophecies that we don't have context for or to nations that no longer exist).

Additionally, I added context within the text to help better explain the events. For example, when the prostitute let down her hair to wash Jesus' feet, this was a sign of intimacy and something women did not do in public. We don't understand this on a surface reading because we are two thousand years removed from these events. This is similar to a modern text describing one roommate leaving a sock on a doorknob to indicate that they have a guest for the evening. Writing that one roommate left a sock on the doorknob communicates far more than just the surface description.

I know that some will look at this book and think that this is an attempt to leave out portions of Scripture that I find inconvenient or unnecessary. That could not be further from the truth. My goal with this project has always been to maintain God's Word but to frame it in such a way that is easier to digest for readers who are thousands of years removed from the original documents.

I fully believe that all Scripture is God-breathed and useful for instruction. I would give my life for its authority and inspiration. I believe that Scripture is how God has revealed himself to humanity and is the sole source of salvation for us all. I affirm all of the historic creeds of the church.

However, not all of the Bible is as useful for us, particularly for those who are new to the Bible or the Christian faith. I believe that this reorganization and paraphrase will make God's truth more accessible for all Christians. My prayer throughout this project is that it brings glory to God and that it doesn't change even an iota of Christian doctrine.

Much as there have been multiple different translations of Scripture to make it easier to understand for a contemporary audience. All I want to do is help people better understand God's message of salvation. I believe this treatment of Scripture succeeds in this aim. The resulting text ends up being less than half the length of the translations we have today.

This book is not for serious bible study. This is a tool to help introduce people to the biblical narrative and aid in our understanding. It is the result of thousands of hours and hundreds of books. I know that I've made decisions about how to word certain

THE WHY AND HOW OF THIS BOOK?

The Bible has been around for nearly 2,000 years, and we have excellent translations that scholars have poured their lives into creating. While we don't have the original manuscripts, we can reconstruct them with astonishing accuracy. We can be highly confident about the Bible we have today.

When I was a young Christian, I would start reading, fly through Genesis, do okay with Exodus, before ultimately losing interest in Leviticus and Numbers. I was frustrated. The problem is that authors wrote the Bible to a specific audience who understood the authors, but we are thousands of years removed from that context. Eventually, I went to a Christian college, grew in my faith, and learned how to read the Scriptures so that I could apply them to my life.

Along the way, I've had the privilege of helping many new believers navigate the text, but it's always like pulling teeth. It's always taken a lot of background work to help them understand. I've also heard many objections to Scripture from critics because of our lack of context for the original texts.

While I was in my twenties, I started working on a harmonization of the Gospels for my personal benefit. I even made hand-bound copies at a local Kinkos that I gave to a few close friends. But then, this project lay dormant for a long time. I pulled it out occasionally but didn't do much with it.

Eventually, I had children of my own, and we faithfully read Bible stories to them. They loved them. But when they became independent readers, they faced some of the same issues I did in my early faith. I thought to myself, "why isn't there an intermediate tool that could help them better understand?" I've utilized The Message in the past. Still, it didn't fully solve the problem of what to do with some of the more obscure passages. I also struggled with some of the paraphrases.

I started making my own paraphrase for myself and my children, and they ate it up. I cleaned up some of the language to make it easier to understand, limiting passive voice and other grammatical issues that come from translation. I had a couple of people encourage me to keep going. In time, I decided to paraphrase the whole Bible with explanatory boxes so that the average person could pick up the text and make sense out of it.

This book is not a translation of the original Greek, Hebrew, and Aramaic, and I do not claim inspiration. I have written this book by paraphrasing English translations (primarily the ESV, NIV, NASB, and NLT) of the original text and expanding when necessary so that the reader can better understand the story.

Wherever there were multiple accounts of an event, I did my best to harmonize them. I looked at the different versions of an event and used logic to determine if they could go together. This is similar to what happens with multiple eyewitness accounts in a

First Five

Reorganized Concise Paraphrased Bible

Book I

By: Obadiah Paulus

INTRODUCTION TO THE FIRST FIVE

This is the first five books of the Bible, the beginning of human history, which is the story of God's glory. While these chapters primarily record human activity, we are not the main characters. Humanity is important, but this book, like the rest of the Bible, is a revelation of God's glory, not our own.

The story starts with God's perfect creation that he gave to humanity as a gift. Everything was as God planned, and nothing bad ever happened. There was no sickness or death, no relational difficulties, no bad weather, no self-esteem issues, nothing that could be considered a failure or deficiency.

But Adam and Eve messed it up with their disobedience, which has eventually led to every bad thing that has ever happened since the Garden. But God graciously did not destroy them in that instant. Instead, he sacrificed some animals so that he could cover their nakedness. He also started his plan to redeem people and bring us into a restored relationship with him.

The first piece of this redemption plan was the ancestors of the faith, Abraham, Isaac, and Jacob. God promised to give them the Promised Land and make their descendants into a great nation who would be a blessing to the entire earth. The story follows their journey into Egypt and captivity and their miraculous deliverance and journey to the Promised Land.

These five books are full of many stories of the fathers of our faith; we need to realize that these are descriptive of what happened and not necessarily prescriptive for what we should do. All the "heroes" of this book are flawed men and women that God chose to use despite their shortcomings. One of the first things that Noah did after the ark landed was to plant a vineyard so he could make wine and get blackout drunk. Abraham and Isaac pimped out their wives for personal gain. Lot slept with his daughters. Jacob was a deceiver and trickster, and his children had all sorts of moral issues. Just because these characters are portrayed with all their warts does not mean that we should imitate all their behaviors, simply that these events happened.

Moses penned this, along with the next four books of the Bible, and although he was not alive for the events of Genesis, God revealed what had happened before his birth. If we accept that God is the author of creation, this type of inspiration by God's hand should not be too difficult to believe. There is a school of thought that rejects Moses as the author of these books, often based on the use of different names for God. However, just because he used different names does not mean that he is not the author of all five books. Other biblical authors in both the Old and New Testament confirm Moses' authorship, and Jesus also attributes the books to Moses.

This book is the beginning of God's story, but it is not exhaustive, nor is it intended to be. The Bible is not a science textbook. However, it is essential to note that no historical or archeological discovery has ever contradicted the information recorded in the Bible. There are many events recorded in this book (as well as other books of the Bible) that we would like to have more information about, but that was not God's purpose for inspiring the Bible. While we may not know precisely who the Nephilim are, where the Garden of Eden was, or how dinosaurs fit into the picture, we can trust that God has given us enough to suit his purposes.

The people in this book gave God many names based on the characteristics and actions that he displayed towards them. I have opted to use either God or the Lord to refer to him to avoid confusion.

MAP OF THE ANCIENT NEAR EAST

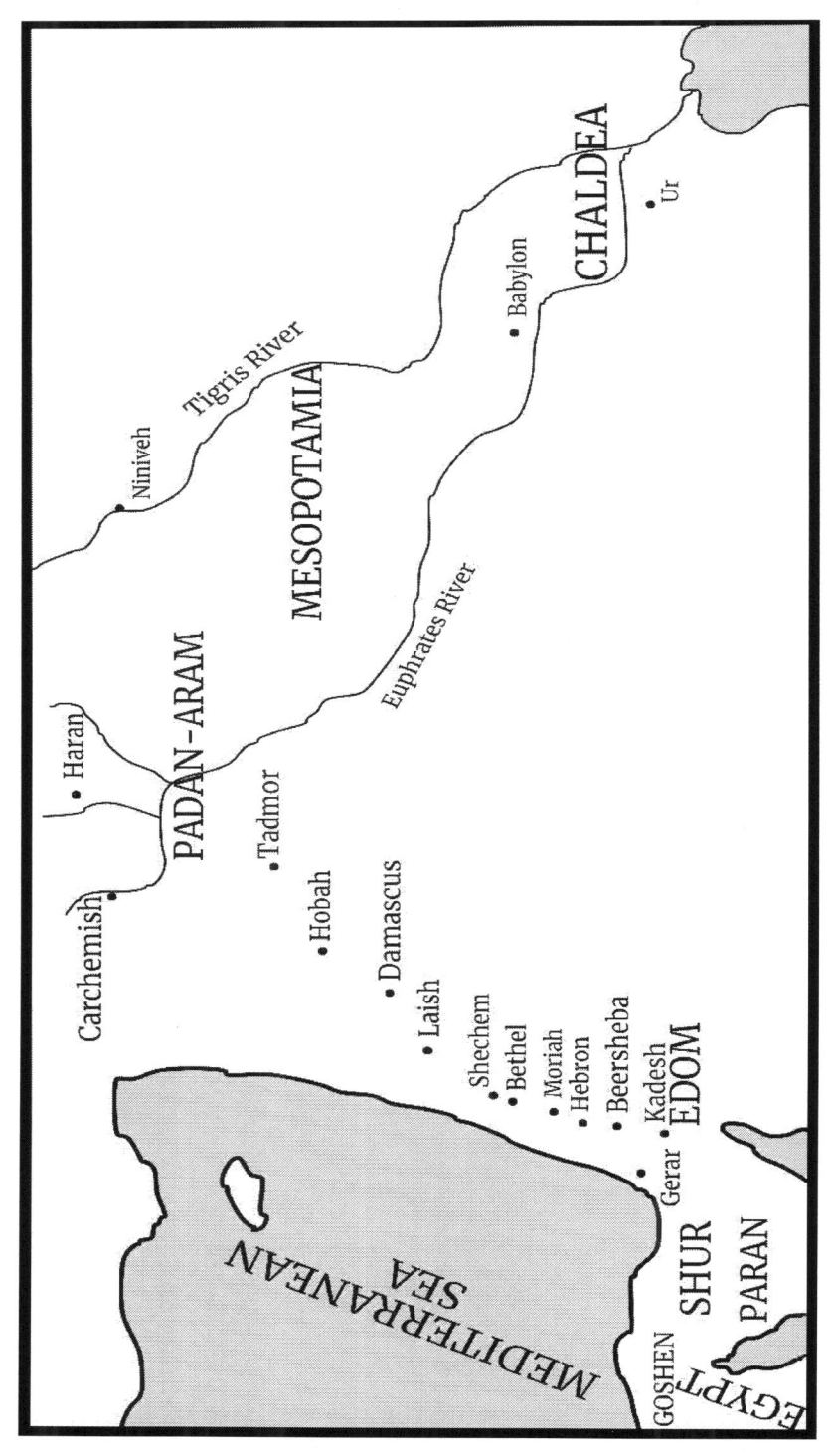

TABLE OF CONTENTS

CHAPTER 1: Creation	1
CHAPTER 2: The Fall	5
CHAPTER 3: Eden to the Flood	7
CHAPTER 4: The Flood	9
CHAPTER 5: End of the Flood	11
CHAPTER 6: Abram	14
CHAPTER 7: God Appears to Abram	17
CHAPTER 8: God Appears to Abram a Second Time	19
CHAPTER 9: Sodom and Gomorrah	22
CHAPTER 10: Isaac's Birth	25
CHAPTER 11: Isaac and Rebekah	28
CHAPTER 12: Jacob and Esau	30
CHAPTER 13: Jacob Steals Esau's Blessing	32
CHAPTER 14: Jacob, Laban, and Jacob's Children	34
CHAPTER 15: Jacob Returns Home	37
CHAPTER 16: Jacob Wrestles an Angel	40
CHAPTER 17: Jacob in the Promised Land	42
CHAPTER 18: Joseph and His Brothers	45
CHAPTER 19: Joseph in Egypt	48
CHAPTER 20: Joseph's Family Comes to Egypt	51
CHAPTER 21: Joseph Reunites with His Family	53
CHAPTER 22: Jacob Goes to Egypt	56
CHAPTER 23: Jacob's Death	58
CHAPTER 24: Moses' Birth	61
CHAPTER 25: God Calls Moses	63
CHAPTER 26: Moses with Pharaoh	66
CHAPTER 27: Plagues One Through Three	68
CHAPTER 28: Plagues Four Through Seven	70
CHAPTER 29: Plagues Eight Through Ten	73
CHAPTER 30: Leaving Egypt	75
CHAPTER 31: Manna from Heaven	78
CHAPTER 32: Water from the Rock and Jethro's Visit	80
CHAPTER 33: Mount Sinai	82
CHAPTER 34: The Golden Calf	85
CHAPTER 35: Second Set of Stone Tablets	87
CHAPTER 36: First Passover in the Wilderness	90
CHAPTER 37: Aaron and Miriam's Jealousy	92
CHAPTER 38: Spying on Canaan	93
CHAPTER 39: Korah's Rebellion	95
CHAPTER 40: Moses' Sin and the Bronze Serpent	97
CHAPTER 41: Balak Summons Balaam	99

CHAPTER 42: Balaam with Balak	101
CHAPTER 43: The Second Census and Fighting the Midianites	103
CHAPTER 44: Reuben and Gad	104
CHAPTER 45: Recounting the Law	105
CHAPTER 46: Moses' Final Benediction	107
CHAPTER 47: The Law	109
CHAPTER 48: Ceremonial Laws	110
CHAPTER 49: Civil and Judicial Laws	113
CHAPTER 50: Moral Laws	115

CHAPTER ONE
CREATION
Genesis 1-2

At the beginning of everything, God created the heavens and the earth out of nothing. Everything was formless and dark; the Holy Spirit hovered over all creation.

Then God said, "Let there be light!" Suddenly, light came into existence. God separated the light from darkness, and he called the light day and the darkness night. There was evening and morning on the first day, and God saw that it was good.

On the second day, God said, "Separate the waters from the space above!" Suddenly, there was a separation between the waters and everything above. God called the expanse above the water the sky. There was evening and morning on the second day, and God saw that it was good.

On the third day, God said, "Let there be land in the midst of all the waters!" Suddenly, land came forth; God called the dry land earth and the waters he called seas. And God saw that it was good. Then God said, "Let there be seed-bearing plants that will each bear fruit according to its kind!" Trees and plants burst forth from the land, each according to its kind. There was evening and morning on the third day, and God saw that it was good.

On the fourth day, God said, "Let there be stars and planets in heaven's expanse to separate the day from the night. These will be a sign for the seasons and to mark the passage of days and years; these will give light in the heavens and earth." God created the sun to rule the day and the moon and stars to rule the night. There was evening and morning on the fourth day, and God saw that it was good.

On the fifth day, God said, "Let there be birds and fish in the sea!" Birds and fish filled the sea, and God blessed them. He said, "Be fruitful and multiply and fill the earth with life!" There was morning and evening on the fifth day, and God saw that it was good.

On the sixth day, God said, "Let the earth be filled with animals and insects!" All the animals and insects came to life and filled the earth. Then God said, "Let us make mankind in our image and let them have authority and rule over all the other animals I have created."

> **Why did God say, "let us make mankind in our image?"**
>
> Some people have problems with the doctrine of the Trinity and argue that a being cannot be three and one simultaneously. Part of the reason we have this problem is that we do not have the words to express God adequately. The Trinity

is one of the great mysteries of the Christian faith and we must remember that God created the universe and our logic. God completely transcends natural laws. Our finite minds cannot grasp what is beyond these laws, and we must recognize that we will never fully comprehend God. Because if we could fully comprehend him, he would cease to be God, or we would become God. Even though it is difficult to understand this concept, the Bible teaches us that God is an undivided being who exists simultaneously as three persons, and all three are fully God.

The word Trinity is not in the Bible, but both the Old and New Testaments imply the doctrine. Some people agree that the Father, Son, and Holy Spirit are equally divine, but they argue that each is a different manifestation of God at different times. However, the use of the plural form and passages like Jesus' baptism show that all three exist simultaneously.

Others agree that the Father, Son, and Holy Spirit are all divine, and all three exist simultaneously, but they argue that God the Father is greater than Jesus, who, in turn, is greater than the Holy Spirit. However, while there may be a subordination of position, there is no subordination of nature. Another way of looking at this is a boss and an employee. The boss may have a greater status than the employee, but the boss is not fundamentally better than the employee. In the same way, God the Father has a superior role to Jesus, but they are equally divine. Each member is fully divine and cannot be subordinate to any being.

Some people have problems with the doctrine of the Trinity and argue that a being cannot be three and one simultaneously. Part of the reason we have this problem is that we do not have the words to express God adequately. Even though it is difficult to understand this concept, the Bible teaches us that God is an undivided being who exists simultaneously as three persons, and all three are fully God.

Before God created humanity, before any plants had grown, a mist rose from the ground to water everything because there was no rain and no one to work the land. God created the first man from the dust of the ground, breathed life into his nostrils, and named him Adam.

God planted a garden that he named Eden and placed the first man, Adam, in that garden. The Lord caused every food-bearing tree to sprout so that Adam would have something to eat. In the middle of that garden, God placed the tree of the knowledge of good and evil that would allow the eater to know the difference between good and evil and the tree of life that would cause the eater to live forever. There was a river that flowed through Eden that split into four rivers (the Pishon, the Gihon, the Tigris, and the Euphrates).

Then God said, "Behold, I have given you every plant yielding seed on the earth, and every tree with seed in its fruit; you will have them for food. I have given every green plant for food to every beast of the earth, bird of the heavens, and everything that creeps on the earth, everything that lives." It was so. Then God saw everything that he made, and it was perfect. There was evening and morning on the sixth day.

God put Adam in the garden and commanded him to work the land and take care of his Creation. God said to Adam, "You can eat from any tree in the garden except for the tree of the knowledge of good and evil because if you eat from it, you will die."

God created every animal, and they all came before Adam so that he could name them. As God watched Adam, he observed, "It is not good for man to be alone; he needs a helper to manage creation. None of these animals are suitable; I will create a helper fit for him."

So, God caused Adam to fall into a deep sleep, took a rib from his side, and closed it up with flesh. From this rib, God formed a woman and brought her to Adam. She was not from his head to rule over him, and not from his foot, to be under him; she was from his side, to be a partner in their work.

When Adam saw her, he sang, "This is bone of my bone and flesh of my flesh; she is a woman, for she was taken from my side." Adam named his wife Eve, for she was the mother of all people. Therefore, a man will leave his parents and become one with his wife. Adam and Eve were both naked, and they were not ashamed.

This is how God created all the heavens and the earth; they were perfect, without flaw or defect. On the seventh day, God rested from all the work that he had done. God blessed the seventh day and made it holy because he rested from all his work in creation.

> **What about dinosaurs?**
>
> While the Bible doesn't mention them by name, there are references and descriptions of huge beasts in the wisdom and poetry literature that do not fit any animal we know. Some of these descriptions are similar to the fossils that we have found of what we now call dinosaurs. Again, the Bible is not an exhaustive science or history book. Dinosaurs existed, became extinct but were not named in Scripture.

So, God created man in his image from the dust of the ground and breathed life into his nostrils; he created both male and female. God blessed them and said, "Be fruitful and multiply, fill the earth and subdue it. Rule over the fish of the sea, the birds of the heavens, and every living thing that moves on the earth."

> **How old is the earth? What about evolution?**
>
> The short answer is, we don't know. If we add up the number of years recorded in the Bible, the earth is less than 10,000 years old. However, there are parts of Scripture where scholars are aware of gaps in the genealogies. The Bible is not a scientific textbook and never intended to establish the age of the earth or an exhaustive record. The Bible tells us the story of God's glory and how we fit into that narrative.
>
> The current popular theory is that species evolved from one to another through various mechanisms and survival of the fittest. We must be careful to avoid

chronological snobbery, where we think that we have all the information available. If we look at the history of science, scientists have discarded many ideas they once believed true. Examples of these include the earth or sun being the center of the universe, alchemy, medieval medicine, atoms being the smallest building block of the universe, the inferiority of the different races, etc.

There is ample evidence of species adapting to their environment and making changes over time. But we have never observed one species changing into another. Furthermore, if evolution is true, it would be the only scientific principle to go against entropy (everything breaks down over time). The theory of evolution is undergirded by the belief that God does not exist and there must be an explanatory principle for the complexity of life we see on earth. If we accept God's existence, we do not need evolution.

This is not to discredit science, but we must approach it with an open mind. Science has done many things to help us better understand the world, God, and the universe around us. We should continue to learn and investigate the world around us because we still have much to learn. Carbon dating is based on what we have observed about our current world, but the variable involved may have changed over time.

If it turns out that evolution is correct and the universe is billions of years old, this doesn't mean that the Bible is flawed or outdated. If these views of science are true, then God is still the author of these processes and the one who is ultimately in control of the universe. This book does not intend to discuss this issue thoroughly, and I recommend further study.

CHAPTER TWO
THE FALL
Genesis 3

Satan had been the most beautiful of angels, but he became proud and wanted to take God's place. God could not tolerate such rebellion and cast him and his followers out of heaven as a punishment. Now, Satan's mission is to deceive people and lead them away from the Lord.

One day, after God had finished creation, Satan took the form of a serpent, the craftiest animal God had made. He came to Adam and Eve and twisted God's words, saying, "Did God really say not to eat the fruit from any of the trees in the garden?"

Eve replied with a slightly twisted version of God's command, "We can eat from any of the trees in the garden, but we cannot eat from the tree in the middle of the garden. We will die if we even touch it."

Satan lied, "You won't die! God knows that eating the fruit will open your eyes, and then you will be just like God, knowing good from evil."

Eve took a second look at the tree, saw how good the fruit looked, and wanted to be like the Creator; so, she took a piece and ate it. Then she handed some to her husband, and he ate it too. In that instant, they became aware and ashamed of their nakedness, so they sewed fig leaves into clothing to cover themselves.

GOD CONFRONTS ADAM AND EVE

A little while later, Adam and Eve heard God walking in the garden during the cool of the afternoon, and they hid from him. But God called to them and said, "Where are you?"

Adam replied, "I heard you walking through the garden, and I hid because I was naked and afraid."

Even though God knew what had happened, he asked, "Who told you that you were naked? Did you eat from the tree I commanded you not to?"

Adam answered, "It's not my fault, the woman you made to be with me gave me the fruit from the tree, and I ate it."

God turned to Eve and said, "What have you done?"

Eve replied, "It's not my fault, the serpent deceived me, and I ate it."

Then God turned to the serpent and said, "You are more accursed than any other animal on earth; you will crawl on your belly and eat the dust of the ground all the days of your life. There will be hostility between you and her offspring, and one day you will bite his heel, but he will crush your head."

God was gracious to Adam and Eve, and he did not destroy them immediately. He turned to the woman and said, "Because you ate the fruit, pregnancy and childbirth will be extremely painful. You will desire your husband's position and authority, but he will rule over you."

> **Eve's curse**
>
> Some look at God's curse for Eve and think that God created a hierarchy between men and women, but this is a result of sin, not God's intention. He made Eve from Adam's rib so that she would be alongside him and rule creation as a partner, not a subservient. In the New Testament, God commands the people to be mutually submissive to each other. Neither men nor women are greater than the other; sexism is a result of the Fall.

To the man, God said, "Because you listened to your wife and ate the forbidden fruit, I am cursing the ground. You will eat the plants of the field, but it will be hard work, and thorns and thistles will make it more difficult. You will labor all the days of your life until you return to the dust of the earth. I made you from dust, and to dust, you will return."

Then God said, "They have become like one of us, knowing good from evil; we cannot let them also eat from the tree of life and live forever." So, he sent them out from Eden to work the ground he used to create them. He made them clothes from animal skins and sent them to the east. Then he placed an angel with a flaming sword that turned every direction to guard the tree of life.

> **Why did God create Satan?**
>
> It seems like life would be much easier if Satan never existed; we trust that God had a reason for Satan's existence. Since God is the greatest possible being, he created the universe to result in the most glory for him. While we may not understand how that works with Satan's existence, we must trust that he has a greater perspective than we do.
>
> One idea for why God would allow Satan's existence is that God wants our love. Love is impossible without choice, so God needed to enable people to choose either him or against him.

CHAPTER THREE

EDEN TO THE FLOOD

Genesis 4-5

After leaving the garden, Adam and Eve had sex, and she became pregnant with her first son, Cain, saying, "God has helped me bear a son." A short while later, she had another son named Abel. Cain grew up to be a farmer, while Abel grew up to be a shepherd.

One day, Cain brought some of his fruits and vegetables as an offering to the Lord, while Abel brought the best of his flock. God accepted Abel's offering, but he disregarded Cain's. This made Cain very angry and he walked around sulking. God came to Cain and asked, "Why are you angry and scowling? If you give from your best with a pure heart, won't you have joy and happiness? But if your heart is not pure, sin is crouching at your door, and it desires to rule over you and become your master. Instead, you must rule over it."

In his anger, Cain went out to the field to speak with his brother, and while he was there, he became so mad that he killed Abel. Later, God came to Cain, and although the Lord already knew, he asked, "Where is your brother?"

Cain scoffed, "How should I know? am I my brother's keeper?"

God replied, "What have you done? Your brother's blood cries out to me. Now, for you, I will curse the same ground you soaked with your brother's blood. When you work the land, it will no longer produce for you. Instead, you will be a fugitive and a wanderer on the earth."

Cain wailed, "My punishment is more than I can bear! You have driven me from the land and will hide from me. I will be a fugitive and a wanderer on the earth, and whoever finds me will kill me!"

God said, "Not so! I will put a mark upon you to protect you, and if anyone kills you, he will receive seven times the punishment!" Cain went further east from Eden to the land of Nod. While he was there, he had his first son, Enoch, and he built a city that he named after his son. Cain's descendants began to form civilization, raised flocks, made bronze and iron tools, and developed musical instruments.

Meanwhile, Adam and Eve had another child she named Seth, saying, "God gave me another son because Cain killed Abel." Seth also had a son, whom he named Enosh. At that time, people began to pray and seek the Lord.

Name	Name Meaning	Year of birth	Age at death	Year of death	Interesting Information
Adam	Man	0	930	930	Saw seven generations after himself
Seth	Appointed	130	912	1042	
Enosh	Mortal	235	905	1140	
Kenan	Sorrow	325	910	1235	
Mahalel	Blessed God	395	895	1290	
Jared	Descending	460	962	1322	
Enoch	Teaching	622	365	987	Righteous man God took to heaven at 365
Methuselah	His death shall bring	687	969	1651	Oldest age recorded in history
Lamech	Despairing	874	777	1651	
Noah	Rest	1056			Flood occurred at 1651

*Note: Year of death is based off time from Creation.

It is interesting to read the names of Adam's descendants in order because we can translate the meanings of the Hebrew names into a gospel message. Man - Appointed - Mortal - Sorrow - Blessed God - Descending - Teaching - His Death Shall Bring - Despairing - Rest. There are debates over the Hebrew names' exact meanings, but this is an interesting interpretation of the genealogy. Also, it appears that both Methuselah and Lamech were alive at the time of the Flood.

Did people really live that long?

The oldest people in the modern world only make it a few decades past 100, yet the Bible says the earliest people lived well past this age, some close to 1,000. There are theories that the atmosphere, the earth, and the human body have changed dramatically after the Flood. All these changes have resulted in a very different world than the one that God created. It is possible that God's original creation was conducive to living longer and growing at a slower rate than we currently do. A slower growth rate and longer life span could also explain how dinosaurs could grow so large.

CHAPTER FOUR

THE FLOOD
Genesis 6-7

As the earth's population grew, the sons of God saw that the women were beautiful and married some of them. Among these sons of God were the Nephilim, and their children were the mighty men of old, the men of legends.

> **Who were the Nephilim?**
>
> The short answer is that we don't know. Some have hypothesized that they were angels. Unfortunately, the Bible is not a complete historical record. While we might want that information, God did not deem it necessary in his story.

Over time, God saw how great humanity's wickedness was and that their thoughts and intentions were always evil. He regretted that he had created them and said, "My Spirit will not stay with them forever because they are just flesh. In 120 years, I will destroy all the people and animals that I have created because I am sorry that I made them."

Despite his sin, Noah found favor in the Lord's eyes.

Noah was a righteous man who was blameless when compared with his generation and he walked with God. As God looked at the earth, he saw that it was corrupt, filled with violence and that everyone had become depraved. Then God said to Noah, "I have decided to put an end to all living things because they have become violent and I am going to destroy the earth in a great flood. But I am going to save humanity through you and your family. Everything else on the planet will die.

"Build an ark out of gopher wood and cover it with pitch so that it will float. Make it 450 feet long, 75 feet wide, and 45 feet tall. Build three separate levels and fill them with different rooms. When you have finished, bring pairs of every living creature onto the ark, a male and a female, to preserve the species. Bring one pair of the unclean animals and seven pairs of the clean. Also, bring all kinds of food to store on the ark for you, your family, and all the animals."

Noah was 500 years old when he began working on the ark, and he faithfully built it over the next century. Noah's friends and neighbors made fun of him because they lived in a desert, and it had never rained before (a mist would rise from the ground to water the whole land). But for an entire century, Noah put up with their mocking because he believed God would fulfill his promise.

When Noah finished the ark, God said to him, "Take your family and all the animals that I have commanded you to gather onto the ark because in seven days I am going to bring rain upon the land for the next 40 days and nights to kill every living thing on the earth."

> **How did Noah get all those animals and food for them on the ark?**
>
> There are several points we must consider when answering this question. First, the dimensions of the ark are like that of a modern ocean liner and would be capable of housing a tremendous number of animals. Second, Noah likely brought on young animals onto the ark, and these would have taken up much less room than full-grown adults. Third, God could have put many, if not most, of these animals into a state of hibernation on the ark. If God can cause a worldwide flood and help Abraham gather all the animals on the ark, he certainly would have the power to keep these animals sedated during their year on the ark. Fourth, it is also likely that Scripture did not use species the same way we use it today. For example, we currently recognize three different elephant species, but there may have only been one on the ark. Therefore, Noah would not need as many types of animals on the ark to preserve life.

Noah took his wife, sons (Ham, Shem, and Japheth), their wives, and all the animals into the ark, and God shut the door behind them. Then they waited for seven days for the rains to come. During this time, Noah was the laughingstock of everyone as he, his family, and countless animals sat in a boat in the middle of the desert, claiming there would be a flood.

But after a week, the flood came. Rain poured from above, and the fountains of water beneath the ground burst forth, and it did not stop for 40 days and nights. The water on the earth rose until even the tallest mountains were more than 40 feet below the water. Every living creature on land drowned except for the animals on the ark. God killed all of them for their exceeding wickedness, leaving only Noah and his family.

CHAPTER FIVE

END OF THE FLOOD
Genesis 8-11

God was watching over Noah, and after 150 days, he sent a strong wind that began to dry up the waters. God stopped the rain and restrained the waters from both above and below. Over the next 150 days, the water receded, and the ark came to rest on Mount Ararat. After another few months, all the tops of the mountains were visible.

One day, Noah sent out a raven and a dove to see if the land had dried up. But they found nowhere to land and they returned to the ark.

He waited another week and sent the dove out again. Later that evening, the dove returned with a freshly plucked olive leaf signaling that the flood was over. After another week, Noah sent the dove out again, and it did not return.

After a year on the ark, Noah opened the door and saw that the ground was dry. God said, "Leave the ark with your family and all the animals that you rescued so that they may be fruitful and repopulate the earth." Noah obeyed and all the animals left the ark.

Noah built an altar and sacrificed some of every clean animal to thank God for saving him and his family. When God saw the sacrifice, he promised Noah and his family, "I will never curse the ground again on account of people because their hearts are evil from birth. I will never kill every animal again, as I did with this flood. While the earth remains, the cycle of the seasons, planting and harvest, day and night will continue."

God blessed Noah and his family, saying, "Be fruitful, and multiply, fill the earth and subdue it. You will rule over every living thing, they will fear you, and you can eat them as food just as I have given you all the plants of the field. But you shall not eat the flesh with the blood, for that is its life. I will require reckoning from anyone who sheds a person's blood.

"Anyone who sheds man's blood will have his blood shed by man because God created mankind in his image."

God continued speaking to Noah and his family, "I am making a covenant with you, your descendants, and every living creature that came out of the ark. I will never again destroy the world with a flood and never again kill all life with a flood. As a reminder of this promise, I will put a rainbow in the sky. Whenever you see a rainbow, know that I remember this promise."

How could there be enough water to flood the entire earth? If there was a worldwide flood, how did people and animals get to the other continents?

A cataclysmic, worldwide flood would cause massive upheaval in the existing geography. The mountains were likely much shorter than they are today. With this in mind, and water bursting forth from the deep, it is imaginable for there to be enough water to cover the face of the earth.

After the floodwaters receded, they likely became groundwater. There was probably a settling period of the tectonic plates moving apart much faster than currently. There is a theory that all the continents used to be one mass of land called Pangea (when we look at a map, we can put the continents together like a puzzle). As the continents moved, people traveled and likely made it to the western world across a land bridge connecting modern Russia with Alaska. They probably made it to islands by sea.

https://commons.wikimedia.org/wiki/Pangea#/media/File:Pangaea_continents.png

AFTER THE FLOOD

After leaving the ark, Noah planted a vineyard and waited for the grapes to grow. As soon they were ready for harvest, he made wine, got drunk, and passed out in his tent naked. One of his sons, Ham, saw that he was naked and did something horrible and then told his brothers about it so they might humiliate their father. Shem and Japheth took a blanket and covered their father's nakedness while averting their eyes to not bring further humiliation.

When Noah woke up, he knew what Ham had done and was furious. He cursed his son, saying, "Cursed is Ham and all his descendants! May God bless Shem, and may Japheth dwell in Shem's tents while Ham's offspring serve them both!" Noah lived another 350 years after the flood.

***

Over time, Noah's sons began to have children of their own; they gradually repopulated the earth and established cities and nations. At this time, everyone spoke the same language, and eventually, they migrated west to the plain of Shinar. Once there, they decided to build a great city with a tower reaching to the heavens so that future generations would remember them and that all people would know of their greatness.

God saw their plans and said, "They are all one people with one language and this is just the beginning of what they will do. If I allow this to continue, then nothing will be impossible for them. I will go down and confuse their language so that they do not understand each other." This was the creation of the world's languages; the inability to communicate made the people disperse and settle in different areas. People called the city Babel because God had confused their language.

CHAPTER SIX

ABRAM

Genesis 12-14

GOD CALLS ABRAM

As the people dispersed, one of Shem's descendants, Terah, had a son named Abram, who took a wife named Sarai. Terah took his family along with Abram and his grandson Lot from their homeland of Ur and traveled along the Euphrates River to the land of Haran (about 600 miles NW of their starting point).

One day, God came to Abram and said, "Leave your home and your family and go to the land that I will show you. I will make you into a great nation, bless you, and make your name great so that you will be a blessing to all the earth's people. I will bless whoever blesses you and curse whoever curses you, and you will be a blessing to all people of the earth."

Even though he was already 75, Abram obeyed God and left Haran. He took his wife, Sarai, his nephew Lot, and all the possessions he had gained and moved 400 miles south to the land of Canaan. When they arrived in Canaan, Abram continued to Shechem, to the great oak of Moreh, a gigantic tree near Mamre. God appeared to Abram and said, "I will give this land to your descendants."

So, Abram built an altar to God since he had appeared there. He continued his journey another 20 miles, made a second altar between Ai and Bethel, and worshiped God again.

At that time, there was a severe famine in the land, and Abram went to stay in Egypt because he heard there was food there. As he and Sarai approached Egypt, he said to her, "You are a beautiful woman, and if the Egyptians think you are my wife, they will kill me so that they can get to you. Please say that you are my sister so that they will treat me well because of your beauty. Then, you will also not have to live without me."

When they entered Egypt, Sarai said she was Abram's sister, and the Egyptians thought she was gorgeous. Word made it to Pharaoh about the new girl in town, and he brought her into his palace, intending to sleep with her. The Egyptians were pleased with this development and they gave Abram lots of livestock and servants as a thank you for bringing his "sister" to them.

Meanwhile, God afflicted Pharaoh and his household with plagues because of Sarai. Pharaoh became suspicious and figured out that she was Abram's wife. He brought Abram in and said, "How dare you do this to me? Why didn't you tell me she was your wife instead of lying to me and calling her your sister so that I would marry her? Take her and all your possessions and get out of Egypt!"

So, Abram left Egypt with Sarai, Lot, and all the wealth he obtained because of his wife and headed back to Bethel, where he had first built an altar, and he called upon the Lord.

ABRAM AND LOT SEPARATE

Abram's nephew, Lot, had also become wealthy, and it became clear that the land could not support both their flocks, herds, and tents. As both of their wealth grew, their servants began to get into fights over the available resources. Abram said to Lot, "We are family and we shouldn't be fighting over such petty matters. The whole land is before you; pick where you want to settle, and I will take the land you don't choose. If you go to the left, I will go to the right; if you go to the right, I will go to the left."

Lot looked at the available land and saw how lush the Jordan Valley was, and it reminded him of the well-watered fields they had seen in Egypt. He chose the land to the east of where they stood. He settled in the Jordan Valley as far as the cities of Sodom and Gomorrah, while Abram went to the west and settled in Canaan. The men of Sodom were evil, much as people had been before God destroyed the world with a flood.

After Lot departed, God came to Abram and said, "Look up from where you are standing in every direction. I will give you all this land to your offspring forever. Even though you don't have any children now, I will make your offspring as numerous as the sands of the sea. Just as there are countless grains of sand, you will have countless descendants. Now, walk throughout all of this land because I promise to give it to you." So, Abram moved his tents to the oaks of Mamre, in Hebron, and he built an altar to the Lord.

ABRAM RESCUES LOT

In those days, there was unrest, and some of the local leaders rebelled against the rulers of their lands. Among these were the leaders of Sodom and Gomorrah, but their rebellion failed. As their army fled, many soldiers fell into tar pits and died while others scattered into the nearby hills. This left Sodom and Gomorrah unprotected; the rulers came and ransacked the cities and took Lot and all his possessions into captivity.

One of Lot's men escaped and he ran to tell Abram that Lot was a prisoner. When Abram heard the news, he gathered all his servants and men from the nearby villages, 318 in total, and pursued Lot's captors 160 miles until he caught up with them. Once he found them, he divided his forces, defeated their enemies, and brought back Lot, his household, and all his possessions.

After they returned home, the leader of Sodom came out to meet Abram to thank him for delivering them. Another local leader, Melchizedek, who was also a priest of God, came out to meet them. He brought bread and wine and then blessed Abram, "May God, the possessor of heaven and earth, bless you! We thank God and praise him for delivering your enemies into your hands!" In response, Abram gave a tenth of everything he had as an offering of praise and worship.

> **Who is Melchizedek?**
>
> We don't know much about his identity, but he is a historical person who worshiped the true God. He arrived to bless Abram and the Book of Hebrews describes him as a "picture of Christ." Abram gave him a gift as an act of worship to the Lord.

Abram could have kept all the plunder and the people he had rescued as servants in this situation. Sodom's leader tried to negotiate with Abram and said, "You can take all the plunder; just let my people go."

Abram replied, "I made a promise to God, the possessor of heaven and earth, that I would not take anything from you, not even a thread of clothing, so that you can't say that you made me rich. I will only take the food that my men have eaten and the share of the profits for the men who went with me; they deserve a reward for the risks they took."

CHAPTER SEVEN

GOD APPEARS TO ABRAM

Genesis 15-16

After Lot's rescue, God came to Abram in a vision, "Abram, don't be afraid, for I am your shield; your reward will be very great."

Abram replied, "What can you give me since I don't have any children, and Eliezer of Damascus is my heir? I am childless."

God answered, "Eliezer will not be your heir; you will have a son of your own." Then God brought him outside and said, "Look up at the stars in the heavens and count them if you can; that's how many offspring you will have."

Abram believed God's promise, and God counted that as righteousness. Then God said, "I am the Lord, your God, who brought you out of Ur of the Chaldeans to possess this land."

Abram replied, "But how do I know I will possess it?"

God replied, "Bring me a three-year-old heifer, a three-year-old female goat, a three-year-old ram, a pigeon, and a turtle dove. Cut the animals in half and put each half on opposite sides of a path, but leave the birds whole."

Abram obeyed, and when birds of prey came to eat the carcasses, he drove them away for the rest of the afternoon. As the sun went down, Abram fell into a deep sleep, and dreadful darkness descended upon him. Then God spoke, "Your descendants will be visitors living in a strange land that is not their home, and they will live for 400 years as servants who are afflicted by their masters. But I will judge their masters and they will come out of that land with great wealth. You will die in peace, and eventually, your offspring will return to this land."

When the sun had finally gone down, a smoking pot and a flaming torch passed between the animals. This was God's way of saying that if he did not follow through, that this is what should happen to him. Thus, God made a covenant with Abram and said, "I give to you and your offspring the land between the Nile and the Euphrates."

What is a covenant?

A covenant is a binding promise where two parties come together to make an agreement. Covenants are like a treaty or contract. These agreements contain promises for what will occur if those involved follow through and what will happen if they do not. In the biblical covenants, God was always the initiator, and he instituted it for the benefit of the person or people involved.

Despite God's promise, Abram's wife had no children. So, she took her servant Hagar, whom she obtained in Egypt, and said to Abram, "Since God has not given me a child, have a baby with Hagar so that I may have children through her." This was a custom at the time that allowed barren women to have children on their behalf but was not God's plan.

Abram was now 85 years old and worried about his ability to father children, so he listened to his wife and took Hagar as a concubine. It did not take long for her to get pregnant, and as soon as she was, Hagar looked at Sarai with great contempt. Sarai was furious and yelled at Abram, "May God judge between us! I gave you my servant, and as soon as she became pregnant, she started looking down on me because I can't have children. I hope God brings this evil back upon you!"

Abram replied, "She's your servant; do whatever you want with her."

Sarai took pleasure in mistreating Hagar, and eventually, Hagar ran away. While she was fleeing, the angel of the Lord found her by a spring of water in the wilderness and asked, "Hagar, where are you going?"

Hagar replied, "I am running away from Sarai. She treats me terribly!"

The angel told her, "Return to Sarai and submit to her. The Lord will also multiply your offspring so that they are a countless multitude. You will have a son; name him Ishmael because God has listened to your affliction. He will be a wild donkey of a man who will have conflict with his relatives and everyone around him."

Therefore, Hagar called the Lord the God who Sees because he had looked after her when she had run away. She returned home to Sarai and submitted herself to her. When Abram was 86, she gave birth to her son, whom they named Ishmael, just as the angel of the Lord had told them.

CHAPTER EIGHT

GOD APPEARS TO ABRAM A SECOND TIME
Genesis 17-18

Thirteen years later, when Abram was 99 years old, God appeared to him and said, "I am the Almighty God, walk before me and be blameless. I will make my covenant with you and give you countless descendants." Abram fell on his face in worship, and God continued, "I have made my covenant with you and you shall be the father of a multitude of nations. Your name is no longer Abram (exalted father); I am changing it to Abraham (father of a multitude). I will make you fruitful; nations and kings will come from you. I will keep my covenant with you and your descendants after you, and it will be an everlasting promise. I will give you and your offspring all the land that I had promised you as an everlasting possession, and I will be their God.

"As for you and your descendants, you will show the sign of this covenant by circumcising the foreskin of every male in your household. When sons are born, you will circumcise them eight days after their birth. You will circumcise every male in your house, whether born there or purchased with money. Circumcision is the sign of our covenant, and I will cut off any male you don't circumcise from his people because he has broken the covenant.

"I am also changing your wife's name from Sarai (contentious) to Sarah (princess). I will bless her, she will have a son, and she will become the mother of nations and kings."

From the ground, Abraham said, "May Ishmael live forever!"

God said, "No. Your wife, Sarah, will have a son, and you will name him Isaac. I will establish my everlasting covenant with him and his offspring after him. As for Ishmael, I have heard your request, and I will bless him and multiply his offspring as well. He will be the father of twelve princes and I will make him into a great nation. But Isaac will be the child of my promise to you, and Sarah will give birth to him one year from now."

God left after he finished speaking to Abraham. Then Abraham stood up and circumcised Ishmael, at the age of 13, along with all the men of his household. He even circumcised himself at the age of 99, despite the pain because he believed God's promise.

***

Not long after this, three men appeared to him as he sat by the door of his tent near the oaks of Mamre (one of them was likely the first appearance of Jesus and the other two were angels who appeared as men). When Abraham saw the men, he ran to them and bowed his face to the ground and said, "Oh, Lord, if I have found favor in your sight, please do not pass by, but rest here. I am your servant; let me wash your feet and feed you so that I can refresh you before you continue."

The three men said, "Do as you said."

Abraham went into his tent and told Sarah to make some bread, and he brought out some milk and cheese from a calf he was preparing and set it before them. Abraham stood by as they ate, and they asked, "Where is Sarah?"

Abraham replied, "She is in the tent, making bread."

The Lord replied, "I will come back a year from now and Sarah will have a son."

Sarah was listening in the tent and she laughed, "I am past menopause and Abraham is old. Will I really have the joy of a son?"

The Lord replied, "Why did Sarah laugh? Is anything too hard for God? A year from now, Sarah WILL have a son!"

Sarah, heard these words, was afraid, and defended herself, "I didn't laugh."

The Lord said, "I heard you laughing."

After they had finished eating, the men turned toward Sodom to leave, and Abraham walked with them. The Lord said, "I have chosen you to be a mighty nation and to bless all people through your descendants. I have chosen you to have offspring so that your children should be righteous and keep my commandments; I will keep my promise to you. Therefore, you should know that I am going down to Sodom and Gomorrah to see if their sin is as great as I have seen."

Abraham knew how wicked Sodom and Gomorrah had become and that God would destroy them. He interceded on behalf of his nephew Lot, who was living there, "Will you kill the righteous with the wicked? What if there are 50 righteous people there? Please spare the city on behalf of the 50 righteous so that they won't die because the rest are evil. Please do justice for the righteous."

The Lord, knowing the hearts of Sodom and Gomorrah, said, "If I find 50 righteous people, I will not destroy the city."

Abraham continued, "I know I'm out of place to speak to the Lord, but what if there are five fewer righteous people? Will you still destroy them if you only find 45?"

The Lord replied, "I won't destroy the city if I only find 45."

Abraham continued, "What if there are only 40 righteous?"

The Lord said, "I will not destroy the city if I only find 40."

Abraham continued his negotiations with requests to spare the city for only 30 and then for 20 until he finally asked, "Lord, please don't be angry with me, but what if you only find ten? Will you still destroy the city if there are even ten righteous people?"

The Lord had agreed to each of Abraham's requests. Knowing their hearts, he said, "Even if there are only ten righteous people in the entire city, I will not destroy it on behalf of those ten." Then the men went their way, and Abraham returned to his tent, terrified that God would not find ten righteous people in all of Sodom and Gomorrah.

> **Does God change his mind?**
>
> Some have used this example that some use to argue that God changes his mind. However, in other places, Scripture is clear that God does not change. This includes changing his mind. While he acquiesced to Abraham's request, he did not change his intent. Even though he lowered the number of righteous people that would spare Sodom and Gomorrah, he did not find enough and destroyed the wicked cities.

CHAPTER NINE

SODOM AND GOMORRAH
Genesis 19-20

The two angels arrived in Sodom, and Abraham's nephew, Lot, greeted them at the city gate, a place of authority. Lot saw them coming and bowed before them and said, "My lords, please come to my house, allow me to wash your feet, and give you a place to sleep before you continue on your journey."

The two angels rejected his initial offer, claiming that they would spend the night in the square. But Lot was persistent, and he convinced the two to stay with him and his family and eat some unleavened bread. Before they went to bed, all the men of Sodom surrounded the house and demanded, "Bring out the men who are staying with you so that we may sleep with them!"

Lot went to the Sodomites and said, "My brothers, I beg you not to act so wickedly. I have two virgin daughters, let me bring them out to you, and you can do whatever you want to them. But please don't do anything to these two men because I have invited them in and am responsible for their safety."

The men of Sodom replied in anger, "Get out of our way! Who do you think you are?! You are a newcomer here and now you want to judge us?! Now we will treat you even worse than we treat them!"

The men pressed forward towards Lot, intending to grab him and break down his front door. The two angels disguised as men reached out from inside, grabbed Lot, pulled him inside, and slammed the door shut. Then the Sodomites were struck with blindness and confusion so that they could not find the front door no matter how hard they tried.

Lot's visitors said to Lot, "Do you have any other family here? Take your sons, daughters, and their fiancés and get out of the city because we are about to destroy it."

Lot was dubious and hesitant to leave his home, so he lingered. But God was merciful, so the two visitors grabbed Lot, his wife, and two daughters by the arms and dragged them out of the city. As they reached the city limits, one said, "Run for your lives! Don't look back and don't stop anywhere until you get out of the valley. Escape to the hills or you might be swept away."

Lot objected, "You have shown me great favor by saving my life, but I don't think I can make it to the hills. There is a small city that is not as far away and I know we can make it there. Let us flee there so that our lives may be spared!"

The man said, "Okay, I will grant your request, and we will not destroy that city. But hurry, we cannot do anything until you get there."

As the sun began to rise, Lot and his family arrived in Zoar, and God rained fire and sulfur down on Sodom and Gomorrah, destroying all the inhabitants and everything that existed in the valley. But Lot's wife looked back, longing for the lifestyle they had left behind in Sodom. God saw the wickedness of her heart and he turned her into a pillar of salt.

Early in the morning, Abraham went out and stood where he had met with the Lord and learned of Sodom and Gomorrah's fate. He saw the smoke rising from the valley from a smoldering fire, but he knew that God had kept his promise to save his nephew from the destruction.

LOT OUTSIDE OF ZOAR

Lot was terrified of what had happened, and he refused to live in Zoar for fear of God's judgment and how the townspeople would view him. So, he lived with his family in a cave in the nearby foothills. They only left when necessary, so the prospects of finding husbands were abysmal for Lot's daughters. One day, the older daughter cooked up a wicked scheme and said to her younger sister, "Our father is old, and there is no way we will find a husband if we stay in this cave forever. Let's get our father drunk and sleep with him so that we can have children."

That night, they got Lot drunk, and the oldest daughter went in to sleep with her father; the next night, the younger daughter copied her sister's evil deed. Lot was drunk enough each night that he had no clue what they had done. Both daughters became pregnant and their children grew up to be separate nations that later caused Abraham's descendants' problems. This was not God's design, but it reflects what the girls had learned to accept from living in Sodom.

> **Descriptive history in the Bible**
>
> Many accounts in the Bible describe what happened that are not examples for us to follow. The men and women in Scripture did both good and evil, and the text records their actions, but that does not mean we should do the same thing. This story of Lot's daughters is an example of this.

ABRAHAM AND ABIMELECH

Abraham decided that it would be good to leave the area for a while, and he traveled west to Gerar and stayed there. As they arrived, Abraham said that Sarah was his sister, just as he had in Egypt because she was still a beautiful woman at 90. The local ruler, Abimelech, sent for Sarah, intending to marry her. God had promised that Sarah would have a child within the year, and this jeopardized his promise. That night, God appeared to Abimelech in a dream and said, "You are a dead man because of the woman you have taken to be your wife because she is already married."

Abimelech had not slept with Sarah yet, and terrified, he replied, "Lord, will you kill an innocent people? They both said they were siblings; I have done this in ignorance and innocence."

In the dream, God answered, "I know that you are innocent and that you have done this with integrity, but I am the one who has kept you from sinning. Return the man's wife and do not touch her, for he is a prophet, and he will pray for you so you will not die. But if you do not return his wife, I will destroy you, your family, and everything in Gerar."

Early the next morning, Abimelech got up and told his servants what had happened, and they were distraught. Then Abimelech called for Abraham and was furious, "What have you done?! What did I ever do to you that you caused me to commit this sin and nearly be destroyed?! You have done something that no one should ever do to anyone else. Why have you done this?!"

Abraham tried to explain, "I did it because I feared for my life. I know how godless this region is, and I was afraid that someone would kill me and take her if he knew she was my wife. Besides, she really is my half-sister, my father's daughter, but not my mother. After we left my father's home, I asked her to tell people she was my sister whenever we came to a new place because I was afraid."

Abimelech was still upset, but he feared that Abraham was a prophet and that God might still destroy him, so he said, "My land is yours; live wherever you want." Then he said to Sarah, "I have given your brother 1,000 pieces of silver to show that I am an innocent and that I'm vindicated of any sin I may have committed against you." Then he also gave them sheep, oxen, and both male and female servants.

God had closed the wombs of all women in Gerar because of Sarah, so Abraham prayed to God. Then God healed Abimelech and all the women of the land so they could once again have children.

CHAPTER TEN

ISAAC'S BIRTH

Genesis 21-23

Then the Lord visited Sarah and fulfilled his promise to her; she became pregnant even though she had already gone through menopause. In nine months, she had a baby boy, and they named him Isaac. On the eighth day, Abraham circumcised him just as the Lord had commanded.

Abraham was 100 years old when Isaac was born and Sarah said, "God has brought me joy and laughter; everyone who hears of this will share my joy. Who would have ever thought that Sarah would ever nurse Abraham's son, yet I have borne him a son in our old age?"

Isaac grew, and when Sarah weaned him, Abraham threw a great feast. There was still great animosity between Sarah and Hagar. Sarah saw her laughing and mocking, so she said to Abraham, "Throw out that servant and her son because there is no way her child should be an heir with my son."

This displeased Abraham because he loved Ishmael, but God said to him, "Do not be troubled because of the boy and Hagar. Do whatever Sarah says because your offspring will be named through Isaac. I will make Ishmael into a nation because he is your child, but he is not the child of the promise."

So, the next morning Abraham gave Hagar and Ishmael bread and water and sent them away. She left and wandered around the wilderness. Once the food and water were gone and they could not find more, she set Ishmael under a bush and went about a half-mile away and sat down because she did not want to watch her child die.

As she wept, God came to her and asked, "Hagar, what troubles you? Do not be afraid; I have heard the boy's cries. Take him by the hand and be strong, for I will make him into a great nation."

Then God opened her eyes and she saw a well of water. She filled her water skin and gave Ishmael a drink. God was with the boy and he grew up and became an expert with the bow. Then they lived in the wilderness and his mother found an Egyptian wife for him when he had grown.

ABRAHAM AND ABIMELECH'S COVENANT

At that time, Abimelech came to Abraham along with the Phicol, the commander of his army, and said, "God is with you in everything you do. Swear to me by God that you will not deal falsely with my descendants or me. I have dealt kindly with you, so please deal kindly with my people and me."

Abraham replied, "I will."

A while later, there was a dispute about a well that Abimelech's servants had seized from Abraham's servants. When Abraham confronted Abimelech about it, Abimelech claimed innocence, "This is the first I'm hearing of this; I did not know anything about this situation until you brought it up." Abraham gave Abimelech sheep and oxen; the two men made a covenant that they would live at peace with each other and that Abraham could utilize the well.

GOD TESTS ABRAHAM

As Isaac grew, God came to test Abraham and said, "Abraham, take your only son, Isaac, the boy you love, to the land of Moriah and offer him on one of the mountains as a sacrifice to me."

Abraham was distraught, but the next morning, he cut wood for the sacrifice, saddled his donkey, and took Isaac along with two male servants. On the third day, Abraham saw the place from a distance and told his servants to stay with the donkey while he and Isaac went further to worship.

Abraham had Isaac carry the wood for the sacrifice while he held the fire and the knife. As they walked, Isaac said, "Dad, we have the fire and the wood, but where is the lamb that we will sacrifice?"

With tears in his eyes, Abraham replied, "God will provide the lamb for a burnt offering, my son." Then they walked on in silence. Even though Abraham had no desire to obey this command, he knew that God had the power to raise the dead, and he believed that God would restore his son to him.

When they arrived at the place God had told him, Abraham built an altar, laid the wood on it, and then bound Isaac and laid him on the altar. Then he took the knife, and as he prepared to slaughter his beloved son, an angel of the Lord shouted, "Abraham! Do not lay a hand on the boy or cause him any harm. Now I know that you fear God because you did not withhold your only son from him."

Abraham gladly put down the knife, and as he lifted his eyes, he saw a ram caught by his horns in some bushes. Abraham took the ram and offered it to the Lord in his son's place, and he named the place The Lord Will Provide.

God called to Abraham and said, "I did not intend for you to harm the boy; now that I have seen that you would not withhold him from me, I swear that I will make your offspring as numerous as the stars in the sky or the sand of the seashore. Because of your obedience, your offspring will conquer their enemies and be a blessing to the whole earth."

So, Abraham returned to his servants with his son Isaac, and they went to the wilderness of Beersheba, near where Hagar and Ishmael lived.

> **Did God really command Abraham to sacrifice his son?**
>
> While God told Abraham to sacrifice his son, this was a test of his faith, and the Lord never intended to have him go through with the act. God is clear that he hates human sacrifice, forbids it in other places, and condemns groups who practiced it.

SARAH'S DEATH

Sarah lived to be 127 and she died in the land of Hebron near where they had first settled after coming from Haran. Abraham wept and mourned over her body and then spoke to the local people, asking for a place to bury his dead wife. They replied, "You are a prince of God among us; bury your dead wherever you like; none of us will withhold a tomb from you."

Abraham bowed before them and said, "If you allow me to bury my dead in your land, I would like to buy the cave on Ephron's property for the full price that it is worth."

Ephron was there and he answered in the way they negotiated sales, "You don't need to give me money; the cave is yours, and the field in front of it. What is 400 pieces of silver between us? In the sight of everyone here, I give you the field."

Abraham listened to Ephron and gave him 400 pieces of silver as a purchase price for the cave and field. This is how Abraham acquired this piece of property, and he buried Sarah in Hebron.

CHAPTER ELEVEN

ISAAC AND REBEKAH

Genesis 24:1-25:10

ELIEZER FINDS A WIFE FOR ISAAC

Abraham was old and God had blessed him in every way. His son Isaac was 40 years old and ready for marriage. Abraham said to Eliezer, his head servant who oversaw everything he owned, "Come, put your hand under my thigh and swear to me by the God of heaven and earth that you will not find a wife for Isaac from these local women. Go to my home country and find him a wife from my people."

Eliezer asked, "What if I find a woman and she isn't willing to come with me to marry Isaac? Should I take him back there to find a wife?"

Abraham replied, "Do not take him back there. The God of heaven and earth who brought me from my homeland and promised to give my offspring this land will go ahead of you and make your journey a success. If the woman refuses to come with you, I release you from this oath; but do not take my son back there." So, Eliezer placed his hand under Abraham's thigh, an ancient sign of making a solemn, binding oath, and swore to Abraham.

Eliezer took ten camels, loaded them with gifts from Abraham, and left for Mesopotamia. When he arrived, he made the camels kneel by a well outside the city in the early evening, when women came to draw water. As he waited, he prayed, "Lord, God of my master Abraham, please grant me success and show him favor. I am standing by the spring and the women are coming out to draw water. Let the woman that offers to water my camels when I ask for a drink be the woman you have chosen to be Isaac's wife. This will be how I know that you have granted me favor."

Before he finished speaking, Rebekah came out with a water jar on her shoulder. She was a beautiful young virgin, and after she drew water, Eliezer ran up to her and asked her for a drink. Rebekah replied, "Drink, my lord." After he had finished drinking, she continued, "I will also draw water until your camels have finished drinking." She emptied her jar into the watering trough and ran back to get more until the camels were finished (camels need lots of water after a long journey). As she worked, Eliezer watched her in silence to learn if God was answering his prayer or not.

When the camels had finished drinking, he gave her a gold ring and two gold bracelets and said, "Who is your father? Is there room for me to stay there tonight?" Rebekah answered that she was from the same people as Abraham and that there was room and plenty of straw and food for Eliezer's animals.

Eliezer bowed his head in worship and said, "I give praise and thanks to the Lord, the God of Abraham, who has not forgotten his love and faithfulness to my master. He has led me to the house of my master's people!"

Rebekah ran home to tell her family what had happened. Her father had died, so her brother Laban was the head of the family. Once Laban saw the jewelry and heard her story, he ran to the well to greet Eliezer. He welcomed him and said, "Why are you standing outside? Come in with me; I have prepared my house for you and a place for the camels." So, Eliezer went to his house, unharnessed and fed the camels, and washed his feet.

Laban brought out food, but Eliezer stopped him, "I will not eat until I tell you why I'm here. I am Abraham's servant and God has blessed him so that he has become a great man. He is wealthy with flocks and herds, silver and gold, servants, and camels and donkeys. In his old age, his wife, Sarah, gave him a son, and Abraham has given all his great wealth to his child. Abraham made me swear that I would not find a wife for his son from the local women but would come back here to find a bride from his people. My master told me that he would release me from my oath if the woman does not want to come with me. I prayed that I would know I had success when a woman gave me a drink and offered to water my camels. Rebekah did me this service, and now I am here asking for her hand in marriage on behalf of my master's son, Isaac. Please let me know if you will allow her to come with me or if I should turn aside to the right or left."

Rebekah's family said, "This thing is from the Lord; we don't have a choice. You may take Rebekah to be Isaac's wife as the Lord has spoken."

When Eliezer heard these words, he bowed to the ground in worship. He then gave Rebekah beautiful jewelry and clothes and her family expensive ornaments. Eliezer and his men ate and drank and then spent the night with Rebekah's family.

The next morning, Eliezer asked to be able to return to Abraham with Rebekah. Her family asked that she might spend at least ten days with them to say goodbye. But Eliezer said, "Please don't delay me because God has granted me success. Send me on my way to my master."

Rebekah's family called for her and asked if she was willing to go with Eliezer, and she consented. So, they sent her and her nurse away with Eliezer saying, "May our sister become the mother of tens of thousands and may they possess the gates of those who hate them."

ISAAC MARRIES REBEKAH

Isaac was meditating in the field one evening when he saw Eliezer and the camels approaching. When Rebekah saw him, she dismounted her camel and asked, "Who is that man walking to meet us?"

Eliezer replied, "It is my master." So, she covered herself with her veil. Eliezer told Isaac the story of his travels, and Isaac brought Rebekah into his mother's tent and married her. This is how he comforted himself after Sarah's death.

After Sarah died, Abraham took another wife, Keturah, and she bore him six sons in his old age. As Abraham came closer to death, he gave gifts to his other children and sent them away to the east. But he gave Isaac everything he owned. He died at the age of 175, and Ishmael and Isaac buried him in the cave where Sarah lay.

CHAPTER TWELVE

JACOB AND ESAU
Genesis 25:11-26:35

Isaac married Rebekah when he was 40 years old and she was barren. After 20 years, he prayed for her; God answered his request, and Rebekah conceived twins. The two children struggled within her womb and Rebekah cried out to God, "Why is this happening?"

God came to Rebekah and said, "Two nations are in your womb, and two people who will end up divided; one will be stronger than the other, and the older will serve the younger."

When she gave birth, the first child came out red and hairy, so they named him Esau. Afterward, his brother came out holding Esau's heel, so they named him Jacob. When the boys grew up, Esau was an outdoorsman and a skillful hunter, while Jacob was a quiet man who preferred to be indoors. Isaac favored Esau because of the game he caught, while Rebekah favored Jacob.

Once when Esau was coming in from the field, exhausted, he saw Jacob cooking a lentil stew. Esau said to Jacob, "Let me eat some of that stew because I am starving to death."

Jacob was crafty, so he replied, "Then sell me your birthright."

Esau was short-sighted in his reply and said, "I am about to starve to death; what good is my birthright?!"

Jacob said, "Then swear to me." So, Esau swore to sell his birthright to Jacob, and Jacob gave him bread and stew. Esau ate and drank and then went on his way; thus, he discarded his birthright.

> **What is a birthright?**
>
> A birthright is a privileged position, usually given to a firstborn son. It provides greater inheritance and a favored position in the family. Essentially, Esau traded a meal for his family's wealth.

There was a famine in the land, much like the one in Abraham's day. Isaac went to Gerar to see Abimelech, king of the Philistines, just as his father had. God came to Isaac and said, "Do not go down to Egypt; stay in the land that I show you. Stay in this land, and I will be with you and bless you. I will give this land to you and your offspring and I will fulfill the promise that I swore to your father, Abraham. I will multiply your descendants like the stars of the heavens and I will give them this land. Your offspring will be a blessing to all the nations of the earth because Abraham obeyed my voice and kept my commandments."

So, Isaac settled in Gerar. When the locals asked about Rebekah, he told them that she was his sister, just as his father had done. He also feared that the people would kill him to have an opportunity with his wife. After they had been there for some time, Abimelech looked out the window and saw Isaac laughing with Rebekah and caressing her cheek like a husband with a wife.

Abimelech was furious and he called Isaac out, "Rebekah is your wife! Why would you lie to us and call her your sister?!"

Isaac replied weakly, "I thought someone here might kill me so that they could have a shot at her."

Abimelech remembered God's threat from when Abraham and Sarah had been there and said, "What were you thinking?! One of my people could have easily slept with her and brought guilt upon all of us!" So, Abimelech warned all his people that anyone who touched Rebekah would die.

Isaac sowed in the fields, and he had a bumper crop, reaping a hundred times what he had planted. The Lord continued to bless Isaac and he became very wealthy. He had many possessions, flocks, herds, and servants, and the locals became very envious.

To harm Isaac, the Philistines stopped up the wells that Abraham had dug. Abimelech could tell that trouble was brewing, so he said to Isaac, "Please leave us because you are so much more powerful than we are." So, Isaac left and camped in the nearby Valley of Gerar.

Isaac re-dug the wells that his father had dug, but the herdsmen of the valley quarreled with Isaac's men claiming that the water was theirs. They dug another well and quarreled over that as well, so Isaac moved farther away. Finally, he found a place where there was no dispute, and he praised God, saying, "God has made room for us in the land, now we will be fruitful and multiply."

As Isaac continued to Beersheba, God appeared to him and said, "I am the God of Abraham. Do not be afraid because I will bless you and multiply your offspring for his sake." So, Isaac built an altar and worshiped the Lord.

Abimelech visited Isaac along with his chief advisor and commander of his army. Isaac said, "What do you want? You hate me and kicked me out of your land!"

The Philistines said, "We see that God is with you in everything that you do. We said to each other that we should make a sworn pact between us that you will not harm us just as we have not harmed you, but sent you away in peace." So, they had a feast, and in the morning, they exchanged oaths and parted ways.

At the age of 40, Esau married a local woman, and their marriage caused Isaac and Rebekah grief.

CHAPTER THIRTEEN

JACOB STEALS ESAU'S BLESSING
Genesis 27:1-28:9

When Isaac was old and could barely see, he called Esau to him and said, "I could die any day now, please take your bow and bring me some savory game so that I can eat and then bless you before I die."

Rebekah was eavesdropping on the conversation; once Esau left, she went to Jacob and said, "Your father just asked your older brother to hunt game and then make a meal so he can eat and then bless him before he dies. Now, listen to what I say and obey me! Bring me two young goats from the flock so that I can prepare food for your father. Then you will bring it to your father so that he can eat and bless you before he dies."

Jacob saw some flaws with this plan and said, "Esau is very hairy, but my skin is smooth. What if my father feels my skin and curses me for mocking him?"

Rebekah replied, "Let your curse be upon me! Just listen to me and get the goats!" Jacob obeyed and Rebekah prepared the food Isaac liked. Then she dressed Jacob in Esau's finest clothing and put goatskins on the backs of his hands and neck.

Jacob took the goats and bread into his father and did his best impersonation of his brother, "I am Esau, your firstborn, I have listened to your words. Sit up and eat my game so that you may bless me."

Isaac was suspicious and asked, "How are you back so quickly? I didn't expect you for quite some time."

Jacob answered quickly, "Because your God granted me success."

Isaac still held his suspicions, so he said, "Come close to me so that I can figure out if you are Esau or not."

Jacob approached his father with apprehension. Isaac smelled Esau's clothing and felt the hair on his hands and back of his neck; it was thick and wiry like a wild animal. Then Isaac said, "You sound like Jacob, but you smell and feel like Esau." Isaac still had his doubts and asked, "Are you really Esau?"

Jacob was committed to the lie and said, "I am Esau." Then he brought him the food and wine so that Isaac could eat and drink and then bless him.

Once Isaac had finished eating, he beckoned his son to come close to kiss him. As Jacob drew near, Isaac said, "My son smells like the earth that God has blessed! May God give you the dew of heaven, the fatness of the earth, and plenty of grain and wine. May peoples serve you and nations bow down before you. May God bless everyone who blesses you and curse everyone who curses you!"

Jacob left after Isaac finished blessing him. Shortly after, Esau came in from hunting. He brought food into his father and said, "Get up and eat so that you can bless me!"

Isaac was confused and asked, "Who are you?"

Esau answered with pride, "I am your firstborn son, Esau!"

Isaac's voice trembled violently, "Who was it that hunted the game and brought it to me? I ate his food and blessed him before you came, and God will bless him indeed."

Esau realized what was happening and wailed, "My father, please, bless me too!"

Isaac replied, "Your brother came deceitfully and stole your blessing."

Esau cried, "He is rightly named Jacob because he has cheated me twice. He took away my birthright and now he has taken my blessing as well. Do you only have one blessing?! Father, please bless me as well!"

Isaac answered, "You will live away from the dew of heaven and the fatness of the land. You will live by the sword and serve your brother. But when you grow restless, you will break his yoke from around your neck."

Esau hated Jacob because he had stolen his blessing; he comforted himself by plotting to murder his brother once Isaac died. Rebekah heard of Esau's plans and told Jacob, "Esau is plotting to kill you! Run to your uncle Laban and stay in Haran with him until your brother's anger subsides. Then I will send for you once he has forgotten this incident. Why should I lose both you and Isaac in one day?"

Then Rebekah said to Isaac, "I hate my life because of these local women. If Jacob marries one of these girls, then my life is worthless! Send Jacob away to find a wife!"

Isaac listened to his wife and called Jacob to him, "Go to Rebekah's household and find a wife. May God bless you to make you fruitful and a great nation. May he give you Abraham's blessing and may you possess all the land he promised him." Jacob listened and traveled to visit Rebekah's brother Laban. Esau saw that his mother hated his wife and that Isaac had sent his brother away, so he took another wife from Ishmael's descendants.

CHAPTER FOURTEEN
JACOB, LABAN, AND JACOB'S CHILDREN
Genesis 28:10-31:2
JACOB'S LADDER

Jacob traveled towards his family in Haran and stayed the night in the wilderness near where Lot had settled. That night he dreamed that there was a ladder reaching heaven with angels going up and down upon it. In the dream, God stood above the ladder and said, "I am the God of both Abraham and Isaac; your children will be like the dust of the earth and spread out in all directions. I will always be with you and bring you back to this land. I will be with you until I have fulfilled the promise I gave to Abraham."

Jacob woke up and said, "Surely God is in this place and I did not know it. How awesome is God and I did not know that this is a gateway to heaven?" So, the next morning, Jacob took the rock that he had used as a pillow, anointed it with oil, and called upon the Lord.

Jacob made an oath to God, "If God is with me and will provide for me so that I make it to Laban's household, then the Lord will be my God, and this stone will be his house, and I will give him a tenth of everything I earn."

JACOB AND LABAN

Jacob continued his journey until he reached the land of his uncle, Laban, and he saw a well where the flocks were waiting for water. Jacob asked the shepherds where they were from, and they replied that they were tending Laban's sheep and that his daughter, Rachel, was coming to water them.

It was the middle of the day and not the time to water animals. But when Rachel arrived with Laban's flock, he was so stricken with her beauty that he moved the large stone covering the well so that she could water her sheep.

Laban heard about Jacob's arrival and how he had removed the giant stone, and he said to Jacob, "You are my nephew; you should stay with me and earn wages for your work."

Laban had two daughters, Rachel, who was beautiful, and her older sister, Leah, who was not attractive. Laban said to Jacob, "You should not serve me for nothing, so name your price."

Jacob had fallen in love with Rachel and he said, "Give me your daughter, Rachel, as my wife in return for the work that I do for you."

Laban said, "I would rather have you marry Rachel than any other man; work for me for seven years, then you can marry her."

JACOB MARRIES LEAH AND RACHEL

Jacob served Laban for seven years and said, "Give me my wife. I have served you for seven years, so allow me to marry Rachel so that I can sleep with her."

Laban gathered all his people together for a wedding feast, but at the end of the celebration, Laban gave his older daughter Leah to Jacob and his servant, Zilpah, as her servant. Since it was dark, Jacob did not realize that it was Leah until the morning.

Jacob was shocked that he had consummated his marriage with Leah, and he said to Laban, "What have you done? I served you seven years for Rachel; why have you lied to me?"

Laban replied, "It is not the custom to marry off the younger before the elder. Serve me for another seven for Rachel's hand in marriage; then, she will be your wife as well."

Jacob loved Rachel so much that he served Laban for another seven years and married her. He loved Rachel so much that the time seemed like nothing, and Laban gave Bilhah to Rachel to be her servant.

Jacob loved Rachel much more than he loved Leah, but Rachel was barren. Leah conceived and she said, "I will name him Reuben because God has looked upon my affliction." She had a second son and named him Simeon because "God has heard that I am hated." She had another son and said, "Since God has given me another son, I will call him Levi." Then she had another son and said, "This time, I will praise the Lord." She named her fourth son Judah and then she stopped having children.

When Rachel saw that she had no children, she was envious, and she said to Jacob, "Give me children, or I will die!"

Jacob was angry and said, "Am I in God's place?"

So, Rachel gave him her servant Bilhah, and Jacob slept with the maid, and she had a son. Rachel said, "God has heard my voice." She named her son Dan. Jacob had a second son with Bilhah and Rachel said, "I have wrestled with my sister and prevailed." So, she called the son Naphtali.

Leah saw that she had stopped having children, so she let Jacob sleep with Zilpah. Zilpah had a son, so Leah called him Gad because God had given her good fortune. Then Zilpah had a second son, and Leah named him Asher because women would call her happy.

In the days of the harvest, Reuben found some mandrakes, an ancient aphrodisiac. Rachel asked Leah for some of the mandrakes and Leah answered, "Is it enough that you should take away my husband? Would you take away my husband's love as well?" Rachel replied that Jacob could sleep with her in exchange for Reuben's mandrakes.

Leah came to Jacob and said, "I have hired you for the night with my son's mandrakes." So, Jacob slept with Leah that night, and she became pregnant with her fifth son. She named him Issachar because God had given a son to her servant. Then she had a sixth son for Jacob and she called him Zebulon because she believed that her husband would honor her. She also had a daughter that she named Dinah.

Then God remembered Rachel and she had a boy whom she named Joseph because God had given her a son.

After Rachel had given him a son, Jacob said to Laban, "Send me away so that I may go to my own country. Give me my wives and my children for whom I have served you so I can start my own life."

Laban replied, "I have learned through divination that God has blessed me because of you. Name your wages and I will give it to you."

Jacob said, "You know how I have served you and how your flocks have fared with me. You did not have much before I served you, now you have much, and God has blessed me wherever I have turned. Shouldn't I now be allowed to provide for my own family?"

Laban replied, "What should I give you?"

Jacob said, "Don't give me anything. I will continue to watch your flocks, and you should give me every spotted, speckled, and black sheep and goats; they will be my wages. That way, you will know my work has been honest. If you find any sheep or goats with me that are not spotted, speckled, or black, they should be counted as stolen."

Laban removed all the spotted, speckled, and black sheep and goats from Jacob and had his sons watch over them. Jacob took his flocks three days away from Laban's flocks and watched over them. As a superstition, he took sticks from poplar and almond trees, peeled them, and set them in front of the herds as they drank water. As they bred, God caused them to bear speckled, striped, and black offspring. Thus, God caused Jacob to prosper until he had large flocks of sheep, goats, camels, and servants.

Jacob heard Laban's sons grumbling, "Jacob has taken all our father's wealth, everything he has come from him." Jacob also saw that Laban no longer treated him with favor, and he became antsy.

CHAPTER FIFTEEN

JACOB RETURNS HOME

Genesis 31:3-32:21

God came to Jacob and said, "Return home where your brother lives and I will be with you."

Jacob called Rachel and Leah into the field where he was watching the flock and he said to them, "Your father doesn't like me as he used to, but the God of my father has been with me. You know that I have served your father with all my strength, but he keeps cheating me and changing my wages. But God has always protected me from his schemes. If he promised me the spotted animals, they all gave birth to spotted offspring; if he promised me the striped, they all gave birth to striped offspring. Thus, God has taken your father's wealth and given it to me. God told me in a dream that he was protecting me from Laban and that it was time for me to go home."

Rachel and Leah answered Jacob, "There is nothing left for us in our father's house; he treats us like strangers. He has sold us and then spent all the money; God has taken his wealth and given it to us. We will do whatever God has told you."

Jacob packed up everything he owned and took his family back to the land of his father, Isaac. Before they left, Rachel snuck in and stole her father's household idols. They went in secret so they could get as far away as possible before Laban came after them.

On the third day, Laban found out that Jacob had fled with his family and possessions, so he took some of his men and chased after his nephew for seven days. As he was about to catch Jacob, God appeared to Laban in a dream and warned him not to say anything good or bad to his nephew.

When Laban finally caught up to Jacob, he said, "What do you think you're doing, taking my daughters away as if you have captured them with the sword? Why did you sneak away when I could have thrown you a great party and sent you away with laughter and singing? Why didn't you allow me to kiss my daughters and grandchildren goodbye? You have made a huge mistake, and I should make you pay for your folly, but your God came to me in a dream last night and warned me not to say anything good or bad to you. I understand why you wanted to go back to your homeland, but why did you steal my household idols?"

Jacob, unaware that Rachel had taken the idols, answered, "I left in secret because I was afraid that you would take your daughters from me by force. As far as your idols? I don't know what you're talking about; we will kill whoever has your idols. With our family as a witness, look through my stuff and tell me what I have that is yours."

Laban went through everyone's tent and didn't find the idols. Rachel had hidden them beneath her camel's saddle and feared being discovered. When Laban came to search her belongings, Rachel apologized, "I am sorry that I cannot rise before you; I have my period."

When Laban didn't find the idols, Jacob became furious, "What is my crime?! What is my sin that you have chased after me like I was a fugitive?! You felt through all my belongings, and what did you find?! Bring it out and put it in front of our family so that they can judge between us. I served you for 20 years and I took excellent care of your flocks. I never took any of them for myself, and if there was any loss, I didn't tell you about it; I paid for it myself. I suffered in the heat of the day and lost sleep at night over your flocks.

"I've served you for 20 years, 14 for your daughters, and six for your flocks, and you have changed my wages ten times. If the God my father and Abraham had not protected me, I'm sure that you would have sent me away empty-handed. But God saw how you afflicted me and he rebuked you last night."

Laban answered, "Your wives are my daughters, your children are my grandchildren, and everything else you have is mine. But what am I supposed to do? Let's make a covenant between us."

So, they both brought stones, made a heap, and they shared a meal. Then Laban said, "This heap of stones is a witness: May God watch between us once we are out of each other's sight. If you oppress my daughters or take other wives, God will see, even though we cannot see each other. This heap is also a witness that neither one of us shall pass this heap to harm the other. May the God of our fathers judge between us."

Jacob swore to the covenant and sacrificed an animal to the Lord. They spent the night in the hills, and the next morning Laban got up early, kissed his daughters and grandchildren, and returned to his home.

Jacob went his way and God's angels met him. Jacob called the place God's camp, and he sent messengers to his brother Esau, saying, "Jacob has been staying with Laban. He has gained oxen, donkeys, flocks, and male and female servants that he would like to give to you to gain favor in your sight."

The messengers returned to Jacob and said, "We delivered your message, and now your brother Esau is coming to meet you with 400 men."

Jacob was terrified, so he divided everyone into two camps thinking that if Esau attacked, at least one group would escape. Jacob cried out in prayer, "God of my fathers Abraham and Isaac, you are the one who told me to return to my family and homeland so that you could bless me. I am not worthy of even the least of the ways you have shown me love and faithfulness all these years. When I first left home, I only had the clothes on my back, and now I have become two separate camps. Please deliver me from my brother's hand because I fear that he will attack me and kill the women and children. Remember your promise to make my offspring as the countless grains of sand on the seashore."

Jacob set up camp for the night and devised a plan to appease his brother's wrath and possibly gain acceptance. He set aside 200 female goats and 20 males, 200 ewes and 20 rams, 30 milking camels and their calves, 40 cows and 10 bulls, and 20 female donkeys and 10 males. He sent these along with five servants, one servant for each type of animal, and instructed them to put some distance between each other and travel to meet Esau. He told them each to tell Esau that they were a gift from his brother and that he was coming to meet him.

CHAPTER SIXTEEN

JACOB WRESTLES AN ANGEL

Genesis 32:22-33:20

That same night, after Jacob sent his wives and children ahead, he was alone. In his solitude, a man came to him, and the two wrestled until daybreak. When the man saw that he could not defeat Jacob, he dislocated Jacob's hip and said, "Let me go, for a new day is dawning."

Through gritted teeth, Jacob replied, "I will not let you go unless you bless me."

The man said, "What is your name?"

Jacob replied, "Jacob."

Then the stranger said, "You will no longer be Jacob; your name is now Israel because you have wrestled with God and man and have prevailed."

Jacob answered, "Tell me your name."

But the man refused and said, "Why do you want to know?" and the man blessed him. So, Jacob named the place Peniel because he had seen God face to face and lived.

> **Jacob or Israel**
>
> Jacob and Israel are interchangeable, but I tend to use Jacob to refer to the individual and Israel to the entire nation.

JACOB AND ESAU'S REUNION

As Jacob limped towards home, he looked up and saw Esau for the first time in 20 years, coming with 400 men. He put Zilpah and Bilhah with their children first, then Leah and her children, and finally Rachel and Joseph in the rear to protect them. Then he went forward and bowed himself to the ground seven times before reaching his brother. But Esau ran to meet him and fell upon Jacob's neck and kissed him, and the two brothers wept.

Eventually, Esau looked up and said, "Who are all these women and children with you?"

Jacob replied through his tears, "These are the children that God has graciously given to your servant."

The three groups of Jacob's family came forward and each of them bowed to the ground. Then Esau said, "What is the meaning of all these other groups of animals and servants that came to me?"

Jacob answered, "I sent them as an apology and a way to find favor in your sight."

Esau said, "My brother, I have plenty, keep your animals and servants."

Jacob replied, "Please, if I have found favor in your sight, accept my gift. I have seen your face, and it is like I have seen God's face because you have accepted me. Please accept my gift because God has been gracious to me and I have more than enough."

Esau accepted Jacob's gift and said, "Then come with me and I will lead us back home."

Jacob did not fully trust his brother yet, so he said, "My lord, you know how frail women and children are, and the nursing flocks have all journeyed a long way. If we keep going at this pace, all the flocks will die. Let us travel at our own pace until we come to your home."

Esau said, "Well, let me take some of the people with me to lighten your burden."

Jacob answered, "There is no need for me to burden you; please let us travel at our own pace."

So, Esau went home to Seir, but once he was out of sight, Jacob went in the opposite direction to Succoth. Even though Jacob had wrestled with God and had been reconciled to his brother, he was not quite ready to believe God's promise to give him the land promised to Abraham and Isaac.

CHAPTER SEVENTEEN

JACOB IN THE PROMISED LAND

Genesis 34-36

Jacob settled in Canaan and purchased some land near the city of Shechem to set up his tents. He built an altar and worshiped God.

Once they had established themselves, one of Leah's daughters, Dinah, went out to meet the local women. While she was with them, one of the princes of the land thought she was beautiful and raped her.

The prince was in love with her and spoke tenderly to her to win her heart. He also went to his father and said, "Go get her for me as a wife."

Jacob heard about the rape but did not do anything about it until his sons came in from watching the flocks. His sons were outraged on behalf of their sister and wanted revenge.

The prince's father approached them and said, "My son longs to marry your daughter, please give her to him as a wife; in exchange, we will open our land to you, intermarry, and trade with each other. Ask whatever you like as a gift for her hand in marriage, and I will give it to you, regardless of the price. But please allow my son to marry her."

Jacob's sons lied, "We cannot give our sister in marriage to anyone who is uncircumcised because that would be a disgrace to our people. If you are willing to circumcise every male in your family, we will allow her to marry your son. Then we will intermarry, dwell with you, and become one people. But if you are not willing to do this, we will take our sister and leave."

Their conditions seemed agreeable, and the men brought the proposal to the other men of their city, saying, "These men want peace, let them live with us and trade because we have plenty of land. Let us intermarry with them because eventually, all their livestock and property will be ours. They have only given us one condition, that we must circumcise all our men. Let us do this one thing and we will profit greatly."

All the men thought this was a good idea and circumcised themselves at the city gate. Then on the third day, when they were at the height of their pain, two of Dinah's brothers, Simeon and Levi, went into the city and killed all the city's men. Then they killed Dinah's rapist and his father, and took their sister back home. Then her other brothers came in and plundered the city, taking all the property and women of the town because there were no men to stop them.

Jacob said to Simeon and Levi, "You have brought me great trouble by making all the locals hate me. We do not have that many people in our number, and if the local people band together, they will destroy us."

"But," they said, "should we just let them treat our sister like a prostitute?"

God came to Jacob and said, "Take your people the 20 miles to Bethel, where I first met you, when you fled from your brother, Esau, and build an altar there."

Jacob was growing in his faith and told his family, "Get rid of your foreign gods, purify yourself and change your clothes. We are going to Bethel to worship the God who has always answered me and helped in my distress."

They listened to their father, gave him all their false gods, and Jacob buried them beneath a tree. Then, they began the journey to Bethel. As they traveled, God made the locals afraid of Jacob and his family, and they were able to travel safely until they reached their destination.

When they arrived at Bethel, God appeared to Jacob and said, "You will no longer be Jacob, from now on, your name is Israel. I am God Almighty, be fruitful and multiply. You will become a great nation and kings will come from your offspring. I will give your descendants the land I promised to Abraham and Isaac."

Once God had finished speaking, Jacob built a stone pillar as a reminder of God's promise and anointed it with offerings of drink and oil.

Around this time, Rachel had become pregnant with a second child; she had a difficult labor and died. As she was dying, she named her newborn son Ben-Oni, but Jacob called him Benjamin.

After establishing themselves in the land, Jacob's oldest son, Reuben, slept with Rachel's servant, Bilhah, and Jacob heard about it.

Jacob traveled to see his father just before Isaac died at the age of 180. Jacob and Esau buried him in the land where he had lived.

JACOB'S SONS

Mother	Child	Notes
Leah	Reuben	Slept with Rachel's servant, Bilhah.
	Simeon	Slaughtered the Shechemites along with Levi after they raped their sister.
	Levi	Slaughtered the Shechemites along with Simeon after they raped their sister.
	Judah	Jesus was a descendent of Judah.
	Issachar	
	Zebulun	

Mother	Child	Notes
Rachel	Joseph	Jacob's favorite son. Given a long-sleeved, multi-colored robe.
	Benjamin	Jacob's last son. Rachel died during his childbirth.
Bilhah (Rachel's servant)	Dan	
	Naphtali	
Zilpah (Leah's servant)	Gad	
	Asher	

CHAPTER EIGHTEEN

JOSEPH AND HIS BROTHERS

Genesis 37-38

Jacob lived in the land of Canaan, where his fathers had lived before him. When Joseph was 17 years old, he went out into the fields to look after his father's flocks with his brothers. Joseph brought back a bad report about his brothers and this made them angry. To make matters worse, Jacob gave Joseph a full-length, long-sleeved, multi-colored robe because Jacob loved Joseph more than any of his other children. This robe was beautiful and ornate and made Joseph look like royalty. Joseph's brothers knew that he was their father's favorite son, and they hated him and couldn't speak to him without starting a fight.

One night, Joseph had a dream, and he shared it with his brothers, "I dreamt that we were out in the field binding up bundles of grain and my bundle stood up tall while your bundles gathered around and bowed down to mine."

This made Joseph's brothers even angrier and they replied, "Do you think you are going to reign over us and become our ruler?!" They hated him even more.

A little while later, Joseph had another dream, and he decided to share this dream with the whole family. He told them, "I had another dream, and this time the sun, moon, and eleven stars were bowing down to me."

This time Jacob became angry and he scolded Joseph, "What is the meaning of this dream? Will your mother, your brothers, and I bow to the ground before you?" These words and Jacob's favoritism made the brothers so angry and jealous that it destroyed their family. But Jacob kept Joseph's dream in mind.

A little while later, Jacob's sons took his flocks to pasture them near Shechem, about 50 miles from where they lived. Jacob said to Joseph, "Your brothers took the flocks to Shechem to graze them. Check on them and see how things are going and then come back to let me know." Joseph sought his brothers where he thought they would be, but a man told him they had gone further to Dothan, an additional 13 miles from home. Joseph continued his journey and found his brothers.

Joseph's brothers saw him coming and plotted to kill him. They said to each other, "Here comes the dreamer. Let's kill him and throw him into one of the nearby pits. Then we can tell our father that a wild animal ate him, and then we will see what becomes of his dreams!"

Reuben, the oldest brother, came to the rescue and said, "Let's not kill him. Let's throw him in a pit, but let's not go so far as to kill him." Reuben planned to rescue the boy out of the pit so that he could take Joseph back to gain their father's favor.

So, when Joseph arrived, they roughed him up and took his fancy robe. Then they threw him into an empty cistern (pit for holding water) before deciding what to do with him. They sat down to eat while Joseph lay in the pit. As they ate, they saw some traveling Ishmaelite merchants on their way to Egypt to sell gum, balm, and perfume. Judah, one of the older brothers, said, "Why don't we make some money off this situation? It doesn't help us out if we kill him. Instead, why don't we sell him to these merchants?" They pulled him out of the pit, and sold him for 20 pieces of silver, and the merchants took Joseph to Egypt.

When Reuben came back to the pit and saw that Joseph was gone, he tore his clothes in grief and yelled, "Now Joseph's gone; what am I supposed to do?! I'm the oldest and I'm supposed to look out for him!"

Then the brothers slaughtered a goat and dipped the robe in the goat's blood. They took the robe back to their father and said, "We found this bloody robe; tell us if this is Joseph's."

Jacob looked at the robe and realized that it was the one he gave his favorite son. He wailed, "This is Joseph's robe! A wild animal has devoured him and he is probably dead!" He tore his clothes in grief and put on mourning garments and mourned his lost son for days.

His family tried to comfort him, but he refused and wept, "Leave me alone and let me die."

JUDAH AND TAMAR

After selling his brother into slavery, Judah needed to be away from the family for a while, so he went off and stayed with a friend named Hirah. While he was there, he fell in love with a local girl, and she gave birth to three sons, Er, Onan, and Shelah.

As his children grew, Judah brought Tamar, a local girl, to marry Er. But Er was wicked and God killed him as judgment for his evil deeds. Judah followed the custom of the time where a younger sibling would marry a deceased brother's wife so that he could raise offspring on behalf of his brother. He told his second son, Onan, "Perform the duty of a brother-in-law and impregnate your brother's wife so that he may live on through the offspring."

But Onan knew that the children would not be his, so he would pull out and waste his semen on the ground every time he slept with Tamar so that he would not give his brother offspring. His refusal to give his brother a descendent was wicked in God's sight, so he put Onan to death, just like his brother.

Judah was afraid that his youngest son would die as well, so he sent Tamar back to her parents' home, saying, "Stay a widow until my youngest son grows up."

A few years later, Shelah was old enough to marry, but Judah had not yet reached out to Tamar to bring her back to marry his son. Judah's wife died and he went to visit his friend Hirah as he processed his grief.

Tamar heard that Judah was making this journey, so she took off her widow's garments, dressed as a local prostitute, and sat by the road where she knew Judah would pass. When Judah saw her, he did not recognize her as his daughter-in-law and offered to pay her for sex. He did not have anything to pay her with, but he promised to send her a goat from his flock, and as a pledge, he left his staff, cord, and signet ring.

Then Tamar returned home and put her widow's garments back on. Judah sent his friend to pay Tamar, but she was no longer there. The locals told Hirah that there had not been a prostitute in the area, so he returned with the goat. Judah was embarrassed by the situation, so he decided to put it all behind him since he had tried to pay her.

Three months later, it turned out that Tamar was pregnant. Judah found out, and was furious, demanding to burn her alive.

As she was brought out, Tamar revealed Judah's staff, cord, and signet ring and said, "The man who owns these things is the father of this child."

Judah was instantly convicted and said, "She is more righteous than I am because I did not give her Shelah as a husband."

When it was time for her to give birth, she had twins. While she was in labor, one son put his hand out, and a midwife tied a string around it to signify that he was the firstborn. But the baby pulled his hand back in and his brother came out first. Tamar named them Perez and Zerah.

CHAPTER NINETEEN

JOSEPH IN EGYPT
Genesis 39-41:45

The Ishmaelites brought Joseph down to Egypt and sold him to one of Pharaoh's officials, Potiphar. God was with Joseph and blessed him, and he gained favor with his new master. Recognizing that God was blessing Joseph's work, Potiphar put the young man in charge of everything in his house. God blessed his household and he did not worry about anything except the food he ate.

In addition to successfully managing his master's household, Joseph was also very handsome. Potiphar's wife noticed Joseph, and one day, she tried to seduce him. But Joseph refused and said, "My master has put everything in his house under my authority and has not kept anything from me except you because you are his wife. How could I commit this great wickedness and sin against God?"

Potiphar's wife was very persistent and she kept after Joseph daily. One day, she grabbed him by his clothing and demanded that he sleep with her. He left his cloak in her hands and ran out of the house. As soon as she saw that he had left his cloak, she called the other servants and said, "This Hebrew has come here to make sport of us! He tried to sleep with me, and I cried out, and then he left his cloak and ran."

She held onto Joseph's cloak until Potiphar came home. She told him the story she had concocted and Potiphar became enraged. He threw Joseph into the king's prison. But God was with Joseph and he found favor in the jailor's eyes. Eventually, the jailor put Joseph in charge of all the other prisoners and everything in the prison. God blessed Joseph and everything he did was successful.

JOSEPH IN PRISON

Sometime later, Pharaoh's chief cupbearer and baker committed offenses, and the king sent them to prison. The jailor put them both under Joseph's supervision and they all were in custody for quite some time.

One night, they both had a dream. When Joseph saw that they were both troubled, he asked, "Why are you sad this morning?"

The baker and cupbearer answered, "We have had dreams, and there is no one to tell us what they mean."

Joseph replied, "Interpretations belong to God; please tell me your dreams."

The chief cupbearer shared his dream first, "I was standing before a vine that had three branches. It grew buds and blossoms and then developed ripe grapes. I held Pharaoh's cup, took the grapes, pressed them, and made wine in Pharaoh's cup. Then I gave Pharaoh the cup and he drank."

Joseph said, "The branches are days. In three days, Pharaoh will restore you to your position as chief cupbearer, and you will give Pharaoh his cup as you used to. When he restores you to your position, remember me and get me out of here. Because I was stolen from my homeland and I have not done anything worthy of being in this pit."

The baker saw that Joseph gave the cupbearer a favorable interpretation and he eagerly shared his dream, "I had three cake baskets on my head, and the one on top was full of all kinds of baked goods for Pharaoh, but birds were eating the bread out of the basket."

Joseph said, "The baskets are days. In three days, Pharaoh will bring you before him and hang you from a tree. Then the birds will come and eat your flesh."

Pharaoh's birthday was three days from then and he made a feast for all his servants. He brought the chief cupbearer and baker up from prison and set them before his servants. Then he restored the chief cupbearer to his position and hanged the baker, just as Joseph had interpreted. But the cupbearer forgot about Joseph.

JOSEPH INTERPRETS PHARAOH'S DREAMS

Two years later, Pharaoh dreamed that he was standing by the Nile River, and seven plump, attractive cows came out of the water and fed on the reeds on the banks. Then seven ugly and thin cows came out of the water and stood next to the attractive, plump cows and ate them. Pharaoh woke up and was troubled by this dream.

He fell back asleep and had a second dream. There were seven plump ears of corn growing on a single stalk, and another stalk grew up next to it with seven thin, weak ears of grain. Then the seven bad ears swallowed up the seven good ears of corn. Pharaoh woke up and his dream troubled him all morning.

Pharaoh called all his magicians and wise men and told the two dreams to them, but none of them could tell him what his dreams meant. Then the chief cupbearer said to Pharaoh, "Today, I am reminded of my past offenses. A couple of years ago, when you were angry, you put me in jail with the baker. One night we each had dreams and the jailor had a young Hebrew servant who interpreted our dreams accurately. You restored me to my position and hanged the baker."

Pharaoh called for Joseph, and they quickly had him shave, change his clothes, and present himself before the Egyptian ruler. Pharaoh said, "I had a dream that no one has been able to interpret, but I've heard that you can give interpretations."

Joseph replied, "I cannot interpret dreams, but God can."

Pharaoh told his dreams to Joseph and the young man said, "The two dreams are the same, and God is revealing what he is about to do. The seven plump cows and seven good ears represent seven good years, and the seven thin cows and seven weak ears represent seven years of blight and famine. There will be seven years of fantastic production followed by seven bad years where the famine will be so severe that people will forget the productive years because of how bad things will get. The fact that there were two dreams means that God declares this is about to happen.

"You should select a wise and discerning man to put in charge of the land. Appoint overseers to collect one-fifth of the produce during the years of plenty so that there will be a reserve of food so Egypt will not perish during the famine."

Joseph had impressed Pharaoh with his proposal, so the ruler said, "Where could we find a man with God's spirit to do this? Since God has revealed all of this to you, who is wiser and more discerning than you? I am putting you in charge of this operation and all Egypt; only regarding the throne will I have more authority than you will."

Then Pharaoh clothed Joseph in fine linen, put a gold chain around his neck, and gave him the royal signet ring. He allowed Joseph to ride in his second chariot and commanded that people should kneel in his presence. He also said, "I am Pharaoh, but no one will lift a finger in Egypt without your consent." He also gave him Asenath, an Egyptian priest's daughter, as a wife, giving the young Hebrew great power and authority.

CHAPTER TWENTY

JOSEPH'S FAMILY COMES TO EGYPT

Genesis 41:46-42:38

Joseph was 30 years old when Pharaoh put him in charge of Egypt and Joseph enacted his plan. During the seven years of plenty, he collected one-fifth of the land's produce and put it into storehouses in all the cities of Egypt. During this time, they gathered so much food that they stopped keeping track of it because it was like the sand of the seashore.

During this time, Joseph and Asenath had two sons. Joseph named the older Manasseh, which means "cause to forget," because God had made him forget his family's pain and hardship. He called the second son Ephraim, which means "very fruitful," because God had made him fruitful in the land of his affliction.

Then the seven productive years ended, and there was a seven-year famine, just as Joseph had predicted. The famine spread to the entire region, but there was food in Egypt. When people became hungry and begged Pharaoh for food, he told them to go to Joseph and do whatever he told them. Then Joseph opened the storehouses and sold grain to the Egyptians and all the people around Egypt.

When Jacob heard there was food in Egypt, he said to his sons, "Why are you standing around staring at each other? I've heard there is food in Egypt; go buy us some grain, so we don't die."

So, ten of Joseph's brothers went down to Egypt, but Jacob kept Benjamin at home for fear that something terrible would happen.

Joseph oversaw the entire land, and when his brothers came before him, they bowed down. He recognized them, although they thought he was a stranger. Joseph spoke roughly to them and asked, "Where are you from?"

Joseph's brothers answered, "We are from Canaan, and we have come to buy food."

Joseph remembered his dreams and said to them, "You are spies! You have come to see our weaknesses so that you can invade!"

Joseph's brothers replied, "No, my lord! Your servants have just come down to buy food. We are honest men, twelve brothers of one man. Our youngest brother stayed home with his father, and our other brother is dead."

But Joseph held firm, "I don't believe you! You are spies, and the only way I will believe you is if one of you returns home to bring your younger brother here while I keep the rest of you here in captivity." Then he threw them all in prison for three days.

JOSEPH SENDS HIS BROTHERS HOME

On the third day, Joseph came to them and said, "I fear God, so if you are honest men, I will keep one of you in prison while the rest of you return home with grain for your family. Then, the rest of you will bring your youngest brother to me so that I will believe that you are not spies. Otherwise, I will hunt you down and kill you!"

The brothers stepped back and whispered to each other, "We are guilty of what we did to Joseph. We saw how distressed he was, and when he begged for his life, we didn't listen. God is finally judging us for our sin."

Reuben said, "Didn't I tell you not to hurt the boy? Now comes the reckoning for his blood!"

Joseph was eavesdropping on their conversation, but they didn't realize that he understood them. Joseph turned aside and wept because he saw their grief over what they had done more than 20 years before. After he dried his eyes, he came back and put Simeon in chains in front of them.

Joseph gave orders to fill each man's sack with grain and return their money at the top of their bags. Then they loaded their donkeys and left. When they stopped to rest and feed their donkeys, one of them opened his sack and saw his money at the top. He told his brothers and all their hearts despaired; they said to each other, "What has God done to us?"

They continued home and told Jacob everything that had happened. They then emptied their sacks, saw that they had their money on top of the grain, and they were terrified.

Jacob was deeply grieved and said to them, "You have taken my children from me. Joseph is gone, Simeon is as good as dead, and now you want to take Benjamin from me? Everything is against me now."

Reuben tried to reassure his father, "If I don't bring Benjamin back, you can kill my two sons. Put him in my care; I will make sure he comes back to you."

But Jacob would not consent and said, "Benjamin is not going down there with you because his brother is dead and he is the only one of Rachel's children I have left. I would die from grief if anything happened to him."

CHAPTER TWENTY-ONE

JOSEPH REUNITES WITH HIS FAMILY

Genesis 43:1-45:15

A little more than a year later, the famine became worse, and Jacob's family ate all the food they had purchased in Egypt. Then Jacob said to his sons, "Go back to Egypt and buy a little more food for us."

Judah protested, "The man warned us that we could not see him again unless Benjamin was with us. If you send him with us, we will go, but if not, there's no point in our journey."

Jacob replied, "Why on earth would you mistreat me and tell him that you have another brother?"

His children answered, "He asked us specific questions about our family. He asked if you were alive and if we had another brother. How would we know that he would ask us to bring Benjamin?"

Judah said to his father, "Send the boy with me so that we can buy some food and not die. I guarantee his safety, and if I don't bring him back, you can blame me forever. If we hadn't been delaying, we could have already gone and returned twice by now."

Jacob finally relented, "If this is the way it must be, then take some gifts of the best things of the land, some balm, honey, gum, fragrances, and nuts. Take double the money so that you can pay him back for what happened last time; maybe it was just an oversight. Take Benjamin with you and buy food. May God grant you mercy when you stand before the Egyptian ruler so that Benjamin might return. If he dies, I guess that's what God has for me."

So, Joseph's brothers took the money, the gifts, and brother down to Egypt and stood before Joseph. When Joseph saw Benjamin with them, he ordered one of his servants to kill an animal so they could have a feast. Joseph's brothers were afraid when they heard they were bringing them to Joseph's house instead of a more neutral location. They said, "They are bringing us to his house because of what happened with the money. He will surely arrest us and take our donkeys in revenge."

When they arrived at Joseph's house, they spoke to his head servant, saying, "My lord, we previously came down to buy food, but when we stopped to rest, we each found that the full amount of our money was in our sacks' mouth. We don't know how it got there, but we have brought that money back along with additional money to buy more food."

The servant replied, "Peace be with you, do not be afraid. Your God has returned your money to you; my records show that I have everything from last time." Then the servant brought Simeon out. After washing their feet and feeding their donkeys, the brothers prepared their gifts for Joseph because they had heard they would have lunch with him.

When Joseph returned home, they brought him their presents and bowed to the ground before him. Joseph had them stand and asked, "How is your father? Is he still alive?"

They told him that Jacob was alive and well and then bowed to the ground again. Jacob looked at Benjamin and asked, "Is this your youngest brother? My son, may God be gracious to you." Then Joseph became overwhelmed with emotion and hurried out of the room so they would not see him weeping.

Once Joseph composed himself, he came back in and had his servants serve the meal. He sat by himself because Egyptians found it abominable to eat with foreigners. To his brothers' amazement, Joseph seated them from oldest to youngest and then gave Benjamin five times as much as the rest of them. Joseph's brothers were extremely relieved to have successfully brought Benjamin to Egypt, secured Simeon's release, and purchased food for their survival.

After they had eaten, Joseph told his servant to fill each man's sack with food and return their money at the top of the bag. He also instructed him to put his personal, silver cup in Benjamin's sack.

Joseph's eleven brothers loaded their donkeys and left at first light the next morning. Not long after they left, Joseph sent his head servant after them and told them to recover his silver cup from his brothers. The servant obeyed and stopped Joseph's brothers just outside the city.

The brothers were angry, "What are these false accusations? When we found the money from our first purchase, we brought it back along with a gift. There is no way that any of us would steal anything from your master. If you find the cup with anyone, that man will die, and the rest of us will become your servants!"

Joseph's servant said, "Whoever has the cup will die, but the rest will be free to go."

One by one, they lowered their sacks, starting with the oldest and continuing to the youngest until they came to Benjamin. They were very concerned when the servant found the money at the top of the sacks but distraught when the cup turned up in Benjamin's sack.

They all tore their clothes in grief and re-loaded their donkeys to return to the city. The short journey seemed to take forever, and when they arrived at Joseph's house, he was furious. He scolded his brothers, "How dare you try to steal from me! Don't you know that a man like me can practice divination? Did you think you could get away with this?!"

Judah had sworn to bring back Benjamin safely and spoke up, "What can we say? How can we defend ourselves? God has judged our guilt, and now we will all be your servants, including the one who stole the cup."

Joseph replied, "I would never punish all of you for one man's sin. The one who stole the cup will stay as my servant, but the rest can return to your father in peace."

Judah stood up and said, "Can I please speak to you in private without you getting angry because you have Pharaoh's power? You asked us if we had a father or another brother, and we told you the truth about our family. We told you that our youngest brother had stayed at home with his father because his brother had died. You said that we had to bring our brother down to you to prove we weren't spies.

"We went home and relayed your words to our father, and he was furious we told you about our brother. We told him we could not appear before you again without bringing him with us, and he said that if we didn't bring him back safely, he would die from grief. We ran out of the food we originally purchased and returned because we were starving. I swore with my own life that I would bring Benjamin back safely. Please let me stay in his place because I don't know what will happen to my father if his youngest son doesn't come home safely."

Joseph could no longer control himself and he ordered all his servants to leave the room. Then he wept so loudly that even those outside his house could hear. He revealed himself to his brothers and said, "It's me, Joseph! Is my father still alive?"

His brothers were speechless when they realized who he was. Joseph approached them and said, "I am your brother Joseph, the one you sold into slavery. Don't be distressed or angry with yourselves because God put me here to save your lives. The famine has been going on for two years, but there are still another five years with neither plowing nor harvest. God sent me here, not you, to preserve our family and allow us to survive. He has caused me to become the ruler of Egypt.

"Hurry home and tell my father that I'm alive and that I have become the ruler of Egypt. All of you will move here to Goshen's fertile land where everyone can be close to me. I can take care of you so you will not die during the five years of famine that are still to come. You can see and believe that I'm your brother Joseph who is telling you this. Tell my father of all the glory and honor I have in Egypt, then move everything you have here."

Then he hugged Benjamin and they wept upon each other's necks. Joseph kissed his brothers and they spent time catching up on the years they had lost.

CHAPTER TWENTY-TWO

JACOB GOES TO EGYPT

Genesis 45:16-47:30

Pharaoh heard that Joseph had reunited with his brothers and was happy. Pharaoh said to Joseph, "Send your brothers home with food and invite them to move here to eat from the best of the land. Send them home with wagons so they can bring everything here; they will not have to worry about anything because they will have the best Egypt has to offer."

Joseph listened to Pharaoh and sent his brothers home with wagons and changes of clothes. But he gave Benjamin 300 pieces of silver and five changes of clothes. Joseph sent them back with wagons and ten donkeys loaded with food and ten more loaded with the best Egypt had to offer. As he sent them away, he told them not to argue with each other but to go home and come back to Egypt quickly.

The eleven brothers went home to Jacob and told him Joseph was alive and had become Egypt's ruler. Jacob was in shock at the news, and at first, he did not believe his sons. But once they showed him everything they had brought back from Egypt and recounted what happened, he perked up and said, "It is enough that Joseph is alive; I will go down to Egypt and see him one more time before I die."

Jacob packed up everything he owned and started the journey to Egypt. On the way, he stopped at Beersheba, a place with spiritual significance to his family, and offered sacrifices to God. That night God came to Jacob in a vision and said, "Jacob, I am the God of your father, do not be afraid to go down to Egypt, because I will make you into a great nation there. I will go to Egypt with you, and I will also bring you back from Egypt; Joseph will close your eyes when you die."

The next morning, they continued the journey to Egypt, carrying everything they owned in Pharaoh's wagons. By this time, Jacob's sons had had children of their own, and a total of 70 people moved to Egypt with him.

Since Judah had stepped into a role of authority by pledging himself for Benjamin's life, Jacob sent him ahead so Joseph could show them the way to Goshen. When Joseph and his father saw each other, they ran to embrace, and wept on each other's necks for quite a while. Then Jacob said, "Now I can die because I have seen your face and I know you are alive."

Joseph told his brothers, "I will go tell Pharaoh that you have arrived. When he brings you before him and asks what your occupation is, tell him that you are livestock herders, and he will allow you to live here in Goshen because they find foreign shepherds detestable."

Joseph brought five of his brothers before Pharaoh and said, "My father and brothers have come from Canaan with their flocks, herds, and everything they own. They are currently staying in Goshen."

Pharaoh said to Joseph, "Your family has come to be with you; all Egypt is before you, settle wherever you like. Goshen is some of the best land we have for livestock, so that is a good place. Let me know if any of them are particularly skilled, and I will put them in charge of the Egyptian flocks and herds."

Joseph brought his father before Pharaoh and Pharaoh asked, "How old are you?"

Jacob replied, "I've lived for 130 painful years. I haven't come close to my fathers' lifespan, but I have seen more than enough evil." Then Jacob blessed Pharaoh.

Joseph settled his father and brothers in Goshen, just as Pharaoh had commanded. Joseph made sure his family had more than enough from all the storehouses to survive the famine.

The famine became worse until there was no food in Egypt or Canaan, except what Joseph had gathered. The people brought money to buy food until Joseph had collected all the money in Egypt and Canaan, and Joseph brought it into Pharaoh's treasury. Then the people came to Joseph and said, "Give us food because we are out of money."

Joseph told them to bring their livestock in exchange for food if they were out of money. They brought their horses, donkeys, herds, and flocks so they could eat for the next year.

The following year, the famine continued, and the people came to Joseph saying, "We have spent our money and our livestock is gone. All we have left is our land and our bodies. Why should we starve to death? Give us food to eat; in exchange, we will give you our land and become Pharaoh's servants."

Thus, Joseph obtained all the land of Egypt for Pharaoh, and all the people became the king's servants. Then Joseph said to the people, "I have purchased you and your land for Pharaoh. Now I will give you seed so you can plant and eventually reap a harvest. Then you will give Pharaoh a fifth of your harvest and keep the rest for food and seed for the following year."

The people said, "You have saved our lives; we will gladly serve Pharaoh." So, Joseph made a law establishing a tax on the Egyptians. Only the priests were exempt from paying.

The Israelites settled in Goshen and they became very fruitful and multiplied greatly. Jacob lived in the land for 17 more years before he died at 147. Before he passed away, Jacob called Joseph to himself and made him swear he would not bury him in Egypt but would take his bones and bury them with Abraham and Isaac.

CHAPTER TWENTY-THREE

JACOB'S DEATH
Genesis 48-50

Not long after, Jacob was on his deathbed, so Joseph brought his sons Manasseh and Ephraim to see their grandfather. Jacob summoned his strength, sat up in bed, and said to Joseph, "The Almighty God appeared to me in Canaan and blessed me. He told me that he would make me fruitful and multiply me until my offspring was a company, and he would give my descendants the land where I lived as a permanent possession. I am claiming your two sons as mine, just as Reuben and Simeon are my children. They will have the same place in the inheritance I leave as your brothers. The children you had after them will be your children and take the same place of inheritance as Manasseh and Ephraim's children." This caused Manasseh and Ephraim to become half tribes of Israel. Jacob did this to give Joseph an even more prominent inheritance.

Jacob was going blind and could not tell who Joseph's children were as they came near to receive a blessing. He hugged and kissed each of them and then said to Joseph, "I never expected to see your face again, but now God has allowed me to see your children."

Joseph bowed himself to the ground and then placed his older son, Manasseh, by Jacob's right (favored) hand and his younger son, Ephraim, by his left hand. Jacob crossed his hands as he stretched out his arms, putting the younger before the older. Then Jacob blessed them, "May the God of my fathers Abraham and Isaac, the God who has been my shepherd and the angel who has redeemed from evil bless these boys. May the Lord carry on my name through them, and may God fulfill his promise to Abraham, Isaac, and myself."

Joseph was displeased when he saw that his father had crossed his hands and tried to switch them so his right hand would be on his firstborn's head. But Jacob refused and said, "I know my son, I know. Manasseh will father a great people, but his younger brother will become greater and have a multitude of offspring." Thus, he put Ephraim ahead of Manasseh.

Jacob said to Joseph, "I am about to die, but God will be with you and bring you to the land of your fathers. I am giving you the town of Shechem as a possession, as opposed to your brothers because they took it by force."

Jacob gathered his sons and said, "Come together so that I can tell you what will happen in days to come:

"Reuben, you are my firstborn, my strength, preeminent in dignity and power. But you are as unstable as water and you will not be first because you defiled your father's bed by sleeping with Bilhah.

"Simeon and Levi are kindred spirits who use their swords for violence. I would never take their council and they will not share my glory because they killed men out of anger. May God curse their fierce anger and cruel wrath. He will divide and scatter their offspring amongst their brothers.

"Judah is a lion's cub who has risen from his prey and then crouched down in readiness. Who would dare to rouse him? The scepter will not leave his family, and the ruler's staff will be between his feet. The people will obey and pay tribute to him. He has made his clothes a dark purple, the color of royalty, by washing them in wine and the blood of grapes. He is handsome, his eyes are darker than wine, and his teeth are whiter than milk.

"Zebulun will dwell by the seashore and be a haven for ships.

"Issachar is like a strong donkey between the safety of sheepfolds. He saw a good resting place in a pleasant land and went to work as a servant at forced labor.

"Dan will judge his people as one of the tribes of Israel. He will be like a serpent by the path who bites at the horse's heels so its rider falls backward. Lord, I pray you save him.

"Foreigners will raid Gad, but he will raid at their heels.

"Asher will have rich food and yield royal delicacies.

"Naphtali is a wild and free doe who bears beautiful fawns.

"Joseph is a fruitful tree by a river with branches running over a wall. People attacked and harassed him, yet he remained unmoved. God made his arms agile and will bless him in every way. His blessings will be greater than his fathers'. May God bless Joseph, the one God set apart from his brothers.

"Benjamin is a ravenous wolf who devours his prey in the morning and divides the spoil in the evening."

After blessing his children, he commanded them, "I am about to die, bury me in the cave Abraham purchased from Ephron in Canaan. Abraham and Sarah are buried there along with Isaac, Rebekah, and Leah." Then he laid down in bed and died.

Joseph fell on his father's body, weeping and kissing him. Joseph commanded his servants to embalm his father and the physicians spent 40 days completing the process.

All Egypt mourned Jacob's death for 70 days, and when that time had been completed, Joseph asked Pharaoh if he could leave to bury his father in the cave that Jacob had instructed.

Pharaoh answered, "Go, bury your father in your ancestors' tomb."

Many Egyptian servants and elders went with Joseph and his brothers to bury Jacob, leaving their adult children and the flocks behind. When they came near the burial site, they stopped and grieved for Jacob for seven days. Then Joseph and his brothers buried their father as he had commanded and returned to Egypt.

After Jacob died, Joseph's brothers were afraid that Joseph had been waiting for their father's death to pay them back for the evil they had done in their youth. So, they sent a false message that Jacob had commanded Joseph to forgive his brothers for the wrong they had done nearly 40 years before.

His brothers fell on their knees before him as they delivered this lie and it made Joseph weep. He said to them, "Do not be afraid; I am not God. What you meant for evil, the Lord used for good so our family could survive and flourish. Do not be frightened; I will provide for you and your children."

***

Jacob's children stayed in Egypt after his death. Joseph lived to the age of 110 and saw many of his offspring before his death. Before he died, he spoke to his brothers, "I am about to die, but God will visit your descendants and bring you out of Egypt to the land he promised to Abraham, Isaac, and Jacob. Embalm me here, but when God brings you out of Egypt, take my bones with you." Then Joseph died.

CHAPTER TWENTY-FOUR

MOSES' BIRTH

Exodus 1-2

Eventually, an Egyptian ruler came to power who did not know Joseph or remember how he had saved them. He said to his people, "There are too many Israelites and they have become too powerful. We need to deal with this situation, or else they will keep multiplying; if we go to war, they might join our enemies and escape." The Egyptians set bosses over the Israelites and afflicted them with the most strenuous labor and heaviest burdens. The Israelites built the store cities of Pithom and Ramses and completed many other works for the king.

But the more the Egyptians oppressed the Israelites, the more they multiplied and spread out in the land. The Egyptians were afraid of the Israelites, so they made them work as slaves. They forced them to build with brick and mortar and labor in their fields.

The king commanded the Hebrew midwives to kill any boy who was born but let the girls live in hopes of neutering Israel's strength. But the midwives refused to follow the order and told the king, "The Hebrew women are not like Egyptians; they have short labors and give birth before we arrive."

God was kind to the midwives, and the Israelites multiplied, becoming very strong. The king was angry at the midwives' disobedience, so he commanded the entire nation to throw all Hebrew boys into the Nile and let the girls live.

A Levite couple had a baby boy, but they were unwilling to throw the child into the Nile, so they hid him for three months. When they could no longer keep their child a secret, his mother made a basket of reeds and covered it with pitch and tar so it would float. Then she put her son in the basket and placed it in the Nile while his sister watched from a distance to see what would happen to her newborn brother.

Pharaoh's daughter came down to the water to bathe while her young women walked along the river bank. She saw the basket floating amongst the reeds and sent one of her servants to retrieve it. Her heart melted when she saw the baby boy and heard him crying. She took pity on him and said, "This is one of the Hebrew children who has been thrown into the river."

The boy's sister saw her brother's basket retrieved from the river, so she approached and asked, "Should I find a Hebrew woman to nurse the baby?"

Pharaoh's daughter approved, and the girl went to get her mother so she could nurse her own child. Pharaoh's daughter promised to pay her to nurse the child and his mother could be with him during childhood. When he grew up, she brought him to court, and Pharaoh's daughter named the boy Moses because she had drawn him out of the water.

MOSES FLEES TO MIDIAN

As a grown-up, Moses observed how the Egyptians mistreated his people and saw an Egyptian beating one of his fellow Hebrews. Moses was outraged, and when he thought no one was watching, he killed the Egyptian and buried the body in the sand.

The next day, he went out and saw two of his countrymen arguing and tried to intervene. One of the men said, "Who made you a prince and judge over us? Are you going to kill me like you did the Egyptian?"

Moses was afraid because he realized his actions had become public knowledge. When the king heard about it, he tried to kill Moses. But the Hebrew fled to Midian and sat down by a well.

A Midianite priest named Jethro had seven daughters who watched his sheep and they came to the well to water the flock. Some of the region's other shepherds drove them away from the well because they didn't like the competition for the limited resources. When Moses saw this, he stood up to intervene and watered the priest's flock.

When the girls came home, their father asked how they had returned so quickly from their day's work. They told him about Moses standing up on their behalf and their father asked, "Where is he? Why did you leave him behind? Go get him so that he can eat with us."

Moses stayed with the Midianite priest and helped tend his flocks. Eventually, he married one of his daughters, Zipporah, and she gave birth to a son that he named Gershom.

After a time, the king of Egypt died, and the people cried out to God for deliverance from slavery. God heard their cry, and he remembered his promise to Abraham, Isaac, and Joseph.

CHAPTER TWENTY-FIVE

GOD CALLS MOSES
Exodus 3-4

While tending his father-in-law's sheep, Moses came to Horeb, God's mountain. There he saw a bush that was on fire but was not consumed. Moses was intrigued and went to see what was happening. God called to Moses from the burning bush, and Moses said, "Here I am."

Then God said, "Stay back and take off your sandals because you are standing on holy ground." He continued, "I am the God of your fathers Abraham, Isaac, and Jacob." Moses hid his face because he was afraid to look at God.

God said, "I have seen my people's affliction in Egypt and know their suffering. I have come to deliver them out of the Egyptians' hands and into Canaan, a fertile land filled with good things. I have heard the Israelites' cry because of the Egyptians' oppression. I am sending you to Pharaoh so I can bring my children out of Egypt."

Moses replied, "Who am I that I should lead Israel out of Egypt?"

God answered, "I will be with you, and when you have brought the people out of Egypt, you will return to this mountain to serve me."

Moses objected, "If I tell the people that the God of our fathers has sent me to deliver them and they ask me your name, what should I say?"

God answered, "I AM WHO I AM. Tell them that I AM sent you. Tell the people the God of Abraham, Isaac, and Jacob has sent you. I AM is my name forever and all generations will remember it. Gather the elders of Israel and tell them that I have seen how they have treated you, and I promise to bring you out of Egypt and into the land of Canaan.

> **God's name**
>
> God reveals himself in many ways throughout the Bible, but here he gives his proper name. However, we don't know the exact name because the Jews would not speak or write his name out of reverence. Whenever they wrote God's proper name, they would only write the consonants YHWH. It is much like writing G-d instead of God. To make it readable, they would write the letters from another of his names, Adonai, and we would have YaHoWaH. This gives us the names Jehovah or Yahweh.

"They will listen, and then you and the elders of Israel will tell Pharaoh that I have commanded that my people go into the wilderness and offer sacrifices to me. But the king of Egypt will not let you go unless he is compelled by a mighty hand, so I will stretch out my hand and strike them with miraculous signs, and then they will let you go. I will also give you favor in the Egyptian's sight so you will not leave empty-handed. Each of you will ask your Egyptian neighbors for jewelry and clothing; thus, you will plunder your captors."

Moses was doubtful and said, "But they will tell me that they don't believe me and argue that the Lord has not appeared to me."

God said to him, "Take the staff in your hand and throw it on the ground." Moses obeyed, and his staff became a serpent. Moses ran away in fear.

God calmed Moses down and told him to grab the serpent by the tail, and when he did, it became a staff again. Then God said, "This will be a sign that the God of Abraham, Isaac, and Jacob has appeared to you."

God commanded Moses to put his hand inside his cloak, and when he took it back out, it was white with leprosy. God told him to put it back inside his cloak, and when he pulled it out, it had returned to normal. Then God said, "If they do not believe the first sign, show them the second, and they will believe you. If they still do not believe you, take some water from the Nile, pour it on the ground, and it will turn into blood."

Moses was still unsure about his mission, so he protested, "I have never been good with words, my speech is slow, and I stutter."

God replied, "Aren't I the one who made your mouth and tongue? Aren't I the one who makes people blind or able to see, deaf, or hear? Go, and I will be with you and give you the words to speak."

Moses was out of excuses and begged, "Lord, please send someone else!"

God's patience was exhausted and he became angry, "Your brother, Aaron is a Levite, and he speaks well. He is on his way to meet you, and when he sees you, he will be overjoyed. You will speak to him and he will be your mouthpiece. I will show both of you what to do and he will speak to the people. Now, take your staff and return to Egypt!"

Moses returned home and told his father-in-law, Jethro, about his meeting with God and asked him to let him go back to Egypt. Jethro blessed Moses and told him to return. Then God said, "Go back to Egypt because the men who wanted to kill you are dead."

Moses took his wife and sons, loaded them onto donkeys, and began the journey back to Egypt. God told Moses, "Go to Pharaoh and perform the signs I have shown you, but I will harden his heart, and he will not allow my people to leave Egypt. Tell him that Israel is my firstborn and that they need to leave to serve me, and if he does not allow my son to leave, then I will kill his firstborn son."

On their return to Egypt, they camped for the night, and God became angry with Moses because he had not circumcised his sons as God had commanded Abraham and his offspring to do. So, Zipporah circumcised his sons with a flint knife, threw their foreskins at Moses' feet, and called him a "husband of blood."

God told Aaron to meet Moses at Mount Horeb, and when they met, Moses kissed his brother and told him everything God had commanded. So, they met with the elders of Israel, and Aaron relayed God's words while Moses showed them the signs that God had given him. The people believed Moses, and when they realized that God had seen their affliction and was preparing to deliver them, they bowed their heads and worshiped.

CHAPTER TWENTY-SIX

MOSES WITH PHARAOH

Exodus 5:1-7:13

When Moses was 80 and Aaron was 83, they went to speak with Pharaoh and said, "The Lord has commanded you to let his people go so that they may have a feast in the wilderness."

Egypt believed in many gods and spirits, so Pharaoh was flippant, "Who is the Lord? Why should I obey him and let Israel go? I do not know your God and I will not let Israel go."

Then they replied, "The God of the Hebrews has met with us, please let us go three days into the wilderness so we may offer him sacrifices, or he may judge us with disease and the sword."

Pharaoh was not swayed and said, "Why are you taking the people away from their work? Get back to your burdens. You people have become numerous and now you are trying to take them away from their jobs!"

He commanded their supervisors, "The Israelites are getting lazy and want a break to worship their God! Don't give them straw for their bricks anymore; make them gather it on their own. But you will still require the same amount of work from them as you have previously. We will break them of their laziness!"

The supervisors went to the Israelites and told them they would no longer receive straw for their bricks, but they must still produce the same amount as before. So, the Israelites scattered throughout the land, searching for stubble to replace the straw they were no longer receiving.

When their production dropped, Pharaoh was angry, and he had the Israelite foremen beaten and scolded for not completing the same amount of work as before. Then they cried out to Pharaoh, "Why are you treating us this way? There is no way for us to complete the same amount of work if you aren't going to give us straw for bricks. This is all your fault!"

But Pharaoh did not budge and said, "You are all lazy! That is why you want to go into the wilderness to worship your 'God!' You will not get any straw, but you still need to make the same number of bricks as you did before!"

The Israelite leaders realized they were in trouble and went out to Moses and Aaron, who were waiting for them, and said, "May God judge you for this! Now Pharaoh hates us and will eventually kill us because we cannot possibly match our earlier production!"

Moses turned to God and yelled, "Lord, why have you done this to your people? Why did you send me on this fruitless errand? Ever since I came to speak to Pharaoh in your name, things have only gotten worse; you have not delivered your people!"

God was patient with Moses and said, "Now you will see what I am going to do with Pharaoh; eventually, he will drive you out of the land with a strong hand. I am the Lord, I appeared to Abraham, Isaac, and Jacob as God, but I did not reveal myself as the Lord until now. I established my covenant with them in the land of Canaan, and now I have heard the cries of my people and will remember my promises to them. Tell the people I will bring them out from under the Egyptians' thumb; I will deliver them from slavery and redeem them with my outstretched arm and judgment. I will take you to the Promised Land, you will be my people, and I will be your God."

Moses relayed God's words to the Israelites, but they didn't want to hear it because their spirits were broken from their harsh slavery. The Lord told Moses to go back in to demand Pharaoh let his people go, but Moses protested, "My people haven't listened to me; why on earth would Pharaoh listen?"

But God spoke to Moses and Aaron and commanded them to talk to Pharaoh again, saying, "I have made you like God to Pharaoh, and Aaron is your prophet. Tell Pharaoh everything that I tell you and demand he let my people go. But I will harden Pharaoh's heart, and even though I do signs and wonders in the land, he will not listen. Then I will judge Egypt and they will know I am the Lord. Then I will bring my people out of the land."

Who hardened Pharaoh's heart?

God used Pharaoh as a tool to show his glory to the Egyptians and the Israelites. Some have complained it seems like Pharaoh did not have a choice because God hardened his heart. But it is essential to realize that God does not cause the initial hardening of people's hearts but allows their free will. He may cause subsequent hardening of the heart and use it for his purposes, but we make the first step.

Moses and Aaron obeyed, and they went in to speak with Pharaoh, but the king said, "Prove yourselves and show me a sign." Then Aaron threw down his staff and it became a serpent. Pharaoh summoned his sorcerers and magicians, and they did the same thing with their dark arts and demonic power. But Aaron's staff swallowed theirs whole, showing that God's power was much greater than the Egyptian's. Yet Pharaoh still refused to listen, just as God had said.

CHAPTER TWENTY-SEVEN

PLAGUES ONE THROUGH THREE
Exodus 7:14-8:19

The Egyptians were very religious people, and they worshiped many gods and spirits. They had magicians and sorcerers who used dark arts and demonic power to perform miraculous signs and control the world around them. Pharaoh dismissed the Almighty God as an unknown deity and did not recognize his authority when commanded to release the Israelites. God used this opportunity to show his power to the Egyptians and his superiority to their gods.

God said to Moses, "Pharaoh's heart is hard and he has refused to release my people. Go out to meet him as he is getting water from the Nile. Say that I have commanded him to let my people go and he has not obeyed. Then take the staff in your hand, strike the Nile with it, and it will turn to blood. All the fish in the Nile will die, the river will stink, and the Egyptians will be unable to drink from it. By this sign, Pharaoh will know that I am the Lord!"

The next morning, Moses and Aaron did as God commanded. Aaron stretched out his staff over the waters of Egypt, Moses struck the river with his staff, and all the waters of Egypt became blood. All the rivers, canals, ponds, and pools of water turned to blood and became unusable. All the fish in the rivers died and a great stench settled over the city.

But Pharaoh's magicians could do something similar with their spells and incantations, so he was not convinced. The Egyptians had to dig to find water because they could not use the water in the river. This first plague lasted seven days and was a judgment against the Egyptian god of the Nile, Hapi. The Nile provided life for Egypt, and God showed that he was more powerful than Hapi and had authority over him.

Then God said, "Go to Pharaoh and tell him that I said to let my people go so they can serve me. If he refuses to let you go, I will plague all of Egypt with frogs. I will cause the Nile to bring forth so many frogs that they fill your homes, bedrooms, and even mixing bowls."

Moses and Aaron went in to speak with Pharaoh, and once again, he refused their request. Then God told Aaron to stretch out his staff over Egypt and make frogs come forward from all the rivers, canals, and pools of water. Aaron obeyed and frogs came forth from every source of water in Egypt. But Pharaoh's magicians were able to do the same thing with their demonic power.

After a couple of days of frogs covering the land, Pharaoh begged Moses and Aaron, "Please end this plague, take away the frogs, and I will let the Israelites go out to the desert and worship."

Moses said, "Let me know when you want it to end, and I will pray to the Lord; then, there will only be frogs left in the Nile."

Pharaoh thought for a moment and said, "Tomorrow morning."

Moses replied, "So you will know there is no one like our God; I will pray, and tomorrow morning the only frogs left will be in the Nile."

Then Moses and Aaron left Pharaoh and cried out to the Lord to end the plague. God listened and all the frogs covering the land died. The Egyptians cleaned up the land and stacked the dead frogs in great heaps until they could figure out what to do with them all. The land was filled with rotting frog carcasses; in some ways, this was worse than the plague of frogs. This plague was a judgment against the Egyptian goddess Heqet. The Egyptians believed she had power over fertility and childbirth.

When Pharaoh saw that the frogs were dead, he hardened his heart and refused to let the Israelites go.

Then God commanded Aaron to stretch out his staff and strike the dust of the earth. Aaron obeyed, and the dust became swarms of gnats covering everything both inside and out. People were constantly swatting at the swarming bugs, trying to see and breathe; everyone was miserable. Pharaoh's magicians tried to replicate this miracle, but they could not. They were terrified and told Pharaoh that this was God's finger that caused this plague. But Pharaoh hardened his heart and refused to let the Israelites leave to worship.

This plague was a judgment against the Egyptian god of the earth, Geb. The Egyptians believed he was the god of all snakes, caused earthquakes, and allowed crops to grow.

CHAPTER TWENTY-EIGHT

PLAGUES FOUR THROUGH SEVEN
Exodus 8:20-9:35

After a few days, the gnats became less severe, and God said to Moses, "In the morning when Pharaoh goes out to the Nile, tell him that I command him to let my people go. If he does not listen, I will send swarms of flies over the entire land. But I will set apart the land of Goshen where the Israelites live so that Pharaoh will know I am the Lord over the entire earth. This sign will happen tomorrow."

Pharaoh still refused to let the Israelites go, and the next morning, swarms of flies covered the land. These swarms were worse than the gnats. Pharaoh saw the plague of flies and said, "You may sacrifice to your God, but you must stay within Egypt."

Moses replied, "I don't think that will work because our sacrifices would be an abomination to the Egyptians and they would stone us to death. We must go three days' journey into the wilderness so we may worship without being disturbed."

Pharaoh relented, "Fine. You may go into the wilderness to worship, but please do not go very far. Pray to your God to take these flies away because we are miserable."

Moses replied, "I will pray as soon as I leave. Tomorrow morning all the flies will be gone and you will have relief. But do not cheat us and change your mind again!"

Moses did as he had said, and the next morning, all the flies were dead; there was not a single fly left in Egypt. This was a judgment against the Egyptian god Khepri, who the Egyptians believed was the god of creation, movement of the sun, and rebirth. He had the head of a fly and this plague showed God's superiority to this deity.

But once the flies were gone, Pharaoh hardened his heart and refused to let the Israelites go.

Then God said to Moses, "Go to Pharaoh and tell him that the Lord says to let his people go so they may serve me. If he refuses, I will cause a very severe plague to fall upon the Egyptian livestock. This will affect all the Egyptian horses, donkeys, camels, herds, and flocks. But, I will make a distinction between Egypt and Israel, and none of Israel's livestock will die."

Once again, Pharaoh refused, and the next morning God killed all the Egyptian livestock, but none of the Hebrew livestock died. This was a judgment against the Egyptian goddess of love and protection, Hathor, who was depicted with a cow's head.

But Pharaoh's heart remained hard and he would not allow the Israelites to go worship.

After the death of the livestock, God said to Moses and Aaron, "Take handfuls of ashes and soot from the fireplace and throw them in the air in Pharaoh's presence.

They will become a cloud of fine dust and cover the entire land, becoming painful sores and boils on all of the Egyptians and their remaining animals."

Moses and Aaron obeyed, and the outbreak of boils and sores was so bad that Pharaoh's magicians could not even stand in their presence. This plague was a judgment on Isis, the Egyptian goddess of medicine and peace.

But God hardened Pharaoh's heart and he would not allow the Israelites to go worship.

As the Egyptians suffered from the boils and sores, God said to Moses, "Present yourselves before Pharaoh tomorrow morning and tell him that I say to let my people go so they may serve me. If he does not listen, I will send all my plagues upon him and the Egyptians, so they will know there is no God like me in all the earth. By now, I could have destroyed them and wiped them from history. I have raised him up so everyone will see my power and proclaim my name in all the earth. Yet, he is still exalting himself against my people and will not let them go.

"At this time tomorrow, I will send hail upon the land as there has never been before. Now get all your livestock and people inside because everyone left outside will die in the storm." Everyone who feared the Lord brought their livestock in and locked their doors to be safe. But those who did not believe ignored the warning.

Then Moses stretched his hand out over the land and a cataclysmic thunder and hailstorm began that destroyed everything left outside. The hail destroyed every plant that had sprouted and severely damaged every tree, but there was no damage in Goshen, where the Israelites lived.

Pharaoh called in Moses and Aaron and said, "This time I have sinned against God; you are right, and we are wrong. Ask God to take the storm away, and I will let you go; I can't handle this any longer."

Moses said, "I will pray as soon as I leave and the storm will stop so that you know God is ruler over the earth. Even though you say these things, I know you do not yet fear God or believe me." This plague was a judgment against Nut, the Egyptian goddess of the sky.

Once Moses left, he prayed, and the storm stopped. When Pharaoh saw that the storm was over, he and his servants hardened their hearts, and they would not allow the Israelites to leave, just as Moses had said.

A little while later, God said to Moses, "Go speak to Pharaoh again, for I have hardened his heart so I may show the Egyptians my power. Then you will be able to tell these stories to your children and grandchildren about my glory."

Moses and Aaron went in to speak with Pharaoh and said, "God wants to know how long you will refuse to humble yourself before him. Let us go so we may serve him. If you continue to refuse, tomorrow God will bring a plague of locusts so thick that they will cover everything in the land. They will eat whatever the hail did not destroy; there will be so many, you won't even be able to see the ground. This will be the worst infestation of locusts in history."

When they left Pharaoh, his servants turned to him and said, "How long will these men be a snare for us? Let them go so they can serve their God. Don't you see that our land is ruined?"

So, Pharaoh called Moses and Aaron back and said, "You may go serve your God, but who will be leaving?"

Moses answered, "We will all be leaving and we are taking our livestock with us so we may worship."

Pharaoh replied, "May the Lord be with you if I ever let all of you go. You have some evil purpose in mind! You can take all the men with you, but everyone else must stay! Get out of my presence!"

CHAPTER TWENTY-NINE

PLAGUES EIGHT THROUGH TEN

Exodus 10-11

When they left, God said to Moses, "Stretch out your hand over Egypt so that the plague of locusts may come forth and destroy the land of Egypt."

Moses obeyed, and a strong east wind came up and blew all night. In the morning, the east wind brought the locusts, and there were so many that they covered the land and blocked out the sun. They ate everything the hail had not destroyed until there was nothing green left in Egypt.

Pharaoh was distraught and called for Moses and Aaron and said, "I have sinned against the Lord. Please plead with him to remove this plague from us." So, Moses prayed, and a strong west wind came and blew all the locusts out to the Red Sea until there were no locusts left in the land.

This was a judgment against the Egyptian god Seth, who was over storms and disorder. But God hardened Pharaoh's heart and he did not let the Israelites go.

God told Moses to stretch his hand over Egypt so that darkness so thick that people could feel it would cover Egypt. Moses obeyed and there was an inky blackness that covered the land for three days. Not even lamps would give forth any light and there was no difference between having one's eyes open or closed. But the Israelites had light where they lived. This was a judgment against Ra, the Egyptian sun god.

Then Pharaoh called for Moses and Aaron and said, "Go and serve your God, but you must leave your livestock behind."

Moses answered, "You are letting us go and offer sacrifices to the Lord; we must take our livestock with us. We are going to serve God, and we do not know what we will need until we get there."

But God hardened Pharaoh's heart and he would not release the Israelites. He said to Moses, "Get away from me and don't ever come back! If I ever see you again, I will kill you!"

Moses replied, "You're the one who said it; I will never see you again!"

Then God said, "I will bring one more plague on Pharaoh, then you will be able to leave. After this, he will drive you out of the land. Tell the Israelites to ask their Egyptian neighbors for silver and gold jewelry." The Lord gave the Israelites favor with their neighbors and the Egyptians gave them great wealth.

Then Moses said, "God says he will to go through Egypt around midnight and kill every firstborn in the land. From Pharaoh to the lowliest slave and even the firstborn of every animal. This will be the greatest tragedy to befall Egypt ever. But not even a dog will growl against an Israelite, so everyone will know that the Hebrews are my chosen people. Then the Egyptians will tell you to get out and never come back. But Pharaoh will not listen to you so that I may show my power in Egypt."

This was a judgment against Pharaoh himself, who people thought was a god and the highest power in Egypt. The Egyptians believed that he was the son of Ra, the most powerful god in Egypt. But Pharaoh's heart was still hard and he would not let the Israelites go.

Plague	**Egyptian deity**	**Notes**
Water to blood	Hapi, god of the Nile	Duplicated by the Egyptians, affected Israelites as well.
Frogs	Heqet, goddess of fertility and childbirth	Duplicated by the Egyptians, affected Israelites as well.
Gnats	Geb, god of snakes, earthquakes, and crops	Not duplicated by the Egyptians, affected Israelites as well.
Flies	Khepri, god of creation	First plague that did not affect Israelites. No further plagues affected them.
Death of livestock	Hathor, goddess of love and protection	
Boils	Isis, goddess of medicine and peace	
Hail	Nut, goddess of the sky	
Locusts	Seth, god of storms and disorder	
Darkness	Ra, god of the sun	
Death of firstborn	Pharaoh and all other Egyptian gods	Required blood on the doorposts.

CHAPTER THIRTY

LEAVING EGYPT
Exodus 12:1-15:21

Then the Lord said to Moses, "From now on, this will be the first month of the year. On the tenth day of this month, every man shall take a perfect, one-year-old male lamb from his livestock and sacrifice it to me. If the family is too small, they will join with their neighbors to make the sacrifice. When you sacrifice the lamb, put some of the blood on the doorposts of your front door. After roasting it, eat it with unleavened bread and bitter herbs. Do not leave any of it until morning. Eat quickly and be ready to leave this country because this is the Lord's Passover.

"Tonight, I am going to pass through Egypt and kill the firstborn in every house that does not have the blood on the doorposts. This is a memorial feast from now on and you will celebrate it every year. For seven days, you will eat unleavened bread to symbolize cleansing yourself from impurity. This is to be the Festival of Unleavened Bread to commemorate my bringing you out of Egypt."

Moses called all the elders of Israel together and gave them instructions for what to have the people do. He also told them to have the people stay in their houses after the meal so that God would not kill them. "In the future, you will tell your children about how God delivered us out of Egypt," Moses said.

At midnight, God struck down the firstborn of every man, woman, and animal in the houses that did not have the blood on the doorposts. There was a great cry throughout Egypt as they mourned their children. Pharaoh called Moses and Aaron to him and was despondent, "Take everyone and everything you have and leave."

The Egyptians were eager to have the Israelites leave because they were afraid they would all die. So, the people quickly prepared their meals as Moses had instructed. Then the people took all their belongings and animals, including the silver and gold the Egyptians had given them, and hurried out of Egypt. About 600,000 men (not counting the women or children) left Egypt and traveled from Ramses to Succoth.

> **Were there really that many Israelites?**
>
> The short answer is that we aren't sure. 600,000 is the number given by interpretation of the best manuscripts. However, there are theories about translation or errors in transcription that may mean far fewer people. The way numbers are written in ancient Hebrew can lead to confusion in understanding the original amount. I use the traditional interpretation throughout this book, although the actual amounts may be much lower. Either a large or small number does not change the text's meaning.

INTO THE WILDERNESS

After they left Egypt, Moses gathered the people together and reminded them of what God had done for them. He taught them the meaning of the Passover and how it was a reminder of God's deliverance from slavery in Egypt. He also commanded the people to consecrate every household's firstborn to the Lord to remind them of their rescue and Pharaoh's stubbornness. They had been there for 430 years and God was finally bringing them into the Promised Land.

> **What does it mean to consecrate the firstborn?**
>
> To consecrate their firstborn meant to set them aside for the Lord. This child represented their offspring, just as the first fruits of their harvest represented the entirety of it. This was a reminder to the Israelites that God was the source of their redemption.

When God led them out of Egypt, he did not take them directly to the Promised Land for fear that the people would lose heart once they saw war. Instead, God led them towards the Red Sea. He put a pillar of fire in front of them at night and a pillar of cloud by day to guide them. Moses also took Joseph's bones with him, just as Joseph's brothers had promised.

Then God said to Moses, "Take the people near the Red Sea and set up camp facing the water. I will harden Pharaoh's heart one last time and he will pursue you thinking the sea traps you. This will be the final way that I show my power over Pharaoh and Egypt."

When Pharaoh heard that the Israelites had left, he and his servants reconsidered, "Why did we let them go? Who is going to serve us now?" Then Pharaoh prepared his chariot and army and set out after the Israelites. They pursued them and caught up to them near the Red Sea.

When Pharaoh's army drew near, the Israelites panicked and cried out to Moses, "Did you bring us out here because there weren't enough graves in Egypt? Why on earth did you bring us out here? It would be much better for us to return to serve the Egyptians than to die out here in the wilderness."

Moses replied, "Do not be afraid, but stand strong and see how God will save you today. This is the last time you will ever see the Egyptians; God is going to fight for you and all you have to do is be silent."

Then God told Moses to have the people march towards the Red Sea and stretch his hand out over the waters. When Moses obeyed, a strong east wind began to blow, and it blew all night, pushing the waters apart so that the ground was dry between them. The angel of the Lord stood guard between the walls of water throughout the night as God made a path through the sea.

That night, the people walked into the midst of the sea on dry ground between the two walls of water. Pharaoh and his army pursued the Israelites into the sea but panicked when they saw the water towering above them. Their wheels clogged in the mud, and their horses became skittish and difficult to control. They instantly realized that God was fighting on behalf of Israel, and they tried to turn around.

God commanded Moses to stretch his hand over the waters again, and when he did, the waters returned to their usual place. All the Egyptians, their horses, and chariots were trapped beneath the sea. This is how God delivered the Israelites from the Egyptians and wiped out Pharaoh and his army. Israel saw God's power and believed in him and his servant Moses.

Moses was so inspired by these events that he burst forth in a song of praise to the Lord. He praised God for the miraculous deliverance and how he had defeated the mighty Egyptian army with wind and water. He worshiped God for his power, might, and holiness. Aaron's sister, Miriam, grabbed a tambourine and led the women in dancing and worship. All the people joined in and they praised God for what he had done.

POSSIBLE PATH OF THE EXODUS

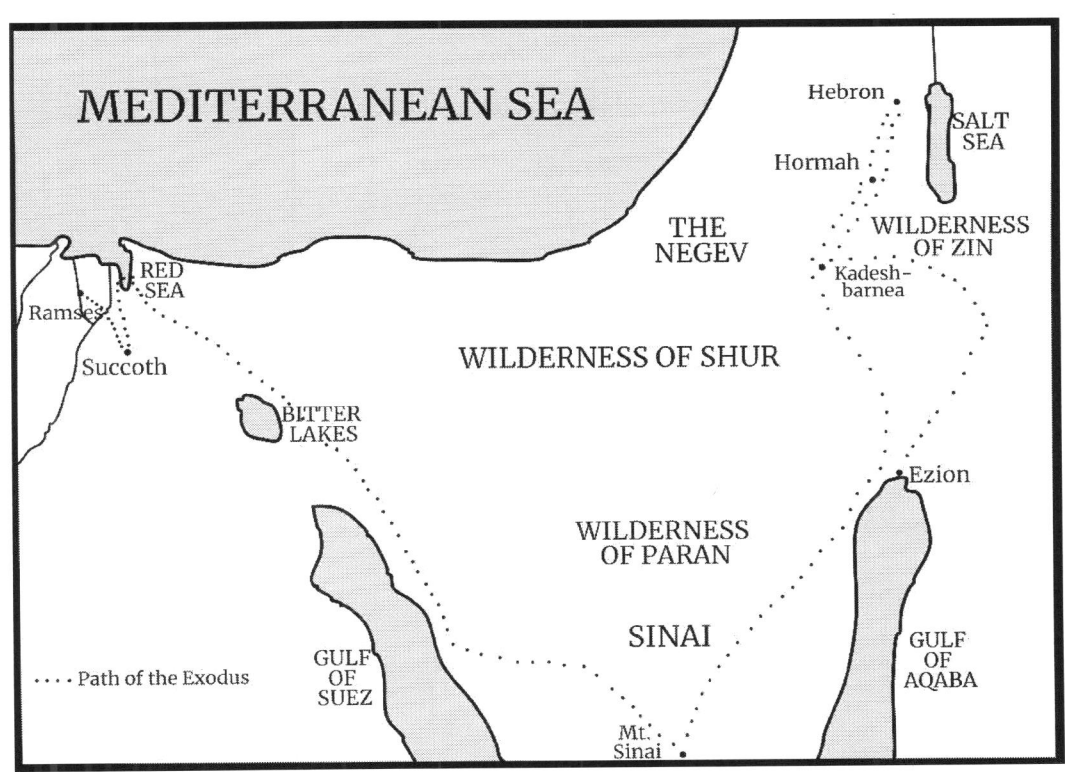

CHAPTER THIRTY-ONE

MANNA FROM HEAVEN
Exodus 15:22-16:36

The Israelites set out from the Red Sea into the wilderness and traveled for three days but couldn't find any water. Finally, they arrived at Marah but could not drink the water because it was bitter. The people grumbled against Moses and he cried out to God to provide them with drinkable water. The Lord showed Moses a log to throw into the spring, and when he obeyed, the water became sweet. There was nothing special about the log, but it symbolized God's intervention.

Then the Lord said to the people, "If you will diligently listen to me, and obey my commandments, then I will protect you from all of the Egyptians' diseases because I am your healer." They drank deeply before moving on to another place where they could find water.

The Israelites continued their slow journey into the wilderness, and a month after they left Egypt, the people started to complain, "It would have been better for us to die in Egypt where we could eat meat and bread until we were full. But now, Moses and Aaron have brought us out to this wilderness to starve to death!"

The Lord heard their complaints and said to Moses, "I am going to rain bread down on the people and I will test you to see if you will obey me. Gather only enough bread for the day, and on the sixth day, gather enough for the seventh day as well."

Moses and Aaron gathered the people and said, "Why are you grumbling about us? Aren't you really complaining about God? But God has heard you and will show you that he is the one who brought you out of Egypt. God said he will give you meat to eat in the evening and bread in the morning, so you will know he is the Lord."

That evening a flock of quail covered the camp, and in the morning, a fine, flaky bread covered the ground. The people were confused by the food on the ground. Moses told them it was the bread God had promised to give them. "God has commanded you to collect this bread each morning, enough for your household," Moses told them. "Eat whatever you gather each day and do not leave any of it as leftovers. Trust the Lord and know he will provide enough for you."

Everyone gathered the bread, and there was enough for everybody to eat and be satisfied. But some people did not listen to Moses. Having been hungry, they tried to save some for the next day because they did not trust that it would happen again. But the following day, it was rotten and filled with worms. Moses was angry with those who did not listen, and he told them to trust God to provide, not themselves.

On the sixth day of the week, Moses told the people, "Today, gather twice as much as usual and prepare it just as you normally would. Tomorrow is a holy day of rest, a Sabbath to the Lord. The double portion you gather and prepare will last an extra day and will not rot as it does on the other days." Some people obeyed, but many did not entirely trust Moses and went out on the seventh day to gather bread.

Then God said to Moses, "How long will you refuse to obey me?! I have given you the Sabbath to be a day of rest; that is why I gave you twice as much on the sixth day of the week. Everyone should rest and not leave their houses." This was the beginning of the Sabbath celebration.

> **What is the Sabbath?**
>
> The Sabbath was the Jewish day of religious observance from sundown Friday to Saturday evening. It was the seventh day and was a symbol of how God rested after creating the universe. The Sabbath was a day of rest so the people could focus on renewal and worship.

The Israelites called the bread that fell from heaven manna and it tasted like crackers with honey. Moses said, "God has told us to keep a day's portion in a jar as a memorial to remember what he fed us after he brought us out of Egypt." The Israelites ate the manna until they were able to enter the Promised Land.

CHAPTER THIRTY-TWO

WATER FROM THE ROCK AND JETHRO'S VISIT
Exodus 17-18

WATER FROM THE ROCK

The Israelites continued their journey into the wilderness and camped at Rephidim, but there was no water for them to drink. The people had still not learned that God would fulfill his promises, and again they accused Moses of bringing them out to the wilderness to die. Moses cried out to God, "Lord, what should I do? The people are ready to kill me!"

"Take some of the elders with you and go to the place I will show you," God replied. "Strike this rock with your staff and water will flow from it." Moses obeyed and the waters flowed.

One of the local nations came out to challenge the Israelites. They had not established any military yet, and Moses told Joshua, "Choose men to fight for us and I will stand on top of a nearby hill with God's staff in my hand."

Joshua led his men into battle while Moses stood with Aaron on top of the hill. Whenever Moses raised his hands, Israel would beat back their enemy, but their opponent prevailed whenever Moses dropped his hands. After a while, Moses tired, and they had him sit on a rock while others held his hands high. Therefore, Joshua and his men defeated their foes.

JETHRO VISITS MOSES

When the plagues in Egypt had become progressively worse, Moses had sent his wife and two sons to live with his father-in-law, Jethro, as a safety precaution. Jethro heard about how God delivered Moses and the Israelites from Egypt, so he brought Moses' family to rejoin them and find out how his son-in-law was doing.

At the joyous reunion, Moses recounted all that God had done for the Israelites. Jethro responded, "Praise the Lord, who has delivered you from the oppression of the Egyptians. Now I know that your God is greater than any other." Jethro offered a sacrifice to God.

The next day Moses sat down to judge the people and settle disputes, and anyone with a complaint gathered around him from morning until night. When Jethro saw all Moses was doing to manage the people, he said, "What on earth are you doing? Why do you sit here and let all the people mob you all day?"

Moses replied, "The people come to me to inquire of God. I settle their disputes and teach them about God's commandments."

"This is a horrible plan," Jethro explained. "There is no way that you can continue to work at this pace and expect to be effective. You cannot do this job alone; you are going to wear yourself out. You can still bring the people's cases to God, and you can still teach them, but you need to get some people to help with the little stuff. Look for wise, honest men who aren't susceptible to bribery and put them in charge of groups of anywhere between ten and 1,000, depending on their ability. They will still bring the weighty matters to you, but they can take care of the petty stuff."

Moses listened to his father-in-law and chose qualified men to be chiefs over different groups of the people. They decided most of the small cases, but anytime there was a thorny problem, they brought it to Moses. After Moses instituted this new hierarchy of leadership, Jethro returned home.

Battling burnout

It is easy to think that we are the only ones who can do things for God; it is essential to remember that he controls everything and will complete his purposes with or without us. Jesus even said that if his followers kept quiet, that the rocks and trees would cry out in worship to him. Moses wanted to serve the people as best he could, but he took on a far too large burden. We can rest in the knowledge that God wants to use us to accomplish his purposes, but it is not ours to bear alone. If we're going to be effective, we must rest and recharge, so we have the energy to work.

CHAPTER THIRTY-THREE

MOUNT SINAI

Exodus 19-31

About three months after the Israelites left Egypt, they camped in the wilderness in front of Mt. Sinai. Moses went up on the mountain and God said to him, "Remind the people of what I did in Egypt and how I brought you out of slavery. If they are willing to keep my commandments, then they will be my treasured possession in all the world because the earth belongs to me. You will be a kingdom of priests and a holy nation."

Moses called the elders to him and repeated God's words to them, and they said in unison, "We will do everything God has commanded us."

The Lord said to Moses, "Tell the people to consecrate themselves today and tomorrow. On the third day, I will come to Mt. Sinai in the sight of everyone. Tell the people to stay away from the mountain, because anyone who touches it will die. Then when they hear the trumpet blow, they will all come to the mountain." Moses went down from the mountain and had the people wash their clothes and consecrate themselves.

On the third day, there was thunder, lightning, a great cloud, and the sound of a trumpet. God descended on the mountain and smoke enveloped it because he came down with fire. As the trumpet blast grew louder and louder, the Lord called Moses up to the mountain, and he went. Then the Lord told Moses to keep the people back so that they wouldn't look at God and die. He also told him to make sure that the priests had consecrated themselves if they came forward. He then told Moses to bring Aaron up to the mountain.

Then God said, "I am the Lord God who brought you out of Egypt. I freed you from slavery because I love you. You will have no other gods; nothing should be more important in your life than me.

"You will not make any likeness or image of me because I am far greater than anything I created. You will not bow down to any created thing to serve or worship it because I am a jealous God. I will judge your great-grandchildren for your sin but will favor those who obey and serve me.

"You will not take my name in vain because I will pass judgment on those who do. Do not misrepresent me.

"Remember the Sabbath day and keep it holy. You may work for six days, but no one in your household should do any work on the seventh, not even your servants. I created the heavens and the earth in six days, and on the seventh day, I rested. When you were in slavery, you had to work every day, but now you are free; your life will not be all about work. Take a day to rest and worship me because I control everything; your labor will not accomplish what I can.

"Honor your father and mother all the days they are alive so you may live long in the Promised Land. Love them and do not dishonor them with how you live your life when you leave home.

"Do not commit murder, but value life and defend it whenever you can.

"Do not commit adultery, but value marriage, protect, and defend it.

"Do not steal, but earn what you have and protect others' rights to have what they have earned.

"Do not lie, but value the truth and fight to defend it.

"Do not spend your time focused on what others have or what you do not. Do not covet anything that your neighbor has that is not yours. Be satisfied with what I have given you and be grateful for the gifts I give."

When the people saw the lightning, smoke, and how the mountain shook, they were terrified and kept their distance from the mountain. Then they shouted up to Moses, "Tell us what God said to you; do not let him speak directly to us, so we don't die."

Moses answered, "Do not be afraid; God is showing you this display of power and might so you will learn to not sin against him."

Everyone stayed away from the mountain while God continued to speak to Moses. "Tell the people that they have seen how I speak to them from heaven. Reject the local practices of making gods out of silver and gold. Make an altar out of the earth and offer sacrifices to me on it. I will bless you in every place where people remember my name."

As the people waited below, God continued to give his commandments and laws to Moses on the mountain. Then Moses came down and shared what God had said to him. All the tribes said in unison, "We will do everything the Lord has commanded."

Moses wrote down everything God had told him and built an altar and twelve pillars to represent the twelve tribes of Israel, and offered animal sacrifices to the Lord. He kept half of the blood in a bowl and threw the other half on the altar. Then he read God's words to the people and they all said, "We will do everything that the Lord has commanded."

Moses sprinkled the rest of the animals' blood over the people as a sign of God's covenant and represented the animal dying in their place for the people's sin. Moses, Aaron, Nadab, Abihu, and 70 of the Israelite elders went up to the mountain and saw God. Underneath the Lord's feet, it seemed like the ground had become clear like a pure sapphire. Even though they saw God, they did not die because the Lord showed them mercy.

They ate and drank in God's presence, and then Moses and his servant, Joshua, went further up the mountain to receive God's commandments on tablets of stone. As he left the camp, he said, "Wait here for us to come back. Put Aaron and Hur in charge while I'm gone; they will settle any disputes."

The glory of the Lord stayed on Mt. Sinai for six days and a cloud covered the mountain. On the seventh day, God called Moses into the cloud, and he remained on the mountain for 40 days and nights.

While he was on the mountain, God gave him instructions to collect a freewill offering from the people to build a sanctuary for God's presence (the Tabernacle or Tent of Meeting). God gave him the dimensions and details for the ark of the covenant and some of the other holy items that would become a part of how the Israelites worshiped God. He also gave him commandments about how the people should prepare for worshiping and serving the Lord on stone tablets.

> **Where did all this all take place?**
>
> We are not sure exactly where all these events took place. There are many theories of where these things happened on the Sinai Peninsula. The exact location of events is not as important as our understanding of what happened. The map at the end of Chapter 30 is one possible interpretation.

CHAPTER THIRTY-FOUR

THE GOLDEN CALF
Exodus 32

When the people saw it was taking Moses a long time to come down from the mountain, they went to Aaron and said, "We have no idea what's happened to Moses, make us gods we can follow now that we have left Egypt."

Aaron told them to give him their gold jewelry and he fashioned it into a golden calf. Then he said to the people, "Israel! This is your god who brought you out of Egypt. Tomorrow we will have a feast to the Lord." Then he built an altar and offered sacrifices on it. The people sat down to eat their feast and then got up to sing and dance to the pagan god that Aaron had made.

Meanwhile, up on the mountain, the Lord said to Moses, "Go down to your people because they have corrupted themselves. They have turned away from my commands in virtually no time and have made a golden calf that they are claiming brought them out of Egypt. I should destroy these stubborn and rebellious people! Stand back so I can destroy them and then make a great nation out of you!"

Moses interceded for his people. "Lord, don't be so angry with the people you brought out of Egypt with your power. If you destroy them, the Egyptians will say that you brought them out of slavery with evil intentions. Remember your promise to Abraham, Isaac, and Jacob to make their descendants into a great nation. Hold back your burning anger and forgive the people for their sake." God listened to Moses and did not destroy the Israelites.

> **Does God change his mind?**
>
> This passage and others seem to indicate that God changed his mind, but this is not the case. The Bible is clear that he does not change his mind or his purposes. If he did, that would imply that he could improve or become worse. Either of these options means that he was not or is not the Ultimate Being. God always hates sin and is ready to judge it, but Moses' intercession restored the people to a right relationship with God. The fact that he relented from his anger is a change in the people, not in him or his intentions.

Moses turned and quickly descended the mountain with the stone tablets in his hands and Joshua at his side. God had written his Law on the front and back of the tablets with his finger. As they approached the camp, Joshua heard the noise of the people worshiping the idol and thought it was a war cry. But Moses corrected him and said that it was neither the cry of victory nor defeat, but the sound of singing.

Once they reached the camp, Moses saw the calf and the people dancing around it and was furious. He slammed the tablets on the ground and shattered them. Then he heated the calf and ground it into dust that he sprinkled across some water and made the people drink it. Then Moses turned to Aaron and said, "What did the people do to you that you have caused them to commit such a horrible sin?"

Aaron tried to defend himself. "Don't be mad at me; you know how the people are. They didn't know if you were dead or ever coming back, so I asked them for their gold, and I threw it in the fire. Then suddenly, a golden calf came out."

Moses saw that people were naked and running wild through the camp because Aaron had lost control. Then he went to the edge of camp and said, "Come to me if you are on the Lord's side!" The Levites gathered around him, and he told them to take their swords and kill those who were worshiping the golden calf. The Levites killed about 3,000 men that day. Their zeal for God was their ordination into service for the Lord.

The next day, Moses said to the people, "You have committed a very great sin, and now I will beg God for forgiveness." Moses went back up to the mountain and spoke to the Lord, "These people committed a great sin when they made this golden idol. Please forgive their sin, and if you are not willing to do so, please pass judgment on me in their place!"

God replied, "I will judge the one who sins against me. But now, lead my people to the Promised Land, and my angel will go before you and drive out all the local nations. But make no mistake, I will judge these people for their sin against me. Go up to a land flowing with everything good, but I will punish them for their sin when the time comes."

Then the Lord sent a plague on the people because of the calf that Aaron had made. The Israelites were alarmed because they feared for their lives heading into the Promised Land. The people all stripped off their ornaments from that moment until they entered the land.

CHAPTER THIRTY-FIVE

SECOND SET OF STONE TABLETS

Exodus 33-40

At that time, Moses would set up a sanctuary for God called the Tent of Meeting or Tabernacle outside the camp. Anyone who needed to seek the Lord would go there. They would line up outside and wait until Moses went into it. Once Moses entered the tent, the pillar of cloud would descend over it, and the Lord would speak with Moses. Whenever the people saw the pillar over the Tabernacle, they would all worship at their tents' door. At these times, the Lord would speak to Moses just as a man would talk to a friend. When Moses returned to the camp, his assistant, Joshua, would stay by the entrance.

Moses said to the Lord, "You have told me to take these people to the Promised Land, but you have not told me who I should take. If I have found favor in your sight, please teach me your ways so that I may teach them to your people that you have chosen."

God replied, "I will go with you, and you will have rest and peace."

Moses said, "If you don't go with me, please don't send me into the Promised Land. How else would I be able to lead these people and know that I have favor in your sight? Your presence is the only way that we will know we are your people and that you will grant us success."

God answered, "I will grant your request, and go before you into the Promised Land because you have found favor in my sight, and I know you by name."

Then Moses begged, "Please show me your glory!"

God replied, "I will go before you into the Promised Land and you will proclaim my goodness to everyone. I will be gracious to whom I will be gracious and show mercy to whom I will show mercy, but you cannot see my face. If you were to see me face to face, you would die because of my glory and holiness. However, there is a place where I will have you stand on a rock. When my glory passes by you, I will cover you with my hand until I have passed by, then you will see my back. But no one will be able to see my face and live."

Then God said to Moses, "Cut out two stone tablets like the original ones you destroyed. Then come up to meet me at the top of the mountain, and I will write my Law on them just as I did previously. Come by yourself and do not let any people or animals near, or they will die."

Moses obeyed and went up the mountain the next morning and the Lord descended just as before. He said to Moses, "I, the Lord God, am merciful and gracious, slow to anger, and full of steadfast love and faithfulness. I am loving to thousands; I forgive sin but will not overlook the guilty. I will judge their sins to their great-grandchildren."

Moses bowed to the ground in worship and said, "If I have found favor in your sight, please go with us into the Promised Land because we are a stubborn people. Forgive our sins and take us as your inheritance."

God said, "I am making a covenant with my people; I will perform miracles in your midst, unlike anything that has ever happened in history. All the people will marvel at what I do for you because it will be astounding.

"Be careful to obey me and I will drive out the local nations before you. But be careful not to make treaties with any of them, or else it will become a problem for you in the future. Destroy their altars and idols because you will not have any other gods besides me. Be careful not to adopt any of their practices or marry their women because they will cause your hearts to stray, and you will whore yourself out to their gods.

"Remember the Passover and celebrate the Feast of Unleavened Bread because it is a reminder of when I brought you out of Egypt. Every firstborn child and animal belong to me, and you must redeem it by sacrifice. Make sure that you keep the Sabbath, work for six days, but rest on the seventh. Whether it is during planting time or harvest, you will relax and do no work.

"You will keep all of the celebrations that I command you and three times a year, every male will present themselves before me. I will drive out the nations and no one will encroach upon your land if you obey me. You will also give me the first and best of all that you produce. Write down my commandments and obey them because I am making a covenant with Israel."

Moses was on the mountain for 40 days and nights and he did not eat or drink the entire time because God sustained him. Moses came down with the tablets God had written his commandments on and his face shone from being in the Lord's presence. He did not realize that his face was shining; everyone was afraid to come near him.

Moses called for them to come near, and eventually, people overcame their fear and gathered. Moses shared all the commandments God had given him. Then he put a veil over his face so that the people would not be afraid. Whenever Moses went to speak to the Lord, he would remove the covering and put it back on when he talked to the tribes.

God had Moses bring Aaron and his sons before the congregation. Moses washed them with water and dressed them in the priestly garments God had commanded. Moses anointed them with oil and consecrated them for service to the Lord. He offered the sacrifices God commanded, and Aaron and his sons were set apart as Israel's priests.

NADAB AND ABIHU

Aaron and his sons presented all the sacrifices God commanded on behalf of the people. But one day, Aaron's sons Nadab and Abihu offered incense that the Lord had not authorized. God was not pleased and he consumed them with fire in his presence.

Aaron stayed silent, afraid that God would consume him with fire as well. He appointed others to take his sons' places and urged the people not to mourn their death, or else they would die as well. He then warned the people that they must be careful to only worship in the way he commanded because he did not want the people to take on the worship practices of the Promised Land's inhabitants.

Once the people set up the Tabernacle, God's glory filled the tent, and Moses could not enter since God was there. Throughout all their journeys, whenever the cloud rose from the Tabernacle, the Israelites would set out, and they would stay put whenever the cloud did not rise from it. When God was there, a cloud filled the tent during the day and fire during the night, and the people were able to see it in the camp. Sometimes, God's presence stayed for a day, sometimes for months on end. Regardless of how long he remained, the Israelites stayed there with him.

CHAPTER THIRTY-SIX

FIRST PASSOVER IN THE WILDERNESS
Numbers 1-11

One year after the people had come out of Egypt, God commanded Moses to count everyone with him. There were a little more than 600,000 men in the census, and they carefully kept track of all the people so that they would know their genealogy and their place within Israel.

> **Were there really that many Israelites?**
>
> The Bible tells us that around 2,000,000 Israelites (including women and children) wandered in the wilderness, but we don't have any significant archaeological findings to support this. Because they were nomadic people, they did not spend a lot of time in one location and did not leave behind many artifacts. When people died, the Israelites buried them in shallow graves, and their remains could not stand against the elements and animals in the land. During their time in the wilderness, God also tells us that he did not allow their shoes to break or clothing to wear out. The Israelites did not leave many artifacts because they did not have much waste they needed to discard.

As the first anniversary in the wilderness approached, God commanded the Israelites to observe the Passover and commemorate how he delivered them from slavery. Some people could not keep the Passover at the appointed time because they were unclean, and God made provisions for them to observe it once they were clean.

After they had celebrated the Passover, God's presence lifted from the Tabernacle, and the people left Mount Sinai. Then the cloud settled in the wilderness of Paran. The people set out in the order that God commanded, with Judah leading. Moses invited his father-in-law to join them, but Jethro declined, opting to stay where he was.

Once the people arrived in Paran, some complained about the conditions and their misfortunes. God heard these complaints and became angry and burned some of the outskirts of the camp. Moses cried out on behalf of the people and the fire subsided.

God still provided manna for the people to eat, but they were ungrateful. The people cried out for meat to eat and began to reminisce about their days in Egypt when they had a great variety of food and meat whenever they wanted it.

Moses complained to God, "Why are you treating me this way? I thought I had favor in your sight, yet these people's complaints wear me out. I did not ask for this job and I did not sign up for this kind of grief! Where am I supposed to get enough meat to satisfy all these people? I cannot bear this burden, and if this is how it's going to be until we enter the Promised Land, then please kill me now, because I cannot take this!"

God said to Moses, "Appoint 70 men to be elders for the nation of Israel and bring them to the Tent of Meeting with you. I will still speak with you, but they will help bear the burden of leading Israel. Then tell the people to consecrate themselves because they will have an entire month's worth of meat tomorrow. They will have so much meat that it will be coming out of their nostrils, and they will be sick of it because they have rejected the Lord who brought them out of Egypt."

Moses answered, "Where am I going to get enough meat to feed 600,000 men, let alone all the women and children? Are we going to slaughter whole flocks of animals or take all the fish out of the sea? There is no way this is possible for one day, let alone an entire month!"

God replied, "Do I not have enough power to fulfill this promise? Now you will see whether or not I fulfill my promises!"

Moses obeyed the Lord and picked 70 men that he brought to the Tent of Meeting with him. God came to speak to Moses and he gave his spirit to the 70 elders. As soon as God's Spirit came upon them, they began to speak on God's behalf. Afterward, they did not continue to have the gift as Moses did.

There were two men Moses had appointed who did not come to the tent, but God still gave them his Spirit, and they began to speak on God's behalf in the camp. Joshua saw what was happening, and he begged Moses to stop them, but Moses said, "Don't be jealous for me; I wish that everyone had this gift!" Then Moses and the elders returned to the camp.

Then God caused a strong wind to bring countless quail and they fell about a day's journey to each side of the camp up to a depth of about six feet. The people spent the next two days gathering the quail and brought them back to camp. Some people were so excited about the meat that they did not wait to cook it. While they were eating the uncooked quail, God struck them with a great plague, and those who could not wait to eat meat died, and the Israelites buried them in the wilderness.

CHAPTER THIRTY-SEVEN

AARON AND MIRIAM'S JEALOUSY
Numbers 12

Not long after God sent the quails, Moses' sister (Miriam) and Aaron became jealous of Moses' leadership. They looked for ways to undermine him and began to publicly criticize the fact he married a foreign woman before God called him to deliver Israel from Egypt. Moses was a very humble man and did not respond to their accusations, but God heard their complaints and was not happy. He called the three of them out to the Tent of Meeting.

When they arrived, God descended in the pillar of cloud and called Aaron and Miriam to stand before him and said, "If there is a prophet among you, I will make myself known to that person in visions and dreams. But it is not this way with Moses because he has been faithful in everything. I speak to him clearly with my voice and he sees my form. Since this is the case, why weren't you afraid to speak against the man I chose to lead the people?" God became angry and left them.

When the cloud left the Tent of Meeting, Miriam became as white as snow with leprosy. Aaron begged Moses, "My Lord, please do not punish us because we have been foolish and sinned. Please do not let her become like one of the dead who has his flesh eaten away." Then Moses cried out to God for her healing.

But the Lord said to Moses, "If her father spit in her face, she would bear her shame for seven days. Let her be shut out of the camp for seven days; then she may return." Miriam was an outcast for seven days and the tribes waited to continue their travels until she was well.

CHAPTER THIRTY-EIGHT

SPYING ON CANAAN
Numbers 13-14; 15:32-36

Then the Lord said to Moses, "Send one man from each of the tribes to spy out the land I'm going to give you." So, Moses selected a chief from each tribe and sent them forth to see if the land was good, where people lived, and if they were strong. He told the spies to be courageous and to bring back some fruit from the land.

The spies went into the land for 40 days and returned with a single cluster of grapes so large they had to carry it on a pole between two men. All of the people gathered eagerly to hear their report and the spies said, "We saw a land filled with every good thing, and this is some of the fruit from it. However, the inhabitants are powerful and live in heavily fortified cities. The men were giants, and we looked like grasshoppers next to them!"

The Israelites were dismayed by this report, but a spy named Caleb spoke up, "We should go occupy the land at once! We will be able to take the land if God is with us!"

But the other spies said, "There is no way we can occupy the land because it will devour us; the people living there will destroy us."

That night, the entire congregation wept and grumbled about Moses and Aaron's leadership. "It would have been so much better for us to die in Egypt or the wilderness," they complained. "Why did God bring us here, where we will die by the sword, and our women and children will become prey? Wouldn't it be better for us to go back to Egypt?" Then they began to discuss amongst themselves who would be best to lead them back into slavery.

> **How did the Israelites forget so quickly?**
>
> It seems difficult to comprehend how quickly the Israelites could forget all God had done for them in the wilderness. We must remember that forgetfulness is a part of the human condition. We run into this problem as well. That's why it's essential for us to continually remind ourselves of what God has done in our lives. We should set up reminders of his goodness and think about the gospel often.

When Moses and Aaron heard these complaints, they fell on their faces before the crowd. Joshua and Caleb had spied out the land, and they joined their leaders on their faces. All four of them tore their clothes and spoke to the people, "The land before us is exceptional, and as God delights in us, he will bring us into this place filled with goodness. Please do not rebel against the Lord and do not be afraid of these people. God has removed their protection and he will deliver them into our hands!"

The people were furious, and they made a move to stone Joshua and Caleb to death. But God's glory covered them at the Tent of Meeting. God said to Moses, "How long will these people reject me? Despite all the signs I have done for them, they still don't trust me. I am going to strike them with pestilence and disown them so I can make you into an even greater nation!"

But Moses interceded on behalf of the tribes, "If you do that, then the Egyptians and the locals will hear about it and say you were not strong enough to deliver the land to us. Everyone around knows you are with us, and if you kill all the people, then all the nations will mock your name as weak. Please keep your promise to us that you are slow to anger and full of steadfast love. Forgive our sins once again, just like you have been doing since we left Egypt."

Then the Lord said, "I have forgiven the people's sin as you have asked. But not one of these people who have seen my power in Egypt and then have still tested me will see the Promised Land. Caleb and Joshua have followed me with all their hearts, and they will be the only ones of this generation to enter the Promised Land. Now take the people back into the wilderness because they are not ready to possess their inheritance."

"How long will you continue to complain about what God has done for you?" Moses exclaimed. "Because you have rejected the land the Lord wanted to give us, none of you will enter the Promised Land. Your children will be shepherds in the wilderness for the next 40 years until you have all died, then your children will be able to enter the land." Then God killed the spies who had brought back a bad report, but he allowed Joshua and Caleb to live.

When Moses told the people what God had said, they were sick at heart. The next morning, they prepared for battle and said, "Here we are! We are ready to enter the Promised Land and we are sorry we sinned."

"Why aren't you listening to what God said?" Moses shouted. "Don't try to enter the land because God is not going with you. You turned your back on him. If you go into battle without him, you will lose." The Israelites would not listen. When they went to fight with the local people, the Canaanites defeated them and chased them for miles.

✱✱✱

While they were in the wilderness, they found a man gathering sticks on the Sabbath, and they brought him before Moses and Aaron. They kept him in custody for a while because God had not commanded what they should do to someone who did not follow the Sabbath. Then the Lord said to Moses, "This man will be put to death so that you will know how serious I am about honoring the Sabbath. All the people will stone him to death outside the camp." The congregation took him outside the camp and stoned him to death, just as God had commanded.

CHAPTER THIRTY-NINE

KORAH'S REBELLION
Numbers 16-17

Eventually, one of the Levites named Korah, and two Reubenites named Dathan and Abiram gathered 250 chiefs and came against Moses and Aaron. Korah said, "You have gone too far! The entire nation has made itself holy and God is in our midst. So, why do you exalt yourself above us as if you were somehow better?"

Moses fell on his face in humility and said, "Tomorrow morning, the Lord will show us who is his and who is holy. He will choose who he wants to bring near to him. We will all burn incense before the Lord and he will show who his holy one is.

"You Levites have gone too far! Isn't it enough that God has set you apart for service in the Tabernacle? Now you want the priesthood too? You are not complaining about Aaron and me; you are complaining about God!"

Moses called for Dathan and Abiram to come up to him, but they refused, saying, "We aren't listening to anything you say. You brought us out of Egypt, a land full of plenty of good things, but now you want to act like a prince over us? You have not brought us into the Promised Land like you said you would. We are done with you!"

Moses was furious, and he told the Lord to disregard their offering because he had never taken anything from the people nor done them any harm. He said to Korah, "Make sure you and your people show up tomorrow with your incense ready."

The next morning, Korah and his people met Moses and Aaron at the Tent of Meeting, ready to burn incense to the Lord. Everyone assembled on one side, with Moses and Aaron on the other in a showdown. Suddenly, God's glory descended and appeared to everyone. God said to Moses, "Get far away from these people because I am about to destroy them!"

Moses and Aaron fell on their faces and pleaded, "Should all of Israel die because of a few men's sins?"

The Lord answered, "Fine, but tell everyone to get away from the homes of Korah, Dathan, and Abiram."

That day, people moved away from the tents where those families were staying. The family members of Korah, Dathan, and Abiram came out and stood in their doorways, defying Moses and the rest of the congregation. Moses said, "If you want proof that God has sent me, here it is. If these men live out the natural course of their lives, that means the Lord has not sent me and everything I'm doing is of my own accord. But, if God causes the earth to open and swallow them and everything they own, then you will know God has sent me."

As soon as Moses finished speaking, the earth opened and swallowed the men, their families, and everything they owned. Then the ground closed over the top of them, and everyone else fled from the site, afraid they would die as well. God sent fire and consumed the 250 men that Korah had brought together to burn incense.

God told Moses to take the plates for burning incense from the fire and hammer them into a bronze covering for the altar. He had decided that even though the men had used the plates for sin, God redeemed them and made them holy. This was also a reminder that only Aaron and his descendants could burn incense to the Lord.

The next day, the Israelites complained about Moses and Aaron, saying they had killed God's people. The people gathered against them by the Tent of Meeting, and the Lord's glory descended. Again, God said, "Move away from these people because I am going to destroy them!"

Moses and Aaron fell on their faces again, and Moses told Aaron to offer incense to atone for the people's sin quickly. Aaron did what Moses said and went to stand amidst the people because God had begun to strike them down. He stood between the dead and the living, and God stopped the killing. Nearly 15,000 died because of Korah's rebellion.

> **Why does God seem so angry in the Old Testament?**
>
> God is always the same. Some have characterized God as angry in the Old Testament and merciful in the New Testament, but this is inaccurate. God is always against sin and looks to be gracious to those who turn to him. God was merciful to all the Old Testament figures and did not destroy them for their sins. The fact that he did kill some people on multiple occasions is still consistent with his character throughout the Bible. Currently, he is patiently giving people time to repent, but when Jesus returns, he will destroy all his enemies.

Then God told Moses he would settle this debate about who he had chosen to lead Israel for the last time. He told Moses to take Aaron's staff and a staff from the leader of each of the twelve tribes. They each wrote their name on their staff and put them in the Tent of Meeting.

The next day Moses went into the tent, and Aaron's staff had sprouted buds, blossoms, and ripe almonds while the rest of the staffs remained the same. Everyone came forward and examined their staffs and saw that only Aaron's had changed. Then God told Moses, "Put Aaron's staff by the tent so it will remind the people not to complain so that I don't kill them."

The people came to Moses and said, "What are we supposed to do? Every time we come to the Lord, we die! We have nothing left, are we all going to perish?"

CHAPTER FORTY

MOSES' SIN AND THE BRONZE SERPENT

Numbers 20-21

MIRIAM'S DEATH AND MOSES' SIN

The tribes migrated into the wilderness of Zin, and while they were there, Miriam died, and the people buried her. Despite how God had provided in miraculous ways, the people began to complain about Moses and Aaron again when there wasn't any water for them to drink. "We wish we would have died with our brothers and sisters earlier," they grumbled. "It would have been better for us anywhere besides here! We could have stayed in Egypt instead of coming here, where we have no food or water!"

Once again, Moses and Aaron fell on their faces at the Tent of Meeting and begged the Lord for deliverance. The Lord appeared to them and said, "Assemble the congregation by the rock of Meribah and then strike it with your staff to bring forth water for you and your animals."

Moses took the staff from before the Lord and gathered the congregation before them at the rock of Meribah. He said to the people, "Listen to me, you rebels, we will bring water from the rock!" He struck the rock with his staff twice and water gushed out.

Moses took credit for the miracle as opposed to giving God the honor. God said to him, "Because you took credit for this miracle and did not uphold me as holy, then you will not have the privilege of bringing the Israelites into the Promised Land."

The tribes moved again. The Edomites were descendants of Esau and the Israelites' distant relatives. Moses asked for safe passage through their territory if they kept to the main highway.

Esau's descendants denied the Israelites' request and threatened war if they came anywhere near their land. The Israelites' responded, "Please let us pass through, and we will stick to the highway. If we take anything, whether it be food or water, we will pay for it." The answer was still no, and Esau's people came out with a large force to prevent them from entering their land. The Israelites were unprepared for war, so they turned away.

AARON'S DEATH

The Israelites journeyed onward from Kadesh and came to Mount Hor. While there, God said to Moses and Aaron, "Aaron is about to die and be buried because I will not allow him to enter the Promised Land because of the incident at Meribah. Bring Aaron and his son, Eliezer, to the mountain and dress Aaron in his holy garments. Then he will die and come to be with me." Moses obeyed, and the three men went to the top of Mount Hor together to complete the transfer of power. When only Moses and

Eliezer came back down, the people knew Aaron had died and wept for him for 30 days.

As they departed from Mount Hor, one of the Canaanite kings attacked them and took some prisoners of war. Furious, the Israelites swore that they would destroy every remnant of that nation once they established themselves in the Promised Land.

As the tribes traveled, they went out of their way to avoid the local nations that had begun to be unfriendly to the Israelites. Once again, the people complained, "Why did you bring us out from Egypt to die in the wilderness? We don't have any real food, just this worthless manna and no water!"

God was angry with their continued ingratitude, and he sent fiery serpents into their midst that bit and killed many. The people came to Moses and said, "We have sinned by complaining about you and the Lord; please pray for us to take these serpents away."

Moses prayed for leniency. "Make a fiery serpent from bronze and put it on top of a pole," God said. "Everyone who comes to look at the bronze serpent will live." Moses obeyed the Lord and told the people how they would survive the serpent bites.

ISRAEL AND THE AMORITES

Israel continued to wander through the wilderness and eventually came near the land of the Amorites and they requested to pass through just as they had asked the Edomites. Just as Esau's offspring refused Israel, so did the Amorites, and they came out to battle the Israelites. But this time, Israel prevailed, and they took possession of the Amorite lands, destroying their cities and overthrowing their government. The Israelites lived in that land for some time and expanded their territory bit by bit.

CHAPTER FORTY-ONE

BALAK SUMMONS BALAAM

Numbers 22:1-35

Israel camped in the plains of Moab, just beyond the Jordan River. Balak, the king of the land, saw what the Israelites had done to the Amorites and was terrified. He said to the Moabite elders, "The Israelites are going to eat us up like an ox eats the grass of a field." So, Balak sent for Balaam, a local holy man, to curse the Israelites.

Balak paid Balaam to curse the Israelites and said, "Come stay with us and then say whatever God says to you."

That night God came to Balaam and said, "Do not go with the men who have given you money to curse the Israelites because I have blessed them."

In the morning, Balaam said to Balak's men, "I cannot go with you. The Lord has forbidden me to curse the Israelites."

Balak's men returned home and relayed Balaam's words to the king. Balak sent higher-level servants who said, "I will give you whatever you want and great honor, but come curse these people for me."

Balaam replied, "It doesn't matter what you pay me. I cannot go against what the Lord God has told me to say. Stay with me tonight and I will tell you what God says to me."

That night, God came to Balaam and said, "Go with these men, but you will only say what I tell you to say." The next morning, Balaam saddled his donkey with his two servants, and went with the Moabites.

While he was on his way to meet Balak, the angel of the Lord stood in his way. His donkey saw the angel with his sword drawn and she turned aside from the road to a field. Balaam beat his donkey until it finally went back to the road.

A little while later, the angel of the Lord blocked the road again, this time next to a vineyard on a narrow path between two walls. The donkey stopped moving forward and leaned into a wall. Balaam was furious and beat his donkey again.

They continued, but the angel of the Lord stood in front of the donkey where there was no room to turn to either side. Balaam was angry and started beating the donkey again. Then God spoke through the donkey's mouth and said, "Why do you keep beating me?"

Balaam didn't think twice about his donkey speaking to him and he replied, "I wish I had a sword in my hand because I would kill you because you keep disobeying me!"

The donkey answered, "Haven't I been your donkey for many years? Do I ever disobey you?"

Balaam replied, "No." Then God opened Balaam's eyes so that he could see the angel with his sword drawn and Balaam fell on his face from fear.

The angel of the Lord said, "Why do you keep beating your donkey? I keep blocking your way because your intentions are wayward and you are only after profit. If she hadn't kept turning aside, I would have killed you by now!"

Balaam answered from the ground, "I have sinned against God! I didn't know that you were there, but if this is an evil journey, I will go back home."

The angel of the Lord said, "Go ahead, but only say what I tell you to say." Then Balaam continued with Balak's men.

CHAPTER FORTY-TWO

BALAAM WITH BALAK

Numbers 22:36-25:18

When Balak heard that Balaam had arrived, he met him and said, "I sent for you twice. Why didn't you come the first time? Don't I have enough to give you great honor?"

Balaam replied, "Isn't it enough that I finally came? But I can only say what God tells me to say." Balaam went with Balak, who offered sacrifices on Balaam's behalf. Together, they went to a place where they could see a portion of the Israelites.

Balaam told Balak to build seven altars and offer seven bulls and rams. Balak did as instructed and then Balaam said, "Stay here and I will say whatever the Lord says to me."

God came to Balaam and told him to say, "You have told me to curse Israel, but how can I curse those who God has not cursed? Who can count Jacob's descendants or even count a fourth of their people? May I die a death like theirs and have the same outcome as they do!"

Balak was angry and yelled, "What have you done?! I asked you to curse them, and instead, you have blessed them!"

But Balaam answered, "I can only say what God has told me to say."

Balak replied, "Come with me to another place so you can see a different portion of them; then you can curse them for me." Balak took him to another place, built seven altars, and sacrificed seven bulls and rams.

God put words in Balaam's mouth and he said, "Listen to me Balak, God is not a man; he won't lie or change his mind. He will do whatever he has said he will do. The Lord has told me to bless them and I cannot do otherwise. There is no misfortune in Jacob and they will not have any trouble within them. The Lord is their God and he has brought them out of Egypt with strength like the horns of a wild ox. There is nothing bad that I can say against them! They are like a lion who does not lie down until it kills its prey and drinks the blood."

Balak asked, "Didn't I ask you to curse them and not give them a blessing?"

Balaam replied, "Didn't I tell you that I can only say what God tells me to?"

Balak said, "Let me take you to the top of a mountain; maybe God will allow you to curse them from there." Balak prepared another seven altars and sacrificed another seven bulls and rams.

Once Balaam saw that God wanted to bless Israel and not curse them, he said, "Oh Israel, your tents are beautiful like a massive grove of palm trees, a beautiful garden by a river, healing aloes the Lord has planted, and a strong cedar tree by water. Their kingdom will prosper and spread far across the earth. God has brought them out of

Egypt with strength like the horns of a wild ox. They will devour their enemies, breaking bones into pieces and piercing with arrows. They lay down like a lion and rest without fear of disturbance. Those who bless Israel will be blessed; those who curse them will be cursed!"

Balak clapped his hands together in anger and said, "I brought you here to curse my enemies, but instead of cursing them, you have blessed them three times! Go home. I told you I would give you great honor, but your God has kept you from receiving it."

Balaam replied, "Didn't I tell you that no matter how much money you gave me, I could only say what God told me to say? I am going home, but before I go, I will tell you what Israel will do to you in the future.

"I see Israel, but not now; in the future, a star will come from Jacob and a scepter from Israel. It will crush you and your people. He will also defeat your neighbors and destroy any survivors." Balaam pronounced destruction for each of the local nations, and then both Balak and Balaam went their separate ways.

> **Who was Balaam?**
>
> Balaam was an itinerant prophet who God used to bless Israel and curse their enemies. He was ultimately motivated by profit (he went to see Balak even though God told him not to). Eventually, he told the Midianites to intermarry with the Israelites to corrupt them.

BALAAM'S ERROR

While Israel lived in the wilderness, Balaam advised the Midianites that one way to take down the Israelites was to send their women to intermarry with them. God's people began to attend Midianite sacrifices and worshiped their gods. Israel yoked themselves to Baal and God became very angry. He said to Moses, "Take all the leaders of the tribes and hang them because you have disobeyed me and worshiped other gods. Then I will turn away my anger."

Moses told the leaders to kill anyone who had yoked themselves to Baal. While the people were weeping by the Tent of Meeting, one of the Israelites brought a foreign woman home to sleep with her in the sight of all the people. When Phineas, the son of Eliezer, the priest, saw them go into their tent, he grabbed a spear and went after them. He went into their tent and stabbed them both through with a single blow. Their death stopped the plague that God had sent on the Israelites. God killed 24,000 people in his wrath.

Then God said to Moses, "Phineas has turned back my anger because he feels the same way about my name that I do, so I did not destroy all of Israel. Therefore, I am making a covenant of peace with him. He and his descendants will be my priests because he was willing to act to atone for the people's sin."

Then God commanded the Israelites to strike the Midianites with the sword because they had become a snare.

CHAPTER FORTY-THREE

THE SECOND CENSUS AND FIGHTING THE MIDIANITES

Numbers 26-31

As the Israelites' time to enter the Promised Land approached, God commanded Moses to take another census. Moses obeyed and found there were just over 600,000 men, just as when they had come out of Egypt.

Then God said to Moses, "Go up to the top of Mount Abiram so you can see the Promised Land Israel is about to enter. After you see it, you will die just as your brother Aaron did because you did not give me glory at Meribah when I caused water to come out of the rock."

Moses replied, "Please appoint someone over Israel to lead them into the Promised Land. They need a leader, so they aren't like a sheep without a shepherd."

God replied, "Your assistant Joshua is full of my Spirit; he will succeed you. Have him stand before Eliezer and the entire congregation and commission him to lead the people. You will transfer your authority to him and the Israelites will listen to his words." Moses obeyed the Lord and put Joshua in charge of the people.

God spoke to Moses again, "I want you to avenge my people against the Midianites, then you will die." So, Moses sent 1,000 men from each tribe along with Phineas, the priest, and the sanctuary vessels. They killed every Midianite male and took their women captive. They took everything that the Midianites owned as plunder and burned their cities with fire. God used the Israelites as his instrument of judgment against the Midianites' sins.

The soldiers brought back the spoils of battle to Moses and Eliezer near the Jordan River in Jericho. When Moses saw all they brought back, he became angry with the army commanders. He said to them, "Did you leave all the women alive? These are the same ones who took Balaam's advice to seduce our men, which led to thousands of deaths. Make sure that you kill every male and every female who has slept with a male. But the young virgins, you can keep for yourself."

Moses commanded the soldiers to stay outside the camp, cleanse themselves for one week, and purify every piece of loot they brought back from the Midianites. Overall, the army brought back 675,000 sheep, 72,000 cattle, 61,000 donkeys, and 32,000 women who had never slept with a man.

When they had been purified, God told Moses to divide the spoils in half, one half for the warriors and one half for the people who stayed behind. He then commanded that one out of every 500 animals from the warriors' portion should go to the priesthood to provide for them. In addition to this, one out of every 50 animals from the people's allotment should go to the priests.

Every Israelite soldier came back from battle alive. They gave about 420 pounds of gold to the priests and the Israelites gained great wealth from the Midianites.

CHAPTER FORTY-FOUR

REUBEN AND GAD
Numbers 32

After destroying the Midianites, the people of Reuben and Gad saw that the Midianite land was suitable for livestock. They went to Moses and asked if they could stay there instead of crossing the Jordan River into the Promised Land. Moses was not pleased with their request and he replied, "Should your brothers go to war while you sit here in peace? Why would you discourage our people this way? This is what your fathers did when they spied on the Promised Land and brought back an unfavorable report. This is the whole reason God kept them from entering the Promised Land.

"Now you are taking their place and rebelling as they did. Every man over 20 who had come out of Egypt died in the wilderness as we wandered around for 40 years. If you continue down this path, we won't be wandering around; God will destroy us!"

They answered, "We will still cross the river to go into battle with our brothers, but we want to settle on this side of the Jordan and build our cities in this land. We will not return here until every one of our brothers has claimed his inheritance."

Moses replied, "If you are willing to cross over and fight alongside your brothers and not come back until we have defeated all our enemies, you can settle on this side of the Jordan. But if you do not follow through, your sin will be discovered."

Moses presented this proposal to Joshua and Eliezer, and they agreed that if Reuben and Gad were willing to fight for the Promised Land with the rest of the people, they could settle east of the Jordan River.

CHAPTER FORTY-FIVE

RECOUNTING THE LAW

Deuteronomy 1-32

Moses pleaded with the Lord to let him enter the Promised Land, but God denied his request. Instead, the Lord took Moses to a high place to see the entire land the Lord was giving Israel. Then God told him to encourage and strengthen Joshua because he had a monumental task before him.

As the people prepared to cross the Jordan, the Lord told Moses to speak to the people. "When you cross the Jordan and enter into Canaan, make sure that you drive out all the inhabitants and destroy their idols and articles of worship," God said. "If you do not drive them out completely, they will be a thorn in your side, and I will do to you what I would have done to them."

Before the tribes entered the Promised Land, Moses recounted the history of their travels and trials since they left Egypt. He reminded them of all God had done for them and how he had shown his power and glory to Israel. He said to the people, "Listen to the commandments and rules that I am teaching you and obey them so you may go into the Promised Land and live. Do not add to any of these commands and do not take away from them. You have seen how God destroyed those who worshiped Baal, but all who held fast to the Lord are still here today. Remember these laws and obey them because this will be a testimony to other nations of your wisdom, understanding, and greatness as a nation.

"Keep your soul diligently, so you don't forget what you have seen, and these words don't depart from your heart. Teach your children and every future generation what the Lord God has done for his people. When your God brings you into the land he promised to Abraham, Isaac, and Jacob, you will take possession of cities you did not build, wells that you did not dig, fields that you did not plant. Ensure that you remember this is a gift from the Lord who brought you out of slavery in Egypt.

"You are going into the land to displace a people far mightier than yourselves. Do not believe that God is bringing you into this land because of your righteousness. God is replacing these nations because of their wickedness and fulfilling his promise to Abraham, Isaac, and Jacob. God is not giving you this good land because you deserve it; you are a stubborn people. Don't forget how you provoked the Lord countless times after he had brought you out of Egypt. God wanted to destroy you, but I prayed on your behalf, and he relented.

"Love the Lord your God with all your heart, soul, and strength. Remember how he first loved you, chose you from all the nations, and brought you out of slavery. Don't ever forget what he has done for you and set up reminders to not forget.

"If you obey God's commands, then he will bless you and give you rain at the appropriate times and a plentiful harvest. He will provide food for your livestock and make you prosper. God will bless your children and every aspect of your life. The Lord will cause your enemies to flee before you. He will establish you as a nation and you will prosper in every way. Other nations will fear you and see what God does for those that he favors.

"But if you go after other gods to worship and serve them, God will be angry with you. He will withhold the rains and the land will not bear fruit for you. None of the good things of blessing will happen, but the opposite will happen. He will strike you with confusion and frustration until you die because you have forsaken the Lord. Your enemies will defeat you and you will be a horror to the entire world. You will not prosper but will be oppressed and robbed by those around you. They will take every good thing from you and consume it in your presence. All these things will happen so the other nations will learn not to disobey his commands.

"But, after all these evils have happened, after God has driven you from your home, and you have become few; if you repent and turn back to the Lord, he will forgive you and restore you. God will have compassion on you and bring you back to your home. If you obey again, he will restore the blessings and transfer his curses to your enemies. God will once again take joy in giving you prosperity if you return to obeying the Lord's commands.

"Remember these commands so that things will go well for you and your future generations. If you carefully obey my commands, the Lord will drive out the mighty nations currently in the land. Every place you set your foot will be your land; no one will be able to stand against you.

"The Lord is setting both a blessing and a curse before us; if we obey, he will bless us. If we don't obey, he will curse us. God is giving you a choice: life or death. Choose life so things will go well with you and your descendants, but know he will not tolerate disobedience.

"God will raise up another prophet for you who is like me and you will listen to him. He will be the Messiah, the Promised One who will speak God's words to you and deal with sin for the last time."

Moses continued, "I am 120 years old and I struggle to get around, though I still am vigorous. I will not be able to cross the Jordan into the Promised Land to lead you. Instead, God will go ahead of you and fulfill his promises to you. Joshua will lead you and you will defeat your enemies. Do not fear them, but be strong and courageous because God will go with you and never leave or forsake you."

Moses wrote all God's commands into a book and gave it to the priests. He had the people gather and the priests read the Law so they would remember his commands when they entered the Promised Land.

Then Moses composed a song to the Lord, and he sang of God's goodness and faithfulness. He sang of how he delivered the people despite their rebellion and sin. He praised God's character, justice, and perfection. He told of how God had chosen Israel out of slavery and delivered them to the Promised Land. He recounted their rebellion and stubborn hearts. He sang of God's curses for their disobedience and how the Lord nearly destroyed them in the wilderness. He praised God for having no equal and for how he would take vengeance on those who hate and reject him.

CHAPTER FORTY-SIX

MOSES' FINAL BENEDICTION

Deuteronomy 33-34

Then Moses blessed the tribes of Israel a final time before his death. He said, "God came to us from Mt. Sinai while we were still in Egypt. He came for us with a flaming fire in his right hand and loved his people. He kept us safe throughout our time in the wilderness. He has been our king and leader since we left slavery.

"Reuben will have a lasting legacy, but his people will be few.

"Judah, may God hear your voice. May he contend against your enemies with his hand and be a help against your enemies.

"Levi, may you keep the holy elements of worship. You have left your family and children to serve the Lord. You will teach Israel God's commands and offer sacrifices on their behalf. May God bless you and the work of your hands; may God crush your enemies' strength, so they are unable to rise against you.

"Benjamin, the Lord loves you, and you will dwell in safety. God will be with you and keep you safe.

"Joseph, may God bless your land with the choicest gifts of creation. May God give you the best because you are a prince amongst your people. You are a firstborn bull and you will gore your enemies as if with the horns of a wild ox.

"Zebulun, rejoice in your work. You will call the people to your mountains, where you will offer proper sacrifices and take the best of the land and the sea.

"Gad chose the best of the land and he crouches like a lion ready to destroy his enemy. He will execute the judgments of the Lord and dole out his justice.

"Dan is a lion's cub that leaps forward.

"Naphtali, may you be satisfied with God's good favor and blessing, and may you possess the lake and land to the south.

"Asher, may your sons be blessed, and may you be a favorite of your brothers. You will have incredible strength, like iron and bronze.

"There is no one like your God who rides through the heavens to help you in his majesty. The eternal God is your dwelling place, and he has thrust out your enemies and told you to destroy them. Israel will live in safety in a place full of the best things. Blessed is Israel because there is no one like you. You are a people God has saved, the shield of your help, and the sword of your victory. Your enemies will fall before you, and you will tread on their backs."

Then God said to Moses, "Go up to Mount Nebo, opposite Jericho. You will be able to see the Promised Land, but you will not be able to enter because you disobeyed me at the Rock of Meribah and did not give me the glory I deserve. Then you will die just as your brother Aaron."

Moses went up to Mount Nebo as God had told him to do and the Lord showed him the Promised Land that the people were to possess. Moses died and the people buried him on the mountain in an unmarked grave.

The people wept for Moses for 30 days because he was the most exceptional leader they had ever had or ever would. There has never been a man like him who could speak with God as Moses did or perform the signs and miracles he did.

Then Joshua took Moses' place of leadership, and the Holy Spirit filled him because Moses had commissioned Joshua to lead by laying his hands upon his assistant. He led the people across the Jordan River and into the Promised Land.

CHAPTER FORTY-SEVEN

THE LAW

As the Israelites came out of Egypt, God gave them rules and regulations to govern their lives. The Israelites were coming out of a very pagan environment into a similar system within the Promised Land. God gave these commandments over the 40 years they were in the wilderness, which fell into different categories. Some of them were ceremonial and governed how the people were to worship. The commandments were different from their previous experience and the people around them. Some were civil and judicial, covering how the nation was to run as God's people. The final category was moral, and these governed how the people were to live with each other.

Most of the ceremonial laws are not in this book because they do not pertain to modern Christians. They were crucial to the Israelites and covered how they were to make worship instruments and offer sacrifices. The sacrifices were a way of covering the people's sins and there were many types God told the people to perform.

Likewise, most civil and judicial laws are not in this book because they do not pertain to us. These governed the way people lived and how they interacted with each other. We can glean some truths from these.

The final category of moral commands applies to us if the New Testament repeats them. This is the most relevant part of the Law for us. However, the commands that matter are in the Life of Jesus and the Spread of the Church.

God did not just give the Law to the Israelites so they knew how to behave. It showed the people the depth of their sin so they would know they needed a solution. It also showed them what it would look like for a people to live in a right relationship with him. This was a revolutionary step forward in the legal codes of the time.

Jesus fulfilled the entire Law in his life, and he became the perfect sacrifice that paid the price for all sins, past, present, and future. The Law exists to point us to Jesus. He is the central figure in our faith, and all of Christianity revolves around his life and ministry.

It is easy to view this as a long list of dos and don'ts, but the Law reflected how redeemed people should live in relationship with each other and the God they served. Even though the people eventually used the Law as a means of legalism, it gave them freedom within certain boundaries. This is much like the rules that we provide to children; they are to protect the child, not confine them or restrict their joy.

CHAPTER FORTY-EIGHT

CEREMONIAL LAWS

The first category of commands God gave was Ceremonial Law, and it covered how the Israelites were to worship in the Promised Land. This was the most significant volume of rules God gave the Israelites, and they governed how they were to worship and serve him. Most of these are not binding today, but we can glean many kernels of truth from them.

Many of these rules set the Israelites apart from the Egyptians and the inhabitants of the Promised Land they were displacing. God used the Israelites as a tool for judgment against the locals who were wicked and practiced things like child sacrifice and other atrocities to appease their local gods.

God's commandments were to be a way to keep the people from false worship practices and to make sure they remembered who he was and what he had done. As humans, our forgetfulness often leads us into problems in our lives and our relationship with him. Obedience to him and his commands were a way to keep the Israelites out of trouble.

To help his people remember him and what he had done, God commanded the people to keep multiple feasts and celebrations throughout the year. He gave specific instructions for these so they would remember his goodness. God had done so much for the people and wanted to make sure they would not fall back into the worship practices or beliefs of the people around them. In modern times, it can be helpful to set up reminders of what he has done through history and our lives.

The Egyptians and original inhabitants of the Promised Land were polytheistic and worshiped many gods. The Lord taught his people he was the only God but existed in multiple manifestations. He revealed himself as God the Father, the Holy Spirit, and promised he would come as Jesus the Son. All three exist as one person and as three separate entities with the same power and status. For more information on the Trinity, see the box in Chapter One.

As a part of their worship, he told them they should not have any carved image to represent him. We still struggle with this today because we find so many things more important than worship and service to the Lord. Even though we may not have images we bow down to; it is easy for us to make possessions, status, accomplishments, activities, or even people as more important than him. All these will be weak and unfulfilling in comparison to living a life devoted to the Lord.

God also commanded the Israelites to keep his name holy and not to profane it in any way. The people were not to claim to be his and then live in an unholy way.

Another of the commandments that God was very serious about was the Sabbath. This reminded the people that they were free and did not need to continue striving to achieve his purpose. God created the heavens and the earth in six days and then rested on the seventh. This was the pattern of work and worship the people were to follow.

While they were in slavery, the Israelite's had to work every day. But in the Promised Land, they were to reserve the seventh day for worship, to remind them he was in control of everything. Even if we work every day or year of our lives, we cannot outdo what God can. He also commanded the people to rest every seventh year, to focus on worship, and remember his sovereignty. During this sabbatical year, the people allowed others to go free from their burdens and debts as a sign of his greatness.

He gave the people precise rules about sacrifices because he wanted the people to be cautious. He commanded the people to make Aaron's descendants the priests for the nation. The Lord also gave meticulous commands about the priesthood so they would be set apart to serve him. This included instructions about the Tabernacle and worship objects. All this was to make sure that the tribes were careful not to allow foreign influence into his worship. These minor infiltrations would eventually lead his people to stray from what he had taught them.

The sacrificial system was an essential part of the Israelites' worship, and all of this was to foretell the coming of Jesus. God is perfect and we cannot approach him unless we are as well. Beginning with Adam and Eve after the Garden of Eden, God shed animal blood to pay for our sins so that we can interact with him.

Every sacrifice the Israelites offered was a picture of what Jesus would do for all people when he died for our sins. God required unblemished animals for offerings because perfection is the only thing that can cover imperfection. The entire system was a way of pushing the people's guilt back until Jesus came to be the ultimate, perfect sacrifice.

Sacrifices were the area God gave the most significant number of commands because he was very interested in saving his people from their sin. A strange rule that was a part of this was not to wear clothing of mixed fiber. God gave this command because the priests wore one garment that of wool and another that was of linen. This prohibition was to help the people remember who the priests were and who could offer sacrifices.

When we look at the volume and types of sacrifice, some interpret that God was a cruel and exacting God, but this was really to show how great our sin is. Even the most minor infraction is enough to separate us from him, and that was the last thing that God wanted. He commanded all the sacrifices because he loved his people and wanted them to be holy so they could have a relationship with him.

The Israelites were to love the Lord with everything they had. He loved them with a never-ending love that acted within their best interests. They were to give their entire lives in service to him because that would give them the best possible life. They were not to put his word to the test but were to follow his commands and live upright lives.

He also gave commands about prophets, those that spoke on his behalf. No one could speak on his behalf unless his words came true or lined up with what he had taught the people. God was very concerned about this because it would have been easy for people to claim to speak on his behalf, gain a following, and then lie. The punishment for speaking falsely in God's name was death.

There were also commands about what made someone clean and unclean. This was to help the people take their worship seriously. Being unclean meant exclusion from the community until they could do what was necessary to become clean so that they could come back and worship the Lord.

CHAPTER FORTY-NINE

CIVIL AND JUDICIAL LAWS

The next area of commands that God gave was the Civil and Judicial Law. These governed the way that people lived and how they interacted with each other. It is essential to remember God gave these commands to specific people more than 3,000 years ago. They dealt with a very different set of circumstances than we are, and these statutes were to help the new nation thrive. For many of the laws to make sense to us, we must understand why God gave the rules rather than take them at face value.

God set up rules for how the Israelites were supposed to run their court and judicial system. They were to have representatives from every community who would be experts in the Law and would be able to help settle differences between citizens. There were rules about who could testify and how they should hear testimony. There were safeguards set up to protect the accused and the accuser. These judges listened to cases on virtually every area of daily life, including transactions, inheritances, property, personal injury, and religious matters. They were to judge regardless of one's wealth, status, or righteousness.

The Lord gave these judges rules for punishment and restitution in all kinds of cases. Generally, the sentence for each offense was to fit the crime. Some penalties involved payment; others involved exile; still, others required physical punishment, even to the point of death.

In all their dealings, God's commands required the Israelites to look out for the underprivileged, widows, and orphans. This was a very different requirement than other nations because the rule of the day was power. Whoever had the most power or money was able to treat anyone with less however they wanted. But God wanted his people to care for those who could not care for themselves.

A unique characteristic was that they could not charge interest to each other or make business deals that took advantage of those who had fallen on tough times. The Israelites were not to defraud or overpower these people if it kept them from living their daily lives or having the necessities to survive.

They also had many rules regarding liability and making sure not to leave property or possessions in a state of disrepair that would endanger others. Examples of this were to build a small retaining wall on the roof of their homes. This was necessary because people often spent time on the dwellings' flat roofs to increase living space (poor households kept animals inside because they could not afford a stable of their own).

A controversial part of the Israelite Law was the treatment of employees, servants, and slaves. In modern times, we have no problem with the treatment of employees, but we cringe at the idea of God condoning slavery. In ancient times, some people would fall so far into debt that they had no way of ever hoping to repay what they owed, and they would sell themselves into servitude. Other times, conquering nations would enslave vanquished foes. But it never had to do with race.

We should not think of Old Testament slavery as we think of what happened in the United States' early history, but rather should view it more like an employment situation. While these workers had to work for their masters, they had rights and privileges their masters could not deny. Slavery was an institution in the ancient world, and the fact that God gave any rules for how to treat people in these circumstances was counter-cultural and groundbreaking. God saw all people as having value and worth; therefore, he commanded slave owners to treat their slaves with dignity and fairness regardless of their social state. Slaves could obtain their freedom, and they could marry and have children. This was a complete departure from their experience with slavery in Egypt, where they had to work seven days a week and were mistreated at the whim of their masters. Under God's law, even slaves were to take the Sabbath day as a day of rest and not work on it.

The Law also covered how the leaders collected taxes, tithes, and offerings. These were necessary to provide for the Levitical priests while they served the Lord. This was a way to further their worship, so there were specific rules for collections.

A tithe was giving ten percent of the best people earned in every area of their lives to show they relied on God for everything. This was to serve as a reminder that God was in control of all things and that this sacrifice would not impair their ability to succeed and prosper.

Freewill offerings were above and beyond the taxes and tithes that the Israelites were to collect. These were to be a show of gratitude for all that God had done for them. The people were not obligated to give these but were worship and thanksgiving for the Lord's blessing and provision. Throughout their history, there were numerous freewill offerings that the leaders collected for various purposes.

CHAPTER FIFTY

MORAL LAWS

God also gave many commands regarding morality. Many of the moral statutes are not surprises to us, and many exist in modern laws. The New Testament repeats many of these, and these are the ones we are to continue to obey. God gave some of them specifically for the Israelites because of their situation. It is important to remember that God gave these commands to a people in a specific time and place, not to us more than 3,000 years later.

Jesus, the Messiah (God in the flesh), was the perfect fulfillment of these moral commands. The statutes not carried down are not binding on us today, but we can still learn from them if we look at the reasons that God gave the Law.

One of the areas of these that seems odd to modern people is the dietary restrictions. He differentiated between clean and unclean animals and provided a list of things the people could not eat. The main reasons for these restrictions were for health and to keep the people separate from pagan worship.

Many of the animals and food that God banned from eating were for health reasons; for example, pigs and some seafood would have been difficult to prepare in a manner ensuring the eater's health. Others kept the Israelites from following pagan worship practices like the prohibition to boil an animal in its mother's milk.

Participation in the community and the family structure was critical in Israel, so there were commands about how it functioned. Parents were to be listened to and respected throughout their lives. Even though God expected people to leave their homes and start their own families, the Israelites were not to live their lives in a way that would dishonor their parents.

The Israelites were not to marry foreigners to protect them from pagan worship practices. Some have used this command to forbid interracial marriage, but that was not the intent. God knew the Israelites were prone to stray in their commitment to him, which was a way to help ensure their faith.

Marriage was to be between one man and one woman and to last for life. God allowed for divorce because of the people's hard hearts, but this was not his design. This is also the first place God forbids incest. This was likely not banned previously because of the gene pool's purity and the scarcity of suitable mates before this time. God also outlawed bestiality and homosexuality.

God commanded the Israelites to wipe out certain people groups; this was his method of judgment against those who had sinned against the Lord. The Israelites could not decide whom they would go to war against or whom they were to kill but were only to fight with those that God commanded. There were some situations where the

Israelites were to destroy even the possessions of those they fought. There were other times that they could take spoil.

God also gave rules concerning a king. He intended Israel to function as a theocracy but knew they would one day demand a king. Knowing this, he gave commands about how a king should act. A king was not to amass wealth for the sake of wealth but was to be a leader who reminded the people of God's commands and what the Lord had done for them.

The Law was a picture of how redeemed people would live in a relationship with God and the people around them, not a long list of dos and don'ts. They were to love each other and treat each other well. They were to help each other whenever possible and act for each other's benefit, not their harm. This was also to carry to non-Israelites.

The Promised Land

Reorganized Concise Paraphrased Bible

Book II

By: Obadiah Paulus

INTRODUCTION TO THE PROMISED LAND

This is Israel's history, covering Joshua through Esther and the events from Israel entering the Promised Land through the end of the Old Testament. This is the story of how God revealed himself to his chosen people. While these chapters primarily record human activity, we are not the main characters. Humanity is important, but this book, like the rest of the Bible, is a revelation of God's glory, not our own.

The story starts with the Israelites entering the Promised Land. Joshua led them into the land and conquered the Canaanite nations as they took possession of what God had promised to Abraham and the other ancestors of the faith. It covers the rule of the judges and the kings of Israel and Judah up through their captivity and return to the land.

The Old Testament is full of many stories of the fathers of our faith, but these are descriptive of what happened and not necessarily prescriptive for what we should do. All the "heroes" of this book are flawed men and women that God chooses to use despite their shortcomings. David was an adulterer and murderer, and most of the other kings were wicked. Just because the Bible portrays these characters with all their warts does not mean that we should imitate all their behaviors, just that these events happened.

Joshua and Ezra are the only two books where we know the authors; both are eponymous. Scholars believe that Samuel, Jeremiah, and Ezra likely wrote the remaining books.

This book covers Israel's history, but it is not exhaustive, nor is it intended to be. The Bible is not a scientific textbook. However, it is essential to note that no historical or archeological discovery has ever contradicted the information recorded in the Bible. There are many events recorded in this book (as well as other books of the Bible) that we would like to have more information about, but that was not the purpose of God inspiring the Bible.

The people in this book gave many names to God based on the characteristics and actions that he displayed towards them. I have opted to use either God or the Lord to refer to him to avoid confusion.

MAP OF ISRAEL

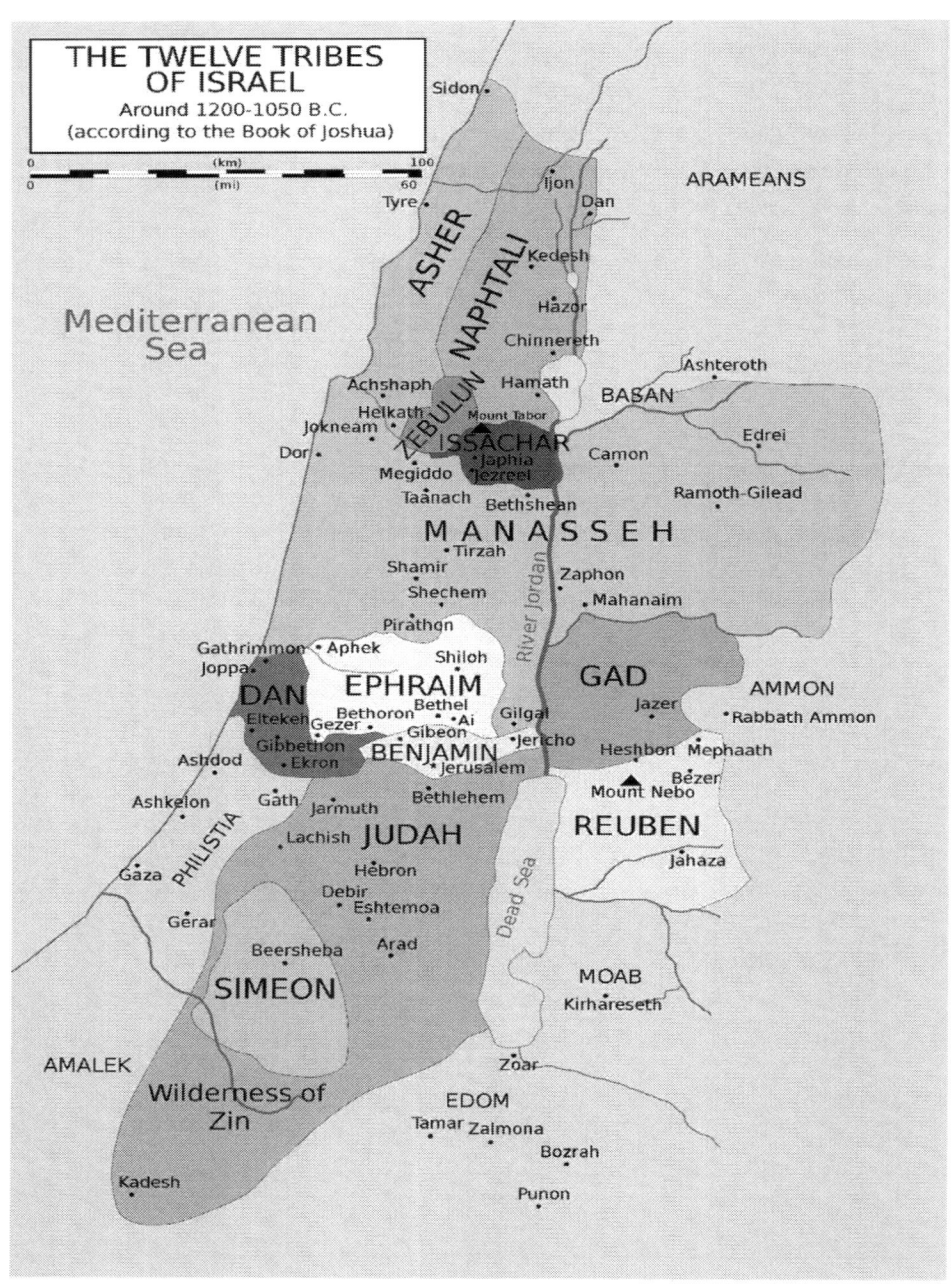

https://commons.wikimedia.org/wiki/File:12_Tribes_of_Israel_Map.svg

TABLE OF CONTENTS

CHAPTER 1: Into the Promised Land — 123
CHAPTER 2: Fall of Jericho — 126
CHAPTER 3: Conquest of Ai — 128
CHAPTER 4: Conquest of Southern Canaan — 130
CHAPTER 5: Conquest of Northern Canaan — 132
CHAPTER 6: The Reign of the Judges — 135
CHAPTER 7: Deborah — 137
CHAPTER 8: Gideon — 138
CHAPTER 9: Abimelech — 142
CHAPTER 10: Jephthah — 144
CHAPTER 11: Samson — 146
CHAPTER 12: Days Without a Judge — 151
CHAPTER 13: Ruth — 153
CHAPTER 14: Samuel — 156
CHAPTER 15: Samuel's Call — 158
CHAPTER 16: The Philistines Capture the Ark — 159
CHAPTER 17: Samuel Judges Israel — 161
CHAPTER 18: Saul to be King — 163
CHAPTER 19: Confirmation of Saul as King — 166
CHAPTER 20: Jonathan Delivers Israel — 168
CHAPTER 21: David's Rise to Prominence — 171
CHAPTER 22: Saul Turns Against David — 174
CHAPTER 23: David Flees from Saul — 177
CHAPTER 24: Samuel's Death, Nabal, and Saul Pursues David — 180
CHAPTER 25: Saul and the Witch — 183
CHAPTER 26: Saul's Death — 186
CHAPTER 27: David Becomes King — 188
CHAPTER 28: David and the Philistines — 191
CHAPTER 29: David and Bathsheba — 194
CHAPTER 30: Amnon and Tamar — 197
CHAPTER 31: Absalom's Rebellion — 199
CHAPTER 32: David's Final Years — 202
CHAPTER 33: David's Census — 204
CHAPTER 34: David's Death and Solomon Becomes King — 205
CHAPTER 35: Solomon as King — 208
CHAPTER 36: Building the Temple — 211
CHAPTER 37: Solomon's Reign — 215
CHAPTER 38: The Kingdom Divided — 217
CHAPTER 39: Asa Rules Over Judah — 221
CHAPTER 40: Elijah and Ahab — 224

CHAPTER 41: Ahab   227
CHAPTER 42: Jehoshaphat's Reign and Elijah's Ascension   230
CHAPTER 43: Elisha   234
CHAPTER 44: Elisha and the Syrians   238
CHAPTER 45: Jehu's Reign   242
CHAPTER 46: Rule to the Assyrian Captivity   245
CHAPTER 47: Hezekiah to the Babylonian Captivity   252
CHAPTER 48: Rebuilding the Temple   257
CHAPTER 49: Rebuilding the Wall   261
CHAPTER 50: Esther   264

CHAPTER ONE

INTO THE PROMISED LAND

Joshua 1-3

After Moses died, the Lord spoke to Joshua, "My servant Moses is dead. Lead these people across the Jordan into the Promised Land. I will give you every piece of land where you set your foot, just as I promised Moses. No one will be able to stand against you while you live. Just as I was with Moses, I will be with you; I will never leave nor forsake you.

"Be strong and courageous because you will lead my people to inherit the land that I promised to their fathers Abraham, Isaac, and Jacob. Be very careful to obey the Law I gave Moses. Do not turn aside from it and you will have great success. My laws will not depart from your mind and you will meditate on them both day and night so that you will obey what I have written. Then you will be prosperous and successful. Be strong and courageous because I am with you; there is nothing that you should fear."

Joshua commanded the officers to go through the camp and have the people get ready to cross the Jordan River into the Promised Land. He reminded the Reubenites, Gadites, and half-tribe of Manasseh that although they were claiming the land east of the Jordan as their own, they still had an obligation to help their brothers drive out the local nations before returning to their home.

> **Why had these tribes settled west of the Jordan River?**
>
> When the Reubenites, Gadites, and half-tribe of Manasseh saw the land east of the Jordan River, they asked their relatives if they could settle there. They agreed that they would still help with the other tribes' conquest of the unclaimed territory.

The tribes answered, "We will do everything you command us and go wherever you send us. We will follow you just like we followed Moses; may God be with you like he was with him. We will kill whoever rebels against you! Be strong and courageous!"

Joshua sent two men to spy on the city of Jericho. They came to the house of a prostitute named Rahab and stayed with her. The king of Jericho found out that the spies had been at Rahab's house, and he went to her and said, "Bring out the spies who stayed with you because they came to find our weaknesses before they invade us."

Rahab had hidden the two men in some stalks of flax that she stored on her roof, and she lied to the king, "It is true that the two men came here, but I didn't know their origin. They left in the evening when they were closing the city gate. If you go quickly, you can probably catch them."

The king's men left to chase after the spies and shut the city gate after leaving. Before the two spies laid down to sleep, Rahab told them, "I know that the Lord is giving you the land. Everyone is afraid of Israel and the people are melting away before you. We heard about what happened at the Red Sea when you left Egypt and how you destroyed the nations east of the Jordan. When we heard these reports of how the Lord God led you, our hearts melted because he rules everything. Since I have treated you kindly, please swear to me that you will treat my family and me kindly as well. Give me a sign that you will spare us when you come to overtake the city."

"May we die if we don't protect you and your family," the spies told her. "Keep our visit a secret, and when the Lord gives us the land, we will deal kindly and faithfully with you and your family."

Rahab lived in a home built into the city wall, and before she let them down by a rope outside Jericho, she told them, "I sent the king's men towards the Jordan. Go the opposite way into the hill country, or they will catch you. Wait three days until the men looking for you have returned, then go on your way."

The men thanked her and said, "We promised that we would save you and your family, but you must do one thing for us. When our army comes, tie a scarlet cord in this window, and gather anyone that you want to save into your house. Whoever is in the house will be safe, but we cannot make promises about anyone who leaves. If you don't tie the cord or if you tell anyone about what we've done here, we are free from our promise."

Rahab agreed and they parted. She did everything they had told her to do. The two men waited three days in the hill country until their pursuers returned to Jericho. Then they returned to Joshua and told him everything that happened and that they were confident the Lord was giving the land into the Israelites' hands.

The Israelites moved their camp next to the Jordan River and stayed there for three days. Then the Israelite officers told the tribes, "As soon as you see the Levites carrying the ark of the covenant, then get up and follow them. Stay about a half-mile behind. The priests will lead you because you do not know where you are going."

Joshua spoke next. "Consecrate yourselves because God will perform wonders in your midst," he told them. Then he directed the priests to take up the ark and lead the people.

The Lord said to Joshua, "Today; I will begin to exalt you so that my people know I am with you just like I was with Moses. Tell the priests carrying the ark to stand still in the water once they come to the Jordan."

Joshua obeyed, and when they arrived at the water, he said to everyone, "Listen to what God has said. You will know that the living God is among you because he will drive out all the local nations and give you their land. The ark of the covenant is going to lead you across the river, and while the priests stand in the river, he will cut off the waters and hold them back in a big heap."

During the harvest, the Jordan River would flood the surrounding areas, but as soon as the priests set foot in the water, the river stopped flowing, and the water piled up about 18 miles upriver. It stayed that way until the priests had led every Israelite across on the dry river bed.

When all the people, including about 40,000 soldiers from the tribes of Reuben, Gad, and Manasseh had crossed the river, God commanded Joshua to appoint one man from each tribe and have them each take a large stone from the Jordan's riverbed. They set these stones up at their camp as reminders of how God brought them into the Promised Land and a sign of how God had cared for them.

That day, God exalted Joshua before the entire congregation, and they held him in high regard just as they had with Moses.

When the priests carrying the ark stepped out of the riverbed, the river flowed again, and it flooded the area, just as it had before. They set up camp near Jericho.

As soon as the local kings heard how God had held back the Jordan and how the Israelites had crossed the river on dry ground, their hearts melted.

God commanded Joshua to circumcise all the men with a flint knife because no one born in the wilderness had been circumcised. All the Israelites who came out of Egypt were circumcised, but they died in the wilderness because of their lack of faith. Joshua obeyed and circumcised all the Israelite males.

CHAPTER TWO

FALL OF JERICHO

Joshua 4-6

After circumcision, all the men stayed in camp until they healed. Then the entire community celebrated their first Passover in the Promised Land.

The day after they celebrated Passover, the people could eat the land's fruit for the first time. The next day, the manna stopped falling from heaven. God had provided manna for 40 years in the wilderness, but it stopped appearing once it was no longer necessary.

One day, as Joshua was looking towards Jericho, he saw an angel standing with his sword drawn. Joshua went to him and asked, "Are you for us or against us?"

The angel replied, "I am the commander of the Lord's army and now I have come."

Joshua fell to the ground and worshiped the Lord. Then Joshua asked, "What do you have to say to your servant?"

The commander of the Lord's army said, "Take off your sandals because you are standing on holy ground."

The people of Jericho were terrified of the Israelites and they shut down the city; no one went in or out. Then the Lord said to Joshua, "I have given Jericho, its king, and its mighty men into your hand. I want you to march around the city with all the soldiers once a day for the next six days. On the seventh day, march around the city seven times. Then have seven priests blow ram's horn trumpets and the people will shout at the top of their lungs. The wall will fall flat so that each man can go straight into the city."

Joshua obeyed the Lord and commanded the people to march around the city without making a sound while the priests blew continuously on the trumpets. They circled the city once a day for six days, and on the seventh, they marched around Jericho seven times in silence. After completing the seventh time around, Joshua yelled, "Shout, for the Lord has given you the city! Destroy everything in the city except for Rahab and everyone who is with her. Bring the gold, silver, bronze, and iron vessels out for God's treasury, but destroy everything else. Don't bring anything else home as plunder, or else you will bring trouble upon us."

The people all shouted, the wall fell flat, and every man ran straight ahead to capture the city. They destroyed all the men, women, children, and livestock just as God had commanded them, but they spared Rahab and her family. They burned the city with fire and brought the gold, silver, bronze, and iron into the Lord's treasury.

Rahab and her family were allowed to live in Israel because she had hidden the spies. Joshua exclaimed, "May God curse the man who tries to rebuild Jericho. May laying the foundation cost him his oldest son and raising the gates cost him his youngest!" God was with Joshua and his fame spread across the land.

> **Why did God command Israel to kill children and livestock?**
>
> Some nations had become so wicked that allowing any remnant of them to exist had the potential to tempt the Israelites to sin. God's people were the means God used to judge the nations and he commanded the Israelites to destroy the nations according to their wickedness.

CHAPTER THREE

CONQUEST OF AI
Joshua 7-8

But not all the soldiers obeyed the command to destroy everything. Achan, from the tribe of Judah, took some of the things they were to destroy, and God's anger burned against the Israelites.

Joshua sent some people to spy out the small town of Ai and they reported back that they could overthrow the town with a few thousand men instead of the whole army. About 3,000 soldiers went up against the town of Ai, were defeated, and then turned and ran. A few dozen Israelites died, and their resolve faltered because such a small town had defeated them.

> **Numbers in the Bible**
>
> Three thousand seems like a large number of troops to send against a small town. This is the number given by interpretation of the best manuscripts. However, there are theories about translation or errors in transcription that may mean far fewer people. The way numbers are written in ancient Hebrew can lead to confusion in understanding the original amount. I use the traditional interpretation throughout this book, although the actual amounts may be much lower. Either a large or small number does not change the text's meaning.

Joshua tore his clothes and fell on his face before the ark of the covenant until evening. He and the elders put dust on their heads and cried out, "Did you bring us over the Jordan to destroy us? If only we could have stayed on the other side of the river! What are we supposed to do if we run from a small town like Ai? Word is going to spread and the strangers will wipe us out! Then what will they say about your great name?"

God replied to Joshua, "Get up. Why are you falling on your face? Israel has sinned by taking some of the things I asked to be destroyed and kept them for themselves. You will not be able to stand before your enemies if you choose those things over obeying me. I will not be with you if you do not destroy what I have devoted for destruction. Get up, consecrate the people, and tomorrow call them out so that you may remove the banned items from your midst and stand before your enemies."

At the Lord's command, Joshua gathered the tribes before him in the morning. They cast lots to choose a tribe, then a clan, then a household, and then man by man. The lot fell on Achan, and Joshua said to him, "My son, give glory and praise to God and tell me what you have done."

Achan answered, "I have sinned against the Lord! When we were destroying the city, I took a beautiful cloak and some gold and silver for myself. I took them home and buried them in my tent."

Joshua sent messengers to Achan's tent and they found the things just as he had described. They brought the items out and laid them before the Lord. Then all Israel took Achan, his family, and everything he owned to a valley. "Why have you brought this trouble on us?" Joshua thundered. "Now, the Lord will bring you trouble!" The people stoned Achan and his family to death with rocks and burned their remains. They raised a great heap of stones over him as a reminder to obey, and God turned away from his burning anger.

Then the Lord said to Joshua, "Do not be afraid or dismayed because I am giving Ai into your hands. Take all the soldiers to Ai and set an ambush in front of the city and behind it. You will do the same thing to them that you did to Jericho. But this time, you will be able to keep the plunder for yourselves."

So, Joshua sent 30,000 men at night to set an ambush behind the city and instructed them to stay close. Then he took the other troops and approached the town from the front. When the men of Ai came out to fight, the Israelites fled as they had previously, and the men of Ai pursued them. Then the hiding soldiers attacked the defenseless city and easily overran it and set it on fire. When the Israelites saw the smoke rising from the city, they stopped their retreat and struck their enemies down until there were no survivors.

The soldiers killed all the inhabitants of Ai, about 12,000 in total, and destroyed all their possessions. But they took the livestock and spoils of the city as their plunder. They captured the king of Ai alive and brought him to Joshua, then hung him from a tree until evening. They made the city into a pile of rubble and heaped stones over the gates.

Joshua built an altar to the Lord on Mount Ebal and they offered sacrifices to God. Then all the people gathered and Joshua read the Law Moses had given them.

CHAPTER FOUR

CONQUEST OF SOUTHERN CANAAN

Joshua 9:1-10:15

When the local kings saw how easily Jericho and Ai had fallen to the Israelites, they banded together to fight against them. But the Gibeonites saw this and acted deceitfully. They dressed in worn-out clothes and took old equipment and stale provisions to meet with Joshua at Gilgal. They came to him and said, "We come from a distant country and have come to make a treaty with you."

Joshua did not trust them, but they said, "We have heard about all that your God has done and how he delivered you out of Egypt. Our elders advised coming to make a treaty with you. We are your servants, and when we left our home, we had new clothes and equipment, and our food was fresh. But now you can see that everything is worn out, and our food is stale."

Joshua made peace with them, but did not consult the Lord, and promised not to destroy them, allowing them to continue living in the land. Three days after the Gibeonites left, the Israelites discovered their deception and went to their cities. But they did not destroy the Gibeonites because they had sworn by God that they would let them live. All the people grumbled against their leaders.

The Israelite leaders said, "We cannot kill the Gibeonites because we swore that we would let them live and we fear God's wrath if we break our oath. They will be our servants and do the menial tasks that we don't want to do."

Joshua went to the Gibeonite leaders and said, "Why did you lie to us and say that you were from a distant country? Now you will be forced laborers for our God."

They answered, "Because we knew that God had given our land into your hands, and we feared for our lives. If you let us live, you can do whatever seems right in your eyes." So, Joshua did not destroy them but forced them to be laborers for the Israelites and the Lord.

When the king of Jerusalem heard about the conquest of Jericho and Ai and the deception of the Gibeonites, he was terrified because Gibeon was a great city. So, he called some of his neighbors and they banded together to fight against the Gibeonites.

The Gibeonites sent men to Joshua, begging him to honor the covenant he made. Joshua took Israelite soldiers and marched all night to battle the coalition attacking the Gibeonites. God said to him, "Do not fear because I have given them into your hand, and none of your enemies will be able to stand against you."

The Israelites took them by surprise, and God threw the coalition into confusion. They chased the soldiers all over the land. As they fled, God threw great hailstones on them; more men died from the hail than the Israelites killed.

As the Israelites pursued their enemies, Joshua asked God, "May the sun stand still until we can exact vengeance on your enemies!" God caused the sun and moon to stop in their places until the Israelites defeated their enemies.

The five kings of the coalition were hiding in some caves. Joshua's soldiers rolled large stones blocking the caves while the Israelites finished wiping out the armies. Returning to the caves, they brought the kings out before all the people. Joshua told the commanders of the army, "Put your feet on their necks. Do not be afraid, but be courageous because this is what God will do to all the enemies that we fight against!"

They killed the kings and hung their bodies from trees until the evening. When the sun finally went down, Joshua threw their bodies into the cave where they had hidden and put boulders over the entrance. The Israelites killed every soldier from the coalition. Israel continued the conquest of the land, and they struck down the people of Libnah, Lachish, Gezer, Eglon, Hebron, and Debir just as they had done to Jericho.

The Israelites killed every living thing from these cities, just as God had commanded. They were able to have such success because God fought for them. After the slaughter, they returned to their camp at Gilgal.

MAP OF THE CONQUEST

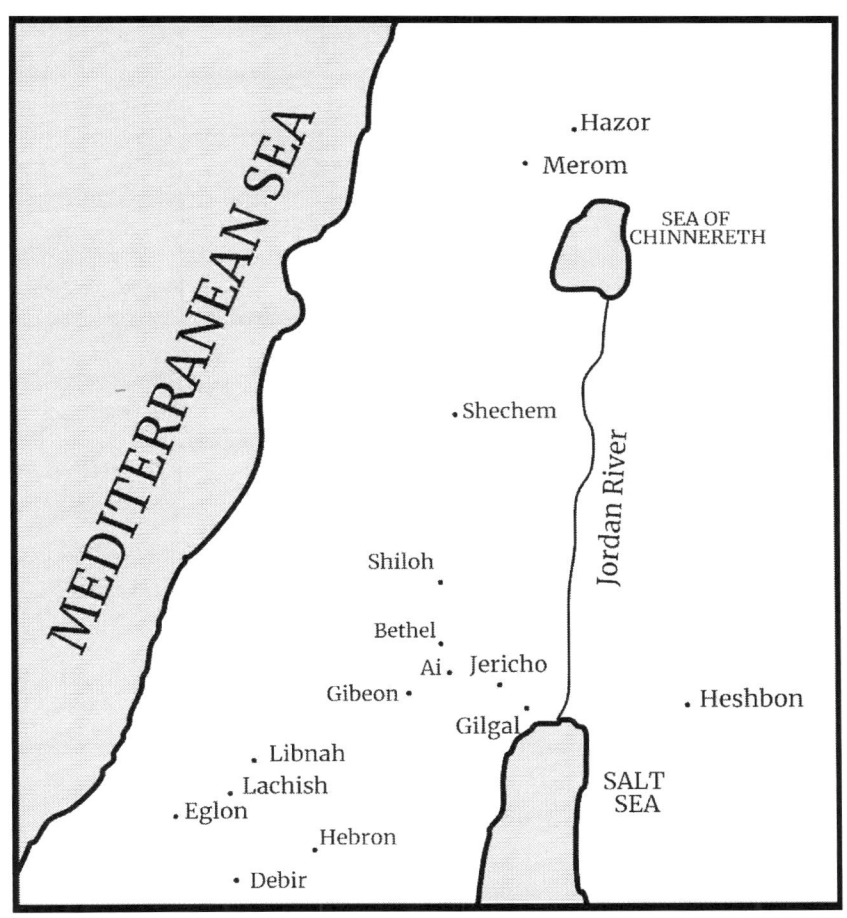

CHAPTER FIVE

CONQUEST OF NORTHERN CANAAN

Joshua 10:16-24:33

When the kings of northern Canaan heard of these events, they came together with many troops, horses, and chariots. Then they advanced on Israel's camp. But God said to Joshua, "Do not be afraid of them, because tomorrow, around this time, you will kill them all. Then you will burn their chariots and hamstring their horses."

Joshua and his men surprised the Canaanite army by attacking when they were not expecting it. The Lord gave the Canaanites into Israel's hands and they destroyed every soldier until there were none left alive. Then Joshua went through their land with the army destroying their cities and taking their spoils as plunder. The Israelites destroyed the capital city of Hazor, just as they had Jericho.

Joshua obeyed the commands that both God and Moses had given him and drove out the local inhabitants. Joshua did not make peace with anyone but the Gibeonites and he destroyed every person from the cities that God had commanded him to kill. Joshua took the entire land, just as God had promised Moses, and the Israelites divided the land according to their tribes. Then there was peace.

Joshua was old and the Lord said to him, "There is still a lot of land left to conquer." They divided the land amongst the tribes as the Lord commanded and set up the cities of refuge. But the tribe of Levi did not receive an inheritance, just as the Lord commanded.

Caleb, one of the original twelve spies who went into Canaan, came to Joshua and said, "You know what God said to Moses about the two of us. I was 40 years old when we went to spy out the land, and we brought back a good report, but our brothers brought back a bad one and made our people afraid. But the Lord promised to give me an inheritance in the land because I followed him.

"God has kept me alive for these 45 years and now I'm 85. But I am still as strong as I was when Moses first sent us to spy out the land. Let me take a part of the hill country with their great, fortified cities. I will drive out the people as the Lord has commanded and this will fulfill the word he spoke to us so long ago."

Joshua blessed Caleb and gave the land of Hebron to him and his family because he had faithfully followed the Lord. Then the Israelites had a period of rest from war and the tribes who took their inheritance to the east of the Jordan River went home to their land.

When the tribes of Reuben, Gad, and Manasseh returned to the east of the Jordan, they built a large altar. When the other Israelites heard about it, they gathered to make war with them because they were not following the laws for worship that God had given them. They went to the eastern tribes and said, "Why have you committed this sin against God by disobeying his commands and making this altar? Haven't we seen enough death because of false worship? We're still trying to cleanse ourselves from it. If you continue with this rebellion, then God is going to be angry with all of us! If your land isn't good enough, cross the river and take a part of our inheritance in our midst. But do not rebel against the Lord by building this altar; many people will die!"

The eastern tribes replied, "The Lord our God, who has brought us into this land with his mighty hand, knows our hearts! If we have sinned or rebelled in any way, then don't spare our lives! We didn't build this altar to offer our own sacrifices; we built it to serve as a reminder for our descendants, so they won't think the Jordan is a boundary and that we have nothing to do with the God of Israel. We are trying to keep our children from forsaking the Lord! So, we decided to build this altar as a reminder, not as a place to burn offerings. Far be it from us to make offerings anywhere but where God has commanded."

Phineas, the priest, returned to the rest of Israel and gave their reasons for building the altar. The people thought it sounded like a good idea, and they stopped talking about making war against Reuben, Gad, and Manasseh.

JOSHUA'S DEATH

Many years later, after Israel had a period of peace, Joshua brought the elders together and said, "I am getting old, and you have seen what God has done to all of these nations on your behalf. He is the one who fought for you. I have doled out your inheritance in both the conquered and unconquered parts of the land. God will defeat the people who are still in the land, just as he has promised.

"Therefore, be very strong and do not stray from the commands that God gave us through Moses, do not turn to the right or left from obeying them. Do not mix with the local nations, do not adopt their gods or practices, but cling to the Lord as you have done to this day. God has driven out nations far stronger than you and no one has been able to stand before us. One Israelite makes 1,000 enemies flee because God is the one who fights for us, just as he promised.

"Be careful to love the Lord, because if you bind yourself with these foreigners and associate with them, then he will not drive them out before you. Instead, they will become a snare and a trap for you, they will be a whip for your backs and thorns in your eyes, and you will not inherit this land that the Lord has given you.

"Now, I am about to die. You know in your hearts that God has not failed on one of his promises. They have all happened; none of them have failed. But just as he has given us all these blessings, he will bring evil upon us if we turn away from him and follow false gods. If you sin against the Lord, he will be angry with us and we will lose the land he has given us."

Then Joshua gathered all the people before him and he recounted the story of what God had done for them. He talked about how God had brought Abraham, Isaac, and Jacob into the land and then the people into Egypt. He reminded them how God had brought them out of slavery in Egypt with great signs and miracles. He told the people of their military conquest of the Promised Land.

He said to the people, "Fear the Lord and serve him with sincere hearts, put away the idols our fathers served and obey God. If serving the Lord doesn't work for you, then choose whom you will serve. But, me and my house will serve the Lord!"

The people answered, "Far be it from us that we would forsake the Lord and serve other gods! He is the one who brought us out of Egypt and he has shown us his power and might through miracles and the way he drove out the local nations. Therefore, we will serve the Lord!"

But Joshua said to them, "You are not able to serve the Lord because he is a holy God. He is a jealous God, and he will not forgive your sins. If you go after foreign gods, he will consume you, just as he has done good for you."

The tribes replied, "No! We will serve the Lord!"

Joshua said, "You are witnesses against yourself that you choose to obey God and serve him. So, get rid of your false gods and idols and turn your hearts towards him!"

The people said, "We are witnesses, and we will serve and obey him only!"

Then Joshua made a covenant with the people and set up rules and regulations for them. Then he took a large stone and set it up by the Tabernacle and told the people it served as a witness that they had declared their love and allegiance to the Lord. Then he sent them to their homes.

Joshua died at 110 and they buried him in the hill country. They also buried Joseph's bones his brothers had brought all the way from Egypt, as they had promised. Aaron's son, Eliezer, also died at this time, and they buried him in the hill country.

CHAPTER SIX

THE REIGN OF THE JUDGES

Judges 1-3

After Joshua's death, the people asked the Lord, "Who will go up for us against the Canaanites?"

God told them to send the tribe of Judah to claim their inheritance. Judah approached the tribe of Simeon and they agreed to drive out the inhabitants of Judah's inherited lands together and then drive out those in Simeon's. The other tribes also made progress in driving out the Canaanites, but not all of them. They put them into forced labor, but they did not destroy them as the Lord had commanded.

Then the angel of the Lord said to the Israelites, "I brought you out of Egypt into the Promised Land. I told you that I would never break my covenant with you and that you shouldn't make covenants with the locals but should destroy their altars instead. But you have not obeyed my voice, what are you thinking?! So, now I am not going to drive them out; instead, they will be a thorn in your side and their gods will be a snare to you." As soon as the people heard these words, they lifted their voices and wept. Then they offered sacrifices to God.

The Israelites had served the Lord all the days Joshua, and the elders who served with him were alive. But once those elders had died, the people lapsed into evil and served other gods. They abandoned the Lord who had brought them out of Egypt. They bowed down to foreign gods and made the Lord angry. So, God sold them out to their enemies, and whenever they fought the foreign nations, they could not defeat them, and their enemies kept plundering their settlements. The hand of God was against them wherever they turned and they were in great distress.

Then the Lord raised up judges to deliver them from their enemies. But the people didn't listen to them and continued to worship foreign gods. They gave up on the way their fathers had obeyed the Lord and ignored God's commandments. God had pity on Israel and would deliver the people while the judge ruled. But once the judge died, the tribes went back to serving other gods. So, God was angry at Israel and said, "Since the people have broken my covenant and have not obeyed my voice, I will not drive out the nations that remained when Joshua died. This is how I will test my people to see if they will listen to me."

God left the Philistines, Hittites, Amorites, Perizzites, Hivites, and Jebusites to test Israel. All these were descendants of Israel's distant relatives, who God had promised to make into nations although they were not his chosen people. So, the Israelites lived among them, married their women, and worshiped their gods.

OTHNIEL

The people debased themselves before foreign gods and cried out to the Lord when foreign nations oppressed them. The first judge that God raised up to deliver the people was Caleb's younger brother Othniel. He gave Israel some military victories and they had 40 years of peace while he served as a judge. But once he died, the people returned to worshiping foreign gods.

EGLON

Then the Lord raised up Eglon, the king of the Moabites, and he afflicted the Israelites. He brought together the Ammonites and the Amalekites and they ruled over Israel for 18 years.

The tribes cried out to God, and he raised up Ehud, a left-handed man from the tribe of Benjamin. He made an 18-inch sword, strapped it to his right thigh, and brought a tribute to Eglon. Most men were right-handed and strapped their weapons to the left thigh, so Eglon's guards did not find it.

Ehud offered his gift and after he had done so, he told the king that he had a secret message for him from the Lord. So, Eglon, an obese man, sent everyone out and met with Ehud in a bathroom to hear the secret message. Ehud took the sword from his right thigh and stabbed Eglon in the belly so deep that his fat closed over the blade's hilt and feces began to leak out.

When Ehud left, he locked the doors after him while Eglon's servants waited outside. They assumed the king was relieving himself and waited an uncomfortable amount of time before getting the key to see if Eglon was okay. When they went in, they found their king dead on the floor.

Ehud was able to escape while they waited outside the bathroom, and he fled to the hill country of Ephraim. He blew a trumpet and told the people, "Follow me because the Lord has given the Moabites into your hands!" Then they went down and killed all 10,000 of the Moabite men.

SHAMGAR

God also raised Shamgar as the next judge to deliver Israel. Shamgar killed 600 people with a cattle prod and saved Israel from their oppressors.

CHAPTER SEVEN

DEBORAH

Judges 4-5

The Israelites had rest for 80 years, but once again, the people began worshiping foreign gods and turned their backs on the Lord. God raised up the Canaanite king, Jabin, to oppress the people. Jabin's military commander, Sisera, tormented the people for 20 years and the Israelites cried out to the Lord to deliver them. God raised up Deborah to judge the people, and she would sit in the hill country of Ephraim and listen to the people's disagreements.

She told Barak that God had commanded him to take 10,000 men from Naphtali and Zebulon and draw Sisera out because the Lord would give the Canaanites into their hands. Barak said, "I will only go if you go with me, but if you are not willing, then I will not do it."

Deborah replied, "I will go with you. But because you did not listen to the Lord, you will not receive the glory. Instead, God will deliver Sisera into a woman's hands."

Barak, Deborah, and their men went to battle against the Canaanites. When Sisera heard about this, he brought his troops and his iron chariots out to meet them. Deborah said to Barak, "Get up and go because this is the day that Lord has given Sisera into your hand! Do not be afraid because God will go before you."

The Lord crushed the Canaanites; Sisera left his chariot and fled on foot. Barak chased them down and killed all their soldiers. Sisera fled to Jael's tent because she was a descendant of Moses' father-in-law, and they were at peace. Jael told Sisera, "Don't be afraid, but come into my tent and I will hide you."

He asked her for some water, but she gave him some milk and then covered him with a rug. Exhausted, he told her to stand at the tent's doorway and tell people that he was not there, then he fell into a deep sleep.

Once she was sure he was asleep, she snuck into the tent and drove a tent peg through his temple until it went into the ground, killing him. Jael went out to find Barak and told him that Sisera was dead in her tent. Barak went in and saw his enemy with a tent peg in his temple. God delivered Israel from Jabin and they battled against him until they destroyed him.

Then Barak and Deborah wrote a song to the Lord about how he had delivered them from Jabin and Sisera. They praised God for his power and recounted how the Canaanites had oppressed the people, but God raised Deborah up to rescue them. They told the story of Jael and how she had killed their enemy through God's power. Then the land had peace for 40 years.

CHAPTER EIGHT

GIDEON

Judges 6-8

Once again, Israel sank to worshiping foreign gods and the Lord raised up Midian to plague them for seven years. They built strongholds in Israel and whenever the Israelites planted crops, the Midianites would devour them so that they had nothing to eat and nothing for their livestock. They came in like locusts and laid waste to the land, leaving nothing for Israel. Then the people cried out to the Lord.

God appointed a prophet to come to Israel and the spokesperson said to the tribes, "God brought you out of the house of slavery in Egypt and brought you into the Promised Land. He is the Lord our God, so do not be afraid of the people who oppress you."

Then the angel of the Lord came to a man named Gideon while he beat out grain in a winepress to hide it from the Midianites. The angel said, "Courageous warrior, the Lord is with you!"

> **Who is the angel of the Lord?**
>
> The angel of the Lord is a title that occurs multiple times in the Old Testament. This is an angel that God uses to carry out special messages or missions on his behalf.

Gideon responded, "If the Lord is with us, then why are all these bad things happening? Where are all the wonderful things our fathers told us about when he brought us out of Egypt? He has forsaken us and given us into the hands of the Midianites."

Then God said to him, "I am sending you to deliver Israel from the Midianites."

But Gideon replied, "How am I going to deliver my people? I am the weakest in my family and come from one of the smallest tribes!"

God said, "I will be with you and you will strike down the Midianites."

Gideon answered, "If I have found favor in your sight, show me a sign that you will be with me. Stay here and I will bring you a gift." So, Gideon went into his tent and prepared a young goat and unleavened bread, and he brought it out in a basket.

The angel of the Lord said, "Put the meat and bread on a rock and pour broth over them." Gideon obeyed, and the angel of the Lord touched the food with the tip of his staff, and the food was instantly consumed. Then he vanished from Gideon's sight.

Gideon realized what was happening and said, "Lord, have mercy on me because I have seen the angel of the Lord face to face!"

God said, "Peace be with and do not be afraid; you will not die." Then Gideon built an impromptu altar to the Lord.

That night, the Lord came to Gideon and said, "Go to the altar your father built to Baal and tear it down along with the idol that he set up beside it. Build an altar to me out of stones and offer two bulls to me, burning them with the wood from the idol." Gideon was afraid to do it during the day, so he took ten men with him and did it at night.

When the town woke up and saw what had happened, they asked each other who had done it and found out that it was Gideon. The men went to Gideon's father, Joash, and said, "Bring out your son so that we may kill him because he tore down Baal's altar and cut down his idol!"

But Joash said to the men, "Are you going to fight for Baal? If he is truly a god, then let him fight for himself!" Then Gideon got the nickname Jerubbaal because he had torn down Baal's altar.

The Midianites and Amalekites crossed the Jordan to raid the Israelite land. The Holy Spirit filled Gideon then, and he sounded a trumpet, and his people came out to meet him. He told them to wait until the Lord told him what to do.

Gideon said to God, "If you will save Israel as you have promised, please show me a sign. I am laying a wool fleece on the floor; in the morning, if the ground is dry, but there is dew on the fleece, then I will know that you will save Israel through my hand as you have told me."

The next morning, the ground was dry and the fleece had enough dew that Gideon could wring out the water into a bowl. But Gideon was still afraid and said, "Please do not be angry with me, but I'm going to put the fleece out one more time. In the morning, if the fleece is dry and the dew covers the ground, I will know that you are sending me." The following day, the fleece was dry, although the ground was wet.

> **Gideon's fleece and God's will**
>
> It is tempting to look at Gideon's laying out a fleece multiple times as a sign of his faith and a way to figure out God's will. However, this was something Gideon did from a lack of faith. God had already commanded him to save Israel and the appropriate response was obedience. Despite his lack of faith, God still was willing to answer miraculously.
>
> When we face difficult situations where we don't know what we should do, we should look to God's word for guidance. If he has not explicitly forbidden a choice, we can choose that option. We then should look at how God has wired us and ask him for wisdom to decide what would best honor him. While God can show us his will through miraculous signs, this is a description of what happened, not a model for how we should make decisions.

Gideon took the men who were with him up by the camp of the Midianites. God told Gideon, "There are too many people with you. I don't want you to think you delivered Israel on your own. Tell the people that if any of them are afraid, that they can go home." Gideon had amassed 22,000 troops, but after he relayed this message, more than half of them went home.

God said, "There are still too many people. Take them down to the water and I will show you who should go with you to defeat the Midianites. Separate the people into two groups, those who kneel to drink and those who put their face in the water to drink."

Only 300 put their face in the water to drink and the rest of the 10,000 knelt. God said, "I am going to save Israel with the 300 men who lapped up water like a dog, send the rest of them home."

So, Gideon had the 300 gather provisions for war and sent the rest of the men home. That same night, God told Gideon to go down to the Midianites' camp because he would deliver them into his hands. The Lord knew that Gideon was afraid, so he told him to take his servant, Purah, with him.

Gideon went to the Midianites' camp and they stretched out like locusts, as far as the eye could see. Gideon heard one of their soldiers tell a dream to his companion, "I had a dream that a piece of barley bread rolled into our camp and hit a tent. Then the tent turned upside down and fell flat."

The other soldier said, "That piece of bread is Joash's son, Gideon! God has given our entire camp into his hands!"

As soon as Gideon heard the interpretation of the dream, he fell on his face and worshiped the Lord. Then he went back to his camp and said, "The Lord has given Midian into our hands!" He divided the 300 men into groups of 100 and gave them all trumpets and empty jars with torches inside. He told the people to follow his lead and blow their trumpets when he blew his, break their jars when he broke his, and shout, "For the Lord and Gideon!"

Gideon and his men approached the camp in the middle of the night, blew their trumpets, and smashed their jars. Then they shouted, "A sword for the Lord and Gideon!"

The men stood in place around the camp and watched the Midianite army flee before them. When they heard the trumpets, God turned the Midianites on each other, and they began killing their countrymen. Then Gideon sent for the Israelites to pursue them to the Jordan River and they defeated their enemies.

GIDEON PURSUES THE MIDIANITES

The next day, the men of Ephraim were angry that Gideon didn't invite them to pursue the Midianites and accused him of making them miss out on the glory. Gideon said to them, "Why are you complaining to me? God has defeated your enemies. What difference does it make if you were able to participate or not?" That calmed the community.

Gideon and his 300 men pursued the Midianites across the Jordan and they were exhausted. They came to the town of Succoth and asked for bread to revive their men.

The men of Succoth were afraid of retribution from Midian and said, "You have already had some success, so why should we help you?"

Gideon replied, "Once we have defeated them, we will come back and whip your flesh with thorns and briars!"

Then Gideon and his army continued their pursuit to the town of Penuel. He asked them for help and they answered the same way that the men of Succoth had. Gideon said to them, "When we come back, we will break down your tower!"

God had already struck down about 120,000 Midianites, but there was still an army of about 15,000 left. The Midianites set up camp because they thought they were secure. Gideon captured their kings, Zebah and Zalmunna, and the remaining army panicked.

Gideon returned home with the two kings. On the way, he encountered a man from Succoth and questioned him. The man gave him the names of the 77 elders from Succoth, and Gideon went back to the town. He put the two Midianite kings before them and confronted the people about not assisting when he asked. Then he whipped the elders with thorns and briars to teach them a lesson. Afterward, he went to Penuel and broke down their tower as he had promised.

Then Gideon turned to Zebah and Zalmunna and asked them about the men they had killed in a previous raid. The two kings tried to get on Gideon's good side by saying that all the men looked like royalty, just like he did. Gideon was furious and said, "They were my brothers! If you had let them live, I would let you live!"

He turned to his firstborn son and told him to kill the two kings, but the man was young and afraid, so he did not obey. Then the two kings challenged Gideon to kill them himself; they didn't think he had the courage to do it. So, Gideon killed them himself and took their camels and the ornaments from their necks.

The men of Israel were so grateful that they tried to make Gideon their king. But Gideon said, "I will not rule over you, nor will my sons. God will rule over you!" Then he asked them to give him the golden earrings from their spoils. They gladly complied and gave him about 50 pounds of gold. Gideon had not fully turned from worshiping false gods and idols, so he made them into a fancy garment, and it became a snare for the people because they bowed down to it in worship. God gave the Israelites rest from Midian and they had peace for about 40 years.

Gideon returned home and enjoyed his fame. He had many wives and girlfriends and fathered 70 sons. The people did a better job obeying the Lord while he was alive, but once he died at a ripe old age, they returned to their pagan practices and worshiped foreign gods and idols. The Israelites did not remember how God had delivered them from their oppressors and did not remain faithful to the Lord.

CHAPTER NINE

ABIMELECH

Judges 9

Once Gideon had died, one of his sons, Abimelech, sent his mother to the local elders and said, "Would you rather have all 70 of Gideon's sons rule over you, or just one? Remember that I am your relative and have your best interests in mind." His mother spread this word around and campaigned for him to be their ruler. The people listened to him and gave him 70 pieces of silver from the treasury that he was to use to consolidate his power.

Abimelech took the 70 pieces of silver and hired worthless men that he was friends with and had him gather his brothers and kill them in a single place. Gideon's youngest son, Jotham, was the only one who escaped, and he hid from his brother. Then, the local elders made Abimelech king (although he was not king over all of Israel).

When Jotham heard this, he called the people to him as he went to a nearby mountain. He stood on it and yelled, "Listen to me, elders of Shechem, so God may also listen to you. The trees went out to look for a king and they asked the olive tree to rule over them, but it declined because it did not want to leave its place of importance as the maker of the oil used to anoint kings. Then the trees asked the fig tree to be their king and it declined because it did not want to leave its sweetness and tasty fruit. Next, the trees asked a grapevine to rule over them, but it refused because it did not want to leave behind making wine. Finally, the trees went to the bramble and asked it to be their leader. The bramble answered that it would be their ruler if they acted in good faith; otherwise, the trees should be cursed."

He continued, "If you have acted in good faith and with integrity in making Abimelech king, then he should rule. If you have treated my other brothers fairly by killing them, if you have justly rewarded them for Gideon's actions and how he delivered us from the Midianites, let us rejoice that Abimelech is our ruler. But if not, may God send down fire to consume him and your elders!" Then Jotham fled the city because he was afraid of his brother.

GAAL'S REBELLION

Abimelech ruled over the Shechemites for three years and then God sent an evil spirit between him and the local elders. The local elders dealt treacherously with Abimelech and they set a trap for him to repay the death of his brothers that he killed. But Abimelech found out about it.

Then an Israelite named Gaal moved into Shechem with all his family and the elders began to trust him. At one of their festivals, the men were drinking wine and slandering Abimelech, and Gaal said, "Who is this clown that we should follow him? Isn't his father the one who tore down our altar to Baal? There are plenty of people we could follow, but why Abimelech? If I were in charge, I would challenge Abimelech to fight and remove him from leadership."

Abimelech's next in command, Zebul, heard these words and became angry. He sent messengers to Abimelech to let him know that Gaal was stirring up the people and plotting an overthrow. He advised Abimelech to set an ambush and attack his men at first dawn to stop the brewing mutiny.

The following morning, Gaal stood at the gate to the city and saw Abimelech's men coming from their ambush down the mountainside. Zebul stood with him and tried to convince him that he only saw tricks of the shadows. But Gaal was insistent that it was groups of men coming down to the city. Then Zebul mocked him, "Where is your big mouth now? These are the people you slandered; go out and fight with them!"

Gaal went out to fight with Abimelech with the Shechemite leaders at his side. Many people were killed and wounded, and Abimelech chased Gaal and his relatives out of the city, forbidding them to live there.

The next day, the Shechemites went out into the fields, and Abimelech heard about it, so he sent his men to set an ambush against them. When Abimelech saw that they had all left the city, he sent people to the gate, and they attacked. There was nowhere for the people to run, and Abimelech and his men slaughtered them. He destroyed the city and covered it with salt so that no one could use the land.

The neighbors of Shechem heard about the attack and quickly banded together. When Abimelech heard that they were gathering forces to defeat him, he and his followers collected wood and went to their stronghold tower. They put the wood around the tower and burned it to the ground, killing nearly 1,000 people.

Abimelech took his men to the neighboring town of Thebez and captured it, but the people fled to a tower for protection. They gathered wood to repeat what they had done at the tower of Shechem. Abimelech went near the tower during the attack, and a woman threw a millstone down and hit him in the head, giving him a mortal injury. He asked his armor-bearer to kill him so that he wouldn't die at the hand of a woman, and the attendant ran Abimelech through with a sword.

Then all the men returned home. God used the people to repay Abimelech's evil and the Shechemites' evil on each other. All their deaths were because of God's judgment on their sins.

CHAPTER TEN

JEPHTHAH

Judges 10:1-12:7

TOLA & JAIR

After Abimelech, God raised Tola, a man from Issachar, to judge the land. He judged the people for 23 years in the hill country of Ephraim and then he died. Then God raised up Jair, and he judged Israel for 22 years, and then he died.

JEPHTHAH

The people returned to their wicked ways and rebelled against the Lord. They worshiped foreign gods and bowed down to idols. God was angry with his people and he allowed the Philistines and the Ammonites to oppress the Israelites. These foreigners ruled over Israel for 18 years and Israel was very distressed. The people cried out to the Lord, confessed their sins, and promised to change their ways.

God came to the people and said, "When you obeyed me, I delivered you from everyone who oppressed you, from the Egyptians to the Midianites. But since you keep rejecting me and worshiping foreign gods, I won't deliver you anymore. Cry out to your new gods and see if they will deliver you."

The Israelites were even more distressed and they said, "You can do whatever seems right to you. But we promise we will get rid of our idols and foreign gods and only serve you."

God saw that the people had repented, and he raised up Jephthah, a man from Gilead, and he was a mighty warrior. Jephthah, an illegitimate child, was driven from the family home, so he lived in the wilderness and surrounded himself with worthless and depraved men.

As the Ammonite oppression became worse, Jephthah's brothers went to him and begged him to deliver them from their enemies. But Jephthah said, "Didn't you drive me out of my home because we had different mothers? Why are you coming to me now that you are distressed?"

But the people continued to beg him to deliver them so he said, "If you let me come home, and the Lord gives the Ammonites into my hand, then I will lead you." The people agreed, so Jephthah went home and became their leader.

He went to the Ammonites and said, "What have we done that you have come to fight against us? When we came out of Egypt, we did not fight against you when you would not allow us to pass through your land. We have not gone to war with you while we've lived here. Why are you coming out to afflict us now? May God judge between Israel and Ammon because we should be faultless in your eyes." But the Ammonites refused to listen.

Jephthah made a vow to God, "If you defeat the Ammonites, I will offer the first thing that comes out of my house as a burnt offering when I return to you." Then Jephthah led the Israelites into battle against the Ammonites and they were victorious.

When he returned home, his only child, a daughter, came out from his house and greeted him with tambourines and music, celebrating how God had delivered Israel from the Ammonites. As soon as he saw her, he tore his clothes in grief and said, "My daughter, you have caused me great grief because I have sworn your life to the Lord, and I cannot take my vow back!"

She replied, "You have sworn to God and you cannot break your vow. You must do whatever you have promised because God has defeated the Ammonites. But give me two months to grieve with my friends because I will die without ever being married."

He granted her request and after two months, she returned, and he sacrificed her to the Lord as a burnt offering. Therefore, it became a custom that the Israelite women would grieve for four days of the year on behalf of Jephthah's daughter.

> **Why did God allow human sacrifice?**
>
> God did not command Jephthah to sacrifice his daughter but allowed this situation to play out because of Jephthah's rash vow. God wanted to deliver the Israelites and Jephthah did not need to make the hasty choice. However, God allowed him to follow through on the promise because it was Jephthah's choice.

The men of Ephraim were upset that Jephthah had not brought them to fight against the Ammonites because they had missed out on the glory. They gathered to burn down Jephthah's home and everything he owned. But Jephthah pointed out they had not volunteered to go against the Ammonites when they knew there was a dispute. Jephthah gathered his men and went to battle against the malcontents.

They captured many of their cities and the land near the Jordan River. When the fugitives from Ephraim tried to cross the Jordan to find a place to stay, the Gileadites asked them to pronounce a word that had a particular regional pronunciation. If they were not able to say the word correctly, Jephthah's men killed them. Around 42,000 people died from this civil war and regional conflict. Jephthah judged Israel for six years.

IBZAN, ELON, AND ABDON

After Jephthah, God elevated Ibzan, who judged Israel for seven years, but allowed his children to marry foreigners. Then God raised up Elon, and he judged Israel for ten years. After him came Abdon, and he judged Israel for eight years.

CHAPTER ELEVEN

SAMSON

Judges 12:8-17:31

Once again, the people turned to foreign gods and rejected the Lord. So, he gave them into the hands of the Philistines for 40 years. There was a man from the tribe of Dan named Manoah, who had no children, and the angel of the Lord appeared to his wife. He said to her, "You will have a son, but make sure that he never drinks alcohol or eats anything unclean. He will be a Nazarite, will never cut his hair, and will begin to save his people from the Philistines."

She told Manoah about what had happened and she prayed to God that it would come true. The Lord listened to her prayer and the angel of the Lord visited her while she was sitting in a field. She went to get her husband, and the angel of the Lord confirmed the message.

Manoah did not realize that it was the angel of the Lord and he said, "Please stay here and we will prepare a meal for you." The angel of the Lord refused and told him to offer the meal to God as a burnt offering. Manoah asked what the stranger's name was and the angel of the Lord refused to give a clear answer. So, Manoah offered the meal as a burnt offering as the angel of the Lord had commanded.

As Manoah and his wife offered the meal, the angel of the Lord went up in the flames. They realized what had happened and they fell on their faces in worship. Manoah was sure that they would die because they had seen God, but his wife reassured him that it would have already happened if he wanted them dead. Nine months later, Manoah's wife gave birth to Samson.

Once Samson had grown, he fell deeply in love with a Philistine woman and asked his father to get her for him as his wife. His parents tried to change his mind and said that he should marry an Israelite woman, but he would not listen. His parents did not realize that God was using this situation to bring judgment on the Philistines.

So, Samson went with his parents to propose marriage. While they were there, a young lion attacked Samson. The Holy Spirit filled Samson, and even though he didn't have a weapon, he killed the lion with his bare hands. He didn't tell anyone what had happened, and he proposed marriage to the Philistine woman.

When he went to marry her, he saw the lion's carcass on the side of the road, and a swarm of bees had made honey in the lion's body. He scraped out some into his hands and ate it as he went and gave some to his parents when he arrived at his destination.

His parents threw a week-long wedding feast and many people came to the party. While they were there, Samson said to the Philistines, "I will give you a riddle, and if you can answer it, I will give you 30 linen outfits, but if you cannot answer it, then you will give me 30 linen outfits."

They agreed to his terms and he said, "Out of the eater came something to eat, out of the strong came something sweet."

The Philistines racked their brains but could not come up with the answer. On the fourth day of the feast, they went to his fiancée and said, "Get Samson to tell you the answer to the riddle; otherwise, we will burn you and your father's household."

So, his fiancée went to Samson and begged him to tell her the answer to the riddle. Samson told her that he had not even told his parents the answer, but she kept after him and wept until the seventh day of the feast. She wore Samson down with her tears, and eventually, he told her the answer.

At sundown on the seventh day of the feast, the Philistines came to him and said, "What is stronger than a lion and what is sweeter than honey?"

Samson was furious and said, "If you had not sent my wife after me, you would have never figured this out!" Then the Holy Spirit filled him, and he went to a nearby town and killed 30 Philistines and brought their clothes back to pay off his bet. He went home because he was so angry, and the girl's father gave Samson's fiancée to the best man as a wife.

After a while, Samson calmed down, and he went to sleep with his wife. But her father wouldn't let him see her and said, "I really thought you hated her, so I married her off to your best man. But you should marry her younger sister; she's better looking anyway."

Samson was furious and he said, "This time, I will be innocent when I hurt the Philistines." Then he caught 300 foxes, lit their tails on fire, and set them loose in the Philistines' fields and olive groves. They were furious and when they found out that Samson had done this because of the situation with his wife, they burned Samson's wife and her father.

Samson said, "If this is how you are going to behave, then I will avenge myself, and then I will quit." He killed many of them, regardless of their guilt, and went out and stayed in the giant crack of a rock.

In retaliation, the Philistines raided the Jewish town of Lehi. When the people of Lehi asked them why they had attacked them, the Philistines told them about what Samson had done. The Israelites sent 3,000 men and confronted him about the raid. Samson replied, "I have only done what they did to me."

The Israelites said, "Don't you know they rule over us? We have come down to tie you up and take you to them."

Samson asked them to promise not to attack him themselves, and he agreed to be tied up and taken to the Philistines. The Israelites tied him up with two of the strongest ropes they had and brought him to Lehi. When the Philistines saw him, the Holy Spirit filled Samson, and he broke the ropes like they were wax. Then he grabbed a donkey's jawbone and killed 1,000 of their men.

After killing the Philistines, Samson was exhausted and extremely thirsty, and he called out to the Lord. God opened the earth and water poured out from it. Then Samson judged Israel for 20 years during the rule of the Philistines.

> **Why was Samson so violent?**
>
> God used Samson as a tool of judgment against the Philistines. The Philistines he killed were punished because of their sin. God commanded this kind of discipline and we cannot use his actions to justify violence. Only God can command this kind of punishment.

SAMSON AND DELILAH

One day, Samson went to Gaza and hired a prostitute. The Philistines heard about it and they set an ambush at the city gate, intending to kill him in the morning. But Samson left the city around midnight. As he departed, he ripped the city gates off their hinges and took them with him.

> **What did city gates signify?**
>
> The city gates were a place of authority for ancient cities. People would come here to meet and have their leaders dispense justice. When Samson tore these down, he was taking away their power and security.

Not long after this incident, Samson fell in love with a Philistine woman named Delilah. The Philistine leaders came to her and said, "Seduce him so we can find out where his great strength comes from, then we can overpower and humble him. If you do this, then we will give you 1,100 pieces of silver as payment."

Delilah asked Samson where he got his strength and he told her, "If you tie me up with seven bowstrings, I will become weak, like any other man." The Philistines gave her seven bowstrings and set an ambush for him. Then she tied him up and told him the Philistines were upon him. But he snapped the bowstrings like they were thread; they did not find out the source of his strength.

Delilah pressed Samson, "You have mocked and lied to me. Tell me how I can overcome your strength." Samson told her that if he was bound with new ropes, he would become like anyone else. One evening, she tied him up with new ropes while the Philistines waited in ambush. She told him the Philistines had come to capture him, but he broke the new ropes like they were thread.

Delilah kept after Samson and asked him how he might be bound. Samson answered, "If you weave the seven locks of my hair like a web and fasten it tight with a pin, I will become weak like any other man." Once he fell asleep, she wove his hair into a web and fastened it with a pin, and she told him the Philistines had come to capture him. When he woke up, he pulled the pin out and was ready for their attack.

She said to him, "How can you say you love me when you keep lying to me? I have asked you three times where your strength comes from and you have lied." She kept asking him every day, and eventually, she wore him down. Samson was too cocky to realize the danger he faced.

One day, he said to her, "I have been a Nazarite from birth and never cut my hair. If you shave my head, my strength will leave, and I will become like anyone else." When she saw Samson had told the truth, she called the Philistine leaders and told them to be ready to capture Samson.

She made Samson fall asleep on her lap. While he slept, she shaved the seven locks of his hair and began to harass him. She woke him up and told him the Philistines had come to capture him. Samson assumed he would be able to fight them off like before, but he did not realize that the Lord had left him because he had broken his Nazarite vow. The Philistines captured him, gouged out his eyes, and brought him down to Gaza in bronze shackles.

The Philistines were thrilled that they had captured Samson, and they offered sacrifices to their god, Dagon. They were praising their god for their deliverance and they decided to bring Samson out to entertain them. His hair had begun to regrow and they made him stand between two support pillars of the house.

Samson asked the young man who led him to put his hands on the two pillars to steady himself. There were nearly 3,000 Philistines in the house to see Samson mocked. Samson called out to the Lord, "God, please remember me and give me strength one more time so I can avenge myself against the Philistines for my eyes." He put his hands on the two pillars supporting the building and pushed against them, crying out, "Let me die with the Philistines." He pushed as hard as he could, the pillars fell, and the house collapsed, killing all 3,000 Philistines who were there.

THE JUDGES

Judge	Notes
Othniel	Caleb's brother, judged Israel for 40 years.
Ehud	Left-handed man who judged Israel for 18 years. Killed Eglon, a Moabite king, in a bathroom with an 18-inch sword.
Shamgar	Killed 600 men with a cattle prod.
Deborah	Female judge who judged Israel for 40 years and helped lead the Israelites against Jabin, a Canaanite king.

Judge	Notes
Gideon	Judged Israel for 40 years. Famous for his prayer with the fleece and beating the Midianites with 300 men. Had 70 sons.
Tola	Judged Israel for 23 years.
Jair	Judged Israel for 22 years.
Jephthah	Judged Israel for eight years and defeated the Ammonites. Sacrificed his daughter to fulfill a rash vow.
Ibzan	Judged Israel for seven years
Elon	Judged Israel for ten years.
Abdon	Judged Israel for eight years.
Samson	Judged Israel for 20 years, he was a Nazarite and the strongest man to ever live. Fought against the Philistines and killed more than 3,000 in his death.

CHAPTER TWELVE

DAYS WITHOUT A JUDGE

Judges 18-21

There was a man from the hill country of Ephraim named Micah. He had taken 1,100 pieces of silver from his mother; he confessed that he had taken the silver and returned it to her. She was happy that he returned the money, so she took 200 pieces of the silver and made it into an idol. Micah kept the idol in his home and he appointed a priest to serve it.

There was no king in those days and people did what was right in their own eyes.

There was a young Levite from Bethlehem who stayed with Micah, and Micah paid him ten pieces of silver and a change of clothes each year to be the priest of his idol. Then Micah was convinced that he would be prosperous because he had a Levite as the priest of his home.

Israel did not have a ruler in those days, and each tribe tried to take their own inheritance in the Promised Land because they had not yet conquered it. The people of Dan sent men to spy out the land and see if they could take it, and they came to Micah's property.

When the Danites realized Micah had a Levite priest, they asked him if their journey would be successful. The priest sent them away in peace because he declared that their mission would be successful. They reported back to their home that the people lived in security and that it would be a good place for them to overthrow.

So, 600 men from the tribe of Dan went into Ephraim's hill country to Micah's home. They took the idol and the Levite priest, saying that it would be better to serve an entire tribe than a single family. After taking the Levite priest, Micah sent his men after them, but they retreated after realizing they were outnumbered. The men from Dan came back and destroyed Micah and his family because they wanted his land.

THE LEVITE AND THE BENJAMINITES

In those days, there was a traveling Levite in the hill country of Ephraim and he had a girlfriend who was unfaithful to him. She left his house and went back to Jerusalem with her father for four months. The Levite went to get his girlfriend back, planning to leave after staying there for three days. The woman's father kept prolonging their stay by insisting they stay until after breakfast and then to wait until after dinner.

But the man would not spend another night with her father, so the two set out from the village and got as far as the city of Gibeah in Benjamin, where they decided to spend the night in the town square. An old man came to them and persuaded them to stay with him.

As they ate together and drank wine, depraved men came to his door and demanded that he bring the travelers out so that they could have sex with them. The old man came and said, "Don't do this wicked thing; here is my virgin daughter and the traveler's girlfriend. Do whatever you want to them, but don't try to have sex with this man."

They grabbed the man's girlfriend and abused her until the morning, but the Levite was too afraid to help. As the morning dawned, they let her go. The Levite went outside and told her to get up so that they could continue their journey. But she did not respond because she was dead. So, he put her on his donkey and returned home. Then, he cut his girlfriend's body into twelve different pieces and sent them to the twelve tribes because he wanted them to know about Benjamin's wickedness. This appalled the Israelites because nothing like this had ever happened in Israel.

Israel sent 400,000 soldiers against Benjamin and they asked how this evil event had happened. The Levite told the soldiers what had happened, and he asked them what they thought should happen. The Israelites decided that they should kill the shameful men of Gibeah. The Benjaminites chose to defend themselves, and they brought out 26,000 men, including 700 left-handed men who were very skilled at slinging stones at their enemy.

The Israelites asked God who should go to battle against the Benjaminites, and he told them to send men from the tribe of Judah. They fought against Benjamin and 22,000 men died. The Israelites still felt like they should destroy the people of Benjamin. They wept before the Lord and asked if they should go into battle with them again. God told them to attack again and this time, 18,000 more men died.

Then, the Israelites fasted and cried out to God and asked if they should attack Benjamin again. The Lord told them that they should go into battle one more time. They set an ambush against Benjamin and killed about 25,000 men from Benjamin on that day.

The people decided that they would not allow anyone to marry anyone from Benjamin and they were deeply distressed. They wept before God and wondered if an entire tribe would be cut off from the Lord.

The next morning, they offered sacrifices to God and asked what they should do because they did not want an entire tribe to die. There were still a few hundred men from Benjamin who had not died, and they told them to take wives from some of the local women so that they would continue to be a tribe.

So, the men from Benjamin took women from the daughters of Shiloh when they came out to dance for the harvest so they would not become an extinct tribe. The men of Benjamin took wives by force and all the Israelites returned to their homes. There was no king in Israel in those days and people did what they thought was right in their own eyes.

Days without a judge

This was one of the saddest periods of the Israelite nation. People followed their own hearts rather than the Lord. This chapter illustrates how poorly the tribes behaved and fared without God's guidance.

CHAPTER THIRTEEN

RUTH

Ruth 1-4

During the judges' reign, there was a famine, and a man from Bethlehem in Judah went to stay in Moab with his wife and two sons. His name was Elimelech, his wife was Naomi, and their two sons were Mahlon and Chilion. Not long after they arrived, Elimelech died, but Naomi stayed there with her sons. They lived there for about ten years and both boys married local women, Orpah and Ruth. Before they had children, both boys died as well, and Naomi was alone.

Naomi decided to head back home to Judah because she had heard that there was food there. Naomi left with her two daughters-in-law, but on the way, she said to them, "Go back to your parents' homes and may the Lord be as kind to you as you have been to me. May each of you find a husband and rest in your home."

She kissed the girls and they all wept. The girls said, "No, we want to go back to your home with you!"

Naomi replied, "Turn back home; there is no reason for you to come with me. I am too old to remarry, and even if I did, I'm done having children. Even if I did, would you wait around for them to be old enough to marry? I am very bitter about this situation on your behalf because God has cursed me."

They cried out again and wept. Orpah decided to leave, but Ruth clung to her mother-in-law. Naomi said, "Follow your sister-in-law back home to your own people and gods."

But Ruth said, "Don't urge me to go home because I am going wherever you go. Your people will become my people and your God will become my God. I will die where you die and be buried with your people, and may God take my life if I don't stay with you." Naomi saw how determined she was and said no more.

The two of them journeyed on to Bethlehem and when they arrived, the entire town was stirred up over Naomi's return. But she said to them, "Don't call me Naomi, call me Mara because the Lord has dealt with me very bitterly. I left full, but I am returning empty. Don't call me Naomi because I am no longer pleasant because of the calamity that God brought upon me."

They arrived in Bethlehem near the beginning of the barley harvest. Naomi told Ruth about one of her husband's relatives named Boaz, who had a field near where they were staying. Ruth said, "Let me go into his field to gather grain for us and see if I find favor in his eyes."

Naomi sent her into the field and Ruth gathered the grain that the harvesters left behind. This was a common practice that allowed for the poorest Israelites to survive.

Boaz came to the field and noticed the young woman and asked the foreman who she was. The servant replied, "She is the Moabite woman who came back with Naomi. She asked to glean the field after the harvesters at morning's light and has been working all day since then."

Boaz went to Ruth and said, "Don't go to any other fields to glean, but only come to mine. Stay close to my young women. Follow my harvesters because I have told them to leave you alone and give you water whenever you are thirsty."

Ruth fell on her face and said, "I am a foreigner. Why have I found favor in your eyes?"

Boaz replied, "I've heard about everything you've done for Naomi since your husband died, how you left home, and came to a strange land so you could take care of her. May God repay you for the good thing you have done!"

Ruth answered, "Thank you for comforting me and treating me kindly, even though I'm not one of your servants."

At lunchtime, Boaz came out to the field and invited her to eat with his servants. She ate until she was full and still had some left over. Then Boaz told his servants to let her glean in their midst and not give her any trouble as she gathered grain. She gathered until evening and had enough for many days' worth of flour.

Naomi was surprised and asked where she had been gleaning, and Ruth told her the exciting news of what had happened that day. Naomi was thrilled and told Ruth that Boaz was one of her family's redeemers, meaning he had the obligation and right to help them out according to God's commands. This was an essential feature of how Israelites were to deal with widows and the powerless. She told Ruth to stay close to Boaz's women so she would be safe and no one would trouble her.

Then Naomi said, "Shouldn't I look out for your good as well? Boaz is our relative and he is going to be working on the threshing floor tonight. Wash up and get dressed and after the men have finished eating and drinking, keep an eye where Boaz lies down. Once he is asleep, follow my instructions."

Ruth listened, and once Boaz was asleep, Ruth uncovered his feet and laid down next to them. Boaz woke up around midnight and was surprised to find Ruth at his feet. When asked who she was, Ruth answered, "I am your servant, Ruth. You are a redeemer; please spread your wings over me."

Boaz replied, "May God bless you! This is even better than what you have done for Naomi because you did not go after young men or money. Do not fear because I will do whatever you ask of me. I will go to the townspeople and tell them that you are an honorable woman. I am indeed a redeemer, but another man has that right before I do. If he refuses to redeem you, then I will do it. Stay here until morning."

She lay by his feet until morning and got up before it was light enough to identify anyone. Boaz didn't want anyone to know that she had been there, but he loaded her up with as much barley as she could carry home. When she arrived, she excitedly told Naomi everything that happened.

That day, Boaz went to sit at the city gate and waited for the relative that he had told Ruth about to pass by. He explained Ruth's situation and gave him the opportunity to purchase Naomi's property and marry Ruth to carry on the family line. Boaz's relative refused because he did not want to jeopardize his own inheritance.

So, Boaz acted in the role of redeemer, and he purchased everything that had belonged to Elimelech and his family. He also married Ruth so that he could carry on Elimelech's family lineage. The townspeople blessed this transaction and verified that it was valid.

Boaz married Ruth and she bore him a son. The women said to Naomi, "Praise the Lord because he did not leave you without a redeemer; may his name be great forever! He will restore your life and nourish you in your old age because Ruth has been better to you than seven sons."

Then the people brought the child to Naomi and she became the child's nurse. They named him Obed, and he was the grandfather of David. Eventually, Jesus came from the line of this foreign woman who was redeemed by a relative according to God's commands.

CHAPTER FOURTEEN

SAMUEL

I Samuel 1-2

Elkanah was a man who lived in the hill country of Ephraim and he had two wives. One of his wives, Hannah, didn't have children, but his other wife did. Every year, Elkanah would go to Shiloh to worship the Lord and offer sacrifices. Eli was the high priest, and two of his sons, Hophni and Phinehas, served as priests at Shiloh. On the day that Elkanah would offer sacrifices, he would give his wives and children gifts. But he always gave Hannah twice as much because he loved her, even though she was barren.

This made Elkanah's other wife angry, so she often looked for ways to humiliate and provoke Hannah. This happened every year they went to Shiloh, and Hannah would weep and refuse to eat. Elkanah tried to comfort her and said, "Why are you so sad? Why do you refuse to eat? Aren't I better to you than if you had ten sons?"

One year, after they had eaten and drunk, Hannah went to pray and she wept bitterly. She was deeply distressed and she vowed, "Lord, I am your servant. If you will look at my affliction and remember me and give me a son, I will devote him to you. A razor will never touch his head as a sign of his dedication to you."

Eli was sitting nearby, and he saw her lips move as she prayed, although she didn't say anything out loud. He thought she was drunk and confronted her about it. Hannah replied, "Please don't think I'm drunk; I am a woman with a troubled soul. I have not had anything to drink; I am just pouring my heart out to the Lord. Please don't think I'm a worthless woman; I have just been praying about my anxiety and frustration."

Eli answered, "Go in peace; God is going to grant your request."

Hannah left and felt much better; she ate some food and was no longer sad. They got up early the next morning, worshiped God, and then went home. Elkanah slept with Hannah and she became pregnant. When her son was born, she named him Samuel because she had asked the Lord for him, and he had answered.

HANNAH BRINGS SAMUEL TO SERVE

The following year, Elkanah and his household went to Shiloh to offer their yearly sacrifice and pay his vow. But Hannah stayed home and said, "As soon as my son is weaned, I will bring him up so that he may be in the Lord's presence and live there the rest of his life." Elkanah agreed and told her to do what seemed best to her.

Hannah nursed Samuel until she weaned him, and then she brought him along with a bull, some flour, and wine to offer to the Lord. Samuel was still very young when she brought him to Eli and she said, "I am the woman who was praying to the Lord in your presence. This is the child that I prayed for and God answered my prayer. Now, I am giving him to the Lord for all the days of his life." Then she gave her offering and worshiped the Lord.

She prayed, "My heart praises the Lord and my strength is for your glory. I ridicule my enemies because I rejoice in your salvation. No one is as holy as the Lord; there is no rock like our God. Do not let me be arrogant because you know all things and judge our actions. You have given the weak strength, the hungry food, and the barren give birth. You give life and take it away; you exalt and bring people low. You raise the poor from the dust and give them a seat of honor. The pillars of the earth are yours and you have set the earth on them. You guard the path of the faithful and cut off the way of the wicked because our might is not enough to save us. You will break your enemies into pieces and judge the entire world. You will give strength to your king and give power to your anointed ones." Then she went home and Samuel served the Lord in the temple while the temple servants raised him.

ELI'S SONS

Eli's sons were worthless men and they did not know the Lord. They would take whatever they wanted from the Israelite's offerings and would save the best for themselves. If people protested that they wanted to offer the best to the Lord, the boys would threaten to take it with force. Their sin was great in God's eyes because they treated his offerings with contempt.

Samuel served before the Lord wearing a linen garment. Every year Hannah would bring him a new outfit when they came to worship the Lord. Then Eli would bless her and Elkanah, saying, "May the Lord give you many children by this woman because of her prayer to God." Then they would return home. God blessed Hannah and she had three more sons and two daughters. Samuel continued to grow and he served the Lord.

Eli was getting very old, and he kept hearing about the evil that his sons were committing and how they were sleeping with the women who served at the Tabernacle. He said to his sons, "Why do you keep doing these evil things? People keep talking; what you are doing is becoming common knowledge. If you sin against a man, the Lord will intercede for you, but if you sin against God, who will intercede?" But they refused to listen and God decided to kill them.

A man of God came to Eli and said, "God revealed himself to your father's household while you were in slavery in Egypt. He chose him from all the Israelites to serve him and be his priest. He gave your family the privilege and honor of offering sacrifices to the Lord, but you are using your position to make yourselves fat and rich. He chose your family, but he will honor whom he wishes, and those he despises will come to nothing. The days are coming where he will cut off your strength and you will no longer have any man in your family who reaches old age.

"You will look on Israel's prosperity with envy, and God will only keep your house alive so it can weep from grief when it sees how your descendants die by the sword. As a sign to you, both Hophni and Phinehas will die on the same day. Then God will raise up a faithful priest who will obey him. The Lord will establish his house, but your descendants will beg him for a piece of silver, a crust of bread, or a job as a priest."

CHAPTER FIFTEEN

SAMUEL'S CALL

I Samuel 3

Samuel served the Lord under Eli's supervision and God rarely spoke or gave visions to the Israelites. Eli was almost 100 and losing his sight. He was in his room while Samuel lay by the ark of the covenant. God called to Samuel and he went to Eli because the boy thought the priest had called. Eli told him to go back and lie down because he had not called him. Samuel did not know God's voice yet and this scenario happened two more times. After the third time, Eli realized that God was calling Samuel, so the priest told him to lie down, and if God called again to say, "Speak, Lord, because your servant is listening."

The Lord called Samuel's name again and the boy said, "Speak, Lord, because your servant is listening."

Then God said, "I am about to do something that will make everyone in Israel's ears tingle when they hear about it. I am going to fulfill my word against Eli and his sons. I will punish his house forever because his sons committed blasphemy against me and he did not stop them. I swear that I will not forgive their sin, even if they offer sacrifices."

Samuel laid back down until the morning and he was afraid to tell Eli what God had said. But Eli asked him directly about God's word and told him that he should withhold nothing. Samuel told him what God had said and Eli replied, "He is the Lord; let him do what seems best."

Samuel continued to grow and serve and all his words came to pass. Eventually, everyone in Israel knew who he was and that God had established him as a prophet. The Lord continued to appear to him at Shiloh and God revealed himself to Samuel.

How does God speak?

The short answer is, however he wants. The primary way he speaks to us today is through the Bible, and it should be our primary source of wisdom. However, if we have faith in him, he has promised to give us the Holy Spirit to live inside us. He can speak through the Holy Spirit to help us know him better and make decisions. God also speaks to his people through other believers, signs, dreams, impressions, and world events. As we try to determine if the message we hear is from God, it is essential to know that he never contradicts what he has taught us in the Bible.

CHAPTER SIXTEEN

THE PHILISTINES CAPTURE THE ARK

I Samuel 4:1-7:2

Israel went out to battle their oppressors, the Philistines, and their enemies routed the tribes. About 4,000 Israelite soldiers died that day and the elders came together to discuss why they had lost. They decided that they should bring the ark of the covenant to the battle to save themselves.

They went to Shiloh and brought the ark along with Eli's sons to their battle camp. When the ark entered the camp, the people shouted so loudly that the earth shook. The Philistines were confused by the shouting, and when they learned the ark had entered the camp, they were terrified. They knew what God had done in Egypt and how he had brought them into the Promised Land. They encouraged each other to fight bravely so that they would not become Israel's slaves.

When they went into battle the next day, the Philistines defeated the Israelites and killed about 30,000 men, including Hophni and Phinehas. They captured the ark of the covenant and all the Israelites fled to their homes.

A messenger from Benjamin ran to Shiloh with his clothes torn, covered in dirt. Eli was sitting by the roadside because he was nervous about the ark and God's message for his family. The man told the city what had happened, and the people wailed. Eli asked the messenger what had happened, and the man told him about Israel's defeat, that his sons were dead, and that the Philistines had captured the ark. When Eli heard about the ark, he fell off his seat and broke his neck because he was old and fat. He judged Israel for 40 years before he died.

Phinehas' wife was pregnant, and when she heard the news about her husband, Eli, and the ark, she went into labor. She had complications and was about to die. The midwives told her that she had given birth to a boy, but she did not respond. They named the boy Ichabod, saying, "Israel has lost its glory."

The Philistines took the ark to Ashdod and set it up in the temple of their god Dagon. The following day, they went into the temple and their idol had fallen on its face before the ark. They set the idol back up and went about their business. The next morning, the idol had fallen again, but this time its head and both hands were cut off and lying at the threshold of the temple.

God's hand was weighty on the Philistines and he afflicted them with tumors and hemorrhoids. When the city elders came together, they decided that the ark could not stay there because God was torturing them. They decided to take it to the city of Gath.

But when the ark arrived in Gath the same thing happened to them that had occurred in Ashdod. There was a great panic and they decided to take the ark to Ekron. But when it arrived, the people said, "You have brought the ark of the God of Israel to kill us." Seeing that they didn't have a place for the ark, they decided to send it back to Israel because they could not stand how God punished them.

The Philistines had the ark for about seven months before they decided to send it back. The Philistine priests advised that they should not send it back empty but should send a guilt offering with it. The priests told them to make five golden mice and five golden tumors to symbolize their nation's five allied cities and represent how God had afflicted them.

They advised the people not to harden their hearts as the Egyptians had but to repent. So, they put the ark on a cart drawn by two milk cows and a box containing the golden images they had made. Then they put the cart on the road back to Israel and let the cows pull it.

God directed the cows and they did not turn away from the road until they reached the Israelite town of Beth-Shemesh. The Philistine lords followed the cart until it came to the town and then they returned home. The Israelites were harvesting wheat when the cart arrived and rejoiced when they saw it. The ark stopped by a field near a giant rock.

The Levites took the ark and the box of golden images off the cart and then used the wood to offer the cows as a sacrifice. Some men tried to get close to the ark and God struck down about 70 of them. The community mourned their loss and sent word to Kiriath-jearim so that they would take the ark there.

Men from Kiriath-jearim brought the ark to their city and put it in Abinadab's house on a hill. Then they consecrated his son, Eleazar, to take care of it. They kept the ark there for about 20 years and all the people lamented after the Lord.

What is the ark of the covenant?

The ark of the covenant was a wooden box inlaid with gold and jewels that the Israelites made in the Sinai wilderness. It was a box that held the Ten Commandments and Aaron's rod that had sprouted buds when the tribal leaders had challenged his authority. It represented God's covenant with his people and the Israelites held it to be one of their most sacred elements. God gave specific commands for building it, carrying it, and using it in worship.

CHAPTER SEVENTEEN

SAMUEL JUDGES ISRAEL

I Samuel 7:3-8:22

Samuel said to the Israelites, "If you are returning to the Lord with all your heart, then put away your foreign gods and idols. Turn your hearts towards him and serve him only, and he will deliver you from the Philistines." The people obeyed and Samuel gathered them all at Mizpah, where he would pray for them.

They drew water and poured it out before the Lord as an offering and fasted that day because they recognized that they had sinned against the Lord. Then Samuel stayed at Mizpah, where he judged the tribes.

When the Philistines heard that the people had gathered at Mizpah, they brought their troops to battle with the Israelites. The people were terrified and begged Samuel to keep praying for them so they would not become the Philistines' slaves. Samuel offered a nursing lamb to the Lord and cried out to God. As he was preparing to offer the lamb, the Philistines approached to do battle, but God answered Samuel's prayer. The Lord threw them into great confusion, and the Israelites struck them down for many miles.

Samuel set up a memorial stone and named it Ebenezer because God had helped them. So, God subdued the Philistines, and they did not enter Israel again all the days of Samuel. They were able to recover the cities that the Philistines had captured and they had peace. Each year Samuel would travel throughout Israel and he would judge the nation.

When Samuel became old, he appointed his sons Joel and Abijah as judges in Beersheba. But they were wicked, and they perverted justice, took bribes, and pursued their own gain. Then the elders of Israel came to Samuel at Ramah and said, "You are getting old, and your sons do not follow in your ways; please appoint us a king to rule over us like the other nations around us." Samuel was not pleased with their request, but they kept after him, and Samuel asked God about it.

God said to Samuel, "Listen to the people because they are not rejecting you; they are rejecting me. Even after everything I have done for them, they keep turning after foreign gods and forsaking me. Now they are doing the same thing to you. Obey them, but make sure to warn them about the dangers of having a king who rules them."

Samuel relayed God's words to the people and said, "If you have a king, he will take your sons and put them into the army. He will make you become farmers for him and keepers of his equipment. Your king will make your daughters perfumers and cooks for his benefit. He will take your best fields, vineyards, and orchards for himself and his servants. Your king will take a tenth of everything you have and the best of your young men and women to be slaves. One day, you will cry out to the Lord because of how your king treats you, but the Lord will not listen to your cries."

But the people refused to listen to Samuel because they wanted to be like the nations around them. Samuel brought the words to the Lord and God told him to listen to the people. Then Samuel sent all the people back to their homes.

CHAPTER EIGHTEEN

SAUL TO BE KING
I Samuel 9:1-12:5

There was a wealthy Benjaminite man with a very tall and handsome son named Saul. The man lost a herd of donkeys and sent Saul to look for them. Saul looked everywhere for animals but could not find them in all the land of Benjamin. Eventually, Saul said to his servant, "Let's go back home, or else my father will stop worrying about the donkeys and become anxious about us."

But before they headed home, Saul said, "There is a man of God in a nearby city that everyone honors, and everything he says comes true. Maybe he can tell us where to look for the donkeys. But we cannot come empty-handed. What should we give him because we don't have any food or provisions left?" His servant told him that he had a small amount of silver, so they decided to see the man.

When they arrived in the town where Samuel lived, Saul asked the local women if he was there. They told him where he was and encouraged him to hurry because he had just offered a sacrifice and was about to sit down to eat.

God had revealed to Samuel that Saul would come to him and that he should anoint him as king because he was the one to deliver the Israelites from the Philistines. When Saul came to see Samuel, God said to Samuel, "The one I told you about is coming to meet you."

Samuel told Saul, "Go up to the high place ahead of me; then I will eat with you. Tomorrow morning, I will tell you everything that is on your mind. Don't worry about the missing donkeys, because they have been found. God is giving everything that one can desire to you and your father's household."

Saul answered, "Why do you say these things to me? I'm from the least important house in Benjamin, the smallest of all the tribes of Israel."

That evening Samuel brought Saul in to have a meal with about 30 other people the prophet had invited and placed him at the head of the table. Samuel set aside the best cut of meat and gave it to Saul and they ate together. He secured a place for Saul to sleep that night and woke him up at dawn the next morning so Saul could be on his way.

Samuel went with him to the edge of the city and then sent Saul's servant ahead of them so that Samuel could tell Saul what God had to say.

Samuel took a flask of olive oil and anointed Saul's head, saying, "The Lord has anointed you to be prince over his inheritance." He continued, "When you leave, you will meet two women as you arrive at the border of Benjamin. They will tell you that they have found the donkeys, but now your father is worried about you. From there, you will continue to the great tree of Tabor and you will meet three men when you get there. One will have three young goats, another will have three loaves of bread, and the third will have a wineskin. They will greet you and offer you two loaves of bread.

"After that, you will continue to Gibeah, where there is a Philistine outpost. You will meet a procession of prophets who will be making music and speaking the word of the Lord. The Holy Spirit will come upon you and you will begin to prophesy. You will become a different person. Once these signs have occurred, continue with your life because God is with you. Wait for me for seven days at Gilgal, and then I will come to you and tell you what you need to do."

As Saul left Samuel, God changed his heart, and all these signs took place that day. When people saw him prophesying, they wondered what had happened because Saul had never been known to be a prophet. Saul's uncle met him, and Saul told him the story of what had happened, but he left out the part about being anointed king.

Samuel called all the people to him at Mizpah and he said, "God brought you out of Egypt and from all the nations who have oppressed you. But now, you have rejected the Lord and asked for a king. Present the twelve tribes before me and God will choose a king for you by casting lots." Samuel selected Saul's tribe, clan, and family; finally, Samuel revealed that Saul would be the king of Israel.

The people searched for Saul, and when the people found out that he was not there, God revealed that he was hiding with the supplies. They brought him out and he was a full head taller than anyone else. Samuel said, "See the man that God has chosen as your king; there is no other Israelite who is like him!"

Then the people shouted, "Long live the king!"

Samuel explained to everyone all the rights and duties of kingship and wrote them down on a scroll. Then he sent them all to their homes. Saul went back to Gibeah with some brave men whom the Lord had filled with the Holy Spirit. But some scoundrels despised Saul and spoke evil about him. Saul heard their talk but didn't say anything about it.

SAUL DELIVERS JABESH

Not long after this, the Ammonites went up to Jabesh, surrounded it, and set siege to it. The people of Jabesh sought to make a treaty with the Ammonites and become their servants, but the foreigners required that they be able to gouge out the Jabeshites' right eyes to disgrace Israel. The people asked for seven days to see if anyone from Israel would deliver them.

Messengers went to Gibeah, and when people heard the news, they wept. Saul was coming in from the field and asked what all the commotion was. They told him and he was furious. The Holy Spirit filled him and he cut a pair of oxen into pieces and sent them throughout Israel, saying, "This is what I will do to anyone who does not follow Saul and Samuel."

People were terrified, and they all came out to follow Saul, 300,000 soldiers in all, including 30,000 from Judah. Saul sent messengers to Jabesh, saying that he would deliver them by midday the next day.

The men of Jabesh were happy and told the Ammonites that they would come out the next day to surrender. Saul divided his men into three separate companies and attacked their enemies late at night. The Israelites caught them by surprise and slaughtered them until the following afternoon.

The people rejoiced and said, "Who spoke ill of Saul? Bring those men out so that we can kill them!"

Samuel stopped them, "No one is going to die today because God has delivered us! Let us go to Gilgal and confirm Saul as king!" So, they went to Gilgal and made Saul their king, and they had a grand celebration.

Samuel spoke to Israel, "I have listened to you and given you a king. I have led you from my youth and now I am an old man. I have served with integrity and have not wronged anyone. The Lord is my witness that I have not taken anything from any of you. Now listen to me because I am going to tell you everything God has done for you and your ancestors."

CHAPTER NINETEEN

CONFIRMATION OF SAUL AS KING

I Samuel 12:6-13:23

The people confirmed that Samuel was faultless in their eyes, and then Samuel proceeded to recite Israel's history from the time they left Egypt to that day. He said to the people, "Even though God has done all these things, you still wanted a king, although God had been your ruler. Here is Saul, the one God has chosen, and he is your king. If you and your leader fear the Lord and serve him, things will go well for you. But if you do not obey him, God will be against you just as he has been against your ancestors. It is harvest time, but God is going to send rain so that you realize the evil you have committed by demanding a king."

When the people realized their sin of rejecting the Lord, they begged Samuel to pray for them. But Samuel said, "Do not be afraid, turn away from your evil. Do not reject the Lord, but serve him with all your heart. Turn away from your worthless idols because they will not be able to do anything for you or rescue you; they are useless. God will not reject you for the sake of his name and because he chose you. I will continue to pray for you and teach you the right thing to do. But be sure to fear the Lord and serve him with all your heart. Remember the great things that he has done for you. But if you continue to do evil, you and your king will perish."

SAUL'S DISOBEDIENCE

Saul was 30 years old when he became king and reigned over Israel for 42 years. He took 3,000 men and sent the rest back to their homes. Then he attacked the Philistine outpost of Geba. The people realized that the Philistines were angry, so they gathered around Saul at Gilgal. The Philistines amassed a massive army to attack the Israelites. People were terrified and they hid wherever they could.

Saul waited for Samuel for seven days as the prophet had instructed, but the people became increasingly afraid and began to scatter. Saul felt like he couldn't wait any longer, so he overstepped his role and offered sacrifices to the Lord. This was a direct violation of what God had set up in the Law.

As he finished the offering, Saul went out to meet Samuel, and Samuel said, "What have you done?"

Saul replied, "You hadn't arrived and I saw how afraid people were as the Philistines were gathering to attack. I thought they were going to attack before I sought the Lord's favor, so I felt compelled to offer him a sacrifice."

Samuel answered, "You have acted foolishly. You have not obeyed the Lord, and if you had, he would have established your kingdom forever. Now your kingdom will not last because God will give it to someone who is after his heart." Then Samuel left and Saul counted the 6,000 men who were still with him.

The Philistines had forbidden the Israelites from having blacksmiths and forced them to bring their farming tools for sharpening. So, the few Israelite soldiers didn't have a single weapon among them. The Philistines regularly sent raiding parties into Israel because they had no weapons to defend themselves.

CHAPTER TWENTY

JONATHAN DELIVERS ISRAEL

I Samuel 14-15

One day, Saul's son, Jonathan, took his armor-bearer to a Philistine outpost without telling his father. Jonathan went through a pass with cliffs on both sides and said to his armor-bearer, "Let us go over to these godless men and maybe the Lord will act on our behalf. Nothing can keep him from saving us, regardless of how few people we have."

Jonathan's armor-bearer told him that he was with him no matter what, and Jonathan said, "We will go over to their camp and let them see us coming. If they tell us to wait for them to come down to us, we will stay where we are. If they call us to come up to them, then we will know that God is giving them into our hands."

The two men walked towards the Philistine camp and their soldiers said, "Look! The Hebrews are crawling out of their holes! Come up here and we will teach you a lesson!"

Jonathan told his armor-bearer to climb up after him, and he went up to the Philistine camp and killed about 20 of their men. God sent the entire Philistine army into a panic and the ground shook. Saul's outposts saw that the Philistines were melting away. Saul called his forces together to see who was there, and they found that Jonathan and his armor-bearer were missing.

Saul called for the ark of God to come to the frontlines and they saw that the panic was becoming worse in the Philistine camp. So, Saul led his men into battle and they found the Philistines attacking each other. Some of the Israelites that had gone into hiding joined Saul and his men when they saw his leadership. God delivered the Israelites on that day.

Saul put the people under an oath that anyone who ate anything before he had vengeance on his enemies would be cursed. They were starving, and when they entered the forest to pursue the Philistines, they saw honey oozing onto the ground. But the people were afraid of Saul's oath, so no one ate any.

Jonathan had not heard his father's oath, so he ate some and had a burst of energy. One of the soldiers told him, "Your father put us under a strict oath, cursing anyone who ate before we defeated our enemies. That is why the people are so faint and no one else is eating."

Jonathan was angry and said, "My father has made trouble for us. See how much more energy I had after just a little taste? We would have slaughtered many more Philistines if we weren't so hungry."

At the end of the day, the soldiers were exhausted and jumped on the spoils with greedy hunger. They were so hungry that they ate the meat raw. Someone pointed out that the people were sinning by eating raw meat, in violation of the Law. Saul told them to bring the animals to a central place to slaughter them so they would no longer sin against the Lord. Then Saul built his first altar to the Lord.

Saul proposed that they continue to pursue the Philistines through the night and into the next day, but one of the priests suggested that they ask God what they should do. Saul asked the Lord if they should continue to pursue, but God was silent.

Saul called the leaders together to see who had sinned and kept God from answering his request. He swore that even if his son had sinned, that he would die. The people listened, but no one said anything about Jonathan and the honey.

Saul set the people on one side and himself and his son on another and prayed that God would show them who had sinned by casting lots. God showed them that the guilt was between him and his son, then God revealed that Jonathan had broken the oath. Saul demanded that he tell him what he had done.

Jonathan told him about the honey he had tasted and accepted that he should be the one to die on behalf of the people. But the soldiers intervened, "Should Jonathan die when he was the one who delivered us? As God lives, no harm will come to him because he rescued us with God's help!" Saul relented and spared Jonathan and the Israelites stopped pursuing the Philistines.

Saul continued to fight against his enemies and punished them wherever he turned. The commander of his army was his cousin, Abner. As long as Saul ruled, whenever he found a brave man, he brought him into the army.

Samuel came to Saul and said, "The Lord is the one who appointed you king, so listen to what he has to say. He wants to punish the Amalekites for attacking his people as they left Egypt. Destroy all the people and possessions they have, do not leave anything of theirs because they are evil in his sight."

Saul summoned 200,000 soldiers as well as 10,000 from the tribe of Judah. He set an ambush against the Amalekites and warned the Kenites to leave the area because of their kindness to Israel. Then Saul attacked the Amalekites and killed all of them except for their king, Agag. They destroyed all their possessions but kept the best of their livestock for themselves.

God was angry with Saul's incomplete obedience and said to Samuel, "It saddens me that I made Saul king because he has not followed all of my commands." Samuel was also angry and he spent the entire night in prayer.

Samuel met Saul the following day and was told that he had set a monument to his own greatness and returned to Gilgal. When Saul saw Samuel leaving, he said, "May the Lord bless you because I have carried out all of his instructions!"

Samuel answered, "Then why do I hear all kinds of sheep and cows around me?"

Saul replied, "We saved the best of the livestock to offer them to the Lord, but we have destroyed everything else."

Samuel was furious and said, "Enough! Last night God told me that he had taken you from your low position to become king over his people. He sent you on a mission to destroy the Amalekites, but you did not listen! Why didn't you obey and completely wipe them out?"

Saul was defensive and said, "But I did destroy them. I only brought back their king and the best of the livestock to offer sacrifices to your God!"

But Samuel replied, "Is the Lord happier with sacrifices or obedience? It is far better to obey than to bring offerings! Disobedience is one of the worst sins; it is just as bad as idolatry or witchcraft."

Saul changed his tactic and said, "I have sinned against God and not listened to your instructions. I was afraid of disappointing the men, so I let them take the best of the livestock. Please forgive me and come back with me so that I may worship the Lord."

Samuel answered, "I will not come back with you because you have rejected the Lord, and now, he is rejecting you as king!"

As Samuel turned to leave, Saul grabbed the hem of his robe, and it tore. Samuel turned to the king and said, "The Lord has torn Israel from your hands and is giving it to one of your neighbors, someone who is far better than you! He is Israel's glory and he does not change his mind like men do."

Saul said, "I have sinned! Please honor me before the elders and Israel by coming back with me so that I may worship your God."

Samuel agreed to go back with Saul and they worshiped the Lord. Then Samuel asked to bring the Amalekite king into his presence. Agag thought he was safe and that Samuel would spare his life. But Samuel said to him, "Just as you have made women childless, now your mother will be childless!" Then the prophet killed him with a sword before God at Gilgal.

Samuel went back to Ramah, and Saul went back to his home in Gibeah. Samuel mourned for Saul from that day on, but he never went to see him until he died. God regretted that he had made Saul king.

Serving God on our terms

Saul wanted to serve God, but he wanted to do it on his own terms. God wants our obedience, not our justifications for our behavior. If he commands us to do something, we should not change his command to make it more palatable.

CHAPTER TWENTY-ONE

DAVID'S RISE TO PROMINENCE

I Samuel 16:1-18:5

The Lord said to Samuel, "How long will you keep mourning over Saul since I have rejected him from being king over Israel? Fill your horn with oil and go to Bethlehem to visit Jesse because I am choosing one of his sons as the next king."

Samuel protested that if Saul heard about this journey, the king would kill him. God told him, "Take a heifer with you to sacrifice to me and invite Jesse to the sacrifice. Once he is there, I will tell you what to do, and you will anoint who I tell you to. Saul will not suspect this errand."

When Samuel arrived in Bethlehem, the people were afraid, but he said to them, "I come in peace to offer a sacrifice to the Lord, consecrate yourselves and join me." Then he invited Jesse and his sons to join him as well.

When Jesse's sons came, Samuel saw the oldest, Eliab, and thought that God would surely choose him. But God said to Samuel, "Do not look at his appearance or height because I have rejected him. People only see the outward appearance, but I see the heart."

Jesse brought each of his sons before Samuel and God rejected each of them. Samuel asked Jesse if he had any more sons and Jesse answered that his youngest son was out watching the sheep. They sent for the boy, and when he came in, he was handsome with beautiful eyes and rosy cheeks. God told the prophet that this was his choice. Samuel anointed his head with oil in his brothers' presence and then returned to Ramah. From that day on, the Holy Spirit filled David. Saul did not know that these events took place.

The Spirit of the Lord had left Saul and God sent an evil spirit to torment him. Saul's servants suggested finding someone who could play music for him whenever he was troubled and Saul agreed.

One of the servants told Saul that David was an excellent musician, had a good character, and the Lord was with him. Saul sent for him and David went with gifts for the king. Saul loved David and he eventually became the king's armor-bearer. Saul told Jesse that David would remain with him, and whenever the evil spirit would come, David would play music to calm Saul down. After a couple of years, David returned home.

DAVID AND GOLIATH

The Philistines gathered for battle in Judah on one side of the Valley of Elah. The Philistines sent out a champion named Goliath from the city of Gath. He was over nine feet tall and carried hundreds of pounds of armor and a massive spear with a head weighing more than 18 pounds. His armor-bearer went with him and he shouted at the Israelites, "Why have you come out to fight against us? I am a Philistine and you are Saul's servants. Choose a champion from your midst and send him to fight me. If he can kill me, we will be your servants, but if I kill him, you will serve us! I defy your army; give me a champion that I can fight!" Saul and the other Israelites heard these words and they were disheartened.

David's three oldest brothers had joined the army and David went back and forth from the battle lines to tend his father's sheep. He would bring food for his brothers and their commanders and bring back word to his father about how things were going.

Goliath came out for 40 days and taunted the Israelites, belittling them and cursing God.

Early one morning, David came out to the battle lines. When he saw what was happening, he left what he had brought with a servant and went out to the front line to check on his brothers. Goliath came out and challenged the Israelites just as he had previously. David heard his curses and saw how terrified the men were as they began to run from the battle line.

David asked the men he was standing with, "What will be done for the man who kills this godless Philistine? How dare he come to us to ridicule the army of the living God!"

The men speculated, "The king will likely make him a wealthy man and give him his daughter's hand in marriage. He will make his father's house rich and powerful in Israel."

David's oldest brother came to him and said, "What are you doing out here? Who's watching our father's sheep? You just came out here so you could watch a battle!"

David was indignant and said, "What did I do? I just asked a question!" Then he went to some other soldiers and repeated his query.

When Saul heard about David's questions, he sent for the boy, and David said to the king, "Don't let anyone be afraid because of this Philistine, I will fight him!"

Saul answered, "You can't fight him, you are just a boy, and he has been a warrior since he was a child."

David was fired up and replied, "I am a shepherd and I have defended my father's flock from lions and bears. Whenever they came to steal a lamb, I chased them down and killed them. This godless Philistine will be like one of them and I will punish him for defying the living God's armies! He delivered me from wild animals and he will deliver me from this man as well."

Saul sighed and said, "Go fight him and may the Lord be with you." Then he tried to give David his armor and sword; however, they were way too big for him.

David tried to walk and was unable, so he said, "I cannot use these because I'm not used to them." So, he took his staff in his hand, chose five smooth stones from a stream, and took them with his sling. Then he walked out to meet Goliath in battle.

Goliath and his armor-bearer approached the Israelites, and when they saw David coming out with no armor and only a sling, the Philistine champion laughed and yelled, "Am I a dog that you are coming out to fight me with a stick?" Then he cursed David.

David answered bravely, "Come fight me and I will give your flesh to the birds as food! You come to me with a sword and a spear, but I come in the name of the Lord, the God of the armies you have ridiculed. He will deliver you into my hand, I will cut your head off, and we will slaughter the Philistines. Then you and all Israel will know that God can deliver without the sword. The battle is his and he will deliver you into my hands!"

Goliath came out to fight as David ran toward the giant. David pulled a stone from his pouch, put it in his sling, and swung it around his head. When he released the stone, it flew and hit Goliath in the forehead. It sunk in, and the giant fell on his face and died. David ran to the fallen giant, grabbed his sword, and cut his head off. When the Philistines saw that their champion was dead, they turned and ran.

The Israelites shouted with joy and pursued the Philistines for miles, killing them as they caught them. Then they came back to the Philistine camp and plundered it. David took Goliath's head back to Jerusalem but put his armor in his tent.

When Saul saw all of this, he asked his commander, Abner, "Who is this boy?" Abner told him that he did not know and Saul told him to find out who his father was. Saul knew who David was, but was surprised by the boy's courage because it was out of context from how he knew him. When David came to the king with Goliath's head, David told Saul he was Jesse's son. Then Saul insisted he come live with him.

As soon as the shepherd finished speaking to Saul, David and Saul's son, Jonathan, became best friends and loved each other as much as they loved themselves. They swore to each other that they would be friends until the day they died. Then Jonathan gave David his robe, armor, and weapons because his shepherd's clothing was not worthy of appearing before the king. This was also a way to show David great honor.

David was successful in everything he did and Saul put him in command of his warriors. The people and all of Saul's servants approved.

CHAPTER TWENTY-TWO

SAUL TURNS AGAINST DAVID

I Samuel 18:6-20:42

One day, as the Israelites returned home from fighting with the Philistines, some women came out to meet Saul and David, dancing and playing music. They sang to one another, "Saul has killed his thousands, but David has killed tens of thousands!" Saul was furious at these words and he feared that David would take the kingdom from him. So, he kept a suspicious eye on him from that day on.

The next day, the Lord sent a harmful spirit to afflict Saul, and the king ranted and raved around his house while David played music to calm him down. Saul was holding a spear and tried to kill David two different times, but he escaped.

> **Why did God send a harmful spirit to afflict Saul?**
>
> The Lord had taken his favor from Saul and was working to remove the kingdom from him. God rules over the universe and has control over all spirits. Some have used this to argue that God is the author of evil, but God did not cause Saul to sin. The king still had his free will and chose to try killing David.

Saul was afraid of David because the king knew that the Lord had left him. So, Saul made David a commander of 1,000 troops to get him away and potentially put the shepherd in harm's way. But David continued to be successful in everything he did and he grew in fame and popularity.

When that plan didn't work, Saul tried to gain the shepherd's favor by giving his daughter, Merab, to David as a wife. The only condition was that he continue to fight for Saul's army. But David refused because he did not think that he was worthy of being the king's son-in-law. So, she married another man.

Another one of Saul's daughters, Michal, loved David, which made Saul happy because he thought he could use the situation against the young shepherd. He asked David to marry Michal and sent some of his servants to help convince David that this was a good idea. But the shepherd protested that he was from a poor family and could not afford a dowry rich enough to pay for a king's daughter.

> **What is a dowry?**
>
> In the Bible, a dowry was something a husband would give to a wife before marriage that functioned like life insurance. Sometimes it was money, livestock, or an act, whatever the family asked.

Saul sent word to David that he wanted the foreskin from 100 Philistines as a dowry. The king hoped the Philistines would kill David. This seemed reasonable to David, so he took his men down to attack the Philistines. He killed 200 of them and brought their foreskins to pay the dowry to marry Michal.

Saul knew that the Lord was with David and that his daughter loved him. He also saw how successful the shepherd was in battle against the Philistines and was terrified of David. But the people continued to love and honor him more and more.

Saul spoke to Jonathan and the royal servants and told them that they needed to kill David. But Jonathan loved his friend, so he told David his father's plans and then set a place to meet once he learned more. Jonathan went to his father and said, "Don't sin against David because he has not sinned against you; he has only worked to help you. He risked his life when he fought Goliath and God delivered the entire nation. You were happy then, so why will you kill David without cause?"

Saul listened to his son and swore that he would not kill David. Jonathan relayed this information to David and his friend returned to Saul's presence as before.

SAUL TRIES TO KILL DAVID

Not long after this, Israel went to war again, and David led them to a great victory. After the army returned, the Lord sent the harmful spirit to afflict Saul and he lost his mind while David played music one day. Saul threw a spear at David and it narrowly missed pinning David to the wall.

Saul sent soldiers to David's house to wait through the night and kill him at first light. David's wife, Michal, warned David that her father would kill him if he didn't run. So, she let him down through the window, and he escaped. To buy some time for her husband, she arranged a statue in the bed, covered it with clothes, and told the soldiers that he was sick.

The soldiers sent a messenger back to Saul to see what he wanted them to do, and the king instructed them to bring David up on his sickbed so that he could kill his adversary. They went in to bring him up to Saul and found the statute in the bed. Saul was furious and yelled at his daughter, "Why have you lied to me and let my enemy go?" She told her father that he had threatened to kill her and then escaped.

David ran to Ramah and told Samuel everything that Saul was doing. They both went and lived in Naioth. Saul sent men to seize David, but as they approached, Samuel was standing with a group of prophets speaking God's word. The men joined the prophets and also spoke on the Lord's behalf. Saul sent another group and the same thing happened. The king tried one more time and had the same result.

Saul was frustrated, so finally, he went himself. When he came close to where Samuel and David were staying, the Holy Spirit came upon him, and he stripped himself naked and prophesied along with the other prophets for an entire day and night.

David fled and met with Jonathan and asked him why his father was trying to kill him. Jonathan wanted to reassure him, "You are not going to die! My father doesn't do anything without telling me and I haven't heard anything about this."

David replied sadly, "Your father knows how close we are, and he has decided to keep this decision from you so that it won't break your heart. I am only a step away from death!"

Jonathan agreed to do whatever David asked him to do. So, David said, "Tomorrow is a new moon and I should be at meals with the king. I will hide for the next three days, and if your father misses me, tell him that I went to my hometown to offer a sacrifice. If he is okay with my absence, he is not trying to kill me. But if he is angry, Saul has decided to end my life. Do me this favor because we are companions, but if you think I'm guilty, please kill me yourself so that we don't have to bring your father into this dispute."

Jonathan decided that he would do this favor and let David know if his father would kill him. They agreed to meet again after three days so that Jonathan could tell David what Saul was going to do. Jonathan made him promise that if Saul killed him, David would not cut off Jonathan's descendants, and they made a covenant with each other. They set up a sign for how and when they would meet and Jonathan returned home.

When the new moon came, Saul sat down to eat with those closest to him, and David's seat was empty. Saul didn't say anything after the first day, but after the second day, Saul asked his son where David was. Jonathan told him the story that David had given him.

Was it okay for Jonathan to lie?

This situation presents an ethical dilemma. At times, we will face problems where we cannot make any choice that isn't a sin. There is no easy answer when we face these choices, but a general rule is to choose what does the least harm. In this instance, Jonathan lied to save a life because life is more valuable than the truth. These are difficult choices for us to make and there is no single rule that we can follow. When we face these situations, we should pray for wisdom and trust in our relationship with God.

Saul was furious and swore at his son, "You son of a perverse, rebellious woman! You have chosen David over me and your family; you should be ashamed! While he is alive, you will never be the king. Bring him to me now because he deserves to die!"

Jonathan answered his father, "Why should he die? What evil has he done?!" Saul was so angry that he threw his spear at Jonathan and tried to kill his son. Jonathan knew that his father intended to kill David, and was so sad that he refused to eat or drink anything.

On the third day, Jonathan went out to the field where he and David had agreed to meet, and he gave the sign that Saul wanted to kill him. Once they were sure that they were alone, David came out of hiding and bowed before his friend three times. They kissed each other and then wept on each other's necks. Then Jonathan said, "Go in peace because we have made a covenant with each other." Then Jonathan went home and David fled.

CHAPTER TWENTY-THREE

DAVID FLEES FROM SAUL

I Samuel 21-24

David went to Nob and met with Ahimelech, the priest who served there. The priest was confused why David was alone, but he told Ahimelech, "Saul has sent me on a secret mission and I am going to meet up with some other men in a little while. Give me five loaves of bread or whatever food you have here."

Ahimelech told David that he only had the holy bread he had dedicated to the Lord and David convinced him to let him have it. Ahimelech gave it to David along with Goliath's sword and the shepherd left. But one of Saul's servants, Doeg, was there and saw everything that took place.

> **Should David have taken the bread dedicated to the Lord?**
>
> Much like Jonathan's choice to lie to save David's life, David chose to break Ceremonial Law to save his men's lives.

David fled to the Philistine city of Gath and they were excited that the Hebrew champion had come into their hands. They brought him to their king, and David behaved as if he were insane, drooling on himself and scribbling on the doorposts. The king was irritated and said, "I have more than enough crazy people; get rid of him."

David left there and hid in a cave. When his family heard about it, they went to him because they feared for their lives. Then everyone who was in distress or disgruntled about Saul's leadership joined him and David became their leader. There were about 400 men in total and they went to the land of Moab and sought refuge there. But the Lord told David to return to Judah and they hid in a forest.

When Saul heard that all of this had happened, he was enraged and said to the men who were with him, "Everyone who thinks that David is going to lead you to great things should listen to me. You all have conspired against your king and no one tells me the truth about what is happening. No one tells me when my son makes a covenant with my enemy."

Doeg spoke up and told Saul what had happened with Ahimelech at Nob. So, Saul called Ahimelech and his whole family and confronted them, asking why they were conspiring against the throne. Ahimelech defended himself, "Who has been more faithful to you than David? This was not the first time that I'd helped David out. I didn't know that you were trying to capture him, so please don't find me guilty."

Saul was too angry to listen to reason, and he commanded his soldiers to kill Ahimelech and his family. But the men were afraid to do anything to God's priest. So,

Saul told Doeg to kill them, and he obeyed. He killed everyone in Nob regardless of age (about 85 people) and slaughtered all the livestock.

But one of Ahimelech's grandsons, Abiathar, escaped, and he went to David and told him what Saul and Doeg had done. David was grieved and he told Abiathar, "When I saw Doeg there, I knew that something bad would happen. I am sorry that I have caused your entire family to die. Stay with me and I will protect you."

While they were on the run, David heard that the Philistines were attacking the city of Keilah. David asked the Lord if he should attack the Philistines and God told him to save the city. The men protested that there was no way they could defeat the Philistines if they were already running from Saul. David asked God again if they should go down to Keilah and the Lord told him to save the city. Then David took his men down and defeated the Philistines.

Saul heard what David had done and that he was in Keilah, so he sent men to attack him. David heard that Saul was coming after him and asked God what he should do. The Lord told David that Saul was coming and that the city's men would hand him over. So, David and his men, which now numbered around 600, left and hid in the wilderness of Ziph. Saul pursued him every day, but he was unable to find him.

While Saul was chasing after David, Jonathan went to meet him and told him, "My father is trying to kill you, but he will not succeed. You will be the king over all of Israel and my father knows this." Then Jonathan went home.

The men of Ziph went to Saul and told him where David was hiding and told him to capture the fugitive. Saul was grateful and told them to return and bring him more details on where he was hiding. Saul followed them to Ziph, and David and his men fled to the wilderness of Maon. As they were getting close, Saul heard that the Philistines were raiding in Israel, so he took his men to defend against them. Then David went and stayed in the wilderness of Engedi.

After Saul had repelled the Philistine attack, he returned to pursuing David and took 3,000 men to Engedi. David and his men were hiding in a cave and by chance, Saul went into the cave to relieve himself. David's men said to him, "This is the day that the Lord has given your enemy into your hands, do whatever seems good to you."

While Saul was pooping, David snuck up behind him and cut off a corner of the king's robe. Afterward, David felt guilty about what he had done and he said, "God forbid that I should do anything against his anointed." He convinced his men not to attack Saul.

After Saul finished, David left the cave and went out to Saul and said, "Why do you listen to people who say that I'm trying to hurt you? God just gave you into my hands, and some of my companions told me to kill you, but I cannot lift a hand against the Lord's anointed."

David held up the corner of Saul's robe and said, "Look, I have the corner of your robe in my hand. I could have killed you, but this is all I did. This is a testimony that I have not sinned against you even though you are trying to kill me. May the Lord judge between us and take vengeance on you if he chooses, but I'm not going to do it. Why are you coming after me anyway? I am nothing more than a dead dog or a single flea! May God judge between us; may he plead my cause and deliver me from you!"

Saul lifted his voice and wept when he heard David's words, "You are more righteous than I am; you have repaid me with good, while I have tried to repay you with evil. You could have killed me when the Lord delivered me into your hands, but you refused. May God reward you with good for the kindness you have shown me this day. I know that you will be king of Israel one day and that the Lord will establish your kingdom. But swear to God that you will not cut off my descendants." Then Saul went home, but David stayed in the wilderness.

DAVID ON THE RUN

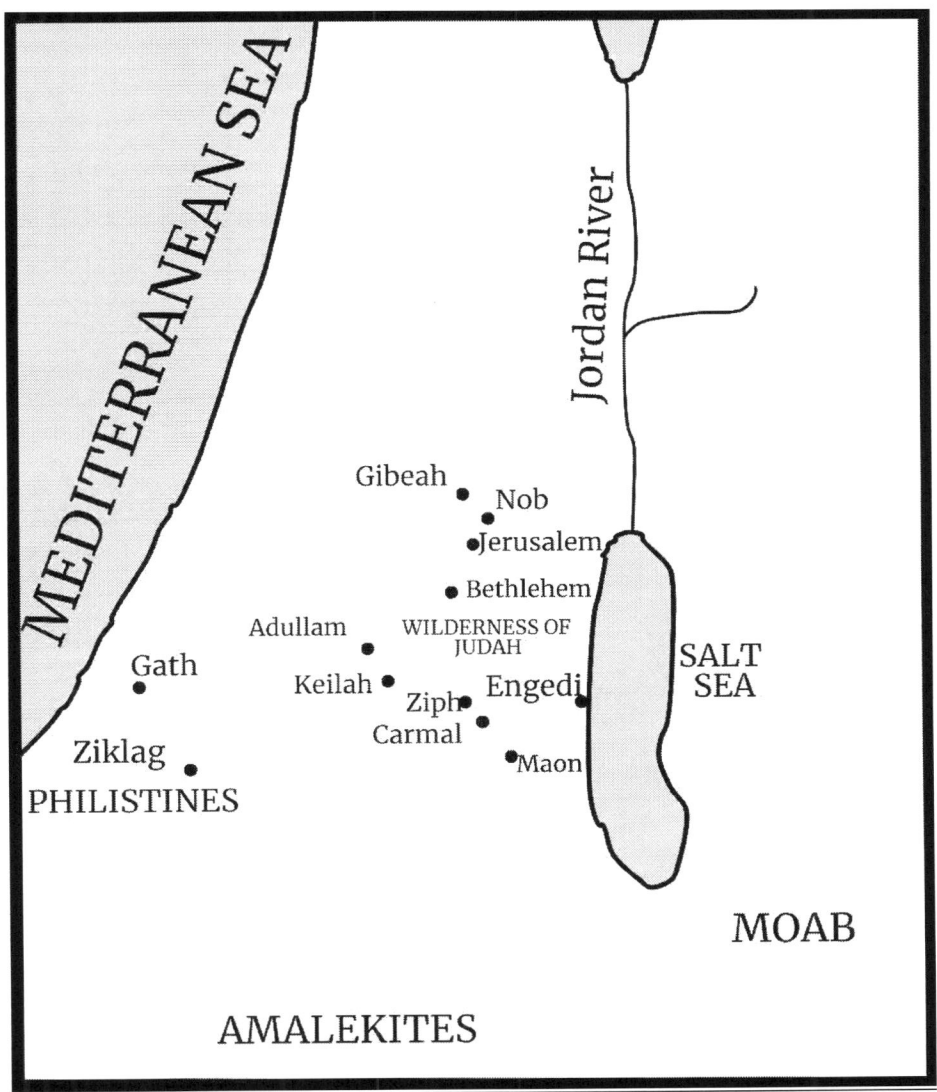

CHAPTER TWENTY-FOUR

SAMUEL'S DEATH, NABAL, AND SAUL PURSUES DAVID
I Samuel 25-26

Samuel died, and all of Israel mourned for him, and they buried him at his home in Ramah. After the prophet's death, David went down to the wilderness of Paran and came across a very wealthy man named Nabal, and his wife, Abigail. Abigail was beautiful and wise, but Nabal was rude and treated people poorly.

David heard that Nabal was shearing his flocks of sheep and sent ten young men to speak on his behalf. They said, "May God grant peace to you, your household, and everything you own. We see that you have sheep shearers here. While your shepherds were in the field, we watched over them and made sure nothing bad happened. If we have found favor in your eyes, please give us anything you can to help sustain David and his men."

Nabal answered David's servants harshly, "I don't know David. How do I know you men aren't lying to me? Many servants are running from their masters; how do I know you aren't trying to escape? There's no way I'm going to take the provisions I've prepared for my men and give them to strangers who are probably lying."

The men went back and told David about the exchange with Nabal. David was furious, so he armed 400 of his men and went to talk to Nabal while the remaining men stayed in their camp. One of Nabal's servants told Abigail about the conversation between her husband and David's men and reminded her how well David had treated them while he was in the area.

Abigail and her servants quickly prepared a large meal for all David's men and sent her attendants to meet him with the food. She followed them, but she did not tell her husband what she was doing. He was drunk and shearing the sheep away from home, so he was unaware of her actions.

David was angry about how Nabal treated his men and decided to kill all the men in his family. But Abigail came to him and intervened. She fell on her face before David and said, "Lord, please let me be the guilty one. Listen to what I have to say and let me explain the situation. My husband is a fool and worthless. I hadn't heard that your men had asked for food, but now I am bringing you a feast.

"Please forgive my transgression because God will establish your house. You are fighting his battles and he will not bring evil upon you all the days of your life. The men who rise against you will be little fools, like my husband, and God will protect you from them. God will surely make you king, and when he does, you will be innocent regarding this issue because the Lord has kept you from avenging yourself on Nabal. Once God deals with him, please remember how I have treated you."

David replied, "Praise the Lord that he sent you to meet me. I praise your discretion and how you have kept me from killing your husband." He took her gift from her and said, "Go home in peace because I have granted your request."

Abigail went home and Nabal was very drunk because he was celebrating the sheep shearing. Once he had sobered up the next morning, Abigail told him what had happened and how she had saved him, then Nabal had a heart attack. He held on for about ten days but then died.

When David heard Nabal's fate, he praised the Lord that he had avenged Nabal's insult but kept him from doing it himself. Then David sent his servants to bring Abigail to him so he could marry her. She quickly consented and went to David with five of her servants. David also married Ahinoam at that time because Saul had given Michal to marry another man.

SAUL PURSUES DAVID AGAIN

After a while, Saul's attitude towards David changed again, and some men from Ziph told the king where David was staying. Saul brought 3,000 men to the hill country near David's camp. When David heard that Saul had brought soldiers after him again, he snuck into their camp at night with one of his men, Abishai.

They found where Saul and Abner were sleeping, and Abishai whispered, "God has given your enemy into our hands. Let me pin him to the ground with this spear."

But David replied, "Do not kill him, because no one can harm God's anointed and not be guilty. He will die when God says it's time, but it will not be by my hand. Let's take the jug of water and spear that are by Saul's head and leave."

God had caused a deep sleep to fall on Saul and his men, so none of them knew that David and Abishai had been in their camp. Then David went to the top of a hill and called out to Saul's commander, Abner, from a great distance, "Abner, you are one of the greatest men in Israel, but why haven't you watched over your king? You have failed at your job because someone came into your camp to kill your lord and king. You deserve to die because you have not watched over God's anointed. Look! I have the water jug and spear that were by his head!"

Saul recognized his voice and David continued, "Why are you chasing me again? What have I done to you and what sin have I committed? If the Lord has caused you to pursue me, then let me make an offering, but if men have caused you to pursue me, then may they be cursed! They have driven me away from my home so that I am practically not an Israelite. Please don't shed my blood away from the presence of the Lord. I am nothing but a single flea."

Saul replied, "I have sinned. Come home; I will not try to hurt you anymore because you valued my life when you could have easily killed me. I have acted like a fool and made a huge mistake."

Then David said, "Here is your spear; send someone over to get it. The Lord rewards people for their righteousness and faithfulness. He gave you into my hands, but I refused to lift a finger against the Lord's anointed. As I spared your life today, may the Lord spare my life and deliver me from trouble."

Saul answered, "You are blessed, my son. You will be successful in many things." Then they each went their way.

CHAPTER TWENTY-FIVE

SAUL AND THE WITCH
I Samuel 27-30

As David reflected on his relationship with Saul, he figured that the king would one day succeed in killing him, so he left Israel and went to the land of the Philistines, thinking that his adversary would eventually get tired of chasing him. So, David took his 600 men to Gath, and they asked the king to let them live there because Saul had driven them out of Israel. The king of Gath allowed them to live in the city of Ziklag, in the countryside. When Saul heard that David was staying in Ziklag, he stopped pursuing him.

David lived with the Philistines for 16 months and he would lead his men on raids of the other local nations. He would kill all the people so they could not report what he had done and then bring the livestock back as plunder. The king of Gath would ask David where he had raided; the young man would lie to the king and tell him that he had attacked a town in Israel. The king of Gath was sure that David had become so repugnant to Saul that David would be a Philistine servant forever.

Not long after Saul and David made peace with each other, the Philistines went to war, and the king of Gath told David that he expected him to bring his forces out to fight against the Israelites. David said that he would bring his men and the king made him his bodyguard.

After Samuel's death, Saul replaced the prophet with psychics and mediums throughout the land. When the Philistines came to fight, Saul was very afraid. He asked God what he should do, but the Lord was silent. So, Saul asked his men to find a medium that he could consult, and they told him there was a witch at En-dor that he could ask.

Saul disguised himself and took two men with him at night to speak with her. Saul asked her to bring up a spirit that would speak to him and he would pay her for her services. She replied, "You know how Saul has outlawed mediums; why are you risking my life?"

> **Are psychics and mediums real?**
>
> There is a spiritual realm that interacts with humans. When psychics and mediums speak to the dead or know things they shouldn't know, they are accessing demonic power. We do not understand these powers, and God tells us not to engage with these forces.

Saul swore to her by the Lord that nothing bad would happen to her and asked her to bring up Samuel's spirit. She called up Samuel's spirit, and when she saw him, she cried out, "Why have you lied to me? You are Saul!"

Saul told her not to be afraid and asked her what she saw. She told him that Samuel was wrapped in a robe and looked like a god coming out of the earth. Saul bowed to the ground and Samuel's spirit asked, "Why did you bring my spirit back?"

Saul replied, "I am in distress because the Philistines are attacking. God will not answer me, so I called for you to tell me what to do."

Samuel's spirit was angry and said, "God has turned his back on you, so why are you asking me? God is doing what he said he would do and is tearing the kingdom from you and giving it to David. He is doing this because you do not obey what he told you to do to the Amalekites. God is giving Israel over to the Philistines, and tomorrow, you and your sons will die."

Saul fell on his face in terror and didn't have the strength to stand because he hadn't eaten anything. The witch was also afraid and said to him, "I did what you asked me to and risked my life in doing so. Now, eat something so that you can regain your strength and be on your way."

Saul refused to eat, but the witch and Saul's men persuaded him to sit on a bed and she prepared them a meal. Then they returned to their camp that night.

DAVID AND THE AMALEKITES

David was in the Philistine camp, and the leaders went through their ranks and stopped when they saw David and his men. They objected that there were Hebrews with their troops and the king of Gath said, "This is David, Saul's servant, and he has been with me for more than a year since he deserted Israel. He has been faithful and never betrayed me."

But the other Philistine leaders were angry and told the king to send him home because they were afraid that he would turn on the Philistines during battle to get back in Saul's good graces. The king of Gath called David to him and apologized for sending him home, explaining why the other leaders had rejected him.

David objected that he had been faithful and the king of Gath said to him, "I know you have faithfully served me, but the other leaders won't let it happen. Take your men and go back home at sunrise. So, David took his men and returned to their home in Ziklag.

It took them three days to get home, and when they arrived, they found that the Amalekites had burned the city and taken everyone captive. David's two wives were among the people captured and the people wept until they had no strength.

The people started to turn on David and there was talk of stoning him. David called for Abiathar and asked the Lord if he should pursue the Amalekites and God told him, "Chase after them because you will catch up to them and rescue your people."

David had not eaten for three days, but he took his 600 men and chased after the Amalekites. A third of the men were too exhausted to continue, so they waited by a stream while David continued with the remaining men. On their way, they encountered an Egyptian who fed them and gave them provisions for their journey.

Once they had eaten and revived themselves, David asked who this Egyptian was. The man replied, "I am a servant of an Amalekite who left me behind because I was sick. We had just come from raiding Ziklag and burning it to the ground." David asked if he would take them to the band of men, and the Egyptian agreed as long as David would not kill him.

David agreed and the man took them to where the Amalekites were staying. The Amalekites were relaxing, eating, and drinking to celebrate their successful raid. David's men attacked and they killed the Amalekites from twilight until the evening of the next day. They killed every one of the Amalekites except for 400 men who fled on camels once they saw they were under attack.

David rescued all the captives, including his two wives. They also recovered everything the Amalekites took and nothing was missing. They also captured a great deal of livestock from the Amalekites and the men set it aside as David's spoil.

When they arrived where their companions were waiting, some of the men who had defeated the Amalekites were angry. They said that their companions should not receive any of the spoil they had won. They said that they should only get back their wives and children.

But David said, "Don't do this, because God is the one who gave us this victory. We are all going to share in the spoils of victory because the Lord is the one who gave it to us. Everyone will have an equal share regardless of whether they stayed or went." David made it a permanent statute that everyone would share in the spoils. Then he sent a portion of the plunder to some of Judah's leaders as a gift.

CHAPTER TWENTY-SIX

SAUL'S DEATH

I Samuel 31-II Samuel 1; I Chronicles 10

The Philistines and Israelites went into battle and Israel was defeated. They fled, and the Philistines pursued them and captured and killed some of Saul's sons. They killed Jonathan, Abinadab, and Malchishua. The battle was intense and Saul was severely wounded by one of the Philistine archers.

Saul called his armor-bearer to him and said, "Draw your sword and kill me so that these godless Philistines don't capture and torture me." But the armor-bearer was afraid to do it because Saul was God's anointed. So, Saul fell on his sword and died. His armor-bearer was afraid and did the same thing that his king had.

When the Israelites heard that Saul was dead, they abandoned their homes and fled. The Philistines captured their cities and lived in them. The next day, the Philistines found Saul's body, cut off his head, stripped off his armor, and sent word to all the Philistines. They put his armor in a temple and nailed his body to the wall.

When the people of Jabesh-Gilead heard what the Philistines had done, they went at night and recovered Saul's body and armor. They brought it back to their city and burned his body. They buried Saul's remains and fasted for seven days.

So, Saul died for his disobedience to the Lord and consulting a witch; then, God turned the kingdom over to David.

A few days after Saul's death, when David had returned to Ziklag after defeating the Amalekites, a messenger came covered in dirt with his clothes torn and told him that Saul and his sons were dead. Hoping that the news wasn't true, David asked the man for more details. The man said, "The Philistines defeated the Israelites and they all fled. They killed many soldiers, and I happened to be on Mount Gilboa when I came across Saul leaning on his spear. He was in anguish, so he begged me to kill him and put him out of his misery. I saw that there was no way he could survive, so I killed him. Then I took his crown and armlet from his body and brought them to you."

David and his men tore their clothes, and they fasted until evening for Saul, Jonathan, and all the Israelites who had died. Then David called for the man who had given him the news about Saul and asked him, "How is it that you weren't afraid to kill God's anointed? Your blood is on your own head because you are the one who told me you killed the Lord's anointed." Then he had his men execute the Amalekite.

> **Who killed Saul?**
>
> Saul committed suicide by falling on his sword. The Amalekite messenger thought that David would reward him for killing Saul and told this story to impress David.

Saul and Jonathan's deaths grieved David and he wrote a song that he taught to the Israelites. His song praised Saul and Jonathan despite how the king had chased after David for many years. He sang about how he would miss his dear friend Jonathan.

CHAPTER TWENTY-SEVEN

DAVID BECOMES KING
II Samuel 2:1-5:16; I Chronicles 11-12

After grieving for Saul and Jonathan, David asked the Lord what he should do next. God told him to go to Hebron. So, he took his two wives and the 600 men who were with him to Hebron, and the people gathered there. The people said to him, "You are one of us. Even when Saul was our king, you were our leader." Then they anointed him king over Judah.

David heard about what the men of Jabesh-Gilead had done for Saul's body and he blessed them. He promised that he would one day repay them for their kindness and told them that the men of Judah had anointed him as their king.

At the same time, Abner, the commander of Saul's army, tried to make Saul's son, Ish-bosheth, king over Israel. They did not recognize David as king. One day, David and his commander, Joab, went to meet Ish-bosheth and Abner at the pool of Gibeon. They each appointed 12 champions to fight for them. As the soldiers came together, they each grabbed the other by the head and stabbed their opponent in the side; then, each pair fell down dead.

There was a fierce battle that day and David's men defeated Abner and his forces, and Ish-bosheth's men fled. Asahel, one of Joab's brothers, chased after Abner and was determined to catch him. Abner tried to convince him to turn away and kill another soldier and take his spoil, but Asahel would not listen.

When Asahel got very close, Abner stopped running and thrust the butt of his spear into Asahel's stomach so deep that it came out his back, and he died. When the other men of Judah came to his body, they stopped and stood still. But when Joab and his other brother Abishai arrived, they kept after Abner.

Joab stood on a hill with his men as the sun set and made an uneasy truce between their two camps. Joab blew a trumpet and his men stopped chasing after Abner and his people. Then each group returned home. That day about 360 of Abner's men died, while only about 20 of Joab's men died.

There was war between David and Saul's houses, and David kept getting stronger. While David was at Hebron, he married more women, and his wives gave birth to six sons. At the same time, Abner gained strength and caused a stir by sleeping with one of Saul's concubines. Ish-bosheth confronted him about it and Abner threatened to defect and help David take control of Israel.

Son's name	Mother
Ammon	Ahinoam

Son's name	Mother
Chileab	Abigail
Absalom	Maacah
Adonijah	Haggith
Shephatiah	Abital
Ithream	Eglah

Abner reached out to David and offered to help him take control of Israel if the new king would make a covenant with him. David agreed to make a covenant with Abner, but only if he restored his first wife, Michal, to him. Abner facilitated her return and her old husband followed after her, weeping the whole way.

Then, Abner went to the elders of Israel and said, "You've wanted David to be your king for quite a while. Make it happen now because the Lord promised that he would use him to deliver his people from the Philistines and all our enemies." Abner also talked with the leaders of Benjamin about making David king.

Abner went to Hebron to meet with David and tell him everything he had been doing and he left to bring the people to Hebron to make David king. Not long after Abner left, Joab and his men came in and heard that Abner had been there but that David had let him go in peace. Joab went to David and said, "What have you done? Abner was here and you just let him go? Whatever he said was a lie and he only came here to spy on you!"

When Joab left, he sent messengers after Abner to bring him back, although David didn't know about it. When Abner returned, Joab pulled him aside as if to speak with him in private, and he killed Abner by stabbing him in the stomach as payback for what he had done to his brother, Asahel.

When David heard what Joab had done, he said, "I am innocent of Abner's blood before the Lord. Let the guilt fall on Joab and his household; may his descendants be cursed before the Lord!"

David told Joab and his men to tear their clothes and mourn Abner's death. David was a part of the funeral procession and all the people wept. They buried Abner's body in Hebron and the people sat to eat a meal. But David refused because he was too sorrowful. Then the people realized that David had not wanted Abner to die, and David prayed that God would repay Joab's wickedness.

When Saul's son, Ish-bosheth, heard that Abner was dead, his courage failed. Abner had two men named Baanah and Rechab, who were captains of raiding bands. They went to Ish-bosheth in the middle of the day, stabbed him in the stomach, and fled. Later in the day, they returned while Saul's son was trying to recover and cut off his head. They traveled overnight to David and gave him their trophy, saying, "Here is the head of your enemy who tried to kill you. The Lord has avenged you!" They thought David would be happy that they had killed the man who threatened his throne.

David was not pleased, "God is the one who has delivered me from my enemies. But, when someone told me that they had killed Saul, I rewarded him with death. What do you think I'm going to do to you when you come to me telling me that you've killed an innocent man?" He commanded his servants to kill the men and cut off their heads, but he buried Ish-bosheth's head in Abner's tomb.

Then all the Israelites came to Hebron and asked David to be the king of the entire nation. Then all the elders of Israel gathered and anointed him as king of Israel. David was 30 years old when he became king and ruled over Israel for 40 years. After ruling in Hebron for seven-and-a-half years, he went to Jerusalem to fight against the Jebusites. They thought that there was no way that David could defeat them, saying, "Our lame and blind will be able to thwart your attack!"

David said to his men, "Whoever is willing to strike the Jebusites, go through their aqueducts and attack them." Joab was the first one to step forward and became the commander of David's army.

After defeating the Jebusites, David rebuilt the city and lived in Jerusalem, and it was called the city of David. The Lord caused him to become greater and greater. Hiram, the king of Tyre, sent messengers to David with gifts of lumber, and David built himself a palace. David knew that the Lord had established him as the king of Israel for the sake of God's name. David took more wives and concubines and had more children. The names of the children born to him in Jerusalem were Shammua, Shobab, Nathan, Solomon, Ibhar, Elishua, Nepheg, Japhia, Elishama, Eliada, and Eliphalet.

While in Jerusalem, he had many champions who distinguished themselves in battle and performed extraordinary feats of bravery while serving David. Joab was the commander of the army. But Josheb-basshebeth, Eleazer, and Jashobeam were his inner three champions, and they served as his bodyguards. Josheb-basshebeth was the most distinguished of David's mighty men and he once killed 800 men in one battle. Eleazer once defended a barley field against the Philistines. He fought so hard and long that once he defeated his foes, he couldn't even release his sword. Jashobeam once killed 300 men in a single battle.

In a lower-tier were Abishai and Benaiah. Abishai was head over the remaining mighty men and nearly had the same honor as the inner three; he once killed 300 men in a single battle as well. Benaiah was also a champion and eventually became the commander of Solomon's army. He once killed a lion in a pit on a snowy day. Another time, he fought an Egyptian champion and killed the man with his own spear.

The others of the mighty men were: Asahel, Eleazer's brother Elhanan, Shammah, Elika, Helez, Ira, Abiezer, Mebunnai, Zalmon, Maharai, Heleb, Ittai, Hiddai, Abi-Albon, Eliahba, Ahiam, Eliphelet, Eliam, Hezroof, Paarai, Igal, Bani, Zelek, Naharai, Ira, Gareb, and Uriah. These men were beasts on the battlefield and helped David rule.

CHAPTER TWENTY-EIGHT

DAVID AND THE PHILISTINES
II Samuel 5:17-8:14; I Chronicles 13:1-18:13

When the Philistines heard that David had been anointed king, they went to fight against him. David asked the Lord if he should go into battle with the Philistines and if he would be victorious. God told him that he should go and that he would win. David defeated the Philistines and said, "The Lord has burst through my enemies like a rushing flood."

The Philistines left their idols behind, and David's men collected them and carried them away as plunder. The Philistines came to fight him again and David asked the Lord if he should go back into battle. This time, God told him to circle around them and attack when they heard the sound of men marching in the trees. David did as the Lord commanded and he struck down the Philistines for many miles. David's fame continued to spread throughout the surrounding lands and all the neighboring nations were afraid of him.

After defeating the Philistines, David decided to bring the ark from Kiriath-Jearim to Jerusalem. He proposed his idea to the people, and they liked it, so he gathered 30,000 of his soldiers and took them to bring back the ark. They put it on a new cart and began the journey to Jerusalem. This was not what Moses had commanded; instead, they should have had the Levites carry the ark on poles between them.

David led a procession of men who were worshiping and making music to the Lord. But at one point in the journey, the oxen pulling the cart stumbled, and Uzzah put out his hand to steady the ark because he was afraid it was going to fall. God became angry, and killed Uzzah on the spot because he touched something holy.

David was angry that God had killed Uzzah and said, "How can I possibly bring the ark to Jerusalem?" So, he left the ark in the house of Obed-edom for three months, and the Lord blessed the man while the ark was there.

DAVID BRINGS THE ARK TO JERUSALEM

When David heard that God had blessed Obed-edom, he attempted to bring the ark to Jerusalem again. This time, he prepared a tent to be a home for the ark and had the Levites carry it on poles between them as Moses had commanded them. Just as during the previous attempt, a procession of men worshiped the Lord before the ark as they entered Jerusalem. David danced at the front of the caravan with all his might, and they sacrificed one ox and one fattened animal every time they went six steps.

As the ark was coming into Jerusalem, Michal (David's wife and Saul's daughter) saw David dancing before the Lord, and she hated him in her heart. They brought the ark to the tent that David had prepared and offered peace offerings to the Lord. When

David had finished offering sacrifices, he blessed the people and gave them all a loaf of bread, a portion of meat, and a raisin cake.

Then David composed a song to the Lord. In his piece, he thanked the Lord and commanded the people to praise God for his wonderful deeds. The king told the people to continually seek the Lord in their weakness because God alone has strength. He told the people to remember the Lord's outstanding works and he recounted what God had done for the people. David sang that they should tell the nations of his mighty deeds because all other gods are nothing but idols. He praised and worshiped the Lord for his holiness and because he had created all things, because he is good and his steadfast love endures forever. He asked God to save them from their enemies so that they could give thanks to his holy name and glory in his praise. All the people joined in and praised the Lord.

David appointed men to watch over the ark and make sacrifices to the Lord in the morning and evening, just as Moses had commanded. Then all the people left and went to their homes.

David returned to his home and as he came close to his house, Michal came out and said sarcastically, "How the king honored himself today, stripping himself down and dancing like a fool!"

David snarled, "God chose me over your father as king of the people and I will gladly rejoice before him. I am willing to be even more undignified than this, and I don't care if you think I'm a fool because the people will honor me for worshiping the Lord." God closed Michal's womb from that day forward, and she did not have any more children.

DAVID WANTS TO BUILD A TEMPLE

David lived in his house and had rest from his surrounding enemies, so he said to Nathan, the prophet, "I live in a cedar house, but the ark lives in a tent." Nathan told the king, "Do whatever was in your heart because God is with you."

But that night, God came to Nathan and said, "Do I need a place to live? Ever since the people came out of Egypt, I've lived in a tent. I've never asked for a house, so why do I need one now? Tell David that I took him from being a shepherd to king over Israel. I have always been with him and defeated his enemies before him. I will make his name great and give the Israelites a home where they will have peace. I will establish his house and establish one of his sons as king over Israel. He will build a house for my name and establish his throne forever. I will be a father to him and he will be my son. When he sins, I will discipline him with the rod of men, but my steadfast love will not leave him as I left Saul. Your house and your kingdom will endure forever and your throne shall be established for all time."

The next day, Nathan relayed all these words to David. The king went in and sat before the Lord and prayed, "Oh Lord, who am I that you have brought me this far? You have promised me an everlasting kingdom, which can instruct all humanity. I cannot say anything else to you because you know me, oh God. You have allowed me to be great because of your heart and promise.

"Therefore, you are great! According to all that we have seen and heard, no one is like you, and there is no God besides you. There is no nation like Israel because we are the only ones you have redeemed us by bringing us out of Egypt and making your name great. You established your people forever and you have become our God. Now, confirm your word that you have spoken and do everything you promised. You will establish your name and my house forever because of your word. I have found the courage to make this prayer because of your revelation. Lord, you are God, and your words are true, and you have given me this great promise.

"May it please you to bless my house so that it will endure forever. You have spoken these things, and with your blessing, the house of your servant will be everlasting."

***

David defeated the Philistines and subdued them. Then he slaughtered the Moabites, killing half of them and putting the other half to forced labor. The Syrians came to help the Moabites, and David defeated them as well. Then, he defeated the Edomites and made them his servants. He took massive amounts of gold, silver, and bronze from these nations, dedicating them to the Lord. God blessed David and gave him victory everywhere he went.

> **Didn't the Israelites already defeat the Philistines?**
>
> The Israelites and Philistines took turns subduing each other for many years. At times, Israel would gain the upper hand; at others, the Philistines would be victorious. It took many years for the Israelites to defeat their enemies completely.

CHAPTER TWENTY-NINE

DAVID AND BATHSHEBA

II Samuel 8:15-12:31; I Chronicles 18:14-20:8

David reigned over Israel and administered justice and equity to all the people. Joab was the commander of his army, Jehoshaphat was his recorder, Seraiah was his secretary, and Zadok, Benaiah, and his sons served as priests.

Then David asked if there were any of Jonathan's descendants still living so he could honor them. One of Saul's servants, Ziba, told David that he still had a disabled son named Mephibosheth. David brought Saul's son before him and said, "Do not be afraid, I will show you kindness for your father's sake, and I will restore all of Saul's land to your family, and you will always have a seat at my table."

Mephibosheth was overwhelmed with gratitude and said, "I don't understand why you would show me such mercy because I am nothing more than a dead dog in your presence."

Then David told Ziba, "Restore everything that Saul had to Mephibosheth and make sure we always take care of his family. But he will always have a seat at my table." Then he made Ziba Mephibosheth's servant, and Mephibosheth lived in Jerusalem and ate at David's table.

After this, the king of the Ammonites died, and his son, Hanun, ruled in his place. David wanted to show him kindness because his father had treated him well, so he sent messengers to console him. But Hanun's servants convinced him that David was sending spies so that he could attack the land. Hanun shaved half the men's beards, cut off their clothing at their hips, and sent them home.

The men were greatly humiliated and David came to meet them as they returned. He told them to stay at Jericho until their beards regrew and were no longer ashamed. When the Ammonites saw that they had made David angry, they hired the Syrians to come and defend them. Joab sent David's mighty men and some of his best soldiers to fight against the Syrians. He put the rest of his men under Abishai's command and sent them to fight against the Ammonites.

Joab said to his brother, "If the Syrians are too strong for me, come help me, and if the Ammonites are too strong for you, I will come help. Be courageous for the people and our country, and may God do whatever he thinks is best."

Joab defeated the Syrians, and when the Ammonites saw this, they retreated. The Syrians gathered their remaining forces and joined with the remaining men of Hadadezer, king of Zobah. David heard that they had joined forces and sent his army to attack them. The Israelites slaughtered them and drove back the Syrians, and the men of Zobah were too afraid to help the Ammonites anymore. Then, Hadadezer made peace with Israel and they became Israel's servants.

DAVID'S SIN

The following spring, when kings went out to battle with their armies, David sent Joab and his men out to fight against the Ammonites, but he stayed home in Jerusalem. Joab struck down the city of Rabbah and captured it for David. He brought David the king's crown, which was about 75 pounds of gold with a massive gem. The Ammonites became Israel's servants and were put to forced labor.

While Joab and the army were at war, David walked around the roof of his home one late afternoon. As he was walking, he saw a beautiful woman bathing on a nearby house's roof. He asked who she was and was told that she was Bathsheba, the wife of Uriah, one of his mighty men. David sent for her, she came to the king, and he slept with her. Then he sent her home after she had purified herself from her uncleanness.

She ended up becoming pregnant and David decided to cover up his sin. He sent a messenger to Joab and asked him to send Uriah back to him. When Uriah arrived, David asked for a report of how things were going and then told him to go home, wash his feet, and return. He hoped that Uriah would sleep with Bathsheba and keep people from discovering his sin.

But Uriah did not go home; instead, he spent the night with David's servants. David asked him why he hadn't spent the night at home. Uriah replied, "The ark of God lives in a tent, and Joab and the servants of the Lord are camping in a field. Why should I eat and drink at home and sleep with my wife? I refuse to disrespect the Lord and my brothers!"

David told Uriah to stay another night and got him drunk, hoping that he would spend the night at home after being impaired. But, once again, the soldier spent the night with David's servants. In the morning, David sent Uriah back to the frontlines with a letter for Joab instructing him to put Uriah in the heat of the battle and then fall back so their enemies would kill him.

Joab obeyed David's letter and sent his men close to the city of Ramah, a move that was a poor battle strategy. Joab sent a messenger with word back to David about how things were going and let him know that Uriah had died.

David told the messenger to encourage Joab that soldiers sometimes die in battle and not let this thing bother him. The king instructed his commander to continue the battle and defeat Rabbah.

When Bathsheba heard that Uriah was dead, she mourned for him. When the time for mourning was over, David married her, and she bore him a son. David's actions displeased the Lord.

The Lord sent Nathan to David and the prophet said, "There was a rich man and a poor man in a city, and the rich man had many flocks, but the poor man had a single lamb that he had bought. The poor man raised the lamb and it grew up with him and his children. It ate and drank with him and was like a daughter to him. One day, a traveler came to the rich man, and he was unwilling to kill one of his sheep to feed the traveler, so he took the poor man's lamb, killed it, and prepared it for the traveler."

David was furious and said, "As the Lord lives, this man deserves to die! He shall pay four times as much for the lamb he took because he had no pity!"

DAVID'S PUNISHMENT

David's Son	Way he died
Unnamed son	First child of Bathsheba who died after Nathan confronted David.
Amnon	Absalom killed David's oldest son after Amnon raped Tamar.
Absalom	Killed by Joab after his rebellion.
Adonijah	Absalom's younger brother, Solomon, had him killed when he tried to usurp the throne.

Then Nathan said, "You are the rich man! God anointed you as king of Israel and delivered you out of Saul's hands. He gave you many wives and all of Israel and Judah. If that weren't enough, he would have given you much more. Why have you rejected God's Word and done this evil? You struck down Uriah with the Ammonite's sword and have taken his wife as well! Therefore, the sword and violence will never depart from your house. God will raise up evil against you from your own house. He will take your wives from you and give them to your neighbor, and he will sleep with them in the light of day. You did this in secret, but God will punish you in midday!"

David confessed, "I have sinned against the Lord."

Nathan replied, "The Lord has forgiven your sin and you will not die. But, because of your sin, your son will!" Nathan went home and the child became deathly ill. David fasted before the Lord all day and night, trying to save his son. The elders of Israel stood beside him and tried to get the king to eat and drink, but he refused.

After seven days, the child died, and the elders were afraid to tell David. If the king was so despondent while the child was still alive, they feared what he would do once he discovered the child had died. David saw them talking to each other and asked if his son was dead. They told him that he had died, and David got up, washed, and changed his clothes. He went to the house of the Lord and worshiped and then went home. He asked for food and ate.

His men were confused by his behavior and they asked him why he acted this way. David answered, "While he was still alive, I fasted and wept before the Lord because he may have been gracious and spared my son's life. But now he is dead, so why should I keep fasting? I cannot bring him back. Someday I will go to be with him, but he will not return to life."

David comforted Bathsheba after the child's death and slept with her. She became pregnant again and had another son, whom she named Solomon. The Lord loved him and sent a message to Nathan, and God called him Jedidiah.

CHAPTER THIRTY

AMNON AND TAMAR

II Samuel 13:1-14:28

Amnon, one of David's sons, fell in love with one of his half-sisters, Tamar (Absalom was her brother). Amnon was so upset about the situation that he made himself sick because it seemed like he couldn't do anything about his feelings. Amnon had a crafty cousin named Jonadab, who advised him to pretend to be ill and ask Tamar to take care of him.

David sent Tamar to look after Amnon and she brought him food. But he refused to eat and sent everyone out of his room except his sister, and he asked her to feed him by hand. When she came close to feed him, Amnon asked her to sleep with him.

She was horrified and said, "My brother, please do not violate me, this is outrageous, and we don't do this kind of thing in Israel. If you do this, I would not be able to bear my shame, and you would be like one of the most outrageous fools in Israel. Please, talk to our father about this!"

But, Amnon was stronger than Tamar, and he raped his sister. After he finished, he was disgusted and kicked her out of his room. She begged him not to throw her out because his rejection would be even worse than the rape. Amnon would not listen to her, and he had one of his servants throw her out and lock the door after her. She was devastated by what had happened. She tore her robe and put ashes on her head, weeping and covering her face as she left.

Her brother, Absalom, heard about this, and he told her not to worry about the situation because Amnon was her half-brother. He gave his sister a place to live in his house and she stayed there as a desolate woman. When David heard about Amnon's actions, he was furious, but Absalom held his tongue.

ABSALOM'S REVENGE

Absalom waited two full years to get his revenge on his brother. He devised a plot to have David send all his brothers with him to oversee the shearing of sheep at Baal-hazor. While they were there and drinking wine, Absalom commanded his servants to kill Amnon, and they did it.

When his brothers saw what Absalom had done to his brother, they all fled, fearing for their lives. While they were running and hiding, news came to David that Absalom had killed all his sons, and the king tore his clothes and fell to the earth in grief. But Jonadab was with the king, and he told David, "Absalom has not killed all of your sons, just Amnon. He has intended to do this since the day Amnon violated Tamar. Do not be upset, my king; only Amnon is dead."

As Jonadab was speaking to the king, his other sons came into view. Then they gathered and wept over their brother Amnon. But Absalom fled and stayed in hiding for three years. David missed his son and wished he could reach out to him after Amnon's death.

ABSALOM RETURNS HOME

Joab knew that the king longed to reunite with Absalom, so he sent a wise woman disguised as a mourner. Joab gave her a story to tell and she went to the king and said, "Save me! I am a widow and my two sons were fighting in a field. There was no one to separate them, and one killed the other. Now, all my family is demanding I hand over my remaining son so that they can kill him. If I do that, I will not have an heir, and my husband's name will be blotted out."

David replied, "Go home, and if anyone says anything more to you about this situation, bring your son to me, and I will handle it." She kept after the king until he promised that not a hair of his head would fall to the ground.

Then the woman continued, "How could you plan a thing like this against God's people? This decision convicts you because you will not bring home the son you have banished. We all deserve to die, but God does not kill us; instead, he makes a way so that the banished does not remain an outcast. I knew that you would listen to my request and give me peace because God has given you the ability to discern good and evil."

David became suspicious and asked her if Joab had put her up to talking to him. She told him that he had. David turned to Joab and said, "I grant you your request; bring Absalom back home."

Joab fell on his face and paid homage to David and said, "Today, I know that I have found favor in your sight because you have granted my request." Then Joab went to bring Absalom back to Jerusalem.

Once Absalom was back, he lived in his own home and did not come into David's presence. All Israel loved Absalom and he was flawless from head to toe. His hair was so thick that it weighed about five pounds when he had his annual haircut. He had three sons and one daughter, named Tamar, after his sister.

CHAPTER THIRTY-ONE

ABSALOM'S REBELLION
II Samuel 14:29-18:33

Absalom lived in Jerusalem for two years without seeing David. Then he sent for Joab to bring him to see his father. But Joab refused to see Absalom twice. Absalom was angry and sent some of his servants to burn one of Joab's fields next to his property.

Joab came to Absalom and asked why he had done this, and Absalom replied, "Because you brought me back to Jerusalem, but you refuse to take me to see my father. It would have been better for me to stay where I was. Take me to see the king, and if he is still angry, then he can kill me." So, Joab took him to see David, and the king kissed Absalom, welcoming him back into the family.

After seeing his father, Absalom obtained a chariot and 50 men to run before him. Every morning, he would go to the city's gate and greet people who came to speak with the king about a dispute. He would listen to their case and give them a judgment. He lamented that David would not appoint him as a judge so he could dispense justice to the people. He would kiss everyone who came to see him and he stole the people's hearts.

ABSALOM USURPS THE THRONE

After four years of doing this, Absalom asked the king if he could go to Hebron to fulfill a vow. David told him to go in peace. While he was on his way, he sent messengers to the people saying that when they heard trumpets, to declare Absalom the new king in Hebron. Absalom took 200 men with him who didn't know about his plot and he continued to grow in power.

A messenger came to Jerusalem and warned David that Absalom had stolen the people's hearts and that he was trying to become king. David gathered his servants, and they decided to flee from Jerusalem because they were afraid of the people who were gathering with Absalom. The king's people said, "We are with you whatever you decide to do." Then David took his household and left the city, but he left ten concubines behind to take care of the palace.

On his way out of town, he stopped at the last house in Jerusalem where Ittai, the Gittite, lived. David had 600 Gittites who were planning on going with him, but Ittai had just arrived in Jerusalem. David said to him, "Why do you want to come with us since you just arrived in Jerusalem? I don't want to make you wander around the wilderness with me. Stay here with your people and may the Lord bless you."

Ittai told David he was committed to the king and would follow him wherever he went. So, the Gittites went with David, and the people wept as the king and his men left the city. They had taken the ark of God with them, and after leaving the city, they set it down to rest.

David said to Zadok, the priest, "Take the ark back to the city. If I find favor in God's eyes, then I will be able to return, but if I don't, then God will do to me whatever he sees fit."

Zadok and Abiathar took the ark back to Jerusalem and David continued his journey into the wilderness barefoot and weeping as he covered his head in shame. They arrived at the Mount of Olives and all the people followed the lead of their king.

David heard that Ahithophel had joined Absalom's ranks as an advisor and he prayed that God would make his advice foolishness. While they were on their way to the summit to worship the Lord, Hushai came to him covered in dirt with his robes torn in grief. David told Hushai to go back to Jerusalem and tell Absalom that he would serve the new king just as he had the old one and to undermine Ahithophel's counsel. So, Hushai returned to Jerusalem just as Absalom was entering the city.

After they had passed the Mount of Olives' summit, Ziba (Mephibosheth's servant) met him with a couple of donkeys and food for his men. He told David, "I have brought these things to feed your men. I have come to you because Mephibosheth thinks God is giving the kingdom back to his family. Now, everything that he has is yours again. I pay homage to you; may I find favor in your sight."

They continued their journey, and while they were on their way, one of Saul's descendants, named Shimei, came out and cursed David as he passed. He threw rocks at him and said, "Get out, you worthless man of bloodshed! God is avenging all the blood you have spilled and he has given the kingdom into Absalom's hands!"

Abishai was irritated by his words and asked David to permit him to cut Shimei's head off. But David said, "What am I going to do with you and your brother? Maybe God has told him to curse me, and if so, then I cannot possibly tell him to stop. My son wants me dead, so it makes sense that this descendant of Saul would curse me. Leave him alone; maybe God will repay me with good for his curses." They continued their journey with Shimei cursing him along the way and they arrived exhausted at the Jordan River.

Absalom arrived in Jerusalem with his men and Ahithophel. Hushai greeted him and said, "Long live the king!"

Absalom asked him why he had not gone with his friend David, but Hushai replied, "No, I will serve whomever the Lord and the people have chosen. Who else would I serve? I will serve you, just as I served him."

Absalom asked Ahithophel what he should do and he replied, "Go into the palace and sleep with your father's concubines and then the nation will see what you have done, and you will strengthen your men." They set up a tent for Absalom on the roof of the palace and he slept with David's concubines in the sight of all of Israel.

Then Ahithophel said to Absalom, "Let me take 12,000 men and I will chase after David tonight. I will come upon him while he is tired and discouraged, then I will throw them into a panic. But I will only kill the king and let the others go. I will bring them all back to you like a bride to her husband and then we will have peace." Absalom liked the advice, but he called Hushai to hear what he had to say as well.

Hushai told Absalom, "Ahithophel's advice is no good this time. You know that your father and his mighty men are like a bear robbed of her cubs. They are experts in war and David will probably not be sleeping with his men anyway. He has probably hidden in a pit or some other place; when our men arrive, David's men will probably slaughter them. Then, people will lose heart and no longer follow you. Gather all the Israelites together and pursue David, and then we will destroy whatever city he is hiding to the ground."

Absalom decided that Hushai's advice was better than Ahithophel's. Then Hushai sent messengers to David, telling him to keep running. David left where he was and crossed the Jordan when he heard the news.

When Ahithophel saw that Absalom had not listened to his advice, he went home, put his affairs in order, and hanged himself. Absalom had set Amasa over his army instead of Joab and they waited to pursue David across the Jordan. Meanwhile, some of the Israelites gave provisions to David and his men.

David put a third of his men under Joab's command, a third under Abishai, and a third under Ittai. David pledged to go with one of the companies, but the men convinced him to stay put because he was worth 10,000 of their lives. He listened to the people and asked them to have mercy with Absalom.

David's men fought and defeated Absalom's army, killing 20,000 Israelites. During the battle, Absalom fled upon his donkey. As he was running from David's men, his hair became caught in an oak tree, and he was left hanging while the donkey ran out from under him. One of David's men saw Absalom swinging by his hair and he went to let Joab know. Joab asked why he hadn't struck him down, and the man replied that he would not strike down the king's son regardless of the reward because David has asked them to show him mercy.

Joab decided to take matters into his own hands and he thrust three spears through Absalom's heart to make sure he died. Then he blew a trumpet to let the people know that Absalom was dead, and he kept his men from killing any more of their countrymen. They threw Absalom's body into a pit and everyone fled to his own home.

Zadok's son Ahimaaz asked to send a message to David, but Joab told him to stay put while he sent word to David to tell him that his son was dead. Ahimaaz decided that he would take word to David regardless of Joab's command and outran Joab's messenger.

David was waiting for news of the battle and he saw both messengers running with information. Ahimaaz arrived first and told the king how his men had defeated Absalom's forces, but he did not know what had happened to Absalom. Then, Joab's messenger arrived and told David that Absalom had died in battle. The news crushed David and he went into a private chamber and wept over the loss of his son.

CHAPTER THIRTY-TWO

DAVID'S FINAL YEARS
II Samuel 19-23

Joab heard that David was grieving over the loss of his son, so he went to the king and confronted him, "Today, you have shamed your servants because they saved your life, but all you are doing is weeping for your son. You have made it clear that they are meaningless because you would rather have Absalom alive than them. Go speak to your people, because if you don't, this will only get worse."

So, David took his place at the city gate, and all the people came to listen to him because they wanted to know what he would do after Absalom's death. He convinced the people to come back to follow him and he returned to Jerusalem.

Shimei came with 1,000 men to beg for David's forgiveness. But Abishai tried to persuade David to kill him because Shimei had cursed him and fought against him. David told Abishai that no one should die because God had established him as king over Israel.

Then David swore to Shimei that he would not die. Mephibosheth also came to David and begged for forgiveness for thinking that God was returning the kingdom to his family.

Barzillai, an 80-year-old man, sent some of his men to escort David to Jerusalem, and he had provided for David while he was away from the capital. David wanted to honor him for his faithfulness and reward him in Jerusalem. But Barzillai asked David to honor him on the other side of the Jordan because he was too old to travel to Jerusalem.

CONFUSION IN ISRAEL

There was much confusion in Israel, and a worthless Benjaminite named Sheba tried to get men to follow him, and the Israelites followed, while the men of Judah kept their allegiance with David.

The king returned to his house in Jerusalem and gave his concubines a place to live, although he did not sleep with them again. David called everyone to him because he feared that Sheba would harm his kingdom more than Absalom did.

David sent Joab to meet with Sheba. Joab met with Amasa, the leader of Sheba's men, and stabbed him in the belly. Those who saw Amasa bleeding out alongside the roadside decided to follow Joab; they pursued Sheba to the city of Beth-maccah, where they set up a siege mound to capture him.

A woman from the city met Joab and asked him why he wanted to destroy the city when only Sheba had sinned against the king. She told Joab that she would throw

Sheba's head over the city's wall to save themselves from David's wrath. She did so, and Joab took his soldiers away from the city.

DAVID'S FINAL YEARS

There was a great famine during David's reign that lasted for three years. David sought the Lord's guidance for what to do and God told him that it was for how Saul had treated the Gibeonites. The king sent a messenger to the Gibeonites and asked them what they wanted. They asked for seven of Saul's descendants to hang and David gave them over. But David spared Mephibosheth because of the oath he had sworn to Jonathan. God relented and allowed the land to grow food again.

There was war between the Philistines and the Israelites. David went down to fight alongside his people but became weary during the battle. Some of David's soldiers defeated some of the Philistines' champions and confirmed their place amongst his mighty men.

After they defeated the Philistines, David sang a song in worship to the Lord. He sang, "The Lord is my rock, my fortress, and my deliverer. I take refuge in him, and he is my shield and the horn of my salvation. I will call upon him because he is praiseworthy, and he saves me from my enemies. I was on the verge of death. I called out to the Lord and he heard me. He became angry, and the heavens and the earth shook from the fierceness of his wrath. Then he sent out his arrows and scattered my enemies. He rescued me from the strength of my enemy because they were too mighty for me. He brought me to a safe place; he rescued me because he delighted in me.

"I have kept his ways and have not departed from his commands. I kept myself innocent of sin and have been blameless before him. He has rewarded me according to my righteousness and cleanness before him. He is merciful to the merciful and we perceive him as we are to others. He saves the humble and tears down the proud. He is my lamp that gives light to my path; he gives me the strength to attack or jump over a wall. He is perfect, and his words are true; he is a shield to all that take refuge in him.

"He is a refuge who has made my way blameless; he has made me as agile as a deer and has set me in a high and secure place. He gives me the strength to bend a bow of bronze. He kept my feet from slipping and allowed me to destroy my enemies. He delivered me from strife with my people and kept me as king. The Lord lives and we should bless and exalt him because he is the rock of my salvation. He gave me victory over my enemies and exalted me over them. I will praise him among the nations because he has shown steadfast love to me and my descendants."

Finally, David realized that he was about to die. He said, "The Lord has told me that when one rules justly in fear of God, he dawns on him like the morning light, like the sun through the clouds, like rain that causes the grass to grow. He has made a promise to me and my descendants, and he will cause them to prosper. But he will throw away worthless men and consume them with fire."

CHAPTER THIRTY-THREE

DAVID'S CENSUS

II Samuel 24; I Chronicles 21

Before David's death, the Lord was angry with Israel, and he incited David to perform a census of the nation. Joab protested David's order, but the king prevailed, and they sent workers out to count the men of Israel and Judah. They found that there were 1,100,00 brave men who could go to war and nearly 500,000 men in Judah who could go into battle.

> **Why was the census a sin?**
>
> When God gave the Israelites the Law, one of the commands was not to take a census unless the Lord ordered it. This was because God did not want rulers to become proud and believe their might had caused them to prosper. David called for this census to have empirical evidence that his kingdom was mighty.

David felt guilty after numbering the people, and he begged God for forgiveness. The next morning, God sent the prophet Gad to speak to him and give him options for his consequence. Gad said, "Would you like three years of famine, three months of running from your enemies, or three days of pestilence and disease?"

David replied, "I am greatly distressed by my sin, let us fall into the hands of the Lord for three days, because he may show us mercy." The Lord sent pestilence and disease on the land and 70,000 people died. The angel of the Lord was at Araunah's threshing floor, ready to destroy Jerusalem. David cried out in distress that God's hand should be against him and not against the people. Then God told the angel to stop.

The prophet Gad told David that God commanded him to build an altar at Araunah's threshing floor. David went to Araunah (also known as Ornan) and Araunah asked why the king was coming to him. David replied, "I have come to buy your threshing floor so that I can build an altar to the Lord for ending the plague against his people."

Araunah tried to give the property to the king and any animals he needed for sacrifices, but David refused to take it for free because he refused to offer sacrifices to the Lord that did not cost him anything. David paid him a fair price and then built an altar and offered God sacrifices for averting his wrath.

DAVID AND ABISHAG

As David became older, he could not keep himself warm, regardless of how many blankets they piled on him. So, his servants looked for a young woman who could help keep him warm with her body heat. They found Abishag, and she would lay with the king to warm him up, but he did have sex with her.

CHAPTER THIRTY-FOUR

DAVID'S DEATH AND SOLOMON BECOMES KING

I Kings 1:1-2:12; I Chronicles 22-29

David's second-oldest son, Adonijah, exalted himself and declared that he would be the next king. He had always had David's favor and he was a very handsome man. He prepared chariots and riders and recruited 50 men to run before him. He consulted Joab and Abiathar and they agreed to help him assume the throne. But the key officials and David's mighty men were not with Adonijah. Adonijah went to offer sacrifices to the Lord and invited all his brothers, but he did not invite David's officials, Solomon, or David's mighty men.

Nathan went to Bathsheba, the mother of Solomon, and said, "Did you hear that Adonijah has become king and David doesn't know about it yet? Let me give you some advice to save your life and Solomon's. Talk to David and remind him that he had promised that Solomon would be king, and ask why Adonijah is taking his place. Then I will come in and confirm your words."

Bathsheba listened to Nathan and spoke to David, adding, "Adonijah has sacrificed many animals with Joab and Abiathar's help but has not invited Solomon to participate. You alone have authority to appoint the next king, and if you don't do something, Adonijah will rule; Solomon and I will be considered outcasts and offenders." As she was speaking, Nathan came in and confirmed everything she said.

David told Bathsheba, "As the Lord lives, who has redeemed me out of adversity, I swore to God that your son Solomon would be king. That will happen today."

Bathsheba bowed to the ground and paid homage to the king. Then David called for Zadok, Nathan, and Benaiah to come to him to anoint Solomon as king. He said to them, "Take my servants, put Solomon on my mule, and ride to Gihon. Zadok and Nathan will anoint Solomon as king of Israel and you will blow the trumpet and yell, 'Long live King Solomon!' Then bring him back here so that he can sit on my throne and rule because I have chosen him to be the next king of Israel."

They listened to David and anointed Solomon king at Gihon. The people followed him, making music and rejoicing loud enough to shake the earth.

Adonijah heard all the commotion and asked what it all meant. Abiathar's son, Jonathan, told him everything that had happened and how Zadok, Nathan, and Benaiah had anointed Solomon king as David ordered. Jonathan also told him that the sound was the people rejoicing and Solomon sat on his father's throne.

Adonijah was very afraid of Solomon and all of Adonijah's followers left him and went home. Adonijah went to the altar, put his hands upon its horn, and begged Solomon to spare his life. Solomon promised that he would not hurt him if he showed himself worthy and not a wicked man. Then Adonijah paid homage to Solomon and went home.

After anointing Solomon as king, David said to himself, "Solomon is a young man, and he will build a magnificent building for the Lord, so I will make preparations and set aside building materials." He gathered craftsmen together and so much building material that they didn't even bother counting or weighing it.

David called for Solomon and charged him to build a house for the Lord, the God of Israel. He said to his son, "I wanted to make a house for the Lord, but God told me I had shed too much blood to build his house. But he promised me that I would have a son and God would give him rest from all his enemies. He told me that you would be that son and that you would build a house for his name. He will be a father to you and establish your kingdom forever.

"May God grant you success in building his house. I have provided tons of building materials, but you will have to obtain even more. I have gathered many skilled workers to help you build. May God be with you!" Then David commanded all the leaders of Israel to help Solomon build the temple because they had peace on every side, and it was time to give the ark a permanent home.

David put all the priests, Levites, musicians, and gatekeepers in order, making sure they understood their duties and responsibilities. He also put leaders over the military divisions and gave them set times to serve throughout the year.

Then David assembled all the leaders and officials of Israel; he stood up and said, "Listen to me, my brothers, I wanted to build a house for the Lord. I made all the preparations for it to happen, but God told me that I would not be the one to build it because I am a man of bloodshed. Instead, he has chosen Solomon out of my many sons to be king over Israel. He will build the temple and God will be a father to him. The Lord promised that his throne would be everlasting if he continues to follow him. So, observe and seek out God's commandments so that you may possess this good land and leave it as an inheritance to your children after you."

He turned to Solomon and said, "Know my God and serve him with a whole heart and a willing mind because he knows every thought and intention. If you seek him, you will find him, but if you forsake him, he will abandon you. He has chosen you to build his house, be strong and do it!" Then, David gave Solomon the temple plans and the worship instruments God had given him.

He continued, "I am about to die. Be strong, and be a man. Follow God's commands and obey his teachings. If you do, then you will prosper in everything you do, and he will establish your throne forever, just as he promised me. Be strong and courageous and complete this work that is before you. The Lord is with you, and he will not leave you."

"You also know how Joab and Shimei treated me and how they treated others, don't let them live out their days in peace. But treat Barzilai well; he helped me when I was on the run. Give him a seat at your table."

Once again, David turned to the people and told them about his preparations for the temple and the building materials he gathered. He added to those materials a freewill offering from his wealth and invited them to do the same. The people gave generously, and everyone rejoiced because they had given willingly and with a whole heart.

Then, David blessed the Lord in front of the people, and he prayed, "God of Israel, our Father, you are blessed forever! All greatness and power are yours because heaven and earth are yours. You are above all, and the kingdom is yours. Riches and honor belong to you and you have all power and might to give strength to all. So, we thank you and praise your glorious name!

"But who am I, and who are these people that we can offer you thanks and praise? We are strangers and aliens, just as our fathers were. We are like a shadow and we will not last. You have given us everything we have and all we will use to build your house. You know my heart and how I have freely given to you; now the people have freely given as well. Direct our hearts to you and give my son a whole heart so that he may obey your commandments and finish your house."

David's final words to Israel were to bless the Lord. Then the people offered sacrifices to God and celebrated with a great party. They anointed Solomon as their king a second time and Zadok as his priest. Solomon took David's place on the throne, he prospered, and all the people obeyed him. All the nation pledged allegiance to him and God made him the greatest king that Israel has ever known.

David, the son of Jesse, ruled over Israel for 40 years, seven-and-a-half in Hebron, and the rest in Jerusalem. He died at a good age, full of days, riches, and honor. Then his son Solomon reigned in his place, and God established his kingdom.

CHAPTER THIRTY-FIVE

SOLOMON AS KING

I Kings 2:13-4:34, II Chronicles 1

Solomon established his kingdom, and God was with him, making him a very great ruler. One day, Adonijah came to Solomon's mother, Bathsheba, and asked to speak to her in peace. She granted him an audience and he said, "You know that the kingdom was mine and that the people were with me. But now my brother reigns and this has come about from the Lord. Please give me one thing, let me marry Abishag, the young woman who was my father's companion in his old age."

Bathsheba took this request to Solomon and the king gave his mother a seat of honor next to him. She asked him to let Adonijah marry Abishag and Solomon was taken aback. He replied, "Why are you making this request? Why don't you ask that he become king because he is my older brother and already has Joab and Abiathar on his side! May God do worse to me if this request doesn't cost Adonijah his life. He will die today!"

Solomon sent Benaiah to kill Adonijah. Then Solomon said to Abiathar, "Go back home because you deserve to die for this rebellion! But I will not kill you because you carried the ark before my father and served him at his lowest point."

When Joab heard what had happened, he was terrified because he had supported Adonijah's throne over Solomon's. He ran to the Tabernacle and grabbed hold of the horns of the altar, begging for his life. Solomon heard that he had fled and he sent Benaiah to kill him. Joab refused to come out of the tent, saying that he would die there, so Benaiah returned to Solomon and asked what he should do.

Solomon said to Benaiah, "Do as he said, kill him and bury him; take the stain of the innocent blood he shed from my family. The Lord is bringing his wicked deeds back on him for killing Abner and Amasa, two men who were better than him. He did this without my father's knowledge, and his blood will be on his head, but David's house will live in peace."

Benaiah returned to the tent, killed Joab, and then buried his body in the wilderness. Afterward, Solomon made Benaiah the commander of his army and Zadok, his high priest. He also called for Shimei and told him to build a house in Jerusalem but never leave it because he would die if he did. Shimei agreed to Solomon's terms and lived in Jerusalem.

SOLOMON'S REQUEST

After three years, two of Shimei's servants ran away to the city of Gath. When Shimei heard where they were, he saddled his donkey and chased them down. When Solomon heard about this, he confronted him, "Didn't you swear to stay in your place and not leave? I warned you that if you left your home, that you would die. Why have you done this? You know what you did to my father in his distress and now God is returning your actions to you. But God will bless my throne and establish David's line forever." Then, Solomon had Benaiah kill Shimei.

Solomon made a strategic alliance with Pharaoh by marrying his daughter, and he brought her to live in Jerusalem until his palace and the temple were complete. Since the temple was not finished, the people would sacrifice to the Lord on the high places. Solomon loved the Lord and walked in the ways of his father David, but he offered sacrifices on the high places as the other people did.

> ### High places
>
> The high places were locations where ancient people would worship. People believed that because the top of a hill was closer to the sky, it was also closer to God. The Israelites adopted this practice, which led to confusion in their worship and tempted them to follow foreign gods.

Solomon went to the tent of meeting in Gibeon, considered the highest of high places, and they set up a bronze altar before the Lord. Then they offered a thousand burnt offerings on it.

That night God came to Solomon in a dream and asked him what he wanted. Solomon replied, "You have shown great and steadfast love to my father, David, and you have made me king in his place. Fulfill your promises to my father because you have made me king over a multitude. Please give me wisdom and knowledge so that I can govern these great people of yours."

God answered, "You could have asked me for anything: riches, honor, long life, or victory over your enemies. But instead, you asked me for wisdom and knowledge so that you could lead my people. I will give you wisdom and knowledge, but I will also give you more wealth and honor than any before or after you." Solomon returned to Jerusalem, stood before the ark of the covenant, and offered sacrifices to the Lord. Then he threw a celebration and the people rejoiced before the Lord.

SOLOMON'S WISDOM

One day, two prostitutes came to Solomon to have him judge a dispute they had. One woman said, "The two of us live in a house together and I gave birth to a child. Three days later, she gave birth to a child as well. The four of us were living together in the house and there was no one else there. In the night, she accidentally smothered her child in her bed. In the middle of the night, she switched our children and went back to bed. When I woke up in the morning to nurse my baby, I saw that the child was dead. But when I looked closely, I realized it was not my child."

The second woman contradicted her story and the two women got into a huge argument. Solomon quieted the women down and asked one of his servants to bring him a sword. He said, "I will cut the living child in half and give each woman a half."

The child's mother spoke up and asked him not to kill the baby but to give it to the second woman. The second woman said, "Cut him in half! Then neither of us will have the child."

Solomon answered, "Do not harm the child; give him to the first woman because she is the mother." All of Israel heard about Solomon's ruling and were in awe because they recognized God's wisdom.

SOLOMON'S REIGN

Solomon appointed officials over the different divisions of government. Zadok, Abiathar (despite his rebellion), Zabud, and Zadok's son Azariah were the priests, Elihoreph and Ahijah were the secretaries, Jehoshaphat was the recorder, Benaiah was commander of the army, Azariah was also over the officials, Ahishar oversaw the palace, and Adoniram was over forced labor.

Israel and Judah prospered greatly under Solomon's reign, the nation was at peace, and all the people had the opportunity to be successful. Solomon gathered a great military of 1,400 chariots, 12,000 horsemen, and 40,000 horses. Each day he prepared generous amounts of food for his court and fed thousands of people. He made gold and silver as common as stones and made cedar as common as sycamore trees. He brought in the best from foreign lands and exported great wealth as well.

God gave Solomon wisdom and knowledge beyond measure and he understood an astonishing breadth of subjects. He wrote 3,000 proverbs and over 1,000 songs on every topic imaginable. He was wiser than any other man who ever lived, and his fame spread across the earth, and people came from everywhere to hear his wisdom.

CHAPTER THIRTY-SIX

BUILDING THE TEMPLE

I Kings 5-8, II Chronicles 2:1-7:10

Hiram, the king of Tyre, sent servants to congratulate Solomon because Hiram had always loved David. Solomon sent word back to Hiram, "You know that my father wanted to build a house for the Lord, but was unable to because he was always at war with his enemies until God put them under his feet. But now we are at peace and prosperous, so I will build a temple for the Lord. This will be a magnificent house because our God is greater than all other gods. Please send lumber and workers to help me build, and I will pay them wages for their labor."

When Hiram heard the message, he replied, "God has made you king over his people because he loves them. Blessed be the Lord, creator of heaven and earth, because he has put a wise man in charge of this building project. My servants will bring lumber to you and work alongside your servants. I am also sending you Huram-abi, a skilled man who is an expert at all forms of design and artistry. Send payment as you have promised and I will send as much lumber as you need."

Solomon had a labor force of 70,000 men to bear burdens, 80,000 to quarry stone, and 3,600 men to oversee them. He also sent 10,000 men a month to Tyre to help harvest lumber. They would return home for two months at a time and a new group of 10,000 would go in their place.

Solomon began building the temple in the 480th year after the people had left Egypt and the fourth year of his reign. He built it at the site of Ornan's threshing floor that David had purchased. This was the site where the angel of the Lord had turned from his wrath after David's census.

The temple took seven years to build and was of such expert artisanship that they could not even insert a piece of paper between the massive foundation stones. Solomon decorated it with precious metal and stones both inside and out.

As the work was coming to a close, God came to Solomon and said, "If you walk in my statutes, obey my rules, and keep my commandments, then I will establish my word with you, just as I did with my servant David."

After finishing the temple, Solomon brought in the ark and gathered all the people. He threw a grand celebration and they sacrificed countless animals as the ark came in. The ark was empty except for the tablets of the Law that Moses had made and Aaron's staff that he had used to lead the people out of Egypt. The people gathered, made music, and sang, "The Lord is good and his steadfast love endures forever!" Then the Lord's presence came into the temple in the form of a cloud and the priests could not remain inside.

THE TEMPLE

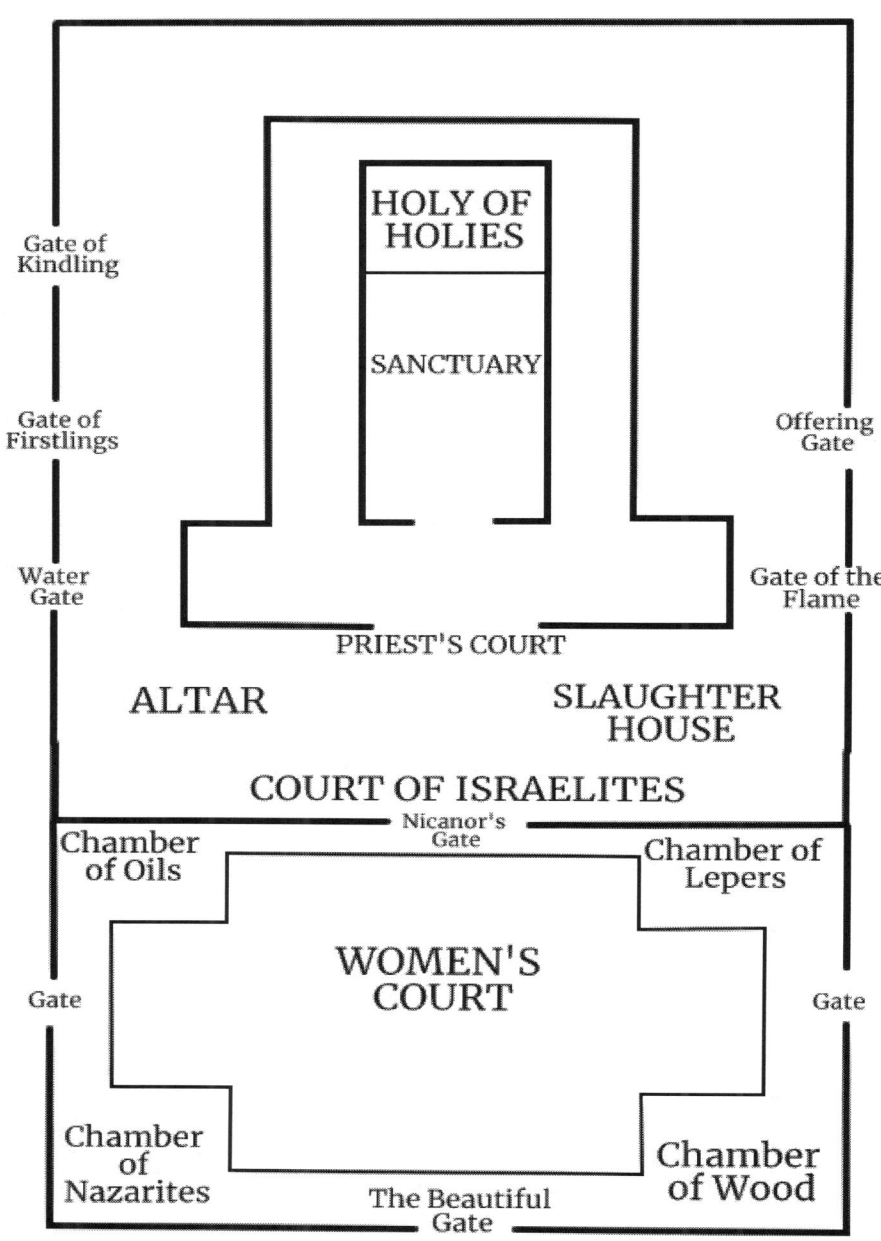

Solomon stood before the people and said, "The Lord said that he would dwell in thick darkness, but I have built him a magnificent house where he can live forever. Blessed be the Lord, God of Israel, who has fulfilled all his promises to my father. David had wanted to build a house for him, but the Lord told him that I would be the one to build a temple. Now, I sit on his throne as the Lord promised, and I have built him a house for the name of the Lord, the God of Israel. And now, the ark has a permanent home!"

Solomon dropped to his knees before the ark, lifted his hands to heaven, and prayed, "Oh Lord, God of Israel, there is no God like you in heaven or on earth who keeps his covenant with his people and shows steadfast love to his servants. You kept your promises to my father and your hand has fulfilled them today. Please keep your word to David that he will not lack a man to sit upon the throne forever if we follow your commandments as he did.

"But will God really live on earth? Even the highest heavens could not contain you, let alone this house! Please listen to your servant's prayer that you will always watch over this house and the prayers offered here. Listen to the people when they ask for forgiveness and forgive them. Hear their prayers and judge, condemning the guilty and vindicating the righteous. When our enemies defeat us, hear our prayers, and deliver us, restoring us to the land. When there is a drought because of our sin, and we repent and turn to you, forgive us, and send rain. When we have no food because of our sin, and we pray, asking for forgiveness, then do for each of us according to the state of our hearts (because you know all hearts). Then we will know that you are God and will walk in your ways.

"Likewise, if a foreigner hears of your great fame and comes to pray toward this house, listen to his request so that your name may be great in all the earth, and they will fear you as Israel does. If we go into battle and pray towards this house, listen to them and maintain their cause. When they sin against you (because everyone sins) and are carried into a foreign land, if they repent with a whole heart and mind, forgive them, and grant them mercy from their captors. Please be attentive to our prayers and see when we turn to you because you set us apart as your people when you brought us out of Egypt.

"Lord, God, go to your resting place, where your ark lives. Clothe your priests with salvation and let your saints rejoice in your goodness. Please do not turn your face from me and remember your steadfast love for your servant David!"

When he had finished praying, he stood before the people and called loudly, "Blessed be the Lord who has given his people rest as he promised. None of the promises he spoke to Moses have failed. May he be with us as he was with our fathers; may he never forsake us! May he incline our hearts to follow him and obey the commandments he gave Moses. May God always listen to my prayer and maintain our cause so that all the earth may know there is no other God besides him. Let your hearts be true to him and keep his commandments as you do today!"

As soon as he finished speaking, fire from heaven came down and consumed the sacrifices, and the glory of the Lord filled the temple. When the people saw the fire consume their offerings, they fell on their faces in worship.

Solomon offered a sacrifice of 22,000 oxen and 120,000 sheep, and all the people dedicated the temple of the Lord. Solomon also consecrated the inner court because the altar was too small to hold all the offerings. They held a great feast and Solomon sent everyone home on the eighth day. All the people rejoiced for what God had done.

> **Why all the sacrifices?**
>
> Solomon offered these sacrifices as an act of worship to God. All these animals would have been costly and Solomon showed his gratitude for God allowing him to complete the temple.

After Solomon finished the temple, he continued building his own house and it took 13 years to complete. He also filled both inside and out with precious metals and jewels and beautiful artistry. He also built a house for Pharaoh's daughter, whom he had married.

CHAPTER THIRTY-SEVEN

SOLOMON'S REIGN
I Kings 9-11, II Chronicles 7:11-9:31

As soon as Solomon finished building the temple and his house, the Lord appeared to Solomon a second time as he had at Gibeon. The Lord said to him, "I have heard your prayer and your request before me, and I have chosen this to be a house of sacrifice to me. If I send drought, famine, or disease and my people humble themselves, repent, and pray to me, I will hear them, forgive their sin, and heal their land. I have consecrated the house that you have built, and my name, heart, and eyes will dwell there for all time.

"As for you, if you walk before me like your father, David did and keep all my commandments, then I will establish your throne forever. If you or your children turn aside from following me and bow down to foreign gods, I will cut off Israel from the Promised Land and cast away the house you built for me. Israel will become an object lesson for the nations and everyone will be astonished when they see the ruins of this house. Then they will know that I brought disaster on you because you abandoned the Lord and followed after other gods."

After 20 years of building, Solomon rebuilt the cities Hiram had given to him as a gift. He drafted all the descendants of the nations in the Promised Land before Israel to be forced laborers. He used them to build cities and storehouses throughout Israel; he completed any project he wanted. Still, he did not put any of the Israelites into forced labor. He also built a fleet of ships on the shore of the Red Sea.

During the Sabbaths, new moons, and three annual feasts (Unleavened Bread, Weeks, and Booths), Solomon would offer a burnt offering to the Lord on the altar that he had built. He provided for the Levites and priests and they were able to serve the Lord as the Law required.

When the Queen of Sheba heard of Solomon's fame and wisdom, she came to test him with difficult questions. She came with a vast entourage, spices, gold, and precious stones. She met with Solomon, asked all her questions, and he was able to answer them all; there was nothing he could not explain. After hearing his wisdom, seeing the temple, the glory of his attendants, and how he provided for his people, she was speechless.

When she regained her breath, she said, "I heard reports of your wisdom and your kingdom's magnificence. I didn't believe them until I saw it with my own eyes. But I only heard a fraction of it; your wisdom and prosperity far surpass anything I heard. Your people are lucky to have you as their king and hear your wisdom. Praise the Lord for making you king! He must love his people to make you king so that you can execute justice and righteousness."

Then she gave Solomon a gift of about a half-ton of gold and many spices and precious stones. King Solomon gave her whatever she desired and she returned to her land with her servants.

SOLOMON STRAYS FROM THE LORD

Each year Solomon would bring in nearly 50,000 pounds of gold and he would use it to build beautiful works of art and decorations for his home and the temple. All his drinking cups were gold because silver was too common. Every three years, he would receive imports from afar of precious metals, ivory, and exotic animals.

Solomon loved many foreign women, including women from the nations that God had commanded his people not to marry. Overall, he had 700 wives and 300 concubines, and they turned his heart away to follow their foreign gods. The things Solomon did were evil in God's eyes and he did not follow the Lord with all his heart, as his father had done. He made places of worship for Ashtoreth, the goddess of the Sidonians, Chemosh and Molech, the gods of Moab, to make his foreign wives happy.

God became angry with Solomon because he had broken his commands about worshiping foreign gods even though he had appeared to Solomon twice. So, the Lord came to him and said, "Since you have not fully obeyed me but have gone after foreign gods, I will tear the kingdom from your hand and give it to your servant. But for the sake of David, I will not do it during your lifetime, and I will leave one tribe for him and one tribe for Jerusalem."

Then, the Lord raised up an adversary for Solomon after many years of peace. Hadad, the Edomite, had fled to Egypt when Joab was destroying the Edomites under David's command. Hadad lived in Egypt and gained prominence, but when he heard that David had died, he asked Pharaoh to send him back home. God also sent Rezon and a marauding band who took up residence in Damascus.

God also began to stir up Jeroboam from the tribe of Ephraim to be a thorn in Solomon's side. During one of the king's construction projects, Jeroboam distinguished himself as industrious and skilled at his work, and Solomon gave him a management position.

One day, as Jeroboam left Jerusalem, Ahijah came to him wearing a new garment and met him in the open country. Then Ahijah tore the garment into twelve pieces and said to Jeroboam, "The Lord is about to tear the kingdom from Solomon's hands, and he will give you ten tribes because they have forsaken him and worshiped foreign gods. But he will not do it during Solomon's lifetime, and he will leave him a single tribe for the sake of his father, David. God will make you king over Israel and you shall have whatever you desire. If you obey the Lord, he will establish you as a house in Israel, just like he did for David. He will afflict David's offspring for this sin, but not forever."

Solomon heard about this encounter, and he tried to put Jeroboam to death. But Jeroboam escaped to Egypt until Solomon finally died. Solomon ruled over Israel for 40 years, then died and was buried in Jerusalem. After that, his son Rehoboam led in his place.

CHAPTER THIRTY-EIGHT

THE KINGDOM DIVIDED

I Kings 12:1-15:8, II Chronicles 10-13

RULERS OF JUDAH AND ISRAEL (931 – 911 B.C.)

Kings of Judah		Kings of Israel	
King and notes	Reign	King and notes	Reign
Rehoboam: Solomon's son, who was an evil king. Kicked all the Levites out of the land and fought against the Egyptians. Shemaiah served as a prophet to him.	17 years	Jeroboam I: A construction supervisor that God raised up to punish Solomon. Set up idols and led the people away from the Lord. Ahijah served as a prophet to him.	20 years
Abijah: Rehoboam's son, who was an evil king. God used him to weaken Jeroboam's power.	3 years		

All Israel went to Shechem to make Rehoboam king; as soon as Jeroboam heard about it, he returned from Egypt. Jeroboam and the Israelites went to Rehoboam and said, "Your father made our burdens heavy, please lighten our load, and we will gladly serve you." He told the people to come back in three days so he could consider their request.

The older men advised him to lighten the people's load, but he ignored their counsel and listened to the young men he kept with him. When the people returned to him on the third day, he said to them, "My little finger is thicker than my father's genitals! I will add to your burdens, and where my father disciplined you with whips, I will discipline you with scorpions!" He spoke these words so that the Lord could fulfill Ahijah's prophecy to Jeroboam.

The people said to each other, "David's house has nothing to do with us! Everyone go home and let Rehoboam rule over his own people!" Then, when Rehoboam sent Adoram to put the people to work, they stoned the servant to death. Rehoboam was afraid of the people and returned to Jerusalem.

The Israelites who were not from the tribes of Judah and Benjamin came together and made Jeroboam their king. Rehoboam gathered his troops together and had 180,000 soldiers to regain the other tribes' loyalty. But God said to them, "Do not attack your relatives, go back home. This is not what I want." The priests listened and did not start a civil war.

Rehoboam lived in Jerusalem and built strongly fortified cities to protect what he still had of the kingdom. Jeroboam kicked all the Levites out of the land and set his own priests up to offer sacrifices. So, they all went to Jerusalem, and Rehoboam put them to work serving the Lord. Everyone who set their hearts to obey the Lord came to Jerusalem to offer sacrifices and Rehoboam was secure in Jerusalem just as Solomon had been.

He followed his father's footsteps and had 18 wives and 60 concubines, and he fathered 28 sons and 60 daughters. He appointed Abijah as his chief priest and ruled wisely over Judah, keeping them safe and secure.

JEROBOAM TURNS AWAY FROM THE LORD (ISRAEL)

Meanwhile, after kicking the Levites out of the land, Jeroboam was afraid that the people would return to Rehoboam. So, he built two golden calves and declared that they were the gods who had brought them out of Egypt. He set one up in Bethel and the other up in Dan, and they became a snare to the people. He made temples on the high places and appointed his own priests to offer sacrifices. He decided that the people needed another festival and set up his own celebration that the Lord had not commanded.

A man of God from Judah came to Jeroboam and confronted him as he stood to make offerings. The man said, "The Lord is going to raise up a king in Judah named Josiah and he will sacrifice the bones of your priests on this altar. As a sign that this will happen, your altar will be torn down, and the ashes inside will be poured out on the earth."

Jeroboam was furious and commanded his men to seize the man of God. As he stretched out his hand to make the command, the Lord caused it to wither. The community was afraid, and they tore down the altar, and poured out the ashes on the earth.

Jeroboam said to the man of God, "Please pray for me so God will restore my hand." The man prayed and the king's hand returned to normal. Jeroboam asked him to come to his home to eat, be refreshed, and receive a reward.

The man of God replied, "Even if you gave me half your kingdom, I would not return with you because the Lord commanded me not to eat or drink until I return home." Then he left Jeroboam and headed home by another way.

There was an old prophet in Bethel who heard about what had happened, and he saddled his donkey and went to meet the man of God from Judah. The prophet asked the man of God to come back to his home and eat and drink with him. The man of God denied his request because God had told him not to eat or drink until he returned home.

The prophet from Bethel lied to him and said, "I am a prophet like you, and an angel told me to tell you to come back with me and eat and drink." So, the man of God from Judah went with him and ate bread and drank water.

As the man of God from Judah was eating, the Lord spoke to the prophet from Bethel, and he cried out, "God just told me that you have disobeyed him and broken the command he gave you. Therefore, you will die and your body will not return home."

Crestfallen, the man of God left Bethel and continued on his trip home. On his way, a lion met him on the road and killed him. He fell on the roadside, and both the donkey and lion stood beside his body. People brought news to the prophet from Bethel about what had happened, and he saddled his donkey and went to retrieve the body.

When he came to the site where the man died, the donkey and lion were still standing by the body, and the lion had not attacked the donkey or eaten the man's body. The prophet took his body back to Bethel and mourned his death. He buried his body in his own tomb and told his sons to bury him next to the man of God.

> **What is happening here?**
>
> This is a strange account of two unidentified men. The first is a prophet who God gave a mission to fulfill. The second man was likely a prophet who had fallen away from following the Lord, and he lied to the prophet from Bethel. This is a warning about incomplete obedience to God. The second man buried the prophet in his tomb out of regret for his actions.

JEROBOAM AND AHIJAH (ISRAEL)

After this, Jeroboam did not turn away from his evil, and he continued to worship his idols and appoint random people to be priests. This was an ongoing sin for Jeroboam's house so God could cut his family off from the face of the earth.

Jeroboam's son became deathly ill at that time, and Jeroboam sent his wife to the prophet Ahijah who lived in Shiloh. He told her to take some bread and honey because he would tell her what would happen to the boy. She disguised herself so that no one would know who she was.

The Lord told Ahijah that she was coming, and when she arrived, he said, "Jeroboam's wife, come in! Why do you pretend to be someone else? I have bad news for you. Go back to Jeroboam and tell him that the Lord exalted him and gave him David's kingdom. But your husband has not been like David and has done evil by setting up false gods and idols for the people.

"Now God is angry, and he is going to cut off every male from Jeroboam's house, and they will be burned up like dung. The dogs will eat the body of anyone who dies in the city, and the birds will eat the body of anyone who dies in the field. When you get home, the child will die because God has not found anything good in Jeroboam. He will shake Israel like a reed and send them into captivity because the Lord is angry with Jeroboam's sin."

Jeroboam's wife returned home and the child died, as Ahijah said. They buried him and mourned him for many days. Jeroboam ruled over Israel for 22 years before he died.

REHOBOAM TURNS AWAY FROM THE LORD (JUDAH)

In Judah, Rehoboam also turned away from the Lord and followed false gods. In the fifth year of his reign, the Lord caused Shishak, the king of Egypt, to attack Israel. They came with a massive army and captured the fortified cities all the way to Jerusalem. The Lord sent the prophet Shemaiah to Rehoboam and he said, "The Lord is abandoning you to Shishak because you abandoned him."

The elders humbled themselves and repented of their sin. Then God said to Shemaiah, "Because the people have humbled themselves, I will not let Shishak destroy them; I will provide some measure of deliverance. But they will become his servants so that they may know what serving foreign countries is like compared to serving me."

So, Shishak came into Jerusalem and plundered the city, taking the temple and palace's treasures away to Egypt. The people served the Egyptians and conditions were very hard in Judah. But God did not destroy them because they had humbled themselves before him.

Rehoboam was 41 when he became king and reigned for 17 years in Jerusalem. He did evil because he did not set his heart to follow the Lord. There was continual conflict between Rehoboam and Jeroboam throughout his reign. When he died, he was buried in Jerusalem, and his son Abijah ruled in his place.

ABIJAH SUCCEEDS REHOBOAM (JUDAH)

Abijah became king during the 18th year of Jeroboam's reign and he ruled for three years in Jerusalem. He did evil just as his father Rehoboam had done and he did not follow in the ways of David. But God did not remove his presence from Judah for the sake of his servant David.

During his rule, he took 400,000 men to fight against Jeroboam and his 800,000 men. As they drew up in battle formation, he stood atop Mount Zemaraim and said to the men of Israel, "Listen to me, Jeroboam and Israel! The Lord, God of Israel, gave David the kingdom through a covenant! But Jeroboam and some worthless men rebelled against their king. Do you really think you can withstand the Lord's army because you have more men and your gold idols? You have appointed false priests to serve idols that are not gods!

"But we have not forsaken the Lord! We have Levites for priests and they make offerings to the Lord every morning. We obey God, but you have forsaken him! God is our head, do not fight against us and the Lord because you cannot possibly prevail!"

Jeroboam had set an ambush behind them, and when they attacked, the men of Judah saw that they were surrounded. They cried out to the Lord and the priests blew their trumpets. When the soldiers shouted the battle cry, God defeated Jeroboam and the Israelites before Abijah and Judah. The men of Israel fled, and Abijah and his men struck down a half-million Israelites that day. Thus, the men of Judah subdued Jeroboam because they relied on the Lord. Abijah pursued Jeroboam and took back some of the cities of Israel. Jeroboam never regained power during the rest of his reign. Abijah had fourteen wives, 22 sons, and 16 daughters. When he died, he was buried in Jerusalem.

CHAPTER THIRTY-NINE

ASA RULES OVER JUDAH
I Kings 15:9-16:34, II Chronicles 14-16

RULERS OF JUDAH AND ISRAEL (911 – 873 B.C.)

Kings of Judah		Kings of Israel	
King and notes	Reign	King and notes	Reign
Asa: Righteous king, who was Rehoboam's son. Relied on the Lord against an Ethiopian horde; however, he did not trust God to deliver him from the Syrians. Hanani and Azariah served as prophets to him.	38 years	Jeroboam I: See previous chapter.	1 year
		Nadab: Evil king, who was Jeroboam's son. Killed by Baasha.	2 years
		Baasha: An evil usurper who supplanted Nadab. Fought against Judah throughout his rule. Jehu served as a prophet to him.	24 years
		Elah: Baasha's son, who led the Israelites astray.	2 years
		Zimri: Murdered Elah and was killed by Omri.	1 week
		Omri: Usurper who did more evil than his predecessors.	12 years
		Ahab: Omri's son, who married Jezebel. See Ch. 42 for more information.	1 year

NADAB AND BAASHA (ISRAEL)

In the 20th year of Jeroboam's reign, Asa became king of Judah, and he reigned for 41 years in Judah. Not long after Asa became king, Jeroboam died, and his son Nadab ruled in his place. Nadab did evil in the Lord's sight just as his father had done. He took his army to besiege the Philistine city of Gibbethon. While they were laying siege to the city, Baasha and some Ephraimites conspired against Nadab and came to kill him. Baasha took Nadab's place and killed all of Jeroboam's sons. This fulfilled God's word through the prophet Ahijah for all the evil Jeroboam had done.

Baasha reigned for 24 years and he fought with Asa throughout his entire rule. He did evil in the Lord's eyes and continued in the sins of Israel's kings, worshiping false gods and idols. To defend himself from Baasha, Asa also allied with Ben-Hadad, the king of Syria, to protect them. Ben-Hadad agreed and removed his support from Baasha and weakened his attack against Asa.

God sent the prophet Jehu to Baasha, and he said, "God exalted you from nothing to become king, but you have continued to walk in the sins of Jeroboam and made Israel sin. Now he is angry and he will sweep away your house just as he did with Jeroboam. Dogs will eat any of your sons killed in the city and the birds will eat anyone who dies in the fields."

GOD DELIVERS JUDAH FROM THE ETHIOPIANS

During the 15th year of Asa's rule, Zerah the Ethiopian brought 1,000,000 men to attack Judah. Asa cried out to the Lord for deliverance and God gave the Ethiopians into his hands. Asa pursued the Ethiopians and slaughtered their entire army. They took a great deal of plunder from them and then attacked some Ethiopian cities and brought even more spoils back to Jerusalem.

After this victory, the Spirit of the Lord came upon the prophet Azariah, and he went to Asa and said, "The Lord is with you as long as you are with him, but if you forsake him, then he will forsake you. Israel has lived without the true God, a teaching priest, and the Law. Israel cried out to the Lord for deliverance in times of trouble, and he answered. We have been without peace and suffered all sorts of afflictions. Take courage and do not let your hands be weak because God will reward your work."

Azariah's words encouraged Asa, and he gathered all Judah and Benjamin to him, along with many people who deserted from Israel because they saw that the Lord was with the king. They took 700 oxen and 7,000 sheep from the Ethiopian spoils and sacrificed them to God. They made a covenant with the Lord to seek him with their whole hearts and that whoever did not agree should die.

Asa did what was right in the Lord's eyes, just as David had done. He took away the foreign idols and high places, broke down the Asherim, and removed the male cult prostitutes. He even removed his mother, Maacah, from being the queen mother because she had done terrible things. He commanded Judah to seek the Lord, the God of their fathers, and obey his commandments.

Asa's heart was wholly committed to the Lord and he brought sacred gifts of precious metals into the temple. He built fortified cities in Judah and had a standing army of 300,000 men from Judah and 280,000 men from Benjamin, and they had peace until the 36th year of his reign.

ASA AND HANANI (JUDAH)

In the 36th year of Asa's reign, the prophet Hanani came to Asa and said, "Because you relied on the king of Syria, instead of the Lord, the Syrians have escaped from your hands. The Ethiopians were a massive army, but the Lord defeated them because you called on his name. God's eyes go throughout the land, looking to support those who are blameless in his eyes. From now on, you will have war!"

Hanani's words made Asa angry, so he arrested the prophet and put him in the stocks. He also began to oppress some of his people and the Lord punished him with a disease in his feet. But he sought the help of doctors instead of God. Eventually, the condition became bad enough to take his life after he ruled over Israel for 41 years. The people buried him in Jerusalem and they mourned his death. Despite his failures at the end of his life, he still followed the Lord with his whole heart.

ELAH, ZIMRI, AND OMRI (ISRAEL)

After Baasha died, his son Elah became king, and he only reigned for two years. One day while he was drunk, his servant Zimri killed him and became king in his place. Then he killed all the males from Baasha's house and his friends. This fulfilled the words that Jehu had spoken because Baasha had caused the people to sin.

Zimri only ruled over Israel for a week before his army rebelled against him. They gave command of the military to Omri and attacked the house where Zimri was staying. He locked himself in a tower, and the army burned the tower, killing all within it.

There was great confusion in Israel, and some of the people followed Omri, but others followed Tibni, who also sought the throne. Eventually, Omri's followers subdued Tibni's followers, and he ruled for 12 years. The king acquired the hill of Samaria and built a city on it. He did more evil than any of his predecessors and ran even further from the Lord than the other kings of Israel had.

AHAB BECOMES KING (ISRAEL)

In the 38th year of Asa's rule, Omri died, and his son Ahab ruled over Israel from the city of Samaria. He sinned even more than his father had and married Jezebel, the daughter of the Sidonian king. He openly worshiped Baal and other false gods and built a house for Baal in Samaria. During his reign, Hiel rebuilt Jericho. Hiel's oldest son, Abiram, died as he laid the foundation, and his youngest son, Segub, died as he erected the gates, just as Joshua had prophesied.

CHAPTER FORTY

ELIJAH AND AHAB
I Kings 17-19

During Ahab's rule, God sent the prophet Elijah to speak against the king. Elijah came to Ahab and said, "As the Lord lives, there will be no rain or dew in Israel for the next three years until I tell the drought to end." Then God told him to flee to the east of the Jordan River, where he could drink from a brook, and ravens would bring him food to eat.

Eventually, the drought dried up the brook, and God told him to go to Zarephath in the land of the Sidonians, where a widow would look after him. As he entered the city, he saw an old woman gathering sticks, and he asked her for a drink. As she came to him, Elijah also asked for some food. The woman replied, "I don't have anything prepared; all I have left is a little flour and oil. Now I am gathering sticks to build a fire, prepare a final meal for myself and my son, and then wait to die."

Elijah answered her, "Don't be afraid, do what you have said you were going to do. But before you make the food for you and your son, make me a cake of bread because God has declared that you will not run out of flour or oil until he sends rain on the earth again."

She did as he asked, and the jar of flour and jug of oil did not run out for many days because God filled them. Elijah stayed with them and the three of them ate as he had promised.

ELIJAH RAISES A WIDOW'S SON

One day, the widow's son died of a sudden illness. The widow said to Elijah, "What do you have against me, you 'man of God?' You have come to remind me of my sin and cause my son's death!"

Elijah asked her to give him her son, and he carried him up to the room where he was staying and laid him on his bed. Then he cried to the Lord, "God, why have you brought trouble to the woman I am staying with by killing her son?" Then he stretched his body out on the child three times and begged the Lord to bring him back to life. God listened to his prayer and brought the boy back to life.

Elijah brought the boy back downstairs and gave him to his mother. The widow was overcome and said, "Now I know that you truly are a man of God and that your words are true!"

ELIJAH AND THE PROPHETS OF BAAL

In the third year of the drought, life had become challenging, and the Lord sent Elijah to speak to Ahab. Obadiah had gone to search for water and grass to feed livestock, and Elijah met him while he was on his journey. Obadiah had hidden 100 prophets in caves and provided for them after Jezebel had cut off prophets of the Lord. Obadiah was afraid that Elijah had come to condemn him, and when they met, he fell on his face. Elijah instructed him to tell Ahab to meet with him, but Obadiah was afraid that Ahab would kill him once he heard the message. He was scared that God would take Elijah to another place because Ahab had been looking to kill him.

When Ahab met with Elijah, the king said, "Is that you, troubler of Israel?"

Elijah replied, "I have not troubled Israel; you and your father's house have because you have forsaken God's commands and worshiped false gods! Now, gather all Israel at Mount Carmel along with the prophets of Baal and 400 prophets of Asherim who eat at Jezebel's table."

Ahab gathered everyone as requested and Elijah said to them, "How long will you waver between two opinions? If the Lord is God, then serve him, but if it's Baal, then serve him!" The people were silent, so he continued, "I am the only prophet of God left, but you have many. Let us each choose a bull, slaughter it, and put it on an altar of wood. Call upon Baal, and I will call upon the Lord, and whoever answers with fire is the true God!"

The people agreed to Elijah's plan and the prophets of Baal went first. They danced around from morning to midday, begging their god to send fire, but nothing happened. At noon, Elijah mocked them, "Yell louder, if he is a god. Maybe he's meditating, on a journey, or maybe he's in the bathroom. Maybe, he's taking a nap and you need to wake him up!"

The prophets of Baal doubled their efforts and cut themselves with knives so that blood gushed out. But nothing happened to the bull and no one answered until the evening sacrifice.

Then Elijah called the people to him and he rebuilt the altar of the Lord with twelve stones to represent the twelve tribes of Israel. Then he dug a trench around the altar and had the people soak the bull and altar with hundreds of gallons of water until the ditch around the altar was full. Then he came to the altar and cried out to the Lord, "Oh God of Abraham, Isaac, and Jacob, make it known that you are the true God and that I am your servant. Answer me so that the people will see your power and turn their hearts back to you."

Fire fell from heaven and consumed the offering, the wood, stones, and even the water in the trench. When the people saw this, they fell on their faces and declared that the Lord was the true God. Elijah commanded them to seize Baal's prophets, take them down the mountain, and kill them all.

Elijah told Ahab to go back home and eat and drink because the sound of torrential rain was coming. Ahab listened and then Elijah bowed in prayer. Then he sent his servant to see if there was anything in the sky, and there was nothing. He repeated this process five more times and the sky was still clear. On the seventh time, the servant returned and said a small cloud was rising from the sea.

Elijah sent his servant to warn Ahab to hurry back to the city of Jezreel so that he wouldn't get stuck in the coming rain. Ahab got in his chariot and drove back home. The sky grew black with clouds and there was a torrential downpour. Elijah ran down the mountain and the Lord carried him to Jezreel so that he arrived before Ahab got there.

ELIJAH FLEES FROM JEZEBEL

Ahab told Jezebel everything that had happened and she was furious. She sent Elijah a message that she would kill him within 24 hours. Elijah was afraid and he fled to Beersheba in Judah. He left his servant there and went a day's journey into the wilderness, sat down under a tree, and asked God to let him die. Then he laid down and went to sleep.

An angel woke him up and told him to get up and eat. A small meal was waiting for him and he ate and went back to sleep. Then the angel woke him a second time and told him to eat a second meal because he had a great journey ahead of him. He ate and drank a second time and then set out on a 40-day trip to Mount Horeb, a journey of 200 miles. He did not eat or drink anything on the journey.

When he arrived, he stayed in a cave, and the Lord spoke to him, saying, "Elijah, what are you doing here?"

Elijah replied, "Lord, I have been very jealous for your name, but your people have forsaken you and killed all your prophets. I am the only one left, and now they want to kill me too."

God told him to leave the cave and stand before him; Elijah obeyed. The Lord passed by, and there was a mighty wind and earthquake, but God was not in the wind or the earthquake. After the wind and earthquake, there was a fire, but God was not in the fire. Then there was the sound of a low whisper, and when Elijah heard it, he wrapped his cloak around his face and stood at the entrance of the cave.

As he stood there, a voice asked him why he was there. As he had before, he replied that he felt like he was the only one left who was still following the Lord. God told him, "Return to the wilderness of Damascus, and when you arrive, you will anoint Hazael to be king over Syria. You will also anoint Jehu to be king of Israel and Elisha to be your successor. Whoever escapes from Hazael, Jehu will put to death, and whoever escapes Jehu, Elisha will kill. Do not be dismayed; I still have 7,000 men who have not bowed their knee to Baal."

ELIJAH APPOINTS ELISHA AS HIS SUCCESSOR

Elijah departed from there and found Elisha plowing a field with twelve oxen. Elijah threw his cloak on him and then passed by him. Elisha asked him if he could kiss his parents goodbye before following him. Elijah responded, "Go back, but don't forget what I've just done to you" Then he sacrificed the oxen, boiled the meat over the wood from the yokes, and they ate. Then he arose and followed Elijah.

> ### What is happening here?
> Elisha was a man of substance, given that he could plow with a dozen oxen. When Elijah threw his cloak over Elisha's shoulders, it was a customary way of eastern teachers appointing a follower to a prophetic office. Elisha asks to say goodbye to his family, and Elijah permits him as long as he came back to follow.

CHAPTER FORTY-ONE

AHAB

I Kings 20-21

Ben-Hadad, the king of Syria, created a coalition of 32 kings and their combined armies came to fight against Samaria. He sent messengers to Ahab, saying, "All your gold and silver are mine. So are the best of your wives and all your children!" Ahab replied in despair that this was true, so Ben-Hadad sent messengers telling him to send these things to him. He also said that his men would come the next day and take whatever they wanted from Israel.

Ahab was distressed and he asked the elders what he should do. They told him he should not consent to his request, and he sent a messenger to Ben-Hadad saying, "I am your servant and will do whatever you want, but I cannot do this thing." They sent a couple more messages back and forth and Ben-Hadad prepared his men to attack.

Then a prophet came to Ahab and said, "The Lord will give this great multitude into your hand so that you may know that he alone is the true God. Send your men into battle and strike first!"

Ahab was only able to muster about 7,000 soldiers and 232 servants of the local governors. They went out to Ben-Hadad at midday while the Syrian king was getting drunk. Ben-Hadad sent men out to see if they wanted to fight or surrender. The Israelites struck down the men who came to meet them and the Syrians fled. The Israelites chased after them and struck a significant blow against the invading army, but Ben-Hadad escaped on horseback.

Elijah came to Ahab and advised him to think carefully about what he would do because the Syrians would come back in the spring to attack again. The Syrians reasoned that the Israelites' gods were gods of the hills; they should make sure that the battle took place in the plains the next time they fought. They refreshed their army and came back the following spring.

> **Who are the Samaritans?**
>
> Samaria is another name for the northern tribes of Israel. The Samaritans were the Israelites of the divided kingdom.

The Syrians fought with the Samaritans again and vastly outnumbered them. Another man of God came to Ahab and said, "Because the Syrians think that God is only over the hills, he will give them into your hands so that they may know that he is God over everything. Then you will know that he is the only true God."

They went to battle and the Samaritans killed 100,000 of their soldiers. The rest of the army fled to Aphek, and the city wall fell upon them, killing 27,000 more. Ben-Hadad fled to an inner chamber in Aphek and his men advised him to beg for Ahab's mercy. His leaders put on sackcloth and came to ask for Ben-Hadad's life. Ahab showed them mercy and Ben-Hadad came out to meet with him. They made a covenant of peace, and Ben-Hadad restored all the cities of Samaria he had captured.

Another prophet went to meet with Ahab, and on his way, he asked a man to strike him on the cheek. The man refused and the prophet declared that a lion would kill him because he had not obeyed the Lord. As soon as he left, a lion met him and struck him down.

The prophet asked another man to strike him, and the man complied and wounded his face. He disguised himself, put a bandage over his eyes, sat down by the road, and waited for Ahab to pass. When he came by, the prophet told Ahab that a soldier had charged him to stand guard over a man and that if he let him die, he would pay with his life. But if he protected his life, then he would receive a reward. Then he told the king that he had lost track of the man.

Ahab told him that he would die because he had failed to keep the soldier's charge. Then the prophet unbandaged his eyes and said, "The Lord says that because you let Ben-Hadad go, your life will go for his and your people for his!" Then Ahab went home, upset about what the prophet had said to him.

> **What is happening here?**
>
> This is a strange account of two unidentified men. The first is a prophet who God gave a mission to fulfill. The second man is likely a different prophet who should have known to obey. Once the unnamed prophet was injured, he set up a ruse to deliver a message to Ahab.

AHAB AND NABOTH

A man named Naboth owned a vineyard next to the palace in Samaria. Ahab wanted it for a vegetable garden and he offered him either money or an equivalent field somewhere else in the city. But Naboth refused because he did not want to give up his family inheritance. So, Ahab moped around the palace and refused to eat.

Jezebel noticed that her husband was sullen and asked what was wrong. He replied, "I asked Naboth for his vineyard, and he refused, even though I offered him money or another field."

She reassured him, "Aren't you the king of Israel? Get up and eat. I will get the field for you." Then she sent letters to the Israelite leaders declaring a feast in Naboth's name. They set Naboth at the head of the table and put two worthless men next to him, who accused him of cursing God and the king. Then they took him outside the city and stoned him to death. Once Jezebel heard that Naboth was dead, she told Ahab to take possession of the vineyard.

Then the Lord came to Elijah and sent him to meet Ahab in the vineyard. When he met the king, Elijah said, "Have you taken possession of this field? The Lord says that the dogs will lick up your blood in the same place where they licked up Naboth's blood!" Ahab was furious and insulted Elijah. Then Elijah continued, "I found you because you have done evil in the Lord's sight. He will burn you up and consume every male from your household! He will make your house like Jeroboam's and Baasha's because you have made Israel sin. He will also kill Jezebel and the dogs will eat her flesh!"

Ahab had done more evil than any other king in Israel because his wife had led him into sin. But when Ahab heard Elijah's words, he tore his clothes, dressed in sackcloth, and walked around depressed. The Lord saw Ahab's repentance and told Elijah that Ahab's house's downfall would not happen during his lifetime but after he had died.

CHAPTER FORTY-TWO

JEHOSHAPHAT'S REIGN AND ELIJAH'S ASCENSION
I Kings 22:1-II Kings 2:14, II Chronicles 17-20

RULERS OF JUDAH AND ISRAEL (870 – 850 B.C.)

Kings of Judah		Kings of Israel	
King and notes	Reign	King and notes	Reign
Jehoshaphat: Asa's son, who began his rule well, but did not always follow the Lord. Made peace with Israel and trusted the Lord for deliverance from the Moabites and Ammonites. Jahaziel served as a prophet to him.	20 years	Ahab: Evil king, who openly worshiped Baal. Micaiah and Elijah served as prophets to him.	16 years
		Ahaziah: Ahab's son, who continued to worship Baal. Elijah served as a prophet to him.	2 years
		Joram: See Ch. 44 for more information.	2 years

JEHOSHAPHAT SUCCEEDS ASA (JUDAH)

Meanwhile, Jehoshaphat had begun to rule Judah during the fourth year of Ahab's reign. Jehoshaphat ruled in Judah and fortified the cities Asa had captured from Israel. The Lord was with him because he followed David's ways and did not worship false gods. The Lord established his kingdom and the people brought tribute to him. He sent priests throughout Judah and they taught the people the Law.

The surrounding nations feared his reign and did not attack him. The Philistines and Arabians brought him gifts and he filled the storehouses and treasuries with many supplies. He had an army of more than a million soldiers and he placed commanders over four military divisions.

JEHOSHAPHAT FIGHTS ALONGSIDE AHAB

After Ahab took possession of Naboth's vineyard, Samaria lived at peace for three years. Then Ahab decided to recapture the city of Ramoth-Gilead from the Syrians. He went to Jehoshaphat and asked him to join forces and attack the Syrians. Jehoshaphat replied, "I am with you; my people and horses are yours. But first, is there a prophet who will ask God what we should do?"

Ahab gathered 400 of his prophets and asked them if he should fight against Ramoth-Gilead, and all his prophets told him that he should because he would succeed. Jehoshaphat asked if there was a prophet of God that they could ask, but Ahab said, "There is one, Micaiah, but I hate him because he never gives me any good news."

Jehoshaphat insisted, and they summoned Micaiah. While they were waiting, Ahab's prophets continued to predict how badly they would defeat the Syrians. As Micaiah came, the king's servants told him all of Ahab's men were prophesying success and that he needed to say something positive. But Micaiah promised he could only say what the Lord said.

When Micaiah came to Ahab, the prophet said dismissively, "Go and triumph because the Lord will give the city into your hand."

Ahab was irritated by his sarcasm and said, "How often have I made you swear only to tell me the truth of what God has said?!"

Then Micaiah replied, "I saw all of Israel scattered on the mountains like sheep without a shepherd. Then the Lord said to let all these people return to their homes because they have no leader."

Ahab instantly said to Jehoshaphat, "See, I told you he would only say evil things about me!"

Then Micaiah continued, "I saw the Lord sitting on his throne surrounded by all his angels and he asked who would convince Ahab to attack Ramoth-Gilead so that Ahab can die in battle. Then one of the angels came forward and said that he would put a lying spirit into the mouths of Ahab's prophets. So, your prophets have heard from this spirit and now the Lord has declared disaster for you!"

Zedekiah, one of Ahab's prophets, slapped Micaiah and yelled, "How did the Spirit of the Lord leave me to speak to you?"

Micaiah snapped back, "You will find out when you hide in an inner chamber!"

Ahab commanded his men to put Micaiah into prison and feed him meager rations until the king returned home safely. Then Micaiah said, "If you return home safely, then the Lord has not spoken through me."

So, the two kings went into battle, and Ahab disguised himself while Jehoshaphat went out in his royal robes. The Syrians' commander told his army only to fight with the king and ignore the other soldiers. When Jehoshaphat saw what was happening, he cried out to the Lord, and God drew the battle away from him. Once they saw that it was not the king of Israel, they stopped pursuing him.

During the battle, a random Syrian arrow hit Ahab. The king's servants took him out of the fight to tend his wound. He sat in his chariot and watched the battle until sunset, when he died. As soon as the people heard that Ahab was dead, they all fled to their own homes. They buried Ahab in Samaria and washed out his chariot at the pool of Samaria. Dogs licked up his blood, and prostitutes bathed in the bloody water, fulfilling God's word. Ahab's son Ahaziah reigned in his place.

JEHOSHAPHAT'S REIGN IN JUDAH

Jehoshaphat began his reign at the age of 35 and he reigned for 25 years. He walked in his father Asa's ways, but he did not remove the high places, and the people continued to offer sacrifices there. He made peace with Israel's king and appointed judges to rule the people, charging them, "Be careful how you judge because you are making decisions for God and not just for men. Execute justice and do not take bribes or show partiality. Judge the people righteously and do not sin. Be courageous and may the Lord be with the upright!"

AHAZIAH SUCCEEDS AHAB (ISRAEL)

Ahaziah ruled in Israel for two years and committed evil just as his father had. He continued to worship Baal and made Israel sin. God was very angry with him and arranged to remove him from the throne.

After Ahab's death, Moab rebelled against Israel and fought with them. One day at the palace, Ahaziah fell through a lattice and was severely injured. He sent his men to ask Baal-zebub, the Philistine god, if he would recover.

The angel of the Lord sent Elijah to meet with Ahaziah's men and he said, "Are you going to Baal-zebub because there is no God in Israel? Therefore, the Lord says that you will never get off your bed and die from your injuries." They went back to Ahaziah and relayed Elijah's message.

When Ahaziah heard these words, he figured out it was Elijah and sent a captain with his 50 soldiers to bring the prophet to him. They found Elijah sitting on top of a hill and told him to come down. He replied, "If I am a man of God, may he send fire from heaven and consume you!" Then fire came down and consumed the soldiers. Ahaziah sent a second group of 50 and the same thing happened.

Ahaziah sent a third group of 50, and this time the captain fell on his knees and begged for his and his men's lives. Then the angel of the Lord told Elijah to go with them, so he got up and went to meet Ahaziah.

When he met with the king, Elijah said, "Because you went to seek Baal-zebub instead of the Lord, you will die from your injuries." Then Jehoram, the son of Jehoshaphat, became king because Ahaziah did not have any children.

MOAB FIGHTS AGAINST JUDAH

The Moabites also rebelled against Judah and went to battle with them as well. Jehoshaphat was afraid, and he called upon the Lord and asked the people to fast and seek the Lord. The entire community fasted and sought God. They prayed, "Oh Lord, God of our fathers, you are God in heaven. You rule over all nations, and you have all power and might so that no one can stand before you. You drove out the nations and gave us the land you promised to Abraham. Solomon built a house for your name and declared that if anyone prays towards the temple, you would hear and deliver us from our enemies. Now, the Moabites and Ammonites are attacking, please deliver us from them. We are powerless before this horde, and we don't know what to do, but our eyes are on you."

They stood before the Lord and waited for him to answer. Then the prophet, Jahaziel, stood up in front of the people and said, "Do not be afraid of this horde, because the battle is not yours; it belongs to God! Tomorrow you will go into battle, but you will not have to fight because God will save you. He will fight for you and the Lord will be with you."

Then they all bowed to the ground and worshiped the Lord. The Levites stood up and praised God with a loud voice. Then everyone prepared to go into battle.

The next morning, Jehoshaphat told them, "Believe in the Lord, and you will be established, believe his prophets, and you will succeed!" Then he went before the army and said, "Give thanks to the Lord because his steadfast love endures!"

People began to sing and praise the Lord. When the Moabites and Ammonites heard their singing, God set an ambush, and Judah routed them. Then the Moabites and Ammonites turned on one other and killed each other.

When the watchmen looked out at the plain, they saw all their enemies lying dead on the ground. Jehoshaphat and his men went out and plundered their enemies. There was so much spoil that it took three days to bring all the goods back home. On the fourth day, they gathered at the Valley of Beracah, and they blessed the Lord. Then they returned home, praising the Lord, and making music.

When the other nations heard what God had done, they were afraid of him, and Jehoshaphat had peace for the rest of his reign. But at the end of his reign, he joined with Ahaziah and acted wickedly. They built ships to go to Tarshish, but God was not pleased, and he destroyed the vessels before they were even launched.

ELIJAH TAKEN UP TO HEAVEN

The Lord was about to take Elijah up to heaven in a whirlwind, and Elijah told Elisha to stay put while he went to Bethel. But Elisha refused and said, "As the Lord lives, I will not leave you." So, they went to Bethel together.

The prophets of Bethel came to Elisha and told him that God was going to take Elijah up to heaven, and Elisha told them to keep quiet because he knew what was going to happen. Elijah went to the Jordan River, and Elisha insisted on going with him, and 50 of the Bethel prophets joined them as well.

When they came to the Jordan, Elijah rolled up his cloak and struck the water with it, and the waters parted so that they could cross on dry land. Once they had crossed the river, Elijah asked Elisha, "What would you have as a gift before I go up to heaven?" Elisha asked for a double portion of Elijah's spirit and Elijah responded, "You have asked for a hard thing, but if you see me taken up from earth, then it will happen."

While they were still talking, God took Elijah up to heaven in a whirlwind, and Elisha didn't see him anymore. He tore his clothing in two and then picked up Elijah's cloak and went back to the Jordan. He stood by the water and said, "Where is the God of Elijah?!" Then he struck the water with the cloak, the waters parted, and he crossed back over the Jordan on dry land.

CHAPTER FORTY-THREE

ELISHA
II Kings 2:15-6:8

RULERS OF JUDAH AND ISRAEL (850 – 849 B.C.)

Kings of Judah		Kings of Israel	
King and notes	Reign	King and notes	Reign
Jehoshaphat: See previous chapter for more information	1 year	Joram: See next chapter for more information.	1 year

When the prophets from Bethel saw him cross the river, they realized that Elisha had Elijah's spirit, and they bowed to the ground. The 50 prophets asked to search for Elijah, but Elisha told them not to look. They continued to urge him until he relented and let them search.

They looked for three days, and then they came back to Jericho, where Elisha was staying. "Didn't I tell you not to look for him?" he said.

Everyone said that Jericho was a pleasant place to live but that the land was barren. Elisha asked for a bowl of spring water. He threw salt into it and said, "The Lord has healed this water; no longer will death or miscarriage come from it." The waters were healed and the land was productive again.

As he left Bethel, some young men came out and made fun of him, calling out, "Go up, you baldhead!" He turned around and cursed them, and two bears came out and attacked the 42 young men. Elisha continued to Samaria by way of Mount Carmel.

> **What is happening here?**
>
> These young men had formed a large angry mob, and they mocked Elisha's ministry, calling him to follow Elijah up into the air. They were likely out of control and the bears saved the prophet from attack.

JORAM SUCCEEDS AHAB (ISRAEL)

In the 18th year of Jehoshaphat's reign, Ahab's son Joram became king and reigned 12 years in Israel. He did evil in the Lord's sight just as his father had done, although he wasn't as bad.

Moab's king was supposed to send a tribute to Israel, but once Ahab was dead, the Moabites rebelled against Joram and refused to send the payment. Joram asked for Jehoshaphat's help and sent troops to go up against the Moabites. They marched along with the king of Edom and his troops for seven days but could not find the Moabite forces, and there was no water for the soldiers.

Jehoshaphat was distressed and cried out that they were all going to die in the wilderness, and he asked if there was a prophet of the Lord that they could ask what they should do. Joram's servants told Jehoshaphat about Elisha, and at first, the prophet refused to talk to the king of Judah.

Jehoshaphat pressed him. Elisha told the king, "If the Lord did not regard you, I wouldn't even speak to you. Bring my musicians and play music." The people obeyed and Elisha said to them, "Even though there will not be wind or rain, the Lord will cause streams of water to spring forth so that you and your animals will be able to drink. This is easy for God, so he will also give the Moabites into your hands, and you shall utterly destroy the land, cutting down every tree and stopping up their wells."

The next morning, the Moabites saw the water in the springs and thought it was blood, and came to plunder the camp. The Israelite coalition fought them and destroyed their army. They overthrew the Moabite cities, threw stones in all the fields, cut down the trees, and stopped the wells so that the land was useless. The Moabite king tried to escape, and when he saw that he could not, he sacrificed his son to appease his gods. Then the Israelites withdrew and returned home.

ELISHA'S MIRACLES

The widow of one of the prophets cried out to Elisha that the creditors were coming to take her two sons into slavery. Elisha asked what she had left in her house and she replied that all she had was a jar of oil. He commanded her to borrow as many vessels as possible from her neighbors and pour the oil into them. She did and the oil lasted until she did not have any containers left. Then she sold the vessels of oil so that she could pay her debts and let her sons live off the rest.

Elisha would often travel through Shunem, and every time he did, he would visit a woman who would feed him a meal. She said to her husband, "Let us build him a small room on our roof so that he has a place to stay whenever he comes through town." Elisha would stay there whenever he passed through the land.

One day, while he was staying there, he had his servant Gehazi bring the woman before him and asked how he could reward her. Gehazi told him that she was childless and that her husband was old. Elisha told her that she would have a son at that time next year. She was afraid that his words would not happen, and she protested, but the following spring, she had a baby boy.

When the child had grown, he went out to work in the field with his father. The boy had a sudden headache that caused him to collapse and his father sent the boy back to be with his mother. He sat on her lap until noon and then died in her arms. She took her only son to Elisha's bed and set out to find Elisha on Mount Carmel.

When Elisha saw her coming, he sent Gehazi to her to see if all was well. She told him all was well, but when she came to Elisha, she fell on the ground and grasped his feet. Gehazi tried to pull her away, but Elisha told him to let her be because she was distressed. Then the widow said to him, "Please don't lie to me. Did I ever ask you for a son?"

Elisha realized that the child had died and said to the woman, "Get up, take my staff, go home, and lay it on the child, and he will be well." But she refused to leave him, so he went with the woman to see the child.

Gehazi went ahead of him and laid Elisha's staff on the boy, but nothing happened. When Elisha came to the house, he went into his room, shut the door behind him, and prayed. He lay on the child, put his face on his face, and stretched his body out over the boy. The dead boy's skin became warm, but he did not revive. Elisha got up, walked around, and came back and laid on the boy again. This time, the child sneezed seven times and opened his eyes. Elisha gave the living boy back to his mother, and she bowed at his feet.

THE POISONED STEW

Elisha went back to Gilgal and there was a great famine in the land. As the sons of the prophets were sitting with him, they made a stew, and one of the men threw some herbs he had found into the pot. When they served the stew, one of the men realized what the herb was and cried out, "Elisha! The stew is poisoned!" And they could not eat it.

Elisha asked for some flour, threw it into the pot, stirred it up, and said, "Now it is okay, give the men some of the stew, and they can eat." Then, the men were able to eat, and no one became sick.

MULTIPLYING BREAD

At that time, a man came with some bread, and Elisha told him to give it to the men. The man protested that he did not have enough to give some to everyone, but Elisha commanded him to break the bread and give it to the men. He started passing out the food and God multiplied it until there was enough for everyone, with some left over.

ELISHA AND NAAMAN

Naaman was the commander of the Syrian army, and he was a fearless warrior, but he suffered from leprosy. An Israelite girl, who had become his slave, said, "If you could meet with Elisha, he could heal your leprosy."

The king of Syria agreed to send Naaman to see Elisha. Naaman went with gifts for the king of Israel along with a message so that the king of Samaria would not think he was invading or spying on the land. When the king of Israel received the news, he tore his clothes and said, "Am I God who has the power to heal? Now the king of Syria sends me his commander to heal him? He is only doing this so that he can have a reason to come attack me!" Elisha heard that the king was distressed and told him to send Naaman to see him.

When Naaman came to meet Elisha, the prophet sent a messenger to him instead of meeting Naaman in person and said, "Go dip yourself in the Jordan River seven times and you will become clean."

Naaman was furious because he thought Elisha would see him or do something miraculous to heal him. He complained that there were cleaner and better rivers that he could dip himself in and that the whole trip was a waste of time.

But his servants said to him, "The prophet has given you something that you can do to be healed. Shouldn't you at least try it and see if it works?" Naaman calmed down and went to the Jordan. After he had dipped himself six times, nothing had happened. But after the seventh time, he came up clean, and his skin was smooth like a newborn baby.

Naaman went back to Elisha and tried to give him a gift as payment for healing him, but Elisha refused even though Naaman wanted to persuade him. Then Naaman asked Elisha if he could bring two loads of dirt home to set up an altar to offer sacrifices to the Lord. He promised he would only burn offerings to God and would pray for his king when he offered sacrifices to other gods. Elisha consented and Naaman left.

After he had left, Gehazi decided to go after him to get a reward from the foreign commander. Gehazi told Naaman that two men had just arrived and that he needed some silver and two changes of clothes for the men. Naaman sent two of his servants back with Gehazi, and they carried two bags of silver and two changes of clothes.

Gehazi took the bags and clothes from the men and hid them in his house. Elisha asked him where he had gone, and Gehazi lied, saying that he hadn't gone anywhere. Then Elisha said, "My heart went with you when you went to meet with Naaman. Is this the time for us to get a reward for serving the Lord? Now, you will have Naaman's leprosy until you die." And Gehazi became a leper with skin as white as snow.

THE AXE HEAD

The men who lived with Elisha proposed they chop down trees to build houses because there was not enough room for everyone. Elisha went with them, and as they were chopping wood, an axe head flew off and landed in the water. The man was distressed because he had borrowed the axe, so Elisha cut off a stick and threw it in the water where the axe head had landed. The axe head floated and the man was able to retrieve it.

CHAPTER FORTY-FOUR

ELISHA AND THE SYRIANS

II Kings 6:9-9:14; II Chronicles 21

RULERS OF JUDAH AND ISRAEL (849 – 841 B.C.)

Kings of Judah		Kings of Israel	
King and notes	Reign	King and notes	Reign
Jehoram: Jehoshaphat's son, who did not follow the Lord. Fought against the Edomites.	8 years	Joram: Ahab's son, who followed in his father's footsteps. Battled against the Syrians. Elisha served as a prophet to him.	8 years
Ahaziah: Jehoram's son, who did evil in the Lord's eyes.	1 year		

Once, when the Syrians were at war with Israel, King Joram decided that he would camp at a specific spot. But Elisha warned him not to go there because the king of Syria would find and defeat him. Thus, God used Elisha to save the king from the Syrians.

The king of Syria was troubled and asked his men if someone had leaked secrets to their enemies. His servants told him that it wasn't their men but Elisha who had warned the king of Israel. He sent his men to capture Elisha, and his men surrounded the city of Dothan, where he was staying.

In the morning, the people of Dothan were terrified to see men surrounding the city. Elisha comforted them and said, "Don't be afraid because we have more men than they do." Then he prayed, and the Lord opened their eyes to see that the mountain was full of horses and chariots of fire all around them.

When the Syrians came to attack, Elisha prayed that the Lord would strike their enemies with blindness, and the Syrians could not see. Then Elisha went to them and said, "Follow me, and I will lead you to the man that you are seeking." The Syrians followed him and he led them into the midst of Samaria.

When they arrived, Elisha prayed for their eyes to open, and they saw that they were surrounded in Samaria. The king asked if he should strike down the Syrians, but Elisha said, "Do not kill them because they are your captives. Set bread and water before them; let them eat and then send them back home." So, they were fed and sent back to Syria. After that, the Syrians stopped their campaigns into Israel.

DELIVERANCE FROM THE SYRIANS (ISRAEL)

Years later, Ben-Hadad, the king of Syria, set up a military blockade against Samaria. There was no food in the land, and people were buying and selling donkey heads and bird poop for food. During the siege, the king walked along the wall, and a woman called out to him for help. She told him that she and another woman had agreed to boil her son for food and that they would cook the other woman's son the next day. They had already eaten her son and now the other woman was hiding her child.

The king was horrified and tore his clothes and cried out, "May God do even more to me if Elisha survives the day!" He sent messengers to bring Elisha, but the prophet barred the door so they would not capture him.

Elisha said, "At this time tomorrow, food will be so plentiful that people will be selling it to each other for virtually nothing." The army captain did not believe him, so Elisha said to him, "You will see this happen, but you will not have the chance to eat from it."

Four lepers sat at the city's gate and they said to each other, "If we go into the city, we will die, and if we stay here, we will die. Why don't we go over to the Syrians? Maybe they will have mercy and let us live?"

They went to the Syrian camp in the evening and found it empty. God had caused them to hear the sound of chariots and horses, and they thought that another army was coming to deliver the Israelites. They left everything and ran for their lives.

The lepers went into a tent and ate and drank until they were full. Then they carried off gold and silver and hid it. They felt guilty about what they were doing and decided to share the news with the others so that God would not judge them.

They sent word to the king, and when he heard it, he thought, "The Syrians are setting a trap for us so that we come out of the city, and then they will come back and get into the city." They decided to send a small scouting party at night to see if the report was accurate. They rode all night and were unable to find any of the Syrians, but they found the ground littered with supplies and clothing that the Syrians had left behind as they fled. Then, they came back and told the king what they had found.

The next morning, the king put his captain in charge of the people so they could go out and plunder the Syrian camp. The people were so excited that they rushed out of the city and trampled the captain to death. They found so much food that it was virtually worthless when they tried to sell it. This fulfilled the word of the Lord that Elisha spoke.

ELISHA RESTORES A WOMAN'S PROPERTY

Elisha said to the Shunammite woman who had built him a room on her roof, "Go stay wherever you can because the Lord is bringing a severe famine on the land that will last for seven years."

She went to stay in the land of the Philistines for seven years, and when she returned, she went to the king to ask for her land back. When she arrived, Gehazi told the king about what the Lord had done through Elisha, and how he had raised a woman's son from the dead. The king ordered her land to be restored to her, along with anything that it had produced over the previous seven years.

HAZAEL BECOMES KING OF SYRIA

Elisha was in the Syrian city of Damascus and Ben-Hadad had become very ill. When he heard that Elisha was there, the king sent Hazael to the prophet to determine if he would recover from his illness. Elisha said to him, "Go tell him that he will live, even though he really will die."

Hazael stared at Elisha for an uncomfortable amount of time and Elisha began to weep. Hazael asked him why he was crying and Elisha said, "Because I know all the evil you will do to the Israelites. You will burn their buildings, kill their young men and children, and rip open their pregnant women. All of this will happen because you will be king of Syria."

When Hazael came to Ben-Hadad, he told him that he would recover. But the next day, he took a wet rag, suffocated the king, and took his place.

JEHORAM SUCCEEDS JEHOSHAPHAT (JUDAH)

After Jehoshaphat had died, his son Jehoram reigned in his place, and he killed all his brothers to keep them from having any claim to the throne. Jehoram was 32 years old when he became king and reigned for eight years in Jerusalem. He walked in Ahab's ways and rebelled against the Lord, but God was unwilling to take the throne from David's line.

During his reign, the Edomites revolted against Judah, but they could not defeat them. Libnah also revolted against Judah because Jehoram did not walk in the way of David. He established high places in the hill country and led the people into sin.

Then, the Lord proclaimed that he would bring a great plague on Jehoram and his people until his bowels came out. The Lord stirred up the Philistines and the Arabians, and they invaded Judah and carried away their possessions. They also killed everyone from Jehoram's house except for his youngest son, Jehoahaz. Then the Lord struck him with an intestinal illness that lasted for two years. He died in great pain and no one mourned his death.

JEHU ANOINTED KING (ISRAEL)

Elisha sent one of the sons of the prophets to anoint Jehu, the commander of the army, as Israel's king. When he arrived in Ramoth-Gilead, he pulled Jehu aside, anointed him with oil, and said, "The Lord is anointing you as king of Israel. You will strike down Ahab's household to avenge all the blood that Jezebel shed. Kill everyone from his house and do not leave any of them alive. Ahab will become like Jeroboam and Baasha, and the dogs of the city will eat Jezebel's flesh."

After he gave the message, the man ran away. When Jehu came out, his men asked, "What did he say?" Jehu tried to dismiss Elisha's words and told his men that the prophet had anointed him king of Israel. The men took his garment, had Jehu stand on it, and then declared him king of Israel.

AHAZIAH SUCCEEDS JEHORAM (JUDAH)

Meanwhile, after Jehoram died, his son, Ahaziah, became king in his place when he was 22 years old, and he only reigned for a year in Jerusalem. He did evil in the Lord's sight, just like Ahab had done because he was his son. He joined with Israel to attack the Syrians, and in one of the battles, Joram, the king of Israel, was injured, and he returned to Jezreel to heal. Ahaziah went to visit Joram in Jezreel.

CHAPTER FORTY-FIVE

JEHU'S REIGN

II Kings 9:16-11:21; II Chronicles 22-23

RULERS OF JUDAH AND ISRAEL (841 – 835 B.C.)

Kings of Judah		Kings of Israel	
King and notes	Reign	King and notes	Reign
Athaliah: Ahaziah of Judah's mother, who ruled as queen and was very evil. Jehoiada served as prophet to her.	6 years	Jehu: Ahaziah of Israel's son, who led the nation to repent from worshiping Baal. Elisha served as prophet to him.	6 years

After his men had declared him king, Jehu made his men swear they would not let anyone know what they had done. Then he got in his chariot and drove furiously to Jezreel. One of the watchmen in Jezreel saw Jehu coming and they sent a messenger to see if he came in peace. Jehu told him to fall in line behind him and continued his approach.

They sent a second messenger to see if Jehu came in peace, and he told him to fall in line behind him as well. The watchman recognized Jehu's furious driving and told Joram what was happening.

Joram went to meet Jehu in the field that Ahab had seized from Naboth. Joram asked if he brought news of peace and Jehu answered, "How can there be peace when the evil and sorceries of your mother exist?!"

Joram turned to run and warn Ahaziah of Jehu's betrayal, but before he could get far, Jehu killed him with an arrow in the back. Jehu told his assistant to throw his body in the field to fulfill God's word.

Ahaziah heard what had happened and tried to run as well. Jehu pursued him and shot him in the back with an arrow. Ahaziah made it to Megiddo before he died. They carried his body back to Jerusalem to bury him.

Jehu went to meet Jezebel and she put makeup on and spoke to him from her window, "Is there peace, you murderer of your master?" He looked up at the window and asked who was on his side in the house. A few eunuchs stuck their heads out a window. "Throw her out," he commanded. They did, and her blood spattered on the wall, and the horses trampled her body.

Then he went into the palace and ate and drank. He sent men out to bury her body because she was a king's daughter. But when they went to retrieve her body, all they could find were her hands and skull because the dogs had eaten her corpse. This fulfilled the Lord's word that Elijah had spoken.

Ahab had 70 sons who lived in Samaria, and Jehu sent a letter to the leaders that his sons should come to fight for their father's throne. Those leaders knew that they could not stand before Jehu, so they told him they did not want to fight for the throne but he should do whatever he thought was right.

Jehu sent a second letter and told them that if they would make him king, they needed to send him all of Ahab's sons' heads in a basket to show their allegiance to him. The Samaritan leaders obeyed and sent the heads in a basket to Jehu. When they arrived, they made two heaps by the city gate.

In the morning, Jehu went out and stood before the people next to the two heaps of heads and said, "You are all innocent because I am the one who conspired against my master. But who killed all of these? Know all God's words will be fulfilled, and this fulfills what he spoke through the prophet Elijah!"

Then, Jehu killed everyone else who was still alive from Ahab's house, including his close friends, so he had no one left who was loyal to him.

Jehu traveled to Samaria, and on his way, he met some people from Ahaziah's house, and he commanded his men to take them captive. Then he took them to a pit and slaughtered 42 men. He also invited Jehonadab to join him to see Jehu's zeal for the Lord.

When Jehu arrived in Samaria, he gathered the people together and said, "Ahab served Baal a little, but I will serve him much! Bring all the prophets, priests, and worshipers together because I will make a great sacrifice to Baal. Don't let anyone be missing, because if they are, I will kill them." He used this ruse to gather them together to kill them all.

He ordered a great feast, and everyone who worshiped Baal came and filled his temple from one end to the other. He dressed them in garments of worship and sent Jehonadab to make sure that no one who worshiped the Lord was with them.

When Baal's worshipers went in, Jehu positioned 80 men outside to cut down any who escaped, or they would pay with their own lives. Then he sent his men in, slaughtered everyone who worshiped Baal, demolished the temple, and made it into a public bathroom.

Thus, Jehu wiped out Baal from Israel. But he still used the golden calves that Jeroboam had set up as objects of worship. God promised that he would allow four generations of his family to rule over Israel because of his zeal for God's glory. But in his later years, he began to worship false gods. During his reign, Hazael led the Syrians into Israel, and they captured some of their territory. Jehu died after ruling for 28 years in Israel and his son Jehoahaz became king in his place.

ATHALIAH BECOMES QUEEN (JUDAH)

After Ahaziah's death, his mother, Athaliah, made a move for the throne, and she set out to kill all the royal family in Jerusalem. One of Ahaziah's sisters hid his youngest son, Joash, in the temple while Athaliah ruled over Judah, and she reigned for seven years.

JEHOIDA PROTECTS JOASH

In the seventh year of her reign, a priest named Jehoiada brought some of the leaders into the temple and showed them Joash. Jehoiada made the men swear that they would not reveal Joash's presence but would guard him no matter where he went. Then, at the appropriate time, they brought him out before the community and put a crown on his head, anointed him, and proclaimed him king, saying, "Long live the king of Israel!"

Athaliah heard all the commotion and went to the temple to see what was happening. When she saw Joash standing in the king's place and heard the people rejoicing, she tore her clothes and yelled, "Treason!"

Then Jehoiada ordered his men to seize Athaliah and kill anyone who tried to stop them. They carried her out of the temple so she would not die in God's house and killed her by the palace.

Jehoiada made a covenant with the Lord and the community to be his people and serve him only. Everyone went to Baal's house in Judah, tore it down, destroyed its altars, and killed the priests. Joash assumed the throne, all the people rejoiced. The city had peace after Athaliah's death.

CHAPTER FORTY-SIX

RULE TO THE ASSYRIAN CAPTIVITY

II Kings 12-17; II Chronicles 24-28

RULERS OF JUDAH AND ISRAEL (835 – 722 B.C.)

Kings of Judah		Kings of Israel	
King and notes	Reign	King and notes	Reign
Joash: Only surviving son of Ahaziah, who became king at 7 years old. Greatly influenced by Jehoiada and he repaired the temple and led the people to repent. However, he strayed at the end of his life. Jehoiada's son, Zechariah, also served as a prophet to him.	40 years	Jehu: See previous chapter for more information.	21 years
Amaziah: Joash's son, who mostly followed the Lord. Fought against the Edomites.	29 years	Jehoahaz: Jehu's son, who did evil in the Lord's sight. Elisha served as a prophet to him.	17 years
		Jehoash: Jehoahaz's son, who continued to do evil. Elisha served as a prophet to him.	16 years
Uzziah: Amaziah's son, who co-ruled with his father for 24 years (beginning at age 16). Defeated the Philistines, Arabians, Meunites, and Ammonites. God struck him with leprosy for his pride.	52 years	Jeroboam II: Joehoash's son, who continued to do evil.	41 years
		Zechariah: Jeroboam II's son, who did evil in the Lord's sight.	6 months
		Shallum: Usurper who killed Zechariah.	1 month
		Menahem: Usurper who killed Shallum. Brutal king who continued to sin.	10 years

Kings of Judah		Kings of Israel	
King and notes	Reign	King and notes	Reign
Jotham: Uzziah's son, who never entered the temple.	16 years	Pekahiah: Menahem's son, who continued to do evil.	2 years
Ahaz: Jotham's son, who did evil in the Lord's sight. Fought against Pekah.	16 years	Pekah: Usurper who killed Pekahiah. Attacked Judah during his reign. Obed served as a prophet to him.	20 years
		Hoshea: Evil king. During his reign, the Assyrians took Israel into captivity.	9 years

JOASH BECOMES KING

Joash began to rule in the seventh year of Jehu and he was only seven years old when he took the throne. He reigned for 40 years in Jerusalem. Jehoiada had a significant influence on the boy because he was so young when he began to rule. He walked in the ways of the Lord all the days of his life, but he did not remove the high places.

As he became an adult, Joash decided to restore the temple to greatness because foreign people had looted it on more than one occasion. He told the priests to gather money from the people through taxes and freewill offerings to repair the temple. He told the priests to act quickly, but they took their time with the repairs.

By the 23rd year of Joash's rule, the priests had still not completed any repairs, so Joash called Jehoiada and the priests together and commanded them to stop collecting money and get to work. The priests agreed, and they gradually began making repairs by giving money to workers and fixing whatever was in disrepair. They did not replace the worship implements because they used the silver and gold to pay the workers. They also did not keep track of the money they paid the workers because they dealt honestly with the priests.

With the repairs complete, they began to replace some of the instruments of worship, but they couldn't replace them all because Hazael attacked Jerusalem. To keep him from laying siege to the city, Joash sent him all the sacred vessels that they had so that he would leave them alone.

While Jehoiada was alive, the people offered regular sacrifices to the Lord and obeyed his commands. But eventually, the high priest died at the age of 130, and was buried in Jerusalem. After his death, Joash listened to some of Judah's young men and strayed from obeying the Lord. They abandoned the temple and went after false gods. The Lord sent prophets to them to pull them back to him, but they ignored God's word.

One of the prophets that God sent was Zechariah (the son of Jehoiada), and he confronted the king for disobeying God's word. Joash was angry, and he sent men to stone the prophet despite how Jehoiada had been so kind to Joash and instrumental in his early rule. As Zechariah lay dying, he yelled, "May the Lord see and avenge me!"

Later that year, the Syrians came to Jerusalem to attack it, and even though it was a much smaller army, God gave them victory over Joash because he had turned from the Lord and killed Zechariah. The Syrians severely wounded Joash in battle, and as he lay in pain, some of his servants, still unhappy about what he had done to Zechariah, killed their king. His son, Amaziah, reigned in his place.

JEHOAHAZ SUCCEEDS JEHU (ISRAEL)

In the same year that Judah began rebuilding the temple, Jehoahaz, Jehu's son, became king in Israel. He reigned for 17 years and he did evil in the sight of the Lord just as his fathers before him had. God was angry and gave them into the Syrians' hands on multiple occasions. One time, after the Syrians had decimated his army, Jehoahaz called on the Lord, and God delivered the Israelites from their enemies. Despite this, Jehoahaz continued to sin, and he did not return to the Lord.

JEHOASH SUCCEEDS JEHOAHAZ (ISRAEL)

After Jehoahaz died, his son Jehoash reigned in his place. He was king over Israel for 16 years. He continued to do evil in the Lord's sight and did not repent from his wicked ways. When he died, the people buried him in Samaria with Israel's other kings. His son, Jeroboam II, reigned in his place.

ELISHA'S DEATH

During Jehoash's rule, Elisha became very sick, and Jehoash wept over him on his sickbed. Elisha commanded him to shoot an arrow out the window to symbolize their victory over their Syrian oppressors. Then he commanded him to take the rest of the arrows and strike the ground with them. Jehoash hit the ground three times and stopped.

Elisha became angry and said, "You should have struck the ground five or six times, and then you would have made an end of the Syrians! But now, you will only strike them three times." After this, Elisha died and was buried.

While they were burying him, the men saw a raiding band and threw another man's body into Elisha's grave. As the corpse touched Elisha's bones, the man instantly came back to life.

The Syrians were against the Israelites throughout Jehoash's reign, and they kept attacking and taking cities captive. But Jehoash kept retaliating and taking back the cities. This happened three times to fulfill Elisha's words.

AMAZIAH SUCCEEDS JOASH (JUDAH)

In the second year of Jehoash's reign, Amaziah, the son of Joash, became king at 25. He ruled for 29 years in Jerusalem, and he did what was right in the Lord's eyes, but not as much as David had done. He allowed the high places to remain and the people continued to offer sacrifices on them.

Once he was in power, he went after the men who had killed his father and put them to death but did not kill their children because he was obeying the Law of Moses, which commanded death only for people for their own sin and not for the sins of their parents or children.

Amaziah gathered his army together to fight against the Edomites. He had 300,000 men of Judah and he hired 100,000 more from Israel to go to war with him. But before he went into battle, a prophet came to him and told him that the Lord was not with the men he had hired. He didn't need their help because God has the power to bring victory or defeat.

Amaziah protested that he had already paid the men, but the prophet told him that God could give him much more than the silver he had paid the Israelite soldiers. So, Amaziah sent them home and allowed them to keep the money he had paid. They felt insulted and were furious with the king.

The king went into battle with the Edomites and killed 10,000. He also captured 10,000 alive and then threw them off the top of a cliff. Meanwhile, the slighted Israelite soldiers attacked some of Judah's cities, killed about 3,000 men, and carried away a great deal of plunder.

After striking down the Edomites, Amaziah brought back their gods and set them up as his own, worshiping them and offering sacrifices. God was angry with Amaziah and sent a prophet to the king, who said, "Why would you worship a god who couldn't even deliver its people from your hand?"

While he was still speaking, Amaziah snapped, "Did I make you one of my royal advisors? Stop talking and don't give me a reason to kill you!" Then the prophet knew that God had decided to punish Amaziah because he would not listen to wise counsel.

Amaziah was upset about the Israelite soldiers' raid, and he tried to meet with Jehoash, the king of Israel. But Jehoash replied, "A weed asked a mighty tree for his daughter's hand in marriage, but then a wild animal stepped on the weed and killed it. Your victory over Edom has made you proud, but you should stay home, or else you will bring about your own downfall as well as Judah's."

But Amaziah would not listen because God was using this situation to punish him for worshiping Edomite gods. They went into battle against each other, and the Israelites defeated the men of Judah, and the men fled to their homes. Jehoash captured Amaziah and brought him back to Jerusalem, where he tore down 600 feet of the wall and took all the gold and silver from the temple and royal treasury back to Samaria.

Not long after this, Jehoash died and was buried. Amaziah ruled for another 15 years before his people conspired and killed him. Then they made his son, Uzziah, king in his place.

JEROBOAM II SUCCEEDS JEHOASH (ISRAEL)

At the same time, Jeroboam II became king of Israel, and he reigned over them for 41 years; he did evil in the Lord's sight and continued to make the people sin. Despite the wickedness in his heart, God gave them some deliverance because of their oppression, and he did not want to blot them out forever. After Jeroboam II died, his son Zechariah ruled in his place.

UZZIAH BECOMES KING (JUDAH)

Amaziah's son Uzziah reigned over Judah for 52 years (24 years as co-ruler with his father), and he did what was right in the sight of the Lord, but he still did not remove the high places, and he let the people offer sacrifices on them. He was a mighty king, and he defeated the Philistines, Arabians, and Meunites, and he made the Ammonites bring him gifts. He fortified the cities and even invented engines that could shoot arrows and throw stones from the tops of the towers.

As Uzziah grew strong, he also became proud, which led to his eventual downfall. One day he went into the temple to burn incense to the Lord even though that was a job reserved for the priests. Eighty of the priests followed him into the temple to rebuke him and the king became angry. As he was about to curse at the priests, God struck him with leprosy, and the priests fled the temple in fear. Then Uzziah lived as a leper for the rest of his life in a separate house, and he never entered the temple again because he was unclean.

CHAOS IN ISRAEL

During the 39th year of Uzziah's reign, Israel went through a tumultuous period where they had three kings in a single year. First, Zechariah, Jeroboam II's son, was king, and he ruled for six months. He did evil in the Lord's sight, and eventually, Shallum conspired against him, killed him, and assumed the throne. Shallum only lasted a month before Menahem killed him and took over the throne.

Menahem was a brutal man, and as he came to power, the city of Tiphash would not accept him, so he attacked the city and ripped open the bellies of their pregnant women. He also took money from the wealthiest Jews and gave it to the king of Assyria to help confirm his position. He was an evil man who continued to walk in his predecessors' sins. Menahem ruled for ten years.

PEKAHIAH BECOMES KING (ISRAEL)

After his death, Menahem's son, Pekahiah, took the throne, and he was evil like his father. He only reigned for two years before Pekah and 50 Israelites conspired against him and killed him. Then Pekah became king and reigned for 20 years over Israel. He continued to sin, and the king of Assyria captured several Israelite cities and made them his own during his rule.

JOTHAM SUCCEEDS UZZIAH (JUDAH)

When Uzziah died, his son, Jotham, became king in his place. He was 25 years old when he became king and ruled for 16 years. He followed most of what his father had done before him, although he never entered the temple. He allowed the people to act corruptly, although he refused to participate. During his time as king, he defeated the Ammonites and forced them to bring him great gifts for three years. Then he died and his son, Ahaz, ruled in his place.

AHAZ SUCCEEDS JOTHAM (JUDAH)

Ahaz was 20 years old when he became king, and he ruled for 16 years in Jerusalem, but he did not do what was right in the Lord's eyes. He sacrificed to false gods on every high place and even went so far as to offer his son as a human sacrifice.

During his reign, Pekah, the king of Israel, attacked and killed 120,000 men of Judah in a single day and took 200,000 people captive. After the attack, the Lord sent the prophet, Obed, to Pekah, and he said, "The Lord, the God of your fathers, was angry with Judah and has given them into your hands as their punishment. You have killed many of them and taken even more captive, and your sins have made God angry as well."

Some of the Israelite leaders also stood up before the returning army and said, "Do not bring these people to Samaria but let them return to their homes. Offer sin offerings to cover our guilt because the Lord is not happy with us." So, the soldiers fed and clothed them and sent them back to their homes.

God was still angry with Ahaz, and the Syrians came to fight against him, but they could not defeat him. While the Syrians were attacking, Ahaz sent a messenger to the king of Assyria and begged him to rescue them. He gave the Assyrians all the gold and silver in the temple and the treasuries, and he also set up an altar for him to offer sacrifices. Then the Assyrians afflicted him as well.

While Ahaz was in distress, he still did not return to the Lord. Instead, he sacrificed to foreign gods because they had defeated him. Then Ahaz died, and they buried him, and his son Hezekiah reigned in his place.

HOSHEA TO THE ASSYRIAN CAPTIVITY

In the twelfth year of Ahaz's rule, Hoshea became king of Israel, and he reigned for nine years. He did evil in the Lord's sight but was not as bad as the kings before him. The Assyrians came to fight against him, and Hoshea became the Assyrian king's servant and paid him tribute. He tried to send to the Egyptians for help, but the Assyrians found out about it and threw him in prison. Then the Assyrians besieged Samaria, and they took it captive, sending all the people into exile.

God sent the people into exile for their idolatry and adopting the local nations' worship practices. They chased after foreign gods and did not obey the commands that God had given them. They did wicked things and provoked God to anger even though he sent prophets to warn them to repent. They burned their children and did so much evil that God could no longer stand it.

When the Lord could not stand it any longer, he sent them into exile and removed them from his sight, leaving only the tribe of Judah. Then the Assyrians sent their people to settle in Samaria. God sent lions into the land and killed many Assyrian occupiers because they did not obey the Lord's commands.

To appease the Lord, the king of Assyria sent a priest back to his homeland to teach the people to obey the Lord. They offered him lip service, but they still worshiped their own gods. The priest tried to get them to follow the Lord, but they never fully devoted their hearts; they still served foreign gods.

CHAPTER FORTY-SEVEN

HEZEKIAH TO THE BABYLONIAN CAPTIVITY
II Kings 18-25; II Chronicles 29-36

RULERS OF JUDAH (722 – 586 B.C.)

King and notes	Reign
Ahaz: See previous chapter for more information.	6 years
Hezekiah: Ahaz's son who repaired the temple and returned to the Lord. Trusted the Lord to deliver him from the Assyrians. God healed him when he was nearly dead. Isaiah served as a prophet to him.	29 years
Manasseh: Hezekiah's son who became the most wicked of Judah's kings.	55 years
Amon: Manasseh's son who refused to repent.	2 years
Josiah: Amon's son who became king at eight years old. Repaired the temple and led the people to repent. Hilkiah and Huldah served as prophets to him.	32 years
Jehoahaz: Josiah's son, who did not follow in his father's footsteps. He was defeated by the Egyptians.	3 months
Jehoiakim (Eliakim or Zedekiah): Jehoahaz's brother who was appointed king by the Egyptian ruler. Did evil in the Lord's sight, and the Babylonians took them into captivity. Jeremiah served as a prophet to him.	11 years

HEZEKIAH SUCCEEDS AHAZ

Hezekiah became king over Judah at the age of 25, and he reigned for 29 years; he did right in the sight of the Lord. He did everything that the Lord commanded and removed the high places and cast out the foreign gods. He served the Lord as David had, and he prospered everywhere he went because the Lord was with him. He rebelled against the Assyrians and struck down the Philistines.

The first thing he did as king was to reopen the temple and repair it. He commanded the priests and Levites to consecrate themselves and the temple so they could once again offer sacrifices to the Lord. They celebrated the Passover, and Hezekiah commanded the people, "Return to the Lord so that you will not become like your brothers the Israelites who have gone into captivity. If you return to the Lord, he is gracious and merciful, and he will not turn his face away from you."

The people listened to the king, put away the foreign gods, and returned to the Lord. Hezekiah prayed for them and the Lord forgave their sins. Then the people came together and offered thousands of animals to the Lord in a show like Solomon's sacrifices. Hezekiah also organized the priests so worship could continue in the way God had commanded.

GOD DELIVERS JUDAH FROM THE ASSYRIANS

In the 14th year of Hezekiah's reign, Sennacherib, the king of Assyria, came against Judah and captured many of their cities. Hezekiah stopped up the water springs so that the Assyrians would not think their land was fruitful and strengthened Jerusalem's fortifications. He told the people, "Be strong and courageous because while they attack us with an arm of flesh, the arm of the Lord defends us!"

While the Assyrians were attacking, Hezekiah told Sennacherib he would give him whatever he wanted to leave their country. Hezekiah had to pay hundreds of pounds of gold and silver. His offering was not enough to satisfy them and Sennacherib sent his man Rabshakeh to Jerusalem to persuade the people to give up.

Rabshakeh said to the men of Jerusalem, "The mighty king of Assyria is against you; what are you relying on? Are you going to trust the Egyptians? They are like a broken reed and will stab through your hand if you lean upon them. You cannot trust the Lord because he has not delivered your brothers, the Israelites, who relied on him. None of the other nations' gods could deliver their people from us, so why do you think your God will deliver you? Even if we gave you 2,000 horses, you wouldn't have enough men to put on them. God has sent us to destroy you!"

Hezekiah's men asked Rabshakeh to speak Assyrian because they understood it. But Rabshakeh insisted on speaking Hebrew so that the people on the wall could understand him. He shouted, "Do not let Hezekiah deceive you, for he will not be able to deliver you! Don't listen to him because the king of Assyria tells you that if you come to him, he will let you live in your own homes and then take you into a land of prosperity where things will be even better than they are here! The gods of the other nations were not enough to deliver them, so your God will not be enough to deliver you!"

The people of Jerusalem did not speak because Hezekiah had commanded them to be silent. Then Rabshakeh sent messengers to the other cities in Judah that insulted the Lord and said similar things.

Upon hearing Rabshakeh's words, Hezekiah tore his robes in grief, and he sent for Isaiah, the prophet. He begged him to pray on behalf of the people because they were afraid of the Assyrians and had no strength to withstand them.

Isaiah reassured the king, "Do not be afraid of the Assyrians and the words they have used to revile me. The Lord will cause him to believe a rumor so that he will return home and die by the sword in his homeland."

Rabshakeh sent more messengers who repeated his original message to Hezekiah to discourage the king. Hezekiah was disheartened, and took the letters to the temple and spread them out before the Lord. He prayed, "God of Israel, you are the only true God, and you have created the heavens and the earth. Please listen to what Sennacherib is saying about you and how he mocks. They have indeed overthrown many nations whose gods could not defend them because they are not real gods. Please save us from the Assyrians so that all nations may know that you alone are God!"

Isaiah came to Hezekiah and said, "The Lord has heard your prayer about Sennacherib and he has heard all the things that he has said to mock God. Even though he has had success, the Lord is the one who made it all happen. The Lord knows everything and has listened to his boasting, so now the Lord will send him back home. He won't even try to attack the city because God will defend us for his own sake and David's sake.

"There will be a remnant in Jerusalem and zeal for the Lord will lead to a band of survivors. You will know this will happen because, for two years, you will live off what the land grows on its own, and then in the third year, you will plant and reap a harvest."

That night, the angel of the Lord killed 185,000 of the Assyrian army, and in the morning, the survivors fled. Sennacherib was worshiping in Nineveh when two of his sons killed him and fled the country. Then his son Esarhaddon ruled in his place.

HEZEKIAH'S ILLNESS

Hezekiah became deathly ill. Isaiah came to him and said, "Put your house in order because you will not recover from this illness." Hezekiah was depressed, and he poured his heart out before the Lord and asked him to remember all the good he had done, and he wept bitterly.

God sent Isaiah back to Hezekiah and he said, "God has heard your prayer and he will heal you. On the third day, go up to the temple, and he will add 15 years to your life. He will heal you and defend this city from the Assyrians for his name and David's legacy." Then Isaiah commanded that they bring a fig cake to lay upon him. Hezekiah asked for a sign that this healing would occur and Isaiah told him the sun would retreat ten spaces during midday instead of progressing forward.

Hezekiah went to the temple on the third day as he had been instructed and was healed. The king of Babylon, Merodach-baladan, sent Hezekiah gifts because he heard he had been sick. Hezekiah showed off all the land's wealth and abundance to impress his visitors.

Isaiah confronted him about showing off his wealth and said to the king, "The days are coming when the Babylonians will come and carry everything you have gained back to their homeland; there will be nothing left in Judah. They will also carry away your sons so that they will be servants in Babylon."

MANASSEH SUCCEEDS HEZEKIAH

Hezekiah was not overly concerned about Isaiah's message because he knew he would have peace while he ruled. Then Hezekiah died and his son Manasseh ruled in his place. He was 12 years old when he became king and reigned for 55 years in Jerusalem. He did evil in the Lord's sight and undid all the reforms his father made. He restored the high places and made sacrifices to all kinds of false gods. He offered his son as a burnt offering and dealt with witchcraft. He even brought idols into the temple and was more wicked than all the nations the Lord had driven out.

The Lord tried to speak to Manasseh and get him to repent, but the king refused to listen. So, God sent his prophets to say, "Because Manasseh has committed these abominations and sinned more than anyone who has been before him, God will bring a disaster upon him that will shock everyone who hears about it. He will wipe Jerusalem away like one wipes a dish clean and then turns it upside down. He will forsake his remnant and give them into the hands of their enemies because they have done evil in his sight and provoked him since they came out of Egypt."

So, the Lord brought the Assyrians to fight against Manasseh, and they captured him and took him as a captive to Babylon. While he was there, he cried out to the Lord and begged for forgiveness. God heard his plea and brought him back to Jerusalem.

Once he returned, he took the foreign gods out of Jerusalem and removed all the altars he had set up on the high places. The people still sacrificed on the high places, but only to the Lord. Then Manasseh died and his son Amon ruled in his place.

AMON SUCCEEDS MANASSEH

Amon was 22 years old when he became king and he only reigned two years in Jerusalem. He did evil just as his father had done at the beginning of his rule. He abandoned the Lord and refused to repent even when God sent prophets to warn him. His people conspired against him and killed him, but Judah's men killed the conspirators.

JOSIAH SUCCEEDS AMON

Josiah was only eight years old when he began to rule Judah, and he began to seek the Lord from his first day as king. He walked in the ways of David and did not turn aside throughout his whole life. In the 12th year of his rule, he began to purge Judah of idols, and he destroyed all the false altars.

It took six years to cleanse the land of the false gods and altars, and then he decided to repair the temple. He put the priest Hilkiah in charge of the repairs, and he paid money to the workmen, but they did not keep track of the funds because the workers dealt faithfully.

While they were making repairs, Hilkiah found the book of the Law and brought it to the king. When it was read to Josiah, he was grieved, and he tore his clothes in despair. He said, "Go ask the Lord what we should do because he is furious that we have not obeyed his commands."

The prophetess, Huldah, said to them, "The Lord will certainly bring disaster upon us and all of the curses from the book of the Law that was read to Josiah. We have forsaken the Lord and worshiped false gods, and he will pour out his wrath upon us. But, because you have repented, you will be gathered to your fathers before he brings this evil upon the nation."

Then, Josiah gathered all the people together, read the book of the Law to them, and made a covenant with the Lord that they would obey his commands. He made the people join with him in the covenant and they continued to walk in the Lord's ways all the days Josiah was king. He continued to purge Judah of idolatry and false worship wherever he found it.

After making this covenant, Josiah kept the Passover and commanded the Levites to prepare themselves to make sacrifices. The people gave generously, and they offered tens of thousands of bulls, lambs, and goats to the Lord. This was the most lavish Passover celebration since the days of Samuel.

Not long after, Neco, the king of Egypt, fought against the Assyrians, and Josiah insisted on meeting with him. Neco tried to dissuade Josiah but still came to meet him. Josiah disguised himself and went to fight, but a random archer mortally wounded the king. His men brought him back to Jerusalem, where he died from his wounds. All the people mourned his death and his son Jehoahaz reigned in his place.

JEHOAHAZ TO THE BABYLONIAN CAPTIVITY

Jehoahaz only ruled for three months and he did evil in the sight of the Lord. He did not follow his father's ways but worshiped false gods. Neco captured Jehoahaz and forced him to pay tribute to him. He replaced him as king with Jehoahaz's brother Eliakim (also known as Zedekiah) and changed his name to Jehoiakim. He taxed the people heavily to pay tribute to Egypt. Jehoiakim was 25 years old when he became king and ruled in Jerusalem for 11 years. He did evil in the sight of the Lord and continued to pursue false gods.

God sent Jeremiah as a prophet to rebuke Zedekiah, but he refused to listen. The people continued to mock the prophets and made their hearts hard until there was no turning back from God's wrath.

During Jehoiakim's reign, God sent Nebuchadnezzar, the king of Babylon, against Judah to punish them for their sin and rebellion. Jehoiakim (Zedekiah) became his servant for three years. After three years, Jehoiakim rebelled against the Babylonians, and they came and laid siege to Jerusalem.

The Babylonians looted the temple and killed many people, regardless of age, gender, or ability to defend themselves. They burned the temple, broke down the walls, and left Jerusalem in ruins. Nebuchadnezzar took all the people who had escaped the sword into captivity in Babylon. This fulfilled Jeremiah's words that the land must have rest for 70 years because the people had not kept the Sabbath commands.

The Babylonians left some of the poorest people in the land to maintain the fields. Nebuchadnezzar appointed Gedaliah as governor over the land, and he told them to live in the land and not to fear the Babylonians. But the people rebelled against Gedaliah, killing him, and then they fled to Egypt because they were afraid of retaliation.

In the 37th year of captivity, Nebuchadnezzar let Jehoahaz out of prison and gave him a seat at his table above all his other servants. Jehoahaz lived out his days in Babylon, never returning home. Jerusalem lay in ruins until the first year of Cyrus, the king of Persia.

CHAPTER FORTY-EIGHT

REBUILDING THE TEMPLE

Ezra 1-10

> **The Book of Ezra**
>
> The Book of Ezra records the Jews' efforts to rebuild the temple after 70 years in captivity. Temple reconstruction took more than two decades to complete and faced intense opposition by the local nations. Ezra arrives about 60 years later, and he helps the people come back into a right relationship with God. This book is closely related to the Book of Nehemiah, both of which were likely penned by Ezra. The events in this book take place between 538-450 B.C.

CYRUS PERMITS TEMPLE RECONSTRUCTION

After 70 years, during the first year that Cyrus ruled over Persia, God fulfilled the word he promised through Jeremiah. The Lord stirred up Cyrus' heart and he made a proclamation, "The Lord of heaven has given me all the kingdoms of the earth and he has told me to build a house for him in Jerusalem. Any Jew who is willing should go back to Jerusalem and rebuild God's house. I will provide whatever they need to complete their task."

God stirred up the hearts of Israel's leaders to return to their homeland and Cyrus gave them what they needed to rebuild the temple. He also gave back most of the holy elements stolen by Nebuchadnezzar.

When the people came to Jerusalem, the first thing they did was rebuild the altar so they could offer sacrifices to the Lord as Moses had commanded. They offered sacrifices to God and kept the Feast of Booths as the Law required.

Next, they collected money to rebuild the foundations. Once the foundation was complete, the priests led a procession, and the people worshiped the Lord for his steadfast and enduring love. Many of the older people who had seen the old temple's glory wept when they saw the foundation laid. The weeping and rejoicing was so great that no one could tell the difference between them, and the sound of their voices resounded throughout the country.

When the Jews' enemies heard that they were rebuilding the temple, they approached Zerubbabel (the Jewish governor) and the other elders saying, "Let us help you build the house of God because we have been sacrificing to the Lord for years."

But Zerubbabel realized they were planning betrayal, so he said, "You have nothing to do with us. We alone will build the house of our God as Cyrus commands." The local nations did everything they could to frustrate the Jews' plans and bribed local officials to thwart them.

They wrote a letter to King Artaxerxes in Babylon saying, "The Jews are rebuilding the wicked city of Jerusalem. Once they have finished, they will rebel and stop paying taxes and tributes, which will hurt your kingdom. Since we benefit from your rule and don't want to see you dishonored, we thought we should let you know. Look through the history books and see how this has been a rebellious city, and that is why the Babylonians destroyed it. If you let the people finish their task, you will lose a great portion of your territory."

King Artaxerxes sent a letter in return that read, "I read your letter, and after searching the history books, I have found that the city has been rebellious and has risen against past kings. Therefore, I command that the Jews stop rebuilding their temple. Act quickly because I do not wish to lose any of my kingdom."

When the locals read the king's letter, they stopped the work by force, and the Jews did not resume work for quite some time.

BUILDING RESUMES

After more than a decade, the prophets Haggai and Zechariah arose and commanded the people to resume their work. Zerubbabel ordered the people to start working again and the locals asked what permitted them to restart building. They also asked for the names of those who oversaw the building project. But God kept them from stopping until word reached the new king, Darius.

The local leaders sent a letter to Darius that said, "The Jews have resumed building a temple for their God. We asked them who gave them the authority to continue this project and who was leading their efforts. They told us that God has given them the authority and referenced a letter that Cyrus had given them to begin rebuilding their temple. Look at the history books and see if such a letter exists."

Darius searched through the records and found Cyrus' letter, so he wrote back, "We found Cyrus' letter and how he commanded them to rebuild their temple. Since it was a royal decree, the work should continue. Give them whatever they need to finish their work and give them whatever animals they need to offer sacrifices to their God. If anyone violates my ruling, impale him upon a timber from his own house, and make his home into a dung heap. May the God who caused his name to dwell there overthrow anyone who stands against this work. May my words be carried out!"

The people continued building God's house until they finished it in Darius' sixth year of rule. Then the Jews held a great celebration and dedicated the temple to the Lord. They offered 100 bulls, 200 rams, and 400 lambs as a sin offering and worshiped the Lord.

The people observed the Passover as Moses had commanded. They slaughtered the Passover lamb and made themselves clean before the Lord. They kept the Feast of Unleavened bread and thanked God that the king of Assyria had facilitated the temple's rebuilding.

EZRA SENT TO JERUSALEM

Artaxerxes sent Ezra from Babylon to the people in Jerusalem. Ezra was a scribe who knew the Law, and the king gave him whatever he asked for because God was with him. The king sent him with some of the other Jews who remained in Babylon, and Ezra set his heart to study the Law.

Darius sent Ezra with a letter reading, "Anyone who wants to go back to Jerusalem has my blessing. You have permission to seek the Lord and I will provide whatever you need to offer sacrifices to God. Do whatever is in your heart, and I command the local rulers to provide whatever you need to worship.

"I give this order so that God's wrath will not be against me. You have permission to charge taxes or fees to make provisions for your worship if necessary. Appoint judges who know your laws to teach them to your people, and if there aren't enough who know the Law, teach it to them. I will execute whatever judgments are necessary for worship."

Ezra blessed the Lord for causing this miraculous turn of events to happen. He took courage from the Lord and recruited the leaders of Israel who had not previously gone to rebuild the temple to go with him.

Ezra was afraid to ask the king for a band of soldiers for protection on their journey to Jerusalem, so he called for a fast to ask the Lord to save them on the way home. God listened to their request and they journeyed safely to Jerusalem. When Ezra arrived, he put things in order for the continued service of the Lord and offered sacrifices to God.

After things had been set in motion, some leaders came to Ezra and told him that the people had not set themselves apart from the locals as God had commanded. They had allowed their children to marry the local nations and broken God's commands. Ezra tore his clothes in grief and ripped some of his hair and beard out.

When the time came for the evening sacrifice, Ezra got up from mourning and prayed, "God, I am ashamed to lift my face to you because our sin has risen over our heads, and our guilt piles up to the heavens. We have sinned so much that you sent us into captivity and now we live in shame. But you have granted us a brief respite from our guilt by allowing us to rebuild your temple. Even though we are still in slavery, you have shown us your steadfast love by enabling us to return to Jerusalem and rebuild its ruins.

"What can we say? We have forsaken your commandments and broken your laws. We have adopted the local nations' abominations as our own and have filled your land with impurity. You told us not to give our children into marriage with them, but we did it anyway. Despite this, you have still blessed us and given us a remnant. We come before you in our guilt and we cannot stand."

While Ezra confessed their sin and wept before the Lord, many people gathered around him, feeling guilty. One of the priests approached Ezra and said, "Even though we have sinned by marrying foreign people, there is still hope for us. Let us put away these foreign wives and children and repent. Get up because this is what you must do and we are all with you."

Ezra got up and made the priests swear they would follow through with this plan, and then he spent the night in prayer and fasting. He sent a proclamation to the people that they all must come to him within three days, or else they would forfeit any land they had within Israel.

All the Jews came to him on the third day and assembled in the open square before the temple. They trembled because of the matter's seriousness and the pouring rain. Ezra commanded the people to put away their foreign wives and children and return to faithfully obeying God's Law.

The people agreed to do what he had asked but asked for time because they needed to do so much, and they could not stay out in the pouring rain for long. Within three weeks, all the people had obeyed his command, and only one man resisted.

CHAPTER FORTY-NINE

REBUILDING THE WALL

Nehemiah 1-13

> **The Book of Nehemiah**
>
> The Book of Nehemiah begins shortly after the end of the Book of Ezra and records the Jews' efforts to rebuild the city of Jerusalem. Nehemiah received permission to rebuild the wall around 445 B.C., and the people quickly finished the task despite intense opposition. This book is closely related to the Book of Ezra, and they describe the Jews' return to the Promised Land after captivity. Ezra was a scribe and wrote both of these books sometime around 430 B.C.

NEHEMIAH'S PRAYER

Nehemiah was a cupbearer to the ruler in the city of Susa. He had been a captive in the capital for 20 years, and one day he asked for a report of how the remnant in Israel was doing. He heard that they were in great distress and trouble because the walls were torn down, and Jerusalem was defenseless.

As soon as he heard the report, he sat down and wept and mourned for many days. He fasted and prayed to the Lord, asking, "Lord, God of heaven, who is awesome and keeps his promises to those who obey his commands, hear my plea! We have sinned against you and broken the Law you gave us through Moses. Remember your promise that even though you scatter us when we are unfaithful, you would restore us to the land if we repented and returned to you. We are your people you have redeemed with your strong hand and great power. Please grant success to your servant in what I am about to do."

ARTAXERXES GRANTS NEHEMIAH'S REQUEST

One day, Nehemiah brought wine to king Artaxerxes, and he looked sad for the first time in his service to the king. Artaxerxes asked what was going on and Nehemiah was afraid. But he gathered his courage and said, "May the king live forever, but I am sad because my hometown is burned and in ruins."

The king asked what he wanted and Nehemiah paused to pray. Nehemiah said, "If I have found favor in your sight, please let me return to Jerusalem and rebuild the city." Artaxerxes agreed to his request and Nehemiah asked the king for materials to rebuild it. This seemed like a good idea to the king and he decided to let it happen.

Nehemiah went to Jerusalem to inspect the city walls and saw how they were in ruins. He told the elders of Jerusalem that he wanted to rebuild the walls and that the king had permitted him to do so; they agreed that they should begin the building project. But some of the local rulers sneered and asked why they were rebelling against the king. Nehemiah replied, "The God of heaven will allow us to prosper, and we will rebuild the walls, but you will have no part of this."

The people came together and began to rebuild the wall, starting with each of the gates. When Sanballat (a local official) saw this, he ridiculed the Jews and made fun of their efforts. One of his companions insulted them by saying that an animal as small as a fox would be able to topple their wall. In response, Nehemiah prayed God would establish and bless their efforts.

The people continued building the wall until it reached half its original height. When Sanballat and his companions saw the progress, they were outraged and came together to fight against the Jews, attacking the workers at the wall's lowest points. The people prayed that God would stop their enemies and Nehemiah put warriors at those places to defend the workers while they rebuilt. He told the Jews, "Do not be afraid of them; remember how great God is and how he will fight for us!"

Encouraged, the people returned to their work. Half the people worked on building while the other half stood ready to defend them. Then they would trade roles back and forth between the two groups. Each worker built while having a weapon with him and they planned to protect the wall wherever their enemies attacked. Each of them took a turn building, followed by a turn guarding the wall.

FINISHING THE WALL

While they were rebuilding the wall, the Jews bickered because each one felt like they were sacrificing more than the others. Some were building, some were providing for those who were building, and everyone was upset. Nehemiah became very angry and held a council of all the people, asking them not to charge interest to those taking out loans to provide for the building or so they could work at building the wall. The people agreed with this request and did what Nehemiah had asked.

During this time, Nehemiah and the other leaders agreed not to partake of their provisions to provide for the workers. Nehemiah also offered an ox, six sheep, and many birds each day for the workers from his own possessions.

The Jews continued to rebuild the wall until there were no gaps left. Sanballat tried to meet with Nehemiah, but instead, Nehemiah sent a message that he was doing a great work for the Lord and couldn't afford to come down to meet with them. They tried to meet with him four more times, and each time, Nehemiah refused.

The fifth time Sanballat and his companions tried to meet with Nehemiah, they told him they had heard he was trying to be king and that Artaxerxes would be angry when he heard about this. But Nehemiah replied that they were wrong in their understanding of what happened. He prayed that God would give them the strength to finish the work that they were doing.

After 52 days of work, the Jews finished rebuilding the wall, and their enemies feared them. But many of the local leaders continued trying to intimidate the Jews.

After they finished the wall, Nehemiah set up guards for the gates and told them not to open them until the afternoon of each day. There were few people to guard the city in those days, but there were many places that they needed to defend. Nehemiah completed a census of all those who had returned to Jerusalem.

EZRA READS THE LAW

Ezra gathered all the people together and read Moses' Law to them, so they would understand what God required. He told the people to go their way and do what was in their hearts because the joy of the Lord was their strength.

They celebrated the Feast of Booths as Moses had commanded. All the people built tents to live in for a week because they had not done so for many years. Each day of the feast, they read the Law and absorbed it into their hearts.

After hearing the Law, the people clothed themselves with sackcloth and ashes because they realized how they had sinned against the Lord. They separated themselves from foreigners and set their hearts to obey God's Law. For the first quarter of the day, they would listen to the Law, and for the second quarter, they would confess their sins to the Lord. Then, the priests would pray for the people, telling the people of Israel's history.

The people made a covenant with the Lord to obey his commandments and not give their children to foreigners. They promised to observe the Sabbath and provide the first fruits of their harvest to God. Then they promised not to neglect the Lord's temple.

***

A little after making this covenant, Nehemiah became very angry when he saw the people breaking God's Law and doing what they had promised not to do. Nehemiah confronted the Jewish leaders and threatened them with violence if they would not obey God's commands. He also beat some of the men who had married foreign women because this was how Solomon had sinned against the Lord. Thus, Nehemiah cleansed the people from evil before God.

CHAPTER FIFTY

ESTHER
Esther 1-6

The Book of Esther

The Book of Esther takes place in between the time of Ezra and Nehemiah, but I chose to put those two together because of their connection. Some Jews had returned to the Promised Land, but many remained in exile like Mordecai and Esther. We don't know who wrote the book, although some have imagined it to be Mordecai. We also don't know when the book was written, but the events took place around 475 B.C. God's name is not in the original text, but his sovereignty is undeniably woven throughout the story.

THE PLAN TO REPLACE THE QUEEN

When Ahasuerus was king of the Medes and Persians, he ruled from his home in Susa. In the third year of his reign, he threw a six-month party to show off his kingdom's wealth and greatness. At the end of this celebration, he threw another week-long party and invited all the men in Susa, and ordered them to partake as each felt right. Queen Vashti threw a party for all the women at the same time.

On the seventh day, Ahasuerus felt merry and ordered the seven eunuchs who attended him to bring his beautiful Queen Vashti to show her off to the men. But Vashti refused to come and Ahasuerus was very angry. He asked his wise men what he should do with his wife, who had embarrassed him.

One of his wise men advised him that not only had she disobeyed him, but she had also set an example for all women in the kingdom to follow. If they copied her actions, women would begin to break commands as they saw fit. He told Ahasuerus to decree that Vashti should never again be allowed to enter his presence and replace her as queen. The king liked this suggestion and sent out a letter to the entire kingdom, describing what he was doing so that every man would continue to rule his home.

After issuing this decree, Ahasuerus was no longer angry, and his young men advised that he bring beautiful young women to see him so he could choose a replacement for Vashti. He liked this idea and commanded his servants to give the young women cosmetics and then bring them to him so he could select a queen.

A Jew named Mordecai, from the tribe of Benjamin, came to Susa when the Babylonians took the people into captivity. He was raising his cousin, Esther, because she was an orphan. When the king's order went out, the servants brought her to the king to participate in the selection process. She quickly gained favor with Hegai, the eunuch, who oversaw the women, and she earned one of the best places in the harem.

But she did not let anyone know she was a Jew because Mordecai had advised her to keep her ancestry a secret.

The women in the harem prepared to meet the king with a six-month beautification process. They could take anything they wanted with them when meeting the king; then, they returned to the harem. Ahasuerus would only see each woman once unless he specifically requested them to come back.

When Esther met with the king, Hegai advised her what to take, and she delighted the king. Ahasuerus chose her to replace Vashti as queen and threw another great celebration.

HAMAN'S PLOT

While the selection process was going on, Mordecai was sitting at the king's gate one day, and he overheard two of the king's servants plotting to kill Ahasuerus. He told Esther about the plot and she relayed the message to the king. They investigated the matter, found the men guilty, and hanged them.

At the same time, Haman rose through the ranks of the king's servants and earned a place of authority over the king's house. The king commanded that all his servants bow in Haman's presence, but Mordecai refused. The king's servants tried to persuade him to pay homage to Haman, but he continued to refuse. This made Haman very upset, and when he found out that Mordecai was a Jew, he decided to destroy all the Jews in the kingdom.

One day, Haman went to Ahasuerus and said, "There is a people group scattered throughout your kingdom who have different laws than we do and it is in your best interest to get rid of them. I will deposit 375 tons of silver into your treasury if you allow me to send out an order to kill them."

Ahasuerus thought this was a good idea and permitted Haman to proceed with his plan. Haman sent letters throughout his kingdom that the people should kill every Jew in a couple of weeks. This threw Susa into chaos because many Jews lived in the city.

When Mordecai heard about the decree, he tore his clothes and put on sackcloth and ashes as he grieved for his people. There was great distress and mourning among all the Jews in the kingdom because they feared for their lives.

Esther heard about the decree and what Mordecai was doing, so she sent clothes for him and messengers asking him what she should do. Esther had not heard this decree because she lived in the palace, so Mordecai explained the situation and asked her to go to King Ahasuerus to beg for her people's lives.

Esther was afraid because the king had not summoned her for more than a month, and anyone who tried to see the king without permission could die. Mordecai sent word to her saying, "Don't think you will escape our fate just because you live in the palace. If you keep silent, we will all die. Who knows, you may have gained this position as queen to deliver us."

Esther sent word back to Mordecai, "Gather all the Jews in Susa and fast on my behalf for three days and nights. I will do the same and then talk to the king even though it is against the law. If I die, then I die, but I will try to save our people." Mordecai did what she asked.

ESTHER DELIVERS THE JEWS

On the third day, Esther put on her royal robes and went to stand by the inner court near the throne room. When the king saw Esther, he was happy and asked her to approach the throne. He extended his golden scepter to her, giving her permission to be there, and said, "Esther, what is your request? I will give you whatever you want, up to half my kingdom."

She was afraid to tell him everything that was on her heart, so she said, "Please bring Haman in so that he can share in the feast I have prepared for us."

The king's men summoned Haman and they ate the meal Esther had prepared. After eating and drinking, the king asked Esther what she wanted, but she was still not ready to share her request, so she asked that Haman come back for a similar feast the next day.

Haman felt good about himself when he left until he saw Mordecai at the king's gate and how he still refused to bow before him. He was furious but didn't do anything about it at that time. Instead, he went home and called his wife and his friends together to hear their thoughts. Haman told them about the great things happening in his life and how the king had invited him to private meals. But he was still frustrated by Mordecai's unwillingness to pay him homage.

His wife told him to make gallows 75 feet high and ask the king to hang Mordecai. This made Haman happy and then he went to bed.

That night, the king couldn't sleep, so he asked his servants to read him the records of the great deeds that had happened in his kingdom. They read him the account of how Mordecai had thwarted an assassination attempt, and when the king asked, his servants told him he had not been rewarded.

When Ahasuerus heard this, he told his men to bring in someone to honor Mordecai. Haman had just come in to ask the king to hang Mordecai, and the king asked him, "What should I do for someone that I want to honor?"

Haman replied, "Who would you want to honor more than me? Whoever you want to honor should receive a royal robe that you have worn, a horse you have ridden, and a crown you have worn. Then one of your officials should dress him up and lead him through the city proclaiming that this is how you honor those you delight in."

Ahasuerus liked the idea and said, "Do it. Take everything you have said and do it for Mordecai, who sits at my gate. Don't leave anything out." Begrudgingly, Haman obeyed the king's command and then went home with his head covered in shame.

Haman told his wife and friends what had happened, and they said, "If Mordecai is a Jew, you will not overcome him; you will surely fall before him." As they spoke, the king's men came to bring Haman to Esther's feast.

Haman went to the feast, and as they were drinking wine after the meal, the king asked Esther what her request was. She drew up her courage and said, "If I have found favor in your sight, please grant me my life and my people's lives. We have been sold and we are all to be killed. If we were merely enslaved, I wouldn't say anything; but our affliction is nothing compared to how this will affect you."

Ahasuerus was troubled by her words and said, "Who has done this and where is he?"

Then Esther replied, "It is the wicked Haman!"

The king was furious, and he stormed out of the room to gather his thoughts, but Haman stayed to beg Esther for his life. When the king came back in, Haman was falling on the couch where Esther was sitting, and the king said, "Will you even assault the queen in my house?!"

As soon as he spoke, the king's men put a sack over Haman's head and led him out of the room. One of the eunuchs told the king about Haman's gallows for Mordecai and the king commanded that they hang Haman on them.

Then the king called Mordecai in and Mordecai revealed that he was Esther's cousin. Then, the king gave him his signet ring, Haman's position, and put him over Haman's house. Esther fell on her face before the king and again begged for her life and her people's lives. She asked him to overturn the decree that he had written concerning the destruction of the Jews.

Ahasuerus answered, "I have given you Haman's house, and hanged him on the gallows he built because he tried to kill the Jews. But I cannot revoke my word because I sealed it with my signet ring."

He called for his men to write letters to his kingdom to allow the Jews to defend themselves from destruction. The king's men carried the message throughout the community; Mordecai left the palace in royal robes. The Jews rejoiced at the good news and held a feast of their own. After that, people feared the Jews, and many proclaimed their allegiance with them.

On the day that Haman had set, the Jews defended themselves from those who sought to destroy them. No one could stand against them and they gained the upper hand over their enemies. In Susa alone, they killed more than 500 men.

When Ahasuerus heard what had happened, he asked Esther if she wanted anything else. She also asked the king to hang Haman's sons from the gallows and to give the Jews another day to defend themselves from their enemies. He granted her request, and the Jews killed another 300 men in Susa, but the Jews did not plunder their enemies. Over the two days, the Jews killed 75,000 of their enemies throughout the entire kingdom, but they did not loot them.

The Jews instituted the feast of Purim to commemorate how God had delivered them from their enemies. Queen Esther sent out her own decree that the people should hold this feast every year and the people agreed to obey.

Mordecai continued to serve as the king's second in command and he did great things for the Jews all the days he served the king.

Poets and Prophets

Reorganized Concise Paraphrased Bible

Book III

By: Obadiah Paulus

INTRODUCTION TO POETS AND PROPHETS

These are the books of poetry and prophecy written to Israel, from Job through Malachi. This is the story of how God revealed himself to his chosen people. While these chapters primarily record human activity, we are not the main characters. Humanity is important, but this book, like the rest of the Bible, is a revelation of God's glory, not our own.

The prophets served an essential role in the history of Israel. A prophet is a spokesperson for God and he appointed these men to speak to his nation on his behalf. They served two roles for Israel, one was to call the people to repentance, and the second was to tell the people what God was going to do. The nation repeatedly struggled with straying from the Lord, and God would send them people to remind them of his goodness and their need to return. God also would tell the people what was going to happen as a sign of his power and omniscience.

The remaining books of this section are Hebrew books of poetry and wisdom literature. These books tackle some of the problematic themes that we deal with as humans and I have reorganized them as user-friendly as possible for the modern reader, including organizing the Psalms and Proverbs by topic. These books can be challenging to understand in English because the original Hebrew is poetry, and we lose meaning in translation. I have changed some of the material to prose to help us pull the purpose from the writers' intent.

The people in this book gave many names to God based on the characteristics and actions that he displayed towards them. I have opted to use either God or the Lord to refer to him to avoid confusion.

TABLE OF CONTENTS

THE PROPHETS:	273
CHAPTER 1: Jonah Sent to Nineveh (Jonah)	274
CHAPTER 2: Social Justice (Amos)	276
CHAPTER 3: God's Faithfulness (Hosea)	279
CHAPTER 4: Isaiah's Commission (Isaiah pt. 1)	283
CHAPTER 5: Ahaz' Failure to Trust (Isaiah pt. 2)	287
CHAPTER 6: God's Judgment on Israel (Isaiah pt. 3)	291
CHAPTER 7: Prophecies from Babylon (Isaiah pt. 4)	296
CHAPTER 8: God Will Judge His Enemies (Micah)	305
CHAPTER 9: Judgment on Nineveh (Nahum)	308
CHAPTER 10: The Day of the Lord (Zephaniah)	309
CHAPTER 11: God's Justice for Foreign Nations (Habakkuk)	311
CHAPTER 12: Jeremiah's Call and God's First Warning (Jeremiah pt. 1)	313
CHAPTER 13: Further Warnings Against Judah (Jeremiah pt. 2)	317
CHAPTER 14: Jeremiah's Warnings to the King (Jeremiah pt. 3)	322
CHAPTER 15: Promise of Restoration (Jeremiah pt. 4)	326
CHAPTER 16: The Fall of Jerusalem and Its Aftermath (Jeremiah pt. 5)	329
CHAPTER 17: Fallen Jerusalem (Lamentations)	334
CHAPTER 18: Judgment for Edom (Obadiah)	336
CHAPTER 19: Daniel's Service to Three Kings (Daniel pt. 1)	337
CHAPTER 20: Daniel's Visions (Daniel pt. 2)	342
CHAPTER 21: Ezekiel's First Visions (Ezekiel pt. 1)	348
CHAPTER 22: Warnings Against Jerusalem (Ezekiel pt. 2)	352
CHAPTER 23: Judgment and Consolation (Ezekiel pt. 3)	356
CHAPTER 24: The Swarm of Locusts (Joel)	362
CHAPTER 25: Temple Reconstruction (Haggai)	364
CHAPTER 26: God Remembers Israel (Zechariah)	365
CHAPTER 27: God's Covenant with Israel (Malachi)	369
THE POETS (Including an index of the Psalms):	371
CHAPTER 28: The Problem of Suffering (Job)	372
CHAPTER 29: Psalms for a Community in Sorrow	383
CHAPTER 30: Psalms for Individuals in Sorrow	389
CHAPTER 31: Psalms of Repentance	405
CHAPTER 32: Psalms of Vengeance	409
CHAPTER 33: Psalms of Thanksgiving	413
CHAPTER 34: Psalms of Trust	420
CHAPTER 35: Worship Psalms	424
CHAPTER 36: Salvation History Psalms	431
CHAPTER 37: Psalms for the King	436
CHAPTER 38: Psalms for Jerusalem and the Temple	442

CHAPTER 39: Wisdom Psalms	446
CHAPTER 40: Torah Psalms	450
CHAPTER 41: The Greatness of Wisdom Over Folly (Proverbs)	454
CHAPTER 42: Fear of the Lord and the Heart (Proverbs)	457
CHAPTER 43: The Tongue (Proverbs)	459
CHAPTER 44: Wisdom in Relationships (Proverbs)	461
CHAPTER 45: Money and Work (Proverbs)	463
CHAPTER 46: The Righteous and the Wicked (Proverbs)	466
CHAPTER 47: Friends, Justice, and Discipline (Proverbs)	469
CHAPTER 48: General Wisdom (Proverbs)	471
CHAPTER 49: Vain Pursuits (Ecclesiastes)	476
CHAPTER 50: Romance (Song of Solomon)	481

THE PROPHETS

ISAIAH – MALACHI

The prophets served an essential role in Israel's history. A prophet is a spokesperson for God and he appointed these men to speak to his nation on his behalf. They served two roles for Israel, the first was to call the people to repentance, and the second was to tell the people what God was going to do. The nation repeatedly struggled with straying from the Lord, and God would send them people to remind them of his goodness and their need to return. God also would tell the people what would happen as a sign of his power and omniscience.

I have put these books in the chronological order of events and the context of what was happening in the nation. It can be helpful to read this in conjunction with The Promised Land (Book II of the RCP Bible). I am aware that there are other timelines of the prophets putting them in a different order. However, this chronology does not do anything to take away from these books' interpretation. I have also omitted repeated portions or messages that pertain primarily to countries that no longer exist.

As we read these books, we must remember that the authors wrote these books to people who lived thousands of years ago and not people in the 21st Century. We can still draw information and application for our lives, but these are not directly to us. One of the most significant lessons we can take away is our need to listen to God's commands and repent from our sins.

CHAPTER ONE

JONAH SENT TO NINEVEH
Jonah 1-4

> **The Book of Jonah**
>
> The Book of Jonah causes many problems for scholars because the elements seem fantastical. Some have struggled with the miraculous accounts of the fish, Nineveh's conversion, and the vine's growth, but if we believe that God can do the supernatural, then we can accept these events. However, Jesus affirms the account of Jonah, and if God in the flesh acknowledges it as true, then we should as well.
>
> The events of Jonah happened during the reign of Jeroboam II and likely took place between 800 and 750 B.C. The book is in the third person, and we do not know who the author was or the exact date of authorship. One of Jonah's major themes is God's right to either anger or compassion on his own terms.

JONAH'S CALL AND THE GREAT FISH

God came to Jonah and said, "Go to the city of Nineveh and tell them that their evil has come up against me." But Jonah fled from the Lord and boarded a ship in the opposite direction. Then the Lord sent a storm against Jonah's boat and it seemed like the ship would break apart. The sailors were afraid for their lives, and they threw all the cargo overboard to make the boat lighter, and they each cried out to their own god.

Jonah was in a deep sleep in the inner part of the ship, and the captain came to him and said, "Why are you still asleep? Call out to your god and perhaps he will deliver us so that we won't die!"

The sailors came together to cast lots to discover who had caused this great storm to come upon them. The lot fell to Jonah and they asked him what he had done to create this great storm. They asked him where he was from and what he did for a living. He answered that he was a Hebrew and feared the Lord, who had made the land and the sea.

The sailors were terrified because they realized that he was fleeing from what God had told him to do, and they asked what they should do to cause the sea to quiet down, because the storm was getting worse.

Jonah told them that he was the reason for the storm and that the sailors should throw him overboard to calm the storm. So, the men threw Jonah overboard, and they offered sacrifices and asked for forgiveness because they were very afraid of the Lord.

Then God appointed a great fish to swallow Jonah, and he was in its belly for three days and three nights. After three days, Jonah cried out to the Lord, "You have cast me into the deep and the seas have surrounded me. You have driven me from your presence, but I will once again look upon your holy temple. Even though the waters have closed over my head, you have redeemed my life from the pit. When I was about to die, my prayer came to you, and you saved me. I will do what I have promised because salvation belongs to the Lord!" Then the fish vomited Jonah out onto dry land.

JONAH'S SECOND CALL

The word of the Lord came to Jonah a second time, telling him to go to Nineveh and give them the message that God gave him. Jonah went to the great city of Nineveh that took three days to cross. Jonah told the people, "In 40 days, God will overthrow Nineveh." The Ninevites believed Jonah, and they repented with sackcloth and ashes.

Hearing Jonah's message, the king commanded all his people to clothe themselves in sackcloth because of their sin, and to fast so that God might turn away from his vengeance against the kingdom. When God saw the people repent, he did not bring about the disaster he had decreed to bring against Nineveh.

> **The real miracle in Jonah**
>
> Many people focus on Jonah living in the fish's belly as the book's main miracle. However, God used a reluctant preacher who preached a sermon consisting of five words in the original Hebrew to cause a wicked city to repent.

Jonah was annoyed that the Ninevites had repented and he prayed to the Lord, "Isn't this what I said you would do when I was at home? I ran away because I knew that you would forgive them. After all, you are a gracious God. Now, please kill me because it is better for me to die than to live!"

Then the Lord said, "Why are you angry?"

God appointed a plant to grow while Jonah watched over the city of Nineveh, and it gave him shade from the heat, and Jonah was happy that the plant was there. But, the next morning, God appointed a worm to attack the plant, it withered as a scorching wind blew, and the sun beat down.

Jonah was suffering and said, "It is better for me to die than to endure this pain. But God confronted Jonah and said, "You are angry about the plant even though you didn't do anything to cause it to grow, and now it's died. Shouldn't I be concerned about the 120,000 people in Nineveh who don't know their right hand from their left, let alone all the cows?

> **Why was Jonah so angry?**
>
> Jonah was angry with God because God did not do what he wanted him to do. Jonah hated the Ninevites and wanted God to judge rather than save them. Jonah's misplaced anger at the withered vine is a betrayal of how he felt about God's mercy. But God showed him that he should be more concerned about the people and even the animals than his comfort.

CHAPTER TWO

SOCIAL JUSTICE
Amos 1-9

> **The Book of Amos**
>
> Amos was a blue-collar prophet who prophesied near the end of Jeroboam II's reign over the northern kingdom and Uzziah's reign over Judah. He lived in a small town south of Jerusalem, worked as a shepherd, and tended sycamore-fig trees. He likely wrote the book between 760 and 750 B.C. This was a relatively prosperous and peaceful time for both kingdoms, but both were full of idolatry, immorality, and corruption. The people felt good about themselves and their standing with God, but the Lord saw past the surface to the people's deeper sin. The people performed the required religious rites, but they lived luxuriously at the expense of the poor. Amos warned the people that God's judgment was imminent because they had ignored social justice.

JUDGEMENT AGAINST FOREIGN NATIONS

The Lord will judge the sins of the nations of Damascus, Gaza, Tyre, Edom, Ammon, and Moab. They keep piling their sins up to the heavens, and he will devour them and send them into exile.

JUDGEMENT AGAINST JUDAH AND ISRAEL

The Lord declares, "I will punish Judah because they have rejected my Law. They believe the same lies their ancestors believed, so I will devour Jerusalem with fire.

"I will punish Israel because they oppress the righteous and the poor, selling them into slavery. They are sexually immoral and flaunt their sin before me, even though I led them out of Egypt and into the Promised Land.

"They have stopped the prophets from prophesying and made the Nazirites break their vows. Therefore, they are a burden to me, and I will press them down like an overloaded cart. None of them will be able to stand, regardless of their strength; rather, they will flee naked and ashamed."

The Lord declares, "I will punish you for your sins because you are my chosen people. I have every reason to punish you because you are guilty; know that I am the source of your disaster.

"I reveal myself through my prophets, so listen to this message. Enemies will surround you and plunder your strongholds because you don't know how to do what's right. But I will save a remnant of the people, just as a shepherd saves whatever he can of a sheep from the lion's mouth.

"On the day I punish Israel's sins, I will tear down the pagan altars and destroy the wealthy's luxurious homes. I will bring them all to an end."

The Lord continued, "Those who have grown rich at the expense of the poor and needy should pay attention. Your punishment is coming, and foreigners will humiliate you as they lead you into captivity. Keep bringing tithes and sacrifices while piling up your sins and see if I listen.

"I have made you hungry, but you still have not returned to me; I have withheld rain and struck you with blight and mildew, but you refuse to come. I have killed your young men, and you still ignore me, so prepare to meet your God. I am the Creator of the heavens and the earth; I am the Lord God of hosts!"

The Lord declares, "Israel will fall and have only a fraction of her power and glory. Seek me and live, do not run to your idols. Seek the Lord, or fire will break out and devour with no one to quench it. I am the one who created everything; I am the Lord. Because you trample the poor and exploit them, your labor will be unprofitable.

"I know your sins and how you afflict the righteous; you will stay silent if you are prudent. Hate evil, love good, and establish justice so that I might be gracious to the remnant of Joseph. There will be wailing and mourning when I pass through your midst.

"Woe to you who long for the Day of the Lord; it will bring darkness and sorrow, not light and hope. It will be like escaping from a lion, only to meet a bear. I hate your feasts, offerings, and gatherings; take away the noise of your songs. But let justice and righteousness roll down like an ever-flowing stream. You did not bring me sacrifices in the wilderness, but turned to idols, so I will send you into exile.

What is the Day of the Lord?

The Day of the Lord is a reference to God's final return when he punishes his enemies and undoes the effects of sin and death. Many Israelites celebrated this day for God's punishment against their enemies. However, they did not realize that God would judge their sins as well.

"Woe to those at ease in Jerusalem and Samaria, you are no better than the foreign kingdoms who enjoy the best of their luxury and wealth. You live a life of comfort and pleasure, but don't care about my people's affliction. You will be the first to go into exile and your prosperity will pass away.

"I hate Israel's pride and their strongholds. I will kill the men of their house and they will be afraid even to speak my name. They should never expect a good result with that kind of behavior, so I will bring an oppressing nation against them. Enjoy what you have while it lasts because your enemies are coming."

HISTORICAL INTERLUDE

Amaziah, the priest of Bethel, reported Amos' prophecy to the king and complained that the people could not handle his message of coming exile. Then Amaziah said to Amos, "Run away from here and find somewhere else to live and prophesy."

Amos replied, "I'm a nobody, just a shepherd, but the Lord sent me to prophesy to his people. Now you're telling me to keep silent? The Lord will make your wife a prostitute, your children will die, and the Lord will divide the land. You will die in an unclean land and Israel will go into exile."

VISIONS OF THE FUTURE

I saw the Lord forming the locusts to devour Israel and fire engulfing the land. I begged him to relent because the calamities would leave the nation desolate. The Lord answered my prayer and granted my request. Then God showed me a plumb line amid the people, promising that he would measure and destroy them.

***

Then the Lord showed me a basket of ripe fruit that was about to spoil and said, "Just as the season is over for fruit, I am done with Israel and I will not overlook their sin any longer. The temple songs will become wailing and the dead will pile up in the streets. I am sick of them eagerly waiting for the end of festivals and the Sabbath, so they can make money by exploiting the poor and needy.

"I will not forget their deeds and the land will tremble on their account. I will make the sun go down at noon and turn their feasts into mourning. The days are coming when I will withhold my Word from the people, the people will search for revelation, but they will not find it."

***

I saw the Lord standing beside the altar and he said, "Strike the people and kill them with the sword; none of them will escape. No matter where they run, I will find them, and I will fix my eyes on them for evil rather than good.

"I am the Lord, who controls the earth, don't think I will not judge you for your sin. My eyes see everything in this evil kingdom, and I will wipe it from the earth, but I will not completely destroy Jacob's house.

COMING RESTORATION

"But, then I will raise up the fallen house of David and repair its walls and rebuild it like the days of old. The days are coming when the land will be fruitful again and I will restore Israel's fortunes. They will live in their land and I will never again uproot them from the land I've given them."

CHAPTER THREE

GOD'S FAITHFULNESS
Hosea 1-14

> **The Book of Hosea**
>
> Hosea began his ministry in the northern kingdom of Israel during Jeroboam II's reign (mid-eighth century B.C.) and continued until just before the Assyrian exile (724-722 B.C.). One of the distinctives of this book is that God commands the prophet to marry a prostitute and uses their relationship as a sign of his interactions with Israel. This gives a picture of the betrayal God felt by his people deserting their first love. Hosea was one of the last prophets to Israel before their captivity. In this book, God condemns Israel for idolatry and spiritual adultery.

HOSEA'S MARRIAGE TO GOMER

When God first spoke to Hosea, the Lord told him to marry a prostitute and have children. This was a picture of how Israel had prostituted itself out by forsaking the Lord and pursuing false gods. So, Hosea married Gomer, and she had a son. God told him, "Name him, Jezreel because I am going to punish King Jehu for the bloodshed at Jezreel and I am going to bring the kingdom of Israel to an end."

Then, Gomer gave birth to a daughter, and God said, "Name her No Mercy because I will no longer have mercy on Israel. I will still have mercy on Judah, and I will save them, but not by their strength."

After Gomer weaned No Mercy, she had another son, and God told Hosea, "Name him Not My People because you are not my people and I am not your God. But Israel will still have as many people as the sand of the seashore. Eventually, they will be my children again, and Judah and Israel will reunite and have one leader, and that will be a great day."

God continued, "Plead with your brothers and sisters, tell them that they are my people, and I will have mercy on them. Plead with your mother because I'm no longer her husband. Tell her to put away her prostitution, or I will strip her naked like the day she was born and make her like a wilderness where she will die of thirst. I will have no mercy on her children because they have played the prostitute and acted shamefully. My children have gone after their foreign gods, so I will surround them with thorns so that they cannot find their paths. She will pursue her lovers, but will not find them.

"Then they will try to come back to me because things were better than they are now. They don't realize that I'm the one who gave them the prosperity they use to worship Baal. But now, I will take everything away so that everyone will see their evil and no one will rescue them. I will put an end to their celebrations and make their land desolate. I will punish my people for worshiping idols."

God continued, "I will bring Israel into the wilderness and speak tenderly to my people. I will give them hope and they will turn to me like they did when they came out of Egypt. They will realize that I am their God and they will no longer chase after false gods. I will take the names of the Baals out of their mouths and renew my covenant with them. They will forever be my betrothed and I will allow them to live in peace. On that day, they will know me; I will answer my people and restore their prosperity. I will have mercy on No Mercy and call Not My People my people and they will call me their God."

Hosea's wife, Gomer, was unfaithful to him and returned to being a prostitute. Then God told Hosea to redeem his wife just as God still loved Israel. The prophet paid money and grain to bring her back home, and he said to her, "You must live with me and no longer play the prostitute with other men." Israel will live for many years without a king, a place to worship, or household gods. Then the children of Israel will seek the Lord again and return to his goodness in the latter days.

THE LORD IS FAITHFUL TO UNFAITHFUL ISRAEL

Children of Israel, listen to the Lord, "There is no faithfulness, love, or knowledge of God in the land; instead, it is full of swearing, lying, murder, stealing, and adultery, and there are no boundaries you have not crossed. Therefore, the land mourns, and its inhabitants do not prosper.

"My contention is with you, the priests, and you will stumble both day and night. My people die because they lack knowledge; I reject you as priests because you deny that knowledge. You have forgotten the Law, so I will forget your children. Like people, like priests, I will punish them for their wickedness. Even though they eat, they will not be satisfied because they rejected me to pursue prostitution and liquor.

"My people have left the Lord, so they ask a piece of wood what they should do. They sacrifice on all the high places because they find comfort there. Because you have left the Lord, your daughters are prostitutes, and your wives commit adultery. But I will not hold them guilty because it is the men leading the way in this sinfulness. Even though Israel is acting like a prostitute, Judah will not become guilty. Let Israel chase her idols and be ashamed of her behavior.

"Pay attention, king, priests, and all of Israel, because this judgment is for you. You have been a trap on every high hill; the rebels have slaughtered many, but I will discipline them all. I know about Israel's prostitution and corruption. Their sins keep them from repentance, a spirit of prostitution is in their hearts, and they do not know God. Their pride testifies against them; both Israel and Judah will stumble and fall.

"They will seek me with their flocks and herds, hoping to buy my love, but they will not find me because I have withdrawn. They are unfaithful and give birth to illegitimate children; I will devour their land. I will punish Israel and Judah because they are determined to cheat and seek filth. Then I will return to my home until they have borne their guilt and seek my face."

Hosea urged his people, "Let us return to the Lord; even though he has torn us to pieces, he will heal us. After two days, he will revive us, and on the third day, he will restore us so that we can live in his presence. Acknowledge him because he will appear as surely as the sun rises."

The Lord said, "What can I do with Israel? Their love is like the morning mist that disappears; therefore, I killed them with the words of my mouth. I desire mercy and not sacrifice, acknowledgment rather than burnt offerings. Like Adam, they have broken my covenant; they are evildoers with bloody footprints carrying out their wicked schemes. Israel is defiled and I am appointing a harvest for Judah where I will restore their fortunes.

"When I would have healed Israel, they revealed their crimes of deceit, robbery, and adultery. They don't realize that I see and remember all their evil deeds. They are all eager for sin and none of them call upon me. Strangers devour their strength and they don't notice how bad things have gotten. Their pride keeps them from returning to me and they foolishly seek help from foreign kings.

"Woe to them because they have strayed from me, I long to redeem them, but they lie about me. They cut themselves to impress their gods, but they turn away from me. Even though I gave them strength, they plot evil against me; their leaders will fall by the sword because of their insolent words.

"Israel claims to acknowledge me, but they reject what is right, set up kings without my consent, and make idols. I reject their idols and will smash them to pieces because they are not gods. They have sown the wind but will reap a whirlwind; Israel has become something that no one wants. Although they have sold themselves to their lovers and gone up to Assyria, I will gather them. They have multiplied their sins and wouldn't recognize my commands, no matter how many I gave. Israel has forgotten their Maker, but I will send a fire upon its cities and devour their strongholds. They will return to captivity."

Israel, do not rejoice like the other nations because you have been unfaithful to your God and love a prostitute's wages. They will not remain in the Lord's land; they will be taken away and unable to worship. Because their sins are so numerous, they call their prophets fools or insane. But the prophets are my lookouts, even though they are hated.

God will reject Israel because they have not obeyed. They will no longer be fruitful, but rather barren, and the Lord will drive them from the land. God will reject them and they will wander among the nations.

Israel was a spreading vine, and as it prospered, it built more altars and gathered more sacred stones. Their heart is deceitful, and they must bear their guilt; the Lord will demolish their altars and destroy their stones. They speak empty words and are oblivious to their folly, so he will punish them when the time is right. They long for their idols, but the Assyrians will take them away, and their king will die.

Sow righteousness and reap the fruit of unfailing love because it is time to seek the Lord. You have planted wickedness, reaped evil, and eaten the fruit of deception.

Because you depended on your strength, your fortresses will be devastated, and your king will die.

The Lord says, "I loved Israel when he was a child, and I called my son out of Egypt, but the more I called, the more he ran. They sacrificed and burned incense to idols and they didn't realize that I was healing them. I led them with kindness and love and I bent down to feed them like a little child. But they keep turning back to Egypt and Assyria because they are determined to turn away from me. Even though they call me God, I will not exalt them.

"But I am compassionate and will not carry out my fierce anger again because I am God and not a man. They will follow the Lord, and I will roar like a lion, then bring them home."

Israel is playing with fire as they multiply their lies and violence. The Lord will bring a charge against Judah and will punish Jacob according to his deeds. He grasped his brother's heel in the womb, and as a man, he struggled with God. He wrestled with the angel and overcame him and begged for his favor with tears.

> **Who was Jacob?**
>
> Jacob was one of the Patriarchs. After spending an entire night wrestling with an angel, the Lord changed his name to Israel. He became the father of the men who became the tribes of Israel.

The Lord declares, "You must return to the Lord, maintain love and justice, and always wait for your God. Do not trust in your wealth or strength because the Lord will see your sin. I have been your God since you came out of Egypt and I will make you live in tents again. I spoke to the prophets through visions and parables; I have always led through them throughout your history.

"The people keep sinning more and more; they make idols and offer human sacrifice. Therefore, you will be like the morning mist that disappears. But I am the Lord your God who brought you out of Egypt and there is no savior besides me. I cared for you in the wilderness and fed you, but you became proud and forgot me. So, I will attack and tear you apart.

"I will destroy you, because you are against me. I gave you a king in my anger and took him away in my wrath. You are like an unborn child who doesn't realize it's time for birth. Should I save you from death? Even though you flourish, you will bear your guilt and face punishment.

"Israel, return to your God because your sins have been your downfall. Ask me to forgive you because Assyria cannot save you. I will heal their waywardness and love them because my anger has turned away from them. I will be like the dew on the grass and you will flourish once again. Be wise and realize that my ways are righteous, and you should walk in them while the rebellious stumble."

CHAPTER FOUR

ISAIAH'S COMMISSION

Isaiah 1-6

The Book of Isaiah

The Book of Isaiah is a collection of the prophet Isaiah's prophecies and teachings from about 740-700 B.C. during the reigns of Uzziah, Jotham, Ahaz, and Hezekiah. Some scholars would like to break the book into two (chapters 1-39 and 40-66) and attribute them to different authors. There is a difference in tone and vocabulary between the two parts, and some of the prophecies seem extraordinary if Isaiah wrote them during his lifetime. However, the first 39 chapters were to a rebellious people that God was going to judge, and the last 27 were to a people in exile that God was going to restore. A different situation and the passage of time can explain the differences in tone and vocabulary. Furthermore, Jesus attributed both parts to Isaiah, and as God in the flesh, Jesus would know. Finally, any fulfillment of prophecy is extraordinary, and if we accept that God can foretell the future, the specificity of the prophecy is no longer an issue.

In addition to speaking against sin and rebelliousness, Isaiah also writes a lot about God's compassion for Israel and the coming Messiah. Some commentators call this book the fifth gospel because of the amount of material that Isaiah wrote about Jesus.

PROPHECIES TO UZZIAH

The Lord says, "I raised my children, but they have rebelled against me. Oxen and donkeys know their masters, but Israel doesn't know me or understand."

Woe to the sinful nation; it is full of wickedness, the offspring of evildoers who act corruptly. They have forsaken the Lord and despised the Holy One of Israel. Why do you keep rebelling and subjecting yourself to beatings? The head is sick, and the heart is faint, covered in bruises from head to toe; sores and raw wounds cover the body. Your country is desolate, your cities burned with fire, and foreigners devour your land in your presence. If the Lord of hosts had not left us a few survivors, we would be like Sodom and Gomorrah.

The Lord says, "What good are all your sacrifices? I've had enough of your offerings; I take no pleasure in the blood of bulls, lambs, and goats. Stop bringing vain offerings; your incense is an abomination to me because I can't stand your worthless assemblies.

"I'm tired of all your feasts and I hate your festivals. I've ceased listening to your prayers because your hands are covered in blood. Wash yourselves and be clean; take your deeds away; stop doing evil, learn to do good; seek justice and remove oppression; stand up for the orphan and the widow.

"Even though your sins are like scarlet, I will make them white as snow, like new wool. If you are willing and obedient, you will eat the fat of the land; but if you refuse, the sword will devour you."

Jerusalem had been full of justice, but now she is a prostitute and a home for murderers. Your silver is tarnished, your wine watered down, your princes are rebels and companions of thieves. Everyone loves a bribe, and you do not stand up for the orphan or the widow.

Therefore, the Lord declares, "I will get relief from my enemies and avenge myself on my foes. I will turn my hand against you and purify you. I will restore your judges and counselors, and then you will be a righteous and faithful city once more."

God will redeem Jerusalem with justice and righteousness, but he will break rebels and sinners, and consume those who forsake the Lord. They will be ashamed of your desires and you will become like a waterless garden. The strong will become fuel and their work a spark, and they will burn together with nothing to quench them.

In the last days, the mountain of the Lord's temple will be established and exalted above the hills, and all nations will run to it. The Word of the Lord will go out from Jerusalem and many people will come so that they may learn his ways. God will judge between the nations and settle disputes. People will change their weapons into tools and stop fighting with each other. Descendants of Jacob, let us walk in the light of the Lord.

Lord, you have abandoned your people because they have adopted the pagan customs of foreigners. The land is full of treasures, wealth, and idols, but they will all be humbled. Hide from the terror of the Lord and the splendor of his majesty because only he will be exalted on that day. God has a day in store for the proud and arrogant, and every lofty thing will be brought low. Humanity will be humbled and their idols will disappear when the Lord comes in the splendor of his majesty. Don't trust in mere humans because they are mortal.

God will cut off supply and support from Jerusalem and Judah: food and water, hero and warrior, judge and prophet, diviner and elder, officers and soldiers, skilled craftsmen and enchanters. Children will be their leaders and infants their rulers; all the people will oppress each other, and the young will disrespect their elders. Merely having a coat will be enough to qualify people to rule over a heap of rubble.

Jerusalem and Judah have fallen because their words and actions defy the Lord's glorious presence. They are proud of their sin and bring evil upon themselves. The righteous will enjoy the fruit of their deeds, but the wicked will be paid back for what they've done. Be careful because your guides lead you astray; the Lord will judge the leaders and hold them accountable.

The Lord says, "The women of Jerusalem are haughty and walk around with flirtatious seductions, but I will judge them!" On that day, God will take away their fancy clothes, jewelry, and adornments and dress them in rags. Their men will die in battle, and the gates of Jerusalem will weep and mourn in the dust. On that day, women will beg any man they can find to take away their disgrace.

On that day, the Branch of the Lord will be beautiful and glorious, and the fruit of the land will be the pride and glory of Israel's survivors. Those left in Jerusalem will be holy when the Lord washes away their filth with a spirit of judgment and fire. Then the Lord will put a cloud by day, a flame by night, and glory as a canopy over the city. He will be a shelter from the heat and a refuge from the rain.

> **Who is the Branch of the Lord?**
>
> The Branch of the Lord is a reference to Jesus, the coming Messiah.

Israel is the Lord Almighty's vineyard and the people of Judah are the vines that delight him. He planted them on a fertile hillside, cleared the land, planted the best vines, and gave them everything they needed to thrive, but they bore bad fruit. Now he will take away the hedge of protection, break down its wall and let it be trampled. It will become a wasteland, and nothing will grow there because when he looked for justice and righteousness, he only found bloodshed and cries of distress.

Woe to those who expand their property as much as possible until there is no more room and you live alone in the land. The Lord has sworn, "The great houses will become desolate and the fine mansions will be empty. The fields will produce far less than expected."

Woe to those who get up early or stay up late to get drunk. They may have a lot of fun, but they don't respect the Lord or his work. Therefore, my people go into exile because they lack knowledge; they are humbled and brought low because of their love for strong drink. But the Lord of hosts is exalted in justice and the Holy God is righteous.

Woe to those who sell evil with lies and haul sin to market; they call for God to act quickly so that they can see it.

Woe to those who call evil good and good evil, who put darkness for light and light for darkness, who put bitter for sweet and sweet for bitter!

Woe to those who are wise and clever in their own eyes!

Woe to heroes at drinking alcohol, who acquit the guilty for a bribe, and rob the innocent of their rights. They will burn up quickly, and their roots will rot away because they have rejected God and despised his word. God is angry with his people and ready to strike with the unrelenting strength of foreign nations. Their arrows are sharp and prepared to strike; their horses and chariots advance like a whirlwind. On that day, they will attack and consume the land.

ISAIAH'S VISION OF THE LORD

In the year King Uzziah died, I saw the Lord exalted on a throne, high and lifted up; the train of his robe filled the temple. There were two angels above him, each with six wings: two were flying, two covered their faces, and two covered their feet. They called to one another, "Holy, holy, holy is the Almighty Lord, the whole earth is full of his glory!"

Their voices shook the foundation and the house filled with smoke. I said, "Woe to me, I am ruined. I have seen the King, the Lord Almighty when I am a man of unclean lips, and I live with people who have unclean lips."

One of the angels flew to me with a burning coal that he had taken from the altar. He touched it to my mouth and said, "This has touched your lips, your guilt is taken away, and your sins are atoned for."

The Lord asked, "Who shall I send, who will go for us?"

I answered, "Here I am! Send me."

He replied, "Tell the people to keep on hearing, but don't understand, keep on seeing, but don't perceive. Make the hearts of these people calloused with dull ears and closed eyes. Otherwise, they might repent and be healed."

> **Did God want the people not to understand?**
>
> No. This was the Lord telling the people to continue in their unbelief, despite God's message. It's not that he wanted them to ignore him, but stating that they would.

I asked the Lord how long and he said, "Until the cities and houses are abandoned and the fields are ruined and ravaged; until I send them far away and the land is forsaken. It will burn until only a tenth remains in it, until it is just a stump. The Messiah is that stump."

CHAPTER FIVE

AHAZ'S FAILURE TO TRUST

Isaiah 7-12, 24-27, (13-23)

PROPHECIES TO AHAZ

When Ahaz was king of Judah, Rezin, the king of Syria, and Pekah, the king of Israel, went to Jerusalem to wage war, but they could not attack it. When Ahaz saw this, his heart and the heart of the people shook with fear.

Then the Lord sent Isaiah to meet Ahaz and say, "Be careful, quiet, and don't be afraid because they will not succeed. Within 65 years, Israel will go into captivity. Stay strong in your faith."

Then the Lord said to Ahaz, "The Lord will give you a sign, a virgin will conceive and give birth to a son, and his name will be Immanuel (God with us). He will eat curds and honey when he is old enough to know right from wrong, but before that, these two kings will be brought low by the king of Assyria."

> **Dual fulfillment of prophecy**
>
> When God spoke to the prophets, they were able to see what God showed them but did not understand when or how God would fulfill them. Some of these prophecies also had multiple fulfillments. This prophecy of a virgin giving birth was fulfilled with Isaiah's child and pointed to the coming birth of Jesus.

"God will call Egypt and Assyria to come against you. The Assyrians will humiliate you by shaving you bald. On that day, people will keep animals alive for milk rather than meat. Briers and thorns will cover the land; the cultivated land will run wild with animals. The people will be in poverty."

Then the Lord told Isaiah to make love to a virgin prophetess, and she gave birth to a son that they named Maher-Shalal-Hash-Baz, and he is a sign of God's promise about Assyria. The Lord said, "The nations should raise a war cry, prepare for battle, and be shattered. They will devise a strategy, but it will fail. God will have the last word in this matter.

"Not everything is a conspiracy and do not fear what they do; you should fear the Lord and regard him as holy. He will be a holy place for both Israel and Judah, and he will be a stone that causes people to stumble and fall. Many will fall and be broken; they will be snared and taken. Seal up this teaching for my followers."

I will wait for the Lord and hope in him who is hiding his face from Israel. When people tell you to consult fortune-tellers and mediums, turn to the Scriptures instead. They will pass through the land, distressed and hungry; they will become enraged and speak against their God. They will look to the earth but will only find distress, darkness, and the gloom of anguish.

But the darkness will not last forever. Previously, the land of Galilee was despicable, but those in darkness will have a light shined on them. A child will be born to us, the government will rest on his shoulder, and he will be called Wonderful Counselor, Mighty God, Everlasting Father, and Prince of Peace. His government and peace will never end, and he will rule from the throne of David with justice and righteousness forever. God's zeal will do this.

> **The promise of the coming Messiah**
>
> Isaiah promises the coming of the Messiah to rule David's throne. He promises that this would be God in the flesh and lead as God always intended. Jesus fulfills this prophecy, and he is the dividing point of history and brings salvation for those who trust in him and condemnation for those who reject him.

The Lord has a message for the proud who believe they will rebuild better than before: the Syrians and Philistines have devoured Israel, but he is still angry and ready to strike. The people are still proud and have not turned to the Lord, so he has cut them off in a single day. The people who guide them have led them astray, and God will not have mercy because they are all godless and evildoers. His hand is outstretched against them. The Lord of hosts has scorched the land and the people will feed upon each other.

Woe to those who make unjust laws, deprive the poor of their rights, withhold justice from the oppressed, and rob widows and orphans. Disaster will come for them and there will be no one to help. God is still angry and ready to strike them.

Woe to the Assyrians, the tool of God's anger. He has sent them against a godless nation to plunder and trample them down like mud in the streets. But they are proud and believe they are greater than they truly are. When the Lord has finished with Jerusalem, he will punish the Assyrian's arrogance. They will believe that their wisdom and strength have given them success, but they are not greater than the Lord. He will send a wasting sickness on Assyria's warriors and they will be devoured. Israel's light will become a fire and his Holy One a flame; it will devour the thorns and briers in a single day.

Then the remnant of Israel and its few survivors will lean on the Lord rather than their oppressors. A remnant of Israel will return to God and he will bring them home. Do not be afraid of the Assyrians because God's fury will end and he will judge them. He will remove their yoke from Israel's neck, and he will bring down their wealth and power.

A shoot will come from the stump of Jesse, and the Branch will bear fruit from his roots. The Spirit of the Lord will rest on him, the Spirit of wisdom, understanding, counsel, might, knowledge, and the fear of the Lord. He will delight in the fear of the Lord, and he will judge with righteousness, not with what he sees or hears. He will strike the earth with the rod of his mouth and kill the wicked with his breath. He will wear righteousness and faithfulness as his garments.

The prey will live with the predator and their young will lie down together. No one in my holy mountain will hurt or destroy each other, for the earth will be filled with the knowledge of the Lord just as the waters cover the sea.

The Root of Jesse (the Messiah) will stand as a signal for all the people, they will turn to him, and his resting place will be glorious. The Lord will extend his hand over the remnant of his people and he will gather them from the ends of the earth. The Lord will restore Israel and destroy its enemies.

On that day, you will say, "I will praise you, Lord. Although you were angry with me, you have turned away your anger and comforted me. The Lord is my strength and defense; I will trust him because he is my salvation.

"Praise the Lord and proclaim what he has done; sing about his glorious works to the entire world. Shout aloud and sing for joy, because the Holy One of Israel is great among you!"

Prophecies against the nations

God also spoke many prophecies against the local nations and how God would execute his judgment on them. I omitted them because they are not as relevant to the modern reader. Among the things that Isaiah foretold were the Medes striking down Babylon, the Philistines facing famine, and other prophecies against Moab, Damascus, Edom, Arabia, Tyre, Egypt, and Cush. One of the more unusual was that Isaiah walked around naked and barefoot for three years to show how the Assyrians would lead away Egypt and Cush.

ISAIAH'S APOCALYPSE

The Lord will devastate the earth and scatter its inhabitants; he will not distinguish between people by class or status. The earth will dry up and wither and the heavens will languish. The people have defiled the land by disobeying the everlasting covenant. A curse consumes it and the people must bear their guilt. There will be no celebration, and the ruined city will be desolate with its gates battered and in ruins.

But some will burst forth in song and praise the Lord from the east to the west. All the earth will glorify his name. Anyone who runs will be caught because the earth trembles and is split open. The Lord will punish his enemies, but he will be glorified.

Lord, you are my God, and I will praise your name because you have done wonderful things planned long ago in perfect faithfulness. You have made the fortified city a ruin that will never be rebuilt; therefore, strong people will honor you. You have been a refuge for the poor and needy and silenced the song of the ruthless.

On this mountain, the Lord will make a feast for his people. He will destroy death forever and wipe the tears from every eye. Those who have waited on him will rejoice in his salvation. God will rest on his holy mountain and trample his enemies.

> **The Messiah will destroy death**
>
> This portion of Scripture promises that Jesus will destroy death and wipe the tears away from every eye. He will undo all the negative effects of sin.

On that day, Judah's people will sing to the Lord, their everlasting rock who humbles the lofty city and lays it in the dust. Trust in the Lord forever, because he is an everlasting rock; he makes the path of the righteous level. We wait for the Lord's judgments and yearn for his presence. The wicked do not learn righteousness or see the Lord's majesty. Lord, consume your enemies with fire and make them ashamed.

Others have ruled over us, but we will only remember God. You alone have increased the nation and enlarged our borders. We were in distress and we whispered a prayer to you. Your dead will rise and sing for joy. The Lord is coming to punish the earth's inhabitants for their sin and it will reveal the blood that has been shed on it.

On that day, the Lord will punish the great dragon with his hand. The Lord's anger will be satisfied and he will protect his people. Jacob will take root and blossom; his guilt will be atoned for when he crushes the idols and incense altars. This people, with no discernment, will return to the holy mountain in Jerusalem from Assyria and Egypt, where they have been driven.

CHAPTER SIX

GOD'S JUDGMENT ON ISRAEL
Isaiah 28-39

PROPHECIES TO HEZEKIAH

Woe to the pride of Israel's drunkards and the fading flower of their beauty; the Lord is appointing a mighty one to bring them down, and he will swallow them whole. The Lord of hosts will be a crown of glory to the remnant of his people and a spirit of justice to him who sits in judgment. They stagger from liquor and stumble in giving judgment. Who are they trying to teach and what are they even saying? They babble on with no meaning, so God will have to speak to them through foreigners.

Therefore, the Lord says, "You think that you have made a deal with death so that you won't face its wrath. I am going to lay a foundation stone in Jerusalem, a precious cornerstone, and those who rely on it will never be stricken with panic. Justice and righteousness will be the measure, and I will sweep away the lies." Then he will cancel the covenant with death when the scourge passes through you. It will be sheer terror to understand the message. You are in a precarious place; you cannot hide from God's wrath.

> **What is the foundation stone?**
>
> The foundation stone is a prophecy of Jesus, the coming Messiah.

Do not scoff at this message, or your bonds will become too strong to break. The Lord has decreed destruction against the whole land. Listen to my message because he does not keep plowing the field forever. Once he levels the field, he will plant seed and not keep beating it. The farmer does not thresh forever and he does not crush the grain. The Lord gives wonderful counsel and excellent wisdom.

Woe to Jerusalem, you will be filled with moaning and lament. You will be attacked and brought low, and your words will rise from the dust. Your enemies will be as numerous as the dust where you lie. The Lord will bring a multitude of nations against you to fight and will rain destruction on you in an instant. It will be like eating in a dream; you won't be satisfied. Your pride has made you drunk, and you stagger, but not with alcohol.

The Lord has poured out a spirit of deep sleep on the prophets and seers, and they will not understand the Lord's message. The Lord says, "Because these people honor me with their lips, but their hearts are far away, the fear of me is only a commandment they've been taught. Therefore, I will do wonderful things before these people and the wisdom of their wise men will perish."

Those who think the Lord doesn't see them have turned things upside down. The pottery cannot talk back to its maker and claim he has no understanding. It will not be long until the deaf shall hear, the blind shall see, the meek will have joy, and they will praise the Holy One of Israel. The ruthless will come to nothing, scoffers will cease, and those who watch evil will be cut off. They will stand in awe of the God of Israel and those who have gone astray will come to understand.

The Lord declares, "Woe to the obstinate children who follow plans that I did not make and pile sin on top of sin; those who turn to foreign nations when I did not tell them. They will become ashamed because those they turn to will be utterly useless. They refuse to listen to my instruction and order their prophets to be silent rather than returning to me.

"Therefore, because you have relied on oppression and deceit, your sin will become like a high wall that will collapse instantly. It will shatter beyond repair and the pieces will not even be big enough to take an ember from the fire.

"Your salvation is in repentance and rest, your strength in quietness and trust, but you reject it. You trust in worldly wisdom, but a thousand of you will flee at the threat of one man."

But the Lord longs to be gracious to you; he will show you compassion because he is a God of justice. He will bless those who wait on him and they will weep no more. He will be gracious if you call out for help and will answer as soon as he hears. Although he has given you the bread of adversity and the water of affliction, he will make his way evident to you. Then you will throw down your idols and get rid of them like trash.

Then the Lord will give you rain for your crops and broad meadows for your cattle. The moon will shine like the sun and the sunlight will be seven times brighter when the Lord binds up his people's wounds. The Name of the Lord comes from afar with burning anger, his lips are full of fury, and his tongue is a consuming fire.

When you sing praises to him, your hearts will rejoice. The Lord will cause people to hear his majestic voice and they will see his mighty arm come down with power. He will strike down his enemies and consume them in a blaze. He has prepared a place for them with eternal fire and sulfur.

Do not rely on Egypt because they are only men and not God. They cannot deliver, but the Lord Almighty will come down to battle Mount Zion and protect Jerusalem like a shield. Israelites, return though you revolted against me. Assyria will not fall at the hands of humans but because of the Lord's power when he puts his terror on them.

A king will rule in righteousness and justice; he will be a shelter to a weary land. All eyes will see and ears will hear. The fearful heart will know and understand; the stammering tongue will be fluent and clear. People will no longer respect fools and scoundrels. They practice ungodliness and spread errors about the Lord; they leave the hungry and thirsty unsatisfied. Scoundrels use wickedness to destroy the poor and needy, but the noble make noble plans.

Those of you who are complacent and at ease, listen to my voice. In just over a year, you will shudder and mourn for your fruitful fields and deserted palace. Weep until he pours out his Spirit from on high and the wilderness becomes fruitful. Then justice will dwell in the wilderness and righteousness in the field. This righteousness will result in peace, quietness, and eternal trust. Then my people will live in peace and security.

Woe to the Assyrians because once you have finished destroying, you will be destroyed. Lord, be gracious to us because we wait for you; be our strength and salvation in times of trouble. The nations will run when you rise up and you will gather your plunder. The Lord is exalted and he will fill Zion with justice and righteousness; he will be our stability, abundance, salvation, wisdom, and knowledge.

The land is desolate, but the Lord says, "I will arise and lift myself up. You will bring forth kindling for the fire of my rage." The sinners in Israel are rightly afraid, but the righteous will live in security and have provision.

You will see the king's beauty in an expansive land. Your heart will wonder where the strong and insolent are, but they will not be there. You will see Jerusalem live in peace, an immovable tent that will never fall. The Lord will provide us with a place of broad rivers and streams that no mortal ship can reach.

For the Lord is our Judge and Lawgiver; he is our King who will save us. You will no longer be bound and will receive your reward. There will be no illness because God will forgive their sins.

Draw near and listen, for the Lord will judge the nations. Their dead will pile up and the skies will roll up like a scroll. The Lord's fury will drink its fill of the blood of his enemies. The Lord has a day of vengeance, and he will turn his enemies' land to burning pitch and sulfur. It will burn forever and be filled with confusion and emptiness. Its princes will be worthless and overrun with wild animals.

Read God's Word, because none of his people will be missing. He has given his command and his people will dwell there forever.

Then the desert and wilderness will rejoice and blossom; they will rejoice, shout for joy, and see the Lord's glory. Strengthen weak hands and steady your knees; be strong and do not fear because God will come with divine retribution, and he will save you.

The blind will see, the deaf will hear, the lame will leap like a deer, and the mute will shout for joy; water will gush forth in the wilderness, and there will be streams in the desert. The burning sand will become a pool and there will be a highway called the Way of Holiness. Only the redeemed and those that the Lord has rescued will walk upon it. They will enter Jerusalem with singing, and everlasting joy will be their crown; gladness and joy will overtake them, and sorrow and sighing will flee.

HISTORICAL INTERLUDE

In the 14th year of King Hezekiah's rule, Sennacherib, the king of Assyria, attacked Judah's fortified cities and captured them. The king of Assyria sent Rabshakeh to Jerusalem with a great army and said to the people keeping watch on the wall, "Do you think that mere words are strategy and power for war? Who do you think will help you stand against us? Are you trusting Egypt? They are nothing more than a broken staff that pierces anyone who leans on it. Your God will not deliver you either. I will make a wager with you, I will give you two thousand horses if you can put riders on them, but you still will not defeat even one of my captains. Your God told me to destroy this land!"

The people asked him to speak in Aramaic so that the common people would not understand what he was saying. But Rabshakeh replied, "My master sent me to let you all know that you are doomed to eat your feces and drink your urine. Don't listen to Hezekiah, make your peace with me and then you will all eat from your own vine and fig tree and drink the water from your own cistern. Then I will take you to a land like your own with plenty of bread and wine. The Lord will not deliver you. None of the gods of any other nations have been able to defeat us; why do you think your God will be able to?" The people on the wall were silent and they relayed Rabshakeh's words to Hezekiah with their clothes torn.

When Hezekiah heard these words, he tore his clothes, put on sackcloth, and went to the temple. He commanded his priests to put on sackcloth as well, and he called for Isaiah to tell him what was happening. Isaiah said, "The Lord says not to be afraid of the king of Assyria because he will put a spirit in him so that he hears a rumor and returns home, then he will fall by the sword in his own land."

Hezekiah heard Isaiah's words and he prayed to God, "Lord of hosts, enthroned above the angels, you are the only God, and you made heaven and earth. Listen to the Assyrian's message. Truly, they have laid waste to all the nations and cast their gods into the fire. They are only idols, so they were destroyed. Save us from his hand so that all the kingdoms of the earth may know that you alone are God."

Then Isaiah told Hezekiah, "Thus says the Lord, I have heard your prayers, and the king of Assyria is trying to mock me. But he doesn't realize that I am making things happen that I planned long ago; I'm the one who brought him to power in the first place. I know he is raging against me, and I will put my hook in his nose, my bit in his mouth, and send him back the way he came. You will know this will happen because you will eat the food that grows by itself. Next year, what grows from that, and then you will sow and reap the third year. Then the surviving remnant of Judah shall again take root downward and bear fruit upward.

"The Lord's zeal will save a remnant from Jerusalem. The king of Assyria will not attack Jerusalem or lay siege to it. He will leave the way he came because I will defend the city for the sake of my servant David."

Then an angel of the Lord went out and killed 185,000 in the Assyrian's camp. Then Sennacherib, the king of Assyria, returned home and lived in Nineveh. While he was worshiping in the house of Nisroch, his god, two of his sons killed him and fled the country. Then his son Esarhaddon ruled in his place.

HEZEKIAH'S ILLNESS

Hezekiah became ill to the point of death, and the prophet Isaiah told him to put his house in order because he was about to die. But Hezekiah prayed to the Lord with tears, "Lord, remember how I have faithfully walked before you with full devotion and done good in your eyes."

God said to Isaiah, "Go tell Hezekiah that I have heard his prayer and seen his tears. I will add fifteen years to his life and defend this city against the king of Assyria. To prove this, I will make the sun go backward ten paces." It happened just as the Lord said.

Then Hezekiah wrote, "In the prime of life I was about to die and see the Lord. He was about to bring me to an end, and I prayed to him that he would spare my life and let me live a bit longer. In his love, he delivered me from death because he has forgiven my sins. Death does not praise or thank him, nor do the dead hope in him. The Lord will save me and we will make music in his house all the days of our lives."

The king of Babylon sent letters and a gift to Hezekiah because he had heard that he had been sick and recovered. Hezekiah gladly received the men bearing the letters and gifts and then showed off all the riches and wonder of his kingdom.

Then Isaiah went to Hezekiah and asked, "Where were those men from, what did they say, and what did you show them?"

Isaiah replied, "They came from Babylon, and I showed them all the riches and wonders of the kingdom; there is nothing I did not show them."

Isaiah answered, "The Lord says that a time will come when Babylon will carry off everything that you have shown off, nothing will be left. They will take some of your descendants there in captivity to become eunuchs in the king of Babylon's palace."

Hezekiah took it well because he thought, "At least there will be peace and security during my life."

CHAPTER SEVEN

PROPHECIES FROM BABYLON
Isaiah 40-66

> **Prophecies of comfort**
>
> After the Israelites went into captivity, God changed the nature of his message to his people. Whereas Isaiah's previous prophecies were warning the people of their coming judgment, the last portion of his writing is how God will restore his people to the Promised Land.

BABYLONIAN EXILE AND DELIVERANCE

The Lord tells me to comfort my people, to speak tenderly to Jerusalem. Her warfare is over, her sin paid for, and the Lord has blessed her. A voice cries in the wilderness, "Prepare the way of the Lord and make a straight path for our God in the desert. Every valley shall be lifted, and every mountain brought low; the uneven ground will become level. The Lord will reveal his glory, and all the world will see it; the Lord has spoken."

> **Prophecy of a forerunner**
>
> This prophecy of a forerunner to the Messiah was fulfilled by John the Baptist.

All flesh is grass, and its beauty like the flowers of the field; they will wither and fade when the Lord blows on them, but God's word will stand forever.

Those who bring good news need to shout it from a high place so all may hear. Our God rules with a mighty arm giving reward and payment where necessary. He will tend his flock like a shepherd, gently gathering them in his arm, close to his heart. The Lord is infinite and beyond measure. The nations are like a drop in a bucket or a speck of dust on a scale; they are worthless compared to him.

What can we compare to God, or what image can we make that is like him? Idols are just metal or wood that people have formed; they can't do anything. The Lord is far above all people and nations, and he sets them up and knocks them down as he pleases. You cannot hide from him because he created everything, he never gets tired, and his understanding is unlimited.

He gives power to the weak. Even youths get tired, and young men become exhausted, but those who wait for the Lord will renew their strength; they will soar on wings like eagles, run and not get tired, walk and not be faint.

The Lord says, "Listen to me in silence while we come together to decide what's right. I am the One who directs the course of history. I am the First and the Last; I have authority over everything. I am God. The earth sees me and trembles, but humanity seeks solace in its idols.

"Israel, you are my servant; descendants of Abraham, I have called you from the farthest ends of the earth. Do not be afraid because I am your God, and I am with you; I will uphold you with my righteous right hand. Those who rage against you will be ashamed and those who oppose you will die as nothing. Your enemies will disappear because the Lord God will be your helper. When the poor and needy cannot find water, I will answer them and not forsake them and give them abundant water to drink so that they understand that I have done this for them."

THE ONE TRUE GOD VERSUS IDOLS

The Lord says, "Idols, make your case and tell us what is going to happen. Tell us about the past so we can understand or tell us about the future to prove that you are gods; do something that inspires fear or terror. You are nothing, and your work is less than nothing, those who worship you are an abomination.

"I am bringing one from the north who will call on my name and stomp rulers into the mud the way a potter works the clay. Did any of you see this coming? I was the One who can proclaim the future. These idols are an illusion and an empty wind.

"Here is my servant whom I have chosen, and I delight in him; my Spirit is upon him, and he will bring justice to the nations. He will not cry out; he will not break a damaged reed or put out a faintly burning flame. He will not falter or be discouraged until he has established justice on the earth.

"I am the Lord, I have called you in righteousness, and I will keep you as a covenant for the people, a light to the nations. I will use you to open blind eyes and free prisoners. I am the Lord, and I do not share my glory with anyone, let alone idols. The past has happened, and now I declare what will happen in the future."

Sing a new song to the Lord and praise him from the ends of the earth. Let all peoples and all nature give glory to the Lord and proclaim his praise! The Lord will march out like a champion and triumph over his enemies.

For a long time, I have kept silent, but now I will cry out. The Lord will dry up the vegetation of the mountains and dry up pools of water. He will lead the blind in a way they don't know; he will turn their darkness into light and the rough places into level ground. Those who trust in idols will be put to shame.

Those of you who think they understand should pay attention because you've missed the main point. The Lord will magnify the Law and make it glorious for the sake of his righteousness. He sees the pain and devastation of his people, and it comes because of sin. But you have not paid attention, so the Lord has set your world on fire.

The Lord says, "Do not fear because I have redeemed you, I have called you by name, and you are mine. I will be with you when you pass through the waters and the fire; they will not destroy you. I am the Lord your God, the Holy One of Israel, your Savior. You are precious in my eyes, and I love you; do not be afraid because I will bring you from every direction of the earth, everyone who I have called for my glory. Bring out the blind and deaf, they will be my witnesses because there is no god before or after me; I am the only Savior.

"For your sake, I will bring them down to Babylon as fugitives; I am your Creator. Forget the past because I'm doing a new thing even though you don't understand. I will make a path in the wilderness and rivers in the desert. The wild animals praise me, but you have not called on me because you were tired. You have brought me your sins instead of offerings, but I will remove your sins for my own sake. Remember who I am and make your case before me. Your ancestors sinned and you have followed in their footsteps.

"Israel, I have chosen you, formed you in the womb, and will help you. Do not be afraid; I will pour out my Spirit on your offspring and my blessing on your descendants. They will spring up like grass in a meadow; this one will say, 'I am the Lord's,' and another will write on his hand, 'The Lord's,' and call himself by Israel.

"I am the First and the Last; there is no God besides me. No one else can declare the future; you are my witnesses of how I have done it in the past. I am the only Rock. Idols are nothing; they are made from metal or wood by someone who is only a man. They use some of the wood to build a house, some to build a fire, and some to build a god that they worship. They are ignorant because God has shut their eyes and hearts. They can't see that they are worshiping a block of wood and lies.

"Remember this because you are my servant, and I won't forget you. I have blotted out your sins; return to me because I have redeemed you. Heavens and earth, sing and shout these things, for the Lord has redeemed Israel. I am the Lord, who made all things and formed you in the womb."

The Lord says, "I will use Cyrus of Persia as my anointed to strip kings of their armor and open doors that cannot be closed. I will give him the treasures of the world and call him by name even though he doesn't know who I am. I will equip him so that people will know that I am the only God who can create light and darkness, well-being and calamity. Turn to me and be saved! Through me, the offspring of Jacob will be justified and glorified.

"I will give you the wealth of the surrounding nations if you follow me, and they will bow down to you and recognize my greatness. I declare what is right and there is no god besides me. Turn to me and be saved because every knee will bow and swear allegiance to my name. I alone will justify and glorify Israel."

SALVATION THROUGH THE LORD'S RIGHTEOUS SERVANT

> **The Lord's righteous servant**
>
> This is a reference to the coming Messiah. This next section contains many references to the person of Jesus.

The Lord called me before I was born; he has spoken my name since I was in my mother's womb. He made my mouth like a sharpened sword, he made me a polished arrow in his quiver. I believed that I labored in vain, but my reward is in the Lord's hand.

It is not too small of a thing for me to rescue Israel; I will also make you a light to the Gentiles so that salvation may reach the ends of the earth. Kings will see you and stand; princes will bow down because the Holy One of Israel has chosen you.

The Lord says, "I will answer in my time of favor and save you; I will make you a covenant for the people to restore the land and free the captives. They will no longer be hungry or thirsty; I will make my mountains a road and raise up the highways.

"Jerusalem may believe that I have forgotten, but I cannot forget you because I have engraved you on the palms of my hands. As sure as I live, you will one day wear ornaments like a bride; although you were desolate, you will be too numerous for the land. Your oppressors will eat their own flesh and drink their own blood like wine. Then all humanity will know that I am the Lord, your Savior, Redeemer, the Mighty One of Jacob.

"I sold you and sent you away because of your sins. When I called you, why didn't you answer? Was my arm too short to save, or do I lack the strength to rescue you? I can dry up the sea or turn rivers into a desert with a word; I can black out the heavens."

The Lord God helps me, and I am not disgraced; he will vindicate me, and he is near. Let my adversary come near because God will help me. They will wear out like a garment and be eaten by moths. Let them lie down in torment.

The Lord says, "Those who pursue righteousness and the Lord, listen to me and look to the rock that you were cut from, to Abraham and Sarah. He was only one man when I called him, but now he is a multitude. The Lord will comfort Jerusalem and look on her ruins with compassion.

"I will give instruction and my justice will become a light to the nations. My salvation is on the way and I will bring justice to the nations. Look to the heavens and earth because they will vanish like smoke, and its inhabitants will die like flies. But my salvation will last forever and my righteousness will never fail. Arm of the Lord, wake up and clothe yourself with strength. You cut Rahab to pieces and parted the Red Sea. Those that the Lord rescued will return and enter Jerusalem with singing and a crown of everlasting joy.

"I am the one who comforts you even though you are mere mortals; you have forgotten your Maker who stretched out the heavens and the earth. The prisoners will soon be set free; they will not die in prison, nor will they lack bread. I am the Lord your God who stirs up the sea, I have put my words in your mouth, and you are my people.

"Jerusalem, you have staggered though you are not drunk. But now I have taken the cup of my wrath away and you will never drink from it again. I will make your tormentors lie prostate and you will walk on them like a street.

HUMILIATION OF GOD'S HOLY ONE

"You were sold for nothing and you will be redeemed without money. My name is blasphemed all day and my people are mocked. But they will know my name because I have foretold it. How beautiful are the feet of those who bring the good news that God reigns! When the Lord returns to Jerusalem, they will see it with their own eyes. Burst into songs of joy because the Lord has comforted his people and redeemed Jerusalem. The Lord will show his holy arm and all the earth will see his salvation. Come out from there and be pure, and the Lord will protect you.

"My servant will act wisely; he will be lifted up and exalted. Many were appalled at him because he was marred beyond human likeness. He will shut their mouths because they will see what they did not see and understand what they have not heard.

"He grew up like a young plant from dry ground; he had no majesty that we should look at him or beauty that we should desire him. He was despised and rejected by men, a sorrowful man who knew grief; we rejected him. He has borne our grief and sorrow, was afflicted by God, but we did not esteem him. He was wounded and crushed for our sin, and his wounds heal us. We have all gone astray like sheep and we have all turned to our own way, but the Lord laid all our sin on him. He was oppressed and afflicted, but he did not open his mouth like a lamb led to slaughter. They killed him with the wicked and buried him with the rich even though he had done no violence and told no lie.

"It was God's will to crush him and make his soul into a guilt offering. He will prolong his days and God's will shall prosper in his hand. He will see and be satisfied out of the anguish of his soul and he will bear our sin. He will divide the spoil with the strong because he poured his soul out to death and was numbered with sinners. He took our sin and intercedes for us."

The Lord says, "Barren women, sing and shout for joy because you have more children than those with husbands. Enlarge your tent because you will prosper, and your descendants will dispossess nations and settle in their cities. Don't be afraid because you will not be ashamed any longer. Your Maker is your husband and Redeemer. I briefly deserted you, but I will bring you back with compassion.

"Just as I swore to Noah that the waters would never again destroy the earth, I swear that I am not angry with you any longer. The mountains and hills may pass away, but my steadfast love will not leave you. I will teach all your children and you will live in peace. You will be established in righteousness and far from terror. No weapon that has been formed will succeed against you and you will refute every tongue that rises against you in judgment.

"All of you who are thirsty and hungry should come to me and drink free water and eat free food. Why waste your money on something that cannot satisfy you? Listen to me and delight in the richest fare, because I will make an everlasting covenant with you. Foreign nations will come to you because the Lord has endowed you with splendor.

"Seek the Lord while you still can; let the wicked turn away from their path and return to God. He will have compassion on you and he will pardon your sins. My thoughts are not your thoughts and my ways are not your ways; as the heavens are higher than the earth, my thoughts and ways are higher than yours. In the same way, the rain and snow come from heaven and cause the land to sprout with seed for the sower and bread for the eater, I speak, and my words accomplish the purpose I intended.

"You will go out in joy and be led in peace; the mountains and the hills will break forth in song and the trees of the field will clap their hands. My word will make an everlasting name for the Lord."

The Lord says, "Maintain justice and righteousness because I will reveal my salvation and deliverance soon. Blessed are those who hold fast, keep the Sabbath, and refrain from doing evil. The Lord will not exclude foreigners or eunuchs but will bring them to his holy mountain and give them joy, for my house will be a house of prayer.

"The righteous die and no one takes it to heart; no one understands that they are taken away to be spared from evil; those who walk uprightly enter peace and find rest in death. Who do you think you're mocking? Your spiritual adultery betrays how you really feel about me. Your works and idols cannot deliver you. But those who trust me will possess the land; I will remove all stumbling blocks from their path."

The Lord says, "I dwell in the high and holy place and with the lowly. I will not always be angry; I struck them because of their sin, I have seen their ways, but I will heal, lead, and comfort them. Peace to the far and near, I will keep them. But the wicked are tossed like the sea and there is no peace for them.

> **Prophecies about the Messiah**
>
> This section of Isaiah contains many prophecies of Jesus' coming. It is meant to comfort the captives in their distress and tells us many things about his birth and ministry.

THE REDEEMER'S KINGDOM

"Cry out and do not hold back, declare their sin to my people. Yet they daily seek me and delight to know my ways as if they were a righteous nation who did not forsake their God. I ignore their fasting because they pursue their own pleasure and oppress their workers.

"The fast I chose is for people to humble themselves, loosen the bonds of wickedness, and break the yoke of oppression. Share your bread with the hungry, house the homeless, and clothe the naked. Then light will break forth like the dawn and I will heal and protect you. I will listen to your prayer if you pour yourself out for them. Then I will guide you and satisfy your desires. You will rebuild your ancient ruins and restore them. If you honor and delight in me, you will ride on the heights of the earth."

The Lord's hand is not too short to save, and his ear is not so dull that it cannot hear, but your sin has separated you from your God, and he has hidden his face from you.

Our hands shed innocent blood, we have spoken lies, and there is no justice in our path. Therefore, justice is far away and we grope around like a blind man. We search for salvation, but our sins are too numerous. They testify against us and are the reason justice and righteousness stand far off.

That's why the Lord was angry; he wondered why there was no one to intercede. Since no one would lead them to righteousness, he did it himself. He put on righteousness as a breastplate and salvation as a helmet. He clothed himself with vengeance and zeal. He will repay his enemies with fury and they will fear his name.

The Lord declares, "A Redeemer will come to Israel; my covenant is with them. My Spirit is upon you, and I will put my words in your mouth forever."

Arise and shine because the glory of the Lord has shone upon you. Darkness will cover the earth, but the Lord will arise upon you, and the world will come to see your light as the Lord brings you back to him. They will rejoice at your abundance and wealth. You will be a source of hope to the world because God has made you beautiful.

Those who afflicted you will bow down at your feet and will recognize Jerusalem as the City of the Lord. While you have been forsaken and hated, I will restore your greatness and give you the best the world has to offer. You will know that the Lord is your Savior and Redeemer. You will no longer have violence and destruction, but your walls will be called salvation and your gates, praise.

You will not need the sun or moon because the Lord will be your everlasting light and glory. Your sun will never go down and your mourning will be over. Your people will be righteous and will inherit the land forever, so that I may be glorified.

The Spirit of the Sovereign Lord is on me because he has anointed me to proclaim good news to the poor, bind up the brokenhearted, proclaim freedom for the captive, and the year of the Lord's favor and God's vengeance. They will be oaks of righteousness and they will rebuild the ancient ruins.

The Lord says, "You will hire workers to do your labor and you will be priests of the Lord. You will feed on the nations' wealth because I love justice and hate wrongdoing; I will reward my people and make an everlasting covenant with them. The nations will know their descendants and they will know that the Lord has blessed them."

I delight in the Lord and my soul rejoices in him. He has clothed me with salvation and righteousness. As the soil makes plants grow, the Sovereign Lord will make righteousness and praise spring up before the world.

I will speak up for Jerusalem's sake until her righteousness shines like a burning torch. The Lord will call you by a new name and you will be God's beautiful crown. The Lord will delight in you and God will rejoice over you as a husband rejoices over his bride.

The Lord has sworn by his power, "I will not allow foreign nations to indulge in the fruits of your labor. Your salvation and reward are coming and you will be the Lord's holy people. I have poured out my vengeance, and now the day of redemption is here. No one else could do this, so I did it myself."

I will tell of the Lord's kindness and compassion for which he is to be praised. They are his children and he has become their Savior. He was distressed by their affliction and he has redeemed them. Yet they rebelled and grieved his Holy Spirit, so he became their enemy and fought against them.

But the Lord remembered his promises to his people; they returned to him and he gave them rest. Look down from your lofty throne in heaven and show your tenderness and compassion. You are our Father, our Redeemer; bring us back to you for your name's sake. We possessed your holy place for a little while, but now our enemies have trampled down your sanctuary.

If only you would tear open heaven and come down so that the mountains would tremble before you; come down and make your enemies and the nations afraid! You have done extraordinary things that we didn't expect; there is no other God besides you who acts on behalf of those who wait for him. You come to the help of the righteous, but when we continued in sin, you were angry.

How can we be saved? We are unclean, and all our righteous acts are like menstrual rags in your sight; we dry up and our sins sweep us away. No one calls on you because you have hidden your face from us and given us over to our sins.

But you are our Father; you are the potter, and we are the clay, the work of your hands. Don't be angry with us or remember our sins forever. Listen to us when we pray because our land is a wasteland and Jerusalem is desolate. Our holy and glorious temple has been burned and lies in ruins. Don't hold yourself back and punish us beyond measure!

The Lord says, "I revealed myself to those who did not ask for me and was found by those who did not seek me. I presented myself to a nation that did not call my name and reach out to a nation pursuing its own gain that continually provokes me. They make themselves unclean but still think they are too holy. They are smoke in my nostrils and I will pay them back in full.

"But I will not destroy all of them, I will bring a portion of them into my land, and my servants will live there. But those who forsake me will taste my wrath. I called for you, but you did not answer; you did evil and displeased me.

"My servants will eat and drink, but you will be hungry and thirsty; they will rejoice, but you will be put to shame. Whoever invokes a blessing in the land will do so by the one true God and I will hide the past troubles from my eyes.

NEW HEAVENS AND EARTH

"I will create new heavens and earth, and the past things will be forgotten. Rejoice in what I create because Jerusalem will be a delight and its people a joy. I will rejoice over Jerusalem and delight in my people; there will be no more tears. Infants will not die and anyone who doesn't live to a hundred will be considered a child. They will enjoy the fruit of their labor and I will bless them. I will answer them before they call, and the predator and prey will live together in peace.

"Heaven is my throne, and the earth is my footstool; nothing you could build for me would suffice. But I will look upon those who are humble and contrite in spirit and fear my word.

"Your empty religious rituals are worthless in my eyes; those who offer an animal may as well kill another person. Just as you have chosen your abominations, I will choose your delusions. I will make your fears a reality because you did not listen when I called you. Your empty platitudes will only bring shame.

"Rejoice over Jerusalem because I will extend peace to her like a river and she will care for you like a newborn baby. I will comfort you in Jerusalem, you will see, and your heart will rejoice. The Lord's servants will know him and he will show indignation against his enemies."

The Lord will come in fire to execute his furious anger and judge all flesh with the sword; he will kill many. The abominable will end because he knows their thoughts, and they will see his glory. The Lord says, "As the new heavens and earth that I make will remain, so will your offspring and name. All will come before me to worship and they will see the bodies of those who rebelled against me. The worm will not die, the fire will not be quenched, and they will be loathed by all."

CHAPTER EIGHT

GOD WILL JUDGE HIS ENEMIES
Micah 1-7

> **The Book of Micah**
>
> Micah was a contemporary of Isaiah and he wrote this book during the Assyrian crisis of the last part of the eighth century B.C. We don't know much about Micah, but he spoke about both Israel and Judah's downfall. Throughout the book, he alternates between oracles of doom and hope, and declares Israel's future glory through the coming Messiah.

JUDGMENT FOR PAST SINS

Listen to me, all people of the world, Judah and Israel's sins have made the Lord angry, and now he is going to leave his throne and stomp the high places of the earth. The mountains will melt beneath his feet, and the valleys will split apart like wax from the flame, like water down a steep incline.

He will make Samaria into a heap in the open country, destroyed and laid bare. God will obliterate all her idols and burn up her wages. She collected them from a prostitute's fee, and thus they shall return.

> **Samaria**
>
> Samaria is another name for the northern tribes of the divided kingdom.

Therefore, I will mourn; I will go about naked, wailing like a jackal or an ostrich. Don't weep for Judah; her wound is incurable. This is inevitable, they are going into exile, and they aren't coming back.

Woe to those who devise wicked schemes while lying in bed and then carry it out in the morning. They seize property and oppress people for their inheritance. But the Lord is devising a disaster against them and he will ruin them.

You have not listened to the prophets, so they stopped speaking. God is not the problem; your sin has brought your punishment. Leave this place because you have ruined it. You would listen to any preacher, regardless of his lies. But the Lord will gather the remnant of his people and shepherd his flock.

***

Leaders of Israel, you should do justice rather than flay the skin from my people and eat their flesh. They will cry to the Lord, but he will not answer because of their evil deeds.

The Lord says, "To the prophets who proclaim peace when they have something to eat and declare war on the hungry. You will have no visions and I will not answer your cries. You hate justice and pervert what is right; you give judgment for a bribe. Yet you think I am in your midst, because you use my name. Jerusalem will be plowed like a field, and it will become a heap of ruins because of you."

PROPHECIES OF FUTURE GLORY

In the last days, the mountain of the house of the Lord will be lifted up, and all peoples will run to it so that God may teach them his paths. He will judge between many peoples, and they will turn their weapons into farm tools, making peace around the world. No one will terrify them and we will walk in the name of the Lord forever and ever.

On that day, the Lord will gather the afflicted and lame and make them into a remnant; then, he will rule over them in Mount Zion for all eternity. But for now, writhe in pain like a woman in labor. You will go to Babylon, but eventually, the Lord will redeem you from the hand of your enemies.

Many hate you and rejoice in your downfall, but they don't understand God's plan to gather his people together. Daughter of Jerusalem, arise because the Lord will make you strong and give you the earth's wealth.

Bethlehem, you are tiny among the clans of Judah, but the Lord's ruler will come from you. He will lead the Israelites, and he will shepherd his flock in the strength and majesty of the Lord, and he will be their peace. He will deliver you from the Assyrians.

> **Jesus' birthplace**
>
> This is a prophecy that the Messiah would be born in Bethlehem; this was fulfilled by Jesus.

Then Judah will be like dew from the Lord and the remnant will be like a lion among the beasts of the forest. God will cut off your enemies' sin and execute his vengeance on the nations that do not obey. On that day, he will cut off your idolatry and tear away your witchcraft.

GOD'S CASE AGAINST ISRAEL

The Lord declares, "How have I failed you? I brought you out of Egypt and redeemed you from slavery. Don't forget how I saved you from your enemies."

The Lord is not pleased with many sacrifices, not even with a firstborn to pay for sin. He has shown you what is good and what he requires: to do justice, love kindness, and walk humbly with your God.

The Lord cries out to the city, "I cannot ignore sin; therefore, I will strike you with a deep blow and make you desolate. Your rich men are full of violence and your mouths are filled with lies; therefore, I will strike you with a grievous blow. You will eat, but still be hungry; save, but not have enough because I will devour it; plant but not reap the harvest. I will make you desolate because you have walked in wickedness."

Woe is me! Our sin has left us impoverished. The godly have died, and there are no upright men left; everyone waits for blood and hunts each other. Their hands do evil; princes and judges ask for bribes. The best of them are no better than thorns; do not trust them. But I will wait for the God of my salvation and he will hear me.

My enemies should not rejoice over me because I will rise when I fall, and the Lord will be a light to me in darkness. I will bear the Lord's anger until he vindicates me because I have sinned. They think God has abandoned me, but a day is coming where he will restore his people.

Lord, shepherd your people and let them graze in peace as in the past. Show them marvelous things so that the nations will be ashamed of their strength and turn in fear to the Lord.

There is no God like you who forgives the sin of his remnant. But you do not stay angry forever because of your steadfast love. You will have compassion on us again and will throw our sins into the depths of the sea. You will show faithfulness to Jacob and everlasting love to Abraham as you swore to our fathers.

CHAPTER NINE

JUDGMENT ON NINEVEH

Nahum 1-3

> **The Book of Nahum**
>
> The Book of Nahum is an exception in the prophets in that it concerned only foreign events. It was a pronouncement of the Lord's judgment against Nineveh and served as an encouragement to Judah's people. Jonah went to the wicked city around a century before, and Nahum writes his prophecy sometime around 650 B.C.

God is a jealous and wrathful God who takes vengeance on his enemies. He is slow to anger and great in power, but he will judge the guilty. He causes the earth to melt before him; who can stand before his indignation? He is good, but no one can stand before him.

The Lord says, "Even though Israel's enemies are at full strength, I will cut them off, and they will not afflict Israel anymore. I will cut off false gods and make them worthless." How beautiful are the feet of those who bring good news and peace? Oh Judah, keep your vows and observe your feasts because God is cutting off the worthless.

Gird yourselves for battle because God is restoring the glory of Israel. God will destroy Nineveh and they will fall. Even though they have great wealth, he will bring them low because the Lord is against them. He will burn their chariots with smoke and devour them with the sword.

Woe to the bloody city of Nineveh because the Lord will bring heaps of dead bodies upon them. God is against them because they have chased after false gods, and he will make them a spectacle amongst all the nations of the world. All who look upon them will be appalled because God will destroy them.

They will fall before their enemies and the sword will devour them. Even though they have many merchants, God will scatter them on the mountains with no one to gather them together. No one can stop their pain and the nations will rejoice because of their suffering.

CHAPTER TEN

THE DAY OF THE LORD
Zephaniah 1-3

> **The Book of Zephaniah**
>
> The prophet Zephaniah was a contemporary of Jeremiah during Josiah's reign in Judah (640-609 B.C.). He likely wrote before 622 B.C. because much of what he wrote mirrors Josiah's reforms that year. He was a person of high social standing and a descendant of Hezekiah, a king of Judah.
>
> One of Zephaniah's central themes is the Day of the Lord, which signifies that the way things were going was ending. He did not specify what this would look like, but it was a clear call to repentance.

The Lord declares, "I am going to sweep away everything from the face of the earth, every person and beast. I am going to stretch out my hand against Judah, and I am going to cut off the remnant of Baal, his idolatrous priests, and those who worship him even though they swear by me."

Be silent before the Lord God! The Day of the Lord is near, he has prepared a sacrifice, and he is preparing to punish those who fill their master's house with violence and fraud. He will punish the complacent who think that God will not act and plunder their wealth.

The great Day of the Lord is coming quickly, and it will be a bitter day of wrath, anguish, devastation, darkness, and a battle cry against fortified cities. He will bring distress to humanity and they will stumble along like the blind because they have sinned against God. Nothing will save them on the day of his wrath and fire will consume the earth.

Those who obey his commands, seek righteousness and humility should seek the Lord before the day of his wrath. Woe to foreign nations because God is going to displace them and restore Israel's fortunes. He will punish the nations for their pride and make them bow down before him.

Woe to Jerusalem, the rebellious and oppressing city, because she refuses to listen or accept correction. She doesn't trust the Lord, and her leaders are violent and treacherous. But the Lord is righteous and just; he will make them listen and accept correction. Wait for him to arise and seize his prey because he will gather the nations together to pour out his anger upon them.

Then he will make his people's speech pure so that they may call upon the Lord and serve him. On that day, we will not be ashamed by our rebellious deeds because God will remove the proud and haughty from our midst. He will leave the humble and lowly, and they will seek refuge in the Lord; they will pursue justice and truth.

Daughter of Jerusalem, rejoice and exult with all your heart because the Lord has taken away the judgments against you and cleared away your enemies. The Lord is in your midst; the mighty one will save you and rejoice over you with gladness. He will quiet you with his love and exult over you with loud singing. At that time, he will deal with your enemies and restore your fortunes before your eyes.

CHAPTER ELEVEN

GOD'S JUSTICE FOR FOREIGN NATIONS
Habakkuk 1-3

> **The Book of Habakkuk**
>
> We don't know much about the prophet Habakkuk. However, we know that he wrote during the transition period between the Assyrians and Babylonians being the region's primary powers. We can estimate that he wrote this book around 630 B.C. and it deals with God's policy for justice for foreign nations. Habakkuk wrestles with how God has not punished the Babylonians' wickedness, but the Lord makes it clear that he will eventually punish their sin.

HABAKKUK'S FIRST PRAYER AND GOD'S RESPONSE

Habakkuk cried out to the Lord, "How long will I cry out to you and you not listen? How long will I cry out 'violence' and you won't save? Why do you allow me to see sin, violence, and oppression and not act? The Law is paralyzed, and the wicked surround the righteous and pervert justice."

Then God answered, "Look among the nations and be astounded because I am doing a work that you would not believe. I am raising up the Babylonians, a dreaded nation who destroy everything in their path. They gather captives like sand and laugh at those who resist them because their might is their god."

HABAKKUK'S SECOND PRAYER AND GOD'S RESPONSE

Habakkuk cried out again, "My God, you are everlasting, and you have ordained them to be our reproof and discipline. You have pure eyes, so why do you allow the wicked to swallow up the righteous. They rejoice over their evil and make sacrifices to their plans to destroy. Will they keep killing forever? I will watch to see what you say and speak whatever I hear."

The Lord answered, "Write down what I say to you because I will answer you with visions that will come true. Their souls are puffed up within them, but the righteous shall live by faith. Their greed is insatiable, and just like the grave, they will never have enough.

"The Babylonians will not last forever because one day, those in their debt will arise, and the Babylonians will become spoils for those that they oppressed. Woe to those who gain by evil to make their houses secure; they have made their own shame because they have forfeited their own lives by cutting off others' lives. They weary themselves for nothing, but the knowledge of the Lord will fill the earth.

"Woe to those who make their neighbors drink because they will have their fill of shame instead of glory. Their violence will eventually overwhelm them. Woe to those who make an idol because they ask advice from either wood or metal; it cannot give wisdom because it has no breath. But I am holy and all the earth will be silent before me."

HABAKKUK'S PRAYER

Then Habakkuk prayed to the Lord, "I have heard of your work, and I fear you; amidst your wrath, remember mercy. You have shown your light, and it has veiled your power, but disease has followed at your heels. You have measured the earth and shaken the nations before you. Everything stands still because of your wrath and you have crushed the house of the wicked. I hear what you have done, and I tremble before you, and I will wait quietly for the day that you have promised.

"Even though trouble will come upon us, I will rejoice in the Lord and take joy in the God of my salvation. God is my strength and he puts me in safe places."

CHAPTER TWELVE

JEREMIAH'S CALL AND GOD'S FIRST WARNING

Jeremiah 1-6

> **The Book of Jeremiah**
>
> The Book of Jeremiah occupies more space than any other book in the Bible, and Jeremiah gives us insight into his struggle with his role as a prophet to a very sinful people. He began his ministry in 625 B.C. as the Babylonians were supplanting the Assyrians in power and Josiah was making his reforms in Judah. In 605, he had his assistant Baruch write down his prophecies, and he continued his ministry until he died in 570.

JEREMIAH'S CALL

The word of the Lord came to me, saying, "I knew you before I formed you in the womb and set you apart to be a prophet to the nations."

I replied, "But Lord, I am too young, and I don't know how to speak."

But the Lord replied, "Don't say you're too young; you must go where I command and to whom I tell you. Don't be afraid because I am with you and will rescue you."

Then the Lord reached out his hand and touched my mouth, saying, "I have put my words in your mouth. I am appointing you over nations and kingdoms to uproot and tear down, destroy and overthrow, build, and plant."

The Lord showed me an almond tree and said, "I am watching that my word is fulfilled."

Then he showed me a boiling pot tilted to the north and said, "I will pour out disaster on the north; I am about to summon all the people of the northern kingdom of Israel. Their kings will set up their thrones at the gates of Jerusalem and come against Judah's towns. I will pronounce my judgments on my people because they have forsaken me and worship false gods.

"Stand up and say what I command you, or I will make you dismayed. Don't be afraid because I am making you like an iron pillar to stand against the kings of Judah and its officials. They will fight against you but will not succeed because I will rescue you."

The Lord came to me and said, "Proclaim to Jerusalem that I remember the devotion of your youth and how you loved me and followed me in the wilderness. Israel was holy to the Lord and I destroyed all her enemies.

"What fault did your ancestors find in me that they turned away and followed worthless idols? I brought you into fertile land with good produce, but you defiled my land and made my inheritance detestable. Your priests did not search for me and they went after false gods.

"Therefore, I will bring charges against you and your children's children. Nations don't change their gods, but my people have exchanged me for worthless idols. They have forsaken me and relied on broken wells that cannot hold water. Israel was not born to be a slave, yet its towns are burned and deserted. You have brought this on yourselves by forsaking the Lord your God.

"Long ago, you broke off the bonds of slavery, but now you have laid down as a prostitute on every high hill and under every broad tree. I had planted you as a choice vine, but you have rebelled and become a corrupt, wild vine. Even if you wash with soap, your guilt is still before me.

"You are defiled and have run after idols; don't run until your feet are bare and your throat is dry. All of you are disgraced, and you worship blocks of wood and ask them to save you. Let your false gods save you if they can! You have not responded to correction and your sword has devoured your prophets like a hungry lion. You have forgotten me for far too long and have stained yourself with innocent blood. Despite all of this, you claim you are innocent, but I will make you ashamed because I reject those that you trust.

"If a man divorces his wife and she marries another man, he should not return to her again. You live like a prostitute with many lovers. Are you going to return to me now? You have defiled the land with your prostitution and wickedness. I have withheld the showers, but you still brazenly refuse to blush with shame. You call me your friend, but you sin as much as possible."

CONDEMNATION OF JUDAH

The Lord came to me again and said, "Israel has gone up on every high hill and under every broad tree to commit adultery. I thought she would return to me, but she did not, and now her unfaithful sister Judah has seen it. I gave Israel a certificate of divorce for her adulteries, and now her sister Judah has gone and done the same thing.

"Faithless Israel is more righteous than unfaithful Judah. Tell Israel to return and I will no longer be angry because I am faithful. Just acknowledge your guilt because you have rebelled and not obeyed me. I am your husband, and I will give you shepherds who follow my heart and lead you with knowledge and understanding.

"In those days, you will no longer need the ark of the covenant because Jerusalem will be the Lord's throne, and the nations will gather there to honor the name of the Lord. They will no longer follow their stubborn, evil hearts. Israel and Judah will rejoin in the Promised Land.

"I want to treat you like my children and give you the pleasant land, the most beautiful inheritance of any nation. I thought you would call me Father and follow me, but you have been unfaithful. Faithless people, return to me, and I will cure you of your backsliding."

Lord, we come to you, because you are our God. Our idolatry is a lie and you alone are our salvation. We have sinned against you just as our ancestors have.

The Lord continued, "If you will return to me, put your idols away, and follow me, then the nations will invoke my blessings and boast in me. Circumcise your hearts or my wrath will burn like fire because of your evil.

"Sound the trumpet in Judah and flee to the fortified cities because I am bringing disaster from the north. Your towns will lay in ruins; therefore, lament and wail because I am angry. Kings and priests will lose heart and be horrified; the prophets will be appalled."

Then Jeremiah said, "Alas, Sovereign Lord! You have deceived the people by proclaiming peace when the sword is at our throats."

The Lord said, "Jerusalem, wash the evil from your heart and be saved. An army is coming from a distant land and will surround Judah's cities because she has rebelled against me. My people are fools; they do not know me, but they know how to sin. The whole land will be ruined, but I will not completely destroy it."

All of this made Jeremiah's heart sick. He cried out, "How long will I have to see this desolation? I saw the earth, formless and void; every person and animal fled and the land was in darkness. The Lord's anger destroyed everything."

> **Jeremiah's depression**
>
> Throughout this book, Jeremiah writes about his sorrow and depression. Sometimes, obeying the Lord does not bring comfort; it results in distress. However, he obeyed, just as we must.

The Lord continued, "Go throughout Jerusalem, and if you can find anyone who deals honestly and seeks truth. If you do, I will forgive this city."

I thought, "Lord, you look for truth; you struck them, and they felt no pain, you crushed them, but they refused correction. These are the poor and foolish; they don't know the Lord or his requirements. So, I will speak to their leaders because surely they know the way of the Lord." But they have torn off their bonds as well.

The Lord declares, "How can I forgive them? I gave them everything they needed, but they have forsaken me and run after false gods. I will avenge myself on this nation because they do not belong to me. They have lied about me and believed they would never see sword or famine. The prophets are like wind and my word is not in them.

"So, I will make my words in your mouth like a burning fire. Tell them that I am bringing a distant nation against them, and they will devour your children and your land. But even in those days, I will not destroy you. I should be feared, yet you have turned away. Your sins have deprived you of good and the wicked among you have waited to trap people to become rich and powerful. They oppress the fatherless and poor. I will avenge myself on a people like this. My people love acting however they want, but what will you do when I bring it to an end?

"I will destroy the beautiful and delicate Jerusalem. An army from Assyria will come to attack because she should be punished for all her oppression. She pours out her wickedness like water, and she is full of violence and destruction. Her inhabitants' ears are closed so they cannot hear me; they are offended by my word. I am full of wrath and cannot hold it in, so I will stretch out my hand on those who live in the land.

"They are all greedy for gain and they are not ashamed by their detestable conduct. They will fall and I will punish them."

STAND AT THE CROSSROADS

The Lord says, "Stand at the crossroads and look, ask for the ancient paths and walk in the good way, then you will find rest for your souls. But you have refused to listen, so I will bring disaster on these people because they have rejected me. Your offerings and sacrifices do not please me, so I will put obstacles before them; parents and children will stumble over them, friends and neighbors will perish. I have rejected them."

Jeremiah heard these words and was depressed. He called for his people to mourn and hide from the coming terror.

CHAPTER THIRTEEN

FURTHER WARNINGS AGAINST JUDAH

Jeremiah 7-19

The Lord told Jeremiah to stand in the temple and proclaim, "Those who come to worship God should listen: change your ways, practice justice, stop oppressing the weak, and stop following other gods, and then I will let you live here. You are fooling yourselves if you think you can steal, murder, commit adultery, lie, and worship other gods and believe I will protect you when you come to this temple. I will throw you out of my presence like I did Israel.

"Do not pray for these people because I will not listen. I will pour out my anger and wrath on this place and burn them with unquenchable fire. I commanded obedience rather than sacrifice and sent my prophets to them every single day. But they didn't listen because they have stubborn, evil hearts. They have done evil by setting up their detestable idols in my house and building the high places to worship; I never even considered commanding them to do that. Beware, because you will become a Valley of Slaughter, and I will make the land desolate.

"Then, the bones of the kings and officials of Judah will be unearthed and lie on the ground like dung. All the survivors of this evil nation prefer death to life.

"When people fall, they get up, and when they turn away, they return; but Israel has turned away and refuses to come back. They refuse to repent and each of them pursues their own desires. Animals know what they're supposed to do, but my people don't know God's requirements.

"How can you think you understand my commands with the way you're acting? The wise will be put to shame and become trapped; since they have rejected me, they don't really have wisdom. Therefore, I will give their wives to other men and their fields to new owners. They are all greedy liars and make people feel at peace when they should be afraid. They should be ashamed, but they don't even know how to blush. Therefore, I will punish them."

Jeremiah was overwhelmed with grief and he wept for his people. The Lord said, "My people do not know me. Don't trust your friends or family because they all tell lies and wear themselves out with their sin. They deserve punishment and I will reduce Jerusalem to a heap of ruins. They have abandoned me and disobeyed my commands. I will feed them with bitterness and poison; I will scatter them in places they've never even heard of and chase them with the sword.

"Weep for Jerusalem and teach your daughters how to wail. Death has crept in through our windows and killed the flower of our youth. Don't let the wise boast in their wisdom, the powerful in their power, nor the rich in their riches. People should boast in knowing that I am the Lord, who demonstrates unfailing love and brings justice and righteousness to the earth. I will soon punish those who are circumcised in body, but not in spirit."

WARNING AGAINST IDOLATRY

The Lord says to Israel, "Do not learn the ways of the nations or be terrified by the signs that terrify them. The people's practices are worthless; they make an idol out of a tree and adorn it with precious metals. They are no better than a scarecrow in a cucumber field; they cannot speak or walk; do not fear them; they are impotent."

Jeremiah said, "No one is like you, Lord; you are great, and your name is mighty. All people should fear you because there is no one like you. You are the true, living God and eternal King; the earth trembles at your anger and no one can endure your wrath. You made the heavens and the earth and causes nature to run its course. Idols are worthless frauds and they will die when judgment comes.

"Lord, we are fools and have not sought you! I know that people's lives are not their own and they do not direct their steps. Do not discipline me in your wrath, or you will destroy me. Pour out your wrath on the nations who do not call on your name."

***

The Lord said to Jeremiah, "Listen to the terms of this covenant and tell it to the people of Judah and Jerusalem. Those who do not obey are cursed, but I will fulfill the oath I swore to your ancestors for those who follow. You had better obey my commands, so that you will be my people and I will be your God."

Jeremiah replied, "So be it, Lord."

The Lord said, "From the time I brought you out of Egypt until today, I have warned you to obey me, but you did not, so I brought all the curses from the covenant on you. Don't even bother praying for these people. The Lord Almighty, who planted you, has decreed disaster for both Israel and Judah because they have done evil by worshiping false gods. I will punish and bring disaster upon them."

JEREMIAH'S COMPLAINT

Jeremiah complained to the Lord, "You are always righteous, but why do the wicked prosper and the faithless live at ease? You know me and my thoughts; drag them off like sheep to be slaughtered! The land is parched and withered because of the wicked; they think nothing will happen to them."

God answered, "If racing against men wore you out, you will not be able to compete with horses, and if you stumbled on smooth ground, you will fall in the thickets. Even your own family has betrayed you; don't trust them.

"I will forsake my house and abandon my inheritance because they have ruined my vineyards and pleasant fields. I will devour them and they will bear the shame of their harvest because of my fierce anger. I will uproot my wicked neighbors who seize Israel's inheritance from their lands, and then I will have compassion and bring Judah back to their own country."

THE RUINED BELT

The Lord told me to buy a linen belt and put it around my waist. Then he told me to take the belt and hide it in a crevice in the rocks. Many days later, he told me to go dig it up, and it was ruined and completely useless.

Then the Lord said, "In the same way I ruin Judah's pride and these wicked people who worship false gods will be like this belt – completely useless! I had bound Israel and Judah to me like a belt is wrapped around the waist, but they have not listened.

"I am going to make this land drunk and smash them against each other to destroy them. Give glory to God before it's too late. If you wonder why this happens, it is because you have forgotten me and run after false gods."

DROUGHT

The Lord sent a drought upon the land and said, "The people search for water and are dismayed when they cannot find it. The animals go hungry and thirsty because of your sin."

Jeremiah replied, "Even though our sins testify against us, act for your name's sake. Don't be a stranger to us. You are in our midst; please do not leave us."

The Lord answered, "These people have always loved to wander, so I cannot accept them. Don't waste your time praying for them, because I am going to consume them by the sword, famine, and disease."

Jeremiah said, "But Lord, the other prophets say that we will have rest and plenty."

The Lord answered, "I did not send them and I didn't tell them to say that. They are worthless and I will pour out their evil upon them. Tell them to weep over the ruin of my people."

Jeremiah replied, "Do you hate us now? Is it not possible for us to heal? We acknowledge our sins and the sins of our ancestors. Don't forsake us forever. Remember your covenant with us because you are our only hope and the only one who can send rain."

Then God said, "Even if Moses and Samuel stood before me, my heart would not go out to these people. Send them away to their destiny: death, sword, starvation, or captivity. I will make them abhorrent to the kingdoms of the earth because of what Manasseh did.

"Jerusalem, no one will pity you or mourn because you have rejected me and keep on backsliding. I am tired of holding back, so I will reach out to destroy you. I will make your widows more numerous than the sand of the sea and destroy the mothers of young men in anguish and terror."

Jeremiah complained, "I am sorry that my mother gave birth to me because everyone curses me. Lord, remember me and care for me, avenge me on my persecutors. You are long-suffering, don't take me away because I suffer reproach for your sake. I ate your words and they gave me joy because I bear your name, Lord God Almighty. I was a loner because your hand was on me and no one wanted to hear what I had to say. My pain has no bounds and wounds are incurable."

The Lord replied, "If they repent, I will restore them that they may serve me; you will be my spokesman if you utter worthy words; they will turn to you, but you must not turn to them. I will make you like a fortified wall of bronze to them; they will fight against you, but they will not be victorious because I will save you from their hands."

JEREMIAH TO BE CHILDLESS

The Lord spoke to Jeremiah, "You must not marry or have children because this land's children will die of deadly diseases, no one will mourn them, and they will lie on the ground like dung. They will die by sword and famine and wild animals will eat their flesh.

"Do not enter houses of either mourning or feasting because I will end all of it. When the people ask why the Lord has decreed this disaster, tell them it's because your ancestors forsook me and worshiped false gods. But you have been more wicked than them, so I will throw you out of this land into a land that none of you have known.

"But days are coming when people will not swear by the God who brought the Israelites out of Egypt, but by the God who brought them back from the north. I will restore them into the land of their ancestors and bring them from everywhere on earth. I see all of their sin and how they have defiled the land with their detestable idols."

Jeremiah replied, "Lord, my strength and fortress, my refuge in distress, our ancestors possessed nothing but false gods that did not help them. Therefore, you will teach them, and they will know your name is the Lord."

TRUST GOD, NOT MAN

The Lord says, "Judah's sin is engraved with an iron tool on their hearts and horns of their altars. You will lose the inheritance I gave you through your own fault, and I will enslave you to your enemies in a foreign land.

"Cursed are those who trust in man and turn their hearts away from the Lord. They will be like a bush in the wastelands and they will not see prosperity. But blessed is the one who trusts in the Lord; they will be like a tree planted by the water that flourishes and never fails to bear fruit.

"The heart is deceitful above all things; the Lord examines it and rewards each person according to their conduct and gives what they deserve."

Jeremiah prayed, "The Lord is the hope of Israel and all who forsake him will be put to shame. Heal me, Lord, and I will be healed, save me, and I will be saved because you are the One I praise.

"I have not run away from being your shepherd; you know I have not desired your despair. Do not terrorize me because you are my refuge on the day of disaster. Let my persecutors be put to shame, but keep me from terror."

***

The Lord said, "People of Judah and Jerusalem, hear the Word of the Lord, do not break the Sabbath by doing work like your ancestors did. But if you are careful to obey me, then the kings will sit on David's throne forever. If you do not obey, I will kindle an unquenchable fire in the gates of Jerusalem that will consume her fortresses."

POTTER AND THE CLAY

The Lord told me to go to the potter's house and I saw him working at his wheel. The pot he was making was defective, so he crushed it and made another one. Then he said, "I can do with Israel just like the potter does with the clay. I can declare any nation to rise or fall that I wish and can reconsider whenever I want.

"People of Judah, I am preparing a disaster for you, so turn from your evil ways and change your actions. But you will refuse because you have forgotten me, so your land will become an object of horror, and all who see it will be appalled."

JEREMIAH'S PRAYER OF VENGEANCE

Jeremiah prayed, "The people have made plans against me. But good should not be repaid evil, so give their children over to famine and the power of the sword. Let their men be put to death because they have dug a pit to capture me. Lord, you know their plots to kill me, do not forgive their crimes, deal with them in your anger."

JEREMIAH SMASHES A JAR

The Lord told Jeremiah to take some of the elders and priests with him to buy a clay jar and then take it to the Potsherd gate and say, "The Lord is going to bring a disaster on this place because they have forsaken me and made this a place of foreign gods and filled it with the innocent's blood. They have built high places to offer their children to idols, something he never thought about commanding. The days are coming when he will call this place the Valley of Slaughter. He will ruin the plans of Judah and Jerusalem and make them fall before our enemies. He will kill our children, and our enemies will eat their flesh."

Jeremiah smashed the jar and said, "The Lord will smash this nation and this city just like I smashed this jar. He will defile the houses of those who burn incense to foreign gods."

Then Jeremiah went into the temple and proclaimed, "The Lord is going to bring disaster on this city because we are stiff-necked and would not listen to his words."

CHAPTER FOURTEEN

JEREMIAH'S WARNINGS TO THE KING
Jeremiah 20-29

JEREMIAH ARRESTED

When the priest Pashhur heard Jeremiah prophesying these things, he had Jeremiah put in the stocks at the Lord's temple. The next day when they released Jeremiah, the prophet said to Pashhur, "The Lord's name for you is Terror on Every Side. The Lord will make you a terror to yourself and your friends, and you will see them fall by their own sword. He will give Judah into the hands of the king of Babylon and he will take the people into captivity along with the city's wealth. You will die there and be buried with all of your friends to whom you have prophesied lies."

JEREMIAH'S PRAYER

Jeremiah prayed, "Lord, you deceived me, I am ridiculed all day long, and everyone mocks me. Whenever I proclaim violence and destruction, I am insulted. But if I don't speak, your word burns in my heart like a fire; I can't hold it in. My friends are all waiting for me to slip, but you are with me like a mighty warrior, so their dishonor will never be forgotten. Show your vengeance on them because I have committed myself to you.

"Sing praises to the Lord because you rescue the needy from the wicked. Cursed be the day I was born; may it be like the towns the Lord overthrew without pity. Why did I ever come out of the womb to see trouble and sorrow?"

> **Jeremiah's range of emotions**
>
> In a single paragraph, Jeremiah praises the Lord and then bemoans his birth. We are allowed to feel whatever our emotions are, and we should talk to God about them.

JEREMIAH AND PASHHUR

The Lord sent Jeremiah to Pashhur and the priest asked Jeremiah to inquire of the Lord what will happen because Babylon was attacking. Jeremiah answered, "The Lord is about to fight against you with an outstretched arm and furious anger. He will strike down those who live in this city and they will die of a terrible plague.

"He will give Zedekiah king of Judah into Nebuchadnezzar's hands, and he will show no mercy, pity, or compassion. He is setting the way of life and death before you, those who stay will die, and those who surrender will live. He is going to do this city harm and he will destroy it with fire.

"Tell the king to administer justice every morning and rescue the oppressed, or his wrath will burn like fire because of the evil you've done. He is against you, Jerusalem, and he will punish your evil deeds."

MESSAGE TO SHALLUM

The Lord sent Jeremiah to Shallum, the king, and he said, "Do what is just and right for the underprivileged and the foreigner. But if you don't, this palace will become a ruin. People will pass by and know that this desolation is because you have forsaken their God's covenant and served other gods. You will die in captivity and never see this land again.

"Woe to those who build their palaces by unrighteousness and injustice, making his people work for nothing. A fancy house doesn't make you any more of a king. Your father did what was right, gave the people justice, and it went well with him; that's what it means to know the Lord.

"But you are greedy and dishonest; you murder the innocent and oppress the poor. So, no one will mourn your death. I warned you, but you did not listen; now I will blow your allies away like the wind, and you will not return to this land."

WARNING FOR THE SHEPHERDS

The Lord says, "Woe to the shepherds who are destroying and scattering my sheep. I will punish you for the evil you have done, and I will gather the remnant of my flock from where they have been driven, and they will flourish again. I will give them shepherds who will care for them, and I will raise up a righteous Branch from David who will reign wisely and do what is just and right in the land. Then people will swear by the Lord who brought his people back from the north rather than Egypt.

> **The Branch from David**
>
> The Branch from David is a reference to the coming Messiah.

"To the prophets and priests, you are godless, and you bring your wickedness to my temple. Your path will become slippery, and you will fall because you prophesy by false gods and lead my people astray. You will eat bitter food and drink poisoned water because of the ungodliness you spread throughout the land.

"Don't listen to the prophets when they fill you with false hopes and claim that you will have peace. The storm of the Lord will burst out in wrath and his anger will not turn back until he fully accomplishes his purpose. I did not send these prophets, but they still claim to speak on my behalf. You cannot hide from me because I fill heaven and earth; my Word is like a fire and hammer that breaks the rock into pieces.

"I will punish false prophets and their households because they distort the words of the living God. I will cast them out and bring on them an everlasting disgrace."

THE BASKETS OF FIGS

After King Nebuchadnezzar exiled the king of Judah, the Lord showed Jeremiah two baskets of figs in front of the temple; one basket had good figs and the other rotten ones. He said, "The good figs are the exiles from Judah. I will watch over them and bring them back to their home. I will give them a heart to know that I am the Lord, they will be my people, and I will be their God. But the bad figs are like Zedekiah and those who remain in this land. I will make them abhorrent and an object of ridicule. I will send sword, famine, and plague against them until they are destroyed."

PROMISE OF BABYLONIAN EXILE

Jeremiah said to the people, "I have prophesied to you for the last 23 years, but you have not listened. Though the Lord has sent the prophets repeatedly, you have not paid any attention to them. They told you to repent, but you didn't listen. Therefore, he will send you to Babylon and destroy this land. This whole country will become a desolate wasteland and will serve the king of Babylon for 70 years. But after that time, he will punish your oppressors for their sins.

"Drink from the cup of God's anger. Get drunk, vomit, and collapse. You don't have a choice; the Lord will punish you. He will roar against the land from heaven and his judgment will reach the ends of the earth. There is nowhere to hide and no way to escape!"

JEREMIAH IN THE TEMPLE COURTYARD

The Lord sent Jeremiah to the temple courtyard to speak to the people in hopes that they would repent. Jeremiah said, "If you don't listen to the Lord and his prophets, then he will make this city a curse among all the nations."

The priests and prophets heard him, and as soon as he was finished, they seized him and said, "You must die! Why do you prophesy that this city will be desolate and deserted?"

The people gathered around him and Jeremiah said, "The Lord sent me to prophesy against this city, now repent, and the Lord will not bring the disaster he has pronounced against you. As for me, I am in your hands; do whatever you think is right. However, if you kill me, you will bring the guilt of innocent blood on yourselves."

The officials yelled that he should be put to death, and some of the elders stepped forward and said, "In the days of Hezekiah, Micah prophesied that Jerusalem would be plowed like a field, and Jerusalem will become a heap of rubble. But Hezekiah did not kill him, he sought the Lord and his favor, and then the Lord relented. Uriah prophesied similar words and Jehoiakim killed the prophet." Then they let Jeremiah go.

JEREMIAH'S YOKE

Early in Zedekiah's rule, the Lord spoke to Jeremiah, "Make a yoke out of straps and crossbars and put it on your neck. I made the heavens and earth; now I will give the nations into Nebuchadnezzar's hands, and they will serve him until the time of his grandson, then many nations will subjugate him. If any nation doesn't bow its neck under his yoke, I will punish them with the sword, famine, and plague.

"Don't listen to your prophets telling you that you won't serve Babylon because they prophesy lies; I have not sent them. Serve the king of Babylon and you will live. He will take the holy things from the temple until the day I come for them and then I will restore them to this place."

Hananiah came to Jeremiah in the temple in the presence of the priests and all the people and said, "The Lord Almighty will break the yoke of Babylon. Within two years, he will bring back the articles from the Lord's house and all the exiles."

Jeremiah replied, "May the Lord do so and bring the exiles back from Babylon. Nevertheless, the prophets who preceded us have prophesied war, disaster, and plague against many countries and kingdoms. But the prophet who prophesies peace will only be recognized as sent by the Lord if his prediction comes true."

Then Hananiah took the yoke from Jeremiah's neck and broke it, saying, "This is how the Lord will break Nebuchadnezzar's yoke from the neck of the nations within two years."

Jeremiah left and the Lord told Jeremiah, "Go to Hananiah and tell him this: you have broken a wooden yoke and replaced it with an iron one. Hananiah, the Lord has not sent you, but you have persuaded this nation to trust in lies. Now, you will die because you have preached rebellion against the Lord." A few months later, Hananiah died.

LETTER FROM EXILE

Jeremiah sent a letter to the people in exile: "Build houses and settle down; marry and have children, increase in number while you are there. Seek the peace and prosperity of the city where you are in exile and you will prosper. Don't listen to the prophets who tell lies because I have not sent them.

"When the 70 years are up, I will fulfill my promise and bring you back to this place. I know the plans I have for you, plans to prosper you and not harm you, plans to give you hope and a future. Then you will pray to me, and I will listen; you will seek and find me when you seek me with all your heart. I will bring you back from captivity, but those who did not come with you will be destroyed because they have not listened to my words."

CHAPTER FIFTEEN
PROMISE OF RESTORATION
Jeremiah 30-35

The Lord told Jeremiah to write everything he had been told in a book, "The days are coming when I will bring my people back from captivity and restore them to the land I gave their ancestors. Jacob is in trouble now, but salvation is coming. I will break the yoke off their necks and tear off their bonds. They will serve the Lord their God and David their king; so, don't be afraid or dismayed because I will bring you back from exile. Even though I destroy the nations where you scatter, I will save you.

"Your wound is incurable and there is no one to plead your cause. All your allies have forgotten you and I have struck you down because of your great guilt. But those who devour you will be devoured and they will be the ones to go into exile. I will restore you to health and heal your wounds. I will restore your fortunes and you will sing songs of thanksgiving. You will be my people and I will be your God."

The storm of the Lord will burst forth in wrath like a driving wind on the heads of the wicked. The fierce anger of the Lord will not turn back until it accomplishes its purpose.

The Lord continued, "I will be the God of Israel and they will be my people. I will give them rest because I love them with never-ending love, and I have drawn them to myself. I will rebuild Israel and they will come to worship again. I will gather them and watch over them as a shepherd watches over his sheep. He will redeem Israel from a mighty nation. They will exchange their sorrow for rejoicing.

"Israel weeps for her children, but I will bring them home; there is hope for your future. Return to me and I will restore you because I alone am God. Israel is still my child, and even though I discipline, I will have mercy. How long will you wander? Come home and I will give rest to the weary. I will make a new covenant with my people and write my words on their hearts. People won't have to teach each other about me because they will all know me; I will forgive their sins. The only way this could possibly fail is if all of nature, that I created, stops its course. The day is coming when I will restore Jerusalem and it will never fall again."

JEREMIAH ARRESTED AGAIN

In the tenth year of Zedekiah, the Babylonian army was besieging Jerusalem and Zedekiah had Jeremiah imprisoned, saying, "Why do you prophesy the way you do? You keep saying that Nebuchadnezzar is going to defeat us and take us captive."

Jeremiah replied, "God is giving this city into the Babylonians' hands. He will keep you there until he decides. Even though you fight against them, you will not succeed."

The Lord told me to buy a field from my uncle because it is my right and duty to buy it. I paid him nearly three weeks' wages and signed all the appropriate paperwork. Then I gave the deed to my assistant Baruch and told him to put it in a clay jar to preserve them because God has told me that we will again buy houses, fields, and vineyards in this land.

Then Jeremiah prayed, "Lord, you have made the heavens and the earth by your outstretched arm; nothing is too difficult for you. You show love to thousands and punish the sinners. You see everything that humanity does and you give rewards according to our actions. You brought your people out of Egypt with signs and wonders and gave them this good land that you had sworn to give their ancestors. They possessed it, but they did not obey you, so you brought this disaster on them. Now the Babylonians are attacking and you will give us into their hands. Despite all this, you told me to buy the field."

Then the Lord spoke to Jeremiah, "I am the Lord, the God of all humanity; nothing is too hard for me. The Babylonians will burn down the city where you aroused my anger by sacrificing to false gods. These people have done nothing but evil from their youth and now I must get them out of my sight.

"But after they have been in Babylon, I will bring them back and let them live safely. They will be my people, I will be their God, and I will give them hearts that will always fear me so that it will go well with them. I will make an everlasting covenant, never stop doing good for them, and they will never turn away from me. People will once again buy and sell fields because I will restore their fortunes."

The Lord spoke to Jeremiah a second time while he was in prison, "Call to me, and I will answer, showing you great and hidden things you have not known. I will restore the fortunes of Israel and Judah and rebuild them as at first. I will cleanse them from their sin and rebellion and make them a place of joy, praise, and glory before all the nations of the earth. Give thanks to the Lord, for his steadfast love endures forever! Once again, I will restore them.

"I will fulfill the promise I made to David a raise to righteous Branch who will execute justice and righteousness in the land. Jerusalem will dwell securely and David will never lack a man to sit on the throne. It is not possible for this covenant to fail and I will multiply his offspring like the sand of the sea. Trust me to fulfill my promises."

JERUSALEM WILL FALL

While Babylon attacked Jerusalem, the Lord sent Jeremiah to Zedekiah, saying, "I am handing the city over to Babylonians. But you will not die by the sword; you will die peacefully, and people will mourn for you just as they mourned for your ancestors."

HEBREW SLAVES

During Zedekiah's reign, the king made a decree and proclaimed freedom for all Hebrew slaves. All the officials and people agreed to free their brothers and sisters, but later changed their minds and enslaved them again.

Then the word of the Lord came to Jeremiah, "I made a covenant with your ancestors when I brought them out of Egypt, and every seventh year, you are supposed to free any fellow Hebrews who have sold themselves to you. However, your ancestors didn't listen to me.

"Recently, you repented and freed your people but then turned around and profaned my name by enslaving them again. So, I will proclaim freedom for you as well, freedom to fall by the sword, plague, and famine. I will give you into your enemies' hands and wild animals will devour your corpses. Judah will become desolate."

CHAPTER SIXTEEN

THE FALL OF JERUSALEM AND ITS AFTERMATH

Jeremiah 36-45, (46-52)

JEREMIAH'S SCROLL

In the fourth year of Jehoiakim's reign, the Lord told Jeremiah to write everything he had said to him on a scroll, from the beginning of his ministry until now, in hopes that the people would repent. Jeremiah had Baruch write down the words while he dictated them.

Then Jeremiah sent Baruch to the temple to read the words to the people because he had been banned from entry. When Micaiah heard Baruch reading from the scroll, he went to where the officials were and told them everything he had heard. None of the people listened.

The officials sent for Baruch and told him to bring the scroll with him. They asked him to read the scroll to them, and when he had finished, they asked him if this was Jeremiah's work. Baruch told them how the scroll came to be and the officials replied, "You and Jeremiah had better hide and not let anyone know where you are!"

The officials took the scroll and brought it to the king, where Jehudi read it to him. After reading three or four columns, the king would cut them off and throw them into the fire until the entire scroll was burned. After it was gone, the king ordered his men to arrest Baruch and Jeremiah.

Then the Lord told Jeremiah to make another scroll just like the first and he dictated the words to Baruch once again.

JEREMIAH ARRESTED

At this time, Jeremiah was free to come and go among the people because he had not been imprisoned yet. Pharaoh's army had marched out of Egypt to help the Israelites, and when the Babylonians heard about it, they withdrew. Then the Lord told Jeremiah to tell the king, "The army Pharaoh is sending to support you will turn around and head back to Egypt. The Babylonians will return and capture this city. Even if you defeated the entire army and they could only attack with wounded men, they would still burn it down."

Jeremiah began to leave the city, but the captain of the guard arrested him, and accused him of deserting to the Babylonians. He brought Jeremiah to the officials who beat him and threw him into a vaulted dungeon, where he stayed a long time.

Eventually, King Zedekiah sent for him and asked if there was any word from God. Jeremiah replied, "Yes, you will be delivered into Nebuchadnezzar's hands." Then he continued, "What crime have I committed to get thrown into prison? Where are your prophets who told you the king of Babylon wouldn't attack? Please don't send me back to my cell, or I will die there." Then Zedekiah gave orders to keep Jeremiah in the guard's courtyard and give him a loaf of bread a day until it was gone.

The soldiers were not satisfied, and they asked the king to put him to death because he was discouraging them. The king gave Jeremiah over to them and they put him into a deep cistern in the courtyard of the guard. There was no water in the pit and Jeremiah sank into the mud.

One of the officials heard what they had done and he appealed to the king to pull him out so he wouldn't die. The king sent 30 men under an Ethiopian named Ebed-melech to pull him out and dress him in rags.

King Zedekiah sent for Jeremiah again and swore not to kill the prophet if he told him the truth of what the Lord said. Jeremiah replied, "If you surrender to the king of Babylon, they will spare your life and not burn down the city. But if you don't surrender, they will burn it down, and you will not escape."

The king answered, "I am afraid that the Babylonians will hand me over to the deserting Jews and they will abuse me."

Jeremiah comforted him, "They will not hand you over, just do what I tell you, and you will live. But if you don't, all the women of the palace will mock you before the Babylonians." The king ordered Jeremiah to keep their conversation a secret. Jeremiah remained a prisoner until the day the Babylonians captured Jerusalem.

THE BABYLONIANS CAPTURE JERUSALEM

In the ninth year of Zedekiah's reign, the king of Babylon and his army marched against Jerusalem, and after an 18-month siege, they broke through the city wall. When Zedekiah saw all the soldiers, he fled towards Jericho; but the Babylonians overtook him and captured the king. They killed his sons and all the nobles of Judah, then they gouged out his eyes and bound him with bronze shackles.

The Babylonians set the royal palace and houses on fire and broke down the wall. They took the people into exile in Babylon, but they left some of the poorest people who had nothing to plunder.

Nebuchadnezzar commanded that his soldiers look after Jeremiah and do whatever the prophet asked of them. Then the Lord spoke to Jeremiah, "Tell Ebed-Melech, the Ethiopian who saved your life, that I am about to fulfill my words against this city in your sight. But I will rescue you and you will escape with your life because you trust in me."

JEREMIAH SET FREE

Nebuzaradan, the commander of Nebuchadnezzar's imperial guard, found Jeremiah in chains among the captives taken into exile. He released Jeremiah from his bonds and said, "The Lord your God decreed this disaster, and he made it happen because your people sinned against the Lord and did not obey him. But I'm freeing you from your chains; you are free to come to Babylon or stay here." Then Nebuzaradan gave Jeremiah provisions and released him.

FLIGHT TO EGYPT

Gedaliah was appointed governor over the people left behind in the land and Jeremiah went to stay with him. The people gathered to Gedaliah and he took an oath to reassure the people, "Don't be afraid to serve the Babylonians, settle in the land, and serve the king, and it will go well with you. I will stay here and represent you to them." The people stayed in Mizpah and gathered the produce of the land.

A man named Johanan went to Gedaliah in secret and said, "Let me kill Ishmael because he is your adversary and wants to kill you. If he succeeds, we will all die." But Gedaliah did not believe him.

A couple of months later, a man named Ishmael was eating with Gedaliah and ten of his men, and he got up and killed Gedaliah. Ishmael also killed all the men of Judah, who were with Gedaliah and the Babylonian soldiers as well.

The next day, before anyone knew about the assassination, 80 men came, with shaved beards and torn clothes, to make offerings to the Lord. Ishmael welcomed them into the city and then killed 70 of them and threw them into a cistern.

While he was slaughtering them, ten of the men begged for their lives because they had stores of supplies hidden in a field. Ishmael let the men live, made all the people in Mizpah captives, and left to cross over to the Ammonites.

When Johanan heard what Ishmael had done, he took some men to attack him for the crimes he had committed. When the people Ishmael had captured saw Johanan, they were glad, and left Ishmael. But Ishmael escaped with eight of his men and fled to the Ammonites. After that, Johanan intended to lead the people to Egypt to escape the Babylonians.

On their way, they stopped to speak to Jeremiah and said, "Pray to the Lord for us so that we can know where we should go and what we should do."

Jeremiah replied, "I will pray to the Lord as you asked and tell you everything he says."

The people said, "Tell us what he says, whether good or bad, and we will do it."

Ten days later, the Lord spoke to Jeremiah, so the prophet called the people together and said, "If you stay in this land, the Lord will build you up because he relents from the disaster he has inflicted on you. Don't be afraid of Nebuchadnezzar because the Lord is with you and will deliver you from his hands. He will show you compassion and restore you to your land.

"But if you go to Egypt for safety, then the sword and famine will follow you there, and you will die. As the Lord poured out his anger and wrath on Jerusalem, he will also pour it out on you when you go to Egypt. You will be a curse, an object of horror, and you will never see this place again. Don't go to Egypt because if you do, you are making a fatal mistake; be sure that you will die if you go there."

When Jeremiah had finished giving them the Lord's message, Azariah, Johanan, and all the arrogant men said to Jeremiah, "You are lying! Baruch is inciting you against us to hand us over to the Babylonians so they can take us into exile."

Then Johanan led the people away to Egypt and took Jeremiah with them. Once they arrived at Pharaoh's palace, the Lord told Jeremiah to take some large stones and bury them under the brick pavement and say, "I will send for Nebuchadnezzar and set his throne over these stones that I have buried. He will attack Egypt and kill those destined for death and take the rest into captivity. He will burn the temples of the Egyptian gods and pick Egypt clean like a shepherd picks his garment clean of lice."

MESSAGE TO THE REFUGEES

Later the Lord spoke to Jeremiah concerning the Judeans who had fled to Egypt, "You saw the disaster I sent on Jerusalem and how the towns in Judah lie in ruins because of their evil. They aroused my anger by worshiping idols and ignored the prophets who warned them to change their ways. But they didn't listen. Therefore, I poured out my wrath on them.

"Don't arouse my anger any further by worshiping Egyptian gods because you will bring a curse on yourselves. Don't forget the wickedness of your ancestors because they refused to obey or humble themselves. Now I am determined to bring disaster on you and all Judah.

"The remnant who has gone to Egypt will die by the sword or famine and become an object of reproach. None of those who have come to Egypt will return to the land except for a handful of fugitives."

The people came together in a large assembly and said to Jeremiah, "We will not listen to your message and we will do whatever we want. We will pour out incense to the Queen of Heaven, just like our ancestors did in Jerusalem. We had plenty of food, and nothing bad happened, but since we stopped burning incense to her, we have all been dying."

Jeremiah replied, "The Lord saw your offerings to her, and when he couldn't bear your wickedness any longer, he cursed your land. You are doing whatever you want; keep it up! Just know that no one from Judah who is now in Egypt will ever again invoke his name because he will kill them by sword or famine. He will deliver the king of Egypt into Nebuchadnezzar's hands; then, you will know whose word will stand, yours or his."

JEREMIAH'S SORROW

In the fourth year of Jehoiakim, Jeremiah said to Baruch, "Woe to me because the Lord has added sorrow to my pain, and I am worn out with groaning and find no rest. The Lord will uproot what he has planted. Don't seek great things for yourself because he will bring disaster on all people, but he will let you escape with your life."

CONCLUSION

The Lord also spoke to Jeremiah and he prophesied about many of the foreign nations surrounding Judah. He prophesied Egypt's downfall at Nebuchadnezzar's hands and spoke against the Philistines before Pharaoh attacked them. He also prophesied to Moab, Ammon, Edom, Damascus, Kedar, and Hazor. He also spoke of Babylon's eventual overthrow.

In the 37th year of their exile, the king of Babylon freed the king of Judah. He gave him a seat at his table, and he lived there until he died, just as Jeremiah had promised.

CHAPTER SEVENTEEN
FALLEN JERUSALEM
Lamentations 1-5

> **The Book of Lamentations**
>
> The Book of Lamentations is a poem mourning the fall of Jerusalem. We are not sure who wrote the book, but it was likely within the first 25 years after the fall of Jerusalem in 587 B.C., and tradition tells us that Jeremiah was the author. The book is a series of five poems, with the first four being acrostics (we lose this structure in translation and conversion to prose). All five capture the grief over Jerusalem's fall and the desecration of the temple, both of which were unthinkable.

Jerusalem was once full of people and is now deserted; she had been a queen and now is a slave. She weeps at night, and there is no one to comfort her; friends have betrayed her and become enemies.

Judah has gone into exile and she finds no resting place. Her enemies are at ease as her sins and masters have brought this grief. Her children are in exile and enemies laugh at her destruction. They took all her treasures and defiled the sanctuary.

No one can compare with my suffering; the Lord put his word in my heart and a fire in my bones. He has taken my strength and given me into the hands of a mighty enemy. The Lord rejected his powerful young men and the Babylonians crushed them. Now I weep and no one can comfort me.

The Lord is righteous, but I rebelled against his command. I turned to my lovers, but they have betrayed me. My enemies rejoice at my misfortune; see their wickedness and deal with them as you have dealt with me.

***

The Lord has covered Jerusalem with the cloud of his anger and ignored his footstool. The Lord is like an enemy; he has swallowed up Israel's palaces and destroyed her strongholds. He has rejected his altar and abandoned his sanctuary; his enemies exult over them.

I have run out of tears, and I am tormented within; my heart is poured out because my people are destroyed. They cry out for their mothers for sustenance, but she has none. Her wound is as deep as the sea and no one can heal it. Her prophets' visions were false and worthless and they did not lead to repentance. Now your enemies rejoice over your downfall.

The Lord has fulfilled his promises and let the enemy rejoice over you. The hearts of the people cry out to the Lord; they pour out their hearts like water. Lift up your hands to him for the lives of your children. Lord, don't treat us like this.

***

I have seen the rod of the Lord's wrath; he has driven me away and made me walk in darkness. My skin and flesh grow old and my bones are broken. He has surrounded me with bitterness and hardship; he has walled me in so I cannot escape.

Even when I cry out for help, he shuts out my prayer and makes my path crooked. He is like a wild animal lying in wait for me. I am the laughingstock of all my people, and I am deprived of peace and have forgotten what happiness is.

But my hope is in the Lord's great love because we are not consumed and his compassion never fails. Great is your faithfulness, it is new every morning, and I wait for you. The Lord is good to those who hope in him and it is good to wait for his salvation. It is best to bear this burden in one's youth and not try to figure out all the reasons why. But no one is cast off by the Lord forever; even though he causes grief, he will have compassion according to his abundant love.

Remember that God is good and is in charge of all things. Let us lift our hands and hearts to heaven and repent from our sins. You have wrapped yourself in anger and made us like the scum of the earth. Our enemies have opened their mouths against us; we are terrified and suffer ruin and destruction. I constantly weep for my people.

My enemies hunted me without cause and they tried to kill me. I called out to the Lord from the depths of the pit and he came near to me. You have taken up my cause and redeemed me! Pay them back what they deserve and destroy them from under the Lord's heavens.

***

The precious children of Jerusalem who were once worth their weight in gold are now like clay pots in the potter's hands. They go hungry and thirsty and no one gives them anything. Our punishment is worse than Sodom's, and our skin has shriveled so much that we are unrecognizable. The dead pity us and it has become so bad that compassionate mothers have even boiled their children for food.

No one would have thought this could happen! Our sin brought this on us and we are so defiled with blood that no one will even touch our garments. The Lord is the one who caused this disaster to overtake us. Jerusalem will one day return from exile, but Edom, your punishment is about to begin.

***

Lord, remember our disgrace because strangers have taken our inheritance, and we are orphans. We cannot even afford water or firewood. Our enemies are at our heels and we have no rest. Our ancestors sinned and died, but we bear their punishment. Our servants have become our masters and our hearts are sick and weary. Our women are raped, elders are dishonored, and our young men are slaves. Our joy has turned to mourning.

Lord, you reign forever; your throne endures forever. Don't forget us, restore us to you, and renew us as in days of old unless you have utterly rejected us and are angry with us beyond measure.

CHAPTER EIGHTEEN

JUDGMENT ON EDOM

Obadiah 1

> **The Book of Obadiah**
>
> The Book of Obadiah is the shortest in the Old Testament, and it is a prophecy against Edom (who descended from Jacob's brother Esau). Obadiah likely wrote this book not long after the fall of Jerusalem in 587 B.C. and it is an indictment against Edom for their role in helping the Babylonians defeat Judah. It also served as a source of encouragement for Israel.

The Lord has sent a messenger to the nations to rise up for battle against Edom. He will make you small and insignificant; you will be despised and rejected. Your pride has deceived you, and although you think that no one can bring you down, God will bring you down from your lofty place. You will have absolutely nothing left, all your wise men will be destroyed, and your young men slaughtered.

You have done violence against your brother, Israel, and you stood by and watched when foreigners invaded and carried off his wealth. Therefore, you will be ashamed, and your people will end. Do not rejoice over Israel's misfortune and distress, and do not seek to profit from their downfall because the Lord's judgment is not far away.

God is going to return all your deeds upon you and he will sweep away the nations like they never existed. But there will be those in Israel who escape, and Israel will once again own its possessions. They will be like a flame that will consume the stubble of your nation and not leave a single survivor. Israel will return to the Promised Land and they shall once again dwell in the land that God has given them.

CHAPTER NINETEEN

DANIEL'S SERVICE TO THREE KINGS

Daniel 1-6

> **The book of Daniel**
>
> Daniel wrote this book describing his life and ministry from 586 until his writing around 530 B.C. Some commentators believe this work to be fictional, but that is from an assumption that predictive prophecy is impossible. Daniel served as a head of state under three different kings, a remarkable feat given that conquering kings always cleaned house and removed the previous regime.

DANIEL TAKEN INTO CAPTIVITY

Nebuchadnezzar, king of Babylon, came to Jerusalem and besieged it; he took the people and Judah's riches to his homeland. He ordered Ashpenaz, chief of his court officials, to bring some of the Israelites into the king's service; young men, without defect, handsome, intelligent, and qualified to serve. He taught them the language and literature of Babylon and gave them food and drink from the king's table. They were to go through years of training before going into the king's service, and Ashpenaz chose Daniel, Hananiah, Mishael, and Azariah. He renamed Daniel, Belteshazzar; Hananiah, Shadrach; Mishael, Meshach; and Azariah, Abednego.

Daniel and his friends decided to retain their Jewish heritage and asked the guard overseeing them for permission to eat and drink what they had as a child. The guard was worried that they would not fare as well as the other young men, and Daniel asked that the officials give them a ten-day trial period of a vegetarian diet and water to see how they did. The Lord granted them favor with the guard, and after ten days, they looked healthier and better nourished than any of the other young men in training. So, the guard allowed them to continue with their diet, and God gave them knowledge, understanding, and great learning; and Daniel could understand visions and dreams of all kinds.

After three years, the king brought them in to serve, and he found that none of the other young men were equal to Daniel, Hananiah, Mishael, and Azariah; they were even more qualified than the Babylonians who served the king. Daniel served Nebuchadnezzar until the first year of King Cyrus.

NEBUCHADNEZZAR'S DREAM

In the second year of his rule, Nebuchadnezzar had a dream that kept him up, and he summoned his wise men to tell him what his dream meant. They asked him to tell him what the dream was so that they could interpret it, but the king refused to share it and replied, "If you don't tell me my dream and what it means, I will kill you and your families. But if you can answer me, then I will give you great honor."

The wise men begged the king to tell him the dream because he asked the impossible, but the king held firm and ordered their execution. The wise men sent for Daniel and he asked the king for a little time to interpret the dream.

Daniel told his friends about the situation and they prayed for God to reveal the dream and its meaning. That night, God revealed the dream and its significance to Daniel, and the young man said, "Praise God forever and ever because he has all wisdom and power. He changes the times and seasons; he raises up and dethrones kings; he knows everything! I thank and praise the God of my ancestors because he has told me the king's dream."

Daniel went to the king's executioner and said, "Do not execute the wise men; take me to the king, and I will interpret his dream."

The executioner brought Daniel before the king and Nebuchadnezzar asked if he could interpret the dream. Daniel replied, "No human can fulfill the king's request, but there is a God in heaven who reveals mysteries. He has shown you what will happen in the days to come and he has revealed it to me so that you might know as well.

"In your dream, you saw a large, beautiful statue with a head of gold, chest and arms of silver, belly and thighs of bronze, legs of iron, and feet part iron and part clay. Then you saw a rock not cut by human hands, and it struck the statue's feet and smashed them. Then the statue crumbled, and the wind swept the pieces away without a trace, but the rock became a huge mountain that filled the whole earth.

"This is what the dream means: God has given you dominion, power, might, and glory; you are the head of gold and rule over everything. After you, another kingdom that is inferior to yours will arise. Then, a third kingdom of bronze that will rule the whole earth. Finally, a fourth kingdom as strong as iron will break and crush the others. This kingdom will then be divided and will be part strong and part brittle; the people will be mixed and no more united than iron mixes with clay.

"But the God of heaven will set up a kingdom that will never be destroyed, and it will crush these kingdoms and bring them to an end. God has shown you what will happen in the future."

The king fell on his face before Daniel, honored him, ordered his servants to present him with an offering and incense, and then put him in charge of all the wise men. At Daniel's request, the king made his Hebrew friends administrators over Babylon while Daniel remained in the royal court.

SHADRACH, MESHACH, AND ABEDNEGO

King Nebuchadnezzar made an image of gold 90 feet high and nine feet wide, and he summoned all the officials of Babylon to come to the dedication. He commanded them to bow down and worship when his musicians began playing music; they would throw anyone who disobeyed into a blazing furnace.

After the dedication, some officials reported that Shadrach, Meshach, and Abednego had not bowed down to worship the golden statue. The king was furious, so he brought the men to him and asked him if the report was accurate, reminding them of his command to throw the disobedient into the furnace.

Shadrach, Meshach, and Abednego replied, "We don't need to defend ourselves; if we are thrown into the furnace, our God can and will deliver us from the king's hand. But even if he doesn't, we will not serve your gods or worship your idols."

Nebuchadnezzar was furious and he ordered his men to heat the furnace seven times hotter than usual. He commanded some of his strongest soldiers to tie the men up and throw them into the furnace fully clothed. The flames were so hot that they killed some of the soldiers who threw the men into the fire.

The king leaped to his feet in amazement when he saw four men walking around in the fire, unbound and unharmed; the fourth looked like a son of the gods (this was likely Jesus or an angel). Nebuchadnezzar called for the men to come out of the fire and they obeyed. All the people were amazed that the three men came out, and not a hair on their heads was singed, their robes were not scorched, and they didn't even smell like smoke.

The king said to them, "Praise the God of Shadrach, Meshach, and Abednego, who sent his angel to rescue his servants. They trusted him and defied my commands and were even willing to die rather than worship anyone other than their own God. Therefore, anyone who slanders their God will be killed, and their house will be turned into rubble because there is no other god who can save like this." Then the king promoted the men.

NEBUCHADNEZZAR'S SECOND DREAM

One day Nebuchadnezzar had another dream that terrified him. He called for his wise men to interpret it, and finally, he called for Daniel to come before him and said, "I saw an enormous tree in the middle of the land that was so tall that it touched the sky and was visible from everywhere on earth. It was beautiful, and it had food for everyone, and it gave shelter to all the animals.

"A holy messenger came down from heaven and commanded that the tree be cut down, its branches stripped, and its fruit scattered. But the stump was to be bound with iron and bronze and left in the field. Then, let him be drenched with dew and live among the plants and animals of the earth; let him have an animal's mind until seven times pass."

Daniel was perplexed and terrified for a while before saying, "I wish this dream was for your enemies. You are the tree you saw; you are great and strong and rule over the earth. But God will drive you away from people to live with the wild animals for seven times until you acknowledge that God is sovereign over all kingdoms, and he gives them to anyone he wishes. But the stump means that God will restore your domain when you acknowledge him.

"Please listen to my advice, renounce your sins, and do right by being kind to the oppressed, then your prosperity will continue."

Twelve months later, the king was walking on the roof of the royal palace, congratulating himself on the greatness of his kingdom and majesty. Even as the words were on his lips, a voice came from heaven, "This is what I decreed for you, your royal authority has been taken away, and you will be driven into the wild where you will live like a wild animal. Seven times will pass until you acknowledge that God is sovereign over all kingdoms and gives power to anyone he wishes."

This happened immediately, and God drove Nebuchadnezzar into the wild; his hair and nails grew long, and he lived like an animal. At the end of that time, he raised his eyes toward heaven, and God restored his sanity. He praised God and gave him honor because the Lord's kingdom endures forever. The king recognized that God does what he pleases, and the Lord returned his glory and splendor. Nebuchadnezzar became even greater than before and exalted God because he is righteous, just, and humbles the proud.

BELSHAZZAR'S VISION

Sometime later, Nebuchadnezzar's son, Belshazzar, ruled Babylon. He gave a great banquet for 1,000 of his nobles. While he was eating and drinking, he gave orders to bring in the gold and silver goblets that his father, Nebuchadnezzar, had taken from the temple in Jerusalem. They brought in the goblets, and as they drank from them, they praised their gods of gold, silver, bronze, iron, wood, and stone.

Suddenly, the fingers of a human hand appeared and wrote on the wall. The king turned pale and his knees knocked in fear. He summoned his wise men and told them that whoever could read and interpret the writing would receive great honor, but none could do it.

The queen came into the banquet hall and told the king about Daniel and all he had done during Nebuchadnezzar's days. So, the king's men brought in Daniel, and they told him the situation. Daniel answered, "Keep your gifts and give your rewards to someone else, but I will read the writing and tell you what it means. God gave your father great power, but the Lord stripped him of his glory when he became arrogant. God drove him into the wild to live like an animal until he acknowledged that God is sovereign over the earth and gives them to whom he wishes.

"But you, Belshazzar, have not humbled yourself even though you know all of this. Instead, you have set yourself up against the Lord of heaven and drank from the goblets you brought from Jerusalem. You did not honor the God who holds your life in his hand but praised false gods.

"He sent the hand that wrote on the wall and it wrote: MENE, MENE, TEKEL, PARSIN. Mene means that God has numbered the days of your reign and brought it to an end; tekel means you have been weighed and found wanting; parsin means that your kingdom will be divided and given to the Medes and Persians."

Belshazzar commanded his men to dress Daniel in purple, give him a gold chain, and named him the third highest ruler in the kingdom. That night, the king was killed, and Darius the Mede assumed the throne at 62.

SERVICE TO DARIUS

Darius appointed 120 officials to rule the kingdom with three administrators over them, one of whom was Daniel. He distinguished himself so much that Darius planned to put him in charge of the entire nation. The other officials were jealous and looked for ways to undermine him but couldn't find any corruption. Finally, they decided that they would only find a way to charge him with something regarding the Law of his God.

They came to him and advised the king to command that anyone who prays to any god or human besides the king over the next 30 days should be thrown into the lions' den. The king liked this proposal, so he put the decree in writing.

Daniel learned about the decree, but he still knelt and prayed to his God three times a day, just as he had done before. The officials found Daniel praying and reported it to Darius. The situation distressed the king, and he looked for a way to rescue Daniel from the judgment, but his officials reminded him that the king's decrees could not change.

So, the king gave the order to throw Daniel into the lions' den, but before he did, he said to Daniel, "May the God you serve rescue you!" The soldiers place a stone over the mouth of the den and the king sealed it with his own signet ring so that Daniel's situation might not change. The king returned to his palace and spent the night refusing food, entertainment, and sleep.

At dawn, the king hurried to the lions' den and called out, "Daniel, has your God rescued you from the lions?"

Daniel answered, "May the king live forever! My God sent his angel and shut the lions' mouths. They have not hurt me because I was innocent in his sight and yours."

The king was overjoyed, and he ordered his men to remove Daniel, and they saw he was not hurt. He commanded his men to throw Daniel's accusers into the lions' den with their wives and children. Before they even hit the ground, the lions overpowered them and crushed all their bones.

Then King Darius wrote to all the nations, "May you prosper greatly! I declare that everyone in my kingdom must give Daniel's God fear and reverence because he is the living God who endures forever, and his kingdom will endure. He rescues, saves, and performs miracles in heaven and on earth. He rescued Daniel from the power of the lions." Daniel continued to prosper through the reign of Darius and Cyrus, the Persian.

CHAPTER TWENTY

DANIEL'S VISIONS
Daniel 7-12

> **Daniel's Visions**
>
> This chapter is difficult for modern readers to understand. It is apocalyptic writing and would have made sense to his contemporary readers, but we have to do some work to understand it. These are organized by the visions as opposed to fitting in with the chronology of the last chapter.

DANIEL'S VISION OF FOUR BEASTS

In the first year of Belshazzar's reign, Daniel had a dream. Daniel said, "In my dream, I saw the four winds of heaven churning up the great sea, and four great beasts came out of the water. The first was like a lion with wings like an eagle. Its wings were torn off, and it lifted from the ground to stand on two feet like a human, and it was given a human mind.

"The second beast looked like a bear, and it was raised up on one of its sides, and it had three ribs in its mouth; it was told to eat its fill of flesh.

"The third beast looked like a leopard and it had four wings on its back; it had four heads and it was given the authority to rule.

"The fourth beast was terrifying and very powerful; it had large iron teeth, ten horns, and it crushed and devoured its victims. As I thought about the horns, a smaller horn came up among them and uprooted three of the horns. The smaller horn had the eyes of a human and spoke boastfully.

> **The beasts from the sea**
>
> Daniel's reference to the sea is the Mediterranean. The four beasts represent four great kingdoms that would rule over the earth. The first beast is the Babylonian empire, the second represents the Medo-Persians, the third is the Greeks, and the fourth is the Roman empire.

"Thrones were set in place, and the eternal God took his seat; his clothes were as white as snow, and his hair was white like wool, and his throne was flaming with fire, and its wheels were ablaze. A river of fire flowed from before him and countless people stood in his presence. The court was seated and the books were opened.

"I kept watching because of the horn's boastful words until the beast was slain and its body was thrown into a blazing fire. The other beasts had been stripped of their authority but were allowed to live for a time.

"Then I saw one who was like a Son of Man coming with the clouds of heaven and he approached God's throne. He was given authority, glory, and sovereign power over the whole earth. His power will not pass away and his kingdom will endure.

"My spirit was troubled and I asked one of the people standing what it all meant. He told me that the four beasts are four kings that will come to power, but the holy people will receive the kingdom forever and ever.

"The fourth beast was a fourth kingdom that will be different from all others and it will trample down the earth and crush it. The horns are ten kings who will come from this kingdom. Then another king will arise, subdue three kings, oppress God's people, and try to change the set times and laws. The people will be given to him for three-and-a-half years, but then he will be destroyed forever. Then the holy people will be given sovereignty, power, and greatness over the earth.

"I was deeply troubled by this, but I kept it to myself."

> **The throne room**
>
> This next portion of Daniel's vision describes God on his glorious throne. It was common for thrones to be on wheels so they could be moved and can also represent God's ceaseless activity. The Son of Man is one of Jesus' favorite titles for himself, and this section describes his coming overthrow of the earthly rulers. The horns represent kingdoms that rise up after Roman rule. We are unsure if these refer to specific domains, if they are yet to come, or merely symbolic. Our takeaway should be that God is sovereign over human history and will one day overthrow the earthly rule of humanity that attempts to rule by its own power rather than God's.

DANIEL'S VISION OF A RAM AND A GOAT

Two years later, I had another vision. I saw a ram with two long horns standing beside a canal, and one horn was longer than the other. It charged in every direction, and no animal could withstand it; the ram did whatever it wanted.

Suddenly, a goat with a prominent horn between its eyes came from the west without touching the ground. It charged the ram in a rage and shattered its two horns; the ram was powerless, and no one could rescue it. The goat became very great, but at the height of its power, the horn was broken off, and four smaller horns grew in its place. Out of one of the smaller horns, another horn grew that started small but kept growing until it reached heaven. It made itself as great as the commander of the Lord's army and it took away the daily sacrifice. He took the Lord's people and prospered in everything it did, and trampled on the truth.

> **The ram and the goat**
>
> The ram with two horns represents the Medes (first horn) and the Persians (second horn). The goat represents the Greek Empire, and the first horn is Alexander the Great. After his death, his four generals (Cassander, Lysimachus, Seleucus, and

> Ptolemy) divided his kingdom. Antiochus Epiphanes was the fulfillment of the final portion when he persecuted the Jewish people.

I heard a holy one ask, "How long until the fulfillment of the vision?"

Another answered, "It will take 2,300 evenings and mornings until the sanctuary is reconsecrated."

> **What are the 2,300 evenings and mornings?**
>
> There are many theories for what this means, and it has given rise to many interpretations. Most likely, it refers to the time between Antiochus Epiphanes persecution (171 B.C.) and the cleansing of the temple during the Maccabean revolt of 165 B.C.

While I was trying to understand the vision, I saw a being who looked like a man, and a voice said, "Gabriel, tell this man the meaning of the vision."

As he approached me, I was terrified and fell on my face before him. But he said to me, "Son of man, this vision concerns the end times. I am going to tell you what will happen later in the time of wrath. The two-horned ram you saw represents the kings of Media and Persia. The shaggy goat is the king of Greece, and the large horn between its eyes is the first king. The four horns that replaced the broken horn are four kingdoms that will come from Greece but won't have the same power.

"Towards the end of their reign, a fierce-looking king who is a master of intrigue will arise. He will become powerful and will succeed in whatever he does. He will destroy the mighty, holy people and cause deceit to prosper. He will consider himself superior and stand up against the Prince of princes. But he will be destroyed, but not by human power. Seal up this vision because it concerns the distant future."

> **Dual fulfillment**
>
> This prophecy likely has a dual fulfillment in the person of Antiochus Epiphanes and the Antichrist at the end of time.

I was appalled by the vision and so worn out that I stayed in bed for several days. Then I got up and went about the king's business, but I still couldn't understand the vision.

DANIEL'S VISION OF 70 WEEKS

In the first year of Darius' rule over Babylon, I understood from the prophet Jeremiah that the desolation of Jerusalem would last 70 years. So, I pleaded with the Lord with prayer and fasting, clothed in sackcloth and ashes. I confessed, "Lord, you are the great and awesome God who keeps his covenant of love with those who keep your commandments; we have sinned and done wrong. We have rebelled and turned away from your commands and laws; we have not listened to the prophets you sent to speak to us.

"You are righteous, but we are ashamed because of our unfaithfulness to you. You are merciful and forgiving even though we are rebellious and have not obeyed your laws. Therefore, you poured out the curses and judgments on us. But we still haven't turned to you and your truth. We have sinned, but in keeping with your righteous acts, turn away your wrath from Jerusalem because those around us scorn us.

"Look on your desolate sanctuary with favor for your sake, Lord. Listen to our prayers and see the desolation of the city that bears your Name. We don't ask because we are righteous but because of your great mercy. Please forgive us and act for your Name's sake."

While I was praying, Gabriel came to me and told me, "I have come to give you insight and understanding. While you were praying, God instructed me to give you a word from heaven. Seventy 'sevens' have been decreed for your people and Jerusalem to finish its sin, atone for wickedness, and bring everlasting righteousness.

"From the time the command to restore and rebuild Jerusalem, there will be seven 'sevens' and 62 'sevens' until the Messiah comes. After the 62 'sevens,' the Anointed One will come and then be killed and have nothing. The people of the ruler who will come will destroy the city and the sanctuary. The end will come like a flood and war will continue until then. He will confirm a covenant with many for one 'seven,' and in the middle, he will put an end to sacrifice and offering. Then he will set up an abomination that causes desolation at his temple until the end that is decreed is poured out on him."

Daniel's 70 weeks

One of the markers of the Bible is the predictive prophecies it contains. Modern scholars struggle with this because they have an assumption that this is impossible. However, if an all-powerful, omniscient God inspired the text, then this is not a problem. Daniel predicted the time of Jesus' arrival hundreds of years before it happened. Some critics interpret Daniel as coming from the Second Century B.C., and even if we accept that assumption, this is still a case of predictive prophecy.

To understand Daniel's 70 weeks, we look at each week as an interval of seven years. The Jews began rebuilding the temple in 457 B.C. and did not complete it for 49 years (the first seven weeks) in 408 B.C. The next 62 weeks lead us to the beginning of the Messianic window (from 26 to 33 A.D.). He was crucified, resurrected, and ascended in the middle of this week. Scholars debate whether the rest of the week has already occurred or if it is still to come before Jesus' Second Coming.

DANIEL'S VISION OF LATTER DAYS

In the third year of Cyrus, king of Persia, I saw a vision of a great war, and I mourned for three weeks afterward. When I was standing on the bank of the Tigris, I saw a man dressed in linen with a golden belt around his waist. His body was like topaz, his face like lightning, his eyes like flaming torches, his arms and legs gleamed like bronze, and he had a booming voice. I was the only one who saw the vision, but those who were with me became terrified and ran away.

I stared at the man and lost all my strength. He stopped my trembling hands and said to me, "Daniel, do not be afraid; God has heard your prayers since the first day you set your mind to gain understanding and humble yourself before him. I have come in response, but the prince of the Persian kingdom resisted me for 21 days until Michael, the archangel, came to help me. I have come to tell you what will happen to your people in the future."

I was speechless, but then he touched my lips, and I said, "I am overcome with anguish because of the vision and I feel very weak. I can barely even breathe; how can I talk with you about this?"

He touched me and gave me strength and said, "Don't be afraid, be strong! I must leave soon to fight against the prince of Persia, but first, I will tell you what is in the Book of Truth.

"Three more kings will arise in Persia and then a fourth who will be far richer than the others. He will stir up everyone against Greece and then a mighty king will arise who will do whatever he wants. But God will break up his empire and give it to others, and there will be conflict between kings in the north and south, and power will go back and forth in war.

"Eventually, the king in the north will become angry against the holy covenant and give favor to those who forsake it. His armed forces will desecrate the temple, end the daily sacrifice, and set up the abomination that causes desolation. He will corrupt those who forsake the Lord, but the people who know their God will resist. Those who are wise will instruct many, although they might be killed or arrested. Some of them will stumble so that they might be refined and made spotless until the end of time.

"The king will do as he pleases, and he will exalt himself above every god; he will succeed until the time for God's wrath is at hand. He will disregard the gods of his ancestors and exalt himself above them all. He will conquer many nations and sweep through them like a flood. But, suddenly, his time will run out, and no one will help him.

Daniel's final vision

This final vision is one of the most specifically fulfilled prophecies in Scripture. Some critics insist this must be history rather than prophecy because they don't believe Daniel could be as precise in his foresight. However, if we accept that God can foretell the future, this is not a problem.

"At that time, Michael will arise to protect you, and there will be a time of distress, unlike any that has ever happened. But everyone whose name is in the book will be delivered. The dead will rise to either everlasting life or everlasting contempt. Those who are wise and those who lead many to righteousness will shine like the brightness of heaven forever.

"Roll up and seal the words of the scroll until the end times. Many will go here and there to increase knowledge."

Then I saw two others who stood before me on each side of the Tigris and I asked how long until these things happen. The man in linen lifted his hands towards heaven and said, "It will be for three-and-a-half years when the power of the holy people has finally been broken; these things will occur."

I didn't understand, so I asked what this would lead to, and he replied, "Go your way. God will purify many, but the wicked will continue to be wicked; they will not understand, but the wise will. The time from the end of the sacrifice to the abomination that causes desolation is 1,290 days. Blessed is the one who waits this long and makes it to the end of 1,335 days. Go your way until the end, then you will rest, and at the end of the days, you will rise to receive your inheritance."

CHAPTER TWENTY-ONE

EZEKIEL'S FIRST VISIONS
Ezekiel 1-7

> **The Book of Ezekiel**
>
> Ezekiel lived during an extremely volatile time in history. He was from Aaron's priestly line, and he had a broad understanding of the Law and the political scene of the time. His ministry extended from 593 to 571 B.C. and his prophecies were a series of short oracles. One of his primary messages was that the people would know that God was the Lord because of his judgments and sovereignty. He gave precise dates for many prophecies and that helps us place his message in a historical context.
>
> One of the distinctives of this book is the seemingly bizarre commands God gave Ezekiel. These served as practical illustrations to grab the attention of the people. The repeated phrase, "you will know that I am the Lord," also demonstrates this.

When I was 30, during the fifth year of King Jehoiachin's exile, the word of the Lord came to me by the Kebar River in Babylon. I saw a windstorm coming from the north, an immense cloud with flashing lightning.

The center looked like glowing metal, and there were four living creatures that looked like humans but had four faces and four wings. Their legs were straight, but they had hooves like a calf and glowed like polished bronze. They had human hands under their wings, and each one's wings touched the wings of another. They all went straight ahead and did not move to the side.

Each one had the faces of a human, lion, ox, and eagle. Two of their wings spread out upward and two wings covered their bodies. Each of them went straight ahead, wherever the spirit would go. The creatures were like burning coals or torches, and fire moved back and forth among them.

Then I saw a wheel on the ground next to each creature that sparkled like topaz and had a wheel inside the wheel. Their rims were high and fantastic, full of eyes all around. They moved in conjunction with the creatures and went wherever the spirit went.

Over the living creatures' heads was something that looked like a vault, sparkling like crystal and awesome. Above that was a throne and above the throne was a figure like that of a man. A brilliant light surrounded him, and from the waist up, he looked like glowing metal, and his legs looked like fire. The radiance around him was like a rainbow on a rainy day. He looked like God's glory, and when I saw him, I fell on my face.

He spoke to me and said, "Son of man, stand up and let me talk to you. I am sending you to the Israelites, a nation that has rebelled against me; they and their ancestors have been in revolt against me to this very day. They are obstinate and stubborn, but tell them everything I say to you so that they will know that a prophet has been among them.

"Do not be afraid of them or their words even though they surround you like thorns and scorpions. Do not be rebellious like they are; open your mouth and eat what I give you."

A hand holding a scroll reached out to me; it had words of lament, mourning, and woe written on both sides. Then he said to me, "Son of man, eat this scroll and then go speak to the people. I am sending you to people who can understand every word you say, but they will be unwilling because they are hard-headed and obstinate. But I will make you just as hard as they are; your forehead will be harder than flint. Go speak my word to them."

I ate the scroll and it was as sweet as honey in my mouth. Then the Spirit lifted me up and I heard the rumbling of the wings of the living creatures from behind me. The Spirit took me away in bitterness, and the anger of my spirit and the strong hand of the Lord was on me. I came to the exiles in Tel Aviv and sat among them for seven days in deep distress.

EZEKIEL TO BE A WATCHMAN

After seven days, the Lord said to me, "Son of man, I have made you a watchman for Israel, so hear my word and warn them. If I tell the wicked that they will die and you don't warn them, they will die for their sin, but I will hold you accountable for their blood. But if you warn them and they don't repent, they will die for their sin, but you will have saved yourself."

> **Son of man**
>
> This is a title that God repeatedly uses to refer to Ezekiel. In this context, it contrasts humanity's low status when compared to the Lord. Jesus used this title during his ministry to demonstrate his connection to all of humanity.

Then the Lord told me to go out to the plain, and when I arrived there, I saw the Lord's glory, and fell face down. The Spirit raised me to my feet and said, "Shut yourself inside your house and they will bind you with ropes so that you cannot go out among the people. I will make your tongue stick to the roof of your mouth so that you will be unable to speak or rebuke these rebellious people. But when I talk to you, I will open your mouth, and you speak my words.

"Put a block of clay in front of you and draw the city of Jerusalem on it. Then lay siege to it, build towers, ramps, and battering rams around it. Then put an iron pan in between you and the city and turn your face toward it. You will besiege the block of clay and it will be a sign for Israel.

"Then lie on your left side and put Israel's sin on yourself; you will lie on your side for 390 days, one day for each year of their sin. Then you will lie down on your right side and bear Judah's sin for 40 days, a day for each year. Turn your face toward the model of Jerusalem's siege and prophesy against her. I will tie you up with ropes so that you cannot roll over until you have finished the days of your siege.

"Store up grain for yourself to make bread that you will eat all the days you lie on your side. Weigh out eight ounces of food and 32 ounces of water to eat and drink each day at set times. Bake your bread in the sight of all the people and use human feces for fuel. This shows how Israel will eat defiled food among the nations where I drive them."

But I protested, "Lord, I have never defiled myself. I have never eaten anything unclean in my whole life!"

The Lord replied, "All right, you can bake your bread over cow poop instead of human. Son of man, I am about to cut off the food supply in Jerusalem, and people will eat and drink with anxiety and despair because they are so scarce.

"When your siege is over, shave your head and beard with a sharp sword and divide it into three parts. Burn a third of the hair inside the city, attack another third with a sword all around the city, and scatter the final third to the wind. But save a few hairs and tuck them into your clothes.

"Burn a couple of these in the fire because a fire will spread from there to all of Israel. I placed Jerusalem in the center of the nations, but in her wickedness, she has rebelled against me and rejected my laws.

"Jerusalem, I am against you, and I will punish you in the nations' sight because of your detestable idols. I will do something that I have never done before and will never do again: parents will eat their children and children will eat their parents. I will scatter your survivors to the winds because you defiled my sanctuary with your detestable idols. Just like Ezekiel, I will shave you myself and will not pity you. A third of your people will die of plague or famine inside the city, a third will die by the sword outside your walls, and I will scatter a third to the winds. Then my anger will cease and I will be avenged; they will know that I have spoken in my zeal.

"When I shoot at you with my deadly and destructive arrows of famine, I will shoot to kill. I will bring more and more famine upon you and cut off your food supply. I will leave you childless and bloodshed will sweep through you."

JUDGMENT ON JERUSALEM

The Lord told me to prophesy against the mountains of Israel and say, "I am about to bring a sword against you, destroy your high places, demolish your altars, and kill your people in front of your idols. Then you will know that I am the Lord.

"But I will spare some of you and scatter you among the nations. Eventually, the exiles will remember me and how their adulterous hearts have turned away from me. They will hate themselves for all the evil they've done and know that I am the Lord because I didn't make empty threats.

"Clap your hands and stamp your feet because of Israel's sin; they will die by the sword, famine, or plague. I will stretch out my hand against them and make them a desolate wasteland. Then they will know that I am the Lord."

***

The word of the Lord came to me again, "The end has come to the four corners of the land and I will unleash my anger against you. I will judge you for your detestable practices and then you will know that I am the Lord.

"Doom has come, and I am about to pour out my wrath on you; I will leave nothing of value. No one will save their life, for my anger is on all of them because of their abominations. Every hand will go limp, every leg will be wet with urine, every face will be covered with shame, and every head will be shaved.

"Prepare the chains for the land is full of bloodshed and the city is full of violence. I will bring in the most wicked nations to displace them and put an end to their pride. Calamity after calamity and rumor after rumor will come upon them. They will search for a vision or prophecy, but there will be none. The king will mourn, the prince will despair, and the people's hands will tremble in fear. Then they will know that I am the Lord."

CHAPTER TWENTY-TWO

WARNINGS AGAINST JERUSALEM
Ezekiel 8-16, (17), 18-19

A little more than a year later, I was sitting in my house, and the elders of Judah were with me. I saw a figure that looked like a man. From the waist down, he was like fire, and from the waist up, he was as bright as glowing metal. He stretched out a hand, lifted me by the hair, and carried me to Jerusalem. The glory of the God of Israel was before me, just as it had been in the vision I saw on the plain.

He showed me an idol inside the inner court of the temple and said, "Son of man, do you see the detestable things the Israelites are doing here that will drive me far from my sanctuary? You will see even worse."

He took me to a hole in the wall and told me to dig deeper into it. I dug into the wall until I saw a doorway there, and he told me to go in and see what they were doing. I saw 70 elders of Israel standing by a wall covered with unclean animals and Israel's idols. Each of the elders held a censer in his hand and a fragrant cloud of incense rose from them. He said, "You can see what the elders of Israel are doing in private; they think the Lord can't see them. But you will see them doing even worse things."

Then he took me to the north gate of the temple and I saw women mourning the god Tammuz. He brought me to the temple's inner court and showed me about 25 men bowing down to worship the sun in the east. He said to me, "Son of man, look at the detestable things they are doing here; they fill the land with violence and then pretend to be holy. I will deal with them in anger and I will not listen to their prayers."

Then he called for those who were going to judge the city. Six men came forward, each holding a deadly weapon, and they were accompanied by a man in linen with a writing kit. They went in and stood beside the bronze altar, and the glory of the God of Israel went up above the cherubim where it had been.

The Lord called to the man in linen and said, "Go throughout Jerusalem and put a mark on the foreheads of those who grieve and lament over the detestable things done here." Then he said to the other six, "Follow him through the city and kill anyone he doesn't mark without pity or compassion. Slaughter the young and old, mothers and children, starting at my sanctuary. Defile the temple and fill the courts with the dead."

They went out and began killing throughout the city. I fell face down and cried, "Sovereign Lord, are you going to destroy the entire remnant of Israel?"

He answered me, "The sin of Israel and Judah is exceedingly great; they are filled with violence and think I don't see it. So, I will not look on them with pity or spare them; I will bring down on their heads what they have done."

Then the man in linen brought back his writing kit and said, "I have done as you commanded."

The Lord said to the man in linen, "Go in among the wheels beneath the cherubim and fill your hands with burning coals and scatter them over the city." Then the glory of the Lord moved to the threshold of the temple, the cloud filled the temple, and the radiance of God's glory filled the court. A cherubim put some coals in the man's hand and then the man left.

Then I saw the four creatures and the wheels I had seen previously by the Kebar River. They went out to the east gate and the glory of the Lord left the temple.

Then the Spirit lifted me up and brought me to the gate where I had seen the 25 men, and the Lord said, "Son of man, these are the men who are plotting evil and giving wicked advice in this city. Tell them that the Lord knows their thoughts and will bring a sword upon them. I will drive them out of the city and deliver them into the hands of foreigners and inflict punishment on them. Then you will know that I am the Lord."

As I was prophesying, Pelatiah, the son of Benaiah, died, and I cried out, "Lord, will you completely destroy the remnant of Israel?"

The Lord answered, "Although I sent them far away, for a little while, I have been a sanctuary for them in the countries where they have gone. I will gather them from the nations and bring them back from the countries where you have been scattered, and I will give them the land again. They will return to it and remove its vile images and idols; I will provide them with an undivided heart and put a new spirit in them, giving them a heart of flesh, removing their heart of stone.

"Then they will follow my laws, they will be my people and I will be their God. I will bring down the heads of those who refuse to leave their detestable idols." Then the vision I was having ended and I told the exiles everything the Lord had shown me.

EZEKIEL PACKS FOR EXILE

The word of the Lord came to me, "Son of man, you are living among rebellious people that do not see and do not hear, so pack your belongings for exile. As they watch you go, perhaps they will understand their rebellion; then dig through the wall and take your belongings with you."

I did as he commanded and the Lord said to me, "Tell the people that you are a sign and as you have done, so I will do to them; they will go into exile as captives. I will spread my net for them and take them to Babylon, where you will die. Then they will know that I am the Lord.

"Son of man, tremble as you eat and drink because the people will live in anxiety and despair for their land will be stripped of everything. Then you will know that I am the Lord. They think it won't happen for a long time, but it is about to happen."

WOE TO THE PROPHETS

The Lord told me to say to the people, "Woe to the foolish prophets who follow their own spirit, but have seen nothing! Your prophets are like jackals among ruins because you have not repaired the breaches in the wall so that it will stand in the battle on the Day of the Lord. Their visions are false even though they claim I have spoken.

"I am against you because of your false words. My hand will be against the false prophets because they lead my people astray. They proclaim peace when there will be none. When the wall falls, you will be destroyed, and you will know that I am the Lord.

"Woe to the women who sew magic charms on their wrists and make veils of various lengths to trap people. You have profaned me among my people for a few scraps of bread, killed those who should have lived, and spared those who should have died.

"I am against your magic charms; I will tear them from your arms and set the people free that you ensnare like birds. I will tear off your veils and save my people from your hands; then, you will know that I am the Lord."

GOD IS AGAINST HIS PEOPLE

Some of the elders sat down in front of me and the Lord said to me, "Son of man, these men have set up idols in their hearts and stumbling blocks before their faces; I won't let them inquire of me. Tell them to repent and turn from their idols or I will set my face against them and remove them from my people. Then they will know that I am the Lord. They will bear their punishment so that they will stop running from me, then they will be my people and I will be their God.

"Even if Noah, Daniel, and Job were here, they could only save themselves with their righteousness. They couldn't even save their children; it will be much worse when I send sword, famine, wild beasts, and plague to kill their men and animals. But there will be some survivors who will console you. Their actions will show you that I have not done this without cause."

***

The Lord spoke to me again, "Son of man, the wood from a grapevine is not as useful as the wood from a tree. It's only good for fuel, and even then, it burns too quickly. Vines are useless both before and after being burned. The people of Jerusalem are like vines growing among the trees of a forest and I will throw them into the fire."

JERUSALEM'S SINS

Another time the Lord said, "Son of man, confront Jerusalem with her sins. Tell her that she is like an unwanted baby that someone abandoned. But I came by and gave her life. I raised her to be a beautiful jewel, and I made a covenant with her when she came of age. I dressed her in fine clothes and jewelry, but she became a prostitute to every man who came along.

"How could this happen? She used her finery to dress up her idols. Then she sacrificed her children to idols, never remembering all I had done for her. Therefore, I have struck her with my fist. But she has gone even further, paying her clients rather than taking payment. So, I will gather your allies, and they will look upon her lewdness and attack. I will do this because of her detestable sins. They will strip you and leave you naked as they cut you to pieces.

"She is just like her pagan sisters, Samaria and Sodom, although she has done far worse than them. Sodom was proud, and the wealthy ignored the needy, so I removed them. She even makes Samaria look righteous. But someday, I will restore her fortunes as well as those of Samaria and Sodom. But until then, you will bear the penalty for your sins.

"I will remember my covenant with her and she will remember the ways of her youth. I will establish my covenant with her and she will know that I am the Lord. I will atone for all her sins."

GUILT FOR INDIVIDUAL SIN

The word of the Lord came to me, "What do you people mean by saying that the parents eat sour grapes and set the children's teeth on edge? Everyone belongs to me; the one who sins is the one who will die. Those who are righteous do what is just and right, don't sin, oppress, or commit robbery. They judge justly and obey my laws; they will live.

"If they have children who sin and do not follow their parents' example, their blood will be on their own heads. Or, if children see their parents sinning and do not follow their example, they will live, and their parents will die. The one who sins is the one who will die. But if the wicked repent, they will live as well.

"I do not take pleasure in the death of the wicked; I am pleased when they repent and live. The Lord is just and will judge each of you according to your ways. Repent and turn from your sin and get a new heart and a new spirit. Repent and live!"

CHAPTER TWENTY-THREE

JUDGMENT AND CONSOLATION
Ezekiel 20-24, (25-32), 33-48

THE ELDERS INQUIRE OF THE LORD

In the seventh year, some of the elders sat down before me and inquired of the Lord, and he said, "I will not let you come to ask of me. On the day I chose Israel, I promised my people in Egypt and told them I am the Lord your God. I swore to them that I would bring them out of Egypt into a beautiful land. I told them to get rid of their idols because I am the Lord. But they rebelled and would not get rid of their false gods, so I poured my wrath out on them. But for my name's sake, I brought them out of Egypt and kept them from being profaned in the sight of the nations.

"I brought them into the wilderness, but they rejected my laws and desecrated my Sabbaths. I did not destroy them for my name's sake and eventually brought their children into the Promised Land. They devoted their hearts to their idols, but I had pity on them and didn't destroy them.

"But their children rebelled against me, and I withheld my hand for my name's sake. Now, you continue to defile yourselves the way your ancestors did. You want to be like the nations around you who serve wood and stone, but what you want will never happen.

"I will rule over you with an outstretched arm and outpoured wrath. As I judged your ancestors, I will judge you as well. I will purge you of those who revolt and rebel against me; then, you will know that I am the Lord.

"You want to be like the nations around you? Go serve your idols, but stop trying to worship false gods and me. On my holy mountain, restored Israel will serve me, and I will accept them. Then you will know that I am the Lord when I bring you into the land I swore to give your ancestors."

JUDGMENT ON JERUSALEM

The Lord spoke to Ezekiel again, "Son of man, I am now Israel's enemy. I will draw my sword and cut off both the righteous and the wicked. Everyone on earth will know that I am the Lord! Every spirit will faint and become as weak as water. I will swing the sword of my anger and slaughter my people and their leaders. I will pour out my fury on Israel and you will be wiped out.

"I am bringing judgment on Jerusalem! They are guilty because of her idols and murders. They hold their parents in contempt, oppress the disadvantaged, and are full of all sorts of sexual sin. They never even think of me or my commands.

"I will scatter them among the nations and purge them of their wickedness. I will purify them with my fiery anger like precious metals are refined. Your priests and leaders devour human lives and disregard my commands. They conspire to take advantage of innocent people and lie; they dishonor my name. I searched for someone to rebuild righteousness and stand in the gap, but I found no one. Now I will pour out my fury and they will bear the full penalty for their sins."

THE TWO SISTERS

The word of the Lord came to me and said, "Son of man, there were two daughters of the same mother who became prostitutes in Egypt. Samaria gave herself to the Assyrians and defiled herself with their idols; therefore, I gave her into their hands.

"They stripped her naked, took away her children, and killed her with the sword. Judah saw this and followed her sister's example and she lusted after the Assyrians as well. But she went further and lusted after the Babylonians in addition to her previous lovers. I turned away from her in disgust just as I had done to her sister, but she kept going and longed for Egypt's lewdness.

"Now, the Babylonians will come against you with weapons and chariots, and I will turn you over to them for punishment. I will direct my anger towards you and deal with you in fury. They will cut off your noses and ears and take away your children in captivity.

"They will deal with you in hatred and take away everything you have made. They will leave you naked and expose the shame of your prostitution. You will drink from your sister's cup and drain it.

"Since you have forgotten me and turned your back on me, you must bear the consequences of your prostitution. They committed adultery with their idols and even sacrificed their children. So, I will end their evil so that all women will learn not to imitate you. Your enemies will attack you with swords and butcher your children. Then you will be repaid for your prostitution and know that I am the Lord."

THE COOKING POT

On the day Babylon laid siege to Jerusalem, the Lord told me to fill a cooking pot with water and pieces of meat and cook them. Then he said, "Woe to the city of bloodshed, cook the meat, mix in spices, and let the bones be charred. Put the empty pot on the coals until it glows hot so that its impurities may be melted and burned away.

"I tried to cleanse your impurity, but you won't be clean until my wrath subsides. I will not hold back, I will not have pity, and I will not relent; I will judge you according to your actions."

EZEKIEL'S WIFE DIES

The Lord came to me and told me that my wife would die and he told me not to mourn my loss. She died, and the next morning I did as I was commanded and did not weep for her, even though my heart broke. The people asked me why I was acting this way.

Then I said to them, "The Lord is about to desecrate his sanctuary and the stronghold that makes you proud. You will do as I am doing; you will not mourn or weep, but waste away because of your sins. I am a sign to you, and when this happens, you will know that he is the Sovereign Lord."

THE KING OF TYRE

The Lord says about the king of Tyre, "You were the picture of perfection, full of wisdom and beauty. You were in the Garden of Eden, adorned in every precious jewel. You were set apart as the guardian angel and lived on God's holy mountain. You were perfect from creation until you chose sin. You were filled with violence, so I threw you down from my holy mountain. Your beauty and wisdom made you proud, so I cast you to the ground. I exposed you to the world, and your sin consumed you. All the world is appalled by your downfall; you have come to a dreadful end and will be no more."

> **The king of Tyre**
>
> This message is one that scholars have seen to have a dual meaning. It is a message to the King of Tyre and a description of Satan's rebellion and God casting him out from heaven.

***

> **Ezekiel's prophecies against the nations**
>
> Ezekiel spoke many prophecies against foreign nations as well. He prophesied judgment on Ammon, Moab, Edom, Philistia, Tyre, Sidon, Egypt, and Nebuchadnezzar for their sins. One of the more unlikely prophecies that Ezekiel made was against the city of Tyre. While I have omitted other prophecies against countries or people who no longer exist in the same form they did more than 2,500 years ago, I will include this one.
>
> God says to Tyre, "I am your enemy and I will bring many nations against you. They will destroy your walls and scrape away your soil until it is a bare rock where fishers spread their nets. They will come against you, destroy your villages, and then lay siege to the city walls. They will plunder your riches and throw the soil and debris from the ruins into the sea. They will destroy you and you will never be rebuilt!"
>
> Tyre had existed as a city for more than 2,000 years and was believed to be impregnable. The stronghold of the city was a rocky island that was immune to regular attack strategies. The rest of the city was on the mainland and various nations had attacked over its history without sustained success.
>
> Thanks to the precise dating in Ezekiel, we know that he made this prophecy on February 3, 586 B.C. King Nebuchadnezzar attacked not long after that, partially fulfilling the prophecy. Over the following years, Syria, Egypt, Rome, Armenia,

> Persia, and Greece all attacked as well. The most fantastic fulfillment came when Alexander the Great attacked in 332 B.C. He easily defeated the mainland, and then in an extremely unorthodox battle strategy, he threw the rubble from the city into the sea to build a siege bridge to the island fortress. Eventually, they overthrew the island, killed the inhabitants, and razed the city.
>
> For years, the island became a place that fishers used for spreading their nets. Over time, the coastline's geography changed with erosion and sand deposits, making the original site of Tyre lost to historians. Given Tyre's history and strategic advantages, this predictive prophecy would have sounded absurd at the time, but it is evidence of God's ability to foretell the future.

EZEKIEL CONFIRMED AS A WATCHMAN

The word of the Lord came to me, "When I appoint a watchman over a land, and he warns them of impending doom, but they don't listen, their blood is on their own heads. If they had listened, they would have been saved. But if the watchman does not warn them, he will be accountable for their blood.

"Son of man, I have made you a watchman for Israel and you must warn them. Tell them that I don't take pleasure in the death of the wicked, repent so that you may live. They claim I am unjust, but I will judge them each according to their deeds."

JERUSALEM'S FALL

In the twelfth year of our exile, a man came to me to tell me that Jerusalem had fallen. Then the Lord opened my mouth and he said, "Because Abraham was an individual who possessed the land, you think that you will retain it because there are so many of you. But you still will not listen to me, so I will make your land a desolate waste; then you will know that I am the Lord.

"My people come to listen to you, but they don't put your words into practice. Their mouths speak of love, but their hearts are greedy for unjust gain. To them, you are nothing more than entertainment. When all your words come true, they will know that a prophet has been among them."

WOE TO THE SHEPHERDS

The Lord spoke to me, "Woe to the shepherds of Israel who only take care of themselves when they should be tending the flock. You have the finest things, but you have not strengthened the weak, healed the sick, or bound up the injured. You have not looked for strays; you have ruled with brutality. They have been scattered and become food for the wild animals.

"Because my flock lacks a shepherd and you care about yourselves and not them, I will hold you accountable for my people. I will track down my scattered sheep and rescue them from the places where they've strayed. I will watch over them in a good pasture and they will lie down in safety. I will bind up the injured and strengthen the weak; I will shepherd with justice.

"As for my flock, I will judge between one sheep and another, between rams and goats. I have given you enough; why destroy the rest of it so that no one else can have any? I will judge between the fat and lean sheep because you shove the weak until you have driven them away.

"I will save my flock and put them in the care of my servant David, and he will be their shepherd. I will make a covenant of peace with them and remove the savage beasts from the land so they can live in safety. I will bless their crops and break the bars of their captivity. Then they will know that I am the Lord their God and that they are the sheep of my pasture."

A HEART OF FLESH

The word of the Lord came to me again, "Son of man, when the Israelites were in their land, they defiled it with their actions and their conduct was like a menstrual rag in my sight. I poured out my wrath on them because of their idols; they profaned my holy name wherever they went.

"It is not for their sake that I've done these things, but for my name. The nations will know that I am the Lord when I prove myself holy through you before their eyes. I will bring you back to your land and cleanse you from your impurities and idols. I will give you a new heart and a new spirit; I will remove your heart of stone and give you a heart of flesh. I will put my Spirit in you and move you to follow my decrees; then you will live in the land I gave your ancestors; you will be my people, and I will be your God."

THE VALLEY OF DRY BONES

The Lord brought me out by the Holy Spirit and set me in the middle of a valley that was full of bones. He led me back and forth among them and the dry bones covered the ground. God asked me if these bones could live again and I replied, "Lord, you are the only one who knows."

He said, "Tell the bones that I will put breath in them and make them come to life. I will attach tendons and flesh and cover them with skin; then, you will know that I am the Lord."

I obeyed, and there was a rattling sound as the bones came together, formed flesh, and were covered with skin. But there was no breath in them, so the Lord told me to call for the four winds to breathe life into the dead so that they could live. Once I did, they came to life and became a great army.

Then the Lord said, "Son of man, these bones are the people of Israel, they are dried up, and their hope is cut off. But I will open their graves and bring them back to the land of Israel. I will put my Spirit in them, and they will live in their land; then they will know that I am the Lord, and I have spoken."

THE TWO STICKS

The Lord told me to take a stick and write "belonging to Judah and the Israelites with him" on it. Then he told me to take another stick and write "belonging to Joseph and all the Israelites associated with him" on it. Then he told me to put them together so that they become one stick in my hand.

The Lord said, "Tell the people that I will join Joseph's stick with Judah's stick and make them one in my hand. I will take the Israelites out of the nations, bring them back to their land, and make them one kingdom again. They will no longer defile themselves with their idols, and I will cleanse them; they will be my people, and I will be their God.

"My servant David will be their king and they will all have one shepherd. They will follow my laws and live in the land I gave to my servant Jacob, the land where your ancestors lived. I will make an everlasting covenant of peace with them and their numbers will increase. Then the nations will know that I made Israel holy when my sanctuary is among them forever."

VISION OF THE FUTURE TEMPLE

In the 25th year of our exile, the Lord showed me a vision of a city on a very high mountain in Israel. I saw a man who looked like bronze standing in the gateway with a linen cord and holding a measuring rod. The man told me to pay close attention and then tell the people of Israel everything I saw.

He showed me a new temple, its gates, courts, and the rooms for the priests. He also showed me the altar and the measurements for all of them. Then I saw the glory of the Lord enter the temple and he showed me how the priesthood would be restored. He then showed me the holy city and the land where the Lord would restore the people.

CHAPTER TWENTY-FOUR

THE SWARM OF LOCUSTS
Joel 1-3

> **The Book of Joel**
>
> We don't know very much about the prophet Joel or when he wrote this book. However, not knowing the details of penmanship does not hinder our understanding of what he wrote. Joel interprets the plague of locusts as God's judgment on his people and sees the restoration of God's favor.

Listen, elders, nothing like this has ever happened before, and you will tell your descendants about this. The locust is coming and is going to destroy everything. An army is coming up against the land with teeth like a lion and it will lay everything to waste.

Go into mourning and proclaim a fast because the Day of the Lord is near. Gather the elders and cry out to the Lord. He will destroy everything and cut off food, you, and gladness. Lord, I call to you because we are devoured, and there will be nothing left. The Day of the Lord is near; let everyone fear because no one can endure it, not even beasts of the field.

Sound the alarm because the Day of the Lord is coming. It will be a day of darkness and fire for his enemies. God's army will be chillingly effective; no one will be able to overcome them. The Day of the Lord will be terrifying; who can endure it?

The Lord declares, "Even now, return to me with all your heart, fasting, weeping, and mourning; tear your hearts and not your clothes."

Return to the Lord your God because he is gracious, merciful, slow to anger, abounding in love, and he relents over disaster; he may relent and bless you. Gather the people together and consecrate them; pray for the Lord to spare you so that you will not become a lesson to the nations. Don't let them ask where your God is.

The Lord became jealous for his land and pitied his people. He answered their prayer and blessed them with grain, wine, and oil, no longer to be a reproach among the nations. He will remove the invaders from your land. Do not be afraid, but rejoice because the Lord has done great things! He will restore the years that the swarming locust has taken and his people will never again be ashamed. He is in Israel; he is the only God and there is no other.

He will pour out his Spirit on all flesh, and our sons and daughters will prophesy, our old men will dream, and our young men will see visions. God will do miracles on earth; the sun will turn to darkness and the moon to blood before the awesome Day of the Lord. The Lord will save everyone who calls on his name.

The Lord will restore the fortunes of Judah and Jerusalem and he will gather his people home. He will pay back those who have stolen his riches from his temple and sold his people into slavery.

Tell the nations to prepare for war and prepare as best they can. It won't matter because God will fight for his people. The Lord roars from Jerusalem, and the heavens and earth quake; he will judge his enemies and be a refuge to his people.

Then you will know that he is the Lord God who dwells in Jerusalem; you will be holy, and strangers will not pass through it again. Judah will flourish, and their enemies will become desolate. Judah will be inhabited forever, and the Lord will avenge their blood.

CHAPTER TWENTY-FIVE

TEMPLE RECONSTRUCTION
Haggai 1-2

> **The Book of Haggai**
>
> The prophet Haggai spoke his message in the year 520 B.C. and was a catalyst for the Jews' rebuilding the temple. His book contains four oracles, all of which motivate the people to get back to work.

HAGGAI'S FIRST MESSAGE

The Lord says, "These people think it's not time to rebuild my house, but is it right for you to live in nice houses while my house is in ruins? Think about it, you work and work, but you never have enough; it's because you have left my house desolate while each of you builds your wealth. Put yourselves to work and rebuild. Nothing is working for you, because you have not obeyed my command." The remnant of Israel obeyed God's voice and began to rebuild the temple because they feared the Lord.

HAGGAI'S SECOND MESSAGE

Several weeks later, the Lord spoke through Haggai again, "If any of you have seen the glory of the former temple, you know that this new one is nothing compared to it. So, get to work because my Spirit is in your midst, and you do not need to be afraid. In a little while, I will shake the nations to bring in treasures to fill my house with glory. All the gold and silver of earth is mine and the glory to come will be greater than the former glory."

HAGGAI'S THIRD MESSAGE

A few months later, the Lord spoke again, "Up until now, things have been difficult because you have been focused on the wrong things. You have brought offerings to me, but they are unclean because you have not turned to me. Things continue to be difficult because you have not obeyed. But from now on, I will bless you."

HAGGAI'S FOURTH MESSAGE

Later that day, the Lord spoke a second time, "I am going to shake the heavens and earth and overthrow the kingdoms, their chariots, and riders. Then I will make Zerubbabel, my servant, like a signet ring because I have chosen you."

CHAPTER TWENTY-SIX

GOD REMEMBERS ISRAEL
Zechariah 1-14

> **The Book of Zechariah**
>
> Zechariah was a member of the priestly family who was born in Babylon during the exile. He returned to Jerusalem with Zerubbabel and was a contemporary of Haggai. He wrote the first portion of the book in 520 B.C. and the latter part sometime after 480 B.C. The primary purpose of his writing was like Haggai's to motivate the people to complete the temple's reconstruction.

ZECHARIAH'S VISIONS

The Lord came to Zechariah, saying, "I was very angry with your ancestors, return to me, and I will return to you. Do not be like your ancestors, who ignored the prophets because my words are eternal. The Lord has dealt with us as he has purposed."

Three months later, the word of the Lord came to Zechariah again, and the prophet said, "I saw a man riding a red horse in the night, and many other horses surrounded him. These patrol the earth and they have seen how the Lord has not had mercy on Judah for 70 years. But now he will have mercy on Jerusalem and build his house there; he will pour out his prosperity on them."

Then I saw the four horns that have scattered Judah, Israel, and Jerusalem. Then the Lord showed me four craftsmen who have come to cast down the horns of the nations that scattered his people.

Then I saw a man with a measuring line in his hand going to measure Jerusalem and the Lord declared, "Jerusalem will be filled with people and livestock, I will be a wall of fire around her, and I will be the glory in her midst. You have been scattered, but I will shake the nations, and you will plunder them. Sing and rejoice because I will live in your midst, and the nations will come to the Lord." All flesh should be silent before the Lord because he has roused himself from his holy dwelling.

Then I saw Joshua, the high priest, standing before the angel of the Lord, and Satan was at his right hand to accuse him. The Lord said to Satan, "I rebuke you, Satan, because this is a brand plucked from the fire."

Joshua was wearing filthy garments and the angel of the Lord said, "I have taken away his sin, clothe him with pure garments and put a clean turban on his head." The angel said, "If you walk in my ways, then you will rule my house, and I will give you the right of access among those standing here. Joshua, you and your friends who sit before you are a sign that I will bring my servant the Branch. I will engrave an inscription on the seven-eyed stone that I've put before Joshua and you will invite your neighbor to recline with you."

The angel who talked with me woke me from a deep sleep and he showed me a golden lampstand with a bowl on top with seven lamps with lips. There were two olive trees on each side of it. Then he said to me, "Not by might or power, but by my Spirit, I will make you a plain, and I will put the stone in the midst of it and people will shout 'grace to it!' Zerubbabel has laid the foundation of this house and he will complete it. These seven eyes are the eyes of the Lord that range through the whole earth. The two trees are the anointed ones who stand by the Lord of the entire earth."

Then I saw a flying scroll 30 by 15 feet, and the angel said, "This is the curse that goes over the land, and everyone who steals will be cleaned out by one side, and the other side will clean out those who swear falsely. It will sneak into their house and consume them."

Then I saw a basket with a woman sitting in it and was told, "This is the land's sin and the woman is Wickedness." Then the angel thrust her back in the basket. Then I saw two women coming forward with the wind in their wings and they took the basket to Babylon where they will build a house for it.

Then I saw four chariots come out from between two bronze mountains; the first had red horses, the second black, the third white, and the fourth dappled. The angel told me, "These are the four winds of heaven going to present themselves before the Lord."

The word of the Lord said, "Take gold and silver from the exiles arriving from Babylon and make a crown for Joshua, the high priest. The Branch will grow from this place and he will build the temple of the Lord and rule from his throne. Those who are far off will come to build the temple and you will know that the Lord of hosts has sent me to you if you obey."

HISTORICAL INTERLUDE

Two years later, the Lord said to Zechariah, "Make true judgments, show kindness and mercy to each other, don't oppress the widow, fatherless, sojourner, or poor. But your ancestors refused to pay attention and stopped their ears so that they might not hear. I called, but they would not hear because their hearts were as hard as a diamond. So, when they called, I did not listen, and I scattered them among foreign nations, and their land was desolate."

Then the Lord said, "I am jealous for Jerusalem with wrath; I will return to it and live there. Once again, people will fill the city, and it will be marvelous in my sight. I will not deal with the remnant as I have in the past, the land will bear fruit, and the remnant will possess it. I will bring my people back to Jerusalem and they will be my people and I will be their God.

"Be strong and finish the temple. I will not treat Jerusalem like I have in the past; I will bless them and not punish them any longer. Do not be afraid because I will save

Judah and Israel, and you will be a blessing. Speak truth to each other and make right judgments and peace, then people will come to seek the Lord of hosts in Jerusalem."

PROPHETIC BURDENS

Rejoice, daughter of Jerusalem, because your king is coming to you with righteousness and salvation, humble and mounted on the colt of a donkey. He will end war and speak peace to the nations as he rules the ends of the earth. He will set your prisoners free and restore your fortunes.

> **The Triumphal Entry**
>
> Jesus fulfilled this prophecy when he entered Jerusalem mounted on the back of a donkey.

He will wield you like a warrior's sword to bring judgment to my enemies. The Lord will go forth like lightning and devour them while he protects you. He will save his people and they will be like the jewels of a crown in the land. He is good and beautiful and he will bless the land.

Ask the Lord for rain, and he will give showers and cause the crops to grow. The household gods speak nonsense and lies and my people wander like sheep without a shepherd. The Lord says, "I am angry with the shepherds and will punish the leaders because I care for my flock.

"I will strengthen Judah and save them; I will bring the cornerstone from them and bring them back to me. I will gather them because I have redeemed them and they will be as numerous as before. They will remember me and return with their children from where they have been scattered. I will make them strong and they will walk in my name.

"Become shepherd of the flock doomed to slaughter, hold them back because their shepherds don't pity them. I will no longer pity the inhabitants of the land and cause them to fall into the hand of their neighbors. So, I became their shepherd, and I tended the sheep with a staff named Favor and another named Union.

"But I became impatient with them and they also hated me. So, I broke the staff named Favor and annulled the covenant I made with them. Then they gave me my wages of 30 silver pieces and the Lord told me to throw it to the potter. Then I broke the staff named Union and annulled the brotherhood between Judah and Israel. Woe to the worthless shepherd who deserts the flock; may the sword strike them.

"I am about to make Jerusalem a cup of staggering to all the surrounding nations. Those who drink from it will hurt themselves. They will gather to attack, but I will strike their soldiers with madness. God will protect Jerusalem and destroy her enemies."

The Lord continued, "I will pour out a spirit of grace and mercy on David's house, and they will look on the one they have pierced and mourn for him as a mother cries over an only child. On that day, I will open a fountain for David's house to cleanse themselves from their sin and uncleanness.

> **Jesus' crucifixion**
>
> This passage is a prophecy of how the Messiah would one day die.

"On that day, I will cut off the idols from the land, and no one will remember them any longer. I will also remove the prophet and spirit of uncleanness; they will be ashamed of what they see.

"Wake up, sword, and strike the shepherd and scatter the sheep. Two-thirds of the sheep will die and I will refine the remaining third; they will call upon my name and I will answer.

"On that day, all the nations will gather to fight against Jerusalem. But the Lord will fight on her behalf. Her enemies will flee as he shakes the earth. God will come and bring all his holy ones with him.

"The Lord will be king over all the earth, and he will strike the people who wage war against Jerusalem. The sun will no longer shine, but there will be continuous light, and the Lord will send life-giving water from Jerusalem. Judah will collect the plunder of the nations and there will be a plague on them. Those who survive will come to Jerusalem to worship God. Every pot in Jerusalem and Judah will be holy to the Lord, and there will no longer be merchants in the Lord's house."

CHAPTER TWENTY-SEVEN

GOD'S COVENANT WITH ISRAEL
Malachi 1-4

> **The Book of Malachi**
>
> This is the last of the prophetic books in the Old Testament and it is the last time that God speaks to his people until Jesus comes. This book was likely written after Nehemiah returned to Persia in 433 B.C. The central theme of this book is that God will come not only to judge his people but also to bless and restore them.

The Lord says, "I have loved Jacob and hated Esau; I have laid his land to waste. Even if they rebuild it, I will destroy their wicked country because I will always be angry with them. You will see this and declare the Lord's greatness.

> **What does this mean about Jacob and Esau?**
>
> This is a reference to Isaac's twin sons, Jacob and Esau. Even though Esau was a couple of minutes older, God chose Jacob to be the one God used to fulfill his covenant. Esau's descendants became the nation of Edom. God is reminding his people that he loves them and has chosen them to be his.

"Sons honor their fathers and servants their masters, but my priests have despised my name. They offer inferior sacrifices, and I wish you would have the courage to stop them because I will no longer accept them. I am not pleased with your worthless sacrifices because you dishonor my name. Cursed are those who promise to offer an acceptable offering and then bring a defective one.

"Priests, if you will not listen, then I will curse you and spread feces on your faces and your children's faces. I made my covenant with your ancestor Levi, and he revered my name; he had true instruction, and he walked with me in peace and righteousness. Priests should guard knowledge and seek guidance from the Lord. But you have turned away and caused my people to stumble. So, I will make you despised before all the people.

"We all have the same Father and Creator, so we should not mistreat each other. But Judah has been faithless and committed abominations by profaning my sanctuary and marrying the daughter of a foreign god. I will cut off any descendant of Jacob who does this and brings me an offering.

"You cover my altar with tears because I don't accept your offerings. Guard your spirit and do not be faithless to your wives. Those who divorce their wives cover themselves with violence. You have wearied me with your words by doing evil in my sight.

"You have worn me out by doing evil in my sight and then asking where I am. So, I am sending my messenger and he will prepare my way. He will refine the sons of Levi and they will bring righteous offerings to the Lord. Then I will judge my people for their sorcery, adultery, lies, oppression, and not fearing me.

"I am the Lord, and I do not change; from your fathers' time, you have turned away from my commands. Return to me, and I will return to you; stop robbing me in your tithes and offerings. Bring the full tithe into the storehouse so that there will be food in my house and I will open the windows of heaven and pour down blessings until there is no more need. I will rebuke the devourer and all the nations will call you blessed.

"You have spoken against me by saying it is vain to serve me and that only evildoers prosper."

Then those who feared the Lord spoke with one another and God listened to them. The Lord says, "They will be mine when I make them my treasured possession and spare them. Then you will see the distinction between the righteous and the wicked."

The Lord says, "The Day of the Lord is coming when all the arrogant and evil will burn like stubble in an oven. But the sun of righteousness will heal those of you who fear my name and you will leap about in joy. You will tread down the wicked and they will be ashes under your feet. Remember Moses' Law and I will send Elijah the prophet before the awesome Day of the Lord comes. He will turn the hearts of fathers to their children and the hearts of children to their fathers."

THE POETS
JOB – SONG OF SOLOMON

The remaining books of this section are Hebrew poetry and wisdom literature. These books tackle some of the problematic themes that we deal with as humans and I have reorganized them as user-friendly as possible for the modern reader. These books can be challenging to understand in English because the original Hebrew is poetry, and we lose meaning in translation. For many sections, I have written in prose to help us pull the purpose from what the writers intended. To further aid in understanding, I've also reorganized the Psalms and Proverbs by topic. As we look at wisdom literature, it is crucial to remember that this is general wisdom, not contractual promises. For example, bringing up a child in the Lord means they will generally continue that path as an adult, but it is not a guarantee.

INDEX OF THE PSALMS

CHAPTER 29 – Community Laments: 12, 44, 58, 60, 74, 79, 80, 85, 89, 90, 94, 123, 126, 129

CHAPTER 30 – Individual Laments: 3, 4, 5, 7, 9, 10, 13, 14, 17, 22, 25, 26, 28, 31, 39, 40:11-17, 41, 42, 43, 52, 53, 54, 55, 56, 57, 59, 61, 64, 70, 71, 77, 86, 120, 139, 141, 142

CHAPTER 31 – Psalms of Repentance: 6, 32, 38, 51, 102, 130, 143

CHAPTER 32 – Psalms of Vengeance: 35, 69, 83, 88, 109, 137, 140

CHAPTER 33 – Psalms of Thanksgiving: (Community) 65, 75, 107, 124, 136 (Individual): 18, 30, 34, 40:1-11, 66:13-20, 92, 108, 116, 118, 138

CHAPTER 34 – Psalms of Trust: 11, 16, 23, 27, 62, 63, 91, 121, 125, 131

CHAPTER 35 – Worship Psalms: 8, 19:1-6, 33, 66:1-12, 67, 95, 100, 103, 104, 111, 113, 114, 117, 145, 146, 147, 148, 149, 150

CHAPTER 36 – Salvation History Psalms: 50, 78, 81, 105, 106, 132, 135

CHAPTER 37 – Psalms for the King: 2, 20, 21, 29, 45, 47, 72, 93, 96, 97, 98, 99, 101, 110, 144

CHAPTER 38 – Psalms for Jerusalem and the Temple: 15, 24, 46, 48, 68, 76, 82, 84, 87, 115, 122, 134

CHAPTER 39 – Wisdom Psalms: 1, 36, 37, 49, 73, 112, 127, 128, 133

CHAPTER 40 – Torah Psalms: 19:7-14, 119

CHAPTER TWENTY-EIGHT

THE PROBLEM OF SUFFERING
Job 1-42

> **The Book of Job**
>
> The Book of Job deals with the universal problem of human suffering. We do not know much about who wrote the book or when it was written. However, this does not nullify the book's inspiration and the importance of the subject matter. Job asks a lot of questions about why he is suffering and doesn't get many answers. We can glean from it that we cannot always give a meaningful analysis of suffering, our suffering is not the result of personal sin, and that God may allow our pain to build our spirituality. A condensed reading is useful because it puts all the arguments together with God's response. Unfortunately, we lose some of the original poetry and imagery, but this gives us an accurate picture of the dialogue. We would often like an answer to our questions, but God does not owe us an explanation, and we may never get one.

JOB'S TESTING

Around the time of Abraham, there was a man in the land of Uz named Job. He was righteous and blameless; he feared God and turned away from evil whenever he could. God had blessed him with seven sons and three daughters, and he had become very wealthy. He had large flocks and herds and many male and female servants; he was the land's richest man. His sons would take turns hosting feasts for their siblings, and after the meal was over, Job would get up early the next morning and offer sacrifices to the Lord in case any of them had accidentally cursed God in their hearts.

One day, Satan came to the Lord, and God asked where he had been. Satan said that he had been roaming around on the earth and observing what was happening. Then God said, "Have you seen my servant Job? There is no one else like him who is righteous and turns away from evil.

Satan replied, "He only fears you because you have protected him and his household from evil and made him prosper. If you take everything away, then he will curse you to your face!"

God said, "Everything he has is in your hand, but do not hurt him physically." Then Satan left the Lord's presence.

JOB'S DOWNFALL

One day, all of Job's children ate and drank wine in the oldest brother's house. A messenger came to Job's home and told him that a raiding party had killed his servants and seized all his oxen and donkeys. As soon as the servant finished speaking, another came and said that fire from God had come from heaven and burned up all his sheep. A third servant told him that another raiding party had come, stolen all his camels, and killed all the servants with them. While he was still speaking, a fourth servant came and told him that a great wind had blown down his oldest son's house, and all Job's children had died.

After hearing all this news, Job tore his clothes, shaved his head, and fell on the ground, and worshiped, saying, "I came from my mother's womb naked and now I will die naked. The Lord gave and now he has taken away; may his name be blessed." In all of this, Job did not sin, and he did not accuse God of wrongdoing.

JOB'S SECOND TESTING

On another day, Satan presented himself before the Lord and told God he had been roaming around the earth and observing what was happening. God said, "Have you seen my servant Job? He is still righteous and holds to his integrity even though you incited me to afflict him without cause."

Satan replied, "He's only righteous because you've blessed him. But a man will give everything he has in exchange for his life; take away his health, and he will curse you to your face." God granted Satan permission to afflict Job if he spared his life.

Satan afflicted Job with sores and painful boils from head to toe. He sat in the ashes of his grief and scraped himself with broken pottery to relieve the pain and itching. His wife shook her head at him and said, "Are you still holding onto your integrity? Curse God and die!"

Job answered her, "You sound like one of the foolish women who go around running their mouths. Should we only accept good from God and not evil as well?" In all these things, Job did not sin with his mouth.

JOB'S FRIENDS COMFORT HIM

Four of Job's friends heard about what had happened to Job, and they decided to visit their friend in his sorrow. Their names were Eliphaz, Bildad, Zophar, and Elihu. When they arrived at Job's house, they didn't recognize him because of how bad he looked. They wept, tore their robes in grief, and threw dust on their heads. They sat with their friend in silence for seven days and nights because they saw how great his pain was.

Finally, Job spoke, "May the day I was born be blotted out from history! I wish that it had never happened and that I had never been born. It would have been better for me to die in childbirth because then I would be at rest. Everyone eventually finds rest when they die, so why couldn't mine have happened a long time ago? Why does God give life to those with no future? It only exposes my misery and longing for death. The things that I fear happen to me and I am never at ease."

Eliphaz spoke up and said, "You have taught many people and strengthened the weak. But now that adversity has come to you, are you upset? Has the innocent ever died, or the righteous ever fallen? Those who plant evil reap the same. God destroys them in his anger regardless of their strength. I had a vision in the night and it made me very afraid. In my dream, someone asked me if anyone can be pure before God or innocent before his Maker. He even judges his angels and convicts them of sin, so how could a mortal man be any different?

"Who will defend you? Affliction comes from somewhere and trouble doesn't just grow out of the ground. If I were you, I would confess my sin to God, who does marvelous things. He sends water on the earth; he elevates the humble and brings the proud low. Blessed are those that the Lord disciplines, so do not be angry with what he is putting you through. Even though he inflicts pain, he will heal, and he will deliver you from destruction. He will remove your pain and restore your good fortune."

Job answered and said, "If only you could weigh my frustration and pain because it would be heavier than all the sand on the seashore. I'm not complaining for no reason; my life is truly bitter. I wish God would get it over with and kill me.

"If I were guilty, I would be happy to have God discipline me. But since I'm innocent, I cannot possibly bear the weight of this wound. But as it is, I don't have anyone willing to help me. You see my pain, but I have still not asked you for anything. Look at me and my life and tell me if you can find any sin within me.

"Life is difficult and we are always looking for relief. I have nothing but emptiness and misery, and I am always looking forward to something else that does not satisfy. I have no hope and will never see good again; I will be gone before you know it.

"Therefore, I will speak; I will let my bitter soul pour out its complaints. Even when I look forward to the joy of sleep, nightmares and visions afflict me. I hate my life and wish I would die. I don't understand why God won't just leave me alone."

Then Bildad said, "How long will you talk like this; you are full of hot air! God does not pervert justice; your sons certainly did something against the Lord. If you seek the Lord and beg for mercy, then he will restore your fortunes. Learn something from history, we are nothing more than a passing shadow, and nothing happens without a cause. God does not reject the blameless and he does not bless evil. Repent, and he will fill your mouth with laughter, and those who hate you will wear their shame."

Job replied, "I know all these things, but how can a man be righteous in God's eyes? If someone wanted to argue with him, how would he even have a case? He is wise and powerful and he created everything we see. He makes the sun rise and sustains the universe. He has done things we cannot understand and more than we can know. He could pass before me, and I wouldn't even notice; I have no way of understanding all that he does.

"How can I possibly answer him even though I have a righteous complaint? Even if he were here, I don't know that I would believe he answered me because I am crushed by affliction without cause and filled with bitterness. Even though I'm in the right, my own words would condemn me. I hate my life and God destroys both the righteous and the wicked. The wicked prosper and he is the one who allows it. Even if I forgot my affliction and put on a happy face, you would still think I was guilty. I am condemned no matter what I do; one could judge between us anyway. If only we had a mediator! I wish he would take his wrath away and then I wouldn't live in terror.

"I hate my life and I will not censor myself. I will tell God my complaint and ask him why he is against me when he knows I'm innocent. He made me and now he has destroyed me. He gave me life and his care has kept me alive. If I am guilty, he will judge me, but if I am right, I still cannot lift my head because I am filled with affliction and misery. Why did he even let me be born? I don't have much time left; I wish that he would leave me alone so that I could find some happiness before I die."

Then Zophar spoke up, "All your words will not go unanswered, your babbling will not shut us up, and you should be ashamed of your mocking. You claim to be pure before God, but I wish he would open his mouth to answer you. He has only given you a fraction of what you deserve. You will never understand the depths of his knowledge; we cannot even measure it. But if you make your heart right, you will reach out to him and remove the sin from your house. Then you will be able to lift your face without shame and you will forget your misery. You will once again have hope and you will be able to rest in peace.

Job answered, "I know that you all have wisdom, but I have understanding too. Everybody knows the things you have told me. I am a righteous man, yet I have become a laughingstock to my friends. It is easy for you to say these things because you are at peace. But, ask the animals and plants; they know these things as well. Wisdom is with the elderly and understanding comes with old age. God alone has wisdom and might. If he tears down, no one can rebuild; whatever he does, no one can undo. He owns everything and he is the one who brings the mighty low.

"I know everything you have told me; I'm not inferior to you, but I still want to argue my case before God. You are all worthless healers; I wish you would shut up and let that be your wisdom. Will you lie on God's behalf? You cannot lie to him without him knowing and he will crush your worthless counsel. Be silent; then I will speak and let the chips fall where they may. Even though God destroys me, I hope in him and give my defense in his presence. I wish that God would withdraw his hand from me and not make me afraid of him. Why has he made my life so hard?

"Our lives are short and we are gone before we know it. God should let us be so that we can enjoy what little time we have here on earth. We don't come back after we die; I wish God would let me hide from his wrath until it was past and then come back. But time keeps moving and you crush my hope just like water erodes the soil."

Eliphaz answered, "You are full of hot air! Should a wise man waste his time arguing against foolishness? You are learning your wisdom from your sin and your own words condemn you. We have just as much wisdom as you do, if not more, so why are you turning your spirit against the Lord? We are far from pure; we are utterly corrupt in God's eyes. The wicked live in pain all the days of their lives and constantly look for something to sustain them. They have defied God, so their lives will be empty, and everything they have will pass away. The company of the godless is barren; they only give birth to trouble and deceit."

Job responded, "You are all worthless comforters; why are you saying this? If I was in your place, I could say similar things, or I could comfort you. God has worn me out and left me a shriveled shell of a man. He has torn me down in his wrath and now my adversaries are ready to destroy me. Men have struck me and God has given me into their hands. I was at ease, but now he has ripped me open, and my guts pour out on the ground. I am permanently clothed in sackcloth, and my eyes are red from weeping even though I am innocent, and my heart is pure. I do not have many years left; I pray that God listens to my case.

"My spirit is broken and the grave is waiting for me while I watch those who mock me. Since you will not listen to me, you are on their side. The righteous are appalled by my situation, but you keep after me. My life is over, and my plans are done; I am ready for death."

Then Bildad answered, "How long are you going to keep defending yourself? Do you think we are stupid? God puts out the flame of the wicked; he shortens his stride and causes his own schemes to come back on him. He is trapped by the earth and terrors frighten him on every side. His roots dry up beneath him and his branches wither overhead. He has no survivor after him and people are horrified by his downfall."

Job answered, "How long will you keep tormenting me? Aren't you ashamed to wrong me? Even if I have sinned, then I must bear that, but you make my misfortune an argument against me even though God is the one who has closed a net around me. I have cried out for help but have not received an answer; the Lord has stripped away my glory and taken the crown from my head. He has kindled his wrath against me and made me his enemy. He has taken my friends and family, and now everyone treats me like a stranger. Everyone despises me and I only survive by the skin of my teeth.

"Have mercy on me! Why do you keep after me like God has? Aren't you satisfied with my flesh? I wish my story were written in a book because my redeemer lives and will rule over the earth. After I die, I will stand before him and make my case."

Zophar spoke up, "I hear your insults and I am compelled to speak from a place of understanding. The victory of the wicked and joy of the godless don't last, they will pass away, and no one will remember them. God will curse the good things they have and they will not enjoy the fruits of their labor. Because they crush the poor and needy, there will be nothing left for them. God will send his burning anger upon them and bring them down. Their possessions will be carried away in the day of God's wrath because he will not allow them to stand."

Job replied, "Keep listening to me, then you can mock all you want. My complaint is with God, not people. Why do the wicked live into old age and become mighty? They live in peace and enjoy life to the fullest. They live in prosperity and then die a peaceful death. You say that God stores up their iniquity for their children, but they should experience the consequences for their sin because they don't care what happens to their stuff after they die. Some die at ease, and some die in great want, but both are buried and eaten by worms. I have seen the prosperity of the wicked, so stop comforting me with your empty lies."

Then Eliphaz took his turn, "Can a man be profitable to God, or is there anything he gains if you are righteous? He judges you because your evil is abundant and there is no end to your sin. You have crushed the needy and sent them away empty-handed. You think that the land belongs to the powerful and privileged. Now, God has seen your deeds, and he is punishing you, and you are terrified. Agree with God's judgment, and you can have peace again, return to him, and he will restore you."

Job answered, "If only I could find God, then I would lay my case before him and fill my mouth with arguments. He would listen to my argument and pay attention because a righteous man can argue with him and be acquitted. I cannot find him, and I don't know where to look for him, but he sees everything I do, and when tested, I will be found pure. I have not departed from his commandments; I have kept them as more precious than food. But God does not change; he does whatever he wants and will finish what he started with me. Therefore, he terrifies me, but I will not be silent.

"Some practice injustice, oppress the needy, and take advantage wherever they can. Meanwhile, the poor struggle and go without, yet God does not charge any with wrong. Some reject the light and wait for darkness so that they can practice their wickedness. But just like drought and heat snatch away the snow, death snatches away those who have sinned. They are forgotten, but God prolongs the life of his mighty by his power. He exalts them for a little while, but then they are brought low, like all others. If I am wrong, prove me a liar!"

Bildad replied, "God rules and makes peace in the highest heavens; there is nothing he cannot do and nothing he does not see. How can a man be right in his sight? The moon is not bright to God, and he does not consider the stars to be pure, how much less a man who is nothing more than a maggot and a worm!"

Job mocked his friends, "How you have helped the powerless and saved the weak. You have counseled the simple and shared so much wonderful knowledge! Where do you think you got the power to speak? There are no secrets to the Lord. He hangs the earth on nothing and makes the clouds hold water; all of heaven and earth are under his power. We see only the tiniest fraction of what he does; how could we possibly understand his full power?

"Even though God has made my soul bitter, as long as I live, I will not speak lies. I cannot agree with you because that would compromise my integrity. Let my enemies be like the unrighteous; when God cuts them off, they will not call upon the Lord. I will teach you about God and you will see that I'm right even though you have lied about him. The wicked have many children so that they can die by the sword or go hungry. Disease consumes those who survive, and the innocent will divide the spoils from his house. His wealth flees from him and terrors overtake him like a flood. The east wind sweeps him away; it claps its hands and hisses at him.

"Men take metal from the dark places of the earth and refine it. Bread comes from the earth, but underneath it is molten fire. Even though we can dig into the earth and do these great things, we cannot find wisdom and understanding. We cannot pay for it or mine it from anywhere on the earth or in death. Only God has wisdom and understanding because he can see all things. When he gave weight to the wind, rain, and waters of the earth, he established wisdom and stated that it was to fear him and turn away from evil."

Job continued, summarizing his defense, "I wish things were like before when God was on my side and my children walked with me. Everything went well for me and I received honor wherever I went. People blessed me and I brought joy to everyone I met. I was clothed in righteousness and I helped the needy. I crushed the unrighteous and thought that I would live out my days in peace. People listened to my advice and I led them as the chief leads his people.

"Now, I am the laughingstock of everyone, even those who weren't worthy of being with my sheepdogs. I am repugnant to the outcast and they spit at me whenever they see me. Since God has humbled me, they no longer hold back; they seek my destruction and bring me trouble. Terrors surround me and my prosperity has fled from me. I am afflicted and doubled over in pain; God has been cruel to me and ignored my cries for help. Even though I have been righteous and helped the needy, God has cast me away from him and given me evil when I had hoped for good to come.

"I have made a covenant with my eyes; I will not look at a woman with lust. God has seen what I do and the path of my life. If I have walked in falsehood or turned aside from righteousness, if any dirt has stuck to my hands, then let me plant, and another man reap the harvest. If I have been unfaithful in my heart or tried to seduce my neighbor's wife, others may sleep with mine in my place.

"If I have rejected the cause of one of my servants when they have a complaint against me, God will know it. If I have withheld anything from the poor and needy that they wanted or took advantage of them because they didn't have the power to oppose me, let my arm fall from its socket and become useless.

"If I have allowed anything else to be a god in the place of the Lord or trusted in anything he has made, then I have sinned and have not been true to God. If I exalted over the downfall of my enemy or tried to hide my sin, then the Lord would know. I wish that he would give me an audience and let me plead my case. If I have done wrong, then I should bear the burden of my sin."

Job and his three friends ceased speaking because Job had made his case, and his friends saw that there was nothing else they could say to make him listen to them. Then the youngest of his friends, Elihu, spoke up, "I was afraid to speak up because I am young; I decided to let wisdom and experience speak before I did. But none of you were able to answer him and I will not repeat your arguments. I have an opinion, and if I don't speak, my words will cause my insides to burst. I will show no partiality because I don't even know how.

"Job, listen to me because my heart will speak knowledge, answer me if you are able. You do not need to be afraid of me because I have listened to everything you have said, and I hear that you believe that you are righteous and that God has wronged you.

Why do you argue against God because he answers those with a complaint against him? He listens to those who pray to him, so listen to me because I will give you wisdom.

"Listen to me, you wise men, and we will decide what is right. Job insists that God has afflicted him, although he is innocent of any sin. He is a scoffer because the Lord does not do wrong but merely gives us the reward of our work. He is just and controls everything on earth, so he cannot be tempted to partiality. He does not need to listen to our arguments to judge; he has all the information he needs and acts justly. God does not punish the innocent. I wish you would have your trial before the Lord because you sound like every other wicked man trying to justify himself and rebelling against God.

"Do you think you are righteous before God? Why do you imagine that doing the right thing doesn't benefit you? Your good deeds or your wickedness don't impact the Lord; he determines your life. Indeed, God does not hear an empty cry; how much less is he listening when you demand that he hears your case? Your words are meaningless and ignorant.

"Listen to me for a little while longer because I have something else to say on God's behalf, and my words are perfect and true. The Lord is mighty in the strength of his understanding, he does not let the wicked prevail, and he gives the afflicted their rights. He watches after the righteous and reproves those who are arrogant. If sinners listen to him, he commands them to repent; if they obey and turn to him, he gives them prosperity. But if they do not obey, they die by the sword. The godless hold onto their anger, they don't cry out to God, and they die in their sin. He called you into a broad place filled with goodness, but now justice has come upon you, so beware that you do not become a scoffer against the Lord.

"Be careful what you ask for and make sure that you do not wish for death because you will get what you ask for and die in your sin. God is exalted in power, and no one can accuse him of doing wrong; we have all seen the wonders of his creation. No one can fully understand him because he is far beyond what we can comprehend. We see him in the weather, and it is a display of his power and might."

As Elihu was speaking, a storm began to gather, and he continued, "My heart is trembling; listen to the rumbling of his thunder, and know that he is speaking against you. He commands the storm, and it obeys him; the clouds, rain, and lightning do whatever he commands. Whether it is for correction or from love, it all does whatever he has planned. You don't know what you are talking about and you cannot do everything that he can. His glory and splendor are coming in the storm, and we cannot possibly understand his power, justice, and righteousness."

GOD'S ANSWER

Then the Lord spoke to Job from the storm, "Who is this that speaks such ignorant words? Brace yourself like a man and I will question you. Where were you when I created the earth? If you talk like this, you surely know all about its dimensions, limits, and how it fits together. Have you commanded the morning since it began? Do you understand the seas or death? Please tell me all about the path to darkness or light. You've been there since the beginning, so you must know.

"You must be able to explain nature and science, how the universe holds together, and how the stars move. Can you command the weather or even begin to tell me how the mind or human consciousness works? Can you provide food for wild animals or keep them all satisfied?

"Are you there when wild animals are born? Do you make sure their generations continue without interruption? Can you explain their behavior or direct their actions? What about the insects that work together with no fear of humans or their strength? What about the birds? Do you direct them as well?

"If you find fault with me, please let me know."

Job answered, "I am nothing; how can I possibly answer? I lay my hand over my mouth; I spoke once, but I won't do it again."

Then God replied out of the whirlwind, "Oh, I'm not finished. Brace yourself like a man and answer my questions. Condemn me if you are in the right. Do you have my strength or the power of my voice?

"Dress yourself with glory and splendor, pour out your anger on your enemies. Bring down the proud and arrogant and destroy them. Then I will acknowledge that you can save yourself. Behold the great dinosaurs and their might and strength, the monsters of both sea and land; I made them.

"Who has given me anything? I made everything that exists and it all belongs to me."

Finally, Job answered the Lord, "I know that you have the power to do anything and no one can stop you. I spoke about things beyond my understanding, about things I can't possibly know. I had heard of you, but now I see you; I reject my claim and repent in dust and ashes."

God's answer to Job

Job repeatedly makes the case that he is innocent before God and that there is no reason for his suffering. When God shows up, he doesn't answer Job but instead points to Job's insignificance in the scheme of the universe. When we deal with pain and suffering, we usually want an answer to why it is happening. Sometimes, the reason for our suffering is apparent, but many times, it is not. When we don't understand why God allows pain and suffering, we should trust that he created everything in the universe. He has a far greater perspective and understanding than we do, and while he has a reason for all of it, he doesn't owe us an explanation. We are the created beings and we don't have the capacity to understand how God uses pain and suffering for his glory.

An example of this from Scripture is the Israelites in captivity in Egypt. They lived in a horrific situation where the government decreed that every baby boy should

> die. The Egyptians oppressed and enslaved the people, taking advantage of them in every way they could. Many people likely questioned God's goodness and purpose for their captivity. But God knew the bigger picture and how he would use their escape for his glory and the good of the people.
>
> As we wrestle with this concept, it can be helpful to remember that all pain and suffering result from sin. Sometimes, it is the direct result of our actions; sometimes, we can trace it to someone else's sin; but there are many times that it is merely because humanity's sin has corrupted the world. God created the world as good, and nothing bad happened until after Adam and Eve sinned. Things like COVID-19, cancer, and natural disasters are examples of situations where bad things happen because of sin's presence in the universe. We can't pin these on any one person or group's sin, and they are not a part of God's original design; they come from sin's corruption of the world.
>
> An infant who needs an operation does not understand that the surgeon's knife will lead to something better. The child only knows it hurts. In the same way, we can't always understand what God is doing in our lives.
>
> However, this answer may not be the best consolation to those in the midst of crisis. When people are hurting, the best response is love and listening. Job's counselors were most effective during their first three days, when they were silent.

The Lord turned to Eliphaz and said, "My anger burns against you and your friends because you have not spoken rightly about me as my servant Job has. Take seven bulls and rams and take them to Job so he can make a sacrifice and pray for you three." Job's friends did as God commanded and the Lord listened to Job.

Then the Lord restored Job's fortunes and gave him twice as much as before. All of Job's friends and family came to Job and comforted him for all the Lord had taken from him. He had even larger herds and seven more sons and three daughters. His daughters were more beautiful than any other women and he gave them an inheritance amongst their brothers. Job lived another 140 years and saw his descendants to the fourth generation; then, he died an old man.

Speaker	Argument
Job	I am sorry that I was ever born, it would be much better if I died because then I would have rest.
Eliphaz	Trouble only comes from our sin and we are all sinful. If you confess your sin, then God will forgive you and restore you.
Job	I am innocent but still afflicted. My frustration and pain are too much to bear, and I wish my life would end. I have no relief and don't understand why God won't leave me alone.

Speaker	Argument
Bildad	Stop resisting and repent. Beg for God's mercy and he will restore your fortunes because misfortune always has a cause.
Job	It doesn't matter what I say because you will think I'm guilty no matter what. God is too powerful for us to understand all he does. I will keep pouring out my complaint to the Lord because I'm already destroyed. I wish that he would let me be so that I can find some happiness before I die.
Zophar	I wish God would answer you because he has only given you a fraction of the punishment you deserve. Repent and God will end your misery.
Job	You aren't telling me anything new. I still want to make my case before God. If God is going to make our lives so hard, he should leave us alone so we can enjoy what we have while we live.
Eliphaz	Why should we waste our time with your words? We are all utterly sinful; of course, God is punishing you.
Job	You are worthless comforters. God has given me into the hand of my oppressors and you are on their side.
Bildad	God punishes the wicked.
Job	God has humiliated me. I wish my story were written down after my death.
Zophar	The prosperity of the wicked is fleeting; eventually, God brings justice.
Job	The wicked prosper until their death.
Eliphaz	Man cannot be profitable to God; you need to repent.
Job	If only I could find God so that I could make my case.
Bildad	God is all powerful; how can you be righteous?
Job	I am blameless, if only God would answer me.
Elihu	I wish you could have your trial before God because he would prove that you are wicked.
God	Who are you to question me?

CHAPTER TWENTY-NINE

PSALMS FOR A COMMUNITY IN SORROW

> **Community laments**
>
> The first grouping of the Psalms was for the Israelites in times of sorrow. We can use these as prayers when we are in times of trouble. It can also be comforting to read about how God worked in the lives of the psalmists.

Psalm 12: "Save Me from the Double-minded"
By David, during Saul's reign.

Oh Lord, save me because the godly and the faithful have vanished.

Everyone is double-minded and lies to his neighbor with flattering lips.

May the Lord cut off their lips because they think they can justify themselves with their words.

They think no one will stop them and that they will lie to their hearts' content.

The Lord will arise because the wicked plunder the poor; the needy groan, and he will give them a place where they can live safely.

The Lord's words are pure and he will keep them from the evil of this wicked generation.

Psalm 44: "Come to Our Help"
By the sons of Korah

Oh God, our fathers have told us about your past deeds, how you drove out the nations and planted Israel.

They didn't win the land with their might, but only by your hand because you loved them.

God, you are my King; save Jacob!

We defeat our enemies through your name and strength; I do not trust my weapons; only you can save us.

We boast in God and give thanks to your name forever.

But you rejected and disgraced us and made us run from our enemies.

You have scattered us among the nations like sheep for slaughter.

Our neighbors taunt us and the nations mock us.

My disgrace is before me, and shame has covered my face.

All this has happened even though we have not forgotten you and we have not left you.

But you have broken us and covered us with the shadow of death.

You would know if we worshiped another god because you know the secrets of the heart.

Yet, for your sake, we are killed all day long.

Don't hide your face from us, and don't forget our affliction and oppression.

Rise up and come to our help; redeem us for the sake of your steadfast love!

Psalm 58: "God Who Judges the Earth"
By David, when Saul turned against him.

Do the rulers decree what is right or judge people with equity?

No, in your hearts, you devise wrong and your hands deal out violence on earth.

The wicked are estranged from birth; they speak lies like a serpent's venom.

God, break the teeth in their mouths and tear out their fangs!

May they vanish like water and their weapons not work; may they be like the stillborn child who never sees the sun.

The righteous will rejoice when he sees the vengeance; he will bathe his feet in the wicked's blood.

Humanity will know that there is a God who judges the earth.

Psalm 60: "He Will Tread Down Our Foes"
By David when he fought against Mesopotamia and Syria.

God, you have rejected us and broken down our defenses; you have been angry, restore us.

You have torn apart the land; repair its cracks because it is tottering.

You have made your people see hard things and given us wine that makes us stagger.

But you have set up a banner for those who fear you.

Give salvation and deliver your loved ones.

The whole world is God's; who will bring me to the fortified city?

God, go forth with our armies and help us against our foes.

With God, we will do valiantly; he is the one who will tread down our enemies.

Psalm 74: "Arise and Defend Your Cause"
By Asaph

God, why do you reject us, and why does your anger burn against the sheep of your pasture?

Remember your people that you purchased long ago; remember Jerusalem, where you lived.

The enemy has destroyed everything in the sanctuary and they roar in your meeting place.

They burned your sanctuary and profaned the dwelling place of your name.

How long will you let your enemies scoff?

Stretch out your hand to destroy them!

God is my king from old, bringing salvation to the earth.

You divided the seas and crushed the heads of the sea monsters.

You split open springs, brooks, and dried up ever-flowing streams.

You own everything and have fixed the boundaries of the earth and the seasons.

Remember how the enemy mocks and dishonors your name.

Have regard for the covenant, and don't let the downtrodden turn back in shame; let the poor and needy praise your name.

God, arise and defend your cause, don't forget the uproar of those who rise against you!

Psalm 79: "Lord, How Long?"
By Asaph, after the Babylonians destroyed the temple.

God, the nations have come into your inheritance and defiled your holy temple.

They have killed your servants and poured their blood out like water all around Jerusalem.

We have become a taunt to our neighbors, mocked by those around us.

Lord, how long will you be angry and your jealousy burn like fire?

Pour out your anger on the nations that don't know you because they have devoured Jacob and his land.

Forget our former sins and be compassionate to us.

God of our salvation, help us for the glory of your name and deliver us from our sins.

Why should the nations ask where you are?

Avenge our blood on the nations and preserve those doomed to die!

We are your people and the sheep of your pasture; we will give thanks to you forever and tell all generations your praise.

Psalm 80: "Restore Us"
By Asaph

God, restore us and shine your face on us and save us!

How long will you be angry with our prayers?

You have fed us with tears and made us a joke to our enemies.

God, restore us and shine your face on us and save us!

You brought a vine out of Egypt, drove the nations out, and planted it.

The vine took root and filled the land, but now you have broken down its walls so that those who pass by may pluck its fruit.

Look down from heaven and have regard for this vine that you planted.

They have cut it down and burned it with fire.

We will not turn back from you; give us life, and we will call on your name.

Restore us and shine your face on us and save us!

Psalm 85: "Revive Us Again"
By the sons of Korah, after the return from Babylonian captivity.

Lord, you restored Jacob's fortunes and forgave all your people's sins.

You turned away your fury and revived us again so that we may rejoice in you.

Show us your steadfast love and grant us salvation.

Your salvation is near to those who fear you so that your glory may dwell in our land.

Unfailing love and faithfulness meet, the Lord will give what is good, and our land will yield its increase.

Psalm 89: "I Will Sing of the Lord's Steadfast Love"
By Ethan the Ezrahite

I will sing of the Lord's steadfast love forever and praise his faithfulness to all generations.

You have made your covenant with David and sworn to establish his offspring forever.

Let the heavens praise your wonders and your faithfulness in the assembly of the holy ones!

No one can compare to you, a God worthy of reverence and awesome above all.

No one is as mighty as you; you rule the oceans and still them; you scatter your enemies with your arm.

Everything is yours because you created it; righteousness and justice are the foundation of your throne, love and faithfulness go before you.

You are the glory of our strength and your favor exalts us.

You are our shield, the Holy One of Israel.

You will crush David's foes before him and strike down those who hate him; you will give him your love and faithfulness.

He will call you his father, God, and the rock of his salvation.

You will make him the firstborn, the highest of the earth's kings.

You will establish his offspring and throne forever.

But you will punish their sin if they do not obey.

But you have cast us off and rejected us; you are angry with your anointed.

You have renounced the covenant with your servant and defiled his crown in the dust.

You have exalted his foes and made his enemies rejoice.

Lord, will you hide forever?

How long will your wrath burn like fire?

Remember how short my time is because no one can escape death.

Lord, where is your steadfast love that you swore to David?

Remember how the nations mock and insult us.

Blessed be the Lord forever!

Amen and amen.

Psalm 90: "From Everlasting to Everlasting"
By Moses

Lord, you have been our dwelling place in all generations; before creation, you have been the everlasting God.

A thousand years are like a day to you; they are like a dream.

They are like the grass that flourishes in the morning and then withers and fades in the evening.

Your anger brings us to an end; your wrath dismays us.

You see even our secret sins and you bring our death with a sigh.

If we are lucky, we live to 80, but our lives are full of toil and trouble.

Teach us to number our days so that we may get a heart of wisdom.

Pity your servants, satisfy with your steadfast love so that we can rejoice and be glad all our days.

Make us happy for as many days as you have afflicted us; show us your work and your glorious power.

Let God's favor be upon us and establish the work of our hands.

Psalm 94: "The Lord Will Not Forsake His People"
By Unknown

God of vengeance, shine forth, arise, and judge the earth, give the proud what they deserve!

How long will you let the wicked exult and pour out their arrogant words?

They crush your people and kill the weak.

They think the Lord doesn't see but understand that he sees everything.

The Lord knows that the thoughts of man are a mere breath.

Blessed is the man that you discipline and whom you teach from your Law.

The Lord will not forsake his people, he will give them justice and righteousness, and the upright will follow it.

If the Lord had not helped me against the wicked, my soul would have lived in the land of silence.

When I thought I would slip, your steadfast love upheld me.

When my heart is burdened, your consolations cheer my soul.

Wicked rulers will not ally with you; they band together against the righteous and condemn the innocent to death.

But the Lord is my stronghold, the rock of my refuge.

He will bring their sin on them and wipe them out.

Psalm 123: "Our Eyes Look to the Lord"
By Unknown: A Song of Ascents for travelers to sing when approaching Jerusalem.

I lift my eyes to God enthroned in the heavens!

As servants look to their master, our eyes look to the Lord until he is merciful.

Have mercy on us because we have had enough of contempt and scorn.

Psalm 126: "Lord, Restore Our Fortunes"
By Unknown: A Song of Ascents for travelers to sing when approaching Jerusalem.

When the Lord brought the exiles back to Jerusalem, it was like we were dreaming.

We laughed and sang for joy.

The Lord has done great things for us; we are glad.

Lord, restore our fortunes!

Those who plant with tears will reap with joyous shouts!

Psalm 129: "Afflicted yet Confident"
By Unknown: A Song of Ascents for travelers to sing when approaching Jerusalem.

Israel has been afflicted since its youth, but her enemies have not prevailed.

The Lord is righteous, and he has cut the cords of the wicked; those who hate Jerusalem will be ashamed.

May they wither like grass on a roof and see no blessing.

CHAPTER THIRTY
PSALMS FOR INDIVIDUALS IN SORROW

> **Individual laments**
>
> The second grouping of the Psalms was for the individuals in times of sorrow. We can use these as prayers when we are in times of trouble.

Psalm 3: "The Lord Is My Shield"
By David, when he was fleeing from his son Absalom.

Oh, Lord! I have so many enemies and they are saying that God will not save me!

But you are my shield, my glory, and the one who lifts my head.

I cried out to the Lord and he answered me from his dwelling place.

I only wake in the morning because the Lord sustains me.

Therefore, I will not be afraid of the countless enemies who surround me.

Arise, oh Lord, and save me!

You strike my enemies and shatter their teeth.

Salvation belongs to the Lord; may he bless his people!

Psalm 4: "How Long, Oh Lord"
Possibly by David

Lord, listen to me when I call.

You gave me relief when I was in anguish, be gracious, and hear my prayer!

How long will men turn my honor into shame?

How long will they love empty words and lies?

Know that the Lord has set the godly apart, and he hears when I call.

Be angry, but do not sin.

Ponder in your heart, and remain silent.

Offer right sacrifices and trust in the Lord.

Many will ask why he hasn't given us more good things.

But God has put more joy in my heart than if I had an abundance of all good things.

I will go to sleep in peace because God allows me to dwell in safety.

Psalm 5: "Hear My Cry"
By David

Lord, listen to my words and notice my groaning because I cry out to you.

I prepare a sacrifice and pray to you in the morning.

You do not delight in evil and you will not allow the proud to stand before you.

You destroy the liar and you detest bloodthirsty and deceitful men.

But your abundant love allows me to enter your house where I bow in holy fear of you.

Please lead me in your righteousness and make my path straight because my enemies want to lead me astray.

Let them bear their own guilt and let their counsel fail because of their many sins against you.

But let everyone who takes refuge in you rejoice; may you protect them, and may they exalt in your name.

Oh Lord, you bless the righteous and cover him like a shield.

Psalm 7: "Defend Me, Lord"
By David

Lord, I take refuge in you; please deliver me from all those who pursue me so that they don't tear my soul apart like a lion tears its prey.

If I have done wrong, if I have repaid good with evil, let my enemies capture me and trample me to dust.

Lord, arise in your anger and defend me against their fury because you are the judge over everything.

Judge me in my righteousness and integrity.

You know all things, so establish the righteous and end the evil of the wicked.

God is my shield; he saves the upright; he is a righteous judge who feels indignation every day.

If a man does not repent, then God is ready with his weapons to make an end of him.

The wicked are full of evil and God causes his wicked plans to come back upon him.

I will thank the Lord for his righteousness and praise the name of the Lord most high!

Psalm 9: "God Remembers"
By David

I will give thanks to the Lord with all my heart and tell the world what you have done.

I will worship you and sing praise to your name.

You have maintained my cause and given righteous judgment.

You have rebuked the nations, you have made my enemies turn back, and have blotted their names out forever!

The Lord has established his throne forever and he judges the nations with righteousness.

He is a stronghold for the oppressed in times of trouble and he has not forsaken those who seek him.

He does not forget the cries of the afflicted.

Sing praises to the Lord and tell the world what he has done!

Lord, be gracious to me and deliver me from death so that I can tell people of your salvation.

God has made himself known and caused the wicked to be caught by their own traps.

All those who forget the Lord will perish, but the needy will not always be ignored.

Arise, oh Lord, and let all the nations know that they are only men and that you will judge them!

Psalm 10: "Do Not Forget the Afflicted"
Possibly by David

Lord, why are you far off and hide in times of trouble?

The wicked arrogantly pursue the poor, let their schemes trap them.

They boast about themselves and curse the Lord; they believe that there is no God.

The wicked man prospers in all he does and thinks that his works will last forever.

He murders the innocent and watches them so that he may ambush them.

He believes that you don't see his evil and that he will never face judgment for it.

Arise, oh Lord, punish the wicked and do not forget the afflicted.

Do not let the wicked get away with their sin; break their arms and judge them.

The Lord is king forever, and he listens to the prayer of the afflicted and will strengthen their hearts.

He will take up the cause of the orphan and the oppressed so that man may no longer strike terror into their hearts.

Psalm 13: "Don't Forget Me"
By David

Lord, will you forget me forever?

How long will you hide your face from me?

How long will I live in sorrow and my enemies exalt over me?

Answer me, or I will die, and my enemies will rejoice over me.

I trust in his steadfast love and I rejoice in his salvation.

I will sing to the Lord because he has dealt bountifully with me.

Psalm 14: "No One Seeks the Lord"
By David

The fool declares in his heart that there is no God.

They are corrupt and do evil; none of them do good.

The Lord looks down from heaven to see if any seek after him, but they have all turned aside and do evil.

They lack knowledge and devour my people like bread.

Now they are in great terror because the Lord is with the righteous.

Oh, that God would save his people and restore the fortunes of Israel.

Psalm 17: "Hear My Prayer"
By David

Lord, hear my cry and keep my lips from lies.

You have tried my heart; you have tested me and found me innocent.

I have avoided the ways of violent men and I have held fast to your paths.

I call upon you; please hear me and show your steadfast love to those who seek refuge from their enemies.

Keep me as the apple of your eye and hide me in the shadow of your wings from my enemies.

They have no pity; they speak arrogantly and want to cast me to the ground.

Arise, oh Lord, confront and subdue them!

Save my soul from the wicked who take their joy in this world.

They have more than enough children and treasure.

But as for me, I am satisfied with your face and your righteousness.

Psalm 22: "Why Have You Forsaken Me?"
By David

> **Jesus' crucifixion**
>
> Jesus quoted this Psalm from the cross, and it refers to the sorrowful aspect of his Messianic fulfillment.

My God, my God, why have you forsaken me?

Why are you so far from saving me?

I cry out to you both day and night, but you don't answer.

But still, you are holy, seated on the throne of your praises.

Our ancestors trusted in you, and you delivered them; they cried out to you, and you rescued them.

I am a worm and not a man; I am scorned and despised.

Those who see me mock and tell me to ask you to save me since I trust you.

But you are the one who caused me to trust you from my youth.

Don't stay away because I'm in trouble and no one is here to help me.

I'm surrounded by those who want to hurt me; they want to devour me.

I am poured out like water, I have no strength, and my heart melts like wax.

My strength is gone; you have laid me in the dust of death.

Evil men surround me; they have pierced my hands and feet, I can feel every bone, and they celebrate my downfall.

They have split my clothes amongst themselves and gamble for them.

Oh Lord, don't be far off, come to my help, and save me!

Deliver me from these evil men and the sword!

I will tell of your power to the congregation; I will praise you.

All who fear the Lord, praise his name because he has not turned away from the afflicted; he has heard those who cry out to you.

I praise you in the congregation; I will serve you before those who fear you.

The afflicted will have relief and those who seek you shall glorify your name.

All the earth will turn to you and worship.

You rule over the nations and all will eventually bow before you.

Future generations will tell of your greatness and your deliverance.

Psalm 25: "A Plea for Help"
By David

Oh Lord, I lift my soul to you! I trust in you; do not let me be ashamed, nor my enemies defeat me.

Those who trust you will not be ashamed, but the treacherous will.

Teach me your ways; lead me into your truth and teach me because you are the God of my salvation.

I will wait for you.

Remember me in your mercy and steadfast love because they have always existed.

Forgive the sins of my youth and remember me for your name's sake.

The Lord is good and upright; he teaches sinners in the way.

He leads the humble into righteousness; all his ways are steadfast love and faithfulness for those who obey him.

Forgive my sins for your name's sake because my guilt is great.

The Lord will teach those who fear him and his offspring shall inherit the land.

He is a friend to those who fear him and he will teach them his covenant.

My eyes are on the Lord and he will save me.

Be gracious to me because I am lonely and afflicted. I am troubled, save me.

Forgive my sins, consider my enemies, and how much they hate me.

Guard my soul and do not let me be ashamed because I take refuge in you.

Let my integrity and righteousness save me; I wait for you.

Psalm 26: "Vindicate Me"
By David

Vindicate me because I have walked in my integrity and trusted the Lord without wavering.

Try me, oh Lord, test my heart and mind.

Your steadfast love is before me and I walk in your faithfulness.

I don't associate with liars or hypocrites.

I am innocent and praise your name and wonderful deeds.

I love your house where your glory dwells, don't sweep my soul away with the wicked.

Redeem me and be gracious; I will praise your name.

Psalm 28: "Lord, My Rock"
By David

Oh Lord, my rock, I cry out to you; do not ignore me, or I will die.

Hear my cries for mercy when I turn to you.

Don't drag me off with the wicked who lie to their neighbors.

Treat them according to their deeds, give them their reward.

They don't care about God's works; instead, they tear them down.

Blessed be the Lord because he has heard my cries for mercy.

He is my strength and shield, my heart trusts him, and he delivers.

I will sing praises to him in response.

The Lord is the strength and savior of his people.

Bless your people and be our shepherd forever.

Psalm 31: "Shelter from Trouble"
By David, when he narrowly escaped from Saul.

Lord, I take refuge in you, don't let me be ashamed, but deliver me in your righteousness.

Hear me now and be my rock of refuge and strong fortress.

You lead and guide me for your name's sake and pull me out of hidden traps.

I commit my spirit into your hands because you have redeemed me.

I reject those who follow worthless idols; I will trust in the Lord.

I will rejoice in your love because you saw my affliction and the anguish of my soul.

You have saved me from my enemy and put me in a secure place.

Be merciful to me because I am sorrowful; even my bones feel weak.

My neighbors and friends run from me because of my enemies; they forget me as if I were already dead.

But I trust in you, Lord, because you are my God.

I am in your hands, deliver me from my enemies and those who pursue me.

Shine your face on me and save me with your unfailing love.

Make the wicked ashamed and silence them with death.

The Lord has stored up an abundance of good things for those who fear and take refuge in him.

He keeps us safe in his dwelling place.

Praise the Lord for the wonders of his love!

When I was afraid, I thought that I was cut off from God, but he heard my cries for mercy.

Love the Lord because he saves those faithful to him and pays back the prideful in full.

Those who hope in the Lord should be strong and take heart.

Psalm 39: "What is the Measure of My Days?"
By David

I will guard my tongue so that I will not sin with my mouth.

I was mute and silent, but my distress grew worse.

My heart burned within me and then I spoke.

Lord, make me know the measure of my days and let me know how fleeting I am.

My days are a few handbreadths and my life is nothing; humanity is nothing more than a breath.

We go about like a shadow and are in turmoil for nothing; we build up wealth for someone else.

Lord, my hope is in you; deliver me from my sin, and do not let fools scorn me.

I am silent because you have done this; stop beating me because you have overwhelmed me.

Your rebuke and discipline consume wealth like a moth; we are just a breath.

Lord, listen to my prayer and see my tears!

I am a guest with you as my fathers before me.

Look away from me so that I can smile again before I die!

Psalm 40:11-17: "Don't Restrain Your Mercy"
By David

Lord, you will not restrain your mercy from me; your love and faithfulness will preserve me.

Countless evils have surrounded me, and my sin has caught up with me; I cannot see, and my heart fails me.

Lord, hurry to help me and let those who want to kill me be ashamed.

But let everyone who seeks you rejoice and proclaim that you are great.

I am poor and needy, but the Lord thinks of me.

You are my help and my deliverance!

Psalm 41: "O Lord, Be Gracious to Me"
By David, when he was sick.

Blessed are those who look out for the poor!

The Lord delivers them in their day of trouble and keeps them alive.

The Lord heals their sickness and restores them to health.

Lord, be gracious to me and heal me because I have sinned against you!

My enemies wait for my death and my visitors speak empty words to me.

Those who hate me whisper with each other and imagine the worst for me.

Even my close friends are against me.

Lord, be gracious to me and raise me up so that I can repay them!

I know that you delight in me because my enemy will not defeat me.

You have upheld me because of my integrity and set me in your presence forever.

Blessed be the Lord, the God of Israel, forever and ever!

Amen and amen.

Psalm 42: "Why are you Cast Down, O My Soul?"
By the sons of Korah

My soul longs for you like a deer pants for water.

My soul thirsts for the living God, and I have fed on my tears day and night while people taunt me, "Where is your God?"

As I pour out my soul, I remember how I would lead the procession to God's house with shouts of praise.

Oh, my soul, why are you so sad and discouraged?

Hope in God because I will praise him again.

I remember you from my past; deep calls to deep at the roar of your waterfalls.

The Lord commands his love by day and a song by night, a prayer to the God of my life.

I ask God why he has forgotten me and allowed me to mourn over the enemy's oppression.

They taunt me all day long, "Where is your God?"

Oh, my soul, why are you cast down and in turmoil within me?

Hope in God because I will praise him again.

Psalm 43: "Send Out Your Light and Truth"
By Unknown

God, vindicate me and defend my cause against an ungodly people; deliver me from the deceitful and unjust man!

I take refuge in you; why have you rejected me and allowed my enemy to oppress me?

Send out your light and truth; let them lead me and bring me to your dwelling place!

Then I will go to your altar and praise you, my God.

Oh, my soul, why are you discouraged and in turmoil within me?

Hope in God because I will praise him again.

Psalm 52: "God's Steadfast Love Endures"
By David, after Doeg told Saul about Ahimelech.

God's steadfast love endures all day, so why do you boast of evil?

Your tongue plots destruction; you love evil more than good, and lies more than the truth.

Your deceitful tongue loves words that devour, but God will break you down forever, and he will uproot you from the land of the living.

The righteous will point out the man who does not make God his refuge but trusts in his wealth and takes refuge in his own destruction!

But I am a green olive tree in God's house; I trust in his steadfast love forever.

I will thank you forever and wait for your name because it is good.

Psalm 53: "No One Does Good"
By David

The fool believes there is no God; they are corrupt and commit abominable sin.

God looks down from heaven on men to see if there are any who understand or seek after God.

They have all fallen away; none of them does good.

Evildoers lack knowledge because they devour my people like bread.

They are terrified when there is no terror because God puts them to shame and rejects them.

When God restores the fortunes of his people, salvation will come out of Jerusalem!

Psalm 54: "The Lord Upholds My Life"
By David, when the Ziphites betrayed David to Saul.

God, save me by your name and vindicate me by your might; hear my prayer.

Strangers rise against me and ruthless men seek my life.

God is my helper; he upholds my life in his faithfulness; he will return evil to my enemies.

I sacrifice to you with a freewill offering and will give thanks to you because you are good.

He has delivered me from trouble.

Psalm 55: "Cast Your Burdens on the Lord"
By David

God, listen to my prayer and hear my plea for mercy!

My enemies make me restless with their oppression.

They give me trouble and bear a grudge against me.

My heart is in anguish and I am afraid of death.

If I only had wings like a dove, I would fly away and rest in the wilderness.

Lord, destroy them and divide their tongues because I see violence and strife in the city.

Oppression and fraud are in the marketplace, and ruin is in its midst.

I could bear it if an enemy taunted me, but it is my friend.

We used to walk together in the temple and listen to his counsel.

Evil is in their dwelling place and heart, may death steal over them.

But I call out to God and he will save me.

I pray all day, and he hears my voice and redeems my soul from the battle I wage.

God will listen and humble them because they won't change or fear God.

My friend has stretched out his hand against me and broken his promises.

His speech was as smooth as butter, but his heart was at war.

Cast your burdens on the Lord, and he will sustain you; he will never let the righteous be moved.

Oh God, cast them down to the pit of destruction; I will trust in you.

Psalm 56: "I Trust in God"
By David, when The Philistines captured him in Gath.

God, be gracious to me because men trample and oppress me all day.

When I am afraid, I trust in you, so I will not be afraid; what can man do to me?

All day long, they injure my cause and think of evil against me.

They stir up strife and wait for my death.

You keep count of my tossing and turning and hold my tears in a bottle.

God is for me, so my enemies will turn away.

I trust in the God I praise, so I will not be afraid.

I will perform my vows and give you thank offerings because you have delivered my soul from death so that I may walk before God in the light of life.

Psalm 57: "Let God's Glory Be over the Earth"
By David, when Saul chased him into a cave.

God, be merciful to me because my soul takes refuge in the shadow of your wings.

I cry out to God Most High, who fulfills his purpose for me; he will save me from heaven and shame those who trample on me.

God will send out his love and faithfulness!

My soul is amid lions and I lie down amid fiery beasts.

God, be exalted above the heavens and let your glory be over all the earth!

They dug a pit for me, but they fell into it.

My heart is faithful; I will sing to the Lord and give thanks among the peoples.

Your steadfast love is great to the heavens and your faithfulness to the clouds.

Be exalted above the heavens and let your glory be over all the earth!

Psalm 59: "Deliver Me from My Enemies"
By David, when Saul sent men to kill him.

God, deliver me from my enemies and protect me from the bloodthirsty men who come to attack me.

They lie in wait for my life even though I'm innocent.

Come to meet me and rouse yourself to punish the nations, do not spare them.

They keep coming back, bellowing with swords in their mouths.

But Lord, you laugh at them and hold all the nations in derision.

I will watch for you because you are my fortress; God will let me triumph over my enemies.

Don't kill them so that people don't forget.

Let their pride trap them for their cursing and lies.

Consume them with your wrath until they are no more so that they know that God rules over Jacob to the ends of the earth.

But I will sing of your strength and steadfast love because you have been a fortress and refuge in my distress.

Psalm 61: "Lead Me to the Rock"
By David

God, hear my cry, and listen to my prayer; lead me to the rock that is higher than me because you have been my refuge and a strong tower against the enemy.

Let me live in your tent forever; let me take refuge under the shelter of your wings!

God, you have heard my vows and given a legacy to those who fear your name.

Prolong the life of the king and make his years endure to all generations!

Appoint your steadfast love and faithfulness to watch over him, and I will sing praises to your name.

Psalm 64: "Hide Me from the Wicked"
By David

God, hear my voice and complaint; preserve my life from dread of the enemy.

Hide me from the secret plots of the wicked who shoot at the blameless.

They maintain their evil purpose and think no one sees them.

They diligently search for injustice, but God shoots his arrow at them.

They are suddenly ruined and those who see them will shake their heads at them.

Let the righteous one rejoice in the Lord and take refuge in him!

Let the upright in heart exult!

Psalm 70: "Lord, Do Not Delay"
By David

God, make haste to deliver me!

Let those who seek my life be ashamed and confused!

May all who seek you rejoice and be glad in you!

May they say God is great!

I am poor and needy; hasten to me because you are my help and my deliverer!

Psalm 71: "Don't Forsake Me When I am Weak"
By David, during Absalom's rebellion.

Lord, I take refuge in you, don't let me be ashamed!

Deliver me and rescue me in your righteousness, save me!

Be my rock of shelter and rescue me from the hands of the wicked.

You are my hope and I have trusted you from birth.

I continually praise you, do not cast me off in my old age, and do not forsake me when I am weak.

My enemies consult together and want to seize me because they think you have left me.

Don't be far away; put my accusers to shame, and consume them with scorn and disgrace.

I will hope in you and praise you more and more; my mouth will tell of your righteous acts and your salvation.

I will remind them of your righteousness because you have taught me from my youth.

Do not forsake me in my old age until I proclaim your might to another generation.

Your righteousness reaches the highest heavens; no one is like you.

You have made me see troubles and calamity and you will revive me again.

You will increase my greatness and comfort me again.

I will sing praise to you with the harp and lyre; my lips will shout for joy.

I will sing of your righteous help all day long because they have been put to shame.

Psalm 77: "I Seek the Lord on the Day of Trouble"
By Asaph

I cry out to God and he hears me.

I seek the Lord on the day of my trouble; my soul refuses comfort.

I moan when I remember God, and my spirit faints as I meditate.

You keep me awake and I am so troubled that I cannot speak.

I think about the past when I taught others to seek you and knew that you would not turn away from me forever.

Your love has not ceased; you have not forgotten your promises; you are still gracious and compassionate.

So, I appealed to you, and I will remind myself of what you have done in the past.

Your way is holy, and no god is great like you; you redeemed your people with your mighty arm.

When the waters saw you, they were afraid, and the deep trembled; the clouds poured out water, the skies thundered, and your arrows flashed on every side.

You led your people like a flock by the hand of Moses and Aaron.

Psalm 86: "Great Is Your Steadfast Love"
By the sons of Korah

Lord, incline your ear to me and answer because I am poor and needy.

Preserve my life and save your servant because I am godly, and I trust in you.

Be gracious to me because I cry to you all day, make my soul glad.

You are kind and forgiving, abounding in love to all who call on you.

I call on you when I'm in trouble because there is no other god like you and none can do what you do.

All the nations will come to you and glorify your name because you alone are God.

Teach me your ways, so I can walk in your truth and fear your name.

I thank you with my whole heart and I will glorify your name forever.

Your steadfast love is great; you deliver me from death.

Insolent men have risen against me and they don't honor you.

You are a merciful and gracious God, slow to anger and abounding in love and faithfulness.

Be gracious to me and give me strength; show me your favor so that those who hate may be ashamed.

Psalm 120: "Deliver Me"
By Unknown: A Song of Ascents for travelers to sing when approaching Jerusalem.

I called on the Lord in my distress and he answered me.

Lord, deliver me from lying lips.

I have lived among those who hate peace for too long; I want peace, but they seek war.

Psalm 139: "Praise to an Omnipotent and Omniscient God"
By David

Lord, you have searched me and known me; you know when I sit down and when I rise; you know my thoughts before I have them.

You know all my ways; you even know what I'm going to say before I say it.

Your hand is upon me; such knowledge is too incredible for me.

Where could I hide from your Spirit or presence?

No matter where I go, you are there!

The darkness is not dark to you; the night is as bright as day.

You formed my inward parts and knitted me together in my mother's womb.

I praise you because I am fearfully and wonderfully made.

My soul knows that your works are wonderful; you wove me together in secret.

Every one of my days was written before any of them took place.

Your thoughts are precious to me, I would count them if I could, but there are more of them than the sand of the sea.

I wish that you would slay the wicked because they take your name in vain!

I reject those who hate you; they are my enemies.

Lord, search me and know my heart!

Try me and know my thoughts and see if there is any evil in me; lead me in the everlasting way!

Psalm 141: "No Compromise"
By David

Lord, I call upon you; listen to my prayer.

Watch over my mouth, and don't let my heart incline to any evil.

Let a righteous man strike me if I am sinning.

My eyes are toward you; I seek shelter in you, don't leave me defenseless!

Let the wicked fall into their own nets while I pass by safely.

Psalm 142: "You Are My Refuge"
By David, when he was in the cave.

I cry out to the Lord with my voice; I plead to him for mercy.

I tell him my troubles and pour out my complaint before him.

He is the only one who knows what I should do.

You are my refuge, my portion in the land of the living.

Hear my cry because I have been brought low; deliver me from my persecutors.

The righteous will surround me, for you will deal bountifully with me.

CHAPTER THIRTY-ONE
PSALMS OF REPENTANCE

> **Psalms of repentance**
>
> The psalmists wrote these poems when they realized their sin and committed to turning back to the Lord. We can use these as prayers to get our hearts right with God.

Psalm 6: "Deliver Me for Your Sake"
By David

Lord, do not rebuke me when you are angry or discipline me when you are upset.

Be gracious to me because I am weak; heal me for even my bones are troubled.

God, how much longer will my soul be troubled!?

Save me and deliver me for the sake of your steadfast love!

The dead do not remember you and they will not give you praise.

My weeping wears me out and I flood my bed with tears.

My eyes pour forth my sorrow because of my many enemies.

But the Lord has heard my prayer and he will shame my enemies and turn them away.

Psalm 32: "The Blessings of Forgiveness"
By David

Blessed is the one whose sin is forgiven and in whose spirit is no deceit.

When I kept silent, my bones wasted away through my groaning all day long.

Your hand was heavy upon me and my strength was dried up.

I acknowledged my sin and confessed it to the Lord, and he forgave me.

Everyone who is godly should pray while you can, you are a hiding place for me, and you save me from trouble.

I will instruct you and teach you how you should go; I will counsel you with my eye upon you.

Don't be like a stubborn mule, or it won't stay near you.

The wicked have many sorrows, but the one who trusts in the Lord is surrounded by steadfast love.

Be glad and rejoice in the Lord, you who are upright in heart!

Psalm 38: "Lord, Do Not Forsake Me"
By David

Lord, don't rebuke me in your anger or discipline me in your wrath because your hand has come down on me.

My flesh is not sound and my bones are weak because of my sin.

My sin has gone over my head and it is a heavy burden that is too heavy for me.

My wounds stink and fester because of my foolishness.

I bow down and go about mourning.

I am feeble and crushed and groan because of the distress of my heart.

Lord, I long for you, and my strength fails.

My friends and companions stand away from me, and not even my close family will come near.

Those who seek my life lay their snares and plan treachery all day long.

But I am like the deaf and mute.

I will wait for you, Lord, because I know you are the one who will answer.

Do not let them rejoice over me when my foot slips because I am about to fall.

I confess my sin; I regret my choices.

Lord, do not forsake me because I pursue good.

Don't be far away from me, but hurry to help me, Lord of my salvation.

Psalm 51: "Create in Me a Clean Heart"
By David, possibly after his sin with Bathsheba and Uriah.

Have mercy on me according to your unfailing love and blot out my sin according to your mercy.

Wash me from my iniquity and cleanse me from my sin.

I know my transgressions because my sin is always before me.

I have only sinned against you and done what is evil in your sight.

I was born in iniquity and my mother conceived me in sin.

You delight in truth in the inward being and you teach me wisdom in the secret heart.

Wash me and I will be whiter than snow.

Let me hear joy and gladness and blot out all my sins.

Create a clean heart in me and renew a right spirit within me.

Don't cast me away from your presence and don't take your Holy Spirit from me.

Restore the joy of your salvation and uphold me with a willing spirit.

Then I will teach sinners your way and they will return to you.

Deliver me from guilt and I will sing of your righteousness.

Open my lips and my mouth will declare your praise.

I would offer sacrifices if it pleased you, but you want a broken spirit and a contrite heart.

Do good to Jerusalem in your good pleasure and build up Jerusalem's walls, then you will delight in right sacrifices and burnt offerings.

Psalm 102: "Do Not Hide Your Face from Me"
By Unknown, a prayer of the afflicted.

Lord, hear my prayer, and do not hide your face from me on the day of my distress!

My days pass away like smoke and my bones burn like a furnace.

My heart is struck; it has withered like grass; I forget to eat.

I lie awake and my bones cling to my flesh.

My enemies taunt me all day long; I eat ashes like bread and mingle tears with my drink.

But you are enthroned forever; you will be remembered throughout all generations.

You will arise and have pity on Jerusalem at the appointed time; nations will fear the name of the Lord because he does not despise their prayer.

Record this for future generations so that they may praise the Lord.

He will sit on your throne forever!

He looked down from heaven on the earth to hear the prisoners' groans, to set those doomed to die free.

He has broken my strength and shortened my days.

God, don't take me away in the middle of my life; you will endure through all generations!

You created the heavens and the earth, they will perish, but you will remain.

You are eternal and always the same.

The children of your servants will live in security and their offspring will be established before you.

Psalm 130: "My Soul Waits for the Lord"
By Unknown: A Song of Ascents for travelers to sing when approaching Jerusalem.

Lord, I cry out to you from the depths; hear my plea for mercy!

No one can stand before you with our sin, but you hold forgiveness so that you may be feared.

My soul waits for the Lord and I hope in his word, for there is steadfast love and redemption with him.

He will redeem Israel from its sin.

Psalm 143: "Hope for the Persecuted Soul"
By David

Lord, listen to my prayer and hear my pleas for mercy!

Answer me in your faithfulness and righteousness!

Don't judge me because there is no one alive who is righteous before you.

My enemies have pursued my soul and crushed me to the ground.

My spirit faints within me; my heart is appalled.

I remember the past and meditate on the work of your hands; my soul thirsts for you like a parched land.

Don't hide your face from me, or I will be like those who go down to the pit.

Let me hear of your steadfast love in the morning and let me know where I should go.

Deliver me from my enemies because you are my refuge!

Teach me to do your will, for you are my God!

Preserve my life and bring my soul out of trouble!

You will cut off my enemies and destroy my soul's adversaries, for I am your servant.

CHAPTER THIRTY-TWO

PSALMS OF VENGEANCE

> **Psalms of vengeance**
>
> The psalmists had times when they called for God to avenge them against their enemies. God tells us to leave room for him to take vengeance, and these are prayers we can use in these situations.

Psalm 35: "Fight Against My Enemies"
By David, probably written about Saul.

Lord, fight on my behalf against my enemies.

Save my soul and put those who seek my life to shame and dishonor.

Let them be disappointed and scattered like dust in the wind; let their path be dark and slippery.

They hid a net and dug a pit for me without cause to capture me; let them fall in their own trap!

Then my soul will rejoice in the Lord and my bones will praise the Lord for my salvation.

Malicious witnesses repay me evil for good even though I looked after them in their distress.

They rejoice when I stumble and mock me.

Lord, how long will you watch?

Rescue me from their destruction and then I will thank and praise you in the great congregation.

Don't let them rejoice over me who are wrongly my foes and hate me without cause.

Lord, do not be silent and don't be far away.

Rise up for my justification according to your righteousness and put them to shame and dishonor.

Let those who delight in my righteousness shout for joy and proclaim your greatness.

Psalm 69: "Save Me"
By David

God save me because the waters have come up to my neck; I have sunk into the mire.

I am weary with tears; my throat is parched; my eyes are dim, waiting for God.

Those who hate me without cause are more than the hairs of my head.

Lord, you know my folly and the wrongs I've done.

Let those who hope in you not be put to shame because of me.

I have born reproach for your sake; I have become a stranger to my brothers.

Zeal for your house has consumed me; when I humbled my soul with fasting, it became my reproach.

I clothed myself with sackcloth, and I became a byword to them; they gossip about me.

But I pray to you, at an acceptable time, answer me in the abundance of your steadfast love.

Deliver me from sinking in the mire and deliver me from my enemies and the deep waters.

Don't let the flood sweep over me, the deep swallow me, or the pit close its mouth over me.

Answer me because your steadfast love is good; answer me quickly because I am in distress.

Redeem me because of my enemies!

You know my reproach, shame, dishonor, and foes.

I am in despair; I looked for pity and comfort but found none.

They gave me poison to eat and sour wine to drink, let their own table become a snare, and their peace become a trap.

Pour out your indignation upon them and let your burning anger overtake them.

They persecute the one you have struck down and recount the pain of those you have wounded.

Add punishment to their punishment and let them be blotted out of the book of the living.

I am afflicted and in pain; let your salvation set me on high!

I will praise the name of God with a song; magnify him with thanksgiving.

This pleases the Lord more than burnt offerings; the humble will be glad when they see it.

Let your hearts revive because the Lord hears the needy and does not despise his prisoners.

Let heaven and earth praise him, for God will save Jerusalem and build up the cities of Judah.

The offspring of his servants will inherit it and those who love his name will live there.

Psalm 83: "God, Do Not Keep Silent"
By Asaph

God, do not keep silent or stay still.

Your enemies are making an uproar, and those who hate you have raised their heads.

They make crafty plans against your people; they consult together against your treasured ones.

They want to wipe us out so that no one will remember the name of Israel anymore.

Lord, make them like the whirling dust in the wind.

Pursue them with a storm and terrify them!

Make them ashamed and die in disgrace so that they know that you are the only God over the earth.

Psalm 88: "I Cry Out to You"
By the sons of Korah, a lamentation.

Lord, God of my salvation, I cry out to you day and night; listen to my cry!

My soul is full of trouble, and I am close to death; I have no strength, like those who are cut off from your hand.

You have put me in the depths of the pit, your wrath lies heavy on me, and you overwhelm me with all your waves.

You have made my friends shun me and I have become a horror to them.

I cannot escape and my eyes grow dim through sorrow.

Every day I call upon you and stretch out my hands to you; the dead cannot praise you.

Why do you ignore me? Death and darkness cannot praise you!

Lord, why do you cast my soul away and hide your face from me?

I have been afflicted and close to death since I was a youth; I am helpless.

Your wrath sweeps over me; it surrounds me like a flood all day long.

Psalm 109: "Vengeance Against My Enemies"
By David

God of my praise, do not be silent because people speak lies about me.

They encircle me with hateful words and attack me for no reason.

They reward me with evil for good and hatred for my love, but I will continue to pray.

Appoint a wicked man to come against him and bring him down.

Cut off his posterity so that his name is blotted out with his grandchildren.

Put them to death because he did not show kindness, and he pursued the poor and needy.

But deal with me on behalf of your name's sake because your steadfast love is good, deliver me!

I am poor and needy, and my heart is stricken within me; my skin hangs off my bones.

My accusers scorn me; save me according to your steadfast love!

Clothe them with dishonor and shame.

I will give thanks to the Lord because he stands by the needy one to save him from those who condemn his soul to death.

Psalm 137: "By the Rivers of Babylon"
By Unknown, during the Babylonian captivity.

We sat down by the rivers of Babylon and wept when we remembered Jerusalem.

Our captors made us sing to them, but how can we sing the Lord's song in a foreign land?

Don't let me forget Jerusalem; I would rather lose the ability to speak.

Blessed be the one who repays Babylon for what he has done to us.

Psalm 140: "Deliver Me from Evil"
By David

Lord, deliver me from evil, violent men who continually stir up wars.

Their tongues are as sharp as a serpent's, and their lips are full of venom.

Lord, guard me against the hands of the wicked who plan to trip my feet.

The arrogant have hidden a trap for me and spread a net in my path.

You are my God; listen to my pleas for mercy.

You are the strength of my salvation; you have covered my head on the day of battle.

Do not grant the desires of the wicked, or they will be exalted!

Let burning coals fall on the heads of those who surround me; don't let the slanderer be established in the land.

The Lord will maintain the cause of the afflicted and execute justice for the needy.

The righteous will give thanks to your name and the upright will dwell in your presence.

CHAPTER THIRTY-THREE
PSALMS OF THANKSGIVING

> **Community thanksgiving**
>
> This section of Psalms is when Israel thanked God for how he had blessed them as a nation. We can use these as prayers for when God has blessed our community.

Psalm 65: "God of Our Salvation"
By David

God, you deserve praise; all flesh will come to you.

When sin prevails against me, you forgive my sins.

Blessed are those you choose to dwell in your courts; we will be satisfied with your goodness and holiness!

You answer our prayers with righteousness through your marvelous deeds; you are the hope of all the ends of the earth.

You established the mountains with your strength and still the waves of the sea so that the whole earth is in awe of you.

You enrich the soil and provide it with grain. You crown the year with bounty and abundance.

Psalm 75: "God Will Judge with Equity"
By Asaph

God, we give thanks to you because your name is near.

You will judge with justice at the appointed time when the earth totters.

You tell the boastful to stop boasting or speaking with pride.

But God executes judgment, putting down one and lifting another.

The Lord gives the wicked a foaming cup of wine and they will drink it down.

But I will sing praise to the God of Jacob.

He will cut off the horns of the wicked but lift the horns of the righteous.

Psalm 107: "Let the Redeemed of the Lord Say So"
By Unknown

Give thanks to the Lord, for he is good; his steadfast love endures forever!

Let the Lord's redeemed declare his goodness.

He has saved them from trouble and delivered them from their distress; let them thank the Lord for his steadfast love and wondrous works.

He satisfies the longing and hungry soul with good things.

Some sat in darkness and the shadow of death because they rebelled against the Lord and despised his counsel.

He bowed their hearts down with hard labor and they fell because there was no one to help them.

Some became fools through their sin and were afflicted to the point of death.

Some went down to the sea and did business on the great waters; the Lord sent a great storm, and the sailors almost died.

Then they cried out to the Lord and he delivered them from their distress.

Let them thank the Lord for his steadfast love and his wondrous works to humanity.

The upright see it and are glad and wickedness shuts its mouth.

Let the wise attend to these things and consider the Lord's steadfast love.

Remember the good things he has done and how he blessed us.

Psalm 124: "The Name of the Lord Is Our Help"
By David: A Song of Ascents for travelers to sing when approaching Jerusalem.

If the Lord had not been on our side, the people would have swallowed us up when they attacked us; the flood would have swept us away.

Blessed be the Lord who has saved us because the maker of heaven and earth has helped us.

Psalm 136: "His Love Endures Forever"
By Unknown

Give thanks to the Lord, for he is good, and he alone does great wonders; his love endures forever.

He created the universe, brought Israel out of Egypt, led his people through the wilderness, and gave them the Promised Land; his love endures forever.

> **Individual thanksgiving**
>
> This section of Psalms is when Israel thanked God for how he had blessed them as individuals. We can use these as prayers for when God has blessed us.

Psalm 18: "Praise After Victory"
By David, after God delivered him from Saul and his enemies.

Oh Lord, I love you because you are my strength, my rock, and my deliverer.

I take refuge in you, my shield and source of salvation.

I call upon the Lord because he is worthy to be praised and save me from my enemies.

I was about to die and I cried out to the Lord and he heard me and became angry about my situation.

He thundered from the heavens, and he sent out his arrows amongst my enemies and caused them to scatter before him.

He drew me out of deep waters; he rescued me from powerful enemies because they were too mighty.

He saved me because he delighted in me and he rewarded me because of my innocence.

I have obeyed his commands and he has found me to be blameless.

God shows himself to be merciful with those who have mercy, he shows himself blameless with those who are innocent, but he is a pain to the wicked.

He saves the humble but brings down the proud.

God lights my lamp and gives me the strength to fight a troop or leap over a wall.

He is perfect and a shield to all who take refuge in him.

He gives me power and defends me so that I can become great.

He gave me a safe place for my feet and allowed me to pursue my enemies until they were consumed.

He made my enemies run from me, and even if they cried out to the Lord, he did not answer them.

He delivered me from strife and made me the head of nations with others to serve me.

Foreigners lost heart and bowed before me.

The Lord lives and blessed be my rock; may the God of my salvation be exalted.

He exalted me above my enemies and rescued me from men of violence.

Therefore, I will praise the Lord and sing to his great name because he has saved me and showed steadfast love to his chosen ones.

Psalm 30: "Dedication of the Temple"
By David

Lord, I will exalt you because you have pulled me out of the depths and did not let my enemies rejoice over me.

I called out to you, and you healed me, saving me from death.

Sing praises to the Lord and give thanks to his holy name.

His anger lasts a moment, but his favor lasts a lifetime; tears may last a night, but joy comes in the morning.

When I feel secure, I know I will not be shaken.

The Lord gives me the strength to stand, but I am dismayed when he hides his face.

I plead to God for mercy because my death doesn't benefit him; while I'm alive, I can praise him and tell of his faithfulness.

He turns my mourning into dancing so that my glory can sing his praise and thank God forever!

Psalm 34: "Praise from the Cave"
By David, when he pretended madness before Abimelech.

I will always bless the Lord and his praise will always be in my mouth.

Magnify the Lord with me and let us exalt his name together!

I searched for the Lord, and he answered me, delivering me from my fears.

Those who look to him are radiant and their faces will never be ashamed.

The poor cried to the Lord, and he saved them; the angel of the Lord protects and delivers those who fear him.

Taste and see that the Lord is good; learn to fear him.

Even young lions go hungry, but those who seek the Lord lack no good thing.

Listen to me and I will teach you the fear of the Lord.

Keep your tongue from evil and lies; turn away from evil and do good; seek peace and pursue it.

The Lord looks upon the righteous and listens to them, but he is against evildoers and will cut them off from the earth.

When the righteous cry for help, the Lord hears them and delivers them from their troubles.

The Lord is near to the brokenhearted and saves those with a crushed spirit.

The righteous may be afflicted, but the Lord delivers them.

Affliction will kill the wicked, but there will be no condemnation for those who take refuge in him.

Psalm 40:1-11: "My Help and My Deliverer"
By David

I waited patiently for the Lord, and he heard my cry; he pulled me out of the pit of destruction, set my feet upon a rock, and made my steps secure.

He put a new song in my mouth; many will see and fear and put their trust in the Lord.

Blessed are those who trust in the Lord, as are those who do not turn to the proud.

Lord, you have done many amazing things, and no one can compare with you.

I will tell the world about them, but there is still more that can be said.

You have not delighted in sacrifice or offerings, but you have listened to me.

I enjoy doing your will; your Law is in my heart.

I have told the congregation how you delivered me, and I have spoken of your faithfulness and salvation.

Psalm 66:13-20: "What God Has Done for My Soul"
By Unknown

Those of you who fear God, listen, and I will tell you what he has done for my soul.

I cried to him with my mouth and praised him; if I held sin in my heart, he would not have listened.

But he heard my prayer.

Blessed be God because he has not rejected my prayer or taken his steadfast love from me!

Psalm 92: "Your Works Are Great"
By Unknown, a meditation for the Sabbath.

It is good to give thanks to the Lord and sing praise to your name, to declare your steadfast love in the morning and your faithfulness by night.

You have made me glad with your wondrous works; your thoughts are profound!

The foolish cannot know or understand that though the wicked sprout like grass and evildoers flourish, they are doomed to eternal destruction.

But Lord, you are on high forever.

Your enemies will perish and evildoers will be scattered.

You have exalted me and poured fresh oil on my head; my eyes have seen my enemies' downfall.

The righteous flourish, they are planted in the Lord's house, and they still bear fruit in their old age.

He is my rock and there is no unrighteousness in him.

Psalm 108: "Praise and Trust from the Past"
By David

My heart is steadfast; I will sing with all my being!

I will give thanks to the Lord and sing your praise to the nations.

Your steadfast love is above the heavens and your faithfulness reaches to the clouds.

Be exalted above the heavens and let your glory be over all the earth so that the ones you love may be delivered!

You rule over the nations, help us against our enemies because their salvation is vain.

We will succeed with God and he will tread down our foes.

Psalm 116: "I Love the Lord"
By Unknown

I love the Lord because he has listened to my pleas for mercy; therefore, I will call on him as long as I live.

The snares of death had surrounded me and I called out to the Lord to deliver my soul.

He is gracious, righteous, and merciful; he preserves the simple, and he saved me when I was brought low.

My soul can rest because he has dealt bountifully with me.

I will walk before the Lord in the land of the living.

I was alarmed and declared that all men are liars; there is nothing I can give to him for all he has done for me.

But I will lift the cup of salvation, call upon the Lord, and pay my vows to him in the presence of his people.

Lord, I am your servant, and you have loosened my bonds.

I will offer you the sacrifice of thanksgiving and call on the Lord.

Praise the Lord!

Psalm 118: "His Steadfast Love Endures Forever"
By David, likely after he consolidated his rule over Israel.

Give thanks to the Lord, for he is good; his love endures forever!

Let those who fear the Lord declare his steadfast love because he is on our side; we should not fear.

The Lord is my help; I will triumph over those who hate me.

It is better to take refuge in the Lord than to trust people.

The nations surrounded me on every side, but I cut them off in the name of the Lord.

The Lord is my strength and song; he is my salvation; I will not die, but I will live to recount his deeds.

He disciplined me severely, but he has not given me over to death.

Open the gates of righteousness so that I can enter them and give thanks to the Lord.

I thank you that you have answered me and become my salvation.

The stone that the builders rejected has become the cornerstone.

This is the day the Lord has made; let us rejoice and be glad in it.

Save us, Lord!

We bless you from the Lord's house.

You are my God, and I will give you thanks to the Lord for he is good and his love endures forever!

Psalm 138: "Give Thanks to the Lord"
By David

Lord, I thank you with my whole heart and sing my praises!

I bow down toward your holy temple for your steadfast love and faithfulness.

You answered my prayer and strengthened my soul.

All the earth's kings will give you thanks and sing to you because they have heard your words.

Even though the Lord is high, he regards the lowly, but he keeps the proud at arm's length.

You preserve my life as I walk amid trouble; you fulfill your purpose for me.

Do not forsake the work of your hands.

CHAPTER THIRTY-FOUR

PSALMS OF TRUST

> **Psalms of Trust**
>
> These are poems that declare trust in the Lord. We can use these psalms as prayers to help build our faith in the Lord.

Psalm 11: "Faith vs. Fear"
By David, as he fled from Saul.

I take refuge in the Lord.

How can you tell me to escape to a place of shelter because if the wicked destroy my foundation, what can I do?

The Lord sits on his throne in heaven; he tests the righteous and rejects the wicked and those who love violence.

May he rain fire upon the wicked and destroy him.

The Lord is righteous, and he loves good deeds; the upright will see his face.

Psalm 16: "Contentment in Troubled Times"
By David

Oh God, I take refuge in you; please save me because I have nothing good apart from you.

I delight in your saints and the sorrows of those who run after false gods will multiply; I refuse to take part in their worship.

The Lord is my lot and he has given me a beautiful inheritance.

I bless the Lord and he instructs my heart in the night.

His ways are before me and I will never be shaken.

My heart is glad, and my whole being rejoices; he will not abandon me to death or let his Holy One undergo decay.

He makes me know the paths of life, and there is joy and pleasures forever in his presence.

Psalm 23: "The Lord is My Shepherd"
By David

The Lord is my shepherd; I shall not want.

He makes me lie down in green pastures and leads me to calm waters.

He restores my soul and makes me righteous for his name's sake.

I will not fear evil even though I walk through the valley of the shadow of death.

His rod and staff comfort me.

He prepares a table for me in the presence of my enemies; he gives me all I need.

Surely goodness and mercy will follow me my entire life and I shall dwell in the house of the Lord forever.

Psalm 27: "Hear Me When I Cry Out!"
By David

The Lord is my light and salvation, the fortress of my life; I shall not be afraid.

When the wicked attack, they will stumble and fall.

Even if an army attacks me, I am confident and will not fear.

I have asked the Lord always to live in his house and behold his beauty.

He will protect me in my time of trouble and set my feet upon safe ground.

God will lift my head above my enemies, and I will worship him and sing before his throne.

Hear me when I cry out! You have told me to seek your face and I have listened.

Do not hide from me; do not forsake me, oh God of my salvation!

Even though everyone leaves me, you will take me in.

Teach me your way and lead me on a safe path.

Do not let my enemies overtake me; they lie about me and threaten violence.

I will see your goodness in the land of the living.

Wait for the Lord; be strong and courageous.

Wait for the Lord!

Psalm 62: "My Soul Waits for God Alone"
By David

My soul waits in silence for God alone because he is the source of my salvation and my fortress; I will not be shaken.

How long will you batter a man and lean on him like a tottering fence?

They take pleasure in lies, they bless with their mouths, but inwardly they curse.

My soul waits in silence for God alone because my hope is in him; he is my rock and salvation; I will not be shaken.

He is the source of my salvation and glory, my mighty rock and refuge.

Trust in him always, and pour out your heart before him.

Those of low estate are just a breath; those of high estate are a delusion; when weighed, they are together lighter than a breath.

Don't trust in extortion or robbery; don't set your heart on riches.

Power belongs to God and he will render to men according to their work.

Psalm 63: "My Soul Thirsts for You"
By David, in the Judean wilderness.

God, you are my God; I earnestly seek you, my soul thirsts for you, my flesh faints for you as in a dry and weary land where there is no water.

I have seen your power and glory; your steadfast love is better than life; my lips will praise you.

I will bless you as long as I live and I will lift my hands.

My soul will be satisfied with rich food and my mouth will praise you with joy.

I will meditate on you in the watches of the night because you have been my help.

My soul clings to you because you uphold me, but those who want to destroy me will go down into the depths of the earth.

But I will rejoice in God and all who swear by him will exult, for he will stop the mouths of liars.

Psalm 91: "My Refuge and Fortress"
By Unknown

Those who dwell in the shelter of the Most High will live in the shadow of the Almighty.

The Lord is my refuge and fortress; I trust in him.

He will deliver us from the hunter and pestilence; he will be our shield.

You will not be afraid of night terrors or arrows.

A thousand may fall at your side and ten thousand at your right hand, but it won't come near you.

You will see the punishment of the wicked because you have made the Lord your dwelling place and refuge.

No evil or plague will come near you.

He will command his angels to guard you in all your ways and they will bear you up on their hands so that you don't strike your foot against a stone.

You will tread on the lion and serpent because he will protect you.

He will answer when you call to him; he will rescue you and give you long life and salvation.

Psalm 121: "My Help Comes from the Lord"
By Unknown: A Song of Ascents for travelers to sing when approaching Jerusalem.

I lift my eyes up to the hills.

My help comes from the Lord, who made heaven and earth.

He will not let your foot be moved because he will not slumber.

Israel's keeper will not sleep because he is our shield.

He will watch over our going out and coming in from now until forever.

Psalm 125: "The Lord Surrounds His People"
By Unknown: A Song of Ascents for travelers to sing when approaching Jerusalem.

Those who trust in the Lord are like Mount Zion, which is immovable.

The Lord surrounds his people from now until eternity and he will not allow a wicked scepter to rest on the land given to the righteous.

Lord, do good to those who are good and to those with upright hearts!

But he will turn aside those with crooked hearts! Peace to Israel!

Psalm 131: "David's Humility"
By David: A Song of Ascents for travelers to sing when approaching Jerusalem.

Lord, I am humble, and I do not worry about things that are too marvelous for me; I have calmed and quieted my soul.

Israel, hope in the Lord from now until eternity.

CHAPTER THIRTY-FIVE
WORSHIP PSALMS

> **Worship Psalms**
>
> The Psalms in this grouping are worship songs that the authors wrote. Many of these have been made into hymns or modern worship songs and we can use these as prayers to worship the Lord.

Psalm 8: "Your Majestic Name"
By David

Oh Lord, our Lord, how majestic is your name in all the earth!

Your glory is above the heavens, and you have used the weak and powerless to establish your strength!

When I look at the night sky and see the glory of your creation, I don't understand why you care for us.

You have crowned us with glory and honor and made us just lower than the angels.

You have made us rulers over everything on earth, over beasts of the field, birds of the air, and fish in the sea.

Oh Lord, our Lord, how majestic is your name in all the earth!

Psalm 19:1-6: "The Heavens Declare God's Glory"
By David

The heavens declare the Lord's glory and the earth pours out the beauty of his works.

Nature proclaims his greatness and shows how awesome he is.

Nature doesn't speak a word, yet it shows us his glory and power.

Psalm 33: "The Great and Awesome God"
By David

Shout for joy in the Lord because praise befits the upright.

Sing new songs of thanks to the Lord with music for the Lord's word is upright and faithful.

He loves righteousness and justice, and his love fills the earth.

The Lord made the heavens with his word; all the earth should fear him and stand in awe.

The Lord frustrates the plans of people, but his plans last forever.

Blessed is the nation whose God is the Lord; he looks down from heaven and sees humanity and their deeds.

Great strength does not deliver kings and warriors, but the Lord's love saves them from death.

Our soul waits for the Lord; he is our help and shield; our joy is in him because we trust in his holy name.

Psalm 66:1-12: "Sing God's Glory"
By Unknown

Shout to the earth, sing the glory of his name, and give him praise!

Tell God how wondrous his deeds are and how great his power is; all the earth worships and sings praises to him.

Come and see what God has done, how he turned the sea into dry land, and they passed through on foot.

We rejoice in him who rules by his might forever, don't let the rebellious exalt themselves.

People, bless our God who has kept our soul among the living and has not let our feet slip.

You have tested us in the way silver is refined.

You laid a crushing burden on our backs and let men trample us; we went through fire and water, but you have brought us into a place of abundance.

Psalm 67: "Shine Your Face Upon Us"
By Unknown

May God be gracious to us, bless us, and make his face shine upon us so that we may know your way on earth and your saving power.

May the people praise you because you judge the earth with equity.

The earth has yielded its increase and he will bless us.

Let the whole earth fear him!

Psalm 95: "Sing Songs of Praise"
By David

Let us sing praises to the Lord; let us make a joyful noise to the rock of our salvation!

Let us come into his presence with thanksgiving and make a joyful noise to him with songs of praise!

The Lord is a great God, a king above all gods.

He holds the world in his hands, let us worship, bow down, and kneel before the Lord, our Maker!

He is our God, the people of his pasture, and the sheep of his hand.

Listen to his voice and do not harden your hearts as your fathers did in the wilderness even though they had seen my work.

He loathed that generation for 40 years, so he swore that they would not enter his rest.

Psalm 100: "His Steadfast Love Endures Forever"
By Unknown

Make a joyful noise to the Lord, all the earth!

Serve the Lord with gladness and come into his presence with singing!

The Lord is God, he made us, and we are his; we are his people and the sheep of his pasture.

Enter his courts with thanksgiving and praise; give him thanks and bless his name!

The Lord is good; his steadfast love endures forever and his faithfulness to all generations.

Psalm 103: "Bless the Lord"
By David

Bless the Lord, oh my soul, and all that is within me, bless his holy name!

Do not forget his benefits because he forgives your sins, heals your diseases, redeems your life from the pit, crowns you with love and mercy, and satisfies you with good things.

The Lord works righteousness and justice for all who are oppressed; he has made his ways known to Moses and his acts to Israel.

The Lord is merciful and gracious, slow to anger, and abounding in steadfast love.

He does not deal with us according to our sins.

For as high as the heavens are above the earth, so great is his steadfast love to those who fear him.

He removes our sin from us as far as the east is from the west.

The Lord shows compassion to those who fear him as a father shows compassion to his children.

He knows our frame and that we are nothing more than dust.

Our days are like the grass and the flowers of the field; it is gone before we know it.

But the steadfast love of the Lord is eternal for those who fear him and obey his commandments.

The Lord established his throne in the heavens and his kingdom rules over all.

Angels who do his work, bless the Lord, and all his works!

Bless the Lord, oh my soul!

Psalm 104: "Lord, You Are Very Great"
By David

Bless the Lord, oh my soul!

You are very great, clothed in splendor and majesty!

He stretches out the heavens like a tent, lays the beams of his chambers on the waters, makes the clouds his chariot, rides on the wings of the wind, and makes his angels a flaming fire.

He set the earth on immovable foundations and covered the deep with a garment.

He directs nature and causes all things to happen.

May the glory of the Lord last forever and rejoice in his works.

I will sing to the Lord while I live; may my meditation be pleasing to him.

Bless the Lord, oh my soul!

Psalm 111: "The Lord's Works Are Great"
By Unknown

I will praise the Lord with my whole heart because his works are great and studied by those who delight in them.

He is full of splendor and majesty; his righteousness endures forever.

The Lord is gracious and merciful; he provides food for those who fear him and remembers his promises forever.

He has shown his power by giving his people an inheritance among the nations.

His works are faithful, and just and his laws are trustworthy.

He sent redemption to his people; his name is holy and awesome!

The fear of the Lord is the beginning of wisdom; those who practice it have a good understanding.

His praise endures forever!

Psalm 113: "Praise the Lord"
By Unknown

Praise the Lord! Bless the name of the Lord from now into eternity!

The Lord is to be praised from the rising of the sun until its setting.

He is high above the nations and his glory is above the heavens.

There is no one like the Lord!

He raises the poor from the dust and the needy from the ashes to make them sit with princes.

He gives barren women a home and the joy of children. Praise the Lord!

Psalm 114: "Water from a Rock"
By Unknown

Oh earth, tremble in the Lord's presence, who turns rock into a pool of water and the flint into a spring of water.

Psalm 117: "The Lord's Faithfulness Endures Forever"
By Unknown

Praise the Lord all the earth!

For his steadfast love and faithfulness toward us endure forever.

Praise the Lord!

Psalm 145: "Great Is the Lord"
By David

I will praise you, my God and King; I will bless your name forever.

The Lord is great and deserves our praise; his greatness is unsearchable.

I will meditate on the glorious splendor of your majesty and your wondrous works.

You are gracious and merciful, slow to anger, and abounding in steadfast love.

You are good to all and your mercy is over everything you have made.

Your works will give thanks to you and your saints will bless you.

They will speak of the glory of your kingdom and your power.

Your kingdom is eternal, and you are faithful and kind in all your words and works.

The Lord upholds those who are falling and raises up those who are bowed down.

We look to you for food in season and you satisfy every living thing.

The Lord is righteous in all his ways and kind in all his works.

He is near to all who call on him in truth.

The Lord fulfills the desires of those who fear him, and he hears their cries; he preserves those who love him, but he will destroy the wicked.

My mouth will praise the Lord and bless his holy name forever and ever.

Psalm 146: "I Will Praise the Lord as Long I Live"
By Unknown

I will praise the Lord as long as I live!

Don't put your trust in princes who cannot save; their plans accompany them to the grave.

Blessed are those who hope in the Lord, maker of heaven and earth, who keeps faith forever.

He executes justice for the oppressed, feeds the hungry, sets the prisoners free, opens the blind eye, lifts those who are bowed down, and loves the righteous.

The Lord watches over the needy but brings the wicked to ruin.

The Lord will reign forever; give him praise!

Psalm 147: "It is Good to Sing Praises to Our God"
By Unknown

Praise the Lord!

It is good to sing praises to our God because he builds up Jerusalem and gathers Israel's outcasts.

He heals the brokenhearted and binds up their wounds; he created and named all the stars.

The Lord is great and abundant in power; his understanding is beyond measure.

He lifts up the humble and casts down the wicked.

Sing to the Lord with thanksgiving!

He covers the heavens with clouds, sends rain, and makes the grass grow; he feeds the animals of the field.

The Lord takes pleasure in those who fear him and those who hope in his steadfast love.

He strengthens Jerusalem's gates and blesses her children; he brings peace and fills her with everything she needs.

He has not dealt with any other nation this way.

Praise the Lord!

Psalm 148: "Let Heaven and Earth Praise the Lord"
By Unknown

Praise the Lord from the heavens; praise him in the heights!

Angels and all his hosts, praise the Lord!

Sun, moon, and shining stars praise the Lord!

He gave the command and created everything; may his creation praise him!

Let all humanity and beasts praise the Lord!

His name alone is exalted and his majesty is above all things.

Praise the Lord!

Psalm 149: "Sing to the Lord a New Song"
By Unknown

Praise the Lord!

Sing to the Lord a new song!

Let Israel be glad in their Maker and let the children of Jerusalem rejoice in their King!

Let them praise his name with song and dance, for the Lord takes pleasure in his people, and he crowns the humble with salvation.

Let the godly exult in glory and sing for joy on their beds.

May the praises of God be in their mouths while a two-edged sword is in their hands to execute vengeance on the nations.

This is an honor for all his godly ones.

Praise the Lord!

Psalm 150: "Praise God in His Sanctuary"
By Unknown

Praise the Lord!

Praise God in his sanctuary and his mighty heavens!

Praise him for his mighty deeds and his greatness!

Praise him with loud instruments; let everything that has breath praise the Lord!

Praise the Lord!

CHAPTER THIRTY-SIX

SALVATION HISTORY PSALMS

> **Salvation history and Covenant Psalms**
>
> The Israelites wrote several Psalms that recounted their salvation history to help them remember what God had done and reminded them of his covenant. When we face hard times, these can be helpful reminders of how God has worked in the past.

Psalm 50: "God is Judge"
By Asaph

God speaks and summons the earth from the rising of the sun to its setting.

God shines forth out of Jerusalem in the perfection of his beauty.

Our God comes and does not keep silent; a devouring fire precedes him and a mighty storm surrounds him.

He calls to the heavens and earth so that he may judge his people.

The heavens declare his righteousness; he is the judge!

Israel, I am your God, and I will testify against you.

I don't rebuke you for your sacrifices because they are constant, but I won't accept an animal from you because every animal is mine, even the cattle on a thousand hills.

If I were hungry, I wouldn't tell you because I own the entire earth.

I don't need the flesh of bulls or the blood of goats; offer me a sacrifice of thanksgiving, fulfill your vows, and call on me on the day of trouble.

Then I will deliver you and you will glorify me.

But to the wicked, you have no right to take my covenant because you hate discipline and cast my words behind you.

You are pleased with thieves and you keep company with adulterers.

You slander your brother and I have been silent; you thought I was like you.

But now I rebuke you and lay a charge before you.

The one who offers a sacrifice of thanksgiving glorifies me; I will show him God's salvation.

Psalm 78: "Tell the Coming Generation"
By Asaph

Listen to my teaching and I will tell you things our fathers taught us in the past.

We will tell the coming generation about the glorious deeds of the Lord and his mighty wonders.

He established a testimony in Jacob and gave fathers a law to teach their children in perpetuity so they would not be stubborn or rebellious.

But they forgot his works and the wonders he showed them; they refused to obey his Law.

He divided the sea and let them pass through it, making the waters stand up on both sides.

He split rocks in the wilderness and gave them water to drink.

But they kept sinning and tested God by demanding the food they craved even though they didn't believe he could do it.

The Lord was full of wrath because they didn't believe in his saving power, but he opened the doors of heaven and gave them manna.

He caused the winds to blow and rained quail on them like the dust of the earth.

Despite all this, they still sinned and refused to believe, so he made their days vanish like a breath.

When he killed them, they repented and earnestly sought God.

They remembered that God was their Rock and Redeemer, but they were not steadfast and eventually broke his covenant.

But God was compassionate and atoned for their sin; he restrained his anger and did not pour his wrath out on them.

They rebelled against him over and over and they did not remember his mighty deeds in Egypt.

He led his people like sheep and guided them in the wilderness like a flock.

He brought them to his Holy Land and drove out the nations before them.

But they tested and rebelled against God and acted just like their ancestors.

They provoked him to anger with their high places and idols.

When God saw this, he rejected Israel and delivered his power and glory into captivity; he gave his people over to the sword and fire.

But he awoke and put his adversaries to everlasting shame.

He chose the tribe of Judah and built his sanctuary there.

He chose his servant David from the sheepfolds and made him shepherd of his people.

Psalm 81: "Sing to the God of Our Strength"
By Asaph

Sing to the God of our strength and make music in his honor.

He took our burden and freed us; he has delivered us from our distress.

There should be no strange god among you and you should not bow down to idols.

I am the Lord your God who brought you out of Egypt.

But my people have not listened or submitted to me.

So, I let them follow their stubborn hearts and do their own thing.

I wish they would listen to me and obey my commands; then, I would subdue and punish their enemies.

But I would feed you with the finest wheat and honey.

Psalm 105: "Tell of All His Wonderful Works"
By David

Give thanks to the Lord, call upon his name, and make his deeds known; sing praises to his name and tell of his wondrous works!

Glory in his holy name and let the hearts of those who seek the Lord rejoice!

Seek the Lord and his strength continually!

Remember what he has done, his miracles and judgments.

He is the Lord our God; his judgments are throughout the earth.

He remembers his covenant forever and his commandments for a thousand generations.

He gave the land of Canaan as an inheritance when his people were small.

He sent a famine on the land, but he sent Joseph ahead of them.

Then Israel came to Egypt and God made them multiply.

But Egypt began to hate his people, so he sent Moses and Aaron, and they performed his signs among them.

He brought them out of Egypt and they were glad when the Jews left.

He spread a cloud for a covering and fire to give light by night.

He gave them quail, bread, and water because he remembered his holy promise to Abraham.

He brought his people out with joy and gave them the nations' lands so they might keep his laws.

Praise the Lord!

Psalm 106: "Give Thanks to the Lord, for He Is Good"
By Unknown

Praise the Lord!

Give thanks to the Lord, for he is good, and his steadfast love endures forever!

His mighty deeds and praise are beyond measure.

Blessed are those who observe justice and righteousness!

Lord, remember me when you favor your people and help me save them so that I might rejoice with them.

When our fathers were in Egypt, they did not remember your love and great works but chose instead to rebel.

But he saved them for his name's sake so that they would know his mighty power; he rebuked the Red Sea and made it like a desert.

He saved them from their enemies; the waters drowned the Egyptians and none of them were left.

They believed and sang his praise, but they forgot his works before long and did not wait for his counsel.

They put God to the test in the desert, and he gave them what they wanted, but also sent a wasting disease among them.

When some of the men became jealous of Moses and Aaron, the Lord opened the earth and swallowed their families.

They worshiped metal idols and forgot their God and Savior, who had done great things in Egypt.

He would have destroyed them if Moses had not stood in between to turn away his wrath.

Then they despised the pleasant land and did not obey the Lord.

Therefore, God swore that none of them would live to see the Promised Land.

Then they yoked themselves to Baal of Peor and God sent a plague.

They angered God at the waters of Meribah and Moses spoke rashly.

When they entered the Promised Land, they did not destroy the nations as God commanded, but they mixed with them and served their idols.

They sacrificed their children to demons and polluted the land with blood.

Their actions made them unclean and the Lord was angry with his people.

He gave them into the hands of the nations and their enemies oppressed them.

The Lord delivered them many times, but they never stopped rebelling.

But he looked upon their distress when they cried out.

He remembered his covenant for their sake and relented out of the overflow of his love.

He made their captors look at them with pity.

Lord, save us and gather us from the nations so that we may give thanks and praise to your holy name.

Blessed be the Lord God of Israel for all eternity!

Psalm 132: "The Promise to David"
By David: A Song of Ascents for travelers to sing when approaching Jerusalem.

Lord, remember all the hardships David endured and how he swore that he would not rest until he found a dwelling place for you.

Lord, arise and go to your temple with the ark of your might.

Let your priests be clothed in righteousness and your saints shout for joy.

Don't turn away from your anointed for the sake of your servant David.

The Lord has chosen Jerusalem for his dwelling place, and he will bless her provisions and satisfy her poor with bread.

He will clothe her priests with salvation and her saints will shout for joy.

The Lord will shine on David's offspring but will clothe his enemies with shame.

Psalm 135: "Your Name Endures Forever"
By Unknown: A compilation

Praise the name of the Lord!

Praise the Lord, for he is good, and it is good to sing to him.

He has chosen Israel as his possession.

The Lord is great, and above all gods, he does whatever he wants.

He makes nature run its course and has struck down many kings and nations.

Lord, your name endures forever; you will vindicate your people and have compassion on your servants.

The nations' idols are man-made; they cannot speak, see, hear, or breathe.

Those who make and worship them become like them.

Praise the Lord!

CHAPTER THIRTY-SEVEN
PSALMS FOR THE KING

Psalm 2: "God's King"
By David

Why are the nations angry and the people make plans that will fail?

Do they think that they can destroy the Lord and his anointed?

Do they think they can escape his rule? Please.

God sits in heaven and laughs at their plans because they will fail.

He will speak to them in his wrath, "I have set my king in Jerusalem!

"The king is like my son!

"I will give you the earth as your possession, and you will break the nations with an iron rod and shatter them like a vase."

Take warning and be wise, you rulers of the earth.

Serve the Lord with fear and rejoice with trembling.

Worship the Son so that he does not become angry, and you die from his fury.

Blessed are all who take refuge in him!

Psalm 20: "Prayer for Lord's Anointed"
By David

May the Lord answer in your day of trouble and may his name protect you!

May he remember your offerings and your sacrifices.

May he grant your heart's desire and fulfill all your plans!

May we rejoice over your salvation and he answer all your prayers!

I know that the Lord saves his anointed and he will answer you from heaven.

Some trust in their strength, but we will trust in the Lord because he will save and answer our prayers.

Psalm 21: "Rulers, Rejoice in the Lord!"
By David

Rulers rejoice in the strength of the Lord because he has fulfilled their desires and answered their prayers.

The Lord has blessed them and given them their position; he has granted them a long life.

If rulers trust in the Lord, his steadfast love will make them immovable.

They will find their enemies and destroy them.

The Lord will swallow them whole and wipe out their opponents.

Even though they plot evil, they will not succeed.

Lord, we praise your power and exalt your strength!

Psalm 29: "God's Voice in the Storm"
By David

Ascribe to the Lord the glory and strength he deserves and worship him in his holiness.

The Lord's voice is powerful and majestic; it thunders over many waters and shatters mighty trees.

He makes mighty nations skip like a calf or young ox.

The Lord's voice strikes with lightning and shakes the desert.

The Lord sits on his throne forever, and he gives strength and blessing to his people with peace.

Psalm 45: "O God, Your Throne is Forever"
By the sons of Korah

My heart overflows with a pleasing theme; I sing to the king; my tongue is like a scribe's pen.

You are the most handsome of men; grace is on your lips; God has blessed you forever.

Put your sword on your thigh and ride out for the cause of truth, humility, and righteousness; let your right hand teach you marvelous deeds!

Your arrows are sharp in the hearts of the king's enemies.

Oh God, your throne is forever and ever; the scepter of your kingdom is uprightness; you love righteousness and hate wickedness.

Therefore, God has anointed you with the oil of gladness beyond your companions.

You have nobles in your presence.

The princess is glorious in her chamber with robes interwoven with gold.

She is led to the king with her virgin companions following her.

They are led into the palace with joy and your sons will replace your fathers.

The Lord will cause your name to be remembered in all generations and the nations will praise you forever and ever.

Psalm 47: "God is King Over the Earth"
By the sons of Korah

Clap your hands and shout to God with loud songs of joy!

The Lord Most High is to be feared, a great king over all the earth.

He subdued peoples under our feet; he chose our legacy for us, the pride of Jacob whom he loves.

God has gone up with a shout and a trumpet; sing praises to God, our King.

He is King over all the earth; he reigns over the nations from his holy throne.

He is highly exalted.

Psalm 72: "Give the King Justice"
By Solomon

God, give the king justice and righteousness!

Let the mountains bear prosperity and defend the cause of the poor and needy; crush the oppressor!

May they fear you throughout all generations and may the righteous flourish.

May his dominion extend from sea to sea and the ends of the earth!

May all the kings fall before him, and all nations serve him because he delivers the poor and needy.

May he live long and become wealthy!

May his name endure forever and his fame as long as the sun shines!

May he bless the people!

Blessed be the Lord God of Israel who does wondrous things; may the earth be filled with his glory!

Psalm 93: "The Lord Reigns in Majesty"
By David

The Lord reigns, robed in majesty with strength as his belt.

He established the world and it will never be moved.

You set your throne from the beginning; you are eternal.

The floods have lifted their voice; they are mightier than the sea; the Lord on high is mighty!

Your decrees are trustworthy; holiness befits your house.

Psalm 96: "Worship in the Splendor of Holiness"
By David

Sing to the Lord a new song; bless his name and tell of his salvation.

Declare his glory among the nations and his marvelous works among the peoples!

The Lord is great and should be praised; he is to be feared above all gods.

The gods of the people are worthless idols, but the Lord made the heavens.

Splendor and majesty are before him; strength and beauty are in his sanctuary.

Ascribe strength and glory to the Lord; bring an offering into his courts!

Worship the Lord in the splendor of holiness; all the earth trembles before him.

Tell the nations that the Lord reigns and will judge the peoples with equity.

Let the heavens be glad, and the earth rejoice; then all the trees of the forest will sing for joy.

He will judge the world in righteousness and faithfulness.

Psalm 97: "Let the Earth Rejoice"
By David

The Lord reigns; let the earth rejoice!

Clouds and thick darkness surround him; righteousness and justice are the foundation of his throne.

He burns up his adversaries with fire, the earth sees, and trembles.

The mountains melt before the Lord like wax; the heavens proclaim his righteousness, and the world sees his glory.

Idol worshipers are put to shame; Jerusalem hears and is glad and rejoices because of his judgments.

The Lord is most high above all the earth, exalted far above all gods.

Those who love the Lord hate evil; he preserves his saints' lives and delivers them from the wicked's hands.

Light is sown for the righteous and joy for the upright.

Rejoice in the Lord and give thanks to his holy name!

Psalm 98: "Make a Joyful Noise to the Lord"
By David

Sing to the Lord a new song because he has done marvelous things!

The Lord has made his salvation known and revealed his righteousness in the sight of the nations.

He has remembered his steadfast love and faithfulness to the house of Israel.

The world has seen his salvation.

Make a joyful noise to the Lord all the earth; break forth in joyous song and praise!

Make music to the Lord with instruments, let the trees clap their hands, and the hills sing for joy to God.

He will judge the world with righteousness and equity.

Psalm 99: "The Lord Our God Is Holy"
By David

The Lord reigns; let the people tremble; he is enthroned above the cherubim!

The Lord is great in Jerusalem; he is exalted over all the earth.

He is holy; let them praise his great and awesome name!

The king loves justice and righteousness, exalt the Lord our God and worship at his footstool, for he is holy!

Moses and Aaron were his priests, and Samuel called upon his name.

They called out to the Lord and he answered them, he spoke to them and they obeyed his commands.

Lord God, you answered them, you are a forgiving God, and you avenge wrongdoings.

Exalt the Lord our God and worship at his holy mountain because the Lord our God is holy!

Psalm 101: "I Will Walk with Integrity"
By David

Lord, I will sing of your steadfast love and justice; I will make music.

I will ponder the blameless way and walk with integrity of heart within my house.

I will not set worthless things before my eyes; I hate the work of those who fall away.

I will know nothing of evil and keep a perverse heart far away.

I will destroy those who slander their neighbors and I will not endure those with an arrogant heart.

I will look on the faithful with favor so that they will dwell with me.

I will not let liars live in my house; I will destroy all the wicked and cut off evildoers from Jerusalem.

Psalm 110: "Sit at My Right Hand"
By David

The Lord says to my Lord, "Sit at my right hand until I make your enemies your footstool."

The Lord sends your mighty scepter forth from Jerusalem, rule amid your enemies!

Your people will offer themselves freely on the day of your power.

The Lord has sworn and will not change his mind, "You are a priest forever after the order of Melchizedek."

The Lord is at your right hand; he will shatter kings on the day of his wrath.

He will judge the nations, filling them with corpses.

Psalm 144: "My Rock and Fortress"
By David

Blessed be the Lord, my rock, who trains my hands for war; he is my steadfast love and fortress, my stronghold and deliverer, my shield and refuge.

Lord, what is man that you regard him, or the son of man that you think of him?

Man is like a breath; his days are a passing shadow.

Stretch out your hand from on high, rescue me, and deliver me from the hand of foreigners who speak lies.

I will sing a new song to you who gives victory to kings.

Deliver me from the hand of liars and establish our children in the land.

Lord, bless us because you are God!

CHAPTER THIRTY-EIGHT
PSALMS FOR JERUSALEM AND THE TEMPLE

> **Psalms for Jerusalem and the temple**
>
> Jerusalem and the temple were two of the primary elements that the Israelites identified as symbols of their relationship with the Lord. They held both as sacred and these are prayers that demonstrate this reverence.

Psalm 15: "Who Can Live with You?"
By David

Oh Lord, who can live with you?

Those who do good and speak the truth in their hearts, who do not slander or do evil to their neighbor.

God is pleased with those who reject evil and walk in integrity, swearing to their own hurt.

Those who do not take advantage of those in need and do these things will never be moved.

Psalm 24: "The Great and Sovereign God"
By David

The earth is the Lord's and everything in it; he has created it all.

Who can stand before the Lord?

Only those with clean hands and a pure heart; only those who are honest.

The Lord will bless and save them.

These are the ones who seek God's face.

Oh, gates of the city, open so that the king of glory may enter!

This is the Lord, strong and mighty in battle.

Open, oh gates of the city so that the king of glory may enter.

The Lord is the king of glory!

Psalm 46: "God is Our Fortress"
By the sons of Korah

God is our refuge and strength, a very present help in trouble.

We will not fear even if the earth gives way and the mountains are thrown into the sea.

There is a river whose streams make God's city.

God is in her midst, and she will not be moved; he will help her when morning dawns.

The nations rage, but when he speaks, the earth melts.

The Lord of hosts is with us; he is our fortress.

See the Lord's works, how he brings desolation.

He causes wars to cease, and he breaks the bow and shatters the spear.

Be still and know that I am God.

I will be exalted among the nations and exalted in the earth!

The Lord of hosts is with us; the God of Jacob is our fortress.

Psalm 48: "Jerusalem, the City of Our God"
By the sons of Korah

Great is the Lord and greatly to be praised!

His holy mountain is the joy of the earth, the city of the great King.

God has made himself known as a fortress; kings came together and the sight astounded them, so they fled.

We have thought about your steadfast love, your praise reaches the ends of the earth, and your right hand is full of righteousness.

God is the Lord forever and ever; he will always guide us.

Psalm 68: "God Will Scatter His Enemies"
By David

God will arise and scatter his enemies; those who hate him will flee like smoke is driven away or like wax melts before the fire!

But the righteous will be glad and rejoice before God with joy!

Sing to God with praises and lift up his name!

He is the father of the fatherless and protector of widows.

He leads his prisoners to prosperity and exiles the rebellious to a parched land.

The earth quaked before him and the heavens poured down rain.

God, you restored your inheritance and flock; you provided for the needy.

You ascended on high and led a host of captives in your train and gave them gifts.

Blessed be the Lord who bears us up; he is our salvation.

He is a God of salvation and he delivers from death.

But he will strike the heads of his enemies, the hairy crown of the guilty.

The Lord will bring them back from exile and the depths of the sea.

Bless God in the congregation, you of Israel's fountain!

God, summon your power and rebuke the beasts of the land.

Trample those who delight in war!

Sing praises to the Lord to him who rides in the heavens.

Ascribe power to God, whose majesty is over Israel, whose power is in the skies.

He is awesome in his sanctuary, the one who gives power and strength to his people.

Blessed be God!

Psalm 76: "Who Can Stand Before You?"
By Asaph

God is known in Judah and his name is great in Israel.

He has made his dwelling place in Jerusalem, where he broke the weapons of war.

You are glorious, more majestic than the mountains of prey.

The stouthearted were stripped of their spoil, and they sank into sleep, unable to use their hands; you stunned the horse and rider.

You are to be feared!

No one can stand before you once your anger is roused.

You uttered judgment from the heavens; the earth feared and was still.

Man's wrath will praise you and you will put it on like a belt.

Make your vows to the Lord and fulfill them; bring gifts to him because he cuts off the spirit of princes and should be feared.

Psalm 82: "Rescue the Weak and Needy"
By Asaph

God has taken his place in the divine council and holds judgment amid the gods.

Give justice to the weak and the fatherless, maintain the rights of the afflicted and destitute.

Rescue the weak and the needy, deliver them from the hand of the wicked.

They do not have knowledge or understanding; they walk about in darkness.

I called them gods, sons of the Most High, but they will still die like men.

God, arise and judge the earth, for you will inherit the nations!

Psalm 84: "My Soul Longs for the Lord's Courts"
By the sons of Korah

Lord of hosts, your dwelling place is lovely!

My soul longs for the Lord's courts; my heart and flesh sing for joy to the living God.

Even swallows are at home at your altar; blessed are those who dwell in your house and sing your praise.

Blessed are those whose strength is in you.

Listen to my prayer and look on the face of your anointed.

One day in your courts is better than a thousand elsewhere.

The Lord is a sun and shield; he bestows favor and honor to the upright.

Psalm 87: "Glorious Things About You"
By the sons of Korah

The Lord loves Jerusalem's gates, the holy mount he founded, more than all Jacob's dwelling places.

Jerusalem is glorious.

Singers and dancers alike find their springs in you.

Psalm 115: "Trust in the Lord"
By Unknown

Glory be to the Lord for your steadfast love and faithfulness, and not to us.

You are in the heavens and you do whatever you want.

Idols are man-made and cannot speak, see, hear, smell, or touch.

Those who make them and those who trust in them will become like them.

Trust in the Lord because he is our help and shield.

The Lord has remembered us and he will bless us.

The heavens are the Lord's, but he has given us the earth.

The dead are silent and do not praise the Lord, but we will bless the Lord until eternity.

Praise the Lord!

Psalm 122: "Let Us Go to the Lord's House"
By David: A Song of Ascents for travelers to sing when approaching Jerusalem.

I was glad when they said, "Let us go to the Lord's house!"

We have been in Jerusalem, where the Lord commanded the tribes to worship and set David's throne.

Pray for Jerusalem's peace and security.

Psalm 134: "the Lord Bless You from Jerusalem"
By Unknown: A Song of Ascents for travelers to sing when approaching Jerusalem.

Those who serve in the temple at night should bless the Lord!

Lift your hands to the holy place and praise the Lord!

May the Lord, Maker of heaven and earth, bless you from Jerusalem!

CHAPTER THIRTY-NINE

WISDOM PSALMS

> **Wisdom Psalms**
>
> Several of the Psalms are like the wisdom we find in the Proverbs. We can use these principles to help us live better lives.

Psalm 1: "Avoid the Wicked"
By David

Blessed is the man who stays away from the wicked and sinners; instead, he delights in God's word, and he meditates on it throughout his days.

He will be like a tree planted by the water that yields much fruit; this man will prosper in everything he does.

The wicked are different, they are driven away like dust, and they cannot stand up to judgment.

The Lord knows the way of the righteous, but the path of the wicked will perish.

Psalm 36: "How Precious Is Your Steadfast Love"
By David

Sin speaks to the wicked deep in their hearts and there is no fear of God before their eyes.

They flatter themselves and believe that the Lord will not discover their sin.

They speak trouble and deceit and no longer do good; they plot evil from the moment they wake up.

Lord, your steadfast love stretches to the heavens and your faithfulness to the clouds.

Your righteousness is like the mighty mountains and your judgments are as deep as the ocean.

The children of humanity take refuge in the shadow of your wings.

You give to them from the abundance of your house.

The fountain of life is with you and you give us light to see.

Don't let me become arrogant or let the wicked drive me away; evildoers fall and cannot rise.

Psalm 37: "He Will Not Forsake His Saints"
By David

Do not fret because of evildoers, and do not be envious of sinners because they will fade away like the grass.

Trust in the Lord, and then you will live in the land and befriend faithfulness.

Delight yourself in the Lord and he will give you the desires of your heart; commit your way to him and he will act.

He will make your righteousness and justice shine like the noonday sun.

Be still and wait patiently for him, and don't worry about the wicked man who prospers.

Stay away from anger and wrath; worry only leads to evil.

In a little while, the wicked will be no more, but those who are meek and wait for the Lord will inherit the land and peace.

The wicked plot against the righteous, but the Lord laughs at them because he knows what is coming.

They will draw their swords to exploit the poor and needy, but they will fall on them.

Better is a little with the righteous than the abundance of many wicked.

The Lord upholds the righteous and will maintain their legacy forever; they even have enough during famines.

The wicked will die and pass away like smoke.

The wicked do not repay their debts, but the righteous are generous and give.

The Lord establishes our steps when we delight in his way; even when we fall, we will get back up because the Lord upholds us.

Turn away from evil and do good so that you will live forever.

The Lord loves justice and will preserve his saints forever while the children of the wicked are cut off.

The righteous will inherit the land and live there forever.

The righteous speak wisdom and justice, God's law is in their hearts, and they do not slip.

The wicked watch for the righteous to kill them, but the Lord will not abandon them.

Wait for the Lord, and he will exalt you, and you will watch when the wicked are cut off.

I saw an evil, ruthless man trying to establish himself, but he passed away, and even though I looked for him, I couldn't find him.

Observe the blameless and upright because there is a future for the peaceful.

But sinners will be destroyed.

In times of trouble, the Lord is the salvation of the righteous and their stronghold; he delivers them from the wicked.

Psalm 49: "I Will Not Fear in Times of Trouble"
By the sons of Korah

Listen to me, inhabitants of the world, I will speak wisdom, and the meditation of my heart will be understanding.

Why should I be afraid in times of trouble when the sin of those who trust their wealth surrounds me?

No one can buy eternal life because it is too costly.

Both the wise and foolish must die and leave their wealth to others.

Their graves are their homes forever, even though they call their lands by their own names.

Men will die just like the beasts of the earth; this is the path of foolish confidence.

Like sheep, they are appointed to die because death is their shepherd, and it will rule over them.

They will be consumed in death with nowhere to live, but God will ransom my soul from the power of death.

Don't be afraid of a man who becomes wealthy and the glory of his house increases.

He will not take anything with him when he dies; even though he counts himself blessed, he will go to the grave like his ancestors.

Psalm 73: "God Is My Strength and Portion Forever"
By Asaph

Truly God is good to Israel and all those who have pure hearts.

But I had stumbled because I envied the arrogant when I saw the wicked's prosperity.

They are fat and sleek and they are not stricken like the rest of humanity.

They wear their pride like a necklace and they wear violence like a garment.

These are the wicked; always at ease, they increase in riches; I have kept my heart clean in vain.

I have been stricken and rebuked every morning.

I couldn't understand this until I went to God's sanctuary, and I learned their end.

You set them in slippery places and make them fall.

You destroy them in a moment when you rise up.

I was like a beast toward you, foolish and ignorant, but you are continually with me.

You guide me with your counsel and receive me to glory.

I have no one else but you, and there is nothing on earth I want more than you.

My heart and flesh may fail, but God is the strength of my heart and portion forever.

Those who are far from you will perish; you put an end to everyone who is unfaithful.

It is good for me to be near to God because I have made you my refuge.

Psalm 112: "The Righteous Will Never Be Moved"
By Unknown

Praise the Lord! Blessed is the man who fears the Lord and who delights in his commands!

His offspring will be blessed and mighty; they will have wealth and enduring righteousness.

It is well with those who are generous and lend, who conduct their affairs with justice.

The righteous will never be moved; they are steady and firm, trusting in the Lord.

They are not afraid; they will triumph over their enemies.

They give to the poor and their righteousness endures forever.

The wicked see it and are angry, but their desire will perish!

Psalm 127: "Unless the Lord Builds the House"
By Solomon: A Song of Ascents for travelers to sing when approaching Jerusalem.

Unless the Lord builds the house, those who build it labor in vain.

Unless the Lord watches over the city, the watchman stays awake in vain.

It is worthless to get up early and stay up late eating the bread of anxious toil because he gives sleep to those he loves.

Children are a legacy of the Lord; the fruit of the womb is a reward.

The children of one's youth are like arrows in the hand of a warrior; blessed is the man who fills his quiver with them!

He will not be put to shame when he speaks with his enemies in the gate.

Psalm 128: "The Blessed Family"
By Unknown: A Song of Ascents for travelers to sing when approaching Jerusalem.

Blessed are those who fear the Lord and walk in his ways!

They will eat the fruit of their labor and it will be well with you.

You will see prosperity, and the Lord will bless you from Jerusalem.

May you see your grandchildren! Peace to Israel!

Psalm 133: "The Unity of Brothers"
By David: A Song of Ascents for travelers to sing when approaching Jerusalem.

It is good and pleasant when brothers live in unity!

It is like the precious oil on the head and running down Aaron's beard.

There the Lord has commanded the blessing and life forever.

CHAPTER FORTY
TORAH PSALMS

> **Torah Psalms**
>
> These Psalms are in praise of God's Word. The psalmist uses the synonyms law, testimonies, precepts, statutes, commandments, rules, word, and ways. All of these refer to what God has spoken to his people.

Psalm 19:7-14: "Keep Me from Presumptuous Sins"
By David

His commands warn his servants and bring me a great reward.

They revive my soul, bringing wisdom and joy.

Keep me from presumptuous sins and I will be blameless in his sight.

Lord, let the words of my mouth and the meditations of my heart be acceptable in your sight.

Psalm 119: "The Greatness and Glory of God's Word"
By Unknown

Your Law:
Lord, your Law is true; I love it and meditate on it day and night.

I delight in your Law; it is better to me than great wealth; blessed are those who obey it.

Open my eyes so that I can see the wonders of your Law and give me understanding so that I may obey.

Your Law brings peace; I long for salvation because your Law is my delight.

See my affliction and deliver me because I don't forget your Law.

The wicked have trapped and derided me, but I will not turn away from your Law.

I am angry because the wicked forsake your Law, rise up, and act because they have broken it.

Grant me mercy because I love your Law, and it has saved me from death.

Keep falsehood and evil far from me and graciously teach me your Law, and I will keep it forever and ever.

I always remember your name and keep your Law close to my heart.

Your Testimonies:
Blessed are those who keep your testimonies and seek you with their whole heart.

I cling to them and will proclaim them before kings, do not let me be ashamed.

I have known your testimonies from my youth; save me so that I may observe them.

Your testimonies are wonderful; they are my delight and counsel.

Take away my scorn and contempt because they are more valuable to me than all riches.

Lord, all my ways are before you; give me life so that I can keep your testimonies.

Incline my heart to them and keep me from seeking selfish gain.

Make me your servant and give me understanding to know your testimonies because they are full of righteousness and faithfulness.

When I reflect on my life, I turn to your testimonies; they are my legacy and the joy of my heart.

Even though I have many adversaries, I will not swerve from your testimonies; I love them with all my being.

They give me more understanding than my teachers because they are my meditation.

Your Precepts:
Make me understand your precepts and I will meditate on your wondrous works.

I long for them because they give life and blessing to those who keep them.

I will never forget nor forsake them, let your hand be ready to help me.

I am a friend to those who keep your precepts because they give understanding.

The wicked lay a trap for me, but I will not stray, redeem me from oppression to keep your precepts.

Make the insolent feel their shame, but I will meditate on your precepts and fix my eyes on your ways.

I am yours; save me, for I seek your precepts.

They are all righteous and I hate every false way.

Though I am small and despised, I do not forget your precepts; they give me more understanding than the elderly.

Consider how I love them and give me life according to your steadfast love.

Your Statutes:
Lord, you are blessed; teach me your statutes!

I will delight in them and I will not forget your word; don't forsake me!

Oh, that my ways may be steadfast in keeping your statutes; hold me up and let me continually regard them.

May my heart be blameless in your statutes so that I may not be put to shame.

Teach them to me and I will keep them to the end.

Even though princes plot against me, I will meditate on your statutes.

It is good that I was afflicted so that I could learn them.

Salvation is far from the wicked because they don't seek your statutes, they go astray, and their cunning is in vain.

Deal with your servant according to your love and teach me your statutes.

I cry out with my whole heart and my lips pour forth your praise; teach me your statutes because you are right and do good.

Your Commandments:
I long for your commandments, lead me in the path, for I delight in them.

I seek you with my whole heart, don't let me wander from your commands; give me understanding so I may learn them.

Teach me good judgment and knowledge, for I believe in them.

All your commandments are true and I love them more than gold.

I seek you with my whole heart, don't let me wander from them; I fix my eyes on you and not be ashamed.

They make me wiser than my enemies, for I keep them with me; I send evildoers away so that I may be obedient.

Even when trouble and anguish find me, your commands are my delight.

I hope for your salvation, and I follow your commands; my tongue will sing of your goodness.

I have gone astray like a lost sheep; find me, for I don't forget your commands.

I find my delight in your commandments, do not hide them from me.

Your Rules:
I will praise you with an upright heart when I learn your righteous rules; my soul is consumed with longing for them.

I praise you for your righteous rules seven times a day; they give me comfort, and I praise you for them.

I choose faithfulness; I set your rules before me.

I will not turn aside from them because you have taught me; I swear to keep them.

Your mercy is great; give me life according to your rules and let my soul praise you.

Don't take the word of truth from my mouth because my hope is in your rules.

Accept my freewill offerings of praise and teach me your rules.

I rejoice at your rules like one who finds great treasure.

The sum of your word is truth and every one of your righteous rules endures forever.

Your Word:
How can a young man keep his way pure? By guarding according to your word.

I have stored up your word in my heart that I might not sin against you; I will not forget your word.

I trust in your word; give me life because it gives me hope.

My soul melts away from sorrow; strengthen me, and give me life according to your word.

Your words are sweet to my taste, sweeter than honey in my mouth.

Your word is a lamp to my feet and a light to my path; you are my hiding place and shield, I hope in your word.

Your word is firmly fixed in the heavens, the sum of them is truth and every one of your righteous rules endures forever.

Deal bountifully with your servant so that I may live and keep your word.

Your Promise:
Confirm to your servant your promise, that you may be feared; let your love come to me and your salvation.

Be gracious to me and comfort me according to your steadfast love; uphold me so that my hope may not be put to shame.

You are my portion; I promise to keep your words.

Keep my steps steady according to your promise, and don't let sin grab hold of me.

Plead my cause and redeem me; give me life according to your promise!

Your Ways:
Blessed are those who do not sin but walk in your ways.

Turn my eyes from looking at worthless things; give me life in your ways.

Turn to me and be gracious, as you do with those who love your name.

CHAPTER FORTY-ONE

THE GREATNESS OF WISDOM OVER FOLLY

> **The Greatness of Wisdom**
>
> Knowledge is correct information, but wisdom is the proper application of that knowledge. These proverbs speak of the greatness of wisdom and the rewards it brings.

Wisdom has built a solid home and prepared a fantastic feast. It has sent out servants, calling to anyone willing to turn into the house and learn. Wisdom has made a compelling invitation to anyone willing to listen.

Wisdom cries out for you to listen; it begs for you to pay attention. It offers truth and a straight path to follow. Wisdom is better than jewels, and nothing you desire can compare with it.

Wisdom cries out to the simple amid a crowded and noisy world. If you seek wisdom, you will find it. But if you ignore it, then misfortune, pain, and anguish will come upon you when you least expect it. If you reject knowledge and do not fear the Lord, you will have the fruit of your choices and schemes. You will die from turning away from wisdom, and complacency will destroy a fool. But those who listen to wisdom will live in security and will not fear disaster.

If you seek wisdom, you will understand righteousness, justice, and equity; it will guard your heart and deliver you from harm. It will protect you from sinners and deliver you from evil. Wisdom will protect you from the adulterous woman who leaves her friends and forsakes the relationship with her God. Her house leads to death and those who go to her do not recover.

Find wisdom, and you will walk with the good and stay on the paths of the righteous. For the upright will live in the land, and the wicked will be cut off and die.

Wisdom is like honey on the tongue; if you find it, you have hope for the future.

Listen to the wise and apply their teaching because it will make your life pleasant.

Listen to your father and mother's wisdom and let their words be like a crown of grace and a pendant around your neck. Keep their words and obey their commandments and live; always keep them before you.

If you listen to their words and treasure their wisdom, if you seek understanding like people seek wealth, then you will understand the fear of the Lord and find the knowledge of God. The Lord gives wisdom; from his mouth comes knowledge and understanding. He stores up wisdom for the upright and guards the path of those who walk in integrity.

Do not forget their teaching, but keep it close to your heart because it will bring you peace and long life. Keep love and faithfulness close to you; then, you will find favor and good standing with God and man. Trust in the Lord with all your heart and don't lean on your own understanding. Acknowledge him in all your ways and he will make your paths straight.

Wise children bring joy to their parents, but fools bring them sorrow.

The wise listen and increase their knowledge; those who understand look for instruction so that they might understand wisdom. The fear of the Lord is the beginning of knowledge, but fools despise wisdom and instruction.

Blessed is the one who finds wisdom because she is more valuable than wealth. She is more valuable than anything you can want; she gives long life, riches, and honor. She brings a pleasant life and peace.

Walk in wisdom, your steps will be safe, and you will not slip. You will not be afraid when you lie down and your sleep will be sweet. Do not be afraid of sudden terror or the ruin of the wicked; the Lord will be your confidence.

Get wisdom and insight, don't turn away from instruction; love wisdom and keep it close because it will protect you. If you value and embrace wisdom, it will lift you up and bring you honor.

Don't think that you are wise; fear the Lord and run from evil because it will bring healing.

You will own either your wisdom or your mocking.

The wise listen to instruction, but fools come to ruin. They speak words of understanding and store up knowledge, but fools bring ruin near.

Wisdom lives in the heart of the wise and it even makes itself known among fools.

The wise follow the path of life and they avoid death.

The wise love their own souls and will find good.

The wise bring down the mighty.

Foolishness is unruly; it is seductive yet knows nothing. It sits by its doorway and calls out to people passing by to join it. Foolishness offers great things, but it leads to death.

Sin is a game for a fool, but wisdom brings the understanding of pleasure.

The wise are praised, but one with a warped mind is hated.

Those who wander away from wisdom will find death.

The Lord made the world in wisdom and it runs through all of creation.

Wisdom is better than gold, and understanding is better than silver.

> **Wisdom vs. folly**
> These proverbs compare the outcome of pursuing wisdom instead of foolishness.

The wise are adorned by their wealth, but the fools by their foolishness.

Wise women build their homes, but the foolish tear it down.

Fools believe everything, but the wise consider what they hear.

The wise are cautious and turn away from evil, but fools are reckless.

Fools inherit folly, but the wise find knowledge.

The wise are slow to anger, but the quick-tempered are foolish.

The mouth of the wise speaks knowledge, but the mouth of fools pour out folly.

Fools think they are always right, but the wise listen to advice.

Fools are annoyed by everything, but the wise overlook insults.

The wise spread knowledge, but not fools.

The heart of the wise seeks understanding, but fools feed on folly.

Fools enjoy folly, but a wise man walks straight.

Wisdom is a fountain of life, but folly brings punishment.

The wise seek understanding, but fools only pursue earthly things.

Fools hate wisdom, they only want to voice their opinions.

Folly brings ruin and is rage against God.

The wise have precious treasure and oil in their homes, but the foolish devour it.

The wise see danger and hide, but fools keep going and suffer.

Do not waste your wisdom on fools because they will not understand.

Fools cannot possibly understand wisdom.

Schemers are fools and people hate a mocker.

Answer fools as they deserve, but be careful, or you will end up like them.

Sending a message with a fool is like cutting off your own feet.

Wisdom in a fool's mouth is useless.

Fools who repeat their folly are like dogs who eat their own vomit.

There is more hope for a fool than those who believe they are wise.

Honor for a fool is like snow in the summer.

When the wise argue with fools, there is no peace.

Fools vent their rage, but the wise hold back.

CHAPTER FORTY-TWO

FEAR OF THE LORD AND THE HEART

> **Fear of the Lord**
>
> One of the great themes of the Proverbs is the fear of the Lord. This does not mean being scared of God but living a life that understands his greatness. It is a sense of awe, respect, and submission to God.

The fear of the Lord is the beginning of wisdom and knowing the Holy One is insight. It will multiply your days and add years to your life. Fools despise wisdom and instruction.

May the wise listen and increase their knowledge; those who understand look for instruction so that they might understand wisdom.

The fear of the Lord is the hatred of evil; reject arrogance, corruption, and perverted speech.

The fear of the Lord brings long life, but the years of the wicked are short and full of trouble.

The fear of the Lord brings confidence and your children will be safe.

A little with the fear of the Lord is better than wealth with trouble.

Humility and the fear of the Lord lead to wisdom, riches, honor, and life.

Do not envy sinners; instead, fear the Lord, and you will have hope.

Those who fear the Lord are upright, but those who hate him are devious.

Fear the Lord and the government and do not rebel against them because who knows what trouble they can bring.

Blessed are those who fear the Lord, but those who harden their hearts will suffer.

Love and faithfulness cover sin, but the fear of the Lord protects from evil.

The fear of man is a trap, but those who trust the Lord are safe.

If you reject knowledge and do not fear the Lord, you will have the fruit of your choices and schemes. My son, if you listen to my words and treasure my wisdom, if you seek understanding like people seek wealth, then you will understand the fear of the Lord and find the knowledge of God. Don't think that you are wise; fear the Lord and run from evil because doing so will bring healing.

> **The heart**
>
> Another theme of the proverbs is the heart. This does not refer to the organ that pumps blood but is a term meaning the whole person. It is the source of our will, intellect, and feelings.

If you seek wisdom, you will understand righteousness, justice, and equity; it will guard your heart and deliver you from evil. It will protect you from sinners and deliver you from harm. Wisdom will protect you from the adulterous woman who leaves her friends and forsakes the relationship with her God. Her house leads to death and those who go to her do not recover.

Trust in the Lord with all your heart and don't lean on your own understanding. Acknowledge him in all your ways and he will make your paths straight.

Blessed are those who fear the Lord, but those who harden their hearts will suffer.

Intelligent hearts seek wisdom and knowledge. Wisdom lives in the heart of the wise and it even makes itself known among fools.

Be vigilant to guard your heart because it is the source of your life.

One's life reflects the heart like a mirror reflects one's face. Only the heart understands its sorrow and joy.

Even children make their hearts known by their actions.

Deferred hope makes the heart sick, but fulfilled desires bring life.

Even in laughter, a heart may be hurting, and grief may follow joy.

A joyful heart is good medicine, but a crushed spirit takes away life. Glad hearts make happy faces, but a sad heart crushes the spirit.

A peaceful heart gives life, but an envious heart rots the bones. Anxiety weighs down the heart, but kind words cheer it up.

The days of the afflicted are painful, but a happy heart has a continual feast.

People believe they have pure hearts, but the Lord weighs tests their motives, just like the fire purifies gold and silver. One's heart is the lamp of the Lord, searching the soul.

Those with evil hearts don't find good; liars get into trouble.

CHAPTER FORTY-THREE
THE TONGUE

> **The tongue**
>
> A significant theme of Proverbs is the words of our mouth. The things we say hold the power of life and death.

The words of one's mouth are deep waters, the fountain of wisdom a rushing stream. They hold the power of life and death.

The righteous tongue is a fountain of life, but the wicked tongue brings violence.

The tongue of the righteous is like silver, but the heart of the wicked is worthless.

The lips of the righteous know what is acceptable, but the wicked mouth only says what is unacceptable.

The words of the righteous bring wisdom, but the perverse tongue will be cut off.

People eat goodness from the fruit of their mouths, but the treacherous desire violence.

A gentle answer turns away wrath, but a harsh word stirs up anger. Kind words are a tree of life, but perversity breaks the spirit.

The wise are discerning and speak gracious words. They are sweet and bring healing to the soul.

The thoughts of the wicked are an abomination to the Lord, but gracious words are pure.

The righteous consider their words, but the wicked speak evil.

Those who cover offenses seek love, but those who keep bringing it up separates close friends.

A fool's mouth brings ruin and begs for a beating.

It is foolish and shameful to answer without knowledge.

Let others praise you and not your own mouth.

Those who flatter are spreading a net for their feet.

Mockers burn down a city, but the wise turn away wrath.

Those who rebuke someone will afterward find more favor than a flatterer.

A fool's mouth lashes out with pride, but the mouth of the wise protects them.

A loud blessing early in the morning is like a curse.

Truth and lies:
Truth lasts forever; lies only last a moment. Truth saves lives, but lies destroy them.

The one who hides hatred has lying lips, but slanderers are fools.

The Lord hates lying lips, but he delights in the trustworthy. Liars hate their victims and they will not go unpunished.

Those who mislead the righteous will fall into their own pit, but the blameless will have a good inheritance.

Those who deceive their neighbors and then claim to be joking are like madmen firing guns in the air.

It is better to be poor than a liar.

Liars mock justice and swallow evil. They listen to mischievous people and bring trouble, but the trustworthy bring healing.

If rulers listen to liars, their officials will be wicked.

Gossip:
Gossips reveal secrets, so don't associate with them. But those with a trustworthy spirit keep things covered.

Gossips spread conflict and separate close friends.

Like a fire without wood is a conflict without gossip.

Argue your case with your neighbor rather than gossip about it.

Wordiness:
Sin is present when there are many words, but the wise consider what to say.

Reckless words pierce like swords, but wise words bring healing.

Those who guard their words preserve life, but those who run their mouths come to ruin.

The wise keep knowledge to themselves, but fools blurt out everything. Even fools who keep silent are thought to be wise and understanding.

Guarding your mouth keeps you out of trouble.

CHAPTER FORTY-FOUR
WISDOM IN RELATIONSHIPS

> **Wisdom in relationships**
>
> The writers of Proverbs wrote a lot about relationships. These teachings can do much to help our lives run more smoothly. They speak extensively about adultery, marriage, and children.

Faithfulness in relationships:

My son, beware of the adulterous woman, her speech is smooth and sweet, but in the end, she is bitter and will lead you to death. She does not consider the path of her life; instead, she wanders aimlessly.

My sons, stay far away from her and don't go anywhere near her house, or you will give away your honor and not receive mercy. Your hard work will only benefit others and your life will be hard.

Wisdom will protect you from the adulterous woman who leaves her friends and forsakes the relationship with her God. Her house leads to death and those who go to her do not recover.

Do not desire the adulterous woman's beauty or let her entice you with her flirting; a prostitute only costs a loaf of bread, but an affair will take your very life. You can't carry fire and not burn your hands or walk on hot coals and not scorch your feet. In the same way, adulterers will be punished. Those who commit adultery lack sense; they destroy themselves. Jealousy makes one furious and the jilted lover will not forgive quickly.

I looked out my window and saw a senseless young man going to her house in the evening. She dresses like a prostitute and comes out to meet him with evil intentions. She is loud and never at home; she kisses him and seduces him, convincing him to go with her. He follows her like a cow going to the slaughter; he doesn't realize that he will die. Do not let your heart desire her or go near her house because she has brought down many, and her ways lead to death.

Adulterous relationships are a bottomless pit; those that the Lord is angry with will fall into it.

An adulterous woman eats, wipes her mouth, and claims to have done nothing wrong.

A beautiful woman with no discretion is like a gold ring in a pig's snout.

Don't spend your strength chasing women or alcohol.

Wives:
A wife of noble character is worth more than precious jewels; her husband has confidence in her and lacks nothing. She works with her hands and handles her household well. She provides food for her family and makes smart money decisions. She works hard and looks out for the poor and needy. She is not afraid of trouble because she is well prepared. She clothes herself with strength and dignity and can laugh at the days to come. She is not idle and manages the affairs of her household well. Charm is deceptive, and beauty is fleeting, but a woman who fears the Lord is to be praised.

Always be satisfied with your wife. Enjoy her beauty and let her love intoxicate you. Don't fantasize about other women because it will only hurt your relationship. The Lord sees everything you think and do and he knows your intentions.

A noble wife is a crown to her husband and a blessing from the Lord. But a disgraceful wife is rottenness in his bones.

Wealth is inherited, but a good wife is a gift from God.

It is better to live in the corner of a roof or the middle of the desert than in a house with an argumentative wife.

Children:
Those who don't discipline their children hate them, but those who love their children discipline them. If you discipline them, there is hope that it will save their future.

Do not withhold discipline from a child; they will not die; it will save them from death.

Teach children to follow the right path, and they will stay on it, even as adults.

Wisdom is the foundation of a home, and it fills the house with rare and beautiful treasures.

Children begin as fools, but discipline leads to wisdom.

An undisciplined child is a disgrace, but discipline imparts wisdom.

A wise child listens to a parent's teaching and makes their parents glad. But a fool does not listen; they make their parents sad and bring their destruction.

Foolish children bring sorrow to their parents.

Those who steal from their parents bring shame and disgrace.

The grave, the barren womb, dry land, and fire are never satisfied.

Grandchildren are the glory of the elderly, and children get glory from their parents.

CHAPTER FORTY-FIVE

MONEY AND WORK

> **Theme of money**
>
> Proverbs also discusses money and gives us guidelines for how we should best use it. God is not as concerned about how much we have but how we gain and use it.

Wealth earned from evil does not profit, but righteousness delivers from death.

Those who trust in wealth will fall, but the righteous will flourish.

There is much treasure in the house of the righteous, but the income of the wicked is trouble.

Better is a little with righteousness than wealth with injustice. It is better to be poor with integrity than a liar and a fool.

A poor man with integrity is better than a crooked rich man. It is better to be humble and poor than rich and proud.

Those who are greedy for unjust gain trouble themselves, but those who hate bribes will live. Those who give bribes believe it will protect them.

Better to have a crust of stale bread with peace than a feasting house with conflict.

Bread gained by deceit tastes sweet but afterward fills the mouth with gravel.

Wealth gained quickly evaporates, but gradual wealth lasts. Those who try to get rich quickly will not go unpunished; their gains will not be blessed.

Wealth gained by lies does not last.

Those who love too much pleasure will become poor.

The stingy are in a rush for wealth, but they don't know they will fall into poverty.

Those who follow worthless pursuits will fall into poverty.

Know the condition of your possessions because wealth does not last.

Do not wear yourself out to get rich because wealth is fleeting; it will fly away like a bird.

Honor the Lord with your wealth and give to him from the first of your income, then he will cause you to prosper.

If you have become liable for another person's debts or made a pledge with a stranger, leave that situation as quickly as possible. Make this your top priority and save yourself from death.

Don't use your possessions to secure debt because if you can't pay, you will lose everything.

Those who put up security for strangers are fools.

The rich rule over the poor, and the lender owns the borrower.

A rich man's wealth is his protection, but poverty brings destruction.

Wealth will not protect on the day of wrath, only righteousness.

The Lord's blessings bring wealth with no trouble.

Wealth threatens the rich, but the poor are not threatened.

Some pretend to be rich but are poor, while others pretend to be poor but are rich.

The wise leave an inheritance for their grandchildren, but the wicked's wealth is saved for the righteous.

Everyone hates the poor, but the rich have many friends. Those who insult the poor and suffering mock God.

The wise are adorned by their wealth, but the fools by their folly.

Wealth brings many friends, but even a poor man's friends leave him.

The poor beg for mercy, but the rich answer harshly.

It is not right for fools to live in luxury.

Buyers claim they got a lousy deal but then boast when they leave.

There is plenty of wealth, but wisdom is even more valuable.

It is better to have a good name and favor than great wealth.

God is the maker of both the rich and the poor.

The generous will be blessed because they share their food with the poor.

Those who oppress the poor to become rich will become poor.

Do not take from the poor because they are poor or crush them in court because God will plead their case and punish those who rob them.

The poor who oppresses the poor is like a storm that leaves nothing behind.

The rich believe they are wise, but a poor man with understanding can see through them.

The greedy stir up conflict, but the Lord will bless those who trust in him.

Do not eat a stingy person's bread because they are not celebrating with you.

Those who get rich from the loss of others gather wealth for those generous to the poor.

Those who ignore the needs of the poor will eventually be ignored as well. Those who are generous to the poor will never want. Those who give to the poor are lending to the Lord and he will repay.

The generous continue to prosper, the stingy come to poverty. People curse a hoarder of wealth, but they pray for God's blessing on those that distribute it.

A secret gift turns away anger and wrath.

Gifts open the door for the giver, and everyone wants to be friends with the generous.

Those who hate their neighbors and oppress the poor insult God, but the generous are blessed.

A little with the fear of the Lord is better than wealth with trouble.

Give me only what I need, not too much or too little, so that I deny the Lord or profane his name by stealing. Don't give me poverty and let me be in want or riches so that I disown the Lord.

> **Work ethic**
> Proverbs also speaks about the way we should work and our work ethic.

If you are lazy, watch the ants and learn wisdom. They gather their food in the summer and harvest time even though no one tells them to. Just a little more sleep, one more nap, a little rest, and poverty will come upon you like a robber.

There is profit in all work, but mere talk only brings poverty.

People's words bring them good things, and the work of their hands brings them a reward. Their labor will bear fruit.

Those who work their land have plenty of food, but those who chase fantasies are fools.

The craving of the lazy will destroy them because they refuse to work. But diligence brings wealth.

An empty manger is clean, but a full manger is a mess while profitable.

Skilled workers will rise to the top of their industry.

The lazy are like drinking vinegar and sting like smoke in the eyes of those who send them.

The lazy don't do anything with their earnings, but the diligent use them.

The soul of the lazy craves and gets nothing, but the soul of the diligent is fed.

The lazy are like those who destroy; they refuse to work when it's time and will go hungry.

The way of the lazy is a rough road, but the path of the upright is smooth.

The lazy become so lazy that they won't even make their own food.

Those who sleep during harvest bring shame.

Don't love sleep, or you will come to poverty.

CHAPTER FORTY-SIX

THE RIGHTEOUS AND THE WICKED

> **Righteous and the wicked**
>
> Another primary theme of Proverbs is the comparison of the righteous and the wicked. Even though doing the right thing may not always lead to immediate gain, overall, God blesses the righteous and punishes the wicked.

Do not envy violent people or choose their ways because the devious are an abomination to the Lord, but the righteous have confidence. The Lord curses a wicked man's house, but he blesses the righteous; the wise receive honor, but fools get disgrace.

Stay away from the path of the wicked and do not walk with sinners. They cannot sleep unless they hurt someone, but the way of the righteous is like the dawn, shining brighter and brighter until midday.

The Lord provides for the righteous, but he frustrates the desires of the wicked.

The righteous earns life; the wicked earns sin.

The memory of the righteous is blessed, but the name of the wicked will rot.

Whoever walks in integrity is safe and blesses their children, but the crooked are eventually discovered. The integrity of the upright will guide them, but the duplicity of the wicked will destroy them.

The malicious cause trouble and a fool who talks too much comes to ruin.

The tongue of the righteous is like choice silver, but the heart of the wicked is worthless.

What the wicked fear will happen, but the righteous have their desires granted.

The hope of the righteous brings joy and good things, but the expectation of the wicked dies in wrath.

The righteous path of the Lord is protection for the blameless but destruction for the wicked.

Wealth will not protect on the day of wrath, only righteousness. The hopes of the wicked die, their desire for wealth dies too.

The righteousness of the blameless makes their paths straight, but the sin of the wicked destroys them; their lust takes them captive.

The righteous are delivered from trouble, but the wicked walk into it.

The godless man destroys his neighbor with his mouth, but knowledge delivers the righteous.

The blessing of the upright lifts people up, but the words of the wicked drag them down.

The wicked earns deceptive wages, but the righteous receive a sure reward.

The righteous earn life, those who pursue evil find death.

The Lord hates the perverse in heart, but he delights in the ways of the blameless.

The wicked will not go unpunished, but the righteous will go free.

The fruit of the righteous is a tree of life and the resolve of the wise saves lives.

If the righteous receive their reward on earth, how much more the ungodly and the sinner!

The Lord gives favor to the good, but he condemns those who make wicked plans.

No one is established by wickedness, but the righteous will not be moved.

The wicked's words lie in wait for blood, but the upright's speech rescues them.

The plans of the righteous are just, but the wicked give deceitful advice.

The house of the righteous stands firm, but the wicked are overthrown.

The wicked desire the strength of the evil, but the root of the righteous endures.

The wicked are trapped by their words, but the innocent escape trouble.

Those who plot evil have deceitful hearts, but promoters of peace have joy.

No harm overtakes the righteous, but the wicked have plenty of trouble.

The righteous choose friends carefully, but the wicked lead them astray.

The light of the righteous rejoices, but the prideful light of the wicked is put out. The righteous hate lies, but the wicked bring shame and disgrace.

The evil ends up bowing down before the good.

The house of the wicked will fall, but the house of the upright will prosper.

Trouble brings down the wicked, but the righteous take refuge in God even in death.

A wicked man's sacrifice is an abomination to the Lord, but he accepts the prayer of the righteous. The Lord is far from the wicked, but he listens to the righteous.

The wicked take secret bribes to pervert justice.

God sees the wicked and eventually brings them to ruin.

Justice brings joy to the righteous and terror to the evil.

Pursuing righteousness and kindness leads to life, righteousness, and honor.

The wicked talk a big game, but the righteous think about their ways.

Do not plunder the house of the righteous because even if they fall seven times, they keep getting back up.

Don't worry about the wicked because they have no future; the Lord will take care of them.

The righteous who give way to the wicked are like a polluted stream.

The wicked run when no one is chasing, but the righteous are as bold as a lion. The wise see danger and hide, but fools keep going. The upright turns away from evil, and it saves their lives.

The wicked want evil and have no mercy for others.

The righteous care for animals, but even the kindest acts of the wicked are cruel.

The unjust are an abomination to the righteous, and the wicked hate the upright.

People rejoice when the righteous succeed, but people hide when the wicked do well.

Righteousness lifts up a nation, but evil brings it down.

A foolish ruler oppresses his people.

Those who only trust themselves are foolish.

The evil are caught by their sin, but the righteous sing and rejoice.

The righteous are concerned with the rights of the poor, but the wicked don't care. The Lord gives light to both the poor and their oppressors.

Do not envy the wicked or long to be with them; their hearts plot violence, and they plot trouble. The wicked are destroyed by their violence and the storms of life, but the righteous are blessed and established forever.

CHAPTER FORTY-SEVEN
FRIENDS, JUSTICE, AND DISCIPLINE

> **Friends and companions**
>
> The friends we choose have a tremendous impact on our lives. Proverbs gives us instructions on how to select our companions.

Walking with the wise brings wisdom, but a friend of fools suffers harm. Avoid fools because they lack knowledge.

Friends always love and brothers are born for adversity.

The righteous choose friends carefully, but the wicked lead them astray.

Do not be friends with people with bad tempers because you might become like them and get yourself in trouble.

Don't hang out with drunkards and gluttons because they become poor.

Gossips reveal secrets, so don't associate with babblers.

Mockers avoid the wise because they hate correction. Get rid of mockers, conflict, and arguments, and abuse will stop.

An offended brother is next to impossible to win over.

Unreliable friends bring trouble, but good friends are better than a brother.

Many people will declare that they are faithful, but few truly are.

An open rebuke is better than hidden love and heartfelt advice refreshes the soul.

Neither death nor the eyes are ever satisfied.

People want true love.

As iron sharpens honor, we sharpen each other.

> **Justice**
>
> The Prophets speak a lot about justice. Proverbs also gives us instructions on why we should pursue this ideal.

If sinners ask you to sin with them, don't listen. If they ask you to steal from the innocent and profit from their misfortune, run away because they set a trap for their own lives. Greed for unjust gain takes away the life of those who seek it.

A false scale is an abomination to the Lord, but he delights in a just one.

It's not good to be partial to the wicked or to keep justice from the righteous.

The Lord prefers righteousness and justice to sacrifice.

Justice brings joy to the righteous and terror to the evil.

Those who plant injustice will reap trouble.

Evil men do not understand justice, but those who seek it do.

> ### Discipline
> Another theme of Proverbs is that of discipline.

Do not hate the Lord's discipline or shy away when he corrects you because the Lord corrects those that he loves, just like a loving parent corrects a child.

Whoever listens to instruction is on the path of life, but those who reject discipline lead others astray. Those who listen prosper, and those who trust the Lord are blessed and live among the wise.

Whoever loves discipline loves knowledge, but whoever hates correction is stupid. Discipline purifies the soul.

Those who ignore many rebukes will suddenly be broken beyond healing. So, listen to advice and accept discipline, and you will be considered wise.

A rebuke has more impact on the wise than a hundred blows on a fool.

Stop listening to instruction and you will stray from wisdom.

Whoever corrects a mocker gets insults, and whoever disciplines an evil man is abused. If you try to teach a fool, he will hate you, but if you correct a wise man, he will love you and grow in knowledge and understanding.

The slow to anger is better than the mighty, and one with self-control is better than a conqueror.

Those who lack self-control are like a fortress with no walls.

CHAPTER FORTY-EIGHT
GENERAL WISDOM

> **General wisdom**
>
> Many Proverbs don't fit into a specific category but still give us instructions for how we should best live our lives.

God has come down from heaven and created all things. All his words are true, he protects all those who take refuge in him. Don't add to his words, or he will rebuke you, and you will be found a liar.

Do not withhold good from those who deserve it when you have the power to do it. Don't tell a neighbor in need to come back later when you can help now.

Do not argue with people when you have no reason to.

Stay away from crooked and devious speech; keep your eyes straight ahead and focus on your path. Think about your life and the decisions you make; do not turn to the right or left, but keep far from evil.

The wicked and worthless have crooked speech; they wink and have secret signals to reveal their true intentions. They have evil plans and are always stirring up conflict. Disaster will come to them quickly and they will be destroyed beyond remedy.

Pride leads to disgrace and brings you low, but humility leads to wisdom and honor.

Pride leads to conflict, but wisdom comes with those who listen to advice.

The Lord tears down the house of the proud, but he looks over the widows.

The Lord rejects the proud; he will surely punish them.

A fool belittles his neighbor, but the wise keep silent.

Without guidance, people fall, but with many wise counselors, there is safety.

Whoever swears for a stranger will suffer harm, but those who hate taking oaths will stay secure.

Kind women gain honor, but ruthless men gain only wealth.

The kind benefit themselves, but the cruel bring about their own ruin.

Gracious women get honor, but cruel men are hurt.

Better to be a nobody with a servant than to pretend to be somebody and have nothing.

Wise servants are favored, but shameful servants receive wrath. They will rule over a disgraceful son and will share in the inheritance.

Do not slander servants to their masters, or they will curse you.

Those who reject instruction will pay for it, but those who listen are rewarded.

The teaching of the wise is a fountain of life that saves from death.

Wise judgment brings favor, but the unfaithful are destroyed.

The wise act with knowledge, but the behavior of fools exposes them.

Those who reject instruction come to poverty and shame, those who listen are honored.

Fulfilled desire is sweet to the soul, but fools will not turn from evil.

Trouble follows sinners, but the righteous receive good things.

Mockers seek wisdom in vain, but the wise find knowledge.

The wise understand their life, but fools do not.

Fools mock reconciliation, but the upright are accepted.

Sometimes a path seems right, but it leads to death.

The Lord sees everything, watching both evil and good.

There is severe punishment for those who turn from God; they will even die.

Better is a humble meal with love than a feast with hatred.

An angry man stirs up conflict, but the patient man smooths it over.

Plans fail without advice, but they succeed with wise counsel.

A wise answer brings joy.

Good news brings refreshment to the soul.

Those who ignore advice hate themselves, but those who listen become wise.

People make plans, but the Lord gives the proper response.

Commit your work to the Lord and he will establish your plans.

The Lord works everything out, even the wicked for their day of disaster.

When the Lord approves one's ways, he makes even his enemies at peace with him.

People plan their ways, but the Lord establishes their paths.

The hunger of a worker drives their labor.

A worthless man plots evil; his speech is a burning fire.

Violent people tempt their neighbors and lead them into evil.

Devious people plot perversity and evil.

Gray hair is a crown of glory gained by a righteous life.

Some choices seem random, but every decision is from the Lord.

The evil rebel against God; they will taste death.

Better to meet an angry bear than a fool.

Those who return evil for good will only receive evil.

The beginning of conflict is like letting out water, so abandon the argument early.

Those who justify the wicked and condemn the righteous are both abominable to the Lord.

Those who love sin love conflict.

Hatred stirs up conflict, but love covers all wrongs.

A thief's accomplice hates his own life.

Those who ruin their families will inherit nothing, and the fool will serve the wise.

Those who cover their sins will suffer, but those who confess and repent will be healed.

Those who forsake the Law praise the wicked, those who obey it work against them.

Even if you grind a fool like grain, you will not remove their folly.

Without the word of God, there is no restraint; those who obey the Lord are blessed.

Punishing the good is evil.

The prudent are wise and understanding.

Those who isolate themselves are selfish and foolish.

Hate comes with evil and disgrace with shame.

The words of a gossip are tasty morsels that go deep into the body.

The Lord is a strong tower and refuge for the righteous.

One can endure illness, but not a crushed spirit.

The first to make a case seems right until you hear both sides.

Flipping a coin can help with decisions between opponents.

Desire without knowledge is bad, and the hasty make mistakes.

Those who obey the Lord save their lives.

Angry people will pay the penalty; if you rescue them, you will have to do it again.

People make many plans, but God's purposes will prevail.

Answer people as they deserve, and wisdom will increase.

Punishment is prepared for mockers and fools.

Keeping from strife is wise, but fools will always argue.

A person's intentions are deep waters; it takes wisdom to find them.

No one is entirely pure from evil.

The Lord has made both the hearing ear and the seeing eye.

Wisdom and advice establish plans.

Don't plan to repay evil; let the Lord take care of it.

We cannot possibly understand our own path because the Lord directs all things.

It leads to trouble to rashly attribute something to God and only inquire after the fact.

Young men's glory is their strength; gray hair is an honor for old men.

The plans of the diligent pay off, but the hasty come to poverty.

There is nothing that can defeat the Lord.

The Lord watches over knowledge and overthrows traitors.

Rescue those who are stumbling towards destruction. Don't pretend you don't see because God knows all things and will judge accordingly.

Do not rejoice when your enemy falls because the Lord will see and turn away his wrath.

Do not show partiality in judgment, and don't claim the guilty are innocent because you will be cursed. It will go well with you if you convict the guilty, and you will be blessed.

Do not testify against another without cause.

False claims about a gift are like clouds and wind that don't bring rain.

Only have a taste of sweets; too much will make you sick.

Don't spend too much time in your neighbor's house, or they will hate you.

Trusting the treacherous in troubling times is a sure way to fall.

Singing songs to the depressed is out of place, like taking a coat off on a cold day.

Give your enemies food and drink, and you will heap burning coals on their heads.

Good news from far away is like cold water to a thirsty soul.

Those who meddle in the conflicts of others are like those who grab strange dogs by the ears.

Don't boast about tomorrow because you don't know what the future holds.

The provocation of a fool is heavier than a stone.

Like a bird leaving its nest are those who run from home.

Those who drink too much end up with sorrow, complaints, and unnecessary problems. Don't long for alcohol because it will harm you and make you confused.

Alcohol is violent and drunkards are fools.

Don't spend your strength chasing women or alcohol.

Every word of God is flawless; he is a shield to those who take refuge in him. Don't add to his words, or he will prove you to be a liar.

Observe nature and learn wisdom. Ants have little strength, but they store up their food in the summer. Rabbits have no power, but they live amidst the rocks. Locusts have no king, but they move together in ranks. Lizards are in kings' palaces even though they are easy to catch.

Stirring up anger produces strife; it is wise to be slow to anger.

Fools have a quick temper and those who plan evil are hated.

Speak up for the voiceless and destitute; defend the rights of the poor and needy.

Do not take advantage of those without power; God will defend them.

CHAPTER FORTY-NINE

VAIN PURSUITS
Ecclesiastes 1-12

> **The Book of Ecclesiastes**
>
> King Solomon wrote the Book of Ecclesiastes as an examination of the meaning of life. It is useful for us in our materialistic culture because it helps us see the emptiness in every pursuit that does not align with the book's final line. Unfortunately, many Christians misjudge the melancholy tone of this book without looking at it all in the context of Solomon's conclusion.

Everything is vanity! What do we gain from all our labor under the sun? Generations come and go, but the earth remains forever. Days come and go, the wind blows, rivers run, and everything continues. Everything is more wearisome than one can put into words; the eyes and ears always want more. Everything that has been will come around again; there is nothing new under the sun. Nothing is new; it has already happened before. People don't remember history and the future will forget us too.

Solomon did his best to find wisdom in everything on earth. All the labor that God has given us ends in unhappiness. He saw everything the world has to offer, and all of it was like trying to grasp the wind. The crooked cannot become straight, and what is missing cannot be counted. Solomon became wiser than anyone else on earth and chased after folly as well. He concluded that all of it was like trying to chase the wind. Wisdom brings sorrow, and knowledge brings grief.

Solomon sought pleasure and found it to be meaningless, laughter, and found it to be madness. He chased after everything that could bring people joy. He drank fine wine, built great houses, vineyards, and gardens. He amassed countless servants, flocks, and wealth. He sought out the finest entertainers and became greater than anyone else on earth. He did not deny himself any possible pursuit of pleasure and counted it as a reward for his labor. But in the end, he found all of it to be meaningless.

He considered wisdom as well as madness and folly. He found that wisdom is better than folly, just like light is better than darkness. But both the wise and the foolish end up dying, so even wisdom is meaningless. Neither one will be remembered; we all die in the end.

So, he hated his work because it was all pointless. He hated all his wealth because he would only leave it for someone else to enjoy. He had no control over what they will do with it; all his work was meaningless. He despaired over all his labor because he was going to leave for one who didn't work for it.

What do people get for all their work, anxiety, and effort? All our work is grief and pain; we can't even turn our minds off at night. The best we can do is to enjoy our lives. Even this comes from God because no one can find enjoyment without him. God blesses those whom he favors and sinners gain wealth to give it to those who please him. Even this is meaningless.

There is an appropriate time for every activity under heaven:

A time to plant and a time to uproot.

A time to kill and a time to heal.

A time to tear down and a time to build.

A time to weep and a time to laugh.

A time to mourn and a time to dance.

A time to scatter and a time to gather.

A time to embrace and a time to refrain.

A time to search and a time to give up.

A time to keep and a time to throw away.

A time to tear and a time to mend.

A time for silence and a time for words.

A time to love and a time to hate.

A time for war and a time for peace.

What do we gain from our work? God has made everything beautiful for its time. He has put eternity into our hearts, but we can't figure out all the works of the Lord. There is nothing better for us than to have joy and do good with our lives. God's works last forever; we cannot add to them or take anything away from them. God is the author of everything so that people will have a healthy fear of him. Everything that is has already existed.

Even in justice, there is wickedness. In time, God will judge the righteous and the wicked. Our fate is the same as that of the animals; we all die. We all have the same fate; everything is pointless. We come from dust and will return to dust. Who knows if our spirits ascend and animals will descend. There is nothing better for a person to enjoy their work because that is our lot.

Solomon observed all the oppressed and there was no one to comfort them. The dead are luckier than living, but those who never lived to see the evil are even better. All work comes from envy of one's neighbor; this is pointless as well. Fools fold their hands and ruin themselves. Better is one handful with peace than two handfuls and chasing the wind.

There was a lonely man with no family. He worked and worked, but he was never content. There was no end to his labor; this was also pointless.

Two are better than one because they will see a better return from their work. If either falls, the other can pick them up; how bad it is to fall alone. If two lie down together, they will keep warm; how can one stay warm alone? One person can be overpowered; two can defend themselves. A cord of three is hard to break.

A poor and wise youth is better than a foolish ruler who does not know how to take advice. There is no end to this cycle. All of this is vanity and chasing after the wind.

Be careful when you go to worship; it is better to listen than to offer a fool's sacrifice because they don't know their own evil. Don't be rash with your mouth or rush to speak to the Lord because he is in heaven and you are on earth. Therefore, let your words be few.

Dreams come when you are occupied, and fools talk a lot. When you promise God something, do it quickly; it's better not to vow than not fulfill it. Don't let your mouth lead you into sin. Why should God be angry and destroy your work? Foolish dreams and too many words are meaningless; so, fear the Lord.

Don't be surprised if you see the oppression of the poor and the denial of rights; because there is always a hierarchy, and those at the top are the ones to profit. If you love money, you will never have enough, and you will never make enough. There will always be people to consume goods and there will never be enough. This is pointless too.

An ordinary worker's sleep is sweet, but the rich can't sleep because they never have enough. Hoarding wealth and riches lost to misfortune are a great evil. We are born naked and die naked; we can't take anything with us. What do we gain since it all ends the same? The best thing we can do is be satisfied with our work and find whatever joy we can from God.

If God gives wealth with the ability to enjoy it, that is a true gift. These people seldom reflect on their lives because God has given them joy.

Another evil is that God gives wealth, but the rich can't enjoy it. No matter how many children and how much wealth, if we can't enjoy it, it doesn't matter. It would be better not to have been born because we all end up dead. We work for appetite, but we never have enough. Whatever exists has already been. The more words, the more foolishness, and it doesn't benefit us because no one knows what will come after our death.

A good name is better than perfume, and the day of death is better than the day of birth. A house of mourning is better than a house of feasting because we all die. Sorrow is better than laughter because a sad face is good for the heart. The wise are in the house of mourning, but fools are in the house of feasting.

It is better to listen to a wise rebuke than the song of fools because the fool's laughter is empty noise. Extortion makes a wise person into a fool, and bribes corrupt the heart. The end of things is better than the beginning, and patience is better than pride. A short temper makes one a fool.

Don't ask why the good old days are better than now because this is foolishness. Wisdom is a shelter and it saves those who have it. No one can straighten what God has made crooked. God has made both good and bad times, and we can't figure out why. The righteous dying in their upstanding, the wicked living a long life; both are meaningless.

Don't be overly righteous; you will destroy yourself; don't be wicked or a fool; both lead to death. It is best to hold both; those who fear God will avoid extremes. Wisdom brings power and no one is perfect.

Don't listen to everything you hear because you will hear others curse you, and you know that in your heart, you have cursed others.

I tried to learn about this in my wisdom, but it was too deep for me. No one can discover the deepest truths. So, I tried to learn everything I could by both wisdom and folly. Adulterous women are traps; those who try to please God will escape, but sinners will be caught. In my search, I didn't find anyone who was truly righteous. God created us all righteous, but we have gone astray.

Wisdom brightens the face and makes us less hardened. Obey rulers because of God's oath; don't be hasty to leave his presence and don't bring an evil cause before them. They can do whatever they want.

Those who follow the Law will be innocent of evil and the wise will know what to do. There is a way and time for everything, even when we are troubled. We can't possibly see the future and we can't cheat death.

The wicked go in and out of the temple, people say good things about them, and then they die. This is also pointless. The evil ones aren't punished immediately and our hearts are wicked. Even though the evil sins a hundred times and continues to live, it will be well with those who fear the Lord. But those who are wicked will not last because they don't fear God.

It is vanity that the righteous and the wicked have the same fate. The best thing for us is to enjoy our work while we live. Regardless of how much wisdom we have, we can never truly find out the reason behind things.

We cannot know what God knows because our deeds are before him, whether motivated by love or hate. It's all the same, for the just and the unjust; we all die. Humanity is full of evil and we all have the same end. But the living has hope because while they know they will die, the dead know nothing, and they are soon forgotten. All their love, hate, and envy have died with them and cannot be shared with the living.

Enjoy your life and what God has granted you, and make the best with what you have. Enjoy the spouse of your youth for all your vain days. Work with all your might at whatever God gives you for all the days of your life because eventually, you will die.

The quick don't win the race, the strong don't win the battle, nor do the intelligent become rich; time and chance happen to them all. We don't know our end, just like animals.

Solomon saw a great king who attacked a small city, and a poor man with wisdom saved the town. Even though no one remembered the poor man, wisdom is better than strength, but one sinner can destroy much good.

Just like dead flies make perfume stink, a little folly outweighs wisdom and honor. Even when fools walk on the road, they lack sense and proclaim their folly to everyone. If a ruler is angry with you, stay in your place because calm can lay an offense to rest.

Many are not in their proper place, fools in authority, and the rich humiliated. If their work harms the workers, there is no benefit. Despite all this, wisdom brings success. Wise words bring favor, but foolishness destroys.

Fools talk too much and no one can tell them anything. Their work wears them out because they don't know how to maximize it. Woe to a nation if its leaders have no wisdom!

Laziness causes a house to fall into disrepair. Bread is for laughter, wine gladdens the heart, and money fixes everything. Don't even think evil thoughts about rulers or the influential because hidden things become known.

Diversify your investments because you don't know what disasters will come.

Nature follows its course and does what it will. If we always wait for perfect situations, we will never work. Just like we don't know how the spirit comes into a body, we don't know all of God's work. Do your work when it is time because you don't know what will be profitable and what will not.

Sunny days are pleasant. Rejoice in all the days of your life, but remember that there will be many dark days. Enjoy the days of your youth and do what makes you happy; just know that God will judge your acts one day. Put away anxiety and bodily troubles because youth and vigor are meaningless.

Remember God while you are young before bad days come and you stop enjoying life. Before you get old and your body begins to fail. Before your body returns to dust and your spirit to God.

Besides his wisdom, Solomon also taught the people and wrote many proverbs. He sought truth and wrote what he found. Wisdom helps keep you on the straight and narrow; beware of anything beyond this. There is no end to what we can learn and too much learning will wear us out. After everything he learned and did, his conclusion was: fear God and obey his commandments because he will judge every deed, whether good or evil.

CHAPTER FIFTY

ROMANCE

Song of Solomon 1-8

> **Song of Solomon**
>
> This book is alternately called Song of Songs. We are unsure if Solomon wrote this book, but it describes the love between the king and a young woman. Two of the key themes of this book are sexual purity and the gift of marriage. Human sexuality is a significant theme in our lives, and this book helps us unpack this topic.
>
> Some commentators have tried to make this book an allegory of God's love for us, but that makes the book weird. When the woman talks about tasting his sweet fruit while sitting in the shade of his tree, that likely refers to oral sex. The navel that is like a rounded goblet is a reference to the young woman's vagina. Hebrew boys were restricted from reading this book until they turned 13.

She: Kiss me with your mouth because your love is more delightful than wine. Your perfumes are pleasant, and your name is like perfume poured out; no wonder the young women love you!

She: Let's hurry away together! Let the king bring me into his chambers. We rejoice and delight in you and praise your love more than wine. I am dark yet lovely; don't stare at me because of my brown skin. My brothers were angry with me and made me take care of their vineyards and neglect mine. Tell me where your flocks graze and where you rest at midday. Why should I be like a veiled woman beside the flocks of your friends?

Beautiful woman, follow the sheep's tracks and graze your young goats by the shepherds' tents.

He: You are like a mare among Pharaoh's chariot horses. Your cheeks are beautiful with golden earrings and your neck with strings of jewels.

She: While the king was at his table, my perfume spread its fragrance; my beloved is like a sachet of myrrh resting between my breasts.

He: My darling, you are so beautiful, your eyes are like doves!

She: My beloved, you are so handsome and charming; the countryside's lush grass is our bed.

He: Our house's beams are of cedar and our rafters are fir trees.

She: I am a rose of Sharon, a lily of the valleys.

He: Compared to other women, my darling is like a lily among thorns.

She: Compared to the other young men, my beloved is like an apple tree among the forest trees, and I delight to sit in his shade and taste his sweet fruit. Let him lead me to the banquet hall and let his banner over me be love. Strengthen me with raisins and refresh me with apples because I am faint with love. He embraces me with both arms and pulls me close. Daughters of Jerusalem, do not arouse or awaken love until it so desires.

My beloved is coming, leaping across the mountains and bounding over the hills. He is like a gazelle or a young stag. He stands behind our wall gazing at me through the windows.

He spoke to me, "Arise, my beautiful darling and come with me. The rains are past and the flowers are in bloom. Fig trees are bearing their early fruit and blossoming vines are spreading their fragrance. Come with me, my beautiful darling."

He: My dove is hiding in the clefts of the rock on the mountainside; show me your beautiful face and let me hear your sweet voice. Catch the little foxes that ruin the vineyards because our vineyards are in bloom.

She: My beloved is mine and I am his; he browses among the lilies. My beloved, turn and be like a gazelle or young stag on the rugged hills until the day breaks and the shadows flee.

All night long on my bed, I looked for the one my heart loves, but I did not find him. I will get up and search the city for him. The watchmen found me as they made their rounds, and I asked if they had seen him.

Then I found him and I would not let him go until I had brought him home to my mother's house. Daughters of Jerusalem, do not arouse or awaken love until it so desires.

Look! Solomon's carriage is coming up from the wilderness like a column of smoke, perfumed with myrrh and incense. Sixty experienced warriors escort him, the noblest in Israel. His carriage is of the most exquisite craftsmanship and its interior is inlaid with love. Come see the king wearing the crown of his wedding day.

He: My beautiful darling, your eyes are like doves, and your hair is like a flock of goats descending the hills. Your teeth are a flock of freshly shorn sheep; they are all in pairs. Your lips are lovely like a scarlet ribbon and your temples are like the halves of a pomegranate. Your neck is like a well-adorned tower, and your breasts like twin fawns that browse among the lilies. You are altogether beautiful; there is no flaw in you.

You have stolen my heart, my sister, my bride with a single glance of your eyes. Your love is delightful, far better than wine, and your fragrance is better than any spice. Your lips are as sweet as honey; milk and honey are under your tongue. You smell fantastic, and you are a sealed fountain and a locked garden growing the best of all plants.

She: North and south wind, wake up and blow on my garden so that its fragrance will spread; let my beloved come into his garden and taste its choice fruits.

Friends: I have come into my garden, my sister, my bride; I have gathered my myrrh with my spice. I have eaten honey and drunk wine and milk. Friends, eat and drink your fill of love.

She: I was asleep, but my heart was awake. My beloved is knocking; I have made myself ready for bed. Do I have to go out again?

My beloved thrust his hand through the window and my heart started pounding for him. I got up to let him in, but he was gone; I searched for him but couldn't find him. The watchmen found me as they made their rounds in the city, beating me and taking away my cloak. Daughters of Jerusalem, if you see him, tell him that I am faint with love.

Friends: How is your beloved better than others?

She: He is radiant and ruddy, the best of ten thousand. His head is like pure gold; his hair is wavy and as black as a raven. His eyes are like doves by streams of water and his cheeks are like beds of spice-yielding perfume. His lips are like lilies dripping with myrrh. His arms are rods of gold set with topaz and his body is like polished ivory. His legs are pillars of marble set on bases of pure gold; he is beautiful. His mouth is sweetness itself and he is altogether lovely.

Friends: Where has your beloved gone?

She: My beloved has gone down to his garden to gather lilies. I am my beloved's and he is mine.

He: You are as lovely as Jerusalem and as majestic as troops with banners. Don't look at me because it's overwhelming. There may be countless other women, but you are my perfect one, unique, your mother's favorite. The young women saw her and called her blessed.

Friends: Who is this that appears like the dawn, fair as the moon, bright as the sun, majestic as the stars in procession?

He: I went down to the tree grove to see the new growth, but before I realized it, my desire set me among the royal chariots of my people.

Friends

He: O Shulamite, come back, that we can see you again!

Your sandaled feet are beautiful and your legs are like jewels. Your navel is a rounded goblet that never lacks wine and your waist is a mound of wheat encircled by lilies. Your breasts are twin fawns of a gazelle. Your neck is like an ivory tower, your eyes like the pools of Heshbon, and your nose like the tower of Lebanon. Your head crowns you like Mount Carmel and your hair is like a royal tapestry.

Your beauty captivates the king. You are like a palm tree, and your breasts are like clusters of fruit; I want to climb the tree and take hold of your fruit. May your breasts be like clusters of grapes on the vine and your breath's fragrance like apples.

She: I belong to my beloved and he desires me. Let us go to the countryside and spend the night in the villages and the vineyards to see if the vines have budded; then we can make love. I have stored up every delicacy for you, both new and old.

If only you were like my brother, then if I found you outside, I would kiss you, and no one would care. I would lead you to my mother's house and give you spiced wine and the nectar of my pomegranates. Daughters of Jerusalem, do not arouse or awaken love until it so desires.

Friends

She: Place me over your heart like a seal because love is as strong as death and its jealousy as unyielding as the grave. No amount of water can quench love's burning fire and no one would trade it for all their wealth.

Friends: We have a little sister, and her breasts haven't grown yet. What should we do for her on the day someone speaks for her? If she is a wall, we will build towers of silver on her; if she is a door, we will enclose her with cedar panels.

She: I am a wall, my breasts are like towers, and I bring him contentment. Solomon had a vineyard that he rented to tenants and each of them was to pay a thousand shekels of silver. But my vineyard is mine to give; the thousand shekels are for you, Solomon, and two hundred are for those who tend its fruit.

He: You who dwell in the gardens with friends in attendance, let me hear your voice!

She: Come away, my beloved, and be like a gazelle or a young stag on the spice-laden mountains.

The Life of Jesus

Reorganized Concise Paraphrased Bible

Book IV

By: Obadiah Paulus

ISRAEL IN JESUS' DAY

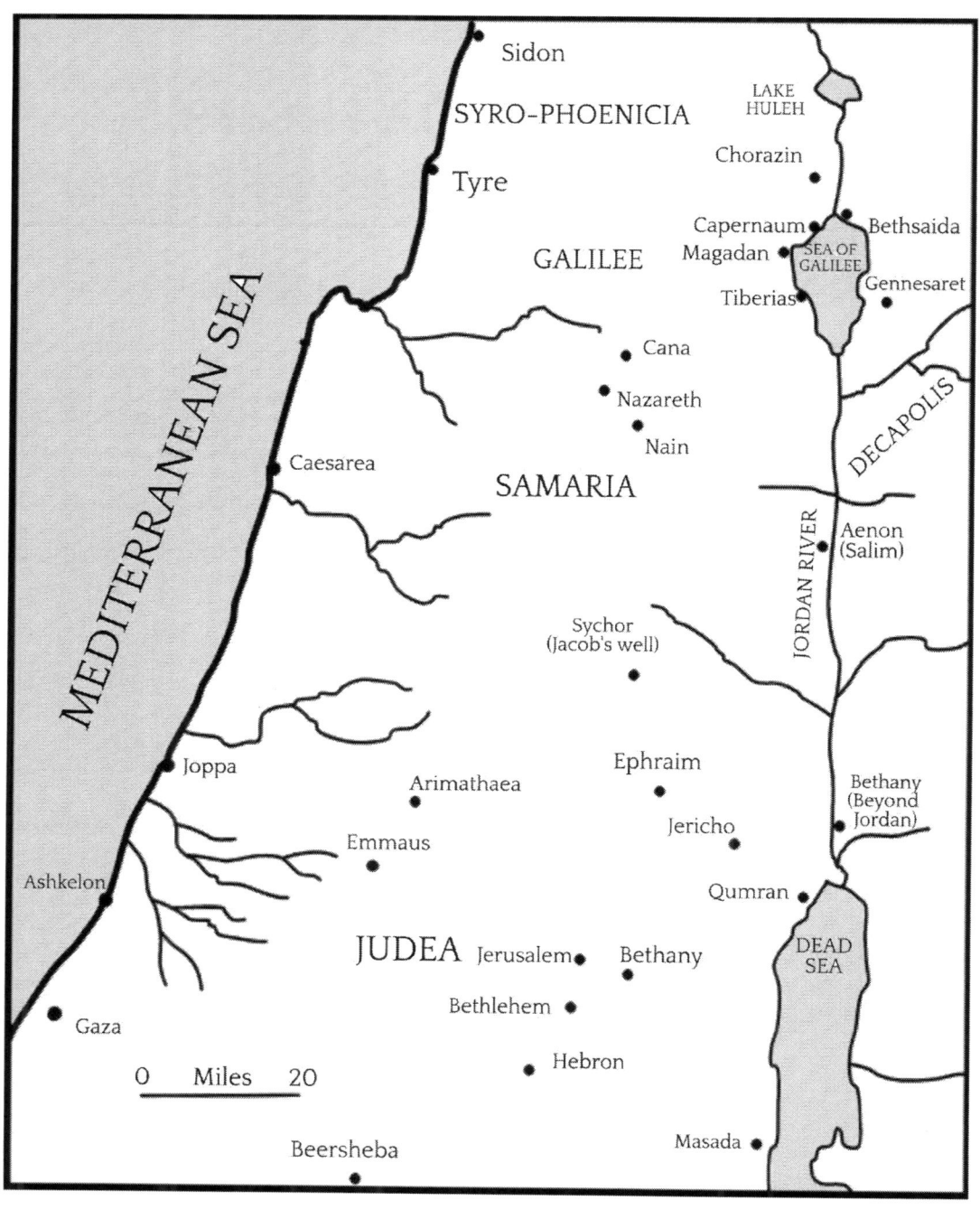

INTRODUCTION TO THE LIFE OF JESUS

The first four books of the New Testament focus on the life of Jesus of Nazareth, the central figure of the Christian faith. Three of these books (Matthew, Mark, and Luke) contain much of the same material, while a fourth book (John) is unique. Outside of these four books, we have very little information about the life of Jesus.

Each book has its distinctions and each presents a different view of the Son of God. The Book of Matthew is written to a primarily Jewish audience and shows that Jesus is the promised Messiah and fulfillment of Jewish expectations. Matthew makes many references to the Old Testament and focuses on Jesus' discourses and sayings.

The Book of Mark records the apostle Peter's viewpoint of the life of Christ and he wrote to Roman Christians. Mark presents Jesus as the suffering servant and strong Son of God. It is the shortest and most compact of the Gospels and focuses on immediate action and his ministry.

The physician Luke's Gospel records the apostle Paul's perspective of Jesus' life. Luke relates Jesus to all of humanity by recording his genealogy back to Adam. This book shows how Jesus reached out to women, children, and the disenfranchised.

The Book of John was the last book written about Jesus' life and it presents many events that the other books do not include. John wrote this Gospel to a broad audience so that all people might believe that Jesus was the Son of God.

While each of these Gospels presents a different view, they all speak about one man's life and actions. This text attempts to look at Jesus' life as a single narrative by integrating the text of all four of the gospel records. This is like the process used in a courtroom where lawyers combine eyewitness testimony to paint an accurate picture of what happened. Each of the four Gospels gives a different perspective in the same way that four witnesses of an event will describe it differently.

Approximate Timeline of New Testament events

4 B.C.	Jesus' birth
26 A.D.	Jesus begins his ministry
30	Jesus' death, burial, and resurrection, the Holy Spirit comes at Pentecost, and the establishment of the Church
35	First persecution of the Church
36	Saul's conversion
40	First Gentile conversion
43	Founding of church at Antioch; book of Matthew written
48	Paul's first missionary journey
51	Paul's second missionary journey
52	I Thessalonians written
53	II Thessalonians written
54	Paul's third missionary journey
57	I Corinthians and Galatians
58	II Corinthians and Romans written; Paul arrested in Rome
59	Book of Luke written
62	Paul's Roman imprisonment; Ephesians, Philippians, Colossians, Philemon, and James written
63	I Peter, book of Acts, Hebrews, I Timothy, and Titus written
64	Book of Mark written
66	II Timothy and II Peter written
67	Paul's death
70	Destruction of Jerusalem
75	Jude written
85	Book of John written
90	John's three letters written
97	Revelation written

TABLE OF CONTENTS

CHAPTER 1: Introduction to the Life of Jesus	491
CHAPTER 2: Intertestamental Period	493
CHAPTER 3: Preparation for Jesus' Birth	495
CHAPTER 4: The Birth of Jesus	498
CHAPTER 5: Jesus' Early Years	500
CHAPTER 6: The Birth of John the Baptist	502
CHAPTER 7: John's Ministry	504
CHAPTER 8: Baptism and Temptation of Jesus	506
CHAPTER 9: Beginning of Jesus' Ministry	509
CHAPTER 10: Meeting with Nicodemus	512
CHAPTER 11: The Woman at the Well	514
CHAPTER 12: Ministry in Galilee	516
CHAPTER 13: Call of the Four & Various Healings	518
CHAPTER 14: Sabbath Controversies and Withdrawals	522
CHAPTER 15: Appointment of the Twelve	526
CHAPTER 16: The Sermon on the Mount	528
CHAPTER 17: Growing Fame	534
CHAPTER 18: First Public Rejection	538
CHAPTER 19: Secrets About the Kingdom in Parables	540
CHAPTER 20: Continuing Opposition	543
CHAPTER 21: Final Galilean Campaign	546
CHAPTER 22: Death of John the Baptist	548
CHAPTER 23: The Bread of Life	549
CHAPTER 24: The Leaven of the Religious Teachers	553
CHAPTER 25: The Great Confession and the Transfiguration	557
CHAPTER 26: Responsibility to Others	560
CHAPTER 27: The Feast of Tabernacles	564
CHAPTER 28: Further Ministry at the Feast of Tabernacles	567
CHAPTER 29: Private Lessons on Service and Prayer	570
CHAPTER 30: Second Debate with Religious Leaders	574
CHAPTER 31: Sabbath Healings and Further Division	579
CHAPTER 32: Principles of Discipleship	584
CHAPTER 33: Further Parables	586
CHAPTER 34: Raising Lazarus	590
CHAPTER 35: Teaching on the Way to Jerusalem	592
CHAPTER 36: Triumphal Entry and the Fig Tree	598
CHAPTER 37: Official Challenge to Jesus' Authority	602
CHAPTER 38: Jesus' Response to Questions	604

CHAPTER 39: Olivet Discourse	607
CHAPTER 40: Arrangements for Betrayal	612
CHAPTER 41: The Last Supper	613
CHAPTER 42: The Upper Room Continued	616
CHAPTER 43: Garden of Gethsemane	620
CHAPTER 44: Jesus' Trial with the Jews	622
CHAPTER 45: Peter's Denials	623
CHAPTER 46: Jesus Before Pilate	625
CHAPTER 47: The Crucifixion	628
CHAPTER 48: The Resurrection	632
CHAPTER 49: Resurrection Appearances	635
CHAPTER 50: Final Instructions	639

CHAPTER ONE

INTRODUCTION TO THE LIFE OF JESUS

Luke 1:1-4; John 1:1-18

Many people have written accounts about the life and actions of the Messiah. The authors of the Gospels carefully investigated the accounts of the early disciples and other eyewitnesses of how God fulfilled his promises. They used these for their source material and then wrote a careful summary to reassure you of the truth of what others have taught. This is a compilation and a synthesis of those eyewitness accounts.

The Word always existed, even at the beginning of the universe. The Word was with God, and he was God; he was with God in the beginning. He created everything that exists and nothing exists that he didn't create. Life was in him, and this life gives light to everyone. His light shines in the darkness, but the darkness did not understand it, nor could it overpower it.

> **What does "Word" mean?**
>
> The Greek word for word here is *logos*. This word represents the principle of divine reason and creative force of God. In this context, it represents the second person of the Trinity, Jesus Christ.

God sent John the Baptist to tell everyone about Jesus so that they might believe. John was not the light; he was just a witness to the light. Jesus, who is the true light and gives light to everyone, had not come yet.

Although the Word made the world, the world didn't recognize him when he came; even his people in his homeland didn't accept him. But to all who accepted and believed in him, he gave the right to become God's children. They are reborn, and this rebirth is from God and not from any human plan.

So, the Word became human and lived on earth with us in the person of Jesus, and he was full of grace and truth. He came so that we might see his glory, which comes from God the Father. John the Baptist testified about him to the people, shouting, "I was talking about Jesus when I said, 'Someone far greater than me is coming because he existed long before I did.'"

God's unfailing love has blessed us over and over. Moses gave us the Law, but Jesus Christ gave us God's unfailing love and truth. No one has ever seen God, but his only Son, who is God and lives with the Father, has told us about him.

Is Jesus really God? Is Jesus really a man?

The answer to both questions is yes. He never became God; he was God from the moment he was born and continued to be God throughout his life, in his death, and after his resurrection. He claimed to be God on multiple occasions (see the box in Chapter 28), and his audience clearly understood his claims (this is why he was killed). Numerous passages state that he is God, including passages in Philippians and Colossians; so, we know his followers understood his nature. He had a miraculous birth and lived a sinless life. He performed miracles, demonstrating his power over nature (which, as God, he created), including raising himself from the dead.

Jesus was also fully man. He was born and suffered all the same things humans do, including hunger, fatigue, and a natural growth process. This can be difficult to reconcile because he was also fully God, but there is nothing in human nature that precludes being God. The Chalcedonian Creed of 451 sums up this position when it says, "in the one person, Jesus Christ, there are two natures, a human nature and a divine nature, each in its completeness and integrity, and that these two natures are organically and indissolubly united, yet so that no third nature is formed thereby."

CHAPTER TWO

INTERTESTIMENTAL PERIOD

God had been silent for roughly 400 years between the last prophet and the birth of Jesus. During this time, God was preparing the earth for his arrival. Israel had some brief independence, but nothing like what they had once enjoyed. The people remembered the promises made to their ancestors. They were anxiously awaiting the arrival of the Messiah, the Anointed One, who would fulfill Old Testament prophecies and restore Israel to prominence.

> **What does Messiah mean?**
>
> The term Messiah means "Anointed One." The Messiah was the promised deliverer of Israel who would restore them to world prominence. Throughout the Old Testament, multiple prophecies told of where he would be born, details of his life and ministry, and resurrection. Jesus fulfilled many of these with his first coming and will fulfill the rest when he returns. In Christianity, we refer to the Messiah as the Christ. Thus, the name Jesus Christ means Jesus the Messiah.

The Romans were in charge and they ruled over most of the known world. There was a common currency, peace, and extensive highway system that allowed for travel and the gospel's eventual spread. The Israelites were desperate for liberation and expected the Messiah to be a military ruler to overthrow the Romans and restore their kingdom. While Jesus will one day come as a conquering king, he first came as a suffering servant. The Israelites focused on the prophecies that told of the Messiah doing what they wanted and ignored the prophecies that spoke of his humble service and sacrifice. Therefore, Jesus confused many of his hearers, and they did not understand why he didn't call the people to arms to defeat the Romans.

When Jesus came, the Pharisees and Sadducees were the chief Jewish religious divisions. The Israelites had lost the Promised Land and the glory of the original temple so, they were determined to keep the Law, the last vestige of God's promises they had left. The Pharisees were so dedicated to following the Law that they set up additional rules around the laws so that they would not even come close to breaking God's commands. While their intentions were good, they ended up loving the rules more than they loved God. Pharisees were typically ordinary people who had formal education in Jewish Law.

The other party was the Sadducees, and they were typically wealthy aristocrats. They wanted to follow God's rules but wanted to adjust them to fit into the culture around them. They changed some of their beliefs to fit in with popular opinion and sacrificed some of their standards to gain popularity with the rulers of the land. They were religious rationalists who denied the existence of miracles and the afterlife.

Jesus' teaching went against both groups' beliefs and they were the groups that Jesus clashed with the most. Jesus taught to love God and others, but the Pharisees and Sadducees were far more worried about following the rules and looking good than loving God and treating the people well. They did everything that they could to maintain public perception and their elevated social standing. Despite their seeming holiness, their hearts were far from God. Jesus' conflict with them was shocking to the people because they held their leaders in high regard.

CHAPTER THREE

PREPARATION FOR JESUS' BIRTH

Matthew 1; Luke 3:23-38; 1:26-56

Jesus was the descendant that God promised to Eve in the garden, to Abraham, and to David. Both Mary, his mother, and Joseph, his adoptive father, were descendants of Abraham and David. Joseph's lineage was through the kings of Israel and Judah, while Mary's ancestors were from David's line, but they did not sit upon the throne.

Some of his ancestors were righteous men of God who were full of faith and love; others were wicked and sinful. We can read many of their stories in the Old Testament, but the most important fact for us is that Jesus was the fulfillment of all of God's promises of a Savior to the Jewish ancestors. He was the solution to our sin and would live a perfect life before becoming the perfect sacrifice for humanity.

Mary was a virgin and had never had sexual relations with any man. But God came to her and she became pregnant with Jesus, who was both fully God and fully human. He needed to be fully God so that he could pay for all of mankind's sin, and he needed to be fully human so that his perfect life and sacrifice could apply to all humanity.

One day, the angel Gabriel came to Mary in the Galilean town of Nazareth. She was engaged to a man named Joseph, a descendant of King David. Gabriel went to her and said, "Greetings, favored one! The Lord is with you!"

Gabriel's words troubled Mary, and she wondered what he meant. But the angel comforted her, "Don't be frightened, Mary, for God is going to bless you! You will become pregnant and have a son, and you are to name him Jesus. He will be very great and will be the Son of God. The Lord will give him the throne of David and he will reign over Israel forever!"

> **Son of God vs. Son of Man**
>
> Son of God and Son of Man are two different titles that the gospel writers used to refer to Jesus. Son of Man focuses on his connection to humanity; Son of God focuses on his connection to divinity. The use of son of means having the same essence, not being a child of what is named. The fact that Jesus used both points to his humanity and divinity. I use the two interchangeably in this book.

Mary asked the angel, "How can I get pregnant since I'm still a virgin?"

Gabriel answered, "The Holy Spirit will come upon you, and God's power will overshadow you. Therefore, your baby will be holy and will be the Son of God. Even your relative Elizabeth has become pregnant in her old age, and although she was barren, she is now in her sixth month. Nothing is impossible with God."

Mary replied, "I am the Lord's servant, and I accept his will. May your words come true." Then the angel left.

A few days later, Mary hurried to her relative's hometown in the hill country of Judea and greeted Elizabeth when she arrived. When Elizabeth heard Mary's greeting, her baby leaped in her womb, and the Holy Spirit came upon her. Elizabeth cried out with a loud voice, "God has blessed you above all other women, and your child is blessed too. It's an honor to have the mother of my Lord visit me! As soon as I heard your greeting, my baby jumped for joy. You are blessed because you believed that the Lord would do what he said."

> **What prophecies did Jesus fulfill?**
>
> There are hundreds of Old Testament prophecies that Jesus fulfilled in his birth, ministry, death, and resurrection. Mathematicians have calculated the odds of just some of these coming true about any individual to be infinitesimally small. To have all of them come true identifies Jesus as the Savior of all humanity that God had promised from the beginning.
>
> Theologians have written entire books on this topic; here is a brief sampling of some of the prophecies that Jesus fulfilled:
>
> - Born of a virgin
> - Born in Bethlehem
> - Descended from King David
> - From the tribe of Judah
> - Would come out of Egypt
> - Sinless life
> - Would be a suffering servant
> - Taught in parables
> - Ministry would begin in Galilee
> - Preceded by a forerunner (John the Baptist)
> - Enter Jerusalem seated on a donkey
> - Betrayed for 30 pieces of silver
> - Crucifixion
> - Resurrection
> - Soldiers would cast lots for his clothes
> - Would not decay in death
> - Mocked and given vinegar to drink at execution

Mary responded and quoted several Old Testament Scriptures, "My soul praises the Lord and my spirit rejoices in God, my Savior! For he noticed his lowly servant girl, and now all generations will call me blessed. For the Lord has done great things for me and his name is holy. He is merciful to all generations, to everyone who fears him. His mighty arm has done tremendous things and he has scattered the proud and arrogant! God has removed rulers from power and lifted the lowly. He has satisfied the hungry with good things and sent the rich away empty-handed. The Lord has helped his servant Israel and has remembered to be merciful. For he promised always to be merciful to Abraham and his descendants."

Mary stayed with Elizabeth and her husband, Zechariah, until Elizabeth's child was born, and then Mary went back home.

Mary returned home to her fiancée, Joseph. She was still a virgin, but she became pregnant by the Holy Spirit. Nazareth was a busy town that was notorious for prostitution, so there were many rumors about whose child it really was. Jewish engagements were very serious and a couple could only break one with divorce. Because Joseph was a righteous man and ashamed of his pregnant fiancée, he decided to quietly break the engagement so he wouldn't disgrace her publicly.

But an angel of the Lord appeared to him in a dream and said, "Joseph, son of David, do not be afraid to marry her because her baby is from the Holy Spirit. She will have a son, and you are to name him Jesus because he will save his people from their sins." All of this happened to fulfill the Lord's message through the prophet Isaiah: "Look, the virgin will have a child! She will give birth to a son, and he will be called Immanuel, which means God is with us."

When Joseph woke up, he did what the angel of the Lord commanded, and he brought Mary home to be his wife. She remained a virgin until her son was born, and Joseph named him Jesus.

CHAPTER FOUR

THE BIRTH OF JESUS

Luke 2:1-39

About that time, Caesar Augustus decreed that there should be a census of the entire Roman Empire (likely 4 BC). People went to their hometowns to register for this census. Since Joseph was a descendant of King David, he traveled about 70 miles from Nazareth in Galilee to Bethlehem in Judea because it was the city of David. He took Mary with him, and when they arrived, there was nowhere for them to stay, so they slept in a barn with the animals. While they were there, she gave birth to Jesus. She wrapped her newborn snugly and laid him in a feeding trough because there was no room for them in the inn.

That night some shepherds were in the nearby fields, guarding their flocks. Suddenly, an angel of the Lord appeared to them, and the Lord's glory surrounded them. The shepherds were terrified, but the angel reassured them, "Don't be afraid, I bring you good news of great joy for everyone! The Savior has been born tonight in Bethlehem, the city of David! He is the Messiah and Lord! You will know it's him because he will be lying in a manger!"

Suddenly, many other angels joined the angel and they all praised God, saying, "Glory to God in heaven, and peace on earth to everyone that God favors."

After the angels returned to heaven, the shepherds said to each other, "Let's go to Bethlehem and see this wonderful thing the Lord has told us about."

The shepherds ran to the village and found Mary and Joseph watching over the baby lying in the manger. Then the shepherds told everyone what had happened and what the angel had told them. Everyone they talked to was amazed, but Mary treasured these things in her heart and thought about them often. Afterward, the shepherds went back to the fields, praising God for everything they saw and heard.

JESUS' EARLY DAYS

Eight days later, Joseph and Mary circumcised the baby and named him Jesus, just as the angel had told them to do.

After 40 days, his parents took him to Jerusalem to present him to the Lord, in obedience to the Law of Moses. Joseph and Mary were poor, but they obeyed God's Law, bringing a pair of turtledoves or pigeons as a sacrifice.

A righteous and devout man named Simeon lived in Jerusalem and the Holy Spirit was in him. He was eagerly expecting the Messiah to come to rescue Israel, and God revealed to him that he would not die until he had seen the Messiah. When Joseph and Mary came to present the baby Jesus to the Lord, the Holy Spirit led Simeon to the temple. When Simeon saw Jesus, he took the child in his arms and praised God, saying, "Sovereign Lord, now I can die in peace! I have seen the Savior that you have given to all people, just as you promised me. He is God's light to all the nations, and he is the glory of Israel!"

Jesus' parents were amazed at what people were saying about their child. Simeon blessed them and said, "People will reject this child, and he will cause grief for many in Israel, but he will cause great joy for many others. He will reveal the deepest thoughts of men, but a sword will pierce your soul."

A very old prophetess named Anna was also in the temple. She was a widow whose husband had died seven years into their marriage. Anna was now 84 years old and she stayed at the temple day and night, worshiping God with fasting and prayer. She came along just as Simeon was talking with Mary and Joseph, and she began thanking and praising God. She told everyone at the temple who had been waiting for the redemption of Jerusalem about Jesus.

CHAPTER FIVE

JESUS' EARLY YEARS

Matthew 2; Luke 2:40-52

A couple of years later, some wise men from eastern lands arrived in Jerusalem and asked, "Where is the newborn King of the Jews? We saw his star in the east, and we have come to worship him."

Their question deeply disturbed Herod, who ruled Judea for the Romans, and the rest of Jerusalem. He called for the leading priests and teachers of religious law and asked them where the Messiah was to be born. "In Bethlehem, according to the prophecies," they replied.

Then Herod secretly called in the wise men to find out exactly when they first saw the star. They told him that they had first seen it a couple of years before their visit. Herod sent them to Bethlehem and said, "Go look for the child; when you find him, come back and tell me so I can worship him, too!"

After talking to King Herod, the wise men went their way and followed the star until it stopped over Bethlehem. When they arrived at the house where Mary, Joseph, and Jesus lived, they bowed down and worshiped the baby. Then they opened their treasure chests and gave him gifts of gold, spices, and incense. But when they left, they went home another way because God warned them in a dream not to return to Herod.

After the wise men left, an angel of the Lord appeared to Joseph in a dream and told him, "Get up and run to Egypt with the child and his mother. Stay there until I tell you to return because Herod is going to try to kill the child." That night the little family left for Egypt and stayed there until Herod died. This fulfilled the prophecy that God would call his son out of Egypt.

Herod was furious when he learned that the wise men had tricked him, so he sent soldiers to kill all the boys in and around Bethlehem under the age of three. This also fulfilled Old Testament prophecy.

RETURN TO NAZARETH

When Herod died a few years later, an angel of the Lord appeared to Joseph in a dream and told him to leave Egypt, saying, "Take Mary and Jesus back to Israel because those who were trying to kill Jesus are dead." So, Joseph returned to Israel with Jesus and his mother. But when he learned that Herod's son Archelaus was the new ruler in Judea, he was afraid. An angel came to Joseph in a dream and told him to return home, so they returned to Nazareth, a small town in Galilee where they had first become engaged. This fulfilled the prophecy that the Messiah would be a Nazarene. Jesus grew up healthy and strong; he was full of wisdom beyond his years, and God blessed him.

> **What prophecy said the Messiah would be a Nazarene?**
>
> There is no explicit Old Testament passage stating that the Messiah would be a Nazarene, but this is a prophecy that was likely in another writing that is not in the Bible. A prophet speaks on behalf of God and some prophets did not have their prophecies recorded in Scripture.

JOURNEY TO JERUSALEM FOR THE PASSOVER

When Jesus was twelve years old, his family traveled the 65 miles from Nazareth to Jerusalem for the Passover festival, just like they did every year. After the festival was over, his parents headed back to Nazareth, but Jesus stayed in Jerusalem. Joseph and Mary thought he was with some of the other travelers, so they didn't miss him at first. But when they couldn't find him, they went back to Jerusalem to look for their boy. Three days later, they found Jesus sitting with the religious leaders in the temple listening to them and asking questions. Everyone there was amazed at his understanding of religious matters.

His parents were astonished when they found him and Mary asked, "Son, why have you done this to us? Your father and I have been frantically searching for you!"

Jesus answered, "You didn't need to look for me! Didn't you know I would be in my Father's house?" Even at twelve years old, Jesus knew his true nature, but his parents didn't fully understand. Jesus went back to Nazareth with them and he continued to obey his parents. Mary stored all that Jesus said and did in her heart. As he grew up, Jesus became wiser and impressed both God and men. He worked with his father as a carpenter and eventually took over the business once Joseph died.

CHAPTER SIX

THE BIRTH OF JOHN THE BAPTIST

Luke 1:5-25, 57-79

Before Jesus began his ministry, God sent John the Baptist to tell everyone about him so that the people might believe. John was not the promised Savior; he was just a witness who pointed people to Jesus. Just as Jesus had a miraculous birth, John also had an extraordinary beginning.

John's father was a Jewish priest named Zechariah and his mother was also from the priestly line of Aaron (both were related to Mary). Both were righteous and carefully obeyed all of God's commandments. But now they were getting old and they had no children because Elizabeth was barren.

One day, Zechariah had a once-in-a-lifetime opportunity to enter the sanctuary and burn incense to the Lord. While he was in the temple, an angel of the Lord appeared, standing to the right of the incense altar. When Zechariah saw him, he was scared. But the angel said, "Don't be afraid, Zechariah, God has heard your prayer. You and Elizabeth will have a son and you are to name him John. He will bring you great joy and gladness, and many will rejoice with you at his birth because your son will be great in the Lord's eyes. He must never drink alcohol, and the Holy Spirit will fill him before he is even born. Your son will persuade many Israelites to return to the Lord their God and he will precede the Messiah in the spirit and power of Elijah (the Old Testament prophet). He will turn the hearts of fathers back to their children and help the disobedient accept godly wisdom; he will prepare the people for the coming of the Lord."

Zechariah recognized all the prophecies the angel referenced, but something troubled him, so he asked, "My wife and I are both old, so how do I know this will happen?"

The angel replied, "I am Gabriel, I stand in God's presence, and he has sent me to bring you this good news! But since you didn't believe my message, you won't be able to speak until the child is born. This is a sign so that you will know that all of this will happen at the proper time."

The people outside had been praying and wondered why Zechariah took so long to come out. When he finally did, he kept gesturing, but he couldn't speak. Then they realized that he must have seen a vision.

Zechariah went home to his wife Elizabeth after finishing his service at the temple. Soon afterward, she became pregnant; then she went into seclusion for five months, saying, "The Lord has dealt with me kindly and taken away my disgrace by giving me this child." It was during this time that her relative, Mary came to visit her.

Elizabeth gave birth to a boy. Her neighbors and relatives shared her joy when they heard about how God had been merciful and kind to her.

On the eighth day after their son had been born, friends and relatives came together to circumcise the child, and they wanted to name him after his father, Zechariah. But Elizabeth protested, "No! His name is John!"

This shocked the crowd and they argued, "But no one in your family is named John." So, they made gestures to Zechariah to ask what he wanted to name the baby. He motioned for a writing tablet, and to everyone's surprise, he wrote, "His name is John." Instantly, he could speak again, and he began praising God.

The whole neighborhood was in awe, and news of these events spread quickly throughout the area. Everyone who heard about it asked how he would turn out because the Lord's hand was with him.

Then the Holy Spirit came upon his father, Zechariah, and he prophesied, quoting numerous Scriptures: "Praise the Lord, the God of Israel, because he has visited and redeemed us. He has sent us a mighty Savior from the royal line of his servant David, just as he promised through his holy prophets years ago. He will save us from our enemies and from all who hate us. God has been merciful to our ancestors by remembering his holy covenant with them, the oath he swore to our ancestor Abraham. God will rescue us from our enemies so that we can serve him without fear, in holiness and righteousness forever.

"My son, you will be called the Prophet of God because you will prepare the way for the Lord. You will tell his people about salvation through the forgiveness of their sins. Because of God's tender mercy, the rising sun from heaven is about to break upon us. It will shine on those who sit in darkness and the shadow of death and guide us to the path of peace."

CHAPTER SEVEN

JOHN'S MINISTRY

Matthew 3:1-11; Mark 1:1-8; Luke 3:1-16; John 1:19-28

John grew up and became strong in spirit, and he lived out in the desert until beginning his public ministry to Israel.

About a year before Jesus began his ministry, the word of God came to John, Zechariah's son, in the wilderness. John started by preaching in the Judean countryside on both sides of the Jordan River. The prophets spoke of John when they said, "I will send my messenger before you, and he will prepare your way. He is a voice shouting in the wilderness: 'Prepare the way for the Lord; make a straight road for him! Fill in the valleys and level the mountains and hills! Straighten the curves and smooth out the rough places, and all people will see God's salvation.'"

This messenger was John the Baptist. He wore clothes made of camel hair with a leather belt and ate locusts and wild honey. People from Jerusalem and all over the Jordan Valley went out to the wilderness to hear him preach. He said, "Repent! Turn away from your sinful thoughts and actions and turn to God because the kingdom of heaven (or kingdom of God) is near." He told the people to show their repentance and receive forgiveness through baptism. After they confessed their sins, he baptized them in the Jordan River.

> **Kingdom of heaven or kingdom of God?**
>
> Matthew's account of Jesus' life speaks of the kingdom of heaven, while Luke's Gospel uses the kingdom of God. The two phrases are basically synonyms, although the kingdom of heaven refers to people on earth, while the kingdom of God includes all of creation. The two writers used different words because of their different audiences. This kingdom of heaven is one where God will rule over all the earth and judge the nations. Although he has not fulfilled all the prophecies in Scripture, Jesus' arrival ushered in the kingdom. He will fulfill the rest of these when he returns to earth. The two terms are interchangeable in this text.

But when John saw some of the Pharisees and Sadducees coming out, he denounced them and exclaimed, "You brood of vipers! Who warned you to flee God's coming judgment? Prove you have repented by the way you live your lives. Don't think you're safe just because you are descendants of Abraham; God can change these stones into children of Abraham if he wants. The axe of God's judgment is ready to cut you off because he will chop down every tree that doesn't produce good fruit and throw it into the fire."

The crowd asked, "What should we do?"

John replied, "If you have two coats, give one to the poor; if you have food, share it with the hungry."

Some tax collectors also came for baptism and asked, "Teacher, what should we do?"

He answered, "Make sure you don't collect more taxes than the Roman government requires."

A group of soldiers asked, "What about us?"

John said, "Don't extort money and don't accuse people falsely; you should be content with your pay."

Everyone was expecting the Messiah, and they wanted to know if it was John. He answered them by saying, "I baptize people with water for repentance, but someone is coming after me who is much greater than I am; in fact, I'm not even worthy to untie his sandals. He will baptize you with the Holy Spirit and with fire. He is ready to separate the good from the bad; he will keep the good and burn up the bad with never-ending fire." John used many such warnings as he exhorted the people and announced the Good News to them.

Eventually, John's popularity became so great that even the Jewish leaders had heard of his ministry and sent priests and temple assistants from Jerusalem to Bethany to ask John if he claimed to be the Messiah. He denied it and said, "I am not the Messiah."

"Well then, who are you?" they asked. "Are you Elijah?"

"No," he replied.

"Are you the Prophet that Moses promised would come?"

"No."

"Then tell us who you are, so we can answer the ones who sent us."

John replied in the words of Isaiah: "I am a voice shouting in the wilderness, 'Prepare a straight path for the Lord!'"

Some of the Pharisees said, "If you aren't the Messiah, Elijah, or the Prophet, what right do you have to baptize?"

John replied, "I baptize with water, but someone you don't know is here who will soon begin his ministry. I'm not even worthy of being his servant."

CHAPTER EIGHT

BAPTISM AND TEMPTATION OF JESUS

Matthew 3:13-4:11; Mark 1:9-13; Luke 3:21-23; 4:1-13; John 1:29-34

The next day John saw Jesus coming and God opened John's eyes to reveal who Jesus was. John said, "Look, the Lamb of God who takes away the world's sin. I was talking about him when I told you that someone much greater than I am was coming because he existed long before me. Even though he is my cousin, I did not recognize him as the Messiah, but I came, baptizing, to reveal him to Israel."

Jesus came from Nazareth, in Galilee, to have John baptize him with the rest of the crowds because he wanted to identify with the people he came to save and to set an example for all. But John protested, "You should baptize me, not the other way around."

But Jesus said, "Let it be for now because it is the right thing to do." So, John baptized him.

As Jesus came up out of the water, the heavens opened, the Holy Spirit descended, and settled on him like a dove. Then a voice from heaven said, "You are my Son, I love you, and I am very pleased with you."

John said, "When God sent me to baptize, he told me that the man I saw the Holy Spirit descend and rest upon, is the Son of God. Well, I saw the Holy Spirit descend like a dove and rest upon Jesus; he is the one you seek. He will baptize you with the Holy Spirit because he is the Son of God."

> **What is the Trinity?**
>
> The Trinity is an essential doctrine to the Christian faith; however, it is tough to understand. A careful examination of Scripture shows us how we derive the doctrine of the Trinity. The Bible clearly shows that God the Father, Jesus the Son, and the Holy Spirit are all divine, and each possesses the full essence of God. However, the Bible also clearly shows us that there is an indivisible unity of God and that he is one in nature (Christians do not believe in three gods). We also see that all three exist simultaneously in Jesus' baptism. With these things in mind, we can conclude that God is an undivided being who exists simultaneously as three persons, and all three are fully God.
>
> The word trinity is not in the Bible, but both the Old and New Testaments imply the doctrine. Some people agree that the Father, Son, and Holy Spirit are equally divine, but they argue that each is a different manifestation of God at different times. However, this passage shows that all three exist simultaneously.

> Others agree that the Father, Son, and Holy Spirit are all divine, and all three exist simultaneously, but they argue that God the Father is greater than Jesus, who, in turn, is greater than the Holy Spirit. However, while there may be a subordination of position, there is no subordination of nature. Another way of looking at this is a boss and an employee. The boss may have a greater position than the employee, but the boss is not fundamentally better than the employee. In the same way, God the Father has a superior role to Jesus, but they are equally divine. Each member is fully divine and cannot be subordinate to any being.
>
> Some people have problems with the doctrine of the Trinity and argue that a being cannot be three and one simultaneously. Part of the reason we have this problem is that we do not have the words to express God adequately. The Trinity is one of the great mysteries of the Christian faith and we must remember that God created the universe and our logic. God completely transcends natural laws. Our finite minds cannot grasp what is beyond these laws, and we must recognize that we will never fully comprehend God. Because if we could fully comprehend him, he would cease to be God, or we would become God. Even though it is difficult to understand this concept, the Bible teaches us that God is an undivided being who exists simultaneously as three persons, and all three are fully God.

JESUS' TEMPTATION

After his baptism, Jesus left the Jordan River. The Holy Spirit led him out into the wilderness between Jericho and Jerusalem so that the Devil could tempt him. After eating nothing for 40 days and nights, Jesus was very hungry. The Devil had been waiting for an opportune time to tempt Jesus, so he said, "If you are the Son of God, change these stones into loaves of bread."

People often have their least resolve when they are tired and hungry, and Satan wanted Jesus to take a shortcut and use his power to circumvent the natural order and make life easier. But Jesus said, "Scripture says, 'People don't live on bread alone; they must feed on every word of God.'"

Then the Devil took Jesus to Jerusalem, to the highest point of the temple, a peak about 250 feet above the floor of the Kidron Valley, and said, "If you are the Son of God, jump off! Scripture says, 'He will command his angels to protect and guard you. They will lift you up with their hands to keep you from striking your foot on a stone.'"

Jesus replied, "Scripture also says, 'Do not test the Lord your God.'"

Next, the Devil took him to the peak of a very high mountain and showed him all the world's nations and their glory. The Devil told him, "I will give it all to you if you will bow down and worship me. You can have all the glory of these kingdoms and authority over them because I can give them to whomever I want."

Taking this path would remove the coming pain and suffering of the cross, but Jesus shot back, "Get out of here, Satan! Scripture says, 'You must worship the Lord your God and serve him only.'"

When the Devil gave up on tempting Jesus, he left until the next opportunity came up. Then the angels came and cared for Jesus.

CHAPTER NINE

BEGINNING OF JESUS' MINISTRY

John 1:35-2:25

After his temptation, Jesus returned to the Jordan River, where John was baptizing. John was standing with two of his disciples when he saw Jesus walking by. John looked at him and declared, "Look, the Lamb of God!" John's two disciples left and followed Jesus.

Jesus saw them following him and he asked, "What do you want?"

They replied, "Teacher, where are you staying?"

"Come and see," he said. It was about four in the afternoon when they went with him, and they stayed with him for the rest of the day.

Andrew was one of the men who followed Jesus that day. The first thing Andrew did afterward was to find his brother Simon and tell him they had found the Messiah.

Andrew brought Simon to meet Jesus, and he looked intently at Simon and said, "You are Simon, the son of John, but I will call you Peter."

The next day Jesus headed for Galilee. On the way, he found a man named Philip and called, "Come, be my disciple."

Philip, who was from Andrew and Peter's hometown, went to find Bartholomew (also known as Nathaniel) and told him, "We have found the one Moses and the prophets wrote about! He is Jesus of Nazareth, Joseph's son."

Nazareth had a reputation as being a backwoods town with little going on. Bartholomew sneered, "Can anything good come from Nazareth!?"

"Just come and see," Philip replied.

As they approached, Jesus said, "Here comes an honest man, a true son of Israel."

"How do you know me?" Bartholomew asked.

Jesus answered, "I saw you under the fig tree before Philip got you."

Bartholomew exclaimed, "Teacher, you are the Son of God, the King of Israel!"

Jesus asked him, "Do you believe all this because I told you I saw you under the fig tree? You will see greater things than this. I tell you the truth, you will see heaven open and the angels of God ascending and descending on the Son of Man."

THE WEDDING IN CANA

The next day Jesus, his mother, and his disciples were at a wedding celebration in the village of Cana. During the party, the hosts made a huge social blunder by not having enough wine for the entire celebration. Mary told Jesus, "They have no more wine, do something to help."

Jesus answered, "Mother, that concerns you, not me. It's not my time."

But his mother told the servants, "Do whatever he tells you."

Six 20- to 30-gallon ceremonial stone waterpots were nearby. Jesus told the servants to fill the jars to the brim with water; after they obeyed, he told them to take a cup full to the master of ceremonies.

When the master of ceremonies drank from the cup (which was now full of wine), he called the groom over. Not knowing where the wine was from, he said to the groom, "Usually a host serves the best wine first and then serves the cheaper wine once everyone has been drinking. But you have kept the best wine until now!"

This was Jesus' first miracle and revelation of his glory. His disciples saw this miracle and believed in him. After the wedding, he went to Capernaum for a few days with his mother, brothers, and disciples.

FIRST CLEANSING OF THE TEMPLE

Around the time of Passover, Jesus went up to Jerusalem. At the temple, he saw merchants selling animals for the sacrifices and money changers behind their counters. Furious, he drove out the animals, overturned the tables, and scattered the moneychangers' coins everywhere. He made a whip from some ropes and chased the merchants out, yelling, "Get this stuff out of here! How dare you turn my Father's house into a marketplace!"

> ### Cleansing the temple
>
> People who came to worship at the temple could only donate money in temple currency and the moneychangers would charge hefty fees to purchase it. Inspectors had to approve animal sacrifices, and they were very picky about outside animals, but there were always pre-approved animals available for a ridiculously high price. These men had figured out how to gouge the worshipers to make a tremendous profit for themselves. Jesus didn't mind people making a reasonable living, but he was furious at how they were making a mockery of Passover and the sacrificial system.

Later his disciples remembered that Scripture said, "Passion for God's house will consume me."

The Jewish leaders were really upset and demanded, "Show us a sign to prove you have the authority to do these things."

Jesus answered, "Destroy this temple, and I will raise it up in three days."

The Jews said, "It took 46 years to build this temple, and you will raise it up in three days?" But what Jesus meant was the temple of his body. After he rose from the dead, his disciples remembered what he'd said, and they knew both Jesus and the Scriptures were true. Many people were convinced that he was the Messiah because of his miraculous signs at the Passover. But Jesus didn't trust them because he knew human nature and their hearts.

CHAPTER TEN

MEETING WITH NICODEMUS

Matthew 4:12; Mark 1:14; Luke 4:14; John 3:1-4:4

One night, a Pharisee named Nicodemus came to speak with Jesus and he said, "Teacher, we know you are from God because you could not do these miracles or have this kind of wisdom if God weren't with you."

Jesus replied, "I tell you the truth, no one can see the kingdom of God unless he is born again." Here Jesus was talking about regeneration, not reincarnation.

Nicodemus thought that Jesus meant a physical rebirth, and he exclaimed, "What do you mean? How can a grown man go back into his mother's womb and be born again?"

Jesus replied, "The truth is, no one can enter the kingdom of God without being born in the flesh and the Spirit. Flesh can only give birth to flesh, but the Holy Spirit gives birth to spirit. You shouldn't be surprised when I say you must be born again. Just as you can hear the wind but cannot tell where it comes from or where it is going, so it is with people who are born of the Spirit."

"What do you mean?" Nicodemus asked.

"You're a respected Jewish teacher," Jesus replied, "and you don't understand these things? We talk about what we know and have seen, but you refuse to believe. If you don't even believe me when I tell you about earthly things, how can you possibly believe me if I tell you about heavenly things? I am the only one who has been to heaven and I have come to earth to tell you about my Father. Just as Moses lifted up the bronze serpent in the wilderness, so the Son of Man must be lifted up. Then, everyone who believes in me will have eternal life.

"For God so loved the world that he gave his only Son so that whoever believes in him will not perish, but have eternal life. God did not send his Son into the world to condemn it but to save it. Those who trust him won't face judgment, but those who don't trust him will face judgment because they reject the light, the only Son of God, and love the darkness. They hate the light because they want to practice their evil deeds in the darkness, and they are afraid that the light will expose their sins. But those who do what is right gladly come to the light, so everyone can see that their deeds have been done through God."

> **What does it mean to be born again?**
>
> Being born again is a spiritual birth where a believer places his or her trust in Jesus for salvation.

JOHN'S TESTIMONY ABOUT JESUS

After this exchange, Jesus and his disciples left Jerusalem for the Judean countryside and spent some time baptizing people there.

Meanwhile, John the Baptist was baptizing at Aenon, near Salim, because there was plenty of water there and people kept coming to him. John's disciples grumbled to him, "Teacher, the man you called the Messiah is also baptizing people, and everybody is going to him instead of us."

John replied, "A man can only receive what God gives him. I told you that I am not the Messiah; I'm just here to prepare the way for him. Remember that the bride belongs to the groom. The best man waits and listens for him, and rejoices with him; I rejoice at Jesus' success. He must become greater, and I must become less.

"He has come from heaven and is greater than anyone else. I am from the earth, and I only understand earthly things, but he understands heavenly things. He tells people about what he has seen and heard. Few people believe him, but those who believe him discover that God is true. God sent him and he speaks the word of God because he gives the Holy Spirit without limit. The Father loves the Son and has given him authority over everything. Whoever believes in God's Son will have eternal life, but God will pour out his wrath on those who reject him."

JOHN ARRESTED

Not long after this, Herod Antipas (not the same Herod who tried to kill the infant Christ) arrested John because he was afraid of his message. Word spread about Jesus, and soon, the Pharisees heard that Jesus' disciples were baptizing and making more disciples than John. When Jesus realized that the Pharisees knew about him and that Herod had arrested John, he left Judea and headed back to Galilee. He took the most direct route through Samaria, propelled by the Holy Spirit's power.

> **Why were there so many Herods?**
>
> Herod was a family name of a group of rulers during the First Century. They all descended from Herod the Great, the one who tried to kill the infant Jesus.

CHAPTER ELEVEN

THE WOMAN AT THE WELL

John 4:5-45

Eventually, Jesus came to the Samaritan village of Sychar near the plot of land that Jacob had given his son Joseph. Jesus was tired from his journey, and he sat down by Jacob's well at about noon while his disciples went into town to buy some food.

Jesus had only been sitting for a little while when a Samaritan woman came out to draw water. Most women came to draw water early in the morning, but this woman came at noon so that she wouldn't have to talk to her neighbors. Jesus was thirsty, so he asked her for a drink. The woman was shocked because most Jews refuse to speak with Samaritans because of their intense hatred for them, so she said, "If you're a Jew and I'm a Samaritan, why are you asking me for a drink?"

> **Jews and Samaritans**
>
> The Jews and Samaritans were both groups descended from Jacob but had very different histories after the division of the Israelite kingdom. The division between them was religious, ethnic, and political. After the Israelite kingdom divided, the Samaritans had made some religious compromises and intermarried with some nations that the Jews found deplorable. The Jews viewed them as half-breeds and wanted nothing to do with them; many Jews wanted the destruction of the Samaritans. The hate flowed both ways and both groups looked down on the other.
>
> The fact that she was not only a Samaritan but also a woman made it unlikely that a Jew, let alone a Jewish teacher, would talk to her. But Jesus loved her and saw her need, not her race. It is also interesting to note that Jesus claimed to be the Messiah very clearly. He was willing to claim to be the Messiah in Samaria, where they did not have as many distorted notions of the Messiah.

Jesus answered, "If you knew the gift that God has for you and who I am, you would have asked me for a drink; and I would have given you living water."

The woman protested, "You don't have anything to get the water with and it's a deep well. Where would you get this living water? Are you greater than our ancestor Jacob, who gave us this well?"

Jesus replied, "Everyone who drinks this water will be thirsty again, but whoever drinks the water I give will never thirst again. The water I give will become a spring of water that gives eternal life."

The woman thought that Jesus was talking about physical water and did not understand that he spoke of a spiritual water, so she said, "I want some of that. It would be great never to get thirsty and not have to come out here to get water."

Jesus said, "Go get your husband and come back."

She answered sheepishly, "I don't have a husband."

Jesus replied, "It's true that you don't have a husband. In fact, you have had five husbands, and you're not even married to the man you live with now."

The woman was shocked. But she saw an opportunity to ask a religious teacher a question because, in her life, she never had access to a teacher. So, she said, "Sir, I can see you're a prophet, so maybe you can answer this question. Our fathers worshiped here on Mount Gerizim, but the Jews say we should worship in Jerusalem. Where should we worship?"

Jesus answered, "Believe me, a time is coming when it won't matter where you worship God. You Samaritans worship what you don't know; we worship what we know, for salvation comes from the Jews. But from now on, true worshipers will worship God in spirit and truth. That's the kind of worshiper God is looking for; God is spirit and we must worship him in spirit and truth."

The woman said, "I know the Messiah is coming, and he will explain everything to us."

Then Jesus declared, "I am the Messiah!"

When his disciples returned, they were surprised to find him talking to a woman, but no one asked why he had been talking to her or about their conversation. The woman left her water jar by the well and went to tell the village, "Come see a man who told me everything I ever did. Could this be the Messiah?" So, the people came out to see Jesus.

Meanwhile, his disciples were urging him to eat. But Jesus said, "I have food to eat that you don't know about."

The disciples asked each other, "Who brought him food?"

Then Jesus explained, "My food is to do God's will and finish the work he sent me to do. Do you think the harvest will only begin when summer ends four months from now? Open your eyes and look at the fields of people coming here; they are ripe for harvest now. The reaper is already earning his wages and his harvest is people who have eternal life. The saying, 'One sows and another reaps' is true. I am sending you out to reap what you have not sowed; others have already done the work and you will gather in their harvest. But the sower and the reaper will share the same joy."

Many of the Samaritans trusted Jesus because of what the woman said, but many more believed he was the Savior after hearing him speak. They came out to him and asked him to stay with them for two days. After that, he left for Galilee, although he knew they would eventually reject him.

CHAPTER TWELVE

MINISTRY IN GALILEE

Matthew 4:13-17; Mark 1:14-15; Luke 4:14-31; John 4:46-54

In Galilee, Jesus received a great welcome because of what he had done at the Passover feast in Jerusalem.

He began to preach, "At last, the time has come. The kingdom of God is near! Turn from your sins and believe the Good News." They all praised him as he taught in their synagogues, and soon everyone throughout the surrounding countryside knew about him.

Around this time, Jesus visited Cana again, where he had turned the water into wine. While he was there, a government official from Capernaum came to see him. When the official found Jesus, he begged him to come heal his son who, was very sick and about to die.

"Must I keep doing miracles and wonders before you people trust me?" Jesus exclaimed.

The official begged, "Please come now before my boy dies."

Then Jesus told him, "Go back home; your son will live." Hoping and believing in Jesus, the government man headed home.

While the official was on his way, some of his servants ran up and told him that his son was better. He asked them what time he got better, and they said, "His fever suddenly left around one in the afternoon." This was the exact time that Jesus had said, "Your son will live." So, the official and his entire household trusted in Jesus. This was Jesus' second miracle in Galilee.

JESUS RETURNS TO NAZARETH

Jesus went to his hometown of Nazareth and entered the synagogue on the Sabbath. In Jewish synagogues, men typically sat to read Scripture while the people stood to listen. Instead of sitting, Jesus stood up to read from the scroll of Isaiah and found where it says, "The Spirit of the Lord is on me because he has appointed me to preach good news to the poor. He has sent me to proclaim that prisoners will be freed, that the blind will see, that the oppressed will be released, and proclaim that the Lord's favor has come." When he finished reading, he rolled up the scroll, gave it back to the attendant, and sat down.

Everyone was confused because he had stood to read and had stopped reading in the middle of a passage. The rest of the passage went on to talk about how God was going to restore the kingdom of Israel and pass judgment on his enemies. They intently stared at him, waiting for him to continue, and he said, "This Scripture is fulfilled before your eyes."

People spoke well of him and his gracious words amazed them. Puzzled, they asked, "Isn't this Joseph's son? How did he get this kind of understanding and authority to teach?"

Then Jesus said, "Surely you will quote this proverb to me: 'Physician, heal yourself. We want to see you do what we heard you did in Capernaum.' I tell you the truth, no prophet is accepted in his hometown.

"There were many needy widows in Israel during Elijah's time when it didn't rain for three-and-a-half years. Yet God didn't send Elijah to any of them but to the widow Zarephath in a foreign land. Or think of the prophet Elisha who healed Naaman, a foreigner, rather than the lepers in Israel."

All the people in the synagogue were furious when they heard this. They understood that he was claiming to be the Messiah, but they wanted a conquering king and were disappointed that he did not meet their expectations. They thought he was blaspheming against God, so they jumped up, drove him out of town, and took him to a cliff to throw him off it. It wasn't Jesus' time to die, so as they neared the cliff, he walked through the crowd and went on his way.

Instead of staying in Nazareth, Jesus went to Capernaum, by the Sea of Galilee. This fulfilled Isaiah's prophecy that a light would shine on those living in the shadow of death in Galilee.

CHAPTER THIRTEEN

CALL OF THE FOUR AND VARIOUS HEALINGS

Matthew 4:18-25; 8:2-4; 9:1-17; Mark 1:16-2:22; Luke 4:31-5:39

One morning, as Jesus was preaching while he walked along the shore of Galilee, people crowded around him to listen to his teaching on the word of God. He saw two empty boats near the water's edge where Peter and Andrew were washing their nets after fishing all night. Jesus got into one of the boats and asked Peter to push it out into the water. Then he sat down in the boat so that the crowds could hear him and he taught the people.

When he had finished speaking, he told Peter, "Go out into deep water, let down your nets, and you will catch many fish."

The middle of the day was not the best time to catch fish, so Peter protested, "Master, we worked hard all night and didn't catch anything, but if you say so, I'll try again." They rowed out and threw their nets into the water. When they tried to pull the nets back in, they were so full of fish that they began to tear. They called their partners in the other boat to come help them, and they filled both boats with so many fish that the boats began to sink.

When Peter realized Jesus' power, he fell to his knees and begged, "Lord, please leave me because I'm a sinful man!"

Jesus replied, "Don't be afraid; from now on, you will catch men." So, the fishermen pulled their boats onto shore and left everything to follow Jesus. The fish they caught would have been extremely profitable and would have provided a comfortable living, but Jesus' words were far more compelling.

Andrew and Peter's partners, James and John, had been sitting in a boat with their father, Zebedee, mending their nets. Jesus called them to follow him too, and they immediately left the boat and their father to follow him.

JESUS CASTS OUT A DEMON

Jesus and his companions stayed in the town of Capernaum, and every Sabbath, he went to the synagogue to teach the people. People were amazed because he taught with so much authority and conviction, unlike their teachers of the religious law.

Once, when he was in the synagogue, a man with an evil spirit cried out, "Leave us alone! What do you want with us, Jesus of Nazareth? Have you come to destroy us? I know who you are—the Holy One of God!"

"Be quiet, and come out of him!" Jesus commanded. The demon that possessed the man screamed and threw the man into a convulsion but came out without injuring him further.

Astonished, all the people could talk about was, "What kind of teaching is this? He has such authority that even the evil spirits obey his commands." News about Jesus spread quickly throughout the surrounding area.

After Jesus and his disciples left the synagogue that day, they went to Peter and Andrew's house, where Peter's mother-in-law was sick with a high fever. "Please heal her," they begged. Jesus went to her bedside, took her by the hand, rebuked the fever, then helped her sit up. The fever left immediately, and she felt well enough to get up and prepare a meal for them.

That evening at sunset, people brought all sorts of sick and demon-possessed people to Jesus. A huge crowd gathered outside to see what would happen. Jesus went to work and healed many sick people and cast out their demons. As they came out, the demons shouted, "You are the Son of God!" because they knew he was the Messiah. But Jesus rebuked those demons and told them to be quiet. All this fulfilled Isaiah's prophecy: "He took our sicknesses and removed our diseases."

> **Demon possession?**
>
> Demon possession is when an evil spiritual being (demon) comes into a person and controls their mind and physical body. The Bible does not tell us how a person can become demon-possessed, but it is only when people open themselves up to Satan's control through their choices and lifestyle. People who trust Jesus cannot be demon-possessed because demons cannot co-exist with the Holy Spirit in a person's soul. However, believers can still be influenced by demons. There are many cases of demon possession in the Bible, and it seems unlikely that it is as common in modern times. Demon possession is different than sickness or mental illness, as shown in this passage.
>
> It is also interesting to note that Jesus told the demons not to identify him as the Son of God. He did this because it was not the right time for this proclamation. Jesus still had much to do before his death and this identification would have accelerated matters too quickly.

FURTHER MINISTRY IN CAPERNAUM

The next morning before dawn, Jesus went out to the wilderness to pray alone. He knew that he needed to stay in constant contact with his Father despite his busy schedule. The people looked all over for him, and when they found him, they begged him to stay.

But Jesus said, "I must preach the good news of the kingdom of God in other places too because that is why I came." So, he traveled throughout Galilee, teaching in the synagogues and preaching everywhere he could. He also healed people with every kind of sickness and disease and cast out many demons.

News about him spread far beyond Galilee so that the sick came from more than 100 miles away for healing. Jesus healed them all: epileptics, paralytics, and the demon-possessed. Large crowds followed him wherever he went.

In one of the towns, Jesus met a man with an advanced case of leprosy. The man came to Jesus and fell face down on the ground, worshiping him. "Lord," he begged, "if you want, you can heal me."

Moved with pity, Jesus reached out and touched the man. Leprosy was an unclean disease in those days, and lepers were outcasts from the community. This was probably the first time anyone had touched him in years. "I am willing," he said. "Be clean!" Instantly the leprosy was gone. Jesus told him, "Go to the priest and let him examine you, but don't talk to anyone along the way. Take the offering that the Law requires for those healed of leprosy, so everyone will have proof of your healing."

But as the man went on his way, he told everyone what had happened. Therefore, so many people crowded around Jesus that he could no longer publicly enter a city. He had to stay out in the secluded places, and people came to hear him preach and for healing. But Jesus often withdrew to the wilderness to pray.

JESUS HEALS A PARALYTIC

Several days later, Jesus took a boat back to Capernaum, and the news of his arrival there spread quickly through the town. Crowds of people came to the house where he was staying and soon, there was no room left, not even outside the door. As usual, there were some Pharisees and teachers of the religious law in the crowd. God's healing power was with Jesus and he preached the word to all of them.

Four men arrived carrying a paralyzed man on a sleeping mat; they tried to push through the crowd to Jesus, but couldn't reach him. Frustrated, they went up onto the flat roof, removed some tiles, and lowered the sick man down into the middle of the crowd. Jesus saw their faith and said to the paralyzed man, "Take heart, my son, your sins are forgiven."

The Pharisees and teachers of the religious law became indignant and said to themselves, "This is blasphemy! Who does he think he is? Only God can forgive sins!"

Jesus knew what they were thinking, so he asked, "Why do you think this is blasphemy? Is it easier for me to say, 'Your sins are forgiven' or 'Get up and walk?' But I will prove to you that the Son of Man has the authority of God to forgive sins." Then he turned to the paralyzed man and said, "Stand up, take your mat, and go home."

The man jumped up, took his mat, and pushed his way through the stunned audience. Fear and amazement swept through the crowd, and they all praised God, exclaiming, "We've never seen anything like this!"

JESUS CALLS MATTHEW

Once again, Jesus went out beside a lake and taught the crowds that followed him. On his way to the lake, he saw Levi, who Jesus renamed Matthew, sitting at his tax collector's booth. Tax collectors were notorious for extortion and people hated them. Levi was also a Jew and that was even worse because the people saw him as a traitor. Jesus said, "Come follow me." Levi got up, left everything behind, and followed him.

That night, the newly renamed Matthew invited Jesus and the other disciples to have dinner with him, his fellow tax collectors, and others of questionable morality. When the Pharisees saw him eating with such sinners (these people were always with Jesus), they complained to his disciples, "Why does your teacher eat with such scum?"

Jesus overheard them and replied, "Healthy people don't need a doctor; sick people do. Learn what this means, 'I desire mercy, not sacrifice.' I have not come to call the righteous but sinners."

Fasting was a common practice of religious men, and it was a way of drawing closer to the Lord. John's disciples and the Pharisees were fasting and they complained that Jesus' disciples were feasting rather than fasting. They came to Jesus and asked, "Why do John's disciples and the Pharisees fast, but your disciples don't?"

Jesus answered, "Should the wedding guests mourn while celebrating with the groom? Of course not; no one fasts when they are with the groom. Someday I will be taken from them and then they will fast."

Then he gave them this illustration, "No one sews an unshrunk patch on an old piece of clothing. If they do, the patch shrinks and pulls away from the clothes, leaving an even bigger hole than before. Also, no one puts new wine into old wineskins. If they do, the wineskin will burst; then they will lose the wine and ruin the wineskin. One must put new wine into new wineskins, and then both the wine and the wineskins are safe. No one who drinks the old wine wants to drink the new wine because they say the old is better."

What about wineskins?

Jesus uses the analogy of wineskins to contrast his teaching and Pharisees' teaching. In modern times, we can look at this as differences in worship styles. The gospel is always the same, but its presentation changes. New generations will express their faith differently and that's valid. We don't need to practice the same as others because we may be happy with our expression of faith. Forcing people to conform will only cause division. Therefore, new churches that express faith differently will reach more people (e.g. traditional versus modern worship).

CHAPTER FOURTEEN
SABBATH CONTROVERSIES AND WITHDRAWALS
Matthew 12:1-21; Mark 2:23-3:12; Luke 6:1-11; John 5

One Sabbath (the Jewish day of worship), Jesus went up to Jerusalem for one of the Jewish feasts. Inside the city, near the Sheep Gate, was the Pool of Bethesda. It had five covered porches where crowds of sick, blind, and paralyzed people lay because when the waters stirred, they could heal people. One man Jesus saw lying there had been there for 38 years! Jesus asked, "Do you want to get well?"

Instead of answering Jesus' question, the man gave an excuse. "I have no one to help me into the pool when the waters are stirred. Whenever I try to get there, someone always gets there ahead of me," the man complained. It soon became clear he was making a living on alms that people gave him.

So, Jesus told him, "Stand up, pick up your mat, and walk." Instantly, the man was healed, picked up his mat, and walked.

Since it was the Sabbath, some Jewish leaders objected and said to the man, "You can't do that, it's the Sabbath and it's illegal to carry that sleeping mat."

The man replied, "But the man who healed me told me to pick it up and walk."

The Pharisees demanded, "Who told you to pick it up and walk?"

The man didn't know who it was because Jesus had disappeared into the crowd.

Later, Jesus found the man in the temple and said to him, "Now that you're healed, stop sinning, or something worse might happen to you." Upset that Jesus had healed him and taken away his means for getting money without working, the man went to the Jewish leaders and told them that it was Jesus who had healed him.

The Pharisees harassed Jesus for breaking the Law by healing the man on the Sabbath. But Jesus replied, "My Father never stops working, so why should I?" Therefore, the Jews tried to kill him because he was not only breaking the Sabbath, but he was calling God his Father, equating himself with God.

Jesus knew their thoughts, so he said, "I tell you the truth, I can do nothing by myself because I can only do what I see my Father doing. Whatever the Father does, I do as well because the Father loves me and tells me everything he is doing. You will see me do even greater things than this healing; just as the Father can raise people from the dead, you will see me raise whomever I wish. Furthermore, the Father has entrusted me to judge the world so that everyone will honor me, just as they honor the Father. In fact, whoever does not honor me, does not honor the Father.

"Whoever listens to my words and believes in God who sent me will have eternal life and won't be condemned. A time is coming and has arrived when the dead will hear the Son of God's voice and live. Just as the Father has the power to give life, he has granted the Son the power to give life; he has given me the authority to judge humanity because I am the Son of Man.

"Don't be amazed; a time is coming when all the dead will hear his voice and rise. Those who have done good will rise to eternal life, and those who have done evil will rise to judgment. But I cannot do anything by myself; I only judge as my Father tells me. Therefore, my judgment is just because it is not mine; it is God's will.

"If I testify about myself, you will say my testimony is not valid. Someone else testifies about me, and his testimony is valid. You asked John and he told you the truth. Human testimony is not always right, but his was. You hold him in high regard and I mention him for your salvation.

"John gave you light and you enjoyed it, but I have a greater witness than John: my teaching and my miracles. My Father has assigned these to me and they testify that he has sent me. The Father has also testified about me, but you have never heard his voice or seen him. His word is not in your hearts because you have not believed me. You study the Scriptures because you think that will give you eternal life. These Scriptures point to me, yet you still refuse to believe.

"I don't receive glory from you because I know you don't have God's love in your hearts. I have come in my Father's name, yet you refuse to accept me; but if someone comes in his own name, you will accept him. How can you believe if you accept praise from each other but don't try to get praise from God?

"But I'm not the one who will accuse you before the Father. Moses will accuse you because you have set your hopes on him. If you trusted Moses, you would trust me because he wrote about me. But since you don't believe what he wrote, why would you believe what I say?"

***

On another Sabbath, Jesus was walking through some grain fields with his disciples. They were hungry, so they broke off the heads of wheat, rubbed off the husks in their hands, and ate the grains. When the Pharisees saw this, they protested, "Don't you know that you're breaking the Law by working on the Sabbath?"

Jesus answered, "Haven't you read what King David did when he and his companions were hungry? He went into God's house with his companions, and they ate the sacred bread that was only for the priests. Or haven't you read in the Law of Moses that the priests work in the temple on the Sabbath? I tell you that one greater than the temple is here. You would not condemn the innocent if you knew the meaning of this Scripture: 'I desire mercy, not sacrifice.' The Sabbath is for the benefit of people, not people for the benefit of the Sabbath. And I, the Son of Man, am the master of even the Sabbath."

***

On another Sabbath, he went into the synagogue and noticed a man with a deformed hand. The Pharisees and teachers of the religious law were looking for a reason to accuse Jesus of some sort of crime, so they watched to see if he would heal the man. They asked Jesus, "Is it legal to heal on the Sabbath?"

But Jesus knew their thoughts and said to the man, "Get up and stand where everyone can see you." So, the man got up. Then Jesus said to his critics, "Which is legal to do on the Sabbath, good or evil, to save life or destroy it? If one of you had a sheep and it fell into a pit on the Sabbath, wouldn't you do work and pull it out? Of course you would, and this man is much more valuable than a sheep. Therefore, it's lawful to do good on the Sabbath."

Jesus looked around at them, distressed by their stubborn hearts. "Stretch out your hand," he told the man. The man stretched out his hand and it was whole again. But the Pharisees were furious and began to talk with Herod's supporters to figure out how they could kill Jesus.

But Jesus knew their plans, so he and his disciples went out by the lake. The news of his miracles had spread, and people came from as far as 50 miles away to see for themselves.

Jesus told his disciples to have a small boat ready for him in case the crowd grew too large. He had healed many people that day, so many more sick people crowded around, trying to touch him. Whenever those possessed by evil spirits saw him, they would fall down in front of him and scream, "You are the Son of God!" But Jesus ordered them not to say who he was. He healed all the sick people but warned them to keep his identity a secret. This fulfilled Isaiah's prophecy, "Look at my Servant, whom I have chosen. I love him, and he pleases me. I will put my Spirit upon him, and he will proclaim justice to the nations. He will not fight or cry out; he won't raise his voice in public. He won't crush the weak or put out hope until he leads justice to victory. His name will be the hope of the entire world."

Jesus and the Sabbath

The Sabbath was the Jewish day of religious observance from sundown Friday to Saturday evening. Jesus was trying to teach the Jews that God made the Sabbath to benefit them, not the other way around. God wanted people to observe the Sabbath so that they would spend time with him and rest, not so that they could have more rules to follow. As a part of their zeal to keep the Law, rabbis created many rules about forbidden activities on the Sabbath. These included travel, preparation of food, and the types of tasks a person could do.

Some of the regulations on work became ridiculous. For example, people could not look in a mirror because they might see a gray hair and pluck it. People also could not move furniture unless it was a ladder, and then they could only move it four paces. While these additions came from a good place, the emphasis became more about the rules than the Sabbath.

One of the Sabbath prohibitions was healing unless the victim was in danger of dying the next day. This man was in no risk of dying. Since Jesus created the Sabbath, his interpretation of permitted activities had far more authority than the religious leaders.

CHAPTER FIFTEEN

APPOINTMENT OF THE TWELVE

Mark 3:13-19; Luke 6:12-19

One evening Jesus went to a mountain to pray, and he spent the entire night in prayer. In the morning, he called his many followers to him and chose twelve of them to be apostles that would spread his message. He sent them out to preach and he gave them the authority to cast out demons. These are the Twelve he chose: Simon (whom he named Peter), James and John (the sons of Zebedee, nicknamed the "Sons of Thunder"), Andrew (Simon/Peter's brother), Philip, Bartholomew, Matthew, Thomas, James (son of Alphaeus), Thaddaeus, Simon (the Zealot), and Judas Iscariot (who later betrayed him).

Disciple	Interesting Notes
Simon (Peter)	Andrew's brother. He was originally a fisherman and became the leader of the early church. The Gospel of Mark records the life of Jesus from his perspective.
James (son of Zebedee)	John's brother. Originally, a fisherman. Commonly, believed to be the first disciple martyred.
John	This was not John the Baptist but James' brother. Possibly, the youngest of the disciples and the only one to die of old age. The Gospel of John records the life of Jesus from his perspective.
Andrew	Peter's brother.
Philip	
Bartholomew	Also known as Nathaniel.
Levi (Matthew)	Had been a tax collector and likely hated by the Jews.
Thomas	Demanded proof that Jesus had really risen.
James (son of Alphaeus)	Possibly Matthew's brother.

Disciple	Interesting Notes
Thaddaeus	Sometimes referred to as Judas, but distinct from Judas Iscariot.
Simon (the Zealot)	Zealots hated Roman rule and often carried blades that they used to kill Romans when given the opportunity. He probably had a tough time with Matthew.
Judas Iscariot	Treasurer for the group; he betrayed Jesus for 30 pieces of silver.

When they came down the slopes of the mountain, the disciples stood with Jesus on a large, level area. Many of his followers and the crowds from all over stood around him because they had come to hear him speak and for healing; Jesus cast out many evil spirits that day. Everyone tried to touch him because power was coming from him and healing them all.

CHAPTER SIXTEEN

THE SERMON ON THE MOUNT

Matthew 5-7; Luke 6:20-49

> **The Sermon on the Mount**
>
> This is a compilation of many of Jesus' teachings and is the longest uninterrupted discourse that he gives in Scripture. In this teaching, Jesus takes many traditional interpretations and turns them on their ear. Most Jewish instruction dealt with actions, but Jesus expanded it to include attitude and heart condition. He also taught that our actions should reflect what is happening inside us and not a way to gain recognition from others. He addressed the legalistic misinterpretation of the Law and resetting their understanding of what God told his people all along.

One day, as the crowds gathered, Jesus went up the mountainside with his disciples and sat down to teach them. A crowd followed and he turned to his disciples and said:

"Blessed are the poor in spirit because the kingdom of heaven is theirs.

"Blessed are the hungry because God will satisfy them.

"Blessed are those who weep because they will laugh.

"Blessed are those who mourn because God will comfort them.

"Blessed are the gentle and lowly because they will inherit the earth.

"Blessed are those who hunger and thirst for righteousness because God will fill them.

"Blessed are the merciful because God will show them mercy.

"Blessed are the pure in heart because they will see God.

"Blessed are those who make peace because they will be children of God.

"Blessed are those who are persecuted for living for God because the kingdom of heaven is theirs.

"Blessed are you when people hate, mock, persecute, reject, and lie about you because you are identified with me, the Son of Man. Rejoice when that happens because a great reward waits for you in heaven. Remember, that's how your ancestors treated the prophets.

"But woe to the rich because they already have their comfort.

"Woe to those who are well-fed because they will go hungry.

"Woe to those who laugh now because they will mourn and weep.

"Woe to you when everyone praises you because that's how your fathers treated the false prophets.

"You are the salt of the earth, but what good is it if the salt loses its flavor? It cannot become salty again; it's worthless and is thrown out and trampled.

"You are the light of the world; a city on a hill cannot be hidden. People don't light a lamp and then put it under a basket; instead, they put it on a stand so everyone can see it. In the same way, let your good deeds shine for all to see so that they will praise your Father in heaven.

"I have not come to abolish the Law or the Prophets; in fact, I have come to fulfill them. I tell you the truth, until heaven and earth disappear, not one letter or pen stroke will pass away until it accomplishes its purpose. Anyone who breaks the least of these commands and teaches others to do the same will be least in the kingdom of heaven, but whoever obeys God's Laws and teaches others to do the same will be great in the kingdom.

"I warn you that unless you are more obedient than the Pharisees and the teachers of the Law, you won't make it into the kingdom of heaven.

> **Jesus and the Law**
>
> Jesus was not invalidating the Old Testament; he was giving a proper interpretation of it. The Pharisees had developed a hierarchy of the commandments, and Jesus shows them that all of it matters. In this next section, he pairs what was considered an important command with a lesser one. He uses these to reveal the heart behind the Law.

"You have heard it said, 'Do not murder' and that 'murderers will be subject to judgment.' But I tell you that if you are angry with someone without cause, you will be subject to judgment. If anyone calls someone else worthless, they will bring him before the court, and whoever calls someone else a fool is in danger of hell.

> **Calling someone a fool**
>
> The Hebrew word for fool went beyond intellect and implied a moral and religious judgment. Jesus warns his audience about calling others fools in the context of unrighteous anger. In other places, Jesus called the Pharisees fools, but as God in the flesh, he knew their hearts and had justifiable outrage.
>
> It's also essential for us to see what Jesus did with his anger. The Gospels tell us that when he was angry, he healed a man and cleansed the temple. Our anger should motivate us to good deeds, not sin.

"Therefore, if you are presenting an offering to God in the temple and remember that someone has something against you, leave your offering and go make things right. Then come back and offer your gift.

"Settle things quickly with your opponent at law on the way to court, or else he may hand you over to the judge, and they will throw you in prison. Then you won't get out until you have paid the last penny.

"You have heard it said, 'Do not commit adultery.' But I say that you have already committed adultery in your heart if you even lust after a woman. If your right eye causes you to sin, gouge it out and throw it away because it is better to lose one part of the body than go to hell. If your right hand causes you to sin, cut it off and throw it away because it is better to lose one part of your body than go to hell.

"You have heard it said, 'Anyone can divorce his wife by giving her a certificate of divorce.' But I tell you that anyone who divorces his wife, unless she has been unfaithful, causes her to commit adultery; anyone who marries a divorced woman commits adultery.

"You have also heard it said, 'Don't break your vows, but keep the oaths you have made to the Lord.' But I tell you not to swear at all. Don't swear by heaven, because it is God's throne; don't swear by the earth, because it is God's footstool; don't swear by Jerusalem, because it is the city of the Great King; and don't swear by your head, because you can't even make one hair white or black. Let your 'Yes,' be 'Yes,' and your 'No,' be 'No.' Anything beyond that is wrong.

"You have heard it said, 'An eye for an eye, and a tooth for a tooth.' But I tell you not to resist an evil person. If someone slaps your right cheek, turn the other cheek as well. If someone wants to sue you and take your shirt, give him your coat as well. If a soldier demands that you carry his gear for a mile, carry it for two. If someone wants something from you, give it to him, and don't try to turn away those who want to borrow things from you.

"You have heard it said, 'Love your neighbor and hate your enemy.' But I say love your enemies, do good to those who hate you, bless those who curse you, and pray for those who persecute you. Doing these things will prove that you are children of your Father in heaven. Remember that he is kind to the unthankful and the wicked. Be merciful just as he is merciful because he gives sunlight to both the evil and the good, and he sends rain on the just and the unjust.

"What good is it if you only love those who love you? Even sinners do that. What good is it if you are only kind to your friends and only do good to those who do good to you? Sinners do that too. Furthermore, everyone lends to others when they expect to get their money back. Do good to your enemies and lend to them without expecting to get anything back. You are to be perfect, just like your heavenly Father is perfect.

"Be careful that you're not just doing good deeds to impress others because you will lose your reward in heaven. When you give to charity, don't shout about it like the hypocrites do, they already have their reward. When you give, don't let your left hand know what your right hand is doing; your giving should be in secret so that your heavenly Father will reward you.

"When you pray, don't be like the hypocrites, who like to pray in public so everyone will see them. Instead, go into your room and pray behind closed doors so that your heavenly Father will reward you.

"Also, don't go on and on with meaningless repetition like some people in other religions. They think their god will listen because of their many words, but remember that your Father knows what you need, even before you ask.

"This is how you should pray: Father in heaven, I honor your name. May your kingdom come, and your will be done on earth like it is in heaven. Give us our bread for today, and forgive our sins, just like we've forgiven those who have sinned against us. Lead us away from temptation, and deliver us from the evil one. For the kingdom, power, and glory are yours forever. Amen.

"If you forgive people who sin against you, your heavenly Father will also forgive you; but if you refuse to forgive others, then God won't forgive you either.

"When you fast, don't make it obvious by looking gloomy and sad. If you do that, you already have your reward from men. When you fast, comb your hair and wash your face so that it won't be obvious that you're fasting. Then your heavenly Father will reward you.

"Don't store up treasures on earth where they will eventually wear out or be stolen. Store up treasures in heaven, where they will never wear out, and they cannot be stolen. Your heart and thoughts will be wherever your treasure is.

"Your eye is the lamp of your body; if your eyes are good, then your whole body will be full of light. But if your eyes are bad, then your body will be full of darkness, and if you think your darkness is light, how deep that darkness is.

> **What did Jesus mean by good and bad eyes?**
>
> This teaching is in the context of material possessions, and we cannot interpret it without considering what is before and after. The eye reveals what we focus on, whether God or money. If our eyes focus on him, then we will be full of light, but on possessions, we will be full of darkness.

"No one can serve two masters. You will hate one and love the other, or devote yourself to one and despise the other. In the same way, you cannot serve both God and money.

"Therefore, don't worry about everyday life and whether you have enough food, drink, or clothes. Isn't life more than these things? Look at the birds; they don't worry about planting, harvesting, or storing up food because their heavenly Father feeds them. You are worth so much more than they are; so, don't worry, because all your worrying won't add a single second to your life.

"Why worry about clothes? See how the lilies of the field grow without hard work, yet not even Solomon dressed as beautifully as they are. If God clothes the grass of the field that will be dead tomorrow, don't you think he will clothe you? Where's your faith?

"So, don't worry about having enough food, drink, and clothing. The world runs after all these things, and your heavenly Father knows that you need them. Make your primary concern the kingdom of heaven, and he will take care of everything else. Don't worry about tomorrow, because tomorrow will have worries of its own; every day has enough trouble.

"Don't judge, or others will judge you by the same standard. Stop criticizing, or it will all come back on you because others will treat you just like you treat them. Others will use your standard for judgment to judge you.

> **Judgment**
>
> Jesus is saying that the standard we use to judge others applies to us as well. Since God will judge us by his standard, it is all right to tell other believers that they are sinning. However, we must also make sure that we are diligently getting rid of sin in our lives. In other places in the Bible, God instructs us to judge our fellow believers to keep them from sinning. We cannot live our lives without making judgments, so Jesus is telling people to make righteous judgments.
>
> However, our job is not to be the morality police for those who do not claim to be Christians. If people do not claim to follow Christ, we should not stand in a place of judgment; God will do that.

"If you forgive others, they will forgive you too; if you give, you will receive. People will give back to you in the same measure that you give. They will pour into your lap as much as they can.

"What good is it for one blind man to lead another blind man? The first will end up leading the other one into a pit. A student is not greater than his teacher but will become like his teacher.

"Don't worry about the speck of sawdust in your friend's eye when you have a log in your eye. How can you even think of saying, 'Let me help you with that speck,' when you can't even get close enough because of the log in your eye? You hypocrite, first take the log from your eye, and then you will be able to deal with the speck in your brother's eye.

"Don't give dogs what is sacred, and don't give pearls to pigs. If you do, they will trample the pearls and then turn and attack you.

"Keep asking, and you will receive; keep looking, and you will find; keep knocking, and the door will be open. Everyone who asks, receives, everyone who seeks, finds, and everyone who knocks has the door open.

"If a child asks for a loaf of bread, parents won't give him a stone instead, and if he asks for a fish, they won't give him a snake. If you, who are evil, know how to give your children good gifts, how much more will God give good gifts to those who ask him?

"Treat others like you want to be treated; this is a summary of everything the Law and the Prophets teach.

"You must enter God's kingdom through the narrow gate. The highway to hell is broad, and the gate is wide, and many will choose that way; but the road to life is narrow, and few people find it.

"Beware of false prophets who come in sheep's clothing but are really wolves that will tear you apart. You can identify them by how they act, just like you can identify a tree by its fruit. A good tree cannot produce bad fruit, and a bad tree cannot produce good fruit. Similarly, a good person does good deeds from a good heart, but an evil person does evil from an evil heart; remember that your heart determines what you are. They will chop down and burn every tree that doesn't produce good fruit.

"Not everyone who sounds religious is godly. They may refer to me as Lord, but they won't enter the kingdom of heaven because they don't obey my Father's commands. On judgment day, they will come to me and say, 'Lord, we prophesied, cast out demons, and performed many miracles in your name.' But I will say, 'I never knew you. Go away, you evildoers.'

"So, why do you call me Lord when you won't obey me? Whoever listens to my teaching and obeys is like a wise person who builds his house with a strong foundation on solid rock. When the rain comes, and the floodwaters rise, it stands firm because of its foundation. But whoever hears my words and doesn't obey them is like a foolish man who builds his house on the sand. When the rain comes, and the floodwaters rise, it will fall with a mighty crash because it has no foundation."

The crowds were amazed at Jesus' teaching because he taught with authority and not like their other religious teachers. Rather than just quoting what other teachers said about God's word, he spoke with authority. So, a great crowd followed him down the mountain, and Jesus went back to Capernaum.

Is this an unattainable goal?

Yes. Jesus even goes so far as to command that we be perfect. Teachings like this show us that we need God's grace and Jesus' death on the cross to justify ourselves before God because we cannot possibly obey all his commands all the time. Just because perfect obedience is unattainable doesn't mean we stop working towards it; following God's teaching draws us closer to him and is evidence of our faith. Jesus meant every word of this teaching and this is what we strive to attain.

CHAPTER SEVENTEEN

GROWING FAME

Matthew 8:5-13; 11:2-30; Luke 7

A Roman officer had a very valuable servant who was sick and dying, so he sent some respected leaders to ask Jesus to come heal his servant. They begged Jesus to come help the man, saying, "If anyone deserves your help, it's him; because he loves the Jews and even built a synagogue for us."

So, Jesus went with these leaders, but before they got to the house, the officer sent some friends to say, "Lord, don't trouble yourself by coming to my home because I'm not worthy of such an honor. In fact, I'm not even worthy to meet you face-to-face; you can heal my servant by just saying the word. I know because I am under authority and have soldiers under me, and when I tell them to come, they come, and if I tell my servants to do something, they do it."

This amazed Jesus; he turned to the crowd and said, "I tell you the truth, I haven't seen such faith in all of Israel. Many will come from the east and west to eat with Abraham, Isaac, and Jacob in the kingdom of heaven, but many Jews will be cast into the outer darkness where there will be weeping and gnashing of teeth."

Then Jesus turned to the officer's friends, "Go home, what you've believed has happened." When the officer's friends got home, they found the slave completely healed.

JESUS RAISES A WIDOW'S SON

Soon afterward, with a huge crowd following him, Jesus went to Nain along with his disciples. As he approached the village, a funeral procession for the only son of a widow was passing by. Jesus had compassion for the woman; he told her not to cry, went over to the coffin, and touched it. The men carrying the coffin stopped and Jesus said, "Young man, get up." The dead boy sat up and began talking to those around him, so Jesus gave him back to his mother.

Fear and awe swept across the crowd, and they all praised God, saying, "A mighty prophet has arisen and we have seen God's hand at work." It wasn't long before news of Jesus' deeds spread all over Judea.

JESUS' MESSAGE TO JOHN THE BAPTIST'S DISCIPLES

Herod Antipas had thrown John the Baptist into prison because John had publicly criticized Herod for marrying his brother's wife, Herodias. John heard about Jesus' deeds while he was in prison, so the Baptist sent some of his disciples to ask Jesus if he was the Messiah. John had identified Jesus as the Messiah, but his arrest made him doubt. John's disciples found Jesus and asked, "John the Baptist wanted us to ask you if you are the Messiah we've been expecting, or should we look for someone else?"

At that time, Jesus cured many people of their diseases, cast out evil spirits, and restored sight to the blind. Jesus said to John's disciples, "Go back and tell John what you have seen and heard, the blind see, the lame walk, lepers are cured, the deaf hear, the dead are raised, and the poor have the good news preached to them. Blessed are those who aren't offended by me." This was a reference to prophecy and told John's followers that Jesus was the Messiah.

As John's disciples were leaving, Jesus talked to the crowd about John, "Did you go out to the desert to see a reed blown around in the wind? Or were you expecting to find a well-dressed man in fancy clothes? People who wear beautiful clothes live in palaces, not in the wilderness. Did you go out to see a prophet? John was more than just a prophet; John is the one Isaiah was talking about when he wrote, 'Look, I'm sending my messenger before you to prepare a way before you.'" Even though John did not fully understand his role, Jesus gave clarity and claimed to be the promised Messiah.

Jesus continued, "I tell you the truth, out of everyone who has ever lived, no one is greater than John the Baptist, but even the most insignificant person in the kingdom of heaven is greater than he is. From the time of John's preaching until now, the kingdom of heaven has forcefully advanced, and violent men attack it. Before John came, all the prophets looked forward to now, and if you are willing to accept it, he is the Elijah that the prophets said would come. Anyone willing to hear should listen to me and understand."

When the people heard this, they all agreed that God's plan was right because John had baptized them. But the Pharisees and experts in the law rejected God's purpose for them because they refused John's baptism.

Who was John the Baptist?

John was the prophet who prepared the people for Jesus' arrival. He was not a reincarnated Elijah, but he served the same function that Elijah did. Elijah was an Old Testament prophet who came to bring reconciliation. The prophet Malachi prophesied that God would send Elijah as a forerunner to the Messiah. John was positionally greater than everyone else because God chose him to do a special task, but he was not better than others.

Then Jesus asked, "How can I describe this generation? They are like a group of children in the marketplace that call out to each other: 'We played happy songs for you and you didn't dance, so we sang sad songs and you didn't cry.' For John the Baptist didn't eat bread or drink wine, and you called him demon-possessed. Then the

Son of Man eats bread and drinks wine, and you call me a glutton, drunkard, and friend of sinners.' But wisdom is shown to be right by the lives of those who listen to it."

Jesus began to denounce the cities where he had done most of his miracles because they had not repented, despite what they had witnessed. "Woe to you, Chorazin and Bethsaida, because if I had done the miracles I did for you in wicked Tyre and Sidon, they would have repented a long time ago. Capernaum, God won't exalt you to heaven; you will end up with the dead. For if Sodom had seen the miracles you have, it would still be here today. It will be much more tolerable for these wicked cities on the Day of Judgment than for those who pretend to be righteous."

> **Who are these cities?**
>
> Sodom was an infamously wicked city that God burned with fire during the time of Abraham. Tyre and Sidon were two cities in the Syro-Phonecian region of the land (just north of Israel) that were famous for their wickedness from the time of the Old Testament prophets through the First Century. Jesus compares the Jewish towns of Chorazin and Bethsaida with these three sinful cities because they had not repented after seeing Jesus' miracles and hearing his teaching.

Jesus prayed, "Father, Lord of heaven and the earth, I praise you because you have hidden these things from the wise and educated, and revealed them to little children. It has pleased you to do it this way.

"My Father has given all things to me. No one knows who I really am except the Father, and no one knows the Father except me and those that I reveal it to."

Then Jesus said to the crowd, "If you are tired and burdened, come to me, and I will give you rest. Take my load and learn from me because I am gentle and humble. You will find rest for your souls because my load is easy and my burden is light."

A WOMAN WASHES JESUS' FEET

Jesus was a popular dinner guest in the early days of his ministry. One of the Pharisees invited Jesus over for dinner; he went and sat down to eat. A sexually immoral woman heard that Jesus was there, so she brought a beautiful jar of expensive perfume. She knelt behind him, started crying, and then began to wet his feet with her tears. Then she wiped up her tears with her hair, kissed his feet, and poured perfume on them. Letting her hair down was a sign of intimacy; the fact that she did this publicly was a sign of worship.

When the Pharisee hosting the meal saw this, he said to himself, "This proves that Jesus is not a prophet, because he would know that this woman who is touching him is a horrible sinner and has slept with many men."

Jesus knew what he was thinking, so he said, "Simon, I have something to say to you."

Simon replied, "Tell me, teacher."

Jesus said, "Two men owed a moneylender money; one owed him 500 days wages, and the other, 50. Neither one of them could pay back the money, so the moneylender forgave both of their debts. Who do you think loved the moneylender more after that?"

Simon answered, "I guess the one who had the larger debt."

Jesus replied, "That's right."

Then he turned to the woman and spoke to Simon, "Do you see this woman? When I came into your house, you didn't offer me water to wash off my feet, but she washed my feet with her tears and hair. You didn't give me a kiss of greeting, but she has not stopped kissing my feet. You didn't give me oil for my head, but she has poured perfume on my feet. Therefore, her many sins have been forgiven, because she loved much; but a person who has only been forgiven a little only loves a little."

Then Jesus said to the woman, "Your sins are forgiven because of your faith; go in peace."

The men at the table said to each other, "Who does he think he is, telling people their sins are forgiven? Only God can forgive sins."

CHAPTER EIGHTEEN

FIRST PUBLIC REJECTION

Matthew 12:22-50; Mark 3:20-35; Luke 8:1-3, 19-21

Not long afterward, Jesus began a tour of the nearby cities and villages to announce the good news about the kingdom of God. He took his twelve disciples with him and some women that he had cured of evil spirits and disease. In the group were Mary Magdalene, from whom he had cast out seven demons; Joanna, the wife of Herod's household manager, Chuza; Susanna; and many others. These women contributed from their resources to help support Jesus and his disciples.

When Jesus returned to the house where he was staying, the crowds began to gather again, begging for teaching and healing. Before long, he and his disciples didn't even have time to eat. When his family heard about this, they tried to bring him home, saying, "He's out of his mind." They didn't believe he was the Messiah and thought he was wasting his time.

A blind, mute, demon-possessed man was brought to Jesus, and he healed the man so that he could both speak and see. The crowd marveled, "Could this be the Son of David, the Messiah?"

But when the Pharisees from Jerusalem heard about Jesus' miracles, they said, "He's possessed by Satan, the prince of demons, and that's where he gets the power to cast out demons."

Jesus knew their thoughts, so he asked, "How can Satan cast out Satan? If a kingdom is at war with itself, how can it stand? If Satan gives me power, then who gives power to your followers when they cast out demons? But if I am casting out demons by the Spirit of God, then the kingdom of God has arrived.

"Let me illustrate my point. You cannot enter a strong man's house and rob him unless you tie him up first. Anyone who isn't helping me is against me and anyone who isn't working with me is against me.

"I tell you the truth, any sin can be forgiven, even blasphemy; but anyone who blasphemes against the Holy Spirit will never be forgiven. Anyone who blasphemes against the Son of Man can be forgiven, but blasphemy against the Holy Spirit won't be forgiven, in this world or the next." He told them this because they were saying he had an evil spirit.

> **What is blasphemy of the Holy Spirit?**
>
> Jesus doesn't explicitly tell us what this means; there is much conjecture about this teaching. The unpardonable sin is a lifestyle of rejecting Christ or ascribing

> the Holy Spirit's work to Satan. Anyone worried that they may have committed the "unpardonable sin" probably hasn't and can still come to Christ.

He continued, "Make a tree good, and its fruit will be good or make a tree bad, and its fruit will be bad because a tree is recognized by its fruit. You brood of vipers! How can you say anything good when you are so evil? People speak what is in their hearts; good people bring forth good things, and evil people bring forth evil. I tell you that on Judgment Day, people will have to give an account for every careless word that they have said. Your words reflect your judgment, and they will either condemn or acquit you."

***

One day some of the Pharisees and teachers of the religious law said to him, "Teacher, we want to see a miracle to prove that you're from God."

Jesus replied, "Only a wicked and faithless generation would ask to see a miraculous sign. The only sign I will show you is that of the prophet Jonah, and just as he was three days and nights in the belly of a huge fish, so the Son of Man will be in the heart of the earth for three days and nights. The people of Nineveh will condemn this generation on Judgment Day because they repented at Jonah's preaching, but something greater than him is here. The Queen of Sheba will also condemn this generation because she came from far away to hear Solomon's wisdom, and now someone greater than Solomon is here, but you refuse to listen to me.

> **Who are Jonah and the Queen of Sheba?**
>
> Jonah was an Old Testament prophet that God sent to warn the wicked Assyrian city of Nineveh to repent. Initially, he ran from God and ended up in the belly of a fish for three days. Jesus used his story as a sign that he would be in the grave for three days. The Queen of Sheba was an Egyptian and Ethiopian queen who visited King Solomon in Israel to see how God had blessed him.

"When an evil spirit leaves a man, it goes into the desert, looking for rest, and does not find it. So, it says, 'I will return to the house I left.' When it arrives, it finds the house unoccupied, swept clean, and put in order. Then the spirit gets seven other spirits that are worse than it is, and they all enter the person and live there. The person is worse off than before; that's how it will be with this evil generation."

As Jesus was speaking to the crowd, his family showed up and wanted to talk to him. They couldn't get to him because of the crowds, so they sent a messenger to let him know that they wanted to see him. But Jesus asked, "Who is my mother, and who are my brothers?" He looked at those sitting around him and said, "These are my mother and my brothers; whoever does God's will is my family."

CHAPTER NINETEEN

SECRETS ABOUT THE KINGDOM IN PARABLES

Matthew 13; Mark 4:1-34; Luke 8:4-18

That same day, Jesus left the house and went down by the lake, where a huge crowd soon gathered. He got into a boat, sat down to teach the crowd, and told many stories like this:

"A farmer went out to plant, and as he scattered his seed, some of it fell on a footpath, and birds came and ate it. Other seed fell on rocky places where there wasn't much soil, and the plants grew quickly until the sun scorched and withered the plants because they didn't have roots. Other seeds fell in the thorns and shot up quickly, but the thorns choked them out, and they didn't produce grain. But some seed fell on fertile soil, and it grew up and produced a crop of 30, 60, or 100 times what was planted. Anyone who is willing to hear should listen and understand."

Later, when Jesus was alone with his twelve disciples, they asked him, "Why do you always speak in parables?"

Jesus answered, "Everything secret will eventually be revealed. God has allowed you to understand the secrets of the kingdom of heaven, but others cannot. Make sure you pay attention to my words because the more open you are to my teaching, the more you will understand it. But those who don't pay attention will never understand. I speak in parables to fulfill Isaiah's prophecy: 'You will hear my words, but you won't understand; you will see what I do, but you won't understand what it means. For these people have hard hearts, they cannot hear with their ears, and they have closed their eyes. Otherwise, they might see with their eyes, hear with their ears, understand with their hearts, and turn to me, and I would heal them.'

> **Why did Jesus not want the people to understand?**
>
> This is a reference to Old Testament prophecies about the Messiah. It's not that Jesus didn't want people to understand, but he was helping his followers comprehend that he was the Messiah and the fulfillment of prophecy.

"But blessed are your eyes because they see and your ears because they hear. Many prophets and godly men wanted access to what you see and hear, but they didn't open their hearts.

"But if you don't understand this story, how will you understand my other stories? This is the explanation of the sower and the seed: The farmer sows God's word and many different people hear it. The seed that falls on the hard ground represents those who hear the good news about the kingdom and don't understand it because the Devil steals it away and prevents them from believing and being saved. The rocky soil represents those who hear the word of God and receive it with joy. But they don't have deep roots, so they wilt under persecution and don't bear any fruit. The thorny ground represents those who accept the good news, but allow the world's worries and cares to keep them from maturing. The good soil represents honest, good-hearted people who truly accept God's word and produce a huge harvest, 30, 60, or even 100 times more than what was planted.

"No one lights a lamp and then puts it under a bowl or a bed; people light a lamp so that they can see. Everything hidden will be made clear and every secret will be brought to light. Anyone that can hear me should listen. Pay attention to what you hear because God will give to you by the same measure that you use, but God will give more. Those who have much will receive more, and those who do not have will lose the little they possess.

"The kingdom of heaven is also like a man who plants seeds in his field. As time goes by, the seed grows because the earth produces crops on its own. The soil produces the grain, first the stalk, then the head, and then the ripened grain; once the grain is ripe, the farmer harvests it.

"The kingdom of heaven is also like a man who plants seeds in his field. But at night, his enemy came and planted weeds among the wheat. When the wheat started to grow, the weeds did too. His servants came to him and said, 'The field you planted with good seeds is now full of weeds.'

"The farmer exclaimed, 'An enemy has done this!'

"'Shall we pull the weeds?' they asked.

"He replied, 'No, you might hurt the wheat. Let them both grow, and when it's harvest time, I'll tell the harvesters to sort it out and burn the weeds.'

"The kingdom of heaven is also like a mustard seed planted in a field. Although it is one of the smallest seeds, it grows into a huge plant where birds can find shelter.

"The kingdom of heaven is like the yeast a woman uses to make bread. She mixes it into a large amount of flour and it permeates every part of the dough."

Jesus told many other stories and said everything to the people in parables. This fulfilled the prophecy that said, "I will speak to you in parables and explain the mysteries hidden since the world's creation." But when he was alone with his disciples, he would explain his parables to them. At one point, they asked him to explain the parable of the weeds in the field.

He answered, "The Son of Man is the farmer who plants the good seed, the field is the world, and the good seed represents the people of the kingdom. The one who planted the weeds is Satan, the weeds are Satan's followers, the harvest is the end of the world, and the harvesters are the angels.

"At the end of the world, it will be just like the harvest. The Son of Man will send his angels to weed out all the evil people and everything that causes sin. Then they will throw it all into the fiery furnace where there will be weeping and gnashing of teeth. After that, the godly will shine like the sun in their Father's kingdom. Anyone who is willing to hear should listen and understand.

"The kingdom of heaven is like a treasure that a man found hidden in a field. After finding it, he hid it again, and then sold everything he had to buy the field.

"The kingdom of heaven is also like a merchant looking for fine pearls. When he found a precious one, he sold everything he owned and bought it.

"The kingdom of heaven is also like a fishing net. When the net is full, the fishermen pull it onto the shore and sort out the good fish from the bad. This is how it will be at the end of the world; the angels will separate the godly from the wicked and throw them into the fire where there will be weeping and gnashing of teeth. Do you understand these things?"

"Yes," they replied.

Then Jesus said, "Every teacher of the religious law who learns about the kingdom of heaven is like a man who brings out of his storehouse both old and new treasures." When he finished these parables, he moved on from there.

CHAPTER TWENTY

CONTINUING OPPOSITION

Matthew 8:18, 23-34; 9:18-34; 13:54-58; Mark 4:35-6:6; Luke 8:22-56

HEALING DEMON-POSSESSED MEN IN GADARENES

One evening Jesus noticed a large crowd growing, so he and his disciples got into a boat and went to the other side of the lake, and many other boats followed them. On the way across, Jesus fell asleep, and while he was sleeping, a storm developed. The wind was fierce and the waves threatened to sink the ship.

The disciples became frantic and woke him up, shouting, "Lord, save us; we're going to drown!"

Jesus woke up and said to the storm, "Be still!" The storm stopped, and there was a great calm, then he turned to his disciples and asked, "Why are you so afraid? Where is your faith?"

The disciples were afraid and stunned, and they said to each other, "Who is this man that even the wind and waves obey him?"

Then they arrived in the land of Gadarenes, across the lake from Galilee. As they were climbing out of the boat, two demon-possessed men ran out to meet them. Homeless and naked, these men had lived in a cemetery for a long time. They were so dangerous that everyone stayed away from that area. People had tried to restrain them with chains and shackles, but they broke them off their wrists. No one was strong enough to control them, and they would roam through the tombs and hills all night, screaming and hitting themselves with stones.

When they got to Jesus, they fell to the ground before him, and one of them shrieked, "Why are you bothering me, Jesus, Son of God? I beg you not to torture us because you have no right to torture us before God's appointed time."

Jesus asked, "What is your name?"

The spirit replied, "Legion, for there are thousands of us." Then the spirits begged him not to send them to the bottomless pit. A large herd of pigs was nearby and the demons said, "If you drive us out, send us into the herd of pigs."

Jesus gave them permission, and the evil spirits went into the pigs. Then the entire herd of 2,000 pigs rushed down the steep bank and drowned in the water.

When the pig herders saw their drowned pigs, they ran to the nearby town and countryside, yelling, and people gathered to see what had happened. The people crowded around Jesus and became frightened when they saw the two formerly demon-possessed men sitting there, fully clothed and sane. The herders told everyone what had happened, and the crowd asked Jesus to leave.

> **Why did Jesus destroy the pigs?**
>
> Some people object to the fact that Jesus allowed the demons to destroy someone else's property, but Jesus did not command the demons to go into the pigs; he allowed them to. Jesus was not responsible for the pigs' destruction; the demons were. Just as God allows us to have free will and commit sin, this does not mean that he is responsible for our actions.

As Jesus was getting back in the boat, the two men begged to go with him. "Go tell your friends what wonderful things God has done for you and how merciful he is," Jesus told them. After that, the two men went through the region of Decapolis, telling the astonishing story of what Jesus had done for them.

JESUS RETURNS TO CAPERNAUM

On the other side of the lake, a large crowd was waiting for Jesus. A local synagogue leader named Jairus fell down and begged Jesus to heal his twelve-year-old daughter, his only child. "She is about to die. Please come and touch her; heal her so she can live!"

Jesus and Jairus went to see the girl, and the crowd followed behind. A woman was in the crowd who had been bleeding for twelve years. She had suffered a great deal through the years and had spent everything she had to pay doctors, but her bleeding had only gotten worse. She'd heard about Jesus and thought to herself, "If I can just touch his clothing, I'll be healed." So, she came up behind him, touched the fringe of his robe, and immediately the bleeding stopped.

Jesus knew that he had healed someone, so he turned around and asked the crowd, "Who touched me?"

His disciples replied, "How can you ask that with such a huge crowd around you?"

But Jesus told them, "No, someone deliberately touched me, and I healed them." So, he kept looking around to see who had done it. When the woman realized that Jesus knew, she fell to her knees and told him what she did. The whole crowd heard about her healing and Jesus said to her, "Daughter, your faith has made you well; go in peace, you are healed."

While he was still speaking to her, messengers came from Jairus' home and said, "The girl is dead, don't bother Jesus anymore."

Jesus ignored them and said to Jairus, "Don't be afraid; just trust me, and she'll be all right." At Jairus' home, he saw the crowd, heard the funeral music, and said, "Stop all this commotion and go away; the girl isn't dead, she's only asleep." But the crowd laughed at him. Jesus finally got the crowd away and entered the house with Peter, James, John, and the girl's parents.

Jesus went in, took the girl by the hand, and said to her in a loud voice, "Get up, my child!" Immediately she got up and walked around, and Jesus told them to give her something to eat. Her parents were overwhelmed. Jesus insisted that they not tell anyone about it, but the report of this miracle spread quickly across the entire countryside.

> **Why did Jesus tell some to spread the news and others to not?**
>
> Jesus told the men in Gadarenes to spread the news because it was not in Israel, and they did not have the same Messianic expectations. He told the Jews in Israel not to spread the story because it was not the right time.

As Jesus was leaving, two blind men followed him, shouting, "Son of David, have mercy on us!"

The men followed him into the house where he was staying and Jesus asked them, "Do you believe I can make you see?"

"Yes, Lord," they replied.

Then he touched their eyes and said, "It will happen because of your faith." Suddenly they could see; Jesus sternly warned them not to tell anyone, but they told everyone about it anyway.

After they left, some people brought him a demon-possessed man who couldn't speak. Jesus cast out the demon, and instantly the man could talk. The crowds were shocked and said, "Nothing like this has ever happened in Israel!"

The Pharisees said, "He casts out demons because the prince of demons gives him power."

***

Jesus left that region and went back to Nazareth with his disciples. The next Sabbath, he taught in the synagogue, and the audience was perplexed. They asked, "Where did he get all his wisdom and the power to perform such miracles? He's just the carpenter, the son of Mary and brother of James, Joseph, Judas, and Simon. All his sisters live with us; what makes him so great?" They were offended and refused to trust him.

"A prophet is honored everywhere except in his hometown and with his family," Jesus told them. Because of their disbelief, he could only heal a few sick people but couldn't do much more; and he wondered at their lack of faith.

CHAPTER TWENTY-ONE

FINAL GALILEAN CAMPAIGN

Matthew 9:35-11:1; Mark 6:6-13, 30; Luke 9:1-6, 10

Jesus traveled through all the cities and villages of that area, teaching in the synagogues, announcing the good news about the kingdom, and healing every disease and sickness. He felt great compassion for the crowds that followed him, seeing that they were helpless and had no one to show them where to go. He told his disciples, "The harvest is great, but there aren't many workers, ask the Lord of the harvest to send more workers into the fields."

Jesus gave them the power and authority to cast out demons and heal every disease and illness. He sent them out in pairs and told them, "Don't go to the Gentiles or the Samaritans but only to the lost sheep of Israel. Tell them that the kingdom of heaven is near, heal the sick, raise the dead, cure those with leprosy, and cast out demons. Give to others, just as you have freely received.

"Don't take anything with you on the journey; don't carry a traveler's bag, food, money, extra clothes, or even a walking stick. Don't hesitate to accept hospitality because workers deserve their wages. Whenever you enter a town, search for a worthy home, and stay there until you leave for the next town. When you enter a house, give it your blessing, and if it is a worthy home, let it stand; if it is unworthy, take the blessing back. If a village doesn't welcome you or listen to you, shake the dust off your feet as you leave that place as a testimony against them. I tell you the truth, Sodom and Gomorrah will face less judgment than that city.

"I am sending you out like sheep among wolves, so be as shrewd as snakes and as innocent as doves. Be on your guard against men, because they will hand you over to the courts and beat you in their synagogues. You will stand trial before government officials because you are my followers and this will be your opportunity to tell the world about me. But don't worry about what you will say in your defense; the Holy Spirit will give you the words to say and will speak through you.

"Family members will turn against each other and turn each other over to be killed. Everyone will hate you because of your allegiance with me, but those who endure to the end will be saved. When one town persecutes you, run to the next. I tell you the truth, the Son of Man will come before you finish going through all the towns of Israel.

"A student is not above his teacher and a servant is not greater than his master. It is enough for the student to become like his teacher and the servant like his master. If they call the master of the house the prince of demons, they will also slander the members of the house. But don't be afraid when they threaten you. A time is coming when everything will be revealed and all secrets will become public. What I tell you in the dark, talk about in the light; what I whisper in your ear, shout from the housetops.

"Don't be afraid of those who can kill you but cannot kill your soul. Instead, fear God who can destroy your body and soul in hell. They sell sparrows for less than a penny, and none of them fall to the ground without your Father knowing about it; you are worth more than a whole flock of sparrows, so don't be afraid. God even knows how many hairs are on your head.

"If anyone publicly acknowledges me here on earth, I will acknowledge that person before my Father in heaven. But if someone disowns me here on earth, I will disown that person before my Father in heaven.

"Don't think that I came to bring peace on earth because I have come to bring a sword. I have come to turn a man against his father, a daughter against her mother, and a daughter-in-law against her mother-in-law. Your enemies will be members of your own family. If you love anyone more than you love me, you aren't worthy of being my disciple. If you don't take up your cross and follow me, you are not worthy of being my disciple. Those who try to keep their life will lose it, and those who lose their lives for my sake will find it.

> **Does Jesus want us to hate our families?**
>
> No. But Jesus wants the highest level of commitment to him. He wants us to love him so much that any other allegiance seems like rejection. Family is important, but if it keeps us from following God, then we must reject them.

"Anyone who welcomes you is welcoming me and whoever welcomes me is welcoming the Father who sent me. If you welcome a prophet as a spokesperson for God, you will receive a prophet's reward, and if you welcome a righteous man, you will receive a righteous man's reward. Also, if anyone gives a cup of cold water to someone because he is my disciple, he will receive his reward."

When Jesus had finished giving these instructions to his twelve disciples, they went off teaching and preaching throughout the country, telling people to turn from their sins. They cast out many demons and healed many sick people, anointing them with olive oil. After they finished their work, they came back and told Jesus what they had done and taught.

CHAPTER TWENTY-TWO

DEATH OF JOHN THE BAPTIST

Matthew 14:3-12; Mark 6:17-29

Around this time, Herod Antipas sent soldiers to arrest and imprison John at his wife Herodias' request. She had been married to Herod's brother Philip but now was married to Herod. John told Herod that his marriage was illegal, and that made Herodias mad. She wanted to kill John but couldn't do anything without her husband's approval. Herod knew John was a good man and was afraid of a riot, so he protected him. Herod even liked to talk to John, although it always disturbed him.

Herodias' chance came on Herod's birthday when he threw a banquet for his government officials, military commanders, and the leading citizens of Galilee. Herodias' daughter, Salome, danced for the men and greatly pleased them, so Herod said to her, "Ask me for anything you want, and I'll give it to you. Whatever you want, even up to half my kingdom."

The girl went out to ask her mother, "What should I ask for?"

Her mother answered, "Ask for John the Baptist's head on a tray!"

So, the girl ran back to Herod and said, "I want the head of John the Baptist on a tray, right now!"

Her request distressed Herod, but he didn't want to break his promise in front of his dinner guests. So, he sent an executioner to bring him John's head. The soldier cut off the Baptist's head and brought it to the girl on a tray; then, she took it to her mother. When John's disciples heard what had happened, they took his body, buried it, and then told Jesus what had happened.

After John's death, Herod kept hearing more about Jesus because everyone was talking about him. These reports troubled Herod because some people said that John the Baptist had come back to life, and that was why he could do such miracles. Others said he was the prophet Elijah or another one of the ancient prophets raised from the dead. Herod was very curious because he had killed John, so he kept trying to see Jesus.

CHAPTER TWENTY-THREE

THE BREAD OF LIFE

Matthew 14:13-36; Mark 6:31-56; Luke 9:10-17; John 6

John's death grieved Jesus and when he saw that a huge crowd was gathering, he said, "Let's get away and rest for a while." So many people were gathering around him that Jesus and his disciples didn't even have time to eat, so they took a boat across the Sea of Galilee towards Bethsaida, looking for a remote area to be alone.

But many people saw them leave and ran ahead to meet them as they landed. A vast crowd gathered as Jesus got out of the boat. Despite his grief, he had compassion for them because they were like sheep without a shepherd. So, he welcomed them, healed their sick, and taught them many things about the kingdom of God.

Then Jesus went up into the hills and sat down with his disciples around him. He saw a great crowd of people coming up the hill, looking for him, so he turned to Philip and asked, "Where can we buy bread to feed all these people?" Jesus was testing Philip, although he already knew what he was going to do.

Philip replied, "It would take about eight months' wages to feed them!"

Then the disciples said, "We're far from town and it's getting late. Send the crowds away so they can go find food and lodging because there is nothing out here in this desolate place."

"They don't need to go away; you feed them," Jesus replied.

"Impossible!" they exclaimed.

"Go find out how much food you have."

They came back and reported, "All we have is a young boy with five barley loaves and two fish. But what good is that with so many people?"

Jesus answered, "Bring them here." Then he had the people sit down in large groups, took the bread, and blessed it. He broke the loaves and fish, gave some to each disciple, and had them hand it out to the people. Everyone ate as much as they wanted, and the disciples still picked up twelve baskets full of leftovers. About 5,000 men and many women and children (around 20,000 total) ate from the five loaves and two fish.

When the crowd realized what had happened, they exclaimed, "He must be the Prophet we've been expecting." Jesus realized that the people wanted to make him king by force, so he made his disciples get back into the boat and go to Bethsaida while he calmed the crowd and sent them home. Afterward, Jesus went up into the hills to pray. He was alone as night came.

PETER WALKS ON WATER

Three or four miles out in the middle of the lake, the disciples were in serious trouble, struggling against the wind and waves. Jesus walked out to them around three in the morning. Jesus started to walk past them, but when they saw him walking on the water, they thought he was a ghost. They were all terrified, but he said to them, "Don't be afraid, it's me."

Peter called out to him, "Lord, if it's really you, tell me to walk out to you."

"Come then," Jesus replied.

Peter climbed out of the boat and walked on the water toward Jesus. But when he saw the wind and the waves, he got scared and started to sink. "Save me, Lord!" he shouted.

Instantly, Jesus reached out and grabbed him. "Where's your faith?" he asked. "Why did you doubt me?" They both climbed back in the boat, the wind stopped, and they were immediately at their destination.

The disciples worshiped Jesus, saying, "You really are the Son of God." They were deeply moved because their hearts had been hard, and they had not understood what was happening with the fish and the loaves feeding all those people.

They anchored the boat at Gennesaret and climbed out. People there recognized Jesus at once, and soon the news of his arrival spread through the entire countryside. Everywhere he went, people brought him the sick for healing. The suffering begged him to let them touch the fringe of his robe, and everyone who touched it was healed.

The next morning, a crowd gathered across the lake, waiting to see Jesus. They knew that his disciples had left before him, and they were hoping to see him again. Several boats from Tiberius had come to see him as well. When they realized that he was not there, they got into boats and went to Capernaum to look for him. Upon finding him they asked him, "Teacher, how did you get here?"

Jesus replied, "You don't want to be with me because of the miracle; you just want to be with me because I fed you. But don't be so worried about perishable food; seek the eternal food that I will give you. That's why God has sent me."

The crowd asked, "What does God want us to do?"

Jesus answered, "God wants you to believe in me as the One he sent."

The crowd replied, "If you want us to believe in you, show us a sign. Our ancestors ate manna in the wilderness, so what will you do?"

"I tell you the truth," Jesus said. "Moses didn't give them bread from heaven; my Father did. Now he has sent the true bread of heaven down and he gives life to the whole world."

The crowd responded, "We want that bread for our lives."

"I am the bread of life," Jesus declared. "Whoever comes to me will never be hungry, and whoever believes in me will never be thirsty. But you haven't trusted me even though you have seen me. I will never turn away anyone my Father sends me. I have come down from heaven to do God's will, not mine. His will is that everyone who believes in me will have eternal life, and I will not lose any of them but will raise them up on the last day."

People began to say to each other, "Isn't this Joseph's son, Jesus? We know his parents, so how can he say he came from heaven?"

Jesus answered, "Stop grumbling. No one can come to me unless the Father who sent me calls him, and I will raise him up on the last day. Just like Scripture says, 'They will all be taught by God.' Everyone who listens to and learns from God comes to me. No one has seen the Father except me. I tell you the truth, whoever believes has eternal life. I am the bread of life; your ancestors ate manna in the wilderness and died. But here is the bread from heaven, and anyone who eats it will not die. I am the living bread from heaven; anyone who eats this bread will live forever. This bread is my flesh, and I will give my life for the world."

Arguments broke out about what he meant, and the people asked, "How can he give us his flesh to eat?"

Jesus said to them, "I tell you the truth, unless you eat the Son of Man's flesh and drink his blood, you cannot have eternal life. If you do these things, I will raise you up on the last day. My flesh is real food, and my blood is true drink; whoever eats and drinks them remains in me, and I in him. God gives me life, and I will give life to those who feed on me. Your ancestors ate manna and died, but whoever eats this bread will live forever."

> **What did Jesus mean by eating his flesh and drinking his blood?**
>
> This does not mean we must literally eat his flesh; Jesus was using figurative language, just as when he says that he is the door, he does not mean he is made of wood and has hinges. He meant that the people must partake in his life and death and live their lives for his glory rather than their own.

Jesus said these things in the synagogue, and his disciples began to say, "This is a difficult teaching; who can understand it?"

Jesus knew that his disciples were complaining, so he asked, "Does this offend you? What will you think when you see the Son of Man return to heaven? The Spirit gives life, but the flesh accomplishes nothing. My words are spirit, and they give life, but some of you don't believe." Jesus knew from the beginning who would not believe and who would betray him. From this time, many of his disciples besides the Twelve stopped following him.

Jesus turned to the Twelve and asked, "Do you want to leave too?"

Peter answered, "Where would we go; you're the only one with eternal life. We trust you and know you are the Messiah, the Holy One of God."

Jesus replied, "I chose twelve of you, but one of you is a devil." He was talking about Judas Iscariot, who would later betray him. Even though Jesus knew this about Judas, he kept him close by and loved him as much as his other followers.

After this, Jesus moved around in Galilee, staying away from Judea because the Jews wanted to kill him.

CHAPTER TWENTY-FOUR

THE LEAVEN OF THE RELIGIOUS TEACHERS

Matthew 15-16:12; Mark 7:1-8:26; John 7:1

Some Pharisees and teachers of the religious law traveled from Jerusalem to confront Jesus. They noticed that some of Jesus' disciples didn't follow the Jewish handwashing ritual before they ate. So, they asked Jesus, "Why don't your disciples follow our customs and eat without first washing their hands?"

Jesus replied, "Isaiah was prophesying about you hypocrites when he said, 'These people honor me with their words, but their hearts are far away. Their worship is a joke, and their teachings are just made-up rules.' You have ignored God's commands and substituted your own traditions.

"You break God's commands to observe your own traditions. For example, Moses said, 'Honor your father and mother' and, 'Anyone who curses his father or mother must be put to death.' But you say that if a man tells his parents, 'I cannot help you because I have dedicated what I could have given you to God.' You allow him to dishonor his needy parents. Thus, you nullify the direct commandment of God to protect your tradition."

> **Clean hands and the Law**
>
> The Jews, especially the Pharisees, did not eat until they had poured water over their cupped hands, as required by their ancient traditions. They also didn't eat anything from the market unless it had been washed. They observed other traditions, such as ceremonial washing of cups, pitchers, and kettles. The washing ceremony was a part of the meticulous rules the Jews made after their captivity under the Babylonians. These were a part of an oral tradition based on an interpretation of Moses' Law until they were recorded in 200 A.D. as the Mishnah (Jewish teachings). Even though this wasn't Scripture, the Jews held it in the highest regard.
>
> Another tradition was that irresponsible children could "dedicate" money to the temple so that they would not have to give it to their parents. However, this dedication did not mean that they had to give it to the temple. This practice was an example of the Pharisees following the letter but not the spirit of the Law.

Then Jesus said to the whole crowd, "Listen and understand, you are not defiled by what you eat; you are defiled by what you say and do."

A little later, his disciples came to him and asked, "Do you realize that you offended the Pharisees?"

Jesus replied, "Every plant my heavenly Father did not plant will be pulled up by the roots. Ignore those blind guides because if a blind man leads another blind man, both will fall into a pit."

Then Jesus went into a house to get away from the crowds, and Peter said, "Explain what you meant when you said people aren't defiled by what they eat."

Jesus replied, "Don't you understand either? Nothing from the outside can make you unclean because it doesn't go to your heart; it goes to your stomach and then out of your body. What comes out of you is what makes you unclean. From men's hearts come evil thoughts, murder, adultery, sexual immorality, theft, lies, greed, wickedness, deceit, lewdness, envy, slander, arrogance, and foolishness. These are the things that make you unclean, but eating with unwashed hands could never make you unclean." By saying this, Jesus declared that all foods are acceptable to eat.

MINISTRY IN TYRE AND SIDON

Heading north to the region of Tyre and Sidon, Jesus tried to keep his arrival secret, but the news spread quickly. A Gentile woman from that region came to him, pleading, "My Lord, Son of David, have mercy on me! My daughter suffers greatly at the hands of a demon."

Jesus ignored her. "Tell her to leave us alone; she's bothering us," the disciples urged.

The woman was a Syro-Phoenician Gentile, so he said to her, "I was only sent to the lost sheep of Israel."

But the woman knelt before him and said, "Lord, help me!"

Jesus replied, "It's not right to take the children's bread and throw it to the dogs."

"Yes, Lord," she replied, "but even dogs can eat the crumbs that fall from the children's plates."

Moved by her faith, Jesus granted her request. Her daughter was instantly healed; when the woman arrived home, her daughter was lying quietly in bed, and the demon was gone.

> **Why did Jesus call this woman a dog?**
>
> Some have interpreted this statement to mean that women are inferior to men. But this was a statement reflecting race relations of the time. Jesus had first come to Israel and his followers would eventually spread the gospel to all people.

JESUS HEALS A DEAF MAN

Jesus left Tyre and went through Sidon, then returned to the Sea of Galilee and Decapolis. Upon his arrival, he climbed a hill and sat down. The crowd brought Jesus a deaf man who could barely talk and begged him to heal the man. Jesus led him away from the crowd and put his fingers into the man's ears. Then he spit on his fingers and touched the man's tongue. Jesus looked up to heaven, sighed, and said, "Be opened." Instantly the man could hear and speak.

The crowd surged up with lame, blind, disabled, mute, and other sufferers, and he healed them all. When the crowd saw these people healed, they were impressed, praising the God of Israel.

Jesus asked the crowd not to tell anyone, but the more he told them not to, the more they spread the news. They kept saying, "He does everything well, he even makes the deaf hear and the mute speak."

FEEDING THE 4,000

Around this time, another large crowd gathered and they ran out of food again. Jesus called his disciples to him and said, "I feel sorry for these people because they've been with me for three days and haven't eaten anything. But if I send them home without feeding them, they will faint on the way because some of them have come from far away."

His disciples asked, "Where will we find enough food for them out here in the wilderness?" Even though they had seen Jesus feed 5,000 men, they still didn't understand his power.

"How many loaves of bread do you have?" Jesus asked.

"Seven, and a few small fish," they replied. Jesus asked all the people to sit down on the ground. He took the loaves and fish, thanked God for them, and began distributing food to his disciples, who gave it to the crowd.

Everyone ate until they were full and there were still seven large baskets of leftovers. That day, they fed about 4,000 men plus women and children (around 16,000 total).

After eating, Jesus sent the people home and he took a boat to Magadan with his disciples.

***

The Pharisees heard about Jesus feeding the people and came to argue with him. They were testing him, demanding a miraculous sign to prove that he was from heaven.

Jesus sighed deeply and replied, "You know the saying, 'Red sky at night, sailor's delight; red sky at morning, sailor's take warning.' You know how to interpret the weather, but you cannot interpret the signs of the times. Only a wicked and faithless generation would ask for a miraculous sign, but the only sign I'll give you is the sign of the prophet Jonah." Jesus got back into the boat and crossed the lake again.

The disciples forgot to bring food, and there was only one loaf of bread in the boat. As they crossed the lake, Jesus warned them, "Beware of the yeast of the Pharisees, Sadducees, and Herod."

The disciples decided that he said this because they hadn't brought any food. But Jesus knew their thoughts and said, "Where's your faith? Why are you worried about food? Are your hearts too hard to learn or understand? You have eyes but cannot see and have ears but cannot hear. When I fed the 5,000 with five loaves of bread, how many baskets of leftovers did you pick up?"

"Twelve," they answered.

Jesus continued, "How many did you pick up when I fed the 4,000 with seven loaves?"

"Seven," they replied.

"Don't you understand?" he asked. "How can you even think I was talking about food? Beware of the yeast of the Pharisees, Sadducees, and Herod."

Finally, the disciples understood that he was talking about false teaching and not food.

When they came to Bethsaida, some people led a blind man up and begged Jesus to touch him. Jesus took the blind man by the hand and led him outside the village. He put spit on the man's eyes, laid his hands on him, and asked, "Can you see anything?"

The man looked up and said, "I see people, but they look like trees walking around."

Jesus put his hands over his eyes again and then the man could see everything clearly. Then Jesus sent him home and said, "Don't go into the village."

CHAPTER TWENTY-FIVE

THE GREAT CONFESSION AND THE TRANSFIGURATION
Matthew 16:13-17:13; Mark 8:27-9:13; Luke 9:18-36

On their way to the villages of Caesarea Philippi, Jesus asked, "Who do people say I am?"

The disciples replied, "Some say you are John the Baptist, some say Elijah, and some say you're one of the other ancient prophets risen from the dead."

Then Jesus asked, "But who do you say I am?"

Peter answered, "You are the Messiah, the Son of the living God."

Jesus replied, "God bless you Peter, because my heavenly Father revealed this to you. I will build my church upon the rock of your confession and the gates of hell will not overcome it. I will give you the keys of the kingdom of heaven; whatever you lock up here on earth will be locked up in heaven, and whatever you open here on earth will be opened in heaven." Then Jesus warned them not to tell anyone he was the Messiah because it was not yet time.

> **Timing**
>
> Jesus told his disciples not to tell people that he was the Christ because the timing was wrong. At times, he may have wanted to keep the crowds small. Other times he may not have wanted the Jews to get the wrong idea because they thought that the Messiah would be a political leader and military conqueror. Finally, Jesus did tell them to spread the word after his resurrection.

From that point on, Jesus began to tell them that the Son of Man must go to Jerusalem, suffer many terrible things, and be rejected by the leaders, priests, and teachers of the religious law. He told them that he would be killed and that he would resurrect on the third day. Jesus talked openly about these things, but Peter took him aside and told him not to say such things.

Jesus turned and looked at his disciples and then sternly told Peter, "Get behind me, Satan! You are a stumbling block; you're only seeing things from an earthly point of view and not God's."

> **Why did Jesus call Peter 'Satan'?**
>
> Peter's attempt to get Jesus to avoid the cross was the same as Satan's temptation to take power in an inappropriate manner when Satan tempted him in the wilderness. Jesus was speaking to Satan, who was using Peter's words as a

> temptation, not Peter. Satan was using Peter as a tool, and we must remember that Satan can tempt in just about any situation. We must deny our interests if they conflict with following Jesus.
>
> It is also interesting to note that Peter had a significant failure only moments after making the great confession. Often our most significant failures will come on the heels of our greatest successes. We always need to make sure to keep our guard up against a growing ego.

Then Jesus called the crowds to him and said, "If any of you wants to follow me, you must deny yourself and take up your cross. Whoever wants to save his life will lose it, and whoever loses his life for me and the gospel will save it. What good is it to gain the whole world and lose your soul? Nothing is as valuable as your soul. If anyone is ashamed of me and my message, then the Son of Man will be ashamed of him when he comes with the angels and his Father's glory to judge people according to their deeds. I tell you the truth, some of you who are standing here will not die before you see the kingdom of God arrive with great power."

THE TRANSFIGURATION

A week later, Jesus took Peter, James, and John to a mountain to pray. As Jesus was praying, his appearance changed so that his face shone like the sun, and his clothes became whiter than any natural process could make them. Just then, Moses and Elijah appeared in glory and began talking to Jesus. They talked about how he was on his way to die in Jerusalem to fulfill God's plan.

Peter, James, and John had fallen asleep while Jesus prayed, but now they were wide awake. As Moses and Elijah were starting to leave, Peter blurted out, "Master, it's good that we're here. Let us put up three shelters, one for you, one for Moses, and one for Elijah."

> ### Who are Moses and Elijah?
>
> Moses and Elijah are two central figures from the Old Testament. Moses represents the Law, and Elijah represents the Prophets. Together, the two represent all Old Testament Scripture.

A cloud appeared and covered them, and they were terrified. A voice from the cloud said, "This is my beloved son whom I have chosen and I am pleased with him; listen to him."

The disciples were terrified and they fell face down on the ground. But Jesus came over, touched them, and said, "Get up and don't be afraid." Then when they looked around, Moses and Elijah were gone.

As they went down the mountain, Jesus told his disciples not to tell anyone what they had seen until after he had risen from the dead. So, they kept it to themselves, but they often spoke of what Jesus meant when he talked about rising from the dead.

They began asking him, "Why do the teachers of the religious law say that Elijah must return before the Messiah comes?"

Jesus replied, "Elijah comes to set everything in order. But I tell you, Elijah has already come, and they treated him as they wished. In the same way, I will suffer and be rejected." Then the disciples understood that he was talking about John the Baptist.

CHAPTER TWENTY-SIX

RESPONSIBILITY TO OTHERS

Matthew 17:14-18:35; Mark 9:14-50; Luke 9:37-50

When they got to the foot of the mountain, they found a great crowd surrounding the other disciples, and some of the teachers of the religious law were arguing with them. Jesus walked up and asked, "What's all this arguing about?" The crowd surged around him with joy.

One man knelt before Jesus and said, "Teacher, my son is possessed by an evil spirit that won't let him talk. Whenever it seizes him, it throws him to the ground; he foams at the mouth, grinds his teeth, and goes rigid. It hardly ever leaves him alone and is always hurting him. So, I brought my son for you to heal him; your disciples tried, but they couldn't cast out the demon."

Jesus rebuked them, "You stubborn, faithless people, how long will I have to stay with you and put up with you? Bring the boy to me."

When they brought the boy to Jesus, the evil spirit threw the boy into a violent convulsion, and he fell to the ground, writhing and foaming at the mouth. Jesus asked the boy's father, "How long has this been happening?"

The man replied, "Since he was very small. The demon has often tried to kill him by throwing him into the fire or water. Have mercy on us and do something if you can."

"What do you mean if I can?" Jesus asked. "Everything is possible for those who believe."

Instantly, the father exclaimed, "I do believe, but help me not to doubt."

When Jesus saw the crowd gathering around, he rebuked the evil spirit and said, "Come out of him, you deaf and mute spirit, and never bother him again."

The demon shrieked, threw the boy into another convulsion, and left him. The boy lay motionless and appeared to be dead. But Jesus took him by the hand, helped him to his feet, and healed the boy.

Jesus went back inside and his disciples asked him, "Why couldn't we drive out the demon?"

He replied, "Because you lack faith. If you had faith as small as a mustard seed you could tell a mountain to move and it would. Nothing is impossible with faith. Plus, this kind of demon only comes out through prayer."

Then they left that region and traveled through Galilee. Jesus tried to avoid the crowds to spend more time with his disciples. He said to them, "Pay attention! I will be betrayed and killed, but I will rise again on the third day." What he was saying was incomprehensible, but they were afraid to ask for clarification.

> **How were the disciples so dense?**
>
> It seems like Jesus was very clear that he would die and rise again, but we must remember that they believed that the Messiah would be a conquering king. It took a long time to undo their misconceptions about the Messiah and what Jesus was accomplishing.

JESUS PAYS HIS TAXES

When they got to Capernaum, tax collectors came to Peter and asked, "Does your teacher pay the two-drachma temple tax?"

Peter answered impulsively, "Of course he does." Then Peter went to ask Jesus about it.

Before Peter had a chance to say anything, Jesus asked him, "Do kings tax their own sons or others?"

"Others," Peter answered.

Then Jesus said, "Ah, so the sons are exempt. But we don't want to offend them, so go down to the lake and throw out your fishing line. Open the mouth of the first fish you catch, and you will find a four-drachma coin. Take it and pay both our taxes."

INSTRUCTION IN CAPERNAUM

As Jesus and his disciples were settling into the house they would stay in while they were in Capernaum, Jesus asked, "What were you discussing on the way here?" Embarrassed, they didn't answer because they had been arguing about which of them was the greatest disciple. He sat down and gathered his disciples around him. He said, "Anyone who wants to be first must be the last and the servant of all."

He called a child over, took him in his arms, and said, "I tell you the truth, unless you repent and become like little children, you will never make it into the kingdom of heaven. Anyone who welcomes a child like this in my name welcomes me, and anyone who welcomes me welcomes the one who sent me. Whoever is least among you is the greatest."

A little while later, John came to him and said, "Teacher, we saw a man casting out demons in your name. We tried to stop him because he's not in our group."

But Jesus said, "Don't stop him because no one can do a miracle in my name and then say something bad about me. Anyone who is not against you is on your side. I tell you the truth, anyone who gives you a cup of cold water because you are my followers will receive a reward.

"But if anyone causes one of these little ones that believes in me to sin, it would be better for that person to be thrown into the sea with a large millstone tied around his neck. Beware that you don't look down on the little ones because, in heaven, their angels are always in God's presence. Woe to the world because of its stumbling blocks. Such things will happen, but woe to whoever causes the stumbling block.

"If your hand or foot causes you to sin, cut it off because it's better to enter life crippled than to go to hell. If your eye causes you to sin, gouge it out because it is better to enter the kingdom of God with one eye than to have two eyes and be thrown into hell 'where the worm does not die and the fire never goes out.'

> **Did Jesus advocate self-mutilation?**
>
> No. We need to be aware of our weaknesses because Satan is very aware of them. If something causes us to stumble, we need to cut it off, no matter how painful it is, so that we won't fall into greater temptation. For example, if we always end up getting into trouble when we hang out with certain friends, it is better to cut them off than maintain relationships that pull us away from God. If we were to take this literally, we would end up cutting off almost every single body part.

"Everyone will be purified with fire. Salt is good for seasoning, but you can't make it salty again if it loses its flavor. Be like salt amongst each other and live in peace.

"If your brother sins against you, go and show him his fault privately. If he listens to you, you have won your brother. But if he refuses to listen, take one or two others with you so that everything may be established by the testimony of two or three witnesses. If he still refuses to listen, tell the whole church; if he refuses to listen to the church, shun him like a pagan or a tax collector.

"I tell you the truth, whatever you bind on earth will be bound in heaven, and whatever you loose on earth will be loosed in heaven. If two of you on earth agree about anything and ask my Father in heaven to do it for you, he will do it. For where two or three come together in my name, I am there with them."

Then Peter came to Jesus and asked, "Lord, how many times should I forgive someone who sins against me? Seven times?" The day's common teaching was to forgive someone three times, but Peter thought that doubling that and adding one would sound impressive.

Jesus answered, "Not seven times, but seventy times seven." Jesus did not mean keeping track until the 490th time, but that there should be no limit to forgiveness.

> **Forgiveness and access**
>
> Jesus teaches us that we need to forgive without limit, but that doesn't mean allowing the same access. If someone violates our trust, we can forgive and restore the relationship, but we do not need to put ourselves in the same position to be hurt again. For example, a business owner may forgive an employee who is stealing from the company, but it does not mean she still has to employ the offending worker.

Jesus continued, "The kingdom of heaven is like a king who wanted to settle accounts with those who borrowed from him. As the settlement began, a servant who owed him millions of dollars came before the king. The servant could not repay his debt, so the king ordered that the servant, his family, and all they owned should be sold to repay the debt.

"The servant fell to his knees before the king and begged him to be patient. The king took pity on him, canceled the debt, and let the servant go.

"But when the servant went out, he found a fellow servant who owed him a few dollars. He grabbed this man and began to choke him, demanding that he pay back what he owed.

"His fellow servant begged him to be patient, but he refused. Instead, he had the man thrown in prison until he could repay his debt. When the other servants saw the situation, they were upset, and they told the king what had happened.

"The king called in the man and said, 'You wicked servant, I canceled all your debt because you begged me to. Shouldn't you have mercy on your fellow servant, just like I had mercy on you?' Then the angry king sent the man to prison to be tortured until he should pay back his debt.

"This is how my heavenly Father will treat you unless you forgive your brother from your heart."

CHAPTER TWENTY-SEVEN

THE FEAST OF TABERNACLES

Matthew 8:19-22; Luke 9:51-62; John 7:2-53

When it was time for the Jewish Feast of Tabernacles, Jesus' brothers urged him to go to Judea for the celebration, saying, "You should go to Judea, so your disciples can see your miracles. You cannot become a public figure if you stay hidden like this. Since you do such wonderful things, you should prove it to the world." They said this because they didn't believe he was the Messiah.

Jesus replied, "Although it's the right time for you, it's not the right time for me. The world cannot hate you, but it hates me because I call it evil. You go ahead to the feast, but it's not my time yet." Jesus stayed in Galilee while his brothers went to Judea.

Once the others had gone, Jesus left for Jerusalem in secret. On the way, he sent messengers ahead to a Samaritan village to prepare for his arrival. But the villagers turned the messengers away because Jesus' men were on their way to Jerusalem. When James and John heard about this, they asked, "Should we call fire down from heaven to burn them up?" But Jesus rebuked them, and they went on to the next village.

As they walked along the road, one of the teachers of religious law said to him, "Teacher, I will follow you wherever you go."

Jesus replied, "Foxes have dens to live in, and birds have nests, but the Son of Man has no place to lay his head."

He said to another man, "Come be my disciple."

The man said, "Let me bury my father first."

Jesus said, "Let the dead bury their own dead, but you go preach the coming of the kingdom of God."

Another person said, "I will follow you, but first, let me say goodbye to my family."

But Jesus told him, "Anyone who puts a hand to the plow and then looks back is unworthy to serve in the kingdom of God."

> **What did Jesus mean?**
>
> These are some difficult statements that Jesus said to people who seemed to want to follow him, but we must remember that he knew their hearts and that they were not ready to commit to follow him. The first man wanted to follow, but Jesus wanted him to know that following would not be a comfortable life and that it would require sacrifice.

> The second man asked to bury his father before he followed Jesus, but, likely, his father was still alive, and the man wanted to wait to follow until a significant life event happened first. Currently, we may substitute a different life event that we are waiting for before committing to follow (graduation, getting a job, having kids, retirement, etc.). Jesus wants our faith now, not when it is convenient for us.
>
> The third man asked to say goodbye to his family, and that seems like a reasonable request. But Jesus answers with a proverb that means that someone beginning a new venture must stay focused and not look back on the past if he wants to be successful.
>
> In all three of these situations, Jesus was questioning their level of commitment. He wanted his followers to know what following him entailed and not change their minds once they realized what they needed to sacrifice.

***

The Jewish leaders tried to find Jesus at the festival; everyone was asking where he was. There was a lot of talk about him, but no one wanted to say anything publicly because they were afraid of the people's divided opinions. Some people said he was a good man, while others said he was deceiving the people.

About halfway through the feast, Jesus began teaching in the temple courts. The Jews were impressed and asked, "How does he know so much without having studied?"

Jesus answered, "My teaching is not my own, but it comes from the one who sent me. If anyone does God's will, he will find out if my teaching is from God or not. Those who speak on their own are looking for praise, but those who seek the glory of the one who sent them are full of truth. Moses gave you the Law, but none of you obey it, so why are you trying to kill me?"

The crowd responded, "Are you crazy? Who's trying to kill you?"

Jesus replied, "I did one miracle and you're all astonished. Moses gave you circumcision, although it really came from Abraham. If you can circumcise a child on the Sabbath so you don't break the Law, why do you condemn me for making an entire man well on the Sabbath? Stop judging by appearances and make a legitimate judgment."

Some of the people who lived in Jerusalem said to each other, "Isn't this the man they're trying to kill? Here he is, speaking in public, and nobody's saying anything to him. Have the authorities decided that he is the Messiah? But that's not possible because no one will know where the Messiah comes from, and we know where he's from."

Jesus was still teaching in the temple courts and he cried out, "You know me, and where I'm from, but I represent one you don't know. I know him and I know that he is true because he sent me."

The authorities tried to arrest him, but no one laid a hand on him; it wasn't his time yet. People in the crowd began saying that the Messiah would not do any more miraculous signs than Jesus was.

The Pharisees heard the crowd whispering so they sent the temple guards to arrest him. Jesus said to them, "I am with you for only a little while longer, and then I will go back to the One who sent me. You will look for me, but won't be able to find me because you cannot go where I am going."

The Jews were puzzled and said to each other, "Where is he going that we won't be able to find him? Is he going to leave Israel and teach the Greeks? What does he mean that we won't find him and that we cannot go where he is going?"

***

On the last day of the festival, Jesus stood up and shouted, "If anyone is thirsty, come and drink. Whoever believes in me will have rivers of living water flowing from within, just as the Scriptures say." By rivers of living water, Jesus meant the Holy Spirit, whom he would give to his followers after his glorification.

Some said, "This man is the Prophet who comes before the Messiah." Others maintained he was the Messiah. Still others said, "He can't be the Messiah because he's from Galilee. The Scriptures clearly say that the Messiah will be born of David's royal line, in Bethlehem, the town where King David was born." People were divided about him, some people wanted to arrest him, but no one touched him.

Finally, the temple guards went back to the chief priests and Pharisees, who asked them, "Why didn't you arrest him?"

"We've never heard anyone talk like him," the guards declared.

The Pharisees replied, "Has he deceived you too? Have any of the rulers or Pharisees believed in him? Of course not; this mob is ignorant and they are cursed."

Nicodemus, a Pharisee who had spoken with Jesus earlier, asked, "Is it legal to convict someone without first giving him a hearing?"

They replied, "Are you a Galilean too? Check the Scriptures and see that no prophet has ever come from Galilee." The meeting broke up; everybody went home and Jesus went to the Mount of Olives.

CHAPTER TWENTY-EIGHT

FURTHER MINISTRY AT THE FEAST OF TABERNACLES
John 8

THE WOMAN CAUGHT IN ADULTERY

Jesus was back at the temple early the next morning. When a crowd gathered around him, he sat down and started to teach. As he was speaking, the religious leaders brought him a woman caught in adultery. They were looking for an opportunity to accuse him of something, so they made her stand in front of the crowd and said, "Teacher, this woman was caught committing adultery. The Law of Moses commands us to stone such women. What do you think we should do?"

Jesus didn't say a word but instead bent down and started to write on the ground with his finger. They kept asking him for an answer, so he stood up and said, "Whoever is without sin should cast the first stone." Then he knelt and started writing again.

When his accusers heard this, they began to slip away one at a time, starting with the oldest, until Jesus was left standing with the woman in the middle of the crowd. Jesus stood up and asked her, "Where are they? Has no one condemned you?"

"No, Lord," she said.

Jesus said, "Neither do I. Go and sin no more."

> **What did Jesus write?**
>
> We don't know what Jesus was writing, but people have suggested that he was listing the Pharisees' sins or writing the names of the Pharisees who had slept with the woman.
>
> Also, we must note that this story is not in the oldest and most reliable manuscripts. It is likely a story that was passed down through oral tradition and then added later.

JESUS CLAIMS TO BE GOD

Later, Jesus said, "I am the light of the world. Whoever follows me will never walk in darkness but will have the light that leads to life."

The Pharisees replied, "You're testifying about yourself, so it is invalid."

Jesus answered, "Even if I testify on my behalf, my testimony is valid because I know where I came from and where I'm going. You judge by human standards, but I don't judge anyone. But if I do judge, my judgment is just because God is with me. The Law says that the testimony of two men is valid; you have me and you have my Father who sent me."

They asked, "Where is your father?"

Jesus answered, "You don't know my Father or me; if you knew me, you would know my Father too." Jesus said these things while teaching near the offering boxes where people made donations, but no one arrested him because it wasn't his time yet.

Then Jesus said again, "I'm going away, and you will look for me, but will die in your sin, because you cannot come where I'm going."

This made the Jews ask, "Is he going to commit suicide? Is that why we cannot go where he's going?"

Jesus continued, "You're from below, but I'm from above; you're from this world, but I'm not. If you refuse to believe in me then you will surely die in your sins."

"Who are you?" they demanded.

Jesus replied, "I am who I have always claimed to be. I have a lot to judge you on, because the one who sent me is reliable, and I tell the world what he tells me."

He could see that they still didn't understand that he was talking about God, so he said, "When you have crucified me, you will know that I am who I said I am. You will also know that I do nothing on my own, but I only say what my Father tells me to. He is still with me and has not deserted me because I do what he wants."

Many people who heard Jesus speak trusted in him, and he said to them, "You are really my disciples if you obey my teachings; then, you will know the truth and the truth will set you free."

They answered, "We are descendants of Abraham and have never been slaves. What do you mean we will be set free?"

Jesus replied, "I tell you the truth, everyone who sins is a slave to sin. A slave doesn't belong in the family, but a son always belongs. If the Son sets you free, you will always be free. I know that you are descendants of Abraham, but you are ready to kill me because you have no room for my word. I am telling you what I heard in my Father's presence, but you are doing what you heard from your father."

"Our father is Abraham," they answered.

Jesus said, "If you were Abraham's children, then you would do what he did. I told you the truth that I heard from God, but you're trying to kill me. Abraham wouldn't do that, so you're doing the things your true father does."

"We're not illegitimate children; God himself is our true father," they protested.

Jesus told them, "If God were your father, you would love me, because he sent me. Why don't you understand what I'm saying? It's because you cannot. Your father is the Devil, and you want to do his will. He was a murderer from the beginning and there is no truth in him. It is natural for him to lie because he is the father of lies, so you don't believe me when I tell the truth. Can you prove me guilty of sin? If I'm telling the truth, why don't you believe me? If you belonged to God, you would hear what he says, but you cannot hear him because you don't belong to him."

"You're a Samaritan and demon-possessed!" the Jews shouted.

Jesus responded, "I'm not demon-possessed, but I honor my Father and you dishonor me. I'm not trying to glorify myself, but God is, so let him be the judge. I tell you the truth, if anyone obeys my word, he will never die."

The Jews called out, "Now we know you are demon-possessed. Abraham and the prophets died, but you say that whoever obeys you will never die. Are you greater than Abraham and the prophets? Who do you think you are?"

"It doesn't matter if I glorify myself," Jesus replied, "but God, whom you say is your father, glorifies me. Even though you don't know him, I do, and I would be a liar like you if I said I didn't. Abraham looked forward to my day with joy and was glad to see it come."

The Jews said, "You're not even 50 years old; how can you say you've seen Abraham?"

Jesus answered, "I tell you the truth, before Abraham was born, I AM!" Then the Jews picked up stones to kill him because they knew that he was claiming to be God, but Jesus hid himself and left the temple.

Did Jesus claim to be God?

Many times, and in many ways, this is the reason that he was ultimately killed. When Jesus says, "I AM," it is a reference to the name God gave for himself (I AM WHO I AM) when he appeared to Moses in the burning bush. Jesus did things that only God could do, like forgive sins and judge people, even when confronted by his opponents. He also accepted worship from his followers. He took on many of the same names and characteristics that only God did in the Old Testament. As a good Jewish teacher, he would not do any of these without understanding that he was claiming to be God. Jesus may not have said the words, "I am God," but everything he said and did pointed to this claim. This is similar to how we may not utter the words, "I am human," but everything about our lives points to this fact.

CHAPTER TWENTY-NINE
PRIVATE LESSONS ON SERVICE AND PRAYER
Luke 10:1-11:13

Jesus chose 70 disciples, including the original Twelve, and sent them in pairs to all the towns and villages that he was about to visit. Before he sent them, he said, "The harvest is ready, but there aren't many workers, so pray that God sends out more workers into the field. I am sending you out like lambs among wolves. Don't take a bag, money, or an extra pair of sandals.

"Don't greet anyone on the road, but bless a house when you enter it. If the man is worthy, your blessing will stand, but if he is not, it will return to you. Don't move around, but stay in one house and take what they give you because a worker is worthy of his wages.

"Heal the sick and tell them that the kingdom of God is near. But if a town does not welcome you, go into its streets and wipe the dust off your feet as a testimony to their coming judgment, reminding them that the kingdom of God is near. Even wicked Sodom will face less judgment than that town.

"Woe to Chorazin and Bethsaida because if Tyre and Sidon saw the miracles they did, they would have repented long ago. It will be more bearable for Tyre and Sidon in judgment than it will be for you. Capernaum won't be lifted to heaven but will go down to death.

"Whoever listens to you, listens to me; whoever rejects you, rejects me; and whoever rejects me, rejects God."

When the 70 returned from their mission, they were elated and said, "Lord, even the demons obey us in your name."

Jesus replied, "I saw Satan fall from heaven like lightning. I have given you the power to overcome the enemy and trample snakes and scorpions without being hurt. But don't rejoice because the spirits obey you; rejoice because your names are written in heaven."

The Holy Spirit filled Jesus and he said, "O Father, Lord of heaven, I praise you for hiding these things from the wise and educated and revealing them to the childlike. It pleases you to do it that way.

"God has pledged all things to me. No one knows me except the Father, and no one knows the Father except me and those to whom I choose to reveal him."

Then he turned to his disciples and said, "You are privileged to see what you've seen because many prophets and kings wanted to hear and see these things, but they could not."

THE GOOD SAMARITAN

One day an expert in the religious law stood up to test Jesus and asked him, "Teacher, what do I have to do to receive eternal life?"

Jesus replied, "What does the Law of Moses tell you?"

The man answered, "'Love the Lord your God with all your heart, soul, strength, and mind,' and, 'Love your neighbor as yourself.'"

"You're right, do this and you will live," Jesus agreed.

But the man wanted to justify himself, so he asked, "Who is my neighbor?"

"Imagine this," Jesus replied. "Suppose a man was going down from Jerusalem to Jericho and on his way, he was attacked by robbers. They beat him up, stole his clothes, and left him for dead on the roadside.

"A Jewish priest came along the road and saw the man, but the priest crossed to the other side of the road. A little while later, a Levite came by and saw him, but he crossed to the other side of the road too.

"Then a Samaritan came along and took pity on the man. He bandaged the man's wounds and gave him some medicine. Then the Samaritan put him on his donkey and took him to an inn, where he cared for the man. The next day the Samaritan had to leave, so he gave the innkeeper some money with instructions to care for the injured man. He also said that if it cost more money, he would pay the rest the next time he came through that way.

"Now, which of these three would you say was a neighbor to the man attacked by bandits?"

The expert said, "The one who had mercy on him."

Jesus told him, "Go, and do the same."

> **The scandal of the Good Samaritan**
>
> The questioner wanted to narrowly define the scope of whom he was responsible to love. But Jesus showed him that we should love everyone we come across who has need. The priest and the Levite in the parable excused themselves from helping because they would have become ceremonially unclean and unable to fulfill their religious obligations. This story also took place on a 17-mile stretch of road that was

a common place for robbers to wait for travelers. But Jesus wanted his audience to view people and their needs as more important than ceremony.

The fact that Jesus made the Samaritan the hero of the story was scandalous because the Jews hated them extremely. The expert in religious law wouldn't even acknowledge that the hero was a Samaritan; he called him "the one who had mercy on him." In modern terms, we can replace the Samaritan with a member from whatever group we view as the lowest or most challenging. God wants us to love even those it's difficult for us to love.

MARY AND MARTHA

As Jesus and his disciples continued to Jerusalem, they came to a village where a woman named Martha welcomed them into her home. Martha was distracted with the necessary preparations to have company, but her sister Mary sat at Jesus' feet and listened to what he had to say. Martha got frustrated, so she came to Jesus and said, "Lord, it's not fair that my sister is making me do all the work; tell her to come help me."

But Jesus said to her, "My dear Martha, you are worried about so many things, but only one thing is essential. Mary has discovered that one thing and I won't take it away from her."

LESSON ON PRAYER

Another day while Jesus was finishing a prayer, one of his disciples asked, "Lord, teach us to pray, just like John taught his disciples."

Jesus said, "This is how you should pray: 'Father, I praise your name, let your kingdom come soon. Give us what we need each day. Forgive our sins, just as we forgive those who sin against us and keep us far from temptation.'"

How does prayer work?

Prayer is the way that we communicate with God; it can be silent or out loud. Through prayer, we praise God, confess our sins, and tell him what we need. God tells us that he answers all our prayers, although sometimes he says no or that we need to wait. One of the primary purposes of prayer is to draw us closer to God. It is like casting a fishing line and catching an island. As we reel the island in, we move closer, not the other way around. When we pray, it draws us closer to him.

He continued, "Suppose you went to a friend's house in the middle of the night to borrow three loaves of bread because you had some company and wanted to feed them. Your friend would say, 'Go away, I'm already in bed and I don't have anything to give you.' Even though he won't give you bread just because you're his friend, he will eventually give you bread if you keep knocking long enough.

"So, keep on asking, and you will receive; keep on seeking, and you will find; keep on knocking, and the door will be opened. Everyone who asks, receives; everyone who seeks, finds; and the door is opened to everyone who knocks.

"Do you fathers give your children a snake if they ask for a fish or a scorpion if they ask for an egg? If you know how to give good gifts even though you are evil, what better gift will your heavenly Father give to those who ask him than the Holy Spirit?"

> **Why doesn't God say 'yes' to every prayer?**
>
> Jesus' teaching seems to indicate that God should say 'yes' to all our prayers. But God is not a sky fairy who exists to grant our wishes like a genie in a bottle. His primary concern is his plan, not what we think we need. Sometimes God says no to our requests because it might end up hurting us in the long term. This is like parents who don't give children everything they want because it is not in their best interest. Sometimes, he tells us to wait because the timing is not right. Ultimately, we must submit to the fact that our lives are about God's glory and not what we might think is best for us.

CHAPTER THIRTY

SECOND DEBATE WITH RELIGIOUS LEADERS

Luke 11:1-13:9

One day, Jesus cast a demon out of a mute man, and the crowd was impressed. But some said he cast out demons because he was the prince of demons. Others demanded another miracle to prove that he was from God.

Jesus knew their thoughts and said, "Any kingdom at war with itself is doomed, and any divided house will fall. If Satan is fighting against himself, how will his kingdom stand? If I drive out demons by the power of Satan, where do your followers get their power? But if I drive out demons by the power of God, then the kingdom of God has arrived.

"When a fully-armed strong man guards his house, his possessions are safe. If someone stronger comes along, that one overpowers him, takes his armor, and carries off his possessions.

"Whoever isn't helping me opposes me; whoever isn't working with me is working against me.

"Now, when a demon leaves a man, it goes through the desert, looking for a place to rest. When it can't find any, it decides to go back. When it gets back, it finds his former home swept and clean, so it takes seven other worse spirits and they all move in. Then the person is worse off than before."

As Jesus was speaking, a woman cried out, "God bless your mother, her womb, and the breasts that nursed you."

Jesus replied, "Rather, God blesses those who hear God's word and obey it."

As the crowd grew, Jesus said, "This wicked generation asks for a sign, but the only sign it will get is the sign of Jonah. As Jonah was a sign for the Ninevites, so I will be a sign for this generation.

"The Queen of Sheba will judge this generation because she came from far away to hear Solomon's wisdom. The Ninevites will also judge you because they repented when they heard Jonah's message. Now someone greater than Solomon and Jonah is here and you refuse to listen.

"No one lights a lamp and then hides it; instead, he puts it on a stand so everyone can see it. Your eye is the lamp of your body, and when your eyes are good, your whole body is full of light. But if your eyes are bad, then your body is full of darkness. Therefore, if your body is full of light and has no darkness, you will be full of light."

***

When Jesus finished speaking, a Pharisee invited him to eat. Jesus went in and reclined at the table. His host was surprised to see that Jesus sat down to eat without first performing the ceremonial washing ritual.

But Jesus said to him, "You Pharisees carefully clean the outside of the cup and the dish, but inside you are full of greed and wickedness! Foolish people, didn't God make the inside as well as the outside? Give what is inside the dish to the poor, and you will be completely clean.

"Woe to you Pharisees, because you tithe the smallest part of your income, but you neglect God's justice and love. You should tithe, but you shouldn't ignore the more important things.

"Woe to you Pharisees, because you love the seats of honor and respectful greetings in the marketplace.

"Woe to you, because you are like unmarked graves that people walk over without knowing it."

One of the experts in the religious law said, "Teacher, you insult us with what you've just said."

Jesus replied, "Woe to you teachers of the religious law because you crush people with impossibly heavy loads but do nothing to help them.

"Woe to you, because you build tombs for the prophets, but your own ancestors killed those prophets. Your actions show that you think your ancestors were right and prove that you would have done the same thing. That's why God said, 'I will send them prophets and apostles, and they will kill some and persecute others.'

"This generation will be responsible for the murder of all God's prophets, from Abel's murder to Zechariah, who they killed between the altar and the sanctuary. You will be responsible for all their blood.

"Woe to you teachers of the religious law, because you hide the key to knowledge from the people. You don't enter God's kingdom yourselves, and you prevent others from entering as well."

This made the Pharisees and teachers of religious law furious. From then on, they grilled him with many hostile questions, trying to trap him in something he might say.

Meanwhile, a crowd of thousands gathered so thickly they were trampling each other. Jesus began to speak to his disciples, saying, "Look out for the yeast of the Pharisees, beware of their hypocrisy. The time is coming when everything will be revealed and all secrets will be made public. Whatever you said in the dark will be heard in the daylight, and what was whispered in your ear will be proclaimed from the rooftops.

"Friends, don't be afraid of those who can kill the body and that's all. Fear him who can destroy the body and throw you into hell.

"Aren't five sparrows sold for a couple pennies? God doesn't forget any of them; so, don't be afraid. You are more valuable than an entire flock of sparrows, so valuable that God knows how many hairs are on your head.

"If someone publicly acknowledges me here on earth, the Son of Man will acknowledge him before God's angels. But if anyone denies me here on earth, I will deny him before God's angels. God can forgive those who speak against me, but God won't forgive anyone who blasphemes against the Holy Spirit.

"When you are brought to trial before synagogues, rulers, and authorities, don't worry about what you will say, because the Holy Spirit will give you words in the moment."

***

Someone in the crowd yelled, "Teacher, tell my brother to divide the inheritance with me."

Jesus retorted, "Who made me a judge to settle such disputes?" Then he continued, "Don't be greedy because life is more than what you own.

"Imagine this. A rich man had a field that produced so much crop that he didn't have room to store it all. So, he decided to tear down his barns and build bigger ones. After making this plan, he decided to take a few years off and enjoy life.

"But God said to him, 'Foolish man, you will die tonight. Now who will get your wealth?' That's what it will be like for people who gain wealth for themselves but aren't rich towards God."

Then he turned to his disciples and said, "Don't worry about food and clothes because life is so much more than that. Look at the ravens; they don't plant, harvest, or store food because God feeds them. You are a lot more valuable to God than a whole flock of birds. All your worrying can't even add a single moment to your life. If it cannot do that, what's the point in worrying over bigger things?

"Look at the lilies and how they grow. They don't work to make their clothing, yet not even Solomon clothed himself with such beauty. If God cares so much for flowers, which will die tomorrow, don't you think he will take care of you? You of little faith, don't worry about what you will eat or drink; God will provide. The world keeps itself busy pursuing such things and God knows that you need them. But make his kingdom your primary concern and he will meet all your needs.

"Don't be afraid, little flock, because God is happy to give you the kingdom.

"Sell your possessions and give to the poor. Store up treasure in heaven where it won't wear out, be stolen, or destroyed. Your heart is wherever you keep your treasure.

"Be ready to serve, like men waiting for their master to come back from a party; then, you will be prepared to open the door as soon as he returns. It will be good for the servants if they are ready to serve, even if their master comes in the middle of the night. I tell you the truth, he will seat them, put on an apron, and serve them as they sit and eat.

"Understand that if a homeowner knows when a thief is coming, he won't let the thief in. Always be ready because the Son of Man will come when you least expect him."

Peter asked, "Are you telling this parable to just us, or everyone?"

Jesus replied, "Consider the faithful, wise servant the master puts in charge of feeding his family. It will be good for the servant that the master finds doing his job when he returns; he will be put in charge of all his master's possessions. But what if the servant thinks his master won't return for a long time and starts to get drunk and beat the other servants? Then, when the master of the house comes back unexpectedly, he will tear that servant apart, and throw him out of the house.

"The servant who knows what to do and doesn't do it will receive severe punishment. The one who doesn't know he is doing the wrong thing will receive light punishment. God requires a lot from everyone who receives a lot; the more he gives, the more he requires.

"I've come to bring a fire to the earth, and I wish I were already finished. I have a terrible baptism ahead of me, and I'm anxious until it's finished. Don't think that I've come to bring peace on earth, because I've come to bring division and strife. From now on, a family of five will disagree with each other, three against two or two against three. Entire families will all be at odds with each other."

Then Jesus turned to the crowd and said, "When you see clouds to the west, you know it's going to rain, and when you feel a south wind, you know it's going to be hot. Hypocrites! You know how to interpret the weather, but you can't interpret this present time.

"Judge for yourselves what is right. If you're going to court with your adversary, try to reconcile on the way, or else the judge will hand you over to the officer and the officer will throw you in jail. Then you won't get out until you have paid the last penny."

***

About this time, someone told Jesus that Pilate had killed some Galileans while they were sacrificing in the temple. Jesus answered, "Do you think these Galileans were worse sinners than all other Galileans because they died that way? No, and you will perish as well unless you repent and follow God. What about the 18 men the Tower of Siloam fell on (a disaster during the First Century)? Were they the biggest sinners in Jerusalem? No, and unless you repent, you will die too."

Then Jesus told this parable, "A man planted a fig tree and was disappointed when he didn't find any fruit on it. Finally, he told his gardener to cut the tree down and plant something else because he hadn't found any fruit on it in three years. But the gardener replied, 'Sir, leave it alone for one more year, and I'll give it special attention and plenty of fertilizer. If it bears fruit next year, fine; if not, cut it down.'"

CHAPTER THIRTY-ONE

SABBATH HEALINGS AND FURTHER DIVISION

Luke 13:10-21; John 9:1-10:39

One Sabbath, Jesus was teaching in a synagogue and he saw a woman who hadn't been able to stand up straight for 18 years because she had an evil spirit. Jesus called her over and said, "Woman, you are healed." Then he put his hands on her, and she stood up straight and praised God.

The leader of the synagogue was indignant because Jesus had healed her on the Sabbath. "There are six days for working; come get healed on one of those days, not on the Sabbath."

Jesus answered, "You hypocrites, doesn't each of you untie your animals and lead them out for water on the Sabbath? Therefore, wasn't it necessary for me to free this woman from 18 years of Satan's bondage, even if it was on the Sabbath?" His enemies were humiliated when they heard these words, and the people rejoiced at the wonderful things he was doing.

Then Jesus asked, "To what can I compare the kingdom of God? It's like a tiny mustard seed planted in the garden that grows up into a tree where the birds of the air can rest. The kingdom of God is also like yeast used for baking bread. Even though there is a lot of flour, the yeast permeates every part of it."

HEALING A MAN WHO WAS BORN BLIND

As Jesus was walking along on another Sabbath, he saw a blind man and his disciples asked him, "Teacher, was it this man, or his parents' sin that caused him to be born blind?"

Jesus answered, "Neither one, but he was born blind so that God's power could be shown in his life. We must do God's work as long as possible, but there is a time coming when we won't be able to work. While I am here, I am the light of the world."

He spit on the ground, made some mud, and put it on the man's eyes. Jesus said to him, "Go wash in the Pool of Siloam." So, the man went and washed, and then he could see.

> **Why do bad things happen?**
>
> Many people have a difficult time understanding why God would allow bad things to happen. Some people use it as a case for why he doesn't exist. If God allows us to have free will, he must let our actions play out. Sometimes, bad things happen because of the choices that we have made, sometimes it is because of the choices

> that others have made, and sometimes it is because creation is under the weight of sin. We don't always know why God allows bad things to happen or how he could use it for his glory, but he has a far greater perspective than we do, and we cannot possibly understand how he makes everything work together. God can use things that we cannot possibly understand to do amazing things in the future.
>
> The disciples had the mistaken notion that all suffering was the direct result of their own or their parents' sin. All suffering is the result of sin, although not always the sufferer's sin (children born with birth defects did not sin before birth).
>
> Suffering came after the fall of Adam and continues today. God always has a purpose for our pain, although we don't always see or understand it. In this instance, the man was born blind for God's glory. God also uses trials and suffering to build our character, to prepare us to comfort others, to discipline us, to further the gospel, or so that we might share in Jesus' suffering. Sometimes the reason for pain is apparent, but in some cases, we may never know why it happened. Our role is not always to understand but to trust God.

Those who knew him as a blind beggar asked, "Is that the same blind beggar we know?" Some said he was, but others disagreed and said he only looked like him.

But the man insisted, "I am that man."

His friends and neighbors asked, "How were your eyes opened?"

He answered, "Jesus made some mud, put it on my eyes, and told me to wash it off in the Pool of Siloam. I did, and now I can see."

"Where is he?" they asked.

"I don't know," the man replied.

His friends and neighbors took him to the Pharisees and they asked him how he could see. The man answered, "Jesus put mud on my eyes, I washed it off, and now I can see."

"This man cannot be from God because he doesn't keep the Sabbath," some of the Pharisees scoffed. But others asked how a sinner could perform such miracles.

Finally, they asked the blind man, "He opened your eyes, so what do you say about him?"

The man replied, "He's a prophet."

The Jewish leaders still didn't believe him, so they called in his parents and asked, "Is this your son? If he was born blind, how can he see?"

The Jewish leaders had decided to kick people out of the synagogue if they said that Jesus was the Messiah, so the parents answered, "He is our son and was born blind, but we don't know how he can see now or who opened his eyes. He's old enough to speak for himself, so ask him."

They called the man who had been born blind back and said, "Tell the truth because we know this man is a sinner."

He replied, "I don't know if he's a sinner or not. All I know is that I used to be blind, and now I can see."

"But how did he heal you?" they kept asking.

The man answered, "I told you once and you didn't listen, so why do you want to hear it again? Do you want to become his disciples?"

Furious, the Pharisees hurled insults at him. "You're one of his disciples, but we're Moses' disciples. We know God spoke through Moses, but we don't even know where this man came from."

Exasperated, the man answered, "That's odd, he opened my eyes, and you don't know where he's from. We know that God doesn't listen to sinners but only to those who do his will. Nobody has ever made a blind man see; if he weren't from God, there's no way that could happen."

"You were born a sinner; how dare you lecture us?" Then the Pharisees kicked him out of the synagogue.

When Jesus heard about this, he found the man and asked, "Do you believe in the Son of Man?"

The man replied, "Tell me who he is, so I can believe in him."

"You've seen him and are talking to him right now," Jesus told him.

"Lord, I believe," he said and he worshiped Jesus.

Then Jesus said, "I have come to judge the world so that the blind might see, and those who see might become blind."

Some Pharisees heard him. "Are you saying that we're blind?" they asked.

Jesus replied, "If you were blind, you would be innocent, but you are guilty because you say that you can see.

"The man who sneaks into the sheepfold instead of coming through the gate is a thief. The man who comes through the gate is the shepherd and the watchman lets him in. The shepherd calls the sheep by name as he leads them out. The sheep listen to him and follow him because they know his voice. They won't listen to a stranger because they don't recognize his voice."

> **Why are we sheep?**
>
> The Bible compares us to sheep, which were animals that all the people were familiar with in Jesus' day. They are some of the dumbest animals alive; they continually need care and attention. This analogy shows that we always need God and that he is constantly watching out for us. We like to think of ourselves as knowing what is best for our lives, but we lack the perspective that God has. We need to stay close to him so that he can provide what we need.

The people didn't understand what Jesus was saying to them, so he said, "I tell you the truth, I am the gate for the sheep. Everyone who came before me was a thief, but whoever enters through me will be saved. The thief comes only to steal, kill, and destroy, but I have come to give life to the fullest.

"I am the Good Shepherd, and I lay down my life for the sheep. The hired hand doesn't own the sheep, so he runs away when he sees a wolf coming; then, the wolf attacks and scatters the flock.

"I know my sheep and my sheep know me, just like the Father knows me and I know the Father, and I lay down my life for the sheep. I have other sheep that aren't from this flock and I must bring them in too. Then there will be one flock and one shepherd.

"The Father loves me because I lay down my life, only to take it up again. No one takes my life from me. I lay it down voluntarily because my Father has given me the power to take it up again."

There was a lot of argument after hearing these words. Some of the Jews said that he was demon-possessed and it was pointless to listen to him. Others argued that a demon-possessed man couldn't open the eyes of the blind.

THE FEAST OF DEDICATION

Winter came and it was time for the Feast of Dedication in Jerusalem. Jesus was in the temple, walking through Solomon's Colonnade, when the Jewish leaders surrounded him and asked, "How long will you keep us in suspense? If you're the Messiah, tell us plainly."

Jesus answered, "I told you, but you didn't believe me. My miracles should tell you that, but you don't trust me because you aren't my sheep. My sheep recognize my voice and they follow me. I give them eternal life, and no one can take them away from me because the all-powerful Father has given them to me. The Father and I are one."

The Jews picked up stones to kill him. Jesus said, "I have done many good deeds from the Father, for which of these are you stoning me?"

They replied, "We aren't stoning you for doing a good deed. We are stoning you for blasphemy because you're just a man, but you're making yourself out to be God."

Jesus answered, "Your own Law calls men gods. So, if those people, who received God's word, were called 'gods,' why do you call it blasphemy if the Holy One says, 'I am the Son of God?' You should only believe me because I do what my Father says. Even if you don't trust me, trust in the works I have done. Then you will realize that the Father is in me, and I am in the Father."

> **Was this a denial of deity?**
>
> Some critics have used this as a denial of deity. But Jesus was not claiming to be a mere man; he was saying that if men were called gods, it was appropriate to call him God. Jesus claimed to be God and the fact that the people wanted to stone him was evidence that they understood his claim to be God.

CHAPTER THIRTY-TWO
PRINCIPLES OF DISCIPLESHIP
Luke 13:22-14:35; John 10:40-42

The Jews tried to arrest him again, but he got away. He crossed the Jordan to where John had been baptizing in the early days. Many people followed him and put their trust in him there. They said to each other, "John didn't do miracles, but all of his predictions about this man have come true."

Jesus taught in the towns and villages on his way to Jerusalem. Someone asked him, "Lord, will only a few people be saved?"

He answered, "Try hard to get in through the narrow door because many will try and fail. Once the owner of the house locks the door, it will be too late. People will stand outside and plead, 'Open the door for us because we ate and drank with you, and you taught in our streets.' But the house owner will answer, 'Get away from me, you evildoers! I don't know you or where you're from.'

"You will weep and grind your teeth when you see Abraham, Isaac, Jacob, and the prophets in the kingdom of God. People will come from all over the earth to take their places, but God will throw you out. Indeed, those who are last will be first, and those who are first will be last."

***

"You should leave because Herod wants to kill you," some of the Pharisees told Jesus. Herod likely sent them because he wanted Jesus to leave the region.

Jesus replied, "Go tell that fox that I will continue to cast out demons and heal the sick today and tomorrow, and then the third day I will fulfill my purpose. I must keep going because no prophet can die outside of Jerusalem."

"O Jerusalem, city that kills the prophets and stones those sent to you. I have wanted to gather your children together like a hen gathers her chicks under her wings, but you wouldn't let me. Now your house is desolate and you won't see me again until you say, 'Blessed is the one who comes in the name of the Lord.'"

***

One Sabbath, Jesus was eating in the home of a prominent Pharisee, and everyone was watching, hoping to find a reason to accuse him. There was a man suffering from edema, so Jesus asked the Pharisees and experts in religious law, "Is it lawful to heal on the Sabbath or not?" When they remained silent, Jesus touched the man, healed him, and sent him home.

Then he turned to the crowd and asked, "If your son or your cow fell into a well on the Sabbath, wouldn't you immediately pull him out?" But they had nothing to say.

When Jesus noticed that they were all trying to sit near the head of the table, he told them, "When someone invites you to a meal, don't head for the best seat. If someone more distinguished than you arrives, the host will tell you to give up your spot. Then you will be embarrassed and have to sit at whatever seat is left. Instead, you should sit at the foot of the table, and then your host will come tell you to sit in a more dignified place. You will be honored in front of the other guests. Everyone who exalts himself will be humbled, and everyone who humbles himself will be exalted."

Jesus turned to his host and said, "When you throw a party, don't invite your friends, relatives, and rich neighbors, because they will pay you back. Invite the outcasts of society because God will reward you for inviting those who couldn't repay you."

A man who heard this said, "Blessed is the man who will share in the kingdom of God."

Jesus replied, "A certain man was preparing a banquet and invited many people. When the banquet was ready, he sent his servant to get his guests.

"But the guests all made excuses. One needed to check on a new field, another wanted to try out his new oxen, and another had just been married.

"The servant came back and told his master they all declined the invitation. His master was upset and told the servant to invite the outcasts of society. The servant told him that they already had, and there was still room. So, his master told him to find whoever they could to fill his house and that the men he originally invited wouldn't get even a single bite of the food he had prepared."

Jesus turned to the crowd following him and said, "If anyone wants to follow me, you must love me more than you love your parents, spouse, children, siblings, and even your own life. If you don't, then you cannot be my disciple. You also cannot be my disciple unless you pick up your cross and follow me.

"If you want to build a tower, you first sit down and figure out how much it will cost to make sure you have enough money to finish. If you only complete the foundation and cannot finish the rest, everyone will make fun of you because you couldn't finish what you started.

"A king who wants to go to war first figures out if he has the strength to fight against the other king. If he doesn't, he sends a delegation to ask for a peace treaty. In the same way, you must give up everything if you want to be my disciple.

"Salt is good, but if it loses its flavor, how will you make it salty again? Flavorless salt is useless and you throw it out. Whoever can hear me should listen to what I say."

CHAPTER THIRTY-THREE

FURTHER PARABLES

Luke 15:1-17:10

SEARCHING FOR THE LOST

A large group of tax collectors and other notorious sinners were crowding around Jesus to listen to him. The Pharisees and teachers of the religious law complained bitterly when Jesus ate with them, angry that Jesus even associated with such wicked people.

Then Jesus told this parable: "If you had 100 sheep and lost one in the wilderness, wouldn't you leave the 99 and look for the lost one? Once you found it, you would joyfully carry it home on your shoulders and throw a party. In the same way, there is more joy in heaven when a lost sinner repents than when 99 righteous people don't sin.

"Or suppose a woman has ten valuable silver coins and loses one. She will light a lamp and clean out the house until she finds it. Once she finds it, she calls her neighbors over to celebrate because she found her lost coin. In the same way, God's angels rejoice whenever a sinner repents."

Jesus continued, "There was a man with two sons, and the younger son told his father to give him his share of the inheritance now. His father agreed and so he divided his property.

"A few days later, the younger son took everything he had and left for a distant country, where he spent all his money on wild living. Around the time he ran out of money, there was a terrible famine and he began to starve. He found a job with a local farmer feeding pigs, and he became so hungry that even the slop he was feeding the pigs looked good.

"After a while, he came to his senses and said, 'All the hired men at home have plenty to eat, but I'm stuck here, hungry. I should go home and apologize to my father and beg him to take me back as a servant.'

"The younger son headed home, and while he was still a long way off, the father saw him coming. His heart broke with compassion, and he ran to his son, threw his arms around his neck, and kissed him. His son said to him, 'Father, I have sinned against heaven and you, I am no longer worthy of being called your son.'

"But his father told his servants, 'Quick! Bring my son the finest robe, put a ring on his finger, and shoes on his feet. Go kill the fattened calf because we're going to celebrate my lost son's safe return.'

"The oldest son heard the party from the fields, so he asked one of the servants what was happening. The servant told him, 'Your brother just came back and your father is throwing a party because he's safe.'

"The oldest son got angry and refused to go to the party. His father came out to ask him to come in but he said, 'I've always worked hard for you and never disobeyed you, but you have never even given me a goat so I could celebrate with my friends. But when your son comes back after wasting all your money on prostitutes, you kill the fattened calf for him!'

"The father replied, 'My dear son, you have always been with me, and everything I have is yours. We're celebrating because your brother was dead, but is alive again; he was lost, but now is found.'"

THE SHREWD SERVANT

Then Jesus said to his disciples, "The manager of a rich man's possessions was accused of wasting his boss's wealth. The rich man called him in to give an account for his work.

"The manager thought to himself, 'What am I going to do if I'm fired? I'm too weak to dig ditches, and I'm too proud to beg.'

"Then he had an idea that would make sure he had a place to stay when he was fired. So, he called in everyone who owed his boss money to discuss their bills. If they owed 800 gallons of olive oil, he made it 400. If they owed 1,000 bushels of wheat, he made it 800.

"The rich man commended the dishonest manager for his shrewdness, and worldly people are far shrewder than the godly are. I tell you, use worldly wealth to make friends so that you will be welcomed into eternal dwellings once it is gone.

"Whoever is trustworthy with a little will be trustworthy with a lot, and whoever is dishonest with a little will be dishonest with a lot. If you haven't been able to handle worldly wealth, why should you get heaven's riches? If you aren't faithful with someone else's property, why should God trust you with your own property?

"No one can serve two masters because you will hate one and love the other, or you will devote yourself to one, and despise the other. Therefore, it's impossible to serve both God and money."

The Pharisees, who loved money, sneered at Jesus, and he told them, "You may justify yourselves before men, but God knows your hearts. God detests what the world values.

"The Law and the Prophets were your guides up until the coming of John the Baptist. Now I preach the kingdom of God and many people are forcing their way into the kingdom. But heaven and earth will disappear before a single part of the Law fails.

"Whoever divorces his wife and marries another woman is committing adultery; anyone who marries a divorced woman is committing adultery.

THE RICH MAN AND LAZARUS

"There was a well-dressed rich man who lived a life of luxury. A beggar named Lazarus used to sit at his gate, longing to eat what fell from the rich man's table. He was covered with sores and the dogs used to come and lick his wounds. Finally, Lazarus died and the angels carried him to Abraham's side. The rich man also died, but he went to Hades and was constantly in torment.

"From a distance, he saw Lazarus at Abraham's side and begged, 'Father Abraham, have pity on me, and send Lazarus to give me a drop of water because I'm in agony.'

"But Abraham replied, 'During your life, you had everything you wanted, and Lazarus had nothing; now he is in comfort, and you are in agony. Besides, no one can cross the great chasm that separates us.'

Then the rich man said, 'Then send him to my family to warn my five brothers so they don't end up in this place of torment when they die.'

"Abraham said, 'They have Moses and the Prophets to warn them.'

"The rich man replied, 'But if they see someone come back from the dead, they will repent.'

"Abraham answered, 'If they don't listen to Moses and the Prophets, they won't listen to someone from the dead either.'"

Hell

Hell is the unpopular concept of a place of eternal punishment and suffering for those who reject Jesus' life and ministry. Jesus talked about hell more than any other figure in the Bible. Scripture describes it as a fiery furnace where there will be weeping and gnashing of teeth, sorrow, torment, unquenchable fire, darkness, and destruction. Popular culture often depicts hell as a mildly warm place where all the "bad kids" hang out and do whatever they want, but this is not the picture the Bible paints.

Some believe that a loving God would never condemn people to an eternal punishment like this, but God's wrath is a part of his nature that we cannot ignore. If God allows sin to go unpunished, then he is no longer holy. If we put our trust in Jesus, then his death pays the debt of our sin. We cannot pick and choose which of God's attributes we like and ignore the others.

Many people wonder what will happen to those who never hear the gospel and never have an opportunity to come to faith. The Bible does not explicitly address what happens in these cases, but we know that God will do the right thing because he is good, righteous, and just. Ultimately, God gives us the choice to say, "your will be done." If we refuse, then he says to us, "your will be done."

STUMBLING BLOCKS

One day, Jesus told his disciples, "Stumbling blocks will come, but woe to the person who causes someone to stumble. It would be better to be thrown in the sea with a large millstone tied around the neck than to cause someone to sin, so watch yourselves.

"If another believer sins, reprimand him; if he repents, forgive him. Even if he sins against you seven times a day and asks for forgiveness, forgive him."

The disciples said to Jesus, "Increase our faith!"

Jesus answered, "If you had faith as small as a mustard seed, you could tell this mulberry tree to uproot and plant itself in the sea, and it would.

"If you have a servant who is out working in the field or looking after the flocks, he doesn't come in and sit down to eat. First, he prepares his master's food and serves him; then, he can eat and drink. The master doesn't even thank the servant for doing this because he's just doing his job. In the same way, when you do what you're told to do, you should say, 'We are unworthy servants who are only doing our duty.'"

CHAPTER THIRTY-FOUR

RAISING LAZARUS

John 11

A man named Lazarus was sick in Bethany, where he lived with his sisters, Martha and Mary (the same Mary who had anointed Jesus' feet). His sisters sent word to Jesus and said, "Lazarus is sick." This was a different Lazarus than the one in the previous chapter.

When Jesus heard this, he said, "His sickness won't end in death; it's for God and the Son of God's glory." Jesus loved Lazarus and his sisters, but he stayed where he was for a couple more days before telling his disciples they should go back to Judea.

His disciples were confused and said, "Teacher, not too long ago, the Jews there wanted to kill you, and you still want to go back?"

Jesus answered, "Every day has twelve hours of daylight. While it is light, people can walk safely. But they will stumble if they walk at night because they don't have light. Our friend Lazarus has fallen asleep, but I'm going there to wake him up."

His disciples said, "If he's asleep, he will wake up." They thought Jesus meant he was literally asleep, but Jesus meant that he had died.

"Lazarus is dead," Jesus told them. "I'm glad that I wasn't there, so you can trust in me. Let's go see him."

Thomas (called Didymus) said to the rest of the disciples, "Let's go die with him."

When they got to Bethany, they found that Lazarus had already been in the tomb for four days. Bethany was only a few miles from Jerusalem, and many Jews had come to console Mary and Martha on their brother's death. When Martha heard that Jesus was coming, she went out to meet him, but Mary stayed at home.

Martha said to Jesus, "Lord, my brother wouldn't have died if you had been here, But I know that God will give you whatever you ask for."

Jesus told her, "Your brother will rise again."

"I know he will rise on the last day when everyone else will," Martha replied.

Jesus said to her, "I am the resurrection and the life; those who believe in me will live, even though they die. Whoever believes in me will never die. Do you believe me Martha?"

"Yes, Lord, I believe that you are the Messiah, the Son of God." Then Martha went to Mary and told her that Jesus wanted to talk to her.

Mary got up quickly and went outside the village to where Martha had met Jesus. When the mourners saw that she was leaving, they assumed she was going to the tomb, and they followed her. When Mary got to Jesus, she fell at his feet and said, "Lord, if you would have been here, my brother would still be alive."

Deeply moved by her grief, Jesus asked, "Where is he buried?"

They led him to the grave and Jesus wept. Some of the Jews said, "See how much Jesus loved him." But others said, "If he can open the eyes of the blind, he could have healed Lazarus."

At the grave, Jesus was profoundly moved and said, "Take away the stone."

But Martha said, "Lord, it's going to stink because he's been in there for four days."

"Didn't I tell you that if you believed, you would see God's glory?" Jesus replied.

So, they rolled the stone away; Jesus looked up to heaven and said, "Father, thank you for hearing me. I know that you always hear me, but I say this out loud so that the people here will believe that you sent me."

Then Jesus shouted, "Lazarus, come out!" The dead man came out with his hands and feet wrapped in linen strips and a cloth around his face. Jesus said, "Unwrap him and let him go."

Many of the Jews who witnessed what Jesus did believed in him. But some went and told the Pharisees about this miracle.

The Pharisees got together and asked each other, "What are we doing? This man is performing many miracles, and if we let him keep going, the whole nation will follow him, and then the Romans will take away our land and freedom."

Then Caiaphas, the high priest, said, "Don't be stupid. Don't you realize that it's better for one man to die than the whole nation?" These weren't Caiaphas' own words, but he prophesied that Jesus would die for the Jews and the Gentiles so that all God's children might become one people.

From that point on, the Pharisees plotted Jesus' death. Therefore, Jesus couldn't move around publicly, so he went to the desert village of Ephraim with his disciples.

How God uses those who don't follow him

God still used the corrupt high priest for his purposes. God will use many different people to work out his plan, even if they are unaware of their role in his overall design. We may not understand how he does this, but that's part of what makes him God.

CHAPTER THIRTY-FIVE

TEACHING ON THE WAY TO JERUSALEM

Matthew 19:1-20:34; Mark 10; Luke 17:11-19:28

JESUS HEALS TEN LEPERS

A short while later, Jesus headed back towards Jerusalem and passed through Samaria and Galilee. As he entered a village, ten lepers cried out, "Master, have pity on us."

Jesus looked at them and said, "Go show yourselves to the priests." As they went, they were healed.

When one of them saw that he was healed, he came back and fell down on his face before Jesus, praising and thanking God.

Jesus asked, "Didn't I heal all ten? Where are the other nine? Does only this Samaritan come to praise God?" Then he said, "Stand up and go; your faith has made you well."

JESUS' RETURN

One day the Pharisees asked when the kingdom of God would come, and Jesus replied, "The kingdom of God doesn't come with visible signs. You won't be able to find it here or there because the kingdom of God is among you."

Later, Jesus talked with his disciples and said, "It won't be long until you will want to see one of the days of the Son of Man, but you won't be able to. People will tell you that he has returned to various places, but don't believe them. It will be obvious when the Son of Man returns, but first, he must suffer many things and have this generation reject him.

"When he returns, it will be just like the days of Noah. People were eating, drinking, and getting married up until the Flood came and destroyed them all.

"It will also be like the days of Lot. People went through their daily routines until the day Lot left, and then God destroyed everything with fire and brimstone.

"Things will go on as usual until the day he returns. When he comes, the person outside shouldn't go inside to pack and the man in the field shouldn't return to town. Remember Lot's wife because whoever tries to keep his life will lose it, and whoever loses his life will save it. Two people may be in one bed, and the Son of Man will take one and leave the other. Two women may be working together, and the Son of Man will take one and leave the other."

The disciples asked, "Lord, where will this happen?"

Jesus answered, "The vultures always gather around a dead animal." By saying this, Jesus meant that his return will be obvious to all.

***

One day Jesus was teaching his disciples that they should always pray. To illustrate his point he said, "There was a godless judge who didn't care about anyone. A widow from his city kept coming to him, begging him to protect her from her enemy. He ignored her for a long time, but finally, he said to himself, 'Even though I don't care about God or people, I will give this woman protection, or else she will wear me out.'

"If this godless judge does this much, won't God bring about justice for his children if they keep asking him. He won't ignore them, but he will make sure they get justice quickly. But will the Son of Man find people with faith?"

Then Jesus told a parable to some people who were self-righteous and looked down on everyone else. He said, "A Pharisee and a tax collector went to the temple to pray. The Pharisee stood up and prayed, 'God, thank you for making me better than other men, especially that tax collector. I don't rob, cheat, or lie; I fast twice a week and give a tenth of my income.'

"The tax collector went off by himself and wouldn't even look up to heaven. He beat his chest and said, 'God, have mercy on a sinner like me.' God was pleased with this tax collector rather than the Pharisee because God humbles the proud and exalts the humble."

After saying these things, Jesus left Galilee and went south to the region of Judea and into the area across the Jordan River. Many people followed him, and he taught them and healed their sick.

Some Pharisees were in the crowd and they tried to trap him by asking, "Should a man be able to divorce his wife for any reason he wants?"

Jesus replied, "Haven't you read the Scriptures? They say that from the beginning, God 'made them male and female' and that 'a man will leave his father and mother and be united with his wife so that the two become one.' Therefore, they are now one flesh, and no one should separate what God has joined."

They asked, "Then why did Moses say a man could divorce his wife?"

Jesus answered, "Moses allowed divorce because of your hard hearts, but that's not how God meant it to be. I tell you that the only acceptable reason for divorce is marital unfaithfulness. Those who get a divorce and marry someone else are committing adultery."

His disciples said, "If this is how it is, it's better not to get married."

Jesus replied, "Not everyone can accept this statement, but only those that God helps. Some people are born eunuchs, others make some that way, and some choose not to marry for the kingdom of heaven. Anyone who can accept this statement should accept it."

CHILDLIKE FAITH

One day some parents brought their children to Jesus so he could bless them, but the disciples tried to stop them. When Jesus saw what was happening, he became upset with his disciples and said, "Don't stop the children from coming to me because the kingdom of God belongs to them. Whoever doesn't have childlike faith will never get into the kingdom of God." Then he took the children in his arms, put his hands on their heads, and blessed them.

JESUS AND WEALTH

One day, a man ran up to him, knelt, and asked, "Good Teacher, what do I have to do to inherit eternal life?"

Jesus turned his question around, "Why do you call me good? Only God is good. If you want eternal life, you must obey the commandments."

> **Did Jesus deny his goodness?**
>
> Jesus did not deny that he was good, but he was trying to get the man to think about his statement. If he was saying that Jesus was good, then he was implying Jesus' divinity.

"Which ones?" the man inquired.

Jesus replied, "Don't murder, don't commit adultery, don't steal, don't lie, don't cheat, honor your father and mother, and love your neighbor as yourself."

The young man said, "Teacher, I've done all of these things since I was a boy. What else do I have to do?"

Jesus felt genuine love for this man as he spoke to him and said, "You only lack one thing. Sell everything you have and give the proceeds to the poor and you will have treasure in heaven. Then come follow me."

When the man heard this, he went away sad, because he was rich. Jesus watched him go and then said to his disciples, "It's tough to get into the kingdom of heaven. In fact, it's easier for a camel to go through the eye of a needle than for a rich person to enter the kingdom of God."

The disciples were amazed and asked, "Then who can be saved?"

Jesus looked at them and said, "It's impossible for men, but everything is possible with God."

Peter answered, "We've left everything to follow you! What do we get?"

> **Wealth and following Jesus**
>
> It's okay to have earthly possessions, but we cannot put them before God, which is what this man had done. Jesus didn't chase him down and make it easier to follow him because he wouldn't water down the gospel. This shocked the Jews because they equated earthly prosperity with divine favor. Neither the poor nor the rich are inherently more righteous; God is more concerned about our hearts. The disciples wondered how anyone could be saved, but Jesus was telling them that people cannot save themselves; only God can do that.

Jesus replied, "I tell you the truth, when the Son of Man sits on his glorious throne, you will sit on twelve thrones and judge the tribes of Israel. Everyone who gives up a home, family, or property for the gospel and me will receive 100 times more than what you left, including persecutions, while on earth. Then you will also receive eternal life. Those who are first will be last, and those who are last will be first.

"The kingdom of heaven is like a landowner who went out early one morning and hired workers for his vineyard. He agreed to pay them a day's wage and sent them to work. Around nine o'clock, he saw some more people standing in the marketplace and he told them to go work in his field and that he would pay them a fair wage at the end of the day. He did the same thing at noon and at three in the afternoon. Finally, at about five, he found some other men doing nothing and he asked them why they had just been standing around all day. They told the landowner that no one had hired them, so he said to them, 'Go work in my vineyard too.'

"When evening came, the landowner had his supervisor pay his workers, starting with the last ones first. The men hired at five got a full day's pay, so the men hired that morning expected to get much more. But they all got the same amount. These men were upset and complained that the men hired at the end of the day got just as much as they did though they hadn't worked as long.

"But the landowner said, 'I'm not being unfair to you, didn't you agree to work for a day's pay? I wanted to give the last workers as much as I paid you. Can't I do whatever I want with my money? Should you get mad because I'm generous?'

"So, the last will be first, and the first will be last."

***

Jesus walked ahead of them on the way to Jerusalem and his followers were afraid because they thought they were going to die. Then Jesus took his disciples aside and told them what would happen, saying, "All the prophecies about the Son of Man will be fulfilled when we get to Jerusalem. The Son of Man will be betrayed to the leading priests and teachers of the religious law and they will sentence him to die. They will mock him, spit on him, beat him, and kill him; but on the third day, he will rise from the dead." But the disciples didn't understand him.

Then James and John's mother came to Jesus with her two sons. She knelt and Jesus asked, "What is your request?"

She replied, "Let my two sons have the places of honor in your glorious kingdom. Put one on the right and one on the left."

Jesus answered, "You don't know what you're asking. Are you able to drink the cup I drink or be baptized with my baptism?"

"We can," they answered.

Jesus said to them, "You will drink from my cup and be baptized with my baptism, but I don't have the right to say who will sit to my right or left. My Father has chosen who will sit in those seats."

When the ten other disciples heard about this, they were angry with James and John. Jesus knew what was happening, so he called them together and said, "You know that the rulers of the Gentiles revel in their authority, but it shouldn't be that way with you. Whoever wants to be a leader should be a servant, and whoever wants to become first must be everyone else's servant. In the same way, the Son of Man didn't come to be served, but to serve and give his life as a ransom for many."

JESUS HEALS TWO BLIND BEGGARS

On their way to Jericho, a great crowd followed Jesus and his disciples. A blind beggar named Bartimaeus was sitting on the side of the road with another blind beggar. When they found out that Jesus of Nazareth was passing by, they shouted, "Jesus, Son of David, have mercy on us!" The crowd tried to get them to be quiet, but they kept shouting louder and louder.

When Jesus heard them, he stopped and told the crowd to bring the men to him. They told the blind men, "Cheer up, Jesus is calling you." So, they jumped up, threw their coats aside, and came to Jesus.

Jesus asked the men, "What do you want me to do?"

The blind men replied, "Lord, we want to see."

Jesus had compassion on them and touched their eyes; instantly, they could see. Then the men followed Jesus down the road, praising God with the crowd.

ZACCHAEUS

Jesus entered Jericho and made his way through the town. A rich man named Zacchaeus lived there and he was one of the most influential Jews in the Roman tax-collecting business. He was too short to see Jesus through the crowd, so he climbed a sycamore tree to watch from there.

When Jesus came by, he looked up and said, "Zacchaeus, come down because I'm going to stay at your house today." So, Zacchaeus came down and welcomed him into his home. But the crowds muttered because he was going to be the guest of a sinner.

When Jesus arrived at his house, Zacchaeus stood and said, "I will give half my possessions to the poor, and if I have cheated anyone, I will pay back four times what I owe."

Then Jesus said to him, "Salvation has come to this home today because this man is a son of Abraham. For the Son of Man has come to seek and save the lost."

PARABLE OF THE SERVANTS

The crowds were listening to everything he said, and he told a parable because the people thought the kingdom of God was going to appear right away. He said, "A nobleman was called to a distant land to be crowned king and then return. He called ten of his servants and gave them money to invest while he was gone. But his people hated him and sent a delegation to say that they didn't want him to be their king.

"However, they made him king and he returned home. When he arrived, he sent for his servants to find out how much money they had earned.

"The first servant reported that he had earned ten times as much. His master was impressed and put him in charge of ten cities as a reward. The second servant reported that he had earned five times as much and his master put him in charge of five cities. Another servant brought the original amount of money and said, 'I hid your money and kept it safe because I know you are a hard man to deal with, taking what you did not put in, and reaping what you did not sow.'

"His master answered, 'You wicked servant, if you knew I was a hard man, why didn't you at least put the money in the bank so that I could have collected it with interest? Take his money and give it to the one who earned the most.'

"His servants replied, 'But master, that servant already has plenty.'

"The man said, 'Those who have will have more given to them, and those who don't have will have everything taken from them. Bring the people who didn't want me to be king and kill them in my presence.'"

After saying these things, Jesus went ahead to Jerusalem.

CHAPTER THIRTY-SIX

TRIUMPHAL ENTRY AND THE FIG TREE

Matthew 21:1-22; Mark 11:1-25; Luke 19:29-48; John 11:55-12:50

It was almost time for the Passover celebration, and people crowded into Jerusalem for the cleansing ceremony. They kept looking for Jesus in the temple and asked each other, "Do you think he will come to the Passover?" The chief priests and the Pharisees were looking for him too and gave orders that anyone who knew where he was should report it so they could arrest him.

Six days before the Passover, Jesus arrived at Lazarus' house in Bethany. People flocked to see him and Lazarus because Jesus had raised him from the dead. Hearing this, the chief priests planned to kill Lazarus too because many of the people believed in Jesus when they heard about that miracle.

The next day, at the Mount of Olives, Jesus sent two disciples ahead of him. He said, "As you enter the village, you will see a donkey tied there with its colt beside it. Bring them to me. If anyone asks what you're doing, say, 'The Lord needs them and will return them.'"

The two disciples found the animals tied outside of a house, just as Jesus had said. As they were untying the animals, some folks nearby said, "Why are you untying that colt?" The disciples answered as Jesus instructed, and the people allowed them to take the animals. When they brought the animals to Jesus, they threw their garments over the donkey and he sat on it. This fulfilled the prophecy, "Your King is coming to you, humble and riding on a donkey."

A huge crowd of Passover visitors spread their coats on the road ahead of Jesus; others cut leafy branches in the fields and spread them on the road. As they reached the place where the road started down the Mount of Olives, his followers began to shout and sing as they walked, "Praise the Lord! Blessed is the One who comes in the name of the Lord! Blessed is the coming kingdom of our ancestor David! Peace and glory in the highest heaven!"

Conquering kings rode on donkeys and spreading coats and palm branches on the road was what people did to show respect for their rulers. The people were half begging and half demanding him to be their king and liberate Israel. At the time, his disciples didn't realize that he was fulfilling prophecy, but after Jesus' glorification, they realized that they had seen Scripture fulfilled.

Pharisees in the crowd said, "Teacher, reprimand your followers for saying things like that."

"If they keep quiet, the stones will burst forth in praise," Jesus replied.

As they got closer to Jerusalem, Jesus saw the city ahead, and began to cry, saying, "I wish that you knew what would bring you peace, but now it's hidden from you. Before long, your enemies will surround you and close in on you. They will crush you and your children to the ground, and they won't leave a single stone in place, because you have rejected God's opportunity."

Those in the crowd who had seen Jesus raise Lazarus from the dead were telling others about it and many more went out to meet him when they heard of the miracle. The Pharisees said to each other, "We've lost; the whole world is following him!"

The blind and lame came to him, and he healed them in the temple. Children ran around praising God. The chief priests became indignant and said, "Do you hear what these children are saying?"

Jesus replied, "Yes, haven't you ever read the Scriptures that say, 'You have taught the children and infants to praise you.'" Then he went back to Bethany with his disciples to spend the night.

CURSING THE FIG TREE

As they were leaving Bethany and returning to Jerusalem the next morning, Jesus was hungry. He saw a fig tree in the distance in full leaf, so he went over to see if there were any figs on it. I was too early for fruit, so there were only leaves on the tree. Jesus cursed the tree in front of his disciples, "May no one ever eat your fruit again!"

SECOND TEMPLE CLEANSING

When they arrived in Jerusalem, Jesus went into the temple and immediately began driving out the merchants and their customers that thronged there, just as he had at the beginning of his public ministry. He knocked over the moneychangers' tables and benches of those selling doves, and he stopped everyone from bringing in merchandise. He said, "It is written, 'My house will be a place of prayer for all nations, but you have made it a den of thieves.'"

After that, he taught daily in the temple. The leading priests and teachers of the religious law heard about what Jesus had done and began plotting how to kill him, but they couldn't think of anything because of all the people surrounding him, hanging on his every word.

***

Some Greeks who had come to Jerusalem to worship at the Passover came to Philip, saying, "Sir, we would like to see Jesus." Philip told his brother Andrew and they both went to tell Jesus.

Jesus replied, "The time has come for the Son of Man to be glorified. I tell you the truth; unless a kernel of wheat falls to the ground and dies, it remains a single seed. But if it dies, it produces many seeds. The man who loves his life will lose it, and the man who hates his life on earth will have eternal life. Whoever wants to be my disciple must follow me because my servants must be where I am, and my Father will honor my servants. Now my soul is deeply troubled, should I ask God to save me from what lies ahead? No, because I came to bring glory to my Father's name."

Then a voice came from heaven, "I have glorified it and will glorify it again." Some in the crowd thought it was thunder and others said that an angel had spoken.

Jesus said, "This voice was for your benefit, not mine. Now it's time to judge the world, and I will drive out the prince of this world. But when I am lifted up, I will draw everyone to myself." He said this to indicate that he would be crucified.

The crowd was confused and said, "The Scripture says the Messiah will live forever, so why do you say that the Son of Man must be lifted up? Who is the Son of Man?"

Jesus replied, "You will only have the light for a little while longer, so walk in the light before darkness overtakes you. Those who walk in the dark don't know where they are going, so put your trust in the light while it is still here, and then you will become sons of light." After he finished saying these things, Jesus hid himself away from them.

***

Despite all his miracles, most would still not trust in him. This fulfilled Isaiah's prophecy, "Lord, who has believed our message and to whom will the Lord reveal his saving power?" The people couldn't believe, and because Isaiah saw Jesus' glory he said, "He has blinded their eyes and hardened their hearts. So, their eyes cannot see, their hearts cannot understand, and they cannot turn to me so I can heal them."

Yet many people, including some of the Jewish leaders, trusted in him. None of them would confess it publicly because they were afraid that the Pharisees would kick them out of the synagogue and they loved the praise of men more than the praise of God.

Then Jesus cried out, "When someone believes in me, he also believes in the one who sent me because when you see me, you see the one who sent me. I have come to this world as a light so that those who believe in me should not stay in darkness. I don't judge people if they hear me and don't obey, because I did not come to judge the world but to save it. But everyone who does not listen to my words will be judged by those same words on the last day. I have only said what the Father has told me to say and his command leads to eternal life."

That evening Jesus and his disciples left the city. The next morning, they passed the fig tree that Jesus had cursed and the disciples noticed that it had withered from the roots. Peter pointed it out and said, "Teacher, the fig tree you cursed has withered! How did this happen so quickly?"

Jesus answered, "Have faith in God. I tell you the truth, if you have faith and don't doubt, you can do this and more. You can even tell a mountain to throw itself into the sea and it will obey. Therefore, you will receive whatever you ask for in prayer if you believe that you have received it. But when you are praying, you must forgive anyone that you have a grudge against so that God will be able to forgive your sins too."

Every night Jesus returned to spend the night on the Mount of Olives, and every day crowds would gather to listen to him teach in the temple.

> **Why did Jesus curse the fig tree?**
>
> Mature fig trees often produce out-of-season fruit and it was likely that Jesus expected to find some of that kind of fruit on the tree. The fig tree is like Israel and the religious leaders at that time. They had the appearance of bearing fruit, but there was no actual substance to them. This was an image of Jesus' condemnation of the religious leaders.

CHAPTER THIRTY-SEVEN

OFFICIAL CHALLENGE TO JESUS' AUTHORITY

Matthew 21:23-22:14; Mark 11:27-12:12; Luke 20:1-19

Jesus continued teaching and preaching the good news in the temple, and the religious leaders came up to him and demanded, "Where did you get the authority to do what you're doing?"

Jesus answered, "I'll tell you where I get my authority if you answer this question. Was John's baptism from heaven, or was it merely human?"

They debated. "If we say it was from heaven, he will ask why we didn't believe him, but if we say it was merely human, the crowd will turn on us because they believe John was a prophet." Finally, they said, "We don't know."

Jesus replied, "Then I won't answer your question either.

"What do you think about this? A man had two sons and he told them both to go work in the vineyard. The older son said he wouldn't, but later changed his mind and went anyway. The younger son said he would go, but then he didn't. Which son obeyed his father?"

"The first," they answered.

Jesus said to them, "I tell you the truth, tax collectors and prostitutes will get into the kingdom of God before you do. John the Baptist came to show you the way of righteousness, and you didn't believe him, but the tax collectors and prostitutes did. Even after you saw this, you refused to repent and believe him.

"Here's another parable. A landowner planted a vineyard, built a wall around it, dug a winepress, and made a lookout tower. He then leased the vineyard to some farmers and went away on a long journey. At harvest time, he sent a servant to the farmers to collect his share of the profits. But the farmers grabbed him, beat him up, and sent him back empty-handed.

"The owner sent another servant, but they beat him and treated him shamefully as well; the farmers killed the next servant he sent. He sent other servants and they were all beaten or killed until only his only son was left. The owner finally sent his son, thinking the farmers would respect his child.

"But when the farmers saw the son coming, they decided to kill the heir and steal his inheritance. So, they grabbed him, took him out of the vineyard, and killed him.

"What will the owner do to those wicked farmers when he gets back?"

The religious leaders answered, "He will put those men to a horrible death and rent the vineyard out to others who will give him his share of the crop after each harvest."

Then Jesus asked them, "Didn't you ever read this Scripture? 'The stone the builders rejected has become the cornerstone. This is God's doing and it is marvelous to see.' Whoever trips over that stone will be broken to pieces and it will crush them. Therefore, the kingdom of God will be taken from you and given to a nation that will produce the proper fruit."

When the delegation of officials heard Jesus, they realized that they were the farmers in the story. They wanted to arrest Jesus, but they feared the crowds' reaction; so, they left him and went away.

Then Jesus told several other parables saying, "The kingdom of heaven is like a king who threw a wedding banquet for his son. He invited many people and when the banquet was ready, he sent his servants to tell everyone that it was time to come; but they refused. So, he sent other servants to tell them to come, but they ignored the servants and went about their daily business. Some of the guests even mistreated and killed some of the servants.

"The king became furious and he sent his army to destroy the wicked men and burn their cities. He said to his servants, 'The wedding feast is ready, but the guests I invited aren't worthy to come; go out to the street corners and invite everyone you find.'

"So, the servants went out and brought in everyone they could find and the banquet hall was full of people. But the king came in and noticed that a man wasn't wearing the proper wedding clothes, even though he had made them available for all his guests. So, he asked him, 'Why did you come without wedding clothes, my friend?' The man was speechless, so the king had his servants tie him up and throw him into the outer darkness where there is weeping and gnashing of teeth. Many are called, but few are chosen."

CHAPTER THIRTY-EIGHT

JESUS' RESPONSE TO QUESTIONS

Matthew 22:15-23:39; Mark 12:13-44; Luke 20:20-21:4

The Pharisees and Herodians got together to come up with a way to trap Jesus. They sent some of their followers to ask him questions. One of them said, "Teacher, we know you are an impartial man of integrity and teach God's word regardless of the consequences. But tell us, should we pay taxes to the Roman government or not?"

Jesus knew their evil intent and said, "You hypocrites! Who are you trying to trick with your questions? Show me the coin used to pay the tax." Someone handed him a coin and he asked, "Whose picture and title is on this coin?"

"Caesar's," they replied.

Jesus replied, "Then give Caesar what belongs to him, and give God everything that belongs to him." Amazed by his answer, they left without saying a word because they hadn't been able to trap him.

That same day the Sadducees, who deny that there is life after death, stepped forward and asked him, "Teacher, Moses told us that if a man dies without children, his brother should marry his widow and have children for him. Once, there were seven brothers, and the oldest married a woman and died without children. The second brother also married her but died childless. This continued until she had married all seven brothers, and none of them had children; finally, she died too. Since she had married all seven of them, whom will she be married to in the resurrection?"

Jesus replied, "You don't understand the Scriptures or the power of God. Marriage is only for people here on earth. Those who rise from the dead are God's children and they will be like angels in heaven that cannot die and don't get married. But since you don't believe in a resurrection, you should read the story of Moses and the burning bush. Even though Abraham, Isaac, and Jacob had died, God said, 'I am the God of Abraham, Isaac, and Jacob.' Since he is the God of the living and not the dead, they are all alive to him. You've made a serious mistake."

When the Pharisees heard that he had silenced the Sadducees, they got together to think up another question. One of them was an expert in the Law and asked, "Teacher, what's the greatest commandment in the Law of Moses?"

Jesus replied, "'The Lord our God is the only God. Love him with all your heart, soul, mind, and strength.' The second greatest commandment is to 'Love your neighbor as yourself.' The rest of the Law depends on these two commandments."

The man who asked the question said, "Well said, Teacher. You're right when you say that there is only one God and that I should love him with all our heart, soul, mind, and strength, and that I should love my neighbor as I love myself. This is more important than all the offerings and sacrifices that the Law requires."

When Jesus saw that he had answered wisely, he said, "You're not far from the kingdom of God."

JESUS CONDEMNS THE RELIGIOUS LEADERS

While teaching in the temple, Jesus asked the Pharisees, "What do you think about the Messiah? Whose Son is he?"

They replied, "He is the Son of David."

Jesus responded, "Then why does David, under the inspiration of the Holy Spirit, call him Lord? David says, 'The Lord said to my Lord, "Sit at my right hand until I make your enemies a footstool under your feet."' If David called him Lord, how can he also be his son?" The crowd was fascinated; no one could answer his question. From then on, no one dared to ask him any more questions.

Then Jesus addressed the crowds and his disciples, saying, "The teachers of the religious law and the Pharisees teach from the Law, so you should obey whatever they say, but don't follow their own example. They don't practice what they teach; they crush you with heavy loads and do nothing to ease the burden.

"Beware of these teachers of the religious law because they do everything for show. They love walking around in flowing robes, greetings in the marketplace, and honor in the synagogues and at banquets. But they cheat widows out of their property and cover it up by making long prayers in public. These men will face severe punishment.

"They love it when people call them 'Teacher,' but don't let anyone call you teacher because you have one teacher, and you are all brothers. Don't call anyone on earth 'Father' because God in heaven is your Father. Don't let anyone call you 'Master,' because the Messiah is the only master. The greatest among you must be a servant because God will exalt those who humble themselves and humble those who exalt themselves.

"Woe to you teachers of the religious law and Pharisees. You hypocrites won't enter the kingdom of heaven, and you don't let others in either.

"Woe to you teachers of the religious law and Pharisees. You hypocrites travel all over to make a single convert and then you make him twice the son of hell that you are.

"Woe to you blind guides. You say that swearing by the temple is meaningless, but swearing by the temple gold is a binding oath. You blind fools, which is greater, the gold, or the temple that makes the gold sacred? You also say that swearing by the altar is meaningless, but swearing by the offering on the altar is a binding oath. But which is greater, the offering, or the altar that makes the offering sacred? When you swear by the altar, you swear by everything on it; when you swear by the temple, you swear by the one who dwells in it; and when you swear by heaven, you swear by God's throne and by him."

"Woe to you teachers of the religious law and Pharisees. You hypocrites give a tenth of everything, but you ignore the important parts of the Law like justice, mercy, and faithfulness. It's good that you tithe, but you need to do the more important things too. Blind guides, you strain out a gnat, but swallow a camel.

"Woe to you teachers of the religious law and Pharisees. You hypocrites carefully clean the outside of a cup, but inside you are filthy and full of greed and self-indulgence. You blind Pharisees should wash the inside of the cup, and then the outside will be clean too.

"Woe to you teachers of the religious law and Pharisees. You hypocrites are like whitewashed tombs, beautiful on the outside, but full of death and uncleanness. On the outside you look righteous, but you are full of hypocrisy and wickedness on the inside.

"Woe to you teachers of the religious law and Pharisees. You hypocrites build tombs for the prophets and decorate the graves of the righteous. You say that you wouldn't have done what your ancestors did if you would have been alive when they were. But you testify against yourselves that you are the descendants of the men who killed the prophets. Go ahead and finish what your ancestors started.

"You snakes and brood of vipers! How will you escape the judgment of hell? I am sending you prophets, wise men, and teachers; you will kill them, beat them, and chase them from town to town. Then you will be guilty of murdering all the prophets, from righteous Abel to Zechariah, whom you murdered between the temple and the altar. You are responsible for the death of every prophet of God. I tell you the truth, all this judgment will come upon this generation.

"O Jerusalem, Jerusalem, city that kills the prophets, and stones God's messengers. I have often wanted to gather your children together, just like a hen protects her chicks under her wings, but you resisted. But now your house is desolate because you will not see me again until you say, 'Blessed is the one who comes in the name of the Lord.'"

THE WIDOW'S OFFERING

While he was in the temple, Jesus sat down and watched the crowd drop their offerings into the collection box. Many rich people put in large amounts, but a poor widow came and put in two coins worth less than a penny. Jesus called his disciples over and said, "I tell you the truth, this poor widow has put in more than everyone else because they gave out of their surplus, but she gave everything she had."

CHAPTER THIRTY-NINE

OLIVET DISCOURSE

Matthew 24:1-25:46; Mark 13; Luke 21:5-38

As Jesus was leaving the temple grounds, his disciples pointed out the various buildings and commented on the beautiful stonework and decorations. Some of the stones were 37 feet long, 12 feet high, and 18 feet deep. One of them said, "Teacher, look at these magnificent buildings and the massive stones."

But Jesus replied, "A time is coming when not a single stone of these buildings will be left on another; they will be completely demolished."

***

Later, Jesus sat on the slopes of the Mount of Olives across from the temple. Peter, James, John, and Andrew came to him and asked, "When will this happen and how will we know it's about to happen?"

Jesus told them, "Don't let anyone deceive you because many will come in my name, claiming to be the Messiah and saying that the time is here. Don't listen to them. Don't be afraid when wars break out all over the place, because these things must happen, but the end won't come right away. Nations will go to war with each other and there will be famines, earthquakes, epidemics, terrifying things, and miraculous signs in the heavens. But all these things are only the beginning of the horrors to come.

"Watch out, because before all this, they will hand you over to the courts, and they will beat, persecute, and kill you in the synagogues and prisons. They will accuse you before governors and kings of being my followers.

"But when they arrest you and put you on trial, don't worry about how you will answer your accusers, because I will give you the right words and wisdom that will confound your opponents. This will be your opportunity to tell the world about me. But know that everyone will hate you because you are my followers and even your family and friends will betray you. They will kill some of you, but not a hair of your head will perish.

"Many false prophets will appear and lead many people astray. Sin will be everywhere, and many will have their love grow cold, but those who endure to the end will be saved. The whole world will hear the good news about the kingdom, and then the end will come.

"You will see 'the abomination that causes desecration' that Daniel described. When you see Jerusalem surrounded by armies, you will know that its destruction is near, and those in Judea will flee to the hills. Those outside their house shouldn't go inside to pack and those in the field shouldn't even go back to get a coat. The people in Jerusalem should escape and those outside the city shouldn't enter it for shelter. These will be days of God's vengeance and the fulfillment of Scripture. They will brutally kill people or take them as captives to other nations and the Gentiles will trample Jerusalem down until the age of the Gentiles ends.

> **What is the desecration that Daniel described?**
>
> There are different views of how we should interpret this portion of Scripture. Some believe that these events already happened with the destruction of the temple in 70 A.D. Others think that this is referring to a future event that has not happened yet. A third possibility is that it refers to both, just as Jesus fulfilled many Old Testament prophecies about the Messiah and will finish their fulfillment at the Second Coming.

"It will be horrible for pregnant women and nursing mothers and you should pray that you don't have to run in the winter or on the Sabbath. These days of distress will be worse than any in history or any to come; unless God relents, he will destroy the entire human race. But he will shorten those days for the sake of his chosen ones.

"Then if people tell you they know where the Messiah is, you should ignore them; if someone says the Messiah is out in the desert or hiding in some secret place, don't bother to go and look. Because many false Messiahs and prophets will arise and perform miracles in an attempt to deceive God's chosen ones. Beware, because I have warned you. But when the Son of Man comes, it will be like lightning, which lights up the entire sky. Just as vultures gather near a carcass, know that these signs indicate that the end is near.

"After those horrible days end, 'The sun will be dark, the moon won't give light, the stars will fall from the sky, and the planets will shake.'

"There will be strange events in the skies and signs in the sun, moon, and stars. On the earth, the nations will be in turmoil and perplexed by the roaring seas and strange tides. People will be afraid of what's happening and there will be great mourning because the heavens will shake. Then everyone will see the Son of Man coming in the clouds with power and great glory. He will send his angels out with the sound of a mighty trumpet and they will gather his chosen ones from all over the earth. When you see these things start to happen, lift your heads, because your salvation is near.

"Learn a lesson from the fig tree: when its buds are tender and it sprouts leaves, you know that summer is close. When you see the things I'm telling you about, know that his return is near. I tell you the truth, the generation living when this happens will not pass away until all these things happen. Heaven and earth will disappear, but my words will remain forever.

"No one knows when these things will happen, not even the angels or myself; only the Father knows. But when I return, it will be just like it was in Noah's day. Before the Flood, people enjoyed parties and weddings until the day Noah got into the ark. People didn't know what was happening until the Flood came and swept them all away; that's how it will be when the Son of Man returns. Two men will be in the field and God will take one and leave the other; two women will be working together and God will take one and leave the other.

"Don't weigh down your hearts with alcohol and the worries of life because the Son of Man's return will come suddenly. Always stay alert and pray that you might be able to escape everything that's about to happen and stand before the Son of Man. It will be like a man who goes on a trip and leaves his servants in charge of his house. They don't know when the owner will come back, so they must constantly keep alert and watch for his return.

> **When will Jesus come back?**
>
> The short answer is that we don't know. There are many books and teachers who claim to know when he will come back based on many different metrics. Jesus promises that he will come back when we are least expecting it and that many will be surprised by his arrival. Our job is to be prepared and use signs of the times to renew our faith and keep us close to God. The fact he did not know his return's exact date is a sign of his humanity, not a limitation of his divinity.

"Know that if a homeowner knew a thief was coming, he would not allow that thief to break into his house. Always be ready because the Son of Man will come when you least expect it.

"Who is a faithful, sensible servant that the master can put in charge of managing his household and feeding his family? The servant will receive a reward if the master finds him doing a good job and the master will put him in charge of the entire house. But if the servant thinks that the master won't be back for a while and begins abusing his authority, then the master will return when least expected. The master will tear him apart and throw him out with the hypocrites where there will be weeping and gnashing of teeth.

"The kingdom of heaven will be like ten bridesmaids who took their lamps and went out to meet the groom. Five were foolish and took their lamps out without bringing extra oil, but five were wise and brought extra oil. But the groom took longer than expected and they all fell asleep.

"They were awakened at midnight with news that the groom had come. The bridesmaids woke up and trimmed their lamps and the foolish ones begged the wise ones to give them some of their oil. But the wise ones said, 'If we give you some, then there won't be enough for both of us. Go buy some of your own oil.'

"But the groom arrived while they were out buying oil and the wise bridesmaids went into the wedding feast and they locked the door behind them. The five foolish bridesmaids came and begged to be let in, but the groom said, 'I don't know you.' So, keep watch, because you don't know when I will return.

"The Son of Man's coming will be like a man going on a journey who entrusted his property to his servants. He gave five bags of gold to one, two bags to another, and one bag to the last; then, he left. The man who received the five bags of gold put it to work and earned five more bags. The servant with two bags of gold did the same and earned two more bags. But the man who received one bag of gold dug a hole in the ground and hid his master's money.

"After a long time, their master returned to settle accounts with them. The first servant brought the ten bags of gold and said, 'Master, you gave me five bags of gold, and I've doubled them.'

"His master was pleased and said, 'Well done, good and faithful servant. Since you've been faithful with a few things, I'll put you in charge of many things. Let's celebrate together.'

"Next came the servant with two bags of gold, and he showed his master that he had doubled his money. The master said, 'Well done, good and faithful servant. Since you've been faithful with a few things, I'll put you in charge of many things. Let's celebrate together.'

"Then the servant with the one bag of gold came and said, 'Sir, I know you're a hard man who harvests where you haven't planted seed, so I was afraid and hid your money in the earth. Here it is.'

"But the master was furious and said, 'You wicked, lazy servant. If you think I'm a hard man, you should have put my money in the bank to earn some interest. Take his money and give it to the man who earned five bags of gold. Those who receive a lot will have even more, and those who don't receive much will have it taken away. Throw this worthless servant into the outer darkness, where there will be weeping and gnashing of teeth.'

"When the Son of Man comes with his angels in his glory, he will sit on his glorious throne in heaven. All the nations will come before him and he will separate them just like a shepherd separates the sheep from the goats. He will put the sheep on his right and the goats on his left. Then the King will say to those on his right, 'Come, you that my Father has blessed, inherit the kingdom prepared for you from the world's foundation. For you fed me when I was hungry, gave me a drink when I was thirsty, invited me in when I was a stranger, clothed me when I was naked, cared for me when I was sick, and visited me in prison.'

"Then the righteous will answer, 'Lord, when did we ever see you in these states?'

"Then the King will tell them, 'Whatever you did for the least of my brothers and sisters, you were doing for me.'

> **Heaven**
>
> Heaven is the place that God is preparing for those who place faith in Jesus and follow him. There are many misconceptions about heaven. We will not become angels and float around on clouds playing harps. We will have a physical body and live for eternity with God. We will not struggle with sin, and everything broken will be made right as God had intended from Creation. Our minds cannot comprehend how amazing this place will be, and we lack the language to describe it accurately. John saw a vision of heaven and he had to use descriptive language to compare how tremendous it will be. For example, he writes that the streets will be paved with gold. This is one of the most valuable substances on earth, and in heaven, it is a common construction material.

"Then the King will turn to those on the left and say, 'Away with you cursed ones, go into the eternal fire prepared for Satan and his demons. You didn't feed me when I was hungry, you didn't give me a drink when I was thirsty, you didn't invite me in when I was a stranger, you didn't clothe me when I was naked, you didn't care for me when I was sick, and you didn't visit me when I was in prison.'

"Then they will reply, 'Lord, when did we ever see you hungry, thirsty, a stranger, naked, sick, or in prison?'

"He will answer, 'Whatever you didn't do for the least of my brothers and sisters, you refused to do for me.' Then they will go away into eternal punishment, and the righteous will go to eternal life."

CHAPTER FORTY

ARRANGEMENTS FOR BETRAYAL

Matthew 26:1-16; Mark 14:1-11; Luke 22:1-6

After saying these things, Jesus told his disciples, "The Passover celebration and the Feast of Unleavened Bread starts in two days, and the Son of Man will be betrayed and crucified."

At this time, the leading priests and teachers of the religious law met at the home of Caiaphas, the High Priest. They tried to figure out how to capture Jesus and put him to death, but they agreed not to do it during the Passover because it would cause a riot.

Meanwhile, Jesus was having dinner in Bethany at the home of Simon, the leper. Martha served them the meal and Lazarus sat at the table with Jesus. Then Mary brought in a beautiful, large jar of expensive perfume and poured it over his head. She also anointed Jesus' feet and wiped them with her hair, and the whole house was full of the fragrance.

Some of the disciples became indignant and scolded her, but Mary was only worried about Jesus. Judas Iscariot, who would later betray him, said, "What a waste of money, she could have sold that perfume for a small fortune and given it to the poor." But Judas didn't really care about the poor; he just wanted to steal from the disciples' funds because he was the one who took care of the finances.

But Jesus replied, "Why are you bothering her? You will always have the poor with you, and you can help them whenever you want to, but I won't be here much longer. She has done what she could to prepare my body for burial. I tell you the truth, her story will be told wherever they preach the good news."

Then Satan entered Judas Iscariot, and he went to the leading priests and captains of the temple guard to discuss the best way to betray Jesus. He asked them how much they would pay him and they agreed on 30 pieces of silver (five weeks' wages). From then on, he looked for an opportunity to betray Jesus so that they could arrest him when the crowds weren't around.

CHAPTER FORTY-ONE

THE LAST SUPPER

Matthew 26:17-35; Mark 14:12-31; Luke 22:7-38; John 13

On the first day of the Feast of Unleavened Bread, the day that Jews sacrificed the Passover lamb, Jesus sent Peter and John ahead to prepare the Passover meal. They asked him, "Where do you want us to go?"

Jesus replied, "As soon as you enter Jerusalem, you will meet a man carrying a pitcher of water, follow him to the house where he's staying. Tell the owner that my time has come and that we will eat the Passover meal at his house. Then ask him where the guest room is and he will show you a large upstairs room that's already set up for us. Prepare for us there." They went into the city and found everything just as Jesus described.

That evening Jesus sat down with the twelve disciples and said, "I have looked forward to eating this Passover with you because I won't eat it again until the kingdom of God comes."

Then they began to argue with each other about who would be the greatest in the coming kingdom. Jesus told them, "In this world, rulers order people around and still call themselves 'friends of the people.' But with you, the greatest should be like the least, and the leader should be like a servant. Normally, the master sits at the table and the servants serve him, but I am here as your servant. You have stood by me in my trials, so I grant you the right to eat and drink at my table in the kingdom just as my Father has given me a kingdom. I tell you the truth, you will sit on thrones and judge the twelve tribes of Israel."

Jesus knew that he had authority over everything and that it was time for him to leave the world and return to his Father, so he decided to show his disciples the full extent of his love. So, he got up from the table, took off his robe, wrapped a towel around his waist, and poured water into a basin. He began to wash the disciples' feet and dry them with the towel around his waist. Most roads in the First Century were unpaved and people walked everywhere in sandals. This meant that their feet were covered with whatever they encountered in the road, including feces. Washing feet was the lowest job one could imagine and it was shocking for Jesus to take on this task.

When Jesus came to Peter's feet, Peter asked, "Lord, why are you washing my feet?"

Jesus replied, "You don't understand what I'm doing now, but someday you will."

Peter protested, "You will never wash my feet."

Jesus answered, "Unless I wash your feet, you have no part with me."

Peter said, "Then don't just wash my feet, but my hands and head as well."

Jesus replied, "A person who has had a bath only needs to wash his feet to be entirely clean. You are clean, but not everyone here is." Jesus said this because he knew that Judas was going to betray him.

When he finished washing their feet, he put his clothes on, sat back down, and asked, "Do you understand what I was doing? You rightly call me 'Teacher' and 'Lord' because that's what I am. I've set an example for you because if I am your Teacher and Lord and I have washed your feet, then you should wash one another's feet as well. I tell you the truth, no servant is greater than his master, and no messenger is greater than his sender. God will bless you if you do these things.

"I'm not saying these things to all of you because I know who I have chosen. But this fulfills the Scripture, 'He who shares my bread has turned against me.' I'm telling you this before it happens so that you will believe I am the Messiah. I tell you the truth, whoever accepts my messengers accepts me; whoever accepts me accepts the one who sent me."

While they were sitting around the table, Jesus was troubled and said, "I tell you the truth, one of you who is eating with me will betray me."

They were very sad, and one by one, they asked, "It's not me, is it?"

Jesus replied, "It's one of you who is dipping his bread with me that will betray me. I must die because it is part of God's plan, but it will be terrible for the one who betrays me. It would be better if he had never been born."

Then Peter motioned for John to ask whom he meant, and Jesus said, "It's the one I give this bread to after I dip it in the dish." Then Jesus dipped a piece of bread and gave it to Judas Iscariot.

Judas looked at Jesus and asked, "It's not me, is it, Teacher?"

Jesus told him, "It's you; go do what you have to do quickly."

No one else there understood what Jesus meant. Most thought that Jesus had sent Judas to buy food or give something to the poor because he was their treasurer and a respected disciple. So, Judas left and went out into the night.

Once Judas was gone, Jesus said, "It's time for the Son of Man to enter his glory so that God may be glorified. I will only be with you for a little longer and then I must leave you. You will look for me, but you cannot come where I am going. So, I give you a new commandment, that you should love one another. I love you, so you should love one another, and this will prove that you are my disciples."

Peter asked him, "Lord, where are you going?"

Jesus replied, "You cannot follow me now, but you will follow me later."

Peter asked, "Why can't I follow you now? I'm ready to die for you."

Jesus told them, "All of you will desert me tonight because Scripture says, 'God will strike the shepherd, and the sheep of the flock will scatter.' But after I rise from the dead, I will go to Galilee to meet you. Peter, Satan has demanded to sift you like wheat, but I have prayed for you so that your faith won't fail. Once you have turned back, you should strengthen your brothers."

But Peter declared, "Even if everyone else leaves you, I won't. I'm ready to go to jail and even die for you."

Jesus replied, "Will you really die for me? I tell you the truth, before the rooster crows twice, you will deny that you know me three times."

"I will never disown you, even if I have to die," Peter insisted. Everyone else agreed.

Then Jesus asked, "Did you lack anything when I sent you out without money, a bag, or extra clothes?"

"No," they answered.

Jesus said, "Now you should take your money and baggage; if you don't have a sword, sell your clothes and buy one. It's time to fulfill the Scripture that says, 'He was counted with the sinners.' Every prophecy about me must be fulfilled."

The disciples replied, "We have two swords."

Jesus said, "That's enough."

As they were eating, Jesus took a loaf of bread and asked God to bless it. After praying, he broke it in pieces and gave it to his disciples, saying, "Take it and eat, because this is my body; do this to remember me." Then he took a cup of wine, thanked God for it, and said, "Each of you drink this because it is my blood and it is poured out for the forgiveness of sins. This cup is the New Covenant in my blood, do this to remember me. I tell you the truth, I won't drink wine again until I drink it with you in my Father's kingdom."

The Last Supper as a marriage covenant

The breaking of bread and sharing of the cup of wine was like a Jewish marriage proposal. When a man proposed to a woman, he would take a cup of wine and say the same words Jesus said to his disciples. Jesus told his followers that he loved them and asked them if they would love him in return.

CHAPTER FORTY-TWO
THE UPPER ROOM CONTINUED
Matthew 26:30; Mark 14:26; Luke 22:39; John 14:1-18:1

Jesus continued, "Don't worry, you trust God; now trust me. My Father's house has many rooms and I'm going there to prepare a place for you. If I prepare a place for you, I will come back to bring you there. Then you will always be with me and you know the way to get there."

Thomas said, "Lord, how can we know how to get there if we don't know where you're going?"

Jesus answered, "I am the way, the truth, and the life; the only way to the Father is through me. If you really knew me, you would know my Father too; but now you know him and have seen him."

Philip said, "Lord, show us the Father and we will be satisfied."

Jesus replied, "Philip, don't you know me after all the time we've spent together? If you've seen me, you've seen the Father, so why do you ask me to show you the Father? Do you think I'm lying? My words aren't my own; they come from my Father because he lives in me and is working through me. Believe that the Father is in me and that I am in the Father, or at least believe the miracles I have shown you. I tell you the truth, whoever believes in me will do what I have done, and even more because I am going to the Father. If you ask for something in my name, it is like asking for something because it is what I would want. I will do whatever you ask in my name so that it may glorify my Father.

"If you love me, you will obey me. Then I will ask the Father to send you the Holy Spirit to be your counselor. The world doesn't accept him because they cannot see him and don't know him, but he will live within you. I promise that I won't leave you as orphans because I will come to you. Soon the world won't see me anymore, but you will still see me, and we will both live. Then you will know that I am in the Father, you are in me, and I am in you. Those who obey me love me and my Father and I will love them and show myself to them."

Thaddeus said, "Lord, why are you going to reveal yourself to us, but not to the world?"

Jesus answered, "If you love me, you will obey me; if you don't love me, you won't obey. If you obey, my Father will love you and we will live with you. Remember that these words aren't mine; they are the Father's. I've told you all these things, but the Holy Spirit will complete your education and remind you of what I've said.

"I give you my peace, but it's not like the world's peace, so don't be afraid. Remember that I'm leaving, but I will come back to you. You should be glad that I'm going back to the Father because the Father is greater than I am. I've told you this beforehand so that you might believe. I don't have much time left to tell you things, because the prince of the world is coming. He has no power over me, but I must do what the Father has commanded so that the world will learn that I love the Father.

"I am the true vine and my Father is the gardener. He cuts off every branch that doesn't bear fruit, and he prunes the other branches so that they will bear more fruit. You're already clean because I've spoken to you. Remain in me and I will remain in you because a branch cannot produce fruit if it is cut off from the vine. In the same way, you cannot bear fruit unless you remain in me.

"I am the vine and you are the branches; those who remain in me will bear much fruit. You cannot do anything on your own because you would be like a useless branch that withers and is tossed in the fire. If you remain in me, ask for whatever you want, and I will give it to you. You glorify my Father if you bear much fruit and prove that you are my disciples. If you do not bear fruit, you are not one of my disciples.

"Just as my Father loves me, I love you, so stay in my love. If you obey me, you will remain in my love, just like I've obeyed my Father and stayed in his love. I've told you these things to bring you joy to the fullest. Therefore, I command you to love each other just like I've loved you. There is no greater love than to lay down your life for someone. You are my friends if you obey me. I don't call you servants anymore because a master doesn't tell his servants what he's doing, but I call you friends because I've told you what my Father is doing. Remember that you didn't choose me, but I chose you to bear lasting fruit. Then the Father will give you whatever you ask for in my name. I command you to love each other.

"Remember that if the world hates you, it's because it hated me first. The world would love you if you belonged to it, but since I chose you out of the world, it hates you. A servant is not greater than his master, so if they persecuted me, they will persecute you; if they obeyed me, they will obey you. They will treat you this way because they don't know the one who sent me. If I hadn't spoken to them, they would be ignorant of their sin, but now they have no excuse. Whoever hates me hates my Father too. If they hadn't seen my miracles, they'd be innocent, but now they've seen these miracles and hated me and my Father. But this fulfills their Law, which says, 'They hated me for no reason.'

"When I send you the Counselor, the Spirit of truth, he will tell you about me. Then you must tell others about me because you've been with me from the beginning.

"I've told you these things so that you won't fall away. Know that they will kick you out of the synagogues and people will think that they are serving God when they kill you. They only do such things because they don't know the Father or me. I've warned you about this now to remind you later; I didn't tell you at first because I was there to protect you.

"Now I am going to the one who sent me and none of you asks me where I'm going. My words bring you grief, but it's good that I'm leaving. If I weren't, the Holy Spirit wouldn't come to you. When I send the Holy Spirit to you, he will convict the world of its unbelief, God's righteousness, and the coming judgment and condemnation.

"I have a lot more to tell you, but you can't handle it right now. When the Spirit of truth comes, he will guide you into all truth. He won't be speaking on his own behalf; he will only tell you what he's heard. He will tell you what's coming and will bring glory to me by telling you what is mine. Everything that the Father has is mine, and that's why I told you that the Spirit will tell you what's mine.

> **Who is the Holy Spirit?**
>
> The Holy Spirit is the third person of the Trinity. He is the promised helper that lives in the hearts of everyone who follows Jesus. The Holy Spirit exists to glorify Jesus and help us better bring him glory and honor. When people put their faith in Jesus, the Holy Spirit lives within them.

"Soon, you won't see me anymore, but you will see me after a while."

Some of the disciples were confused and said to each other, "What does he mean we won't see him and then we will see him and that he's going to the Father? What does he mean after a while? What is he talking about?"

Jesus realized that they wanted to ask him questions, so he said, "Did I confuse you? I tell you the truth, you will weep and mourn while the world rejoices, but your grief will turn to joy when you see me again. A woman in labor forgets her pain because of her joy when her child is born. In the same way, this is your time of grief, but you will rejoice when I see you again, and no one will take away your joy. Then you won't need to ask me for anything because my Father will give you whatever you ask for in my name. You haven't asked for anything in my name, but now, ask and you will receive; then you will rejoice.

"I've spoken to you in parables, but a time is coming when I will tell you plainly about my Father and then you will ask the Father in my name. I'm not saying I will ask the Father on your behalf because the Father loves you, and you love me and believe that I came from God. Now I must return to him."

Then the disciples said, "We understand you now that you're not speaking in parables. We understand that you know everything and don't need anyone to tell you anything; thus, we know that you came from God."

"Finally, you trust me," Jesus answered. "But very soon, you will all scatter to your own homes. You will all leave me alone, but I'm not alone because my Father is with me.

"I've told you these things to give you peace. You will have trouble in the world, but take heart, because I have overcome the world."

After saying this, Jesus looked to heaven and prayed, "Father, the time has come. Glorify your Son, so that he may glorify you. You've given me authority over all people so that I might give eternal life to all those you've given me. Eternal life comes from knowing you and me, the Messiah, the one you sent. I've glorified you by finishing the work you've given me, so Father, bring me into the glory we shared at the beginning of the world.

"I've told these men about you because you gave them to me. They have obeyed your word and now they know that everything I have is a gift from you. I gave them your words, and they accepted them; they know I came from you, and they believed my words. I pray for them because they belong to you. We share everything and they've brought me glory. Now I'm coming home to you, but they will remain in the world. Holy Father, I don't pray that you take them out of the world, but protect them by the power of your name so that they may have unity. I've kept them safe while I was here, and the only one I lost was the one that the Scriptures said was doomed to destruction.

"Now I'm coming to you, but I say these things to them so that they might have joy. I've given them your word, and the world hates them because they're not from this world, and neither am I. Purify them and make them holy by teaching them your words. Just as you sent me into the world, I'm sending them into the world, and I give myself to you that they might also be entirely yours. I'm also praying for those who will believe them, and I pray that they will have unity and the world will believe that you sent me.

"I've given them the glory that you've given me that they may have the same unity that we do. Cause them to have complete unity so that the world will know that you sent me and love them.

"Father, I want them to be with me so that they can see the glory you've given me because you loved me before the beginning of the world. Righteous Father, the world doesn't know you, but I do; and these disciples know that you've sent me. I've revealed you to them and will continue to reveal to them so that they may know the love that you have for me."

They sang a hymn and went out to the Mount of Olives across the Kidron Valley.

CHAPTER FORTY-THREE

GARDEN OF GETHSEMANE

Matthew 26:36-56; Mark 14:32-52; Luke 22:40-53; John 18:2-12

Then Jesus brought them to an olive grove called Gethsemane and told them, "Pray that you won't fall into temptation. Sit here while I go over there and pray." Then he took Peter, James, and John with him, and he was distressed. He told them, "I'm sorrowful to the point of death, stay here and watch with me."

He went about a stone's throw away and fell facedown, praying, "Daddy, Father, you can do all things. If possible, please take this cup of suffering from me; but not my will, but your will be done." An angel from heaven came to strengthen him and he prayed so fervently that his sweat fell to the ground like great drops of blood.

Jesus returned to his disciples and found them sleeping. "Peter," he said. "Are you asleep? Couldn't you stay awake and watch for me for an hour? Stay awake and pray so that temptation won't overwhelm you. The spirit is willing, but the flesh is weak."

Again, he stepped away and prayed, "Father, if I must drink this cup, your will be done." He came back to his sleeping disciples; they had nothing to say. So, he went back a third time and prayed the same thing.

When he returned, they were still asleep, exhausted from grief, so he said to them, "Why are you still sleeping and resting? Enough! It's time for the Son of Man's betrayal into the hands of sinners. Let's go, my betrayer is here."

As he said this, Judas Iscariot arrived with a mob. Judas knew where they were meeting because Jesus had gone there with his disciples many times. The leading priests and Pharisees had sent a battalion of Roman soldiers and temple guards with Judas with blazing torches, lanterns, and weapons. Judas told them that he would kiss Jesus and that they should take him away.

Jesus realized what was going to happen, so he stepped forward and asked, "Who are you looking for?"

"Jesus of Nazareth," they replied.

Jesus told them, "I'm the one you're looking for." As he said this, they all fell backward to the ground because of the authority of his words. Then he asked them again, "Who are you looking for?"

Again, they replied, "Jesus of Nazareth."

Jesus said, "I told you that I'm the one you seek. Since you want me, let these others go." He said this to fulfill his statement, "I have not lost a single one of those you gave me."

Jesus said to Judas, "Friend, do what you came for."

Judas stepped forward and as he kissed him, he said, "Greetings, Teacher!"

But Jesus said, "Judas, how can you betray the Son of Man with a kiss?" Then the temple guards grabbed Jesus and arrested him.

When the other disciples saw what was happening, they exclaimed, "Lord, should we fight? We have the two swords!" Without waiting for an answer, Peter drew a sword and cut off the right ear of Malchus, the high priest's servant.

Jesus looked at Peter and said, "Put away your sword, because those who live by the sword will die by the sword and I must drink from the cup that the Father has given me." Then he touched the place where Malchus' ear had been and healed him. "Don't you realize that if I ask the Father, he will give me thousands of angels to protect us? But if I did, how would we fulfill the Scriptures that say it must happen this way?"

Then Jesus turned to the leading priests and captains of the temple guard and said, "Am I a dangerous criminal leading a rebellion? Is that why you've come to arrest me with swords and clubs? Why didn't you arrest me in the temple when I was teaching every day? But this is the time that darkness reigns and all of this fulfills the words of the prophets."

Meanwhile, all his disciples ran away. There was a young man (likely Mark) wearing a linen nightshirt following behind them, and when the mob tried to grab him, he left his clothes behind and ran away naked.

CHAPTER FORTY-FOUR

JESUS' TRIAL WITH THE JEWS

Matthew 26:57-68; Mark 14:53-65; Luke 22:54, 63-65; John 18:13-23

First, the mob took him to Annas because he was the high priest Caiaphas' father-in-law. Even though Caiaphas had replaced Annas, many still viewed Annas as the real high priest. It was Caiaphas who had told the Jewish leaders that it was better for one man to die for the nation than to have the entire nation perish.

Inside Annas' house, they began asking Jesus about his followers and his teaching. Jesus replied, "I've spoken openly in the synagogues and the temple. Everyone has heard me clearly, so why are you asking me these questions? Ask the people who heard me; they all know what I said."

One of the temple guards hit Jesus in the face and demanded, "Is that any way to answer the high priest?"

Jesus answered, "Tell me if I've said something wrong. But if I've told the truth, why did you hit me?"

Then Jesus' accusers took him to Caiaphas' house to stand before the teachers of the religious law and the other Jewish leaders.

The leading priests and Sanhedrin (group of Jewish elders) were seeking witnesses who would lie about Jesus so that they could kill him. Even though they found many people to lie, their testimony contradicted each other. Finally, they found two men to say, "He said, 'I will destroy this temple of God and rebuild it in three days.'" But even then, they couldn't agree on their testimony.

The high priest stood up before the crowd and addressed Jesus, "Aren't you going to defend yourself against what these men are saying?" Jesus just remained silent. Finally, the priest demanded, "In the name of the living God, tell us whether or not you are the Messiah, the Son of God!"

Jesus replied, "I am, and in the future, you will see the Son of Man sitting at God's right hand and coming back on the clouds of heaven."

Outraged, the high priest tore his clothes and shouted, "Blasphemy! We don't need any more witnesses. You all heard his blasphemy! What's your verdict?"

"Guilty!" they shouted. "He must die!"

They blindfolded Jesus and some spit on him and punched him. "Tell us who hit you, Messiah," they jeered. They continued to beat and insult him as they led him away to the courtyard.

CHAPTER FORTY-FIVE

PETER'S DENIALS

Matthew 26:69-27:10; Mark 14:66-72; Luke 22:54-71; John 18:15-27

Meanwhile, Peter and John followed along far behind because they wanted to see what would happen to Jesus. John knew the high priest Caiaphas, so John was allowed into the courtyard with Jesus. Peter stood anxiously just outside the gate. John got the woman at the gate to let Peter in, and together they warmed themselves around a fire, with the guards and household servants.

A servant girl who worked for the high priest stared at Peter in the firelight and said, "You are one of Jesus' followers."

But Peter denied it in front of everyone, saying, "Woman, I don't know what you're talking about." Then he went out into the entryway.

Later, one of Malchus' relatives, who served the high priest asked, "Didn't I see you in the olive grove with Jesus of Nazareth? You are definitely one of them." But Peter denied it, and immediately a rooster crowed.

Peter denied it again with an oath, saying, "I don't even know him."

A little later, some other people came over to him and said, "You must be one of them because of your Galilean accent."

Peter began to call down curses on himself and he swore to them, "I swear to God that I don't know him." A rooster crowed a second time and at that moment, Jesus turned and looked at Peter. Suddenly, Peter remembered Jesus' words, and he left the courtyard, weeping bitterly.

Very early in the morning, the leading priests, the teachers of the religious law, the other leaders, and the whole Sanhedrin met again to discuss how to persuade the Romans to put Jesus to death.

They brought Jesus out, demanding, "Tell us if you are the Messiah."

Jesus replied, "You won't believe me if I tell you and you won't answer if I ask you a question. But from now on, the Son of Man will sit at God's right hand."

They all shouted, "Are you the Son of God?"

Jesus answered, "You are right to say that I am."

They said to each other, "We don't need other witnesses; we heard him say it ourselves."

Judas realized that they condemned Jesus to die, and he was sorry. So, he took the 30 pieces of silver back to the leading priests and said, "I've sinned because I've betrayed an innocent man."

But they retorted, "We don't care; that's your problem." So, Judas threw the money onto the temple floor and went out and hanged himself. The leading priests picked up the money and said, "It's against the Law to put it in the treasury because it's blood money." After discussing what to do with it, they decided to buy the Potter's Field and make it a cemetery for foreigners. After that, they called it the Field of Blood. This fulfilled Jeremiah's prophesy "They took the 30 pieces of silver that Israel paid for him and purchased the Potter's Field as the Lord directed."

CHAPTER FORTY-SIX

JESUS BEFORE PILATE

Matthew 27:11-26; Mark 15:1-15; Luke 23:1-25; John 18:28-19:16

Jesus' trial with Caiaphas ended in the early morning hours, and the Sanhedrin bound him and took him to Pilate, the Roman governor. His accusers waited outside because they didn't want to defile themselves and be unable to participate in the Passover feast. So, Pilate went out and asked, "What's your charge against this man?"

They replied, "We wouldn't have brought him here if he weren't a criminal."

"Then go judge him by your own laws," Pilate said.

The Jewish leaders answered, "But only the Romans can execute him." This statement fulfilled Jesus' prediction about how he would die. Then the Jewish leaders made their case, saying, "This man has been trying to ruin our people by telling them not to pay their taxes and claiming to be the Messiah, a king."

Pilate turned to Jesus and asked, "Are you the King of the Jews?"

Jesus answered, "Are you asking me yourself, or did others tell you about me?"

Pilate replied, "I'm not a Jew; it was your own people and their priests that brought you here. What have you done?"

Jesus answered, "I'm not an earthly king; otherwise, my servants would have fought to prevent my arrest. My kingdom is not of this world."

"So, you are a king," Pilate said.

Jesus said, "You're right when you say that I am a king and that's why I was born. I came to bring truth to the world and everyone who loves the truth will recognize that I speak the truth."

"What is truth?" Pilate asked. Then he went out to the people and said, "He's not guilty of any crime. I find nothing wrong with this man."

The mob became desperate and said, "But he's stirred up trouble all over Judea, from Galilee to Jerusalem."

Jesus remained silent while the Jewish leaders accused him of many crimes. Pilate was surprised and said, "Don't you hear them? You should answer these charges." But Jesus said nothing.

After listening to their charges, Pilate asked if Jesus was a Galilean. When he found out that Jesus was, Pilate sent him to Herod Antipas because he was in Jerusalem, and Galilee was under Herod's authority.

Herod was delighted to see Jesus because he had heard about him and wanted to see him perform a miracle. He asked Jesus many questions, and the leading priests and teachers of the religious law made many accusations, but Jesus refused to answer any of them. Herod and his soldiers mocked and ridiculed Jesus; they put a royal robe on him and sent him back to Pilate. That day Herod and Pilate became friends, where they had previously been enemies.

Every Passover, the governor would release one prisoner the crowd wanted. This year, a notorious prisoner named Barabbas was in jail for murder during an insurrection. Pilate called the Jewish leaders together and said, "You brought me a man that you accuse of leading a revolt, but I have examined him in your presence and I find him innocent. Herod found him innocent as well, and there is no reason to put him to death. So, I will flog him and then release him. I will bring him out to you now, but know that I don't find him guilty."

When they brought out Jesus, Pilate said, "Here he is! Who do you want me to release, Barabbas, or Jesus, the Messiah?"

The leading priests and other leaders persuaded the crowds to ask for Barabbas instead of Jesus. When Pilate asked again, "Who do you want me to release to you?" the crowd shouted, "Barabbas!"

Pilate asked, "But if I release Barabbas, what should I do with the man you call the King of the Jews?"

The crowd shouted, "Crucify him!"

Pilate answered, "You crucify him, I find him innocent."

The Jewish leaders replied, "Our Law says that he should die because he called himself the Son of God."

When Pilate heard this, he was afraid and took Jesus back inside. "Where are you from?" he demanded, but Jesus was silent. Then Pilate continued, "Don't you realize that I can release or crucify you?"

Finally, Jesus said, "You wouldn't have any power unless God gave it to you, so the ones who brought me to you are the greater sinners."

Pilate tried to release him, but the Jewish leaders insisted, "You're not a friend of Caesar if you release this man because anyone who calls himself a king is rebelling against Caesar."

Pilate brought Jesus out to the mob again and sat down on the judgment seat on the platform known as the Stone Pavement. It was about noon on the day before the Passover. As Pilate was sitting on the judgment seat, his wife sent a message, saying, "Leave that innocent man alone because I had a terrible dream about him last night."

"Here's your king!" Pilate said to the people.

"Away with him! Crucify him!" the crowd yelled.

Pilate asked, "Do you want to crucify your king?"

The leading priests shouted, "Our only king is Caesar."

Pilate demanded, "Why should I crucify him? What crime has he committed?"

But the crowd only roared louder, "Crucify him!"

Pilate demanded a third time, "What crime has he committed? There's no reason for me to put him to death, so I will flog him and let him go."

But the crowd shouted louder and louder, and Pilate realized that a riot was starting. So, he sent for a bowl of water and washed his hands, saying, "I am innocent of this man's blood; you take responsibility."

The people yelled back, "Let his blood be on our children and us."

Pilate wanted to please the crowd, so he released Barabbas and had Jesus flogged with a lead-tipped whip 39 times (this was one short of a lethal sentence). Then he sentenced Jesus to die and he gave him over to the Roman soldiers to crucify him.

Some of the governor's soldiers took Jesus into their headquarters and brought out all the other soldiers. They stripped him and put a scarlet robe on him. They also made a crown of long, sharp thorns and put it on his head, and put a stick in his right hand as a scepter. They knelt before him and mocked him, yelling, "Hail the King of the Jews!" Then they spit on him and beat him with the stick they gave him.

When they got tired of mocking him, they took off the robe, put his clothes back on, and led him away to be crucified.

CHAPTER FORTY-SEVEN

THE CRUCIFIXION

Matthew 27:27-66; Mark 15:16-47; Luke 23:26-66; John 19:16-42

On their way out, they met a man from Cyrene named Simon, and forced him to carry Jesus' crossbeam, a piece of wood weighing between 30 and 40 pounds. Then they went to a place called Golgotha, or the Place of the Skull, and great crowds followed behind. Jesus turned to some of the grief-stricken women in the crowd and said, "Don't weep for me, but weep for yourselves and your children because they will soon say that the childless are blessed. People will beg the mountains to fall on them and for the hills to bury them. If men do these things when the tree is green, what will happen when it is dry?"

The soldiers gave him some wine mixed with bitter gall; this was a painkiller given to those condemned to die. But once he had tasted it, he refused to drink it. Meanwhile, the soldiers led out two criminals that were also being executed that day.

The soldiers nailed Jesus to the cross about nine in the morning and Jesus said, "Father, forgive them; they don't know what they're doing."

> **Crucifixion**
>
> The Romans were experts at torture and death and one of the primary methods they used for execution was crucifixion. While this technique predates the Romans, they perfected the art. The condemned would have their hands tied or nailed to a crossbeam attached to a vertical pole. Prisoners had a small platform to stand on or had their feet nailed to the pole. Eventually, victims would become exhausted and the bodyweight would cause them to asphyxiate and die.
>
> When Jesus was executed, he had two spikes nailed through his wrists between his radius and ulna. He also had a spike hammered through the tops of his feet close to his ankles. He had to alternate between holding his body weight on his feet and pulling himself up with his arms to breathe. This was an excruciating way to die.

After they nailed him to the cross, the soldiers divided his clothes among the four of them. They cast lots to decide who would get his undergarment because it was a seamless robe and would be worth a small amount of money. This fulfilled the Scripture that said, "They divided my garments amongst them and cast lots for my clothing."

Then the soldiers sat around and kept watch as he hung there. They fastened a sign in Aramaic, Latin, and Greek above his head that read, "This is Jesus of Nazareth, the King of the Jews."

The leading priests went to Pilate and said, "Change it to say that he claimed to be the King of the Jews."

Pilate replied, "I've written what I've written."

Jesus' mother, his aunt, Mary (the wife of Clopas), and Mary Magdalene were standing near the cross; when Jesus saw his mother standing next to John, he said to her, "Mother, here is your son." Then he turned to John and said, "Here is your mother." From then on, John took her into his home.

***

The people who passed by mocked him, saying, "So you can destroy the temple and rebuild it in three days? If you're the Son of God, save yourself and come down from the cross!"

The leading priests and Jewish leaders also mocked Jesus, saying, "He saved others, but he cannot save himself. If he is the Messiah, he should come down from the cross so that we can all believe in him. If he trusts in God, let God come save him since he said he is the Son of God."

The soldiers also mocked him by offering him some sour wine. They called out, "If you're the King of the Jews, you should save yourself."

One of the criminals next to him scoffed, "If you're the Messiah, prove it by saving yourself and us."

But the other criminal protested, "Don't you fear God? We deserve to die, but this man is innocent." Then he turned to Jesus and said, "Remember me when you come into your kingdom."

Jesus replied, "I tell you the truth, you will be with me in paradise today."

At noon, darkness fell across the whole land for three hours. Then Jesus called out, "*Eli, Eli, lama sabachthani?*" which means, "My God, my God, why have you forsaken me?" This is the first line of the 22nd Psalm and showed that this was the fulfillment of Scripture.

Some of the bystanders thought he was calling for the prophet Elijah and one of them said, "Let's see if Elijah will come save him."

Jesus knew that everything was finished, and to fulfill Scripture, he said, "I'm thirsty." Someone soaked a sponge in a jar of sour wine, put it on a hyssop branch, and held it up to his lips. These were the sponges that servants used at public toilets to clean the wealthy users' backsides and the wine was what they used to disinfect the sponges. When Jesus tasted it, he said, "It is finished! Father, I entrust my spirit into your hands!" With those words, he breathed his last and died.

> **What happened when Jesus died?**
>
> When Jesus died on the cross, God the Father was pouring out all his wrath and judgment on Jesus instead of us. A sacrifice means something set aside from everyday life as a gift to make things right between two parties, like parents will sacrifice money, time, and privacy to raise happy, healthy children. Jesus had lived a perfect life and was the perfect sacrifice for all past, present, and future sins that people would commit to make things right between God and man. Jesus willingly went to the cross because he loves us and wants us to spend eternity with him rather than be separated from him in judgment.

At that moment, the thick veil hanging in the temple was torn in two, from top to bottom, and there was a great earthquake. Many tombs opened and the bodies of many holy people came back to life. These people went into Jerusalem and many people saw them.

The Roman soldiers handling the execution were terrified. When the captain of the guard saw how Jesus died, he said, "Certainly this was a righteous man; truly he was the Son of God!"

When the crowd saw what had happened, they beat their breasts and went home in despair. Many women who had been with Jesus since Galilee were watching from a distance. Among them were Mary Magdalene, Mary (the mother of James the younger and Joseph), Salome, and Zebedee's wife (the mother of James and John).

This all happened on Friday, the day before the Sabbath, and this Sabbath was going to be special because it was also the Passover. The Jews didn't want the bodies to hang overnight, so they asked Pilate to break their legs and take them down. The soldiers broke the two criminals' legs, but when they came to Jesus, they saw he was already dead, so they didn't break his legs. However, John saw them put a spear in his side, and blood and water flowed out. These things fulfilled the Scripture that reads, "None of his bones will be broken" and, "They will look on the one they pierced."

> **Did Jesus really die?**
>
> The Romans were experts at death, and if they declared Jesus to be dead, he was undoubtedly dead. If they declared victims to be dead when they were not, they forfeited their own lives, so there was tremendous motivation to be accurate with their judgments. When people die, the water in the blood begins to separate, so this is a sign that Jesus really was dead.
>
> There are theories against the resurrection that Jesus did not really die, but none of these are realistic when we look at the brutality he suffered. There is no way he could have gone through everything he did and then convinced his disciples that he

> Had risen from the dead. He would have been very weak from blood loss and barely able to stand if he had just revived in the cool of the tomb.

JESUS' BURIAL

As evening approached, Joseph of Arimathea, a member of the Sanhedrin, gathered his courage and asked Pilate for Jesus' body. Joseph was a secret disciple of Jesus because he was afraid of the Sanhedrin. He was waiting for the kingdom of God and disagreed with the actions of the other religious leaders. Pilate verified that Jesus was dead and gave Jesus' body to Joseph.

Nicodemus, the man who had come to Jesus at night, came with Joseph and brought 75 pounds of embalming ointment made from myrrh and aloes. They wrapped Jesus in linen cloth with the spices according to the Jewish burial custom. Joseph owned a new tomb in a nearby garden and they put Jesus' body there and rolled a large stone over the entrance.

Mary Magdalene and the other Mary were watching where they buried Jesus, and then they went home and prepared more spices and ointments to embalm him. But they rested on the Sabbath in obedience to the Law.

The next day the leading priests and Pharisees went to see Pilate and told him, "That deceiver we just killed once said, 'After three days I will rise again.' We ask that you guard the tomb until the third day so that the disciples won't be able to steal the body. If they do, their lies will be worse than his."

Pilate replied, "Take a guard and make the tomb as secure as you know how." So, they put a seal on the stone and posted guards to protect it.

> **Who killed Jesus?**
>
> Multiple parties are responsible for his death and we cannot pin it on one person or people group. The Romans are the ones who carried out the execution and were guilty. The Jews rejected him as Messiah and were also responsible. Jesus died for our sins as well, so we bear the guilt for his death too. Finally, God is the one who is ultimately responsible, and if Jesus had not wanted to die, he would not have. He chose to go to the cross because of his love for us.

CHAPTER FORTY-EIGHT

THE RESURRECTION

Matthew 28:1-15; Mark 16:1-11; Luke 24:1-12; John 20:1-18

The following evening, when the Sabbath had ended, Mary Magdalene, Mary, James' mother, and Salome bought spices to anoint Jesus' body. Early Sunday morning, while it was still dark, there was a great earthquake because an angel of the Lord rolled away the stone and sat on it. The guards shook with fear and became like dead men when they saw him because his face shone like lightning, and his clothing was as white as snow.

> **Three days in the grave?**
>
> Some people object that Jesus only spent about 36 hours in the grave (Friday evening to Sunday morning) and not the three days that Scripture claims. However, in Jewish accounting of time, any part of a day counted as a day. He was in the grave Friday evening, Saturday, and Sunday morning, thus making three days.

Not long after that, Mary Magdalene came to the tomb and found the stone rolled away. She ran and found Peter and John and said, "They've taken the Lord's body out of the tomb and I don't know where they've put him."

Peter and John ran to the tomb, and John got there first. He looked in and saw the linen cloth on the ground, but he didn't go in. Peter arrived, went inside, and saw the linen cloth on the ground and Jesus' head covering folded on the side. Then John went in and believed because he finally understood that Scripture had said that the Messiah would rise from the dead.

Peter and John both went home, but Mary, who had followed them, lingered outside the tomb. She cried as she looked in the tomb and she saw two men sitting where Jesus had been. One of them asked her, "Why are you crying?"

She replied, "Because they've taken away my Lord, and I don't know where they've put him."

She looked over her shoulder and saw Jesus standing there, but she didn't recognize him. He asked Mary, "Why are you crying? Who are you looking for?"

She thought he was the gardener, so she said, "Sir, if you've taken him away, tell me where you've put him, and I'll go get him."

Jesus said, "Mary."

She recognized his voice, turned to him, and exclaimed, "Teacher!"

Jesus said, "Don't cling to me because I haven't returned to the Father yet. Go find my brothers and tell them that I'm returning to our God and Father."

Mary Magdalene, the woman that Jesus had cast seven demons from, was the first to see the risen Lord. She went and found the other disciples and told them that Jesus was alive. They didn't believe her and continued to weep and grieve. Despite their unbelief, she insisted that she had seen the Lord, and she gave them his message.

Meanwhile, as the new day was dawning, the other women went out to the tomb with the spices. On the way they talked about who would roll the stone away. When they got to the tomb, they saw that the large stone covering the entrance was already rolled away. They were puzzled when they entered the tomb and couldn't find the body. They saw two men in dazzling robes and the terrified women bowed before them.

One of the men said, "Don't be afraid. You're looking for Jesus of Nazareth, but he isn't here because he's risen from the dead. Don't you remember that he told you that the Son of Man would be betrayed, crucified, and rise on the third day? Come look where they put his body and then tell his disciples and Peter that he has risen and is going ahead of them to Galilee. You will see him there just as he said before his death." They then recalled that Jesus had indeed said this.

The bewildered women ran from the tomb, trembling, yet elated. They were too frightened to talk, and they rushed to find the disciples and give them the angels' message. As they went, Jesus met them and said, "Greetings." Then they ran to him, touched him, and worshiped him. Jesus said, "Don't be afraid! Go tell my brothers that I will meet them in Galilee."

Jesus and women

Women were not treated well during the First Century. They were not even allowed to give legal testimony. Jesus did much to change and elevate the status of his female followers, as evidenced by listing the women who helped in his ministry and saw his crucifixion. He also made his first appearances to women, giving them an elevated position in the resurrection story.

As the women entered the city, some of the men who had been guarding the tomb went to the leading priests and told them what had happened. The religious leaders decided to bribe the soldiers, telling them to say that the disciples came while they were asleep and stole the body. They also said, "We'll stand up for you if the governor hears about you falling asleep." The soldiers agreed and the story became widespread among the Jews.

The women who went to the tomb, Mary Magdalene, Joanna, Mary, the mother of James, and several others, rushed back to tell everyone what happened. They told the disciples their story, but they didn't believe them because it sounded like gibberish.

However, Peter ran back to the tomb and saw the linen wrappings. Then he went home again, wondering what had happened.

> **Did Jesus really rise from the dead?**
>
> Many have tried to discredit Jesus' resurrection because they don't like the implications. This is the crucial component of Christianity, and if he did not rise from the dead, then our faith is worthless. Jesus appeared multiple times to multiple people, ate food, and had his followers touch his physical body.
>
> People present many arguments that try to deny the resurrection, although it is interesting that none of Christianity's early opponents tried to refute it. When we examine the various attempts to explain away the resurrection, none of them hold water. The first hypothesis is that the disciples stole the body. However, this does not explain why the disciples would later die for their faith (people do not die for what they know is a lie).
>
> Another view is that the Roman or Jewish authorities stole the body. However, this view does not make sense because these authorities had nothing to gain by stealing the body. The authorities could have stopped the resurrection story by producing his body.
>
> A third possibility is that the disciples went to the wrong tomb. Again, the authorities could produce Jesus' body to stop the resurrection story. Also, Joseph of Arimathea, the tomb's owner, would not have gone to the wrong tomb.
>
> Another view is that Jesus never really died but rather fainted and then revived in the tomb. However, if Jesus, weakened by blood loss and lack of food and water, could get himself out of the 75 pounds of burial wrappings, move the stone by himself, and get past the guard, he would not inspire great confidence in his disciples. Furthermore, the Romans were experts at putting people to death, and they knew Jesus was dead.
>
> A final theory is that Jesus' followers had a group hallucination. However, 500 people do not have the same hallucination at once, hallucinations do not suddenly stop (Jesus left after 40 days), and hallucinations only come from what is already in the mind (the disciples did not believe that Jesus would resurrect). If the hallucination theory is true, then the authorities could have produced the body and stopped the disciples' story from spreading. When we look at the evidence, which even the harshest critics agree with, the only option that makes sense is that Jesus physically rose from the grave.

CHAPTER FORTY-NINE
RESURRECTION APPEARANCES
Mark 16:12-15; Luke 24:13-43; John 20:19-21:25; I Corinthians 15:5-6

That same day two of Jesus' followers were walking to Emmaus, a village about seven miles from Jerusalem. As they were walking, Jesus joined them, but God kept them from recognizing him.

Jesus asked, "What are you talking about?"

They stopped walking, looking heartbroken. One of them named Cleopas replied, "You must be the only person in Jerusalem who doesn't know what's happened over the last few days."

"What things?" Jesus asked.

They replied, "The things that happened to Jesus of Nazareth, the prophet who did wonderful miracles and was a mighty teacher. We had hoped that he would redeem Israel, but our leaders sentenced him to death and crucified him. It's the third day since his death and some of our women have told us that they were at his tomb and couldn't find his body this morning. Some of our friends went to the tomb and found it just like the women said, but they couldn't find his body."

Then Jesus said, "You foolish men, why don't you believe what the prophets wrote? Didn't the prophets say that the Messiah must suffer all these things before he could enter his glory?" Then Jesus explained to them what the Scriptures said about him. Still, the men did not recognize Jesus.

They were getting close to Emmaus, and Jesus acted like he would go further, but they begged him to stay because it was evening. So, Jesus stayed with them.

When they sat down to eat, he took a loaf of bread, gave thanks, broke it, and gave it to them. Suddenly they recognized him, but he disappeared. They turned to each other and said, "Didn't our hearts burn within us while he explained the Scriptures to us?"

They got right up and ran back to Jerusalem, where the other followers of Jesus were meeting behind closed doors, fearing the Jewish leaders. When the two followers arrived, they told the disciples, "The Lord has risen and appeared to Peter." Then they told the story of how Jesus had come to them and how they had recognized him when they broke bread together.

Just as the two men were finishing their story, Jesus himself appeared and said, "Peace be with you." The whole group was frightened because they thought they were seeing a ghost. But Jesus continued, "Why are you scared and why do you doubt? Look at my hands and feet, and here is my side. Touch me, because a ghost doesn't have a body like I do."

They still didn't believe it because they were in shock. Jesus rebuked them for not trusting him and asked, "Do you have anything to eat?" They gave him a piece of broiled fish and watched him eat it.

When they finally realized that it really was him, they were euphoric. Jesus said, "Peace be with you. Just as the Father sent me, I am sending you." Then he breathed on them and said, "Receive the Holy Spirit. If you forgive anyone's sins, they are forgiven; if you don't forgive them, they aren't forgiven."

***

Thomas was not with the disciples when Jesus came, and they told him, "We've seen the Lord!"

But he replied, "I won't believe it unless I see the scars and touch them."

They were all meeting together a week later and this time, Thomas was with them. Although the doors were locked, Jesus appeared in their midst and said, "Peace be with you."

Then he turned to Thomas and said, "See my hands and my side and touch them. Stop doubting and believe."

Thomas exclaimed, "My Lord and my God!"

> **Did people think Jesus was God?**
>
> Yes, and there are many examples of him receiving worship from his followers. Jesus would not have allowed them to do this if he were not God. Other New Testament writers also claimed that he was God and all of this would be blasphemy and a capital crime if they were not 100% sure.

Jesus said, "You trust because you have seen me, but blessed are those who believe even though they haven't seen me."

***

A little while later, Peter went fishing in the Sea of Galilee with Thomas, Bartholomew, James, John, and two other disciples. They went out and caught nothing all night. At dawn they saw a man standing on the beach and he called out, "Friends, have you caught any fish?"

"No," they replied.

Jesus said, "Throw your net on the right-hand side of the boat, and you'll catch some." They did, and they were unable to pull in the net because there were so many fish.

John realized that the man on the beach was Jesus, and he turned to Peter and said, "It's the Lord!" Peter put on his coat (he had stripped for work), jumped into the water, and swam to shore. Since they were only about 100 yards out, the others stayed in the boat and pulled the net to the shore. When they landed, Jesus was cooking fish on a fire, along with some bread.

"Bring some of the fish you just caught," Jesus said. Simon dragged the net onto the shore, and although there were 153 large fish, the net was not torn by their weight.

"Let's have some breakfast," Jesus said, serving out the bread and fish. None of the disciples asked if he was really Jesus because they were all sure.

After breakfast, Jesus asked Peter, "Peter, do you love me more than these?"

Peter answered, "Yes, Lord, you know that I love you."

Jesus said, "Feed my lambs."

Jesus repeated the question, "Peter, do you love me?"

Peter replied, "Yes, Lord, you know I love you."

Jesus said, "Take care of my sheep."

Once more, Jesus asked, "Peter, do you love me?"

Peter was sad that Jesus asked him a third time and said, "Lord, you know all things, and you know that I love you."

> **Why did Jesus keep asking Peter if he loved him?**
>
> Throughout this exchange, Jesus and Peter are using different words for love. Jesus is using the word *agape*, which is an unfailing love that the Father has for us. Peter was using *phileo*, which is brotherly love, or affection that's not nearly as deep. However, the third time Jesus switched and used the same word that Peter had been using.

"Then feed my sheep. I tell you the truth, when you were young, you dressed yourself and went where you wanted, but when you are old, you will stretch out your hands, and someone else will dress you and take you where you don't want to go." Jesus said this to indicate how Peter would glorify God in his death. Then he said, "Follow me."

Peter turned and saw John following them and asked, "Lord, what about him?"

Jesus replied, "What difference does it make to you if I want him to stay alive until I return?" The rumor spread that John wouldn't die, but Jesus had only said that it didn't matter to Peter if he wanted John to stay alive.

"I told you that everything in the Law, the Prophets, and the Psalms must come true." Then he opened their minds so that they could understand the Scriptures and he said,

"They wrote that the Messiah must suffer, die, and rise again on the third day. Preach this message to all the nations, beginning in Jerusalem, because you are witnesses of these things.

"Now, I will send the Holy Spirit that my Father promised. But stay here in Jerusalem until you are clothed with power from heaven."

CHAPTER FIFTY

FINAL INSTRUCTIONS

Matthew 28:16-20; Mark 16:15-20; Luke 24:44-53; Acts 1:3-12

During the 40 days after his crucifixion, he appeared to his disciples, proving that he was alive and talking to them about the kingdom of God. One time he appeared to more than 500 of his followers at one time, and another time, he appeared to his half-brother James.

In one of these meetings, they were eating a meal, and he told them, "Don't leave Jerusalem until the Father sends the Holy Spirit. John baptized with water, but I will baptize you with the Holy Spirit in a few days."

The disciples kept asking him, "Are you going to free Israel and restore our kingdom?"

Jesus replied, "The Father sets those dates, and they're not for you to know. But when the Holy Spirit comes upon you, you will receive power and will tell people about me in Jerusalem, Judea, Samaria, and to the ends of the earth."

Then Jesus led them to Bethany, lifted his hands, and blessed them, saying, "I've been given complete authority on heaven and earth. Go into the entire world and preach the good news to everyone you meet. Make disciples of all the nations, baptizing them in the name of the Father, the Son, and the Holy Spirit. Teach them to obey everything that I've commanded you and know that I'm with you always, even to the end of the age."

While he was blessing them, he went up into the sky while they were watching, disappeared into a cloud, and sat down at God's right hand.

His disciples were staring at the sky when two white-robed men appeared and said, "Men of Galilee, why are you standing here, staring at the sky? Jesus has gone back to heaven, and someday he will return in the same way he left." Then they worshiped Jesus and joyfully walked the half-mile back to Jerusalem.

JESUS' RESURRECTION APPEARANCES

Mary Magdalene	At the empty tomb, early Sunday morning. Physically touched Jesus.
Mary and the other women	Outside the tomb after hearing he had risen. Physically touched Jesus.
Peter	Saw the burial clothing in the empty tomb.

Two disciples	On the road to Emmaus. Jesus ate a meal with them.
Ten disciples (not Thomas)	Appeared amid their meeting. Saw his wounds, touched him, and watched him eat.
Eleven disciples	Saw wounds, and Jesus invited Thomas to touch him.
Seven disciples	Came on the shore while they were fishing. They watched him eat food.
All disciples	Gave the Great Commission.
500 believers at one time	Paul reports the largest appearance to many people.
James	Jesus' half-brother
All disciples	Jesus' ascension. Ate a meal with him.
Paul	Jesus taught Paul individually after conversion.

After that, the disciples spent their time in the temple, praising God. Then they went out preaching the good news everywhere and God confirmed their words with many miracles.

> **The Second Coming**
>
> The first time Jesus came to earth, he was a suffering servant who died and rose again to pay for our sins. He will come back a second time as a conquering king who will judge his enemies and rule forever with those who have put their faith in him. There is a lot of controversy about when he will return and the events surrounding his return, but the most crucial piece for us is that he is coming back, and this should be a source of encouragement and comfort to us. With much of the world's chaos around us, it is easy to believe that his return is right around the corner, but every generation since Jesus ascended into heaven believed they would witness his return. He could come back tomorrow, 100 years from now, or 1,000 years from now.

Spread of the Church

Reorganized Concise Paraphrased Bible

Book V

By: Obadiah Paulus

INTRODUCTION TO SPREAD OF THE CHURCH

Other than the four gospels, the 23 other books of the New Testament record the spread of the Christian church. The Book of Acts is a historical document of how Jesus' followers shared the gospel with the Jews and Gentiles of the Ancient Near East. The next 21 books are letters from church leaders to local churches dealing with specific issues they faced. The final book, Revelation, is a vision that the apostle John saw that is an unveiling of what was to come.

We do not have the original manuscripts of the New Testament, but we have an overwhelming amount of evidence that allows us to reconstruct the original text. We have over 5,300 Greek manuscripts (including 10,000 Latin copies and at least 9,300 ancient copies in other languages) of the New Testament. Many of these were copied not long after the original was written. We have far fewer copies for other important ancient documents, and the copies we have are much farther from the original date than the copies we have for the New Testament.

The translations of the Bible that we read today are based on what we believe was in the original manuscripts. There are differences in some copies, but scholars can use a logical process to figure out which of the different options are most likely to have been the original. Using the manuscripts we have and textual criticism, we are confident that 99.5% of what we have is an accurate copy of the original documents. None of the material that is in question affects significant doctrine.

We do not have a precise timeline for the events of the spread of the church after Christ's ascension, but the following is a good approximation of when events took place and gives us an outline for the book's organization.

Approximate Timeline of New Testament events

30 A.D.	Holy Spirit comes/establishment of the church
35	First persecution of the Church
36	Saul's conversion
40	First Gentile conversion
43	Founding of Antioch church; Book of Matthew written
48	Paul's first missionary journey
51	Paul's second missionary journey
52	I Thessalonians written
53	II Thessalonians written
54	Paul's third missionary journey
57	I Corinthians and Galatians
58	II Corinthians and Romans written; Paul arrested
59	Book of Luke written
62	Paul's Roman imprisonment; Ephesians, Philippians, Colossians, Philemon, and James written

63	I Peter, Acts, Hebrews, I Timothy, and Titus written
64	Book of Mark written
66	II Timothy and II Peter written
67	Paul's death
70	Destruction of Jerusalem
75	Jude written
85	Book of John written
90	John's three letters written
97	Revelation written

MAP OF THE SPREAD OF THE CHURCH

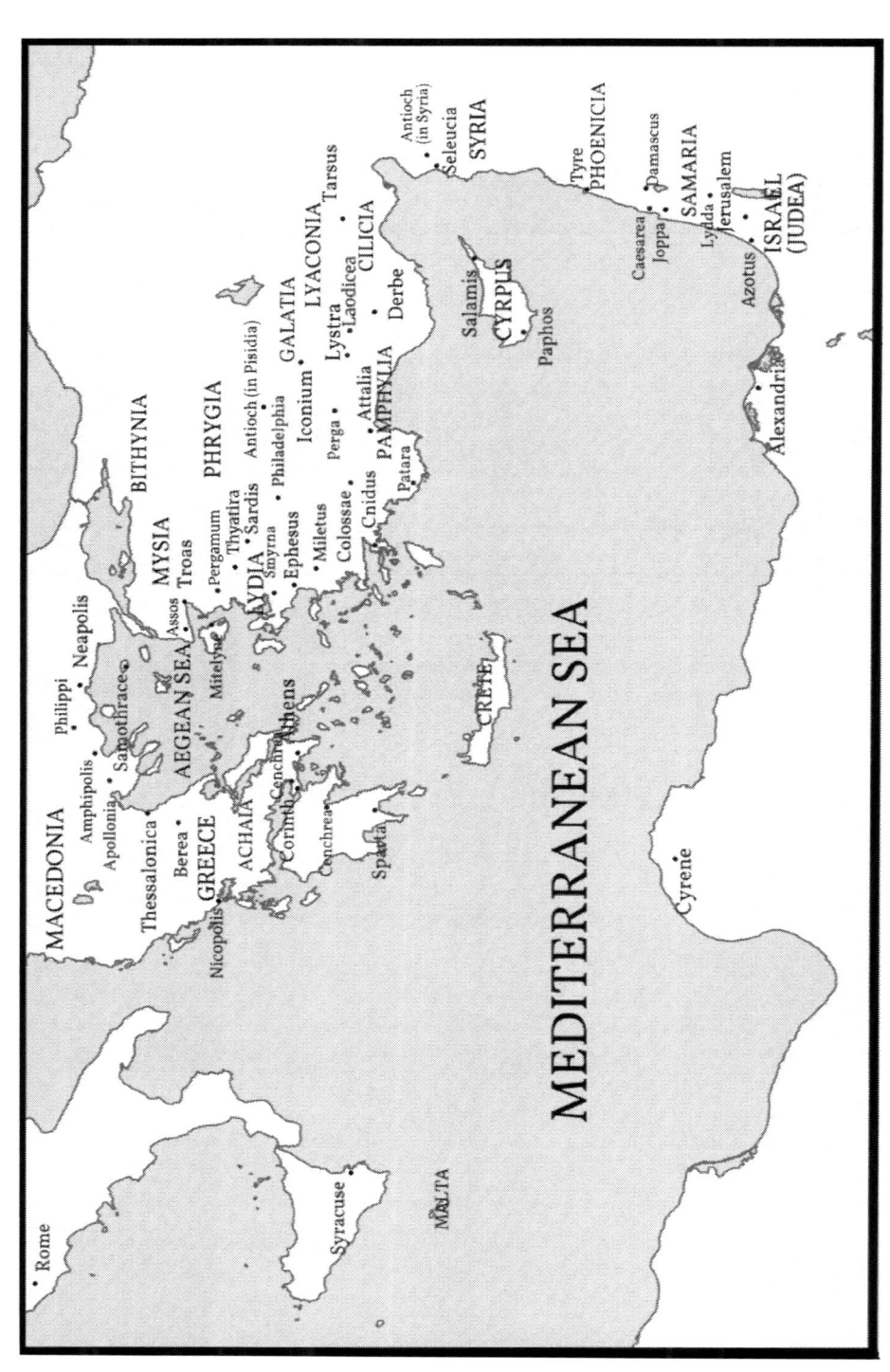

TABLE OF CONTENTS

CHAPTER 1: Beginning of the Church (Acts pt. 1)	647
CHAPTER 2: First Conflict with Jewish Leaders (Acts pt. 2)	650
CHAPTER 3: Ananias and Sapphira and Persecution (Acts pt. 3)	653
CHAPTER 4: Stephen Martyred (Acts pt. 4)	655
CHAPTER 5: Philip and the Ethiopian Eunuch (Acts pt. 5)	658
CHAPTER 6: Saul's Conversion (Acts pt. 6)	660
CHAPTER 7: First Gentile Converts (Acts pt. 7)	662
CHAPTER 8: The New Gentile Church (Acts pt. 8)	665
CHAPTER 9: Paul's First Missionary Journey (Acts pt. 9)	667
CHAPTER 10: Paul's Second Missionary Journey (Acts pt. 10)	671
CHAPTER 11: Paul's Third Missionary Journey (Acts pt. 11)	675
CHAPTER 12: Holy Living and the Second Coming (I Thessalonians)	678
CHAPTER 13: Clarification on Jesus' Return (II Thessalonians)	681
CHAPTER 14: Paul's Response to Corinthian Problems (I Cor. pt. 1)	683
CHAPTER 15: Marriage and Questionable Things (I Cor. pt. 2)	688
CHAPTER 16: Spiritual Gifts and the Resurrection (I Cor. pt. 3)	692
CHAPTER 17: Justification by Faith in Christ (Galatians)	698
CHAPTER 18: Paul's Ministry and Collection for the Saints (II Cor. pt. 1)	702
CHAPTER 19: Paul's Defense of His Ministry (II Cor. pt. 2)	706
CHAPTER 20: The Problem of Sin (Romans pt. 1)	708
CHAPTER 21: Salvation Through Faith (Romans pt. 2)	711
CHAPTER 22: Results of Salvation (Romans pt. 3)	714
CHAPTER 23: Jews and Gentiles (Romans pt. 4)	718
CHAPTER 24: A Transformed Life (Romans pt. 5)	721
CHAPTER 25: Paul's Arrest (Acts pt. 12)	724
CHAPTER 26: Paul Transferred to Caesarea (Acts pt. 13)	727
CHAPTER 27: Paul's Journey to Rome (Acts pt. 14)	730
CHAPTER 28: Our Riches in Christ (Ephesians)	732
CHAPTER 29: Rejoice in the Lord (Philippians)	737
CHAPTER 30: Christ's Supremacy (Colossians)	741
CHAPTER 31: Reconciliation with Onesimus (Philemon)	745
CHAPTER 32: True and Practical Religion (James)	746
CHAPTER 33: Proper Living During Suffering (I Peter)	750
CHAPTER 34: Superiority of Christ (Hebrews pt. 1)	754
CHAPTER 35: Superiority of the New Covenant (Hebrews pt. 2)	759
CHAPTER 36: Exhortations (Hebrews pt. 3)	761
CHAPTER 37: Leading a Church (I Timothy)	765
CHAPTER 38: Stay Strong (Titus)	770
CHAPTER 39: Finish Your Ministry (II Timothy)	772
CHAPTER 40: Steadfast in Christ (II Peter)	775

CHAPTER 41: Warning Against False Teaching (Jude)   778
CHAPTER 42: Jesus Came in the Flesh and Gives Eternal Life (I John)   780
CHAPTER 43: John's Second and Third Letters (II & III John)   784
CHAPTER 44: John's Vision and Letters to the Churches (Rev. pt. 1)   785
CHAPTER 45: The Seven Seals and the First Five Trumpets (Rev. pt. 2)   789
CHAPTER 46: The Sixth and Seventh Trumpets (Rev. pt. 3)   793
CHAPTER 47: The Great Dragon and Bowls of Wrath (Rev. pt. 4)   795
CHAPTER 48: Judgment of Babylon (Rev. pt. 5)   800
CHAPTER 49: The Final Battle (Rev. pt. 6)   802
CHAPTER 50: The New Jerusalem (Rev. pt. 7)   805
EPILOGUE: What's the Point?   807

CHAPTER ONE

BEGINNING OF THE CHURCH
Acts 1:13-2:47

After Jesus ascended to heaven, the disciples returned to Jerusalem and entered the Upper Room to pray with the women who followed him. One day Peter stood up in their midst (about 120 people total) and said, "Brothers and sisters, the Scriptures had to be fulfilled about Judas betraying Jesus. He was one of us and shared in our ministry and now we must appoint someone to take his place. It should be one of the men who has been with us throughout Jesus' whole ministry, from his baptism until his ascension, so that he can tell people of all that Jesus said and did."

They put forward Joseph (also known as Barsabbas or Justus) and Matthias as potential candidates. Then they prayed and asked God to show them who should take Judas' place and then cast lots. The lot fell to Matthias and he became an apostle with the other eleven.

> **What is an apostle?**
>
> In the First Century, an apostle was a messenger sent to bear the message of the sender. With the commissioning of the Holy Spirit, Jesus' eleven remaining disciples and Matthias became apostles. Jesus' remaining disciples were Peter, James (Zebedee's son), John, Andrew, Philip, Bartholomew, Matthew, Thomas, James (Alphaeus' son), Thaddeus, and Simon. Later, Paul became an apostle through Jesus' commissioning as well.

When the Day of Pentecost came, the believers gathered in the Upper Room, and a mighty rushing wind filled the entire house. Tongues of fire rested upon them, and the Holy Spirit filled them, giving them the power to speak in other languages.

There were devout Jews from all over the region who had come to Jerusalem to worship; they came together when they heard the mighty, rushing wind. They were amazed when they saw a group of Galileans speaking in languages that the crowd understood as their native tongues. Some wondered what this meant, but others mocked them, thinking that they were drunk.

> **What is Pentecost?**
>
> Pentecost is the Greek name for Shavuot, the spring festival for the Jewish harvest. This was the seventh Sabbath (50 days) after Jesus' death just before Passover. Passover was the Jewish festival where the Jews commemorated God leading them out of Egypt.

Peter stood up with the other eleven apostles and said, "These men are not drunk; it is only nine in the morning! This is a fulfillment of the prophet Joel who said that God would pour out his Holy Spirit in the latter days and that his people would have visions and prophesy. He will show mighty wonders and save all who call upon his name.

"Men of Israel, Jesus of Nazareth, who did signs and wonders in your midst, was crucified by godless men to fulfill God's predetermined plan. God raised him from the dead because death couldn't hold him down. Our former king, David, said that he saw him seated on high. This gave him hope because God will not allow him to undergo decay. God made him know the paths of life and he rejoiced in his presence.

"David died, was buried, and we know where his tomb is. The Lord had promised that David would have a descendant to sit upon the throne forever, and he prophesied about the Resurrection and that Jesus would not undergo decay. Jesus rose from the dead and we are all witnesses of this fact. Now God has exalted him to the right hand of God and he has poured out the Holy Spirit on us as you have seen.

"David did not ascend to heaven, but he says, 'God said to my Lord to sit at his right hand until he makes his enemies a footstool beneath his feet.' God has made Jesus, whom you crucified, both Messiah and Lord."

What does Christ mean?

Christ is the Greek word for Messiah, the promised Savior of Israel and the world. The name Jesus Christ means Jesus the Messiah. The Old Testament promised that the Messiah would be God in the flesh and eventually deliver Israel and bless the world.

Peter's message convicted the people and they asked Peter and the other apostles what they should do. Peter told them, "Every one of you should repent and be baptized in the name of Jesus Christ for the forgiveness of sins so that you may receive the Holy Spirit. This promise is for everyone who hears the message and God calls to himself." He continued to preach to them and give them evidence that they need to repent for salvation. About 3,000 of them believed and the apostles baptized them that day.

What is baptism? How does it work?

Baptism is the public act where we identify with Jesus' death, burial, and Resurrection. It is an outward act that is a public profession of what God has done in our hearts. This is like a married person wearing a wedding ring. The literal translation for the Greek word for baptism is to dip or immerse. Baptism should be one believer fully submerging another believer who is proclaiming their faith in Christ.

Jesus commanded baptism, so it is a requirement, but it does not save us. The Bible is clear that God saves us through our faith, by grace, and there is no physical action necessary. Believers who understand their decision should be baptized to identify their internal faith.

The newly born church devoted themselves to the apostles' teaching, fellowship, sharing meals, and prayer. Everyone was in awe and the apostles performed many signs and wonders amongst them. All the people were together and shared all their possessions, selling belongings so that they could give money to whomever had need. They met daily in the temple and shared their meals with glad and generous hearts, praising God and gaining favor with all the people. God added people to their number every day.

> **What is the church?**
>
> The church is more than just a building where Christians meet on Sundays. The church is a group of people who worship Jesus as Lord and Savior and gather. This is the way that Jesus has chosen to spread the good news of his death, burial, and Resurrection to the world around us. The church exists on two levels, the universal and the local. The ultimate purpose is to glorify God, and it helps people know, grow, and go in Christ for God's glory.

CHAPTER TWO

FIRST CONFLICT WITH JEWISH LEADERS

Acts 3:1-4:35

One day, Peter and John were on their way to the temple for afternoon prayers when they saw a disabled man who begged at the temple entrance every day. He saw the two men coming and expected to receive some money from them, but Peter looked at him and said, "I don't have any money, but I will give you what I have. In the name of Jesus Christ, stand up and walk!"

Peter took him by the hand, pulled him to his feet, and immediately God healed his legs, so that he could walk. He jumped around, praising God, and all the people who saw him were full of wonder and amazement because they recognized him as the lame beggar who daily sat at the temple gates.

The people all gathered around. Peter said, "Why are you amazed as if we made this man walk by our power? The God of our fathers has glorified Jesus, whom you crucified and rose again from the grave; Jesus has made him well. Faith in Jesus is what made this man well even though you rejected Jesus when Pilate tried to set him free. I know that you acted in ignorance, but God foretold that this would happen. Therefore, repent from your sins so that he may forgive you and refresh you with the Holy Spirit.

"Moses said that a prophet like him would arise from you and that you should listen to that man and that whoever does not listen would be destroyed. All of the prophets spoke about Jesus, and now God has raised him up to bless you by turning all of you from your wickedness."

As the disciples spoke to the people, some of the religious leaders came to listen and grew very annoyed upon hearing the teaching about Jesus and his Resurrection from the dead. This message went against their core beliefs and undermined their authority. The religious leaders arrested Peter and John and held them in jail overnight. But many more people believed and their number came to about 5,000.

The next day, the religious leaders gathered with the high priest and members of his family. They had Peter stand in their midst and asked him on what authority he did these things. Peter was filled with the Holy Spirit and he replied, "If we are on trial for a good deed that we did for a disabled man and you want to know how he was healed, listen to me. By the name of Jesus Christ of Nazareth, whom you crucified, and God raised from the dead, is this man healed and able to stand before you. Even though you rejected Jesus, he has become the cornerstone, and there is salvation with no one else but him, for there is no other name under heaven that can save us."

> **Prescriptive vs. descriptive**
>
> As we read through the Bible, we must remember that the authors wrote these books to a historical people group. While many parts of Scripture apply to our lives, we must differentiate which parts are prescriptive and descriptive.
>
> Descriptive passages describe what happened, and we can draw instruction from the reason beneath the event. For example, when Peter and John healed this man, it is a description of what happened. While God still has the power to heal, not everyone we tell to "be healed" will experience healing. This is a descriptive passage of what occurred. We can use this to teach us that miracles are possible and the power to heal is from God.
>
> Prescriptive passages tell both the original audience and us what is true or what we should do. For example, when Peter tells the people that "there is salvation with no one else but him," that is prescriptive for us as well. Generally, material from the Book of Acts is descriptive, while material from the letters is prescriptive. However, there are exceptions to this rule.
>
> To know whether a passage is prescriptive or descriptive, we must determine how the original audience would understand the text. While this book has added boxes to help with this process, it will require study beyond this text's scope. One thing we can do is to look at all of Scripture to see if there is information that helps us determine if the message is for all people or just the original audience.

The religious leaders were astonished because they realized that these uneducated men had been with Jesus. They could not say anything to oppose Peter and John because they saw the formerly disabled man standing in front of them. They sent them out of the council and talked with each other to decide what they should do because there was no denying that a miracle had occurred. They called Peter and John back in and told them to no longer preach in the name of Jesus.

But Peter and John replied, "You decide if we should listen to you rather than God, but we cannot stop preaching what we have seen and heard." The leaders threatened them, but could not find a reason to punish them because all the people were praising God for what had happened. The man who was healed had been unable to walk for over 40 years.

After their release, Peter and John went to their friends and told them what the chief priests had said to them. When the people heard it, they lifted their voices and said, "Sovereign Lord, maker of heaven and earth, our father David wondered why the Gentiles raged and plotted in vain against the Lord and his anointed. The people of Jerusalem, Herod, Pilate, and the Gentiles fought against Jesus and the plan that you made. See the threats that they have made against us and give us boldness and power to heal through your servant, Jesus." While they were praying, the place where they gathered shook, and they were all filled with the Holy Spirit and continued to speak the Word of God with boldness.

All the people who believed were of one heart and soul, and they shared all their possessions with each other and had all things in common. The apostles were performing great acts and were testifying of what Jesus had done. There was not a needy person among them because many of them were selling their possessions and laying the proceeds at the apostles' feet.

CHAPTER THREE

ANANIAS AND SAPPHIRA AND PERSECUTION
Acts 4:36-5:42

At this time, a follower named Joseph, also known as Barnabas (which means son of encouragement), sold a field and brought the proceeds to the apostles. A man named Ananias and his wife Sapphira also sold a piece of property. They brought a portion of the profit to the apostles but said that they gave the entire amount. Peter said to Ananias, "Why has Satan filled your heart and convinced you to lie to the Holy Spirit? While you owned the property, it was in your hands, and you could do whatever you wanted with it. Why are you trying to convince us that you have done some great thing? You have not just lied to us; you have lied to God!" When Ananias heard these words, he fell down and died, and everyone was terrified. The young men took his body to bury him.

> **The Holy Spirit is God**
>
> This is one of the clearest places where the Bible establishes the Holy Spirit as the third person of the Trinity. Peter tells Ananias that he has not just lied to them, but by lying to the Holy Spirit, he has lied to God. See the note in Chapter 30 for more information about the Trinity.

Three hours later, Sapphira came in, not knowing what had just happened. Peter asked her if they had brought the full profit to the apostles, and she said that they had. Then Peter said, "Why have you and your husband agreed to lie to us? The men who buried your husband are outside and now they will bury you!" Then she fell down and died as well. The young men took her out and buried her with her husband. The congregation was very afraid.

> **Why was God so harsh?**
>
> From our perspective, it seems like God overreacts to Ananias and Sapphira's lie to the church. Some might even say they accomplished much good while only telling a "white lie." God was so harsh because the church was just starting, and he needed to communicate how much he hated sin so that his followers understood how important the church was. He acted this way with the Hebrews when they first came out of Egypt as well.
>
> Some don't like that God has wrath, but that is a part of his nature that we cannot ignore. God's reaction to Ananias and Sapphira's lie is what he should do anytime we sin. However, he rarely punishes our sin the moment we commit it. If God allows sin to go unpunished forever, then he is no longer holy. If we put our trust in Jesus, then his death pays the debt of our sin. We cannot pick and choose which of God's attributes we like and ignore the others.

ARREST OF THE APOSTLES

The believers gathered regularly at Solomon's porch in the outer courts of the temple where any person could enter. While there, they performed many great signs and wonders. All the people spoke well of them, but many were afraid to join them. But people continued to join their numbers every day. They brought many sick people hoping that Peter's shadow would even fall upon them, and the apostles healed them all.

The high priest and Sadducees were jealous, so they arrested the apostles and threw them into prison. But in the middle of the night, the angel of the Lord freed them and sent them back to the temple to preach the gospel. At daybreak, they went into the temple and preached the good news to anyone who would listen.

When the high priest came in, he called for the soldiers to bring the apostles out of prison. However, the jailors reported that the doors were locked, but that their cells were empty. The high priest was perplexed, and then some people said they were preaching the gospel just as they had previously. The officials asked the apostles to speak to them but were afraid to bring them in by force because they thought the people would riot.

The high priest asked them why they were continuing to preach when they had been commanded not to, and Peter answered, "We must obey God rather than men. The God of our fathers raised Jesus, whom you crucified, and has exalted him to his right hand as the Lord and Savior to bring Israel to repentance. We are witnesses of these things, and so is the Holy Spirit, whom God has given to those who obey him."

Furious, the council wanted to kill them all, but a Pharisee named Gamaliel stood up and said, "Men of Israel, be careful what you do with these men. Remember how Theudas claimed to be somebody, and about 400 men followed him. But once he died, they scattered, and it came to nothing. Then Judas from Galilee arose during the census. Some people followed him, but then his followers scattered once he died. Leave these men alone, because if this is not from God, this movement will fizzle out. But if this is from God, you will not be able to stop them, and you may even end up fighting against the Lord!"

The council took his advice, beat the apostles, and then let them go, commanding them to stop preaching about Jesus. The apostles left, rejoicing that they had been worthy to suffer for the name of Jesus. They continued preaching every day about Jesus and kept meeting from house to house.

CHAPTER FOUR

STEPHEN MARTYRED

Acts 6:1-8:2

As the number of Christians increased, some Jewish believers complained because they felt the church was overlooking them in the daily distribution of food. The twelve apostles gathered and decided that it would be best for them to use their time preaching the gospel and praying. So, they advised the people to choose seven men who were full of the Holy Spirit to take over the church's day-to-day operations.

The people liked this idea, so they chose Stephen, Philip, Prochorus, Nicanor, Timon, Parmenas, and Nicolas, men full of the Holy Spirit. They presented them to the disciples who prayed for them and commissioned them into service. Thus, the Word of God continued to spread rapidly in Jerusalem, and several Jewish priests came to faith.

Stephen, one of the men appointed to serve, was full of God's grace and performed great wonders and signs before the people. However, Jews from the Synagogue of Freedmen opposed Stephen and began to argue with him; but they could not stand against the wisdom that the Spirit gave him.

Finally, they persuaded some men to give false testimony that Stephen had blasphemed against God and Moses. The Jews stirred up the people to grab Stephen and bring him in front of the Sanhedrin (Jewish ruling council). The false witnesses said, "This man never stops speaking against the holy place and our laws. He keeps saying that Jesus of Nazareth will destroy the temple and change the customs that Moses handed down to us." After hearing these accusations, the Sanhedrin stared at Stephen and saw that his face was like an angel's.

The high priest asked Stephen, "Are these charges true?"

Stephen replied, "Brothers and fathers, listen to me! God appeared to our father Abraham when he was still in Mesopotamia and told him to leave his home and people and go to the land God would show him. So, after his father died, Abraham left home for the land where we now live. God never gave him an inheritance here, but the Lord promised Abraham that his descendants would inherit the land, even though Abraham was childless at the time. God told him that his descendants would spend 400 years in slavery, but eventually, he would punish their captors and bring Abraham's people into the Promised Land to worship the Lord. Then God gave Abraham the covenant of circumcision.

"Eventually, Abraham became the father of Isaac, and he circumcised his son on the eighth day. Isaac became the father of Jacob, and Jacob became the father of the twelve Patriarchs, including Joseph. Joseph's brothers were jealous of him and they sold him into slavery in Egypt. But God was with him and rescued Joseph from his troubles.

He gave Joseph wisdom and allowed him to gain Pharaoh's favor, eventually becoming ruler over the land and the palace.

"Then, a famine struck the land, bringing great suffering, and our ancestors could not find any food. When Jacob heard that there was food in Egypt, he sent his sons to buy some. On their second visit, Joseph told his brothers who he was, and Pharaoh learned about Joseph's family. Joseph brought the 75 members of his family to Egypt, where they all eventually died. Our ancestors carried their bodies out of Egypt and buried them in the tomb Abraham had purchased.

"As the time came for God to fulfill his promises, our people had multiplied, and a new king who did not know Joseph came to power. He oppressed our ancestors and forced them to kill their newborn babies. During this time, Moses was born, and his family hid him for three months. When Moses' mother placed him in the Nile, Pharaoh's daughter found him and adopted him. He learned all the wisdom of the Egyptians and became mighty in word and deed."

Stephen continued, "At age 40, Moses visited his people and saw an Egyptian mistreating one of the Israelites, so Moses killed the Egyptian. Moses thought the Israelites would realize that God was using him to deliver them from the Egyptians, but he was wrong. The next day, he tried to intervene in a fight between two Israelites, but one of them pushed him away and said, 'Who made you ruler and judge over us? Are you going to kill me like you killed the Egyptian yesterday?' When Moses heard this, he fled to Midian, where he lived as a foreigner. Eventually, he had two sons.

"After 40 years in the desert, an angel appeared to Moses in a burning bush near Mount Sinai. Astounded, he went to get a better look, and the Lord spoke to him from the flames, 'I am the God of your fathers, Abraham, Isaac, and Jacob. Take off your sandals because you are standing on holy ground. I have seen the suffering of my people in Egypt and heard their groans; now, I am sending you back to Egypt to lead them to freedom.' Moses was terrified, but he returned to Egypt and led his people out, performing signs and wonders in Egypt, at the Red Sea, and in the wilderness over the next 40 years.

"Moses told the Israelites that God would raise up a prophet like him from within them. He received God's Words on Mount Sinai and brought them to our ancestors. But they refused to obey; instead, they rejected Moses and turned their hearts back to Egypt. They told Aaron, Moses' older brother, to make a god to lead them because they weren't sure what had happened to Moses. They made a golden calf into an idol, brought it sacrifices, and reveled in their hands' work.

"God turned away from them and let them worship the sun, moon, and stars. Therefore, the prophets wrote, 'Did you bring me sacrifices and offerings the 40 years you were in the wilderness? You have taken up the false gods of the local people, so I will send you into exile beyond Babylon.'

"The Lord directed Moses to build the tabernacle according to God's specifications and our ancestors carried it with them in the wilderness. Joshua took the tabernacle with them as God drove the nations of the Promised Land out before the Israelites.

It stayed there until the time of David, who enjoyed God's favor and asked to build the Lord a permanent home. However, David's son Solomon built the temple even though the prophets tell us that no building can house God, no created thing can contain him.

"You stubborn people! Your hearts and ears are not able to hear God!" Stephen continued, "You are just like your ancestors, always resisting the Holy Spirit. They persecuted every prophet and even killed those that predicted the coming of Christ. Now, you have betrayed and murdered him; you have received the Law, but you have not obeyed it!"

When the Sanhedrin heard this, they were furious and raged against Stephen. But he was full of the Holy Spirit, and he looked to heaven, seeing God's glory and Jesus standing at the right hand of God. He said, "Look, I see heaven opened and the Son of man standing at the right hand of God!"

This was the last straw, and the Sanhedrin covered their ears and rushed at him, screaming at the top of their lungs. They hated that he proclaimed that Jesus was the Messiah. They dragged him out of the city and threw him to the ground. The men threw their coats at the feet of a young man named Saul, signifying that he approved their actions. Then they began to throw stones at Stephen. While they were stoning him, he prayed, "Lord Jesus, please receive my spirit and do not hold this sin against them." Then he died.

Stephen's murder started widespread persecution against the church in Jerusalem, and all the believers scattered throughout Judea and Samaria. Godly men buried Stephen and the church mourned for him. Meanwhile, Saul made war against the church, going house to house, and arresting anyone who claimed to believe in Jesus.

CHAPTER FIVE

PHILIP AND THE ETHIOPIAN EUNUCH
Acts 8:3-40

PETER AND SIMON

Those who had scattered preached the gospel wherever they went. Philip went to Samaria and preached there and the people listened to his message when they saw the signs he performed. He healed the lame and paralyzed and cast out many shrieking demons, and the people rejoiced.

For some time, a man named Simon had impressed people by practicing sorcery throughout Samaria. He claimed to be a great man, and all the people listened to him, proclaiming that he was the Great Power of God. They had followed Simon for a long time, but they were baptized when they believed Philip's message. Even Simon believed, was baptized, and followed Philip everywhere.

When the apostles in Jerusalem heard that the Samaritans had believed the gospel, they sent Peter and John. When the men arrived, they prayed that the believers would receive the Holy Spirit because although the people had been baptized, they had not yet received the Spirit. When they laid their hands on the people and prayed, the believers received the Holy Spirit. Simon saw this, and he offered Peter and John money, begging for the same power.

Peter answered, "May your money die with you because you thought you could buy God's gift! You have no part of this ministry because your heart is not right. Repent from your sin and pray that God would forgive you for having such a thought. I can see that you are still full of bitterness and a slave to sin!"

Simon replied, "Pray for me that nothing you've said will happen to me." Peter and John continued to testify about Jesus and returned to Jerusalem, preaching the gospel.

PHILIP AND THE ETHIOPIAN EUNUCH

An angel of the Lord told Philip to head south along the desert road from Jerusalem to Gaza. As he started out, he met a eunuch who was a treasurer for the Ethiopian queen. This man had gone to Jerusalem to worship, and on his way home, was sitting in his chariot, reading the prophet Isaiah's words. The Holy Spirit told Philip to go up to the chariot.

Philip ran up to the eunuch and asked him if he understood what he was reading. The eunuch answered, "How can I understand unless someone explains it to me?"

Philip sat down with the man, and the eunuch was studying the passage that reads, "He was led like a sheep to slaughter, and as a lamb is silent before its shearer, he did not speak. In his humiliation, he was deprived of justice. Who can speak of his descendants, for his life was taken from him?"

The eunuch asked Philip, "Is the prophet talking about himself or someone else?"

Philip began with that passage and explained the good news about Jesus. As they traveled along the road, they saw some water, and the eunuch asked what kept him from baptism. They stopped the chariot, and Philip took the eunuch down to the water and baptized him.

When they came up out of the water, the Holy Spirit took Philip away; and although the eunuch did not see him any longer, the Ethiopian went on his way rejoicing. Philip immediately appeared in Azotus and he traveled on to Caesarea, preaching as he went.

CHAPTER SIX

SAUL'S CONVERSION

Acts 9:1-31

Meanwhile, Saul was still breathing murderous threats against the Lord's disciples. He went to the high priest and asked him to send word to Damascus' synagogues to give permission to arrest any professing Christians and bring them back to Jerusalem. As he neared Damascus, a bright light from heaven flashed around him. He fell to the ground and heard a loud voice saying, "Saul, Saul, why are you persecuting me?"

Saul replied from his knees, "Who are you, Lord?"

The voice from heaven answered, "I am Jesus, whom you are persecuting! Now get up and go into the city where I will tell you what to do." Saul's traveling companions stood by him, speechless because although they heard the sound, they did not see anyone speaking.

Saul got up from the ground and opened his eyes but couldn't see anything. So, his friends took him by the hand and led him to Damascus. Once he was there, he did not eat or drink anything for three days.

There was a believer in Damascus named Ananias whom the Lord told in a vision, "Go to Judas' house on Straight Street and ask for Saul of Tarsus because he is there praying. He saw you in a vision come place hands upon him to restore his sight."

Ananias replied, "Lord, I have heard many reports about this man and all the damage he has done to Christians in Jerusalem. Now, he has come here with authority from the chief priests to arrest anyone who trusts in your name."

But the Lord insisted, "Go! I have chosen him to proclaim my name to the Gentiles, their kings, and the people of Israel. I will show him how much he must suffer for me."

Ananias obeyed and went to Judas' house. He put his hands on Saul, saying, "Brother Saul, the Lord Jesus appeared to you on the road here; now he has sent me so that you can regain your sight and be filled with the Holy Spirit." Immediately, something like scales fell off Saul's eyes, and he could see again. Saul got up and was baptized; he ate and regained his strength.

Saul spent several days with the believers in Damascus and immediately started to preach in the synagogues that Jesus was the Son of God. The people were stunned because they recognized Saul as the one who persecuted the church and arrested Christians. Yet, he continued to grow more powerful and baffled the Jews in Damascus by proving that Jesus was the Messiah.

After a while, some of the Jews conspired to assassinate Saul because they were angry that he proclaimed Jesus as the Messiah. They kept watch day and night at the city gates so that they could catch and kill him. Saul learned of the plan, and one night, his followers lowered him over the wall in a basket so he could escape.

Saul traveled to Jerusalem, and when he arrived, he tried to join the other disciples. But they refused because they didn't believe he was a true follower of Jesus. Barnabas took Saul under his wing and stood up for him, telling the other brothers about Saul's experience on the road to Damascus and how he had preached the gospel.

Saul stayed in Jerusalem and freely moved about the city, fearlessly preaching Jesus. He debated the Jews, and eventually, they plotted to kill him. When the other believers discovered this, they sent him to his home city of Tarsus. After Saul's departure, the church enjoyed a time of peace and growth. They lived in fear of the Lord, and the Holy Spirit strengthened and encouraged them.

CHAPTER SEVEN

FIRST GENTILE CONVERTS

Acts 9:32-11:18

PETER RAISES TABITHA FROM THE DEAD

Peter traveled about the country, visiting the Christians in Lydda. While he was there, he found a man named Aeneas who had been paralyzed for eight years. Peter looked at him and said, "Jesus Christ heals you. Get up and roll up your mat." Immediately, he got up and picked up his mat. All the people in Lydda and Sharon saw him and turned to the Lord.

In Joppa, there was a disciple named Tabitha who was always doing good and helping the poor. She died from an illness, and the other Christians washed her body and placed her in an upstairs room. Joppa was near Lydda, so when the believers heard that Peter was there, they sent two men who urged him to come at once.

Peter went with them and entered the upstairs room. The widows stood around the room, weeping and holding out articles of clothing that Tabitha had made. Peter sent them all out of the room and then knelt and prayed. Turning towards her, he said, "Tabitha, get up." She opened her eyes, saw Peter, and sat up. Peter took her by the hand and brought her to other believers, and presented her alive. Word of this miracle spread throughout Joppa and many people trusted in the Lord. Afterward, Peter stayed in Joppa with a man named Simon.

PETER AND CORNELIUS

At Caesarea, there was a centurion in the Italian Regiment named Cornelius. He and his family were devout and feared God, giving generously to the needy and praying regularly. One day, at about three in the afternoon, he saw an angel who called to him. Surprised, Cornelius said, "What is it, Lord?"

The angel answered, "Your prayers and gifts to the poor have come before the Lord as a memorial offering. Send men to Joppa to bring back a man named Peter, who is staying with a man named Simon." When the angel left, Cornelius called two soldiers, including one of his attendants, and told them what the angel had said. He sent the men to Joppa to bring back Peter.

Around noon the following day, Peter was praying on the roof as the two men approached Simon's house. While lunch was prepared, Peter fell into a trance. He saw heaven open and something like a large sheet coming down by its four corners. It contained all kinds of animals, including both clean and unclean birds and reptiles. A voice told him to get up and eat, but Peter protested that he had never eaten anything unclean.

> **Unclean food**
>
> In the Old Testament, God gave the Jews many rules about what they could eat. Forbidden food was considered unclean. Most of the foods that God declared unclean were because they were difficult to prepare healthily. God used the laws about unclean food as an analogy for people. The Jews considered Gentiles (non-Jews) unclean, but God was showing his people that all people were worthy of his love.

The voice spoke to him, "Don't call anything unclean that the Lord has made clean." This vision happened three times and then the sheet went back into heaven. While Peter wondered what the vision meant, Cornelius' men arrived at Simon's house and asked for Peter. As he continued to ponder, the Holy Spirit told him to go with the men without misgivings.

Peter went down and asked the men why they had come. The two soldiers told him, "We have come from Cornelius, a God-fearing centurion who all the Jewish people respect. An angel had told him to send for you so that he can hear what you have to say."

Peter invited them into the house as his guests. The next day, Peter went with the men and some of the other believers from Joppa. Cornelius, along with many of his friends and family, was expecting them. When Peter arrived, Cornelius bowed down to worship him, but Peter said, "Stand up, I'm just a man like you."

Peter saw the gathered people and said, "You all know that it is unlawful for a Jew to visit or associate with anyone from another nation, but God has shown me that I should not call any person common or unclean. So, here I am. Why did you send for me?"

Cornelius answered, "Four days ago, I was praying around three in the afternoon when I saw a man in bright clothing who told me that God had heard my prayers and that I should send for you in Joppa. Now that you are here, we have all gathered to hear what God has told you to say."

Peter opened his mouth and said, "Now I understand that God does not show partiality, and he accepts anyone who fears him and does what's right. You all know the good news that God sent to Israel, proclaiming peace through Jesus Christ. How, beginning with John's baptism, God anointed him with the Holy Spirit and power; he went around doing good and healing those under the Devil's control because God was with him. We are all witnesses of what Jesus did amongst the Jews in both the country and Jerusalem. They crucified him, but on the third day, God raised him from the dead, and he appeared to those that he chose to be his witnesses. Not everyone saw him, but we ate and drank with him after his Resurrection.

"Jesus commanded us to preach to the people and testify that God has appointed him to judge the living and the dead. All the prophets spoke of him and wrote that all who trust in him have their sins forgiven."

While Peter was still speaking, the Holy Spirit fell on his audience. The circumcised believers with Peter were amazed that the Gentiles had the Holy Spirit as they heard them speak in tongues and praise God. Peter said, "They have received the Holy Spirit, just as we have, surely we cannot keep them from being baptized." Then Peter commanded them to be baptized. The new believers asked Peter to stay with them for several days.

The apostles and other Christians in Judea heard that the Gentiles had received the Word of God. So, when Peter returned home, the circumcised believers criticized him for eating with uncircumcised men. But Peter told them the entire story of his vision and visit to Cornelius in Caesarea. He argued that if God had given them the same gift, the church couldn't stop it. When the other believers heard this, they had no further objections, and they glorified God, saying, "God has granted life-giving repentance to even the Gentiles."

CHAPTER EIGHT

THE NEW GENTILE CHURCH
Acts 11:19-12:25

The believers who had scattered during the persecution after Stephen's death traveled throughout the known world, spreading the message only to Jews. But some men from Cyrene and Cyprus went to Antioch (a Gentile city in Syria) and preached to them as well. The Lord's hand was with them, and many people believed and turned to the Lord.

This report came to the church in Jerusalem and they sent Barnabas to Antioch. When Barnabas arrived, he was glad to see God's grace, and he encouraged the people of Antioch to remain strong in their faith and purpose. He was a good man, full of the Holy Spirit and faith, and he helped lead many people to the Lord.

Barnabas went to Tarsus to look for Saul and brought him back to Antioch. They stayed with the new church for a year, teaching many people. Antioch was the first place that believers were called Christians; it was meant to be an insult, like "little Christs."

During this time, some prophets came to Antioch from Jerusalem. One of them, named Agabus, stood up and foretold the famine during the reign of Claudius (around 45 A.D.). Thus, the Antioch Christians determined to send support and relief to those living in Judea. After collecting what they could, they sent it to the elders in Jerusalem with Saul and Barnabas.

PETER ARRESTED

Around that time, King Herod began violently persecuting the church by arresting some of them. He had James, John's brother, executed. When Herod saw that this made the people happy, he arrested Peter during the Festival of Unleavened Bread. Herod imprisoned Peter intending to bring him to trial after Passover; the king put him under 16 soldiers' care to ensure there was no chance for escape. While Peter was in jail, the church prayed for him.

On the night Herod was going to bring Peter out to trial, the king chained the prisoner to two soldiers with two others standing watch at the door. Suddenly, an angel appeared in the cell, along with a bright shining light. The angel woke Peter by hitting him in the side and said, "Get up and get dressed quickly." The chains fell off Peter's hands, and he quickly put on his clothes, sandals, and cloak.

Peter followed the angel, not knowing if what was happening was real or a dream. The angel led Peter past the two soldiers guarding the prison to the iron gate to the city. The gate opened for them on its own, and they walked out and then down the street when the angel suddenly left them.

When Peter finally realized what was happening, he said, "Now I know the Lord has rescued me from Herod and everything the Jews expected to happen."

He hurried to Mary's house, the mother of John Mark (a believer who wrote the Book of Mark), where many believers had gathered to pray. He knocked on the door and a servant named Rhoda answered. She recognized his voice, but in her joy, she ran to tell the others instead of letting him in. They told her that she was out of her mind and that it was only Peter's angel. Peter kept knocking, and when they finally let him in, the believers were astonished. Peter motioned for them to be quiet, and then he told them how the Lord had led him out of prison.

When morning came, the soldiers were frantic over what had become of Peter. After Herod searched for Peter and could not find him, he questioned the guards and then ordered their execution. Peter left for Caesarea and spent time there.

HEROD'S DEATH

Herod was angry with the people of Tyre and Sidon and forbade food exports to them. The people persuaded Blastus, the king's chamberlain, to give them an audience with Herod because they depended on royal provisions of food. On the appointed day, the king put on his robes and gave a speech to the gathered masses.

When he finished, the people roared in approval and chanted, "The voice of a god and not a man!" Immediately, an angel of the Lord struck Herod down because he did not give God the glory; worms ate his insides, and he died.

***

The gospel continued to spread and more people believed. Once Saul and Barnabas had finished their work, they returned to Antioch from Jerusalem, bringing John Mark along with them.

CHAPTER NINE

PAUL'S FIRST MISSIONARY JOURNEY

Acts 13-15

There were prophets and teachers at the church in Antioch: Barnabas, Simeon (also called Niger), Lucius of Cyrene, Manaen (a member of Herod the tetrarch's court), and Saul. They worshiped the Lord and fasted, and the Holy Spirit told them to send Barnabas and Saul on a special mission. After more fasting and prayer, they laid their hands on Barnabas and Saul and sent them off.

After being set apart by the Holy Spirit, Saul and Barnabas went to Seleucia with John Mark, and together they sailed for Cyprus. When they arrived at Salamis, they preached in the synagogues. They made their way through the whole island as far as Paphos and came across a Jewish false prophet named Elymas (also known as Bar-Jesus), who practiced the magic arts. A local governor, Sergius Paulus, an intelligent man, called for Saul and Barnabas to hear the Word of God. But the magician tried to stop them because he wanted to keep political power.

Saul (who was now going by Paul) looked at Elymas and said, "You son of the Devil! You are the enemy of righteousness, full of evil and lies! When will you stop perverting God's ways?! Now his hand is on you and you will be completely blind for a time!" Immediately, mist and darkness fell upon Elymas, and he stumbled around, looking for someone to guide him. When Sergius Paulus saw what had happened, he believed, astonished by the Word of the Lord.

PAUL IN ANTIOCH

After this, Paul and his companions sailed from Paphos to Perga in Pamphylia. John Mark left them, but the rest continued to Antioch (in Pisidia). One Sabbath, they went to the synagogue and sat down. After the reading of Scripture, the leaders asked them if they had any words of encouragement.

Paul stood up, quieted the crowd, and said, "Men of Israel and those who fear God, listen to me. The God of Israel chose our fathers and made them great while they were in Egypt and then led them out with his power. God put up with them in the wilderness for 40 years before driving out seven Canaanite nations and gave them the land as an inheritance.

"They lived there for 450 years and God gave them judges until the prophet Samuel. Then our ancestors asked for a king, and God gave them Saul, a Benjamite, for 40 years. When God removed Saul, he raised up David, the son of Jesse, a man after God's heart who would do his will. From this man's offspring, God brought Israel a Savior in Jesus, as he promised. Before Jesus came, John the Baptist preached a baptism of repentance to all Israel. As John was finishing his ministry, he testified that he was not the Messiah and was unfit to untie the Savior's sandals. Fellow Israelites and God-fearing Gentiles, he has sent us this message of salvation.

"The people of Jerusalem and their rulers did not recognize the Savior or understand their prophets that they hear every Sabbath; they fulfilled the prophets' message by condemning the Messiah to death. Even though he hadn't committed any crime, Pilate had him crucified. When they had fulfilled all the prophecies about him, they took him off the cross and buried him in a tomb. But God raised Jesus from the dead and he appeared for many days to his followers who now testify about him.

"Now we bring you the good news of what God promised our fathers, that he fulfilled by raising Jesus from the dead. The second Psalm promised, 'You are my Son and I am your Father.' God raised him from the dead to not rot; God gave him the holy blessings promised to David. After David served God's purpose, he died, and his body rotted; but the same is not true of Jesus.

"Now, I proclaim to you the forgiveness of sins through Jesus, and he can free you from everything that the Law couldn't. Beware that what the prophets warned doesn't come true about you. He will do an amazing work in your time, and you won't even know it if someone told you about it."

As the people left, they begged that Paul and Barnabas would come back the next week to tell them more. The men encouraged the Jews and converts to continue in God's grace.

The next Sabbath, almost the entire city came out to hear God's Word. But when the Jews saw the crowds, they were jealous and began to contradict and revile Paul and Barnabas. But the men spoke out boldly, "You needed to hear God's Word first. But since you think you are unworthy of eternal life, we are turning to the Gentiles. God has commanded us to be a light to the Gentiles so that we can spread salvation to the whole earth."

When the Gentiles heard this, they rejoiced and glorified God, and as many as he appointed to eternal life believed.

The Word of the Lord spread throughout the region. But the leading men and women stirred up the people, persecuted Paul and Silas, and drove them out of the city. Paul and Silas shook the dust off their feet and went to Iconium and the Holy Spirit filled the disciples with joy.

PAUL IN ICONIUM

In Iconium, Paul and Barnabas went to the synagogue and preached so effectively that many Jews and Gentiles accepted the gospel. But the unbelieving Jews stirred up the Gentiles and poisoned their minds against these new ideas. Paul and Barnabas stayed there for a long time, preaching boldly about God's grace, and performing miracles by his power.

The city was divided; some sided with the Jews and some with Paul and Barnabas. When they learned they were to be stoned, Paul and Barnabas fled to Lystra and Derbe, preaching the gospel throughout the region.

In Lystra, they met a man disabled since birth. As he listened, Paul looked at him, saw that he had the faith for healing, and said in a loud voice, "Stand on your feet!" Immediately, he jumped up and began walking.

When people saw this, they cried out in their native language, "The gods have come down to us as men." They called Barnabas Zeus and Paul Hermes because he was the primary speaker. The temple of Zeus was near the city gates and the local priest brought out garlands and oxen to sacrifice.

When Paul and Barnabas realized what was happening, they tore their garments and rushed into the crowd, crying out, "Men, why are you doing this? We are humans, just like you! We bring you good news so that you would turn away from these false gods to the living God who created everything. In the past, he allowed people to do their own thing, but he did not leave himself without witness; he gave you rains and fruitful seasons of harvest, satisfying you with good things." Even with this, they barely stopped the people from offering them sacrifices.

Some Jews from Iconium and Antioch (in Pisidia) came to Lystra and incited the crowds to stone Paul and leave him for dead outside the city. But as the disciples gathered around him, Paul got up and went back into town.

The next day, Paul and Barnabas left for Derbe. While there, they preached the gospel and made many converts. Then they returned to Lystra, Iconium, and Antioch, strengthening and encouraging the believers. They appointed elders in each church and taught them that they must face many trials as they entered the kingdom of God.

Paul and Barnabas continued their journey through Pisidia, Pamphylia, Perga, and Attalia before returning to Antioch. They gathered the church together and told them all that God had done during their travels, and they stayed there for quite some time.

***

Some men came to Antioch from Judea, teaching the new Christians must be circumcised to be saved. Paul and Barnabas debated with them, and eventually, they decided to send some men to Jerusalem to ask the apostles and other elders about this issue. As they passed through Phoenicia and Samaria, they told the believers how the Gentiles had come to faith, and everyone rejoiced together.

RETURN TO JERUSALEM

When they arrived in Jerusalem, the church welcomed them, and the men from Antioch told them everything that had been happening. Some of the Pharisees who had become believers stood up and protested that all Christians need to be circumcised to keep Moses' Law. Peter gathered the apostles and elders to discuss the matter.

After much debate, Peter stood up and said, "Brothers, you know that God decided that the Gentiles would believe the gospel when I preached to them. God knows the heart, and he bore witness to their faith by giving them the Holy Spirit, just like he gave to us. He made no distinction between them and us because he cleansed their hearts by faith. Now, why are you testing God by putting a yoke on these brothers that none of us have been able to bear? We believe that they will be saved by the grace of God alone, just as we will."

Then Paul and Barnabas told them everything God had done through them with the Gentiles. Once they finished, James said, "We have heard how God visited the Gentiles to make a people for his name. The prophets agree with this when they write that God said, 'I will return to rebuild the fallen tent of David, so that the rest of the world may call on the Lord and be saved.'

"Therefore, I think we should not make it any harder for Gentiles who turn to God. We should write a letter telling them to stay away from things polluted by idols, sexual sin, meat from strangled animals, and blood. For the Law of Moses has been proclaimed in every city and is preached every Sabbath in the synagogues."

The church in Jerusalem sent Paul, Barnabas, Judas Barsabbas, and Silas to the church in Antioch with a letter summarizing their decision. The people rejoiced in the message; they rejoiced because of its encouragement. Judas Barsabbas and Silas strengthened the church with many words and then returned to Jerusalem. But Paul and Barnabas stayed in Antioch, preaching the gospel with many others.

CHAPTER TEN

PAUL'S SECOND MISSIONARY JOURNEY
Acts 16-18

After a while, Paul told Barnabas that he wanted to go back through the cities where they had preached to see how the believers were doing. Barnabas and Paul argued about bringing John Mark with them; finally, they separated. Barnabas went with John Mark to Cyprus while Paul went through Syria and Cilicia with Silas.

Paul and Silas traveled through Derbe to Lystra, where they met a disciple named Timothy, who had a believing Jewish mother and a Greek father. He had a good reputation with the churches in Lystra and Iconium because of the work he had done there. Paul wanted to bring Timothy with them, so Paul circumcised him so it wouldn't be an issue with the Jews who knew his father was a Greek. Even though it wasn't necessary, Paul wanted to avoid the arguments. They delivered the apostles' letter to the churches they visited, strengthening their faith and increasing their numbers.

PAUL GOES TO MACEDONIA

The Holy Spirit forbade them to preach in Asia, so they went through Phrygia and Galatia. They attempted to go to Bithynia, but the Spirit did not allow them, so they went to Troas. One night, a vision appeared to Paul of a Macedonian man urging him to help them. Paul concluded that God wanted him to preach the gospel in Macedonia, so they went there. Luke began traveling with Paul at this time.

They made their way to Philippi, sailing through Samothrace and Neapolis, staying there for many days. One Sabbath day, they went outside the city gate to the river, where a group of women had gathered to pray. One of the women named Lydia was from Thyatira; she sold expensive goods and worshiped the Lord. God opened her heart to believe and she was baptized along with the rest of her household. After this, she urged Paul and Silas to stay at her house as her guests.

One day, on their way to the place of prayer, they met a servant girl who communicated with demons and had made her masters lots of money by fortune-telling. She followed them, crying out, "These men are servants of the Highest God and they proclaim the way of salvation!" She kept this up for many days.

Eventually, Paul became so annoyed that he turned to the girl and said, "I command you in the name of Jesus Christ to come out of her!" The evil spirit left her.

When her masters saw that their potential to profit was gone, they seized Paul and Silas and dragged them into the marketplace before the city leaders. The men accused Paul and Silas of disturbing the city and advocating breaking Roman law. The crowd joined in with some of the leaders, tearing Paul and Silas's clothes off and ordering some soldiers to beat them. After many blows, they threw Paul and Silas into the city's highest security jail cell.

Around midnight, Paul and Silas sang praises to God loud enough for all the jail to hear. Suddenly, there was a great earthquake, all the prison doors opened, and the shackles fell off the prisoners. When the jailer saw this, he drew his sword to kill himself, thinking that the prisoners had escaped. But Paul cried out, "Don't hurt yourself; we are all here!"

The jailer called for lights and fell down in fear at Paul and Silas' feet. He brought them out and asked, "What must I do to be saved?"

Paul and Silas replied, "Trust in the Lord Jesus and he will save you and your household." They continued to share the good news with them and the jailer believed. Within the hour, he was baptized, and then he tended to Paul and Silas's injuries and gave them food to eat. He celebrated with his family that he had believed in Jesus.

In the morning, the city leaders gave the order to set Paul and Silas free. When the jailer tried to let them go, Paul said, "They publicly beat two Roman citizens without a trial and then threw us in prison; now they want to let us out secretly? No, they need to let us out themselves!"

The police reported Paul's words to the city leaders, and they were afraid when they found out that Paul and Silas were Roman citizens. The leaders went to them, apologized, and begged them to leave the city. Paul and Silas left the jail and went to visit with Lydia. After encouraging the other believers there, Paul and Silas left the city.

PAUL IN THESSALONICA

They passed through Amphipolis and Apollonia on their way to Thessalonica, where there was a synagogue. For three consecutive Sabbaths, Paul went into the synagogue to reason with the Jews. He explained from the Scriptures that the Messiah must suffer and die and that it was Jesus. Some Jews were convinced and joined Paul and Silas, including many devout Greeks and leading women.

But the Jews were jealous; they formed a mob with some worthless men, set the city in an uproar, and attacked one of the members of Jason's house where Paul and Silas were staying. When the mob discovered Paul and Barnabas weren't there, they dragged Jason and some of the believers before the city authorities yelling, "These men have turned the world upside down and now they've come here to stay with Jason. They are breaking Caesar's laws by claiming that Jesus is king!" Hearing this threw the crowd into an uproar. Jason posted bond and they let them go.

As soon as it was night, the church sent Paul and Silas to Berea, where they went to the synagogue. These Jews were nobler than those in Thessalonica; they heard the Word with gladness, daily examining the Scriptures to see if this message was true. Many people believed, including many influential Greek women and men.

But when the Jews from Thessalonica heard that Paul had gone to Berea, they came there too and stirred up the crowds. The brothers immediately sent Paul away by boat, leaving Silas and Timothy to stay. Paul sailed as far as Athens and sent the ship back for Silas and Timothy, while Paul remained.

PAUL IN ATHENS

While Paul was waiting for them in Athens, he saw that the city was full of idols, which provoked his spirit. He reasoned with Jews and devout Greeks in the synagogue and whoever would listen to him in the marketplace. Some of the philosophers gathered to listen to Paul. Some thought he was insane, and others saw him as a preacher of foreign gods because he proclaimed Jesus and the Resurrection.

So, Paul stood up in the Areopagus (a local meeting place) and said, "Men of Athens, I see that you are very religious. I've seen your objects of worship; I even saw a plaque to the unknown god. I proclaim to you the God you don't know. The God who made heaven, earth, and everything in it does not live in man-made temples, nor is he served by humans as if he needs anything since he made everything. He made all the nations of the earth from one man, and he set forth their allotted times and boundaries so that they might search for God and find him. He is not far from us because, 'in him, we live, move, and have our life' and even as some of your poets have said, 'we are his children.'

"Being God's children, we should not think of God as gold, silver, stone, or anything else that can be made by human hands or from our imagination. God has overlooked our times of ignorance, but now he commands all people everywhere to repent because he will one day judge the world by the righteousness of Jesus, whom he raised from the grave."

When he spoke of resurrection, some mocked, but some desired to hear him again. Paul left them, but some people believed, including an Athenian aristocrat named Dionysus and a woman named Damaris.

After this, Paul left Athens and went to Corinth. He met a Jew named Aquila, who had recently come from Italy with his wife Priscilla because Claudius had kicked all Jews out of Rome. They were tentmakers by trade, so Paul stayed and worked with them. Every Sabbath, he went to the synagogue and reasoned with both Jews and Greeks. When Silas and Timothy arrived, Paul devoted himself exclusively to preaching the Word, testifying that Jesus was the Messiah. When the Jews opposed him, he shook out his coat in protest and said, "Your blood be on your heads! I am innocent. From now on, I will only preach to the Gentiles."

He left there and went to the house of Titius Justus, a man who worshiped God and lived next to the synagogue. Crispus, the synagogue leader, believed in the Lord, along with his entire household. He gave him a place to preach, and many people believed and were baptized.

One night, the Lord spoke to Paul in a vision and said, "Don't be afraid, keep speaking because I am with you and will protect you; I have many people in this city." So, Paul stayed there for 18 months, teaching the Word of God.

PAUL IN EPHESUS

But when a man named Gallio became a trusted advisor to the governor of Achaia, the Jews made a united attack against Paul. They brought him to court, accusing him of breaking the Law by teaching people to worship God.

When Paul opened his mouth to defend himself, Gallio said, "Jews, if this were a matter of some vicious or actual crime, I would listen. But since this is an issue of your Law, figure it out yourselves. I refuse to be the judge of such things." He kicked them out of court, and the Jews grabbed Sosthenes, the new head of the synagogue, and beat him in front of the court. But Gallio paid no attention.

Paul eventually left for Syria with Priscila and Aquila. When he arrived at Cenchreae, Paul cut his hair because he was keeping a vow. When they arrived in Ephesus, he left his companions and went to the synagogue to reason with the Jews. They begged him to stay longer, but he declined, saying, "If God wills, I will return."

When he got to Caesarea, he greeted the church and then proceeded on to Antioch. He spent some time there and then went on through the regions of Galatia and Phrygia, strengthening the believers.

A Jew named Apollos, a native of Alexandria, came to Ephesus. He spoke well and knew the Scriptures. Apollos had learned the way of the Lord and being fervent in spirit, he taught accurately about Jesus, but he only knew about John's baptism. He boldly preached in the synagogue, but when Priscila and Aquila heard him, they took him aside and better explained the gospel. When Apollos wanted to go to Achaia, the church encouraged him and wrote letters to support his mission. When he arrived, he helped those who had believed by the grace of God. He powerfully refuted the Jews by proving that Jesus was the Messiah.

CHAPTER ELEVEN

PAUL'S THIRD MISSIONARY JOURNEY

Acts 19-20

PAUL IN EPHESUS

While Apollos was in Corinth, Paul traveled inland until he came to Ephesus, where he found a group of about twelve believers. He asked if they had received the Holy Spirit, and they answered that they didn't know about it. When Paul heard this, he asked about their baptism, and they told them that they only knew of John's baptism. So, Paul said, "John preached a baptism of repentance telling people to believe in Jesus, who came after John." Upon hearing this, they were baptized in the name of the Lord Jesus. Paul laid his hands on them, the Holy Spirit filled them, and they began speaking in tongues and prophesying.

Paul went into a synagogue and spent three months boldly proclaiming the gospel, trying to persuade people about the kingdom of God. But some people were stubborn and refused to believe. They even maligned the faith to others in the congregation; so, Paul took the believers and taught them daily in the hall of Tyrannus. They met for about two years, and eventually, all the Jews and Greeks in Asia heard the gospel.

God was doing amazing miracles through Paul; even the handkerchiefs and aprons he had touched were able to heal people and cast out demons. There were seven sons of a Jewish high priest named Sceva who were traveling around casting out demons. They saw that the name of Jesus had power over evil spirits. They tried to cast out a demon in "the name of Jesus whom Paul proclaims."

But the demon possessing the man replied, "I know Jesus, and I recognize Paul, but who are you?" Then the possessed man jumped on the seven men and gave them such a beating that they ran out of the house naked and bleeding. This story became known to all the residents of Ephesus; they were frightened and spoke highly of the Lord.

Many new believers publicly confessed their sins and many who had practiced magic arts brought their books and publicly burned them. The total value of their books was worth the annual wages of about 160 people. The Word of the Lord continued to increase.

***

After this, Paul decided to go through Macedonia and Achaia on his way to Jerusalem and eventually Rome. Before leaving, he sent Timothy and Erastus to Macedonia and stayed a little longer in Asia.

Before Paul could leave, there was another controversy. A silversmith named Demetrius, who made shrines to Artemis, met with his fellow craftsmen. He said, "Men, you know that we have made lots of money from making shrines to Artemis, but Paul is preaching all over the world that any god people can make is not worthy of worship. We run the risk of losing our profession and having the temple of Artemis and our beloved goddess becoming irrelevant."

This made the craftsmen furious and they began crying out, "Great is Artemis of the Ephesians!" The city was in chaos, and a mob dragged Gaius and Aristarchus (two Macedonians traveling with Paul) into the local theater.

Paul wanted to go into the theater to defend himself and his friends, but the other disciples and some of the locals urged him not to. There was a lot of confusion and most people didn't even know why they were there. Some Jews prompted a man named Alexander to come forward and he tried to calm the crowd down to explain the situation. But when the people recognized that he was a Jew, they chanted, "Great is Artemis of the Ephesians!" for about two hours.

Finally, the town clerk was able to settle the people down, and he said, "Men of Ephesus, everyone knows that we Ephesians are the keepers of Artemis' temple and the sacred stone that fell from the sky. Since this is common knowledge, don't do anything rash. You have brought these men here even though they haven't committed any crimes against our goddess. So, if Demetrius or the craftsmen want to file a complaint, let them do it in court. We are in great danger of being accused of rioting today and we really don't have a reason for this commotion." Then he dismissed the crowd.

Once things calmed down, Paul encouraged the other believers and then left for Macedonia. He encouraged the local churches as he passed through until he reached Greece. Paul stayed there for three months until he uncovered a plot against him. Retracing his steps through Macedonia, he sent several of his companions ahead of him to Troas and caught up with them after the Feast of Unleavened Bread.

***

One Sunday, the church gathered in an upper room to eat together, and Paul talked with them until late in the evening. Around midnight, a young man named Eutychus was sitting in a third-floor window, and he fell into a deep sleep. As Paul went on, Eutychus fell out of the window and died when he hit the ground.

Paul went out, bent over the young man, and then told the crowd that he was okay because his life was still in him. Paul took communion and continued to talk with people until he left in the morning. The people welcomed Eutychus back and were very comforted.

Paul went to Assos and then boarded a ship to Mitylene. While there, he called for the elders of Ephesus to come to him because he wanted to get to Jerusalem by Passover. When they arrived, Paul said to them, "You know how I lived with you from the first day I arrived. I served the Lord with humility and tears and how the Jews plotted to destroy me. You know how I kept teaching you anything profitable from house to house. I preached to everyone I could about repentance toward God and faith in the Lord Jesus.

"Now I'm headed to Jerusalem, and I don't know what will happen except that the Holy Spirit has told me that I will face imprisonment and persecution everywhere I go. However, I don't value my life; I only want to finish the race and ministry given to me by Jesus to share the gospel of God's grace.

"I know that I will never see any of you again. I am innocent of everyone's blood because I never shied away from preaching the gospel. Watch out for yourselves and the church that God has made you elders of because he bought it with his blood. After I leave, savage wolves will come in to attack the church, and men from your midst will come to draw away believers. Therefore, be alert! Remember that for three years, I never stopped warning each of you with tears. Now I commend you to God and the Word of Grace, which can build you up and give you an inheritance with those who are holy.

"I never took anything from anyone; instead, I worked to provide for myself. In everything I've done, I've shown you that by working hard and helping the weak, we remember the words of Jesus, 'it is more blessed to give than receive.'"

After saying this, he knelt and prayed for them all. There were many tears, and they all hugged Paul, sad that they would never see him again. Then they accompanied him to his ship.

CHAPTER TWELVE

HOLY LIVING AND THE SECOND COMING
I Thessalonians 1-5

> **Paul's first letter to Thessalonica**
>
> The first letter to the Thessalonians was the first letter written to a congregation during the spread of the church. Paul founded the church during his second missionary journey when he had the vision of a Macedonian man asking for his assistance. The church was in its infant stages and Paul (along with Silas and Timothy) wrote within a year or two after leaving. Paul sent Timothy back to Thessalonica to check on them and this letter was Paul's response to Timothy's report.
>
> Thessalonica was the capital of Macedonia, located on a harbor with a significant highway. The church was a mix of Jews and Gentiles. It struggled in its infancy because some of the Thessalonian Jews were so set against Christianity that they had started a riot during Paul and Timothy's first visit.
>
> Timothy's report was mostly good, although the church was unsure of their standing in Christ and matters of Jesus' Second Coming. Paul wrote to them about holy living as believers and instructed them on Christ's return.

We always thank God for you when we pray because of the work your faith and love have produced and your endurance in the hope of our Lord Jesus Christ. We know that he chose you because the gospel came to you with power, the Holy Spirit, and deep conviction. You imitated our lives as we imitate the Lord, and now many believers follow your example in suffering. We don't need to tell others about you because news has spread about your faith and service to God.

Our visit to you was productive after our suffering in Philippi because, with God's help, we preached boldly. Our appeal to you is not a mistake or deceit; on the contrary, we speak as God has approved us to preach the gospel. We aren't trying to please men or seek their approval; God is our witness that we didn't use flattery or a mask to cover our true intentions. As apostles, we could have asserted our authority over you; but instead, we cared for you as a mother cares for her children. We loved you so much that we shared our lives with you as well as the gospel.

You remember our toil and hardship as we worked without stopping so that we wouldn't be a burden to anyone while we preached. You and God know how holy, righteous, and blameless we were; how we treated you like a father treats his children, encouraging, comforting, and urging you to live a life worthy of God who called you.

We continually thank God because you accepted our teaching as God's Word. You imitated God's churches in Judea and suffered the same things they were experiencing at the hands of those who killed the Lord Jesus. These oppressors displease God and oppose humanity to keep us from preaching and saving people. They are heaping guilt upon themselves until God pours out his wrath on them at the end.

We are apart from you for a while, and we've tried to visit you, but Satan stood in our way. You are our hope, joy, and the crown of glory that Jesus will give us when he comes again. When we couldn't stand it anymore, we sent Timothy to you to strengthen and encourage your faith so that our trials wouldn't unsettle you. We were destined for this and we told you this would happen. We were afraid that Satan had tempted you and that our work might have been in vain.

Now that Timothy has returned to us, he has brought good news to us about your faith and love and given us pleasant memories of our time with you. During our persecution, your faith encouraged us since you are standing firm in the Lord. We cannot thank God enough because of the joy you give us. We continuously pray for you that we might see you again and strengthen your faith. May he cause your love to overflow for others just as our love overflows for you. May he strengthen your hearts so that you will be blameless and holy before our God and Father when Jesus comes again.

INSTRUCTIONS ON HOLY LIVING

As for other matters, we instructed you how to please God, just as you have been. Now we ask you to go even further because God wants you to be holy, avoid sexual immorality, and control your body in an honorable manner. Don't live in lust like the pagans who don't know God and take advantage of each other. God has called you to holiness and not impurity; anyone who ignores this is ignoring the Holy Spirit.

I don't need to tell you anything about brotherly love. God has already taught you this and you are already doing it. Keep going and aspire to live quietly, minding your own business and doing your work as we showed you. Then you may behave properly and live independently.

We want to inform you about those who have died so that you don't grieve like others who don't have hope. Since we believe Jesus died and rose again, we think that he will bring them with him. The Lord declares that those who are still alive when Jesus returns will not precede those who have died.

Jesus will descend from heaven with a commanding cry, the voice of an archangel, and God's trumpet. The dead in Christ will rise first, and then those who are still alive will join with them in the clouds to meet the Lord. Then we will be with him forever. Encourage each other with these words.

The Day of the Lord will come like a thief in the night when people least expect it. But you are not in the dark; you are children of the light and should not be surprised by his return. Stay awake and be sober because people sleep and get drunk in the dark. Since we belong to the Lord, be sober, put on faith and love as a breastplate, and the hope of salvation as a helmet.

God did not appoint us to suffer wrath, but for salvation through Christ; he died for us so that we can live with him whether we are dead or alive. Encourage and build each other up with these words.

Respect those who work hard at caring for you in the Lord. Esteem them with love because of their labor. Warn those who are idle and disruptive, encourage the fainthearted, help the weak, live in peace, and be patient with everyone. Do not repay evil with evil, but do good to everyone. Always rejoice, pray without ceasing, and give thanks in every circumstance because this is what God wants from you. Do not despise prophecy, but test everything; hold onto the good and abstain from evil.

> **How does prayer work?**
>
> Prayer is the way that we communicate with God; it can be silent or out loud. Through prayer, we praise God, confess our sins, and tell him what we need. God tells us that he answers all our prayers, although sometimes he says no or that we need to wait. One of the primary purposes of prayer is to draw us closer to God. It is like casting a fishing line and catching an island. While it seems like we are reeling the island in, we move closer, not the other way around. When we pray, it draws us closer to him.

May the God of peace sanctify you so that your whole body, soul, and spirit may be blameless when Jesus comes again. God who calls you is faithful and he will do it. Pray for us and greet all the brothers and sisters warmly. Read this letter to the church, and may the grace of our Lord Jesus Christ be with you.

CHAPTER THIRTEEN

CLARIFICATION ON JESUS' RETURN
II Thessalonians 1-3

> **Paul's second letter to Thessalonica**
>
> Paul, Silas, and Timothy wrote this second letter to the church in Thessalonica within a year of the first. There was some confusion about Christ's return and they wrote to clarify some of these points. Someone had circulated a forged letter from Paul after his first letter leading some church members to believe that the Second Coming was imminent. Some of these believers had become fanatics and Paul found it necessary to correct their misconceptions.

We always thank God for you because of your faith and love for each other continue to grow. Therefore, we boast about your perseverance in faith and afflictions. All of this is evidence of God's righteous judgment, and as a result, you will be worthy of God's kingdom.

When our Lord Jesus comes from heaven in blazing fire with his mighty angels, he will repay those who trouble you and give you relief. He will punish those who do not know God or obey his gospel. They will suffer eternal punishment away from the glory of God's power on the day he comes for glorification in his holy people because you believed our message. So, we always pray that God would make you worthy of his calling and accomplish every good work of faith by his power. Then you may glorify our Lord Jesus' name according to his grace.

Do not let the teaching that allegedly comes from us that Jesus has already returned unsettle or alarm you. Don't be deceived; that day will not come until the man of lawlessness, the son of destruction comes. He opposes and exalts himself against every so-called god or object of worship, even claiming to be God himself. I told you this when I was with you and you know that God is holding him back until the right time.

> **Who is "the man of lawlessness"?**
>
> The "man of lawlessness" that Paul writes about is the Antichrist that will come just before Jesus returns. He will be a man who denies God and seeks to lead people away from devotion to the Lord.

When the lawless one comes, he will do miracles that serve the lie and do evil until the Lord Jesus destroys him when he returns. God will allow him to deceive people so that those who didn't believe the truth will face condemnation.

We should always thank God for you because he chose you as the first fruits of salvation by the Spirit and faith. He called you through our gospel so that you may obtain the glory of our Lord Jesus Christ. So, stand firm in what we taught you. Then our God and Father who loves and comforts us through the hope of grace may comfort your hearts and establish you in every good work and word.

EXHORTATIONS TO HOLY LIVING

Finally, pray for us that the gospel may continue to spread rapidly, just as it did with you. Pray that he would deliver us from wicked people; the Lord is faithful and will strengthen you and protect you from Satan. We know that you are doing what we command and will continue to obey. May the Lord direct your hearts to God's love and Christ's perseverance.

In the Lord Jesus Christ's name, we command you to stay away from every idle believer who is disruptive and does not follow our teaching. Just as we were not idle when we were with you and did not eat anyone's food without paying for it. We worked nonstop so that we wouldn't be a burden to any of you. We had every right to compensation, but we did this as an example because anyone unwilling to work should not eat.

We have heard that some of you are idle and disruptive; they are not busy, they are busybodies. We urge such people to settle down and earn their keep. Don't tire of doing good, and refuse to associate with idle and disruptive believers so that they might be ashamed. They are not your enemies; warn them as brothers or sisters.

May the Lord of peace always be with you and grant you grace and peace.

> **Jesus' Second Coming**
>
> The Bible talks about Jesus' Second Coming in multiple places. Jesus speaks to his followers about it in his final instructions to his disciples, Paul writes about it in his two letters to the Thessalonians, and John writes about it in the Book of Revelation.
>
> The first time that Jesus came to earth, he was a suffering servant who died and rose again to pay for our sins. He will come back a second time as a conquering king who will judge his enemies and rule forever with those who have put their faith in him. There is a lot of controversy about when he will return and the events surrounding his return. However, the most crucial piece for us is that he is coming back; this should be a source of encouragement and comfort. With much of the world's chaos around us, it is easy to believe that his return is right around the corner; every generation since Jesus ascended into heaven has believed the same. He could come back tomorrow, 100 years from now, or 1,000 years from now.

CHAPTER FOURTEEN

PAUL'S RESPONSE TO CORINTHIAN PROBLEMS

I Corinthians 1-6

> **Paul's first letter to Corinth**
>
> Paul wrote to the Corinthian church in conjunction with Sosthenes, one of Paul's co-workers. The two men had a long-standing relationship with the church. Paul founded the church during his second missionary journey between 49 and 52 A.D. There is a lost letter to the Corinthians that Paul wrote, asking the church to dissociate from professing believers who lived sinful lives. Paul wrote this surviving letter in 55 A.D. from the city of Ephesus during his third missionary journey. He wrote it in response to a message that the church had sent to him.
>
> Corinth was located on the Isthmus of Greece between the Aegean and Mediterranean Seas, about 50 miles west of Athens. Nearly 400,000 people lived in Corinth. There was a lot of travel and trade through the city and people could find every imaginable vice there.
>
> Corinth was a pagan city with a reputation for extreme wickedness. People even invented the word Corinthianize which meant to live a promiscuous lifestyle. It was a cosmopolitan city made up of retired soldiers, freemen, Jews, and people from all over the region. It was a mainly Gentile church with little background in Judaism, as evidenced by some of the members' extreme behavior. Paul wrote about the nature and unity of the church. He dealt with issues ranging from factions, worldly wisdom, unethical conduct, marriage and celibacy, idols, female leaders, communion, spiritual gifts, and the Resurrection.

Grace and peace to you from God, our Father, and the Lord Jesus Christ. I always thank God because of his grace for you in Jesus. He has enriched you in both speech and knowledge, just as Christ confirms his testimony in you. Therefore, you do not lack any spiritual gift as you eagerly await our Lord's return. God has called you into fellowship with his Son and he is faithful.

I ask that you agree with each other so that there are no divisions and that you are united in thought and purpose. Chloe's people made it clear that there are quarrels among you, and each of you claim to follow Paul, Apollos, Peter, or Christ. Is Christ divided? Was Paul crucified for you, or were you baptized in the name of Paul? I thank God that I didn't baptize very many of you. For Christ didn't send me to baptize, but to preach the gospel plainly so that Christ's cross might not be powerless.

The message of the cross sounds foolish to those on the road to destruction, but to believers, it is God's power. He will destroy the wisdom of the wise and set aside the cleverness of the clever. There is no wise man, scholar, or debater who can stand before God. The world's wisdom doesn't lead to God, so he was pleased to save those who believe through the foolishness of our preaching. Jews ask for miracles, and Greeks seek wisdom, but we preach Christ crucified. The cross is a stumbling block for Jews and nonsense to Greeks, but to everyone who has been called, Christ is the power and wisdom of God. Even God's foolishness is wiser than us and his weakness is stronger than our strength.

Consider yourselves; the world wouldn't call many of you wise, powerful, or noble. But God chose the foolish things of the world to shame the wise and the weak to shame the strong. He chose the lowly and despicable things of the world to nullify that which is important so that no one can boast before God. He is the source of your life in Jesus Christ, who has become our wisdom, righteousness, holiness, and redemption. Therefore, whoever boasts should boast in the Lord.

When I came to you, I did not have eloquence or superior wisdom as I preached the gospel. While I was with you, I decided to know nothing except Jesus and his crucifixion. I came to you in weakness, fear, and trembling. My message and preaching didn't consist of wise and persuasive words but with a demonstration of the Spirit's power so that your faith would not rest on men's wisdom but God's power.

We speak wisdom to the mature, but not the world's wisdom or the world's rulers because they are becoming irrelevant. We speak God's secret wisdom that he predestined for our glory, the wisdom which none of the world's rulers have understood. If they had, they would not have crucified Jesus.

No eye has seen, no ear has heard, and no one has ever imagined all that God has prepared for those who love and trust him. But the Lord has revealed them to us through his Spirit, for the Spirit searches everything, even the depths of God. Who can know what a person is thinking except that man's spirit? In the same way, no one knows God's thoughts except his Spirit. We have not received the world's spirit but God's so that we may understand what he has graciously given us.

We speak in words taught by the Spirit, not human wisdom, and we explain spiritual matters to spiritual people. But those who do not have the Spirit do not accept the things from God, for they seem foolish to them, and they cannot understand them because that requires spiritual judgment. But those who have the Spirit judge all things, but no one judges them. We cannot know all that God knows, but we understand these things because we have the mind of Christ.

I could not address you as spiritual men, but only as worldly, mere infants in Christ. I gave you milk instead of solid food because you weren't ready for it; you're still not prepared because you are still worldly. Where there is jealousy and strife, you are worldly and acting like mere people. When you take sides with Paul or Apollos, you are acting like mere people. Apollos and I are only servants who preached the gospel to you. I planted, Apollos watered, but God was causing the growth. Neither the one who plants nor the one who waters are anything, but only God who causes the growth. The one who plants and the one who waters have the same purpose, and each will receive a reward according to their work. For we are God's workers, and you are his field or building.

By God's grace, I laid a foundation as an expert builder, and someone else is building on it. But we should be careful how we build because no one can lay a foundation other than Jesus Christ. Regardless of what we use to build with, God will test our work with fire on the day he returns. If our work remains, we will receive a reward. If our work burns up, we will suffer loss, although God will save us by the skin of our teeth. We are his temple and he lives within us; if anyone destroys this temple, God will destroy him because his temple is sacred.

Don't be deceived; if you think you are wise by the world's standards, you should become a "fool" so that you may become wise. For the world's wisdom is foolishness to God. Scripture tells us that the Lord knows that the thoughts of the wise are worthless; therefore, do not boast about spiritual leaders! Everything belongs to you: Paul, Apollos, Peter, the world, life, death, the present, and the future. It all belongs to you, and you belong to Christ, and Christ belongs to God.

We are Christ's servants, and God has entrusted his truth with us; we must be faithful. I don't care if you judge me; my conscience is clear; it is the Lord who judges me. Wait for the Lord to come, and he will bring everything to light, including the heart's hidden motives; then, we will all receive our praise from God.

I have applied these things to myself and Apollos for your benefit so that you would not become proud and arrogant towards each other. None of us are any better than each other; we have received everything we have from God, so we should not boast. You have already become rich and are beginning to reign; we wish to reign with you.

But it seems like God has put us, apostles, at the end of the line, like those condemned to die in the gladiator arena. We are fools for Christ, but you are wise; we are weak, but you are strong; we have no honor, but you do. We are hungry and thirsty, dressed in rags, mistreated, and homeless. We work hard with our own hands; when people curse us, we bless; when persecuted, we endure; when slandered, we answer with kindness. We have become the scum of the earth, the trash of the world.

I don't want to shame you but to warn you as my children. Even if you have countless other guides in Christ, I am your father. Imitate me; that is why I sent you Timothy, to remind you what I have taught in every church. I have heard that some are arrogant as if I am not coming, but I will come to find out about their power if the Lord wills. Because the kingdom of God does not consist in talk but power. You choose if I should come with a spirit of discipline or love and gentleness.

SEXUAL IMMORALITY

I've heard that there is sexual immorality among you that not even the pagans tolerate, a man sleeping with his step-mother. You are proud of your tolerance, but you really should mourn! Kick this man out of your church; even though I'm not there, I've already judged him. With the power of our Lord Jesus, hand him over to Satan so that while God destroys his body, he will save the man's soul.

Your pride is not good; don't you know that a little yeast leavens the whole lump of dough? Get rid of the yeast (pride) so that you may be a new, unleavened batch as you already are. Christ, our Passover Lamb, has already been sacrificed; observe the rest of the festival with the unleavened bread of sincerity and truth and not the old bread of malice and wickedness.

> **What did Paul mean?**
>
> Paul used the analogy of yeast in bread to show that their pride would spread and affect their entire lives. He ties this in with the Jewish Passover Feast that commemorated God delivering the Israelites from Egyptian slavery.

I wrote to you in my previous letter not to associate with sexually immoral people. I didn't mean everyone who is wicked, greedy, cheaters, nor idolaters; otherwise, you would have to leave the world. But do not associate with anyone who claims to be a believer and practices these things; don't even eat with them. If God will judge the outside world, shouldn't you judge those in the church?

If any of you have a dispute with another believer, don't take it to court; settle the matter amongst yourselves. God's people will one day judge the world; can't you decide trivial issues? One day, you will judge angels. Can't you figure things out without having the church's name dragged through the mud? The fact that you can't settle disputes is shameful; it is better to be wronged or cheated. Instead, you cheat and wrong each other.

Sinners will not inherit the kingdom of God. Don't be deceived; the sexually immoral, idolaters, adulterers, homosexuals, thieves, the greedy, drunkards, slanderers, and swindlers will not inherit the kingdom. That's what some of you were, but now the Holy Spirit has washed, sanctified, and justified you in our Lord Jesus Christ's name.

All things are permissible, but not everything is good for you; don't let anything master you. People say that sex is for the body and that the body is for sex, but the body is not meant for sexual sin, the body is meant for the Lord, and the Lord is for the body. By the Lord's power, God raised Jesus from the dead, and he will raise us as well. Our bodies are members of Christ; we should not join them with a prostitute. Anyone who unites themselves with a prostitute becomes one with her because, as Moses wrote, "the two become one flesh."

Whoever unites with Christ is one with him in spirit. Run from sexual immorality; all other sins are outside the body, but sexual sin is against the body. Your bodies are temples of the Holy Spirit who lives inside you. You are not your own; God bought you with a price, so honor him with your bodies.

> **What is sexual immorality?**
>
> Sexual immorality is any form of sex or sexuality that is outside of marriage. This includes extra-marital sex and pornography. Our current culture is hyper-sexualized

and there is temptation in every direction we turn. The answer is not to adopt the world's morality around us but to cling to the way God designed sex before sin entered the world. Sex is a gift from God and it is best if we practice it in the way he intended, between a husband and wife, in a committed covenant marriage. The world tells us that what we do with our bodies does not affect our souls, but this is not true.

CHAPTER FIFTEEN

MARRIAGE AND QUESTIONABLE THINGS

I Corinthians 7:1-11:1

When you wrote, you asked if it was okay for people to have sex. Since sexual immorality is happening, people should only have sex with their spouses; each should fulfill their marital duty to each other. Neither has authority over their bodies, so do not deprive each other except by mutual consent so that you can devote yourselves to prayer. Then come together again to avoid temptation. This is more of a concession than a command; I wish you were all single like me, but we all have our own gifts.

To the single and widows, I think it is better to stay single, but if you can't control yourself, it is better to marry than to burn with lust. The married should stay married, and if they divorce, they should remain single or reconcile with their ex. If anyone is married to an unbeliever, try to stay married unless they want to leave. For the believing spouse sanctifies the unbelieving spouse, and they make the children holy. It's okay if the unbelieving spouse files for divorce; you are not bound in this situation because God has called you to peace. You may even end up saving your unbelieving spouse.

Let each person live the life that God has given them. Whether circumcised or uncircumcised, don't try to change it because neither one matters, only obedience to God. If you were a slave when called, try to become free, but don't worry if you can't. Regardless of your status, you are free in Christ. Whatever your situation when God called you, stay in it.

> **Slavery**
>
> The New Testament talks about slavery without condemning it, but it is essential to know that it is not like the slavery we think of in modern terms. Slavery in the First Century resulted from a conquering nation enslaving their enemies or a way that people who had nothing could survive and keep from extreme poverty. It had nothing to do with race, class, or national origin. We should not equate it with what happened in the United States during the 17th through 19th centuries. Some masters mistreated their slaves, but we should not look at this as justification for degrading fellow humans.

I don't have a specific command concerning those who are engaged, but I think you should stay as you are. Considering the current situation, I think both the married and single should stay that way; but anyone who gets married is not sinning. Married people must deal with marital issues and I want to spare you of that. Our time is short, this world is passing away; we should focus on the work we have to do for the Lord. I don't want to put a burden on you; I only want you to live a life with undivided devotion to the Lord. You will be fine whether you marry or stay single, but I think you will be happier if you stay as you are.

QUESTIONABLE THINGS

Concerning food sacrificed to idols, we know that knowledge puffs up, but love builds up. If you think you know something, you don't know everything; our knowledge should not make us proud. But whoever loves God knows himself. So, regarding food sacrificed to idols, we know that there is only one God and that they are nothing. However, because of some people's past association with idols, they believe that eating food sacrificed to idols is sinful.

> **Meat sacrificed to idols**
>
> Idols were a significant problem in the First Century and they continue to be today. Merchants in most major cities would sell the meat sacrificed to idols in the marketplace. Some Christians viewed eating this meat as participating in idol worship.

It doesn't help or hurt us if we eat food sacrificed to idols; just be careful that you are not an obstacle to the weak. If people with a weak conscience see you eating this food, it could destroy their faith. When you hurt them like this, you hurt Christ. Therefore, if what I eat causes another believer to sin, I will never eat meat again so that I won't cause them to fall.

I am free, I have seen Jesus, and you are the seal of my apostleship. In defense to those who accuse me, we all have the right to eat, drink, and get married. Do only Barnabas and myself have to work for a living? Whoever works deserves a wage, and we should get paid if we preach the gospel. If we have sown spiritual seed among you, we should be able to reap a material harvest.

Those who preach the gospel should earn a living from it. We have not made use of these rights, and I'm not begging you for a salary; I would rather die. I must preach the gospel, so I cannot boast; if I preach voluntarily, I have a reward, but if not voluntarily, I'm just doing my job. My reward is that I can preach free of charge.

Even though I'm free, I have made myself a servant to everyone so that I may lead as many as possible to Christ. I have lived like a Jew to win the Jews; to those under the Law, I have lived under the Law; to those without the Law, I have lived like one without the Law; to the weak, I have become weak, to win as many as possible. I do everything for the sake of the gospel so that I can share in its blessings.

> **Becoming like other groups**
>
> Paul did whatever he could to make the gospel more palatable to his audience without compromising his message. Many times, when people become Christians, they withdraw from the world and lose contact with those outside the

> church. This is not the way it should be. We need to protect ourselves from sin, but we need to be still engaged with the world around us to tell them about the grace that Jesus offers us. Whatever your interests are, use them to bring God glory and tell similar people about God's love.

Every runner runs the race, but only one wins; run so that you might win the prize. Every athlete exercises self-control to win a perishable wreath, but we compete for an imperishable one. I discipline my body and control it so that I am not disqualified after I preach.

Our ancestors lived under a cloud, and they all passed through the sea; they were baptized into Moses in the cloud and the sea. They all ate the same spiritual food and drank the same spiritual drink that flowed from the rock of Christ. But God was not pleased with most of them and their relatives buried them in the wilderness. These things are an example for us to keep us from setting our hearts on evil as they did.

Don't be idolaters or sexually immoral as some of them were; God killed 23,000 in one day. We should not put Christ to the test like they did, and snakes killed them. We should not grumble as some of them did, and an angel killed them. These are all examples for us so that we wouldn't repeat their folly.

If you think you are standing, be careful that you don't fall. Nothing that is uncommon to people has tempted you; God is faithful, and he will not allow you to face any temptation beyond what you can resist. With every temptation, he will also provide a way to resist so that you can endure.

Therefore, run from idolatry. The communion we take is Christ's body and blood, and since we all share in it, even though there are many of us, we are one body. The Israelites who ate the sacrifices participated in the altar, but that doesn't mean that food offered to idols or the idol itself is anything. I don't want you to participate in what the pagans offer to demons. You cannot partake of both the Lord and demons; we are not stronger than God is.

All things are lawful, but not everything is helpful, nor does it build us up. Don't just look out for your own good, but also the good of your neighbor. You can eat whatever you find in the market without asking questions for the sake of your conscience. If someone invites you to dinner, eat whatever they serve without asking questions for the sake of your conscience. But if someone tells you that some food has been sacrificed to idols, don't eat so that you don't hurt someone else's conscience. No matter what you do, do everything for God's glory. Try not to offend anyone so that many might know God. Follow my example as I follow Christ's example.

> ### Questionable things
>
> There are many things that the Bible does not prohibit us from partaking in that are problems for some people. In Corinth, one of the most significant issues was food sacrificed to idols. In modern times, we can substitute things like alcohol, tobacco,

marijuana, gambling, etc. For some people, these things are sinful because they can lead to other sins. For others, they can participate without sinning. We need to decide for ourselves if we can partake in these with a clean conscience.

We also need to choose how we partake in these questionable things. If we do it in such a way that leads other believers into temptation, we must proceed with caution. Our freedom is not worth leading someone else into sin. We can be legalistic in our behavior, but we cannot apply this standard to others. While some believers may choose not to partake, they cannot force others to follow the same rule.

CHAPTER SIXTEEN

SPIRITUAL GIFTS AND THE RESURRECTION
I Corinthians 11:2-16:24

I commend you because you remember what I taught you, but I want you to understand that God is the head of Christ, Christ is the head of every man, and the husband is head of his wife. Every man who prays or prophesies with his head covered dishonors his head, but every wife who prays or prophesies with her head uncovered dishonors her head. A man should not cover his head because he is God's image and glory, but the woman is man's glory. God created woman from man; that is why a wife should have a symbol of authority on her head. However, neither is independent of the other because just as a God created woman from a man, now men are born from women, and all things are from God.

> ### Men and women
>
> Some use this passage to argue that men are better than women, but that is not Paul's purpose. Head coverings were a cultural sign like a wedding ring today. Men and women need each other in life and God's kingdom. Also, in other places, Paul writes about mutual submission. As believers, we must submit to each other and look out for other believers' best interests.

THE LORD'S SUPPER

When it comes to the Lord's Supper (communion), I do not commend you. I've heard that there are divisions when you gather, and I believe it because you have an unspoken hierarchy among believers. When you meet for the Lord's Supper, some have private meals and get drunk, while others go hungry. Don't you have homes where you can eat and drink? You are rejecting God and humiliating the poor. What should I say?

> ### What is the Lord's Supper?
>
> The Lord's Supper, or communion, is the Christian rite that commemorates Jesus' death, burial, and Resurrection. The night before he was crucified, Jesus shared a meal with his disciples and gave them this celebration to remember his sacrifice.

On the night Jesus was betrayed, he took bread, gave thanks, and said, "This is my body, which is for you; do this to remember me." He also took the cup and said, "This cup is the New Covenant in my blood; whenever you drink it, remember me."

As often as you eat the bread and drink from the cup, you proclaim the Lord's death until he comes. So, whoever eats the bread and drinks from the cup in an unworthy manner sins against Christ's body and blood. Examine yourself before taking the Lord's Supper because you bring yourself into judgment if you don't.

Therefore, you are weak and sick, and some of you have died. If we were more discerning, we would not come under such judgment. The Lord disciplines us when he judges us like this so that he won't condemn us with the world. When you take the Lord's Supper, wait for each other. If you're hungry, eat at home; I will give further instructions when I come.

SPIRITUAL GIFTS

I want you to know about spiritual gifts. Once, when you were pagans, mute idols led you astray. But you must understand that no one who has the Holy Spirit can ever say Jesus is accursed, and no one can call Jesus Lord who does not have the Spirit.

There are different kinds of gifts, but the same Spirit gives them. Different types of service and works, but the same Lord who is at work through them. Each of you has a gift from the Holy Spirit for the good of the church. Some have gifts of wisdom, knowledge, faith, healing, miraculous powers, prophecy, discernment, speaking in tongues, or interpreting tongues. But all of these come from the same Spirit as he desires.

> ### What are spiritual gifts?
>
> The Bible teaches us that they are many different spiritual gifts, and no individual has them all. These are divine empowerment to do work so the church can function correctly. All these gifts are for building up the church and glorifying God. The Holy Spirit gives each believer gifts as he sees fit, and we all have them in different measures. All of them are necessary for both the local and universal church to function as God wants it to, and whatever gifts we have, we should use them in love. Scripture lists many spiritual gifts, including administration, teaching, prophecy, miracles, service, wisdom, knowledge, faith, discernment, tongues, interpretation of tongues, evangelism, giving, leadership, mercy, and encouragement.

Even though the body has many members, they are all one, just as it is with Christ. We were all baptized into one body and all drank from the same Spirit. But the body consists of many members. The foot isn't a hand or an ear, and it can't see; that doesn't make it any less a part of the body. If the body was only eyes or ears, it couldn't smell or walk. God put all the members of the body together as he chose so that it could work. As there are many parts, but one body, no part can tell the others that it doesn't need them. Instead, the parts that seem weaker deserve greater honor, which the seemingly greater parts don't need.

There should be no divisions among you and you should care for one another. If one member suffers, you all suffer; if one member is honored, you should rejoice; you are all individual members of Christ's body. God has appointed apostles, prophets, teachers, miracle workers, healers, servants, administrators, and those who speak in tongues. Not everyone has all the gifts but eagerly desire the greater ones.

> **What is prophecy?**
>
> Prophecy is not just making predictions about the future; it is also speaking on behalf of God. While God does sometimes speak through his followers to reveal what will happen, most of the time, it is delivering a message from God to his people. When people prophesy, it will never contradict what God has revealed in the Bible.

But I want to show you a more excellent way.

If I speak in the tongues of people but don't have love, I'm just making noise. If I have every gift, know everything, can move mountains, or become a martyr, but I don't have love, it is worthless.

Love is patient, kind, does not envy or boast, is not arrogant or rude. It does not insist on its own way, is not irritable or resentful, does not rejoice in sin, but rejoices in the truth. Love bears all things, believes all things, hopes all things, and endures all things. Love never ends. Everything else will pass away; we only know in part, but when Jesus returns, the partial will pass away. When I was a child, I spoke, thought, and reasoned like a child; but I had to put the childish away once I grew up.

Now we see as if in a fogged mirror, but we will know everything like we are fully known when we see him face to face. Faith, hope, and love remain, but love is the greatest of these.

> **Love, our underlying motivation**
>
> Love should be the underlying motivation for everything we do. This is not romantic love but a choice to put the needs of others above our own.

Pursue love and earnestly desire spiritual gifts, especially prophecy. Those who speak in tongues speak to God and not to men because no one can understand them. But those who prophesy speak to everyone for their strengthening, encouragement, and comfort. Those who speak in a tongue strengthen themselves, but those who prophesy strengthen the church.

I wish you all spoke in tongues, but even more to prophesy. Those who prophesy are greater than those who speak in tongues unless there is someone to interpret. No one benefits from tongues, but you will only benefit if I bring you a revelation, knowledge, prophecy, or teaching. If a musician doesn't play specific notes on an instrument, no one will know the tune. The same is true of you; if you speak unintelligible words, no one knows what you are saying. There are many languages in the world, but it is meaningless if the listener doesn't understand. Seek to build up the church; pray for the ability to interpret, so you are not just praying with your spirit.

If you pray with both your spirit and mind, you will be able to worship with both. How can anyone agree with your praise unless they know what you're saying? Then they can also be strengthened. I thank God that I pray in tongues, but I would much rather speak five words with my mind to instruct than many words in a tongue.

Stop thinking like children, be innocent of evil, but mature in your thinking. Tongues are a sign for unbelievers, but prophecy is for believers. If the whole church speaks in tongues, then outsiders will think you are insane. But if everyone is prophesying, then God will convict them; they will worship the Lord and declare that he is in your midst.

> **What are tongues?**
>
> Tongues are one of the spiritual gifts that the Holy Spirit gives to some believers. For some, this is the ability to speak natural languages that they do not otherwise know, and for others, it is a prayer language that we speak to God. This is a mysterious gift that we don't fully understand, but it builds up the church and edifies believers. Many people with this gift use it in their private communication with God. We should not expect everyone to speak in tongues, and the Bible tells us to have someone to interpret if we speak in the church.

When you meet, each of you brings a song, revelation, tongue, or interpretation; everything must be to build up the church. Only a few of you should speak in a tongue and there must be someone to interpret. If there is no one to interpret, the one who speaks in a tongue should keep quiet and only talk to God. Two or three prophets should speak and the others should evaluate the message. If God gives a revelation to one who is sitting, then the speaker should be silent.

Prophesy one by one so that everyone can learn and be encouraged because God is not a God of disorder, but peace. Women should remain silent in church and stay in submission. If they have questions, they should ask their husbands at home.

If anyone thinks they are a prophet or have a gift from the Spirit, let them acknowledge that these aren't just my opinions, I'm writing the Lord's commands. If anyone ignores this, ignore them. Be eager to prophesy and allow tongues, but let everything be orderly.

> **Orderly worship**
>
> One of the more controversial teachings in the Bible is that women cannot speak in church. This was meant for the church in Corinth because some women would jump up and talk over everyone else. Worship services in Corinth were often chaotic. Women are not inferior to men and are allowed to be a part of worship services. Still, no matter what happens, church meetings need to be orderly so that outsiders don't have ammunition to speak ill of God and his congregation.

THE RESURRECTION

I want to remind you of the gospel I preached to you. It is what saves you if you hold to it; otherwise, you believed in vain. Christ died for our sins, was buried, and then rose on the third day according to the Scriptures. Then he appeared to Peter and the other apostles and then to more than 500 believers (most of whom are still living, but some have died). Then he appeared to James and the other apostles; last, he appeared to me even though I persecuted the church. But, by God's grace, I am what I am, and his grace toward me was not in vain. It was God's grace working, regardless of who preached to you.

If we preach that Christ rose from the dead, how can you say there is no resurrection? If there is no resurrection, then not even Christ has risen, then our preaching and your faith are in vain. Then we are even lying about God if he didn't rise from the dead.

If Christ has not risen, then your faith is futile, and you are still in your sins; and those who have died in Christ will remain dead. If we only have hope in this life, then we are pitiful fools. But if Christ rose from the dead, he is the first fruits of those who died.

Since death came from one man, then resurrection also comes from one man. As Adam led to our death, Jesus leads to our life. When he comes again, everyone who belongs to him will rise from the dead; then he will hand over the kingdom to God the Father after destroying his enemies. He will reign until he has put all his enemies under his feet, and the last enemy he will destroy is death. When he does this, then Christ will put himself in submission to God. If you believe there is no resurrection, then why are some of you baptized for the dead? If there is no resurrection, suffering for the gospel is worthless. We should eat and drink because we may die tomorrow.

> **Baptism for the dead**
>
> Baptism for the deceased was a First Century practice that some people performed, but it is not something that God ever commanded Christians to do. Paul referenced this as an argument to show the necessity of belief in the resurrection.

Don't be deceived; bad company corrupts good morals. Wake up from your drunken stupor and stop sinning.

Some will ask what kind of body we will have when we rise, but that's a foolish question. Seeds only grow if they die; our current bodies are like seeds that God plants. When we die, he will raise it as he determines. Every living being has its own kind of flesh; there are earthly bodies and heavenly bodies, and their splendor is different. So it will be with resurrection from the dead. We are sown perishable and raised imperishable; sown in dishonor and weakness, and raised in power and glory.

If there is a natural body, there is also a spiritual body. The first Adam became a living being; the second Adam (Jesus) became a life-giving spirit. The first is from the earth and natural; the second is from heaven and spiritual. Just as we bear Adam's image, we will one day bear Christ's.

> **Adam as a "type"**
>
> Adam was the first human God created and Paul references him as a "first" to his readers. Adam was a first for all people and Jesus was a first for all spiritual people.

Flesh and blood cannot inherit the kingdom of God, nor does the perishable inherit the imperishable. We will not all die, but we will all change in the twinkling of an eye. When the last trumpet sounds, the dead will rise imperishable. We will change; this mortal body will put on immortality, and victory will swallow up death. The sting of death is sin, and the power of sin is the Law; thanks be to God that he gives us the victory through our Lord Jesus Christ. Therefore, stand firm and don't let anything move you; give yourselves entirely to God's work knowing that it is not in vain.

COLLECTION FOR THE SAINTS

Like I directed the Galatian churches, put aside money, and save it for when I come so that you won't have to do an additional collection. When I arrive, I will send it on to Jerusalem along with anyone you would like to send.

I hope to see you soon and spend some time with you, maybe even a whole winter, if the Lord allows. But I am staying in Ephesus until Pentecost because God has allowed me to minister there. When Timothy comes, put him at ease, for he is doing the Lord's work like I am.

Concerning Apollos, I urged him to visit you, but the time wasn't right; he will come when he gets the chance.

Watch out, stand firm in the faith, and be mature; do everything in love. Be subject to your spiritual leaders and other workers for the gospel because they have devoted themselves to serving the church. They have refreshed our spirits, give them recognition.

Let those who don't love the Lord be accursed! May he come quickly! May the Lord's grace be with you. I love you, brothers and sisters.

CHAPTER SEVENTEEN

JUSTIFICATION BY FAITH IN CHRIST
Galatians 1-6

> **Paul's letter to Galatia**
>
> The Galatian region in what is now modern-day Turkey was an area where the early church flourished. This letter is not to an individual congregation but a group of local churches in the Galatian region. It was intended to be circulated to multiple congregations. Paul likely wrote this letter around 55 A.D during his time in Ephesus.
>
> In this letter, Paul writes in defense of his apostleship and against a false gospel that some were preaching. As the early church grew, one of the first issues that arose was that some taught that Christians needed to add elements to the gospel. These people were known as Judiazers, and they wanted Christians to adhere to both the Old Testament and Jesus' teachings.

I am astonished that you are so quickly deserting God's grace and turning to a different gospel. There is no other, but there are some who are trying to distort Christ's gospel. But even if an angel from heaven or we should preach a different message, let them be accursed. I am not trying to please people, but God, otherwise I wouldn't be Christ's servant.

> **Jesus is the only gospel.**
>
> Jesus is the central figure of the Christian faith. He is the ABCs and the graduate level of the faith. Some people want to add other things to the gospel for many different reasons. We must keep our focus on him rather than getting sidetracked by secondary issues. We need to reject any teaching that pulls us away from Jesus.

I am not preaching a manufactured gospel; I am teaching what Christ taught me. You know about my former life, how I violently persecuted the church, and was advancing in Judaism beyond my peers. But God, who had set me apart before birth, called me by grace to know Jesus and preach his gospel. Afterward, I didn't consult with anyone but went to Arabia, where God taught me. After three years, I went to Jerusalem and stayed with Peter for 15 days; while I was there, I didn't see any other apostles besides James. I was preaching in Syria and Cilicia while I was still unknown to the church. They praised God that I was now preaching the gospel and no longer trying to destroy the church.

Fourteen years after that first visit, I returned to Jerusalem with Barnabas and Titus to clarify what God had revealed. I only met with the church leaders so that it wouldn't become a public issue magnified by racial tensions and risk my current ministry. Even Titus, who is not a Jew, did not go along with their pressure.

While we were there, some false believers snuck in to spy on our freedom and enslave us. But we did not give them the time of day because we wanted to preserve the gospel's truth. I don't care about their reputation, and neither does God; they had nothing to add to our message. Soon it was clear that God had given me the same ministry with the Gentiles that he gave Peter to the Jews. The leaders of the church agreed to accept Barnabas and me if we kept looking after the poor.

Later, when Peter came to Antioch, I confronted him because he refused to associate with the Gentiles. He gave into the pressure from people who preached circumcision. The rest of the believers, including Barnabas, followed this hypocrisy. When I saw that this was contrary to the gospel, I called them out on it.

We may be Jews by birth and not Gentiles, but we know that faith in Christ justifies us and not the Law, which cannot make us right with God. But if we still sin, that doesn't make Christ a servant of sin. If I rebuild what I tore down, then I only prove that I'm a sinner. I died to the Law so that I might be alive to God; I have been crucified with Jesus, and it is no longer I who lives, but Christ who lives in me. I live in him by faith in the Son of God, who loved me and gave his life for me. I don't nullify God's grace because if the Law could make us righteous, then Christ died for no reason.

You foolish Galatians, who tricked you? You know Jesus was crucified, and you received the Holy Spirit by faith and not the Law. After starting with the Spirit, are you going to finish with the Law? You know that God works miracles among you by the Holy Spirit's power and not the Law. You are Abraham's children because of the same faith that God credited to him as righteousness. Scripture prophesied that Abraham's descendants would bless the world through this faith.

Those who don't obey the whole Law are cursed, but those who live by faith will be right with God. Christ rescued us from the Law by taking our place when he was crucified. God redeemed us through Christ to receive the promise of the Spirit and fulfill the prophecies in Scripture.

No one can change the terms of a contract after the fact; in the same way, the promises made to Abraham were through a singular person and not through many. The Law that came 430 years later did not do away with the promise because the inheritance depends on the promise and not the Law.

The Law came to expose sin until Jesus came. This doesn't mean it is against God's promises; the Law merely locked everything under sin until Jesus came to give faith to everyone who believes. The Law was our guardian until Christ came to justify us; we don't need that guardian anymore. In Christ, you are all God's children; your faith and baptism are in him.

There is no longer Jew nor Gentile, slave nor free, male nor female because you are one in Christ. If you belong to Christ, then you are children of Abraham and heirs according to the promise.

> **Equality in Christ**
>
> Paul makes a compelling statement here that there are no longer racial, class, or gender distinctions. Some have used the Bible to justify racism, classism, sexism, and just about any other form of -ism imaginable. These are all distortions of the gospel. God views us as equals, and no human is better than another, regardless of the classification. As followers of Christ, we must fight against these hierarchies wherever we find them.

While heirs are children, they are no different from servants even though they own everything until parents declare otherwise. When we were spiritual children, we were under the Law until Jesus came to free us and adopt us as his heirs. God has sent the Spirit of his Son into our hearts so that we can call him Father and Daddy. You are no longer slaves but God's children and heirs.

When you did not know God, those who are not gods enslaved you. But now that you know God and he knows you, how can you return to the worthless promises of the world and enslave yourselves again? I am afraid that I may have preached to you in vain; I beg you to become like me in your faith.

I first preached to you because of an illness, and although it was a burden, you didn't look down on me. Instead, you treated me like an angel or even Christ himself. You would have even given me your own eyes if you could have. I'm not your enemy; those trying to convince you of a different gospel are only trying to alienate us from each other. It's fine to be zealous for good, but you should act this way even if I'm not with you. My children, I wish I could be with you because I'm perplexed and worried about you.

Abraham had two sons, Ishmael, through a slave woman, and Isaac, through a free woman. The slave's son was born according to the flesh, while the free woman's son was born through the promise. Hagar, the slave, represents the Law and corresponds to earthly Jerusalem because she was enslaved with her children. But Sarah, the free woman, corresponds with the Jerusalem from above; she is our mother. You are like Isaac, the children of the promise. Just as Ishmael persecuted Isaac, those under the Law want to oppress you now. But we should cast out the slave woman and her son because we are children of the freewoman.

> **Abraham and his children**
>
> Abraham was the first of the Jewish ancestors that he revealed himself to in the Old Testament. God promised him a son even though Abraham and his wife were past child-bearing age. In a lapse of faith, he had a son named Ishmael with a slave girl named Hagar. Later, God fulfilled his promise with a son named Isaac with his wife, Sarah.

Christ has set us free, so don't enslave yourselves any longer. If you accept circumcision to justify yourselves, then Christ can't help you because you must obey the whole Law. If you are trying to justify yourselves with the Law or anything else, you are alienated from Christ and have fallen from grace. We eagerly await the hope of righteousness through the Spirit and faith; neither circumcision nor uncircumcision matters, only faith working through love.

You were doing so well, don't stop now because this temptation isn't from God; beware because a little yeast leavens the whole batch. I am confident that you will agree with me because the one causing confusion will bear the penalty. If circumcision mattered, I shouldn't face persecution because the cross has been abolished. I wish these people would go all the way and not just circumcise but emasculate themselves.

God called you to be free, but don't use your freedom to indulge the flesh. Use it to serve one another humbly in love. The entire Law is summed up in the command to love others as yourself. If you bite and devour each other, you will destroy one another.

Walk in the Spirit, and you won't gratify the flesh's desires, for the flesh is against the Spirit and vice versa. They war against each other, so don't do whatever you want; the Spirit leads you and is not under the Law. The acts of the flesh are sexual immorality, impurity, sensuality, idolatry, witchcraft, hatred, discord, jealousy, fits of rage, selfishness, dissensions, factions, envy, drunkenness, orgies, and the like. People who indulge in these acts will not inherit the kingdom of God.

The fruit of the Spirit is love, joy, peace, patience, kindness, goodness, faithfulness, gentleness, and self-control; there is no law against them. Those who belong to Jesus Christ have crucified the flesh along with its passions and desires. Since we live by the Spirit, let's walk by the Spirit and not become conceited, provoking, and envying each other.

If you see people caught in sin, those who are spiritual should restore them with a gentle spirit. Watch yourselves so you won't be tempted as well. Bear each other's burdens and fulfill the Law of Christ. If you think you are something when you are nothing, you are fooling yourself. Test your work, and then you won't take credit for someone else's work; you must bear your own load. If you are taught the Word, you must share with the one who teaches.

Do not be deceived; you cannot mock God. You will reap whatever you plant. If you plant according to the flesh, you will harvest corruption; if you plant according to the Spirit, you will harvest eternal life. Don't get tired from doing good because, in time, you will gather a harvest. Do good if you have the chance, especially for other believers.

Those who want to impress people through the flesh want you to be circumcised and are only trying to avoid persecution. But they don't even keep the Law themselves; they only want you to be like them so they can boast. I will only boast in the cross of our Lord Jesus Christ; the world is dead to me and I'm dead to it. Neither circumcision nor uncircumcision matters, only a new creation. If you live by this rule, peace and mercy are on you and the God of Israel. Don't cause me any more trouble because I bear the scars of the gospel on my body.

May the grace of our Lord Jesus Christ be with you all.

CHAPTER EIGHTEEN

PAUL'S MINISTRY AND COLLECTION FOR THE SAINTS
II Corinthians 1-9

> **Paul's second letter to Corinth**
>
> With all the issues in Corinth, Paul's first letter was not enough to fix their problems. Paul had a painful visit between his first and second letters to the Corinthians, and there is evidence of a sorrowful letter he wrote them in between the two letters. He wrote this letter from Macedonia, and it gives us the best insight into how Paul felt about himself as an apostle. He co-wrote this letter with Timothy.

Praise God, the Father of our Lord Jesus Christ, who is the source of all compassion and comfort. He comforts us in our troubles so that we can help others who go through problems. Just as we share in Christ's sufferings, we also share his comfort with others. Whether we suffer or are comforted, it is for your benefit as you patiently endure the same sufferings we do. Our hope for you is strong because we know that you will share in our comfort just as you share in our sufferings.

We were under enormous pressure when we were in Asia, far beyond what we could endure, and we despaired of life itself. We thought God had given us a death sentence, and we trusted he was using that to get us to rely on him who raises the dead. But he delivered us from danger and he will do it again; we set our hope on him to deliver us. Please pray for us that our labor might be fruitful and cause many to rejoice.

We have behaved with simplicity and godly sincerity, showing you God's grace and not earthly wisdom. Don't look for hidden meanings; we have only written simple truth. We want you to be as proud of us as we are of you when we stand before Jesus.

I intended to visit you twice, but I couldn't. I wasn't trying to make false promises, just as our message wasn't fake. I didn't make it to you to spare you pain, not to manipulate you. We work with you for your joy so that you can stand firm in your faith.

Another visit would have been painful for both of us; that's why I wrote what I did (this refers to the missing letter); I thought that was best. But it turned out that I wrote with many tears because I love you so much. It's time to forgive the one who caused both of us so much pain. His punishment has been enough; if you keep piling on, you could destroy him. It's time to love this brother and that's why I last wrote. I have already forgiven anyone you forgive, and this is for your sake so that Satan might not outwit us.

PAUL'S DEFENSE OF HIS MINISTRY

When I arrived in Troas, I found an open door for the gospel, but I couldn't relax without finding Titus there. So, I went to Macedonia, looking for him to reassure me about you because God causes us to give off a sweet fragrance of Christ to both believers and those who are perishing. We are not like some preachers of God's Word who water it down to make it acceptable; we preach from a sincere heart as God has commissioned us.

We aren't patting ourselves on the back or seeking your approval; your lives are all we need. You are a letter from Christ, written by the Spirit on human hearts. Only God could write this kind of letter and it authorizes us to carry out this New Covenant. The Law kills, but the Spirit gives life; the Law came on stone tablets with such glory that the Israelites couldn't even look at Moses in the face. If the ministry of condemnation brought glory, the ministry of righteousness will far outshine it. The glory of righteousness far surpasses the Law, and it is permanent.

With this hope, we are much bolder than Moses was, who put a veil over his face. But the Israelites' minds were hardened, and even now, when they read the Law, the veil remains over their hearts because only Christ can take it away. But when people turn to the Lord, God takes away the veil, and they see that he is a living Spirit and that the old, restrictive Law is obsolete. We are free! We will behold the Lord's glory without a veil as he transforms us from one degree of glory to another as we become more like him.

Having this ministry, we do not lose heart; we have renounced disgraceful, underhanded ways. We refuse to tamper with God's Word. Our lives are a statement of our clean conscience in God's eyes. Even if our gospel is veiled, it is only veiled to those who are perishing because Satan has blinded their hearts. We don't proclaim ourselves; we proclaim Jesus and ourselves as his servants; he shines in our hearts so that people may know God's glory in the face of Jesus Christ.

We have this treasure in fragile jars to show that this power belongs to God and not us. We are afflicted in every way, but not crushed; perplexed, but not despairing; persecuted, but not forsaken; struck down, but not destroyed. We carry his death with us so that Jesus might be manifested in our lives. Our lives are always at risk for his sake, making his life even more evident in us.

While our lives are horrible, yours are extraordinary. We have the same spirit of faith and we know that the one who raised Jesus will raise us too. All of this is for your sake so that more people might believe. Even though we are wasting away, God is renewing our souls. This momentary pain does not compare to the eternal glory God will give us. The things we see are nothing, but what we cannot see will last forever.

We know that if God destroys the tent of our earthly home, he has a building for us that he made in heaven. We long for our heavenly dwelling, waiting to be fully clothed so that life would swallow up death. God has prepared this building for us and has given us the Holy Spirit as a promise. We are confident that while we are at home in this body, we are away from the Lord.

We live by faith and not sight. I would rather be with him than here in my body; so, we make it our goal to please him wherever we are. One day, we will all stand before the judgment seat of Christ so that we will receive what we deserve, whether good or bad.

Since we know what it means to fear the Lord, we try to persuade others, and I hope you know the same. We want to give you the chance to take pride in us so that you can answer those who trust in the visible rather than the heart.

If we sound insane, it's for God; if we are in our right mind, it's for you. Christ's love controls us because he died for us so that we might live for the one who died and rose again. We no longer regard anyone from a worldly point of view. We once saw Christ in this way, but not anymore because if we are in Christ, we are a new creation; the old has gone, the new has come!

This is all from God, who has reconciled us to himself through Christ and given us this ministry to preach that God forgave people's sins through his death. We are Christ's ambassadors, and we implore you, on his behalf, to be reconciled to God. For our sake, God made Jesus, who knew no sin, to become sin so that we might become God's righteousness in him.

Do not receive God's grace in vain; he is calling you; now is the day of salvation.

We don't want to put obstacles in anyone's way. Instead, as God's servants, we endure trouble, hardship, persecution, beatings, imprisonments, riots, hard work, sleepless nights, and hunger. We face these hardships in purity, understanding, patience, kindness, the Holy Spirit, love, truth, and God's power. We hold the weapons of righteousness in both hands through glory and dishonor, good and bad reports, those who are genuine but believed to be dishonest, known yet unknown, dying while we live, beaten but not killed, sad but rejoicing, poor but making many rich, having nothing but possessing everything. We have opened our hearts to you and spoken freely about Christ; open your hearts to us.

PAUL'S APPEAL TO THE CORINTHIANS

Do not be partners with unbelievers because light has nothing to do with darkness, and God's temple has nothing to do with idols. We are the temple of the living God; he lives with us and makes us his people. The Lord tells us to leave them and be separate, to leave unclean things behind. He will be a father to us and we will be his children. Therefore, let us purify ourselves from everything that defiles us.

> **Partners with unbelievers**
>
> Paul warns the Corinthians not to become partners with unbelievers, which is good advice for us as well. In situations like marriage and business, it can be difficult to have successful relationships because our motivation should be God's glory while they focus on other objectives.

Please accept us in your hearts; we have not wronged, corrupted, or exploited anyone. I have spoken frankly; I take great pride in you; in fact, we would live or die with you. We were greatly distressed in Macedonia and Titus comforted us when he came and told us how you longed for us.

I don't regret any sorrow I caused you because it only hurt for a little while. Your grief led to a repentance that leads to salvation. Your pain brought an earnest desire to justify yourselves and prove your innocence. My letter showed God how devoted you are to us, and your response encouraged me.

I bragged to Titus about you and you proved me right. His affection for you grew because of your obedience and how you received him with fear and trembling.

We want you to know about what the gift the Macedonian church sent has done. During their affliction and extreme poverty, their generosity has brought them great joy. They gave beyond their means to help other believers, but first, they gave themselves to the Lord and then to us. As you excel in faith, speech, knowledge, earnestness, and love, excel in the collection for other believers. I am not commanding you to do this, but asking so that you may prove your genuine love.

You know about Christ's grace and how he became poor for your sake so that you might become rich in his poverty. You started this work a year ago, finish strong out of fairness to those who have also given. Let your prosperity supply others' needs so that everyone may have enough. Right now, you have plenty and can help those in need; later, they will share with you if you have need.

I thank God that he gave Titus the same concern that I have for you. He is coming to see you because he misses you, and the churches have chosen him to administer this gift. We want to avoid criticism and do what is right. Titus is my co-worker with you; show these men the proof of your love and the reason for our pride in you.

I don't need to write about this because I know how eager you are to help, and your attitude has caused others to give. I am sending these brothers to you so that you will be ready when the Macedonians arrive. So, I urge you to finish the work you started so that your generous gift won't be a grudging duty.

Whoever plants a little will harvest a little, and whoever plants a lot will harvest a lot. Each of you should give what you've decided, not reluctantly or under compulsion, because God loves a cheerful giver.

God can bless you abundantly so that you will always have enough. God, who supplies the seed and food, will also increase your harvest of righteousness. He will bless you so that you can be generous and magnify God's glory. Your service not only supplies your needs but also gives an avenue for praising God. Thank God for his indescribable gift!

CHAPTER NINETEEN

PAUL'S DEFENSE OF HIS MINISTRY
II Corinthians 10-13

I appeal to you in humility and gentleness because I know I am timid in person but bold in my letters. I hope that I don't have to be so bold when I come. Though we live in the world, we do not wage war as the world does; we fight with divine weapons strong enough to destroy strongholds.

We destroy arguments and lofty opinions against God; we take every thought captive and make it obedient to Christ. Then we may punish the disobedient once you obey. If you are confident in your faith, remember that we are his as well. Even if I boast too much about my authority in Christ, my goal is to build you up, not tear you down.

I'm not trying to scare you with my letters because I know some of you think my writing is severe, but my speaking is unimpressive. You should know that my actions will match my letters when I arrive. I'm not speaking out of turn; I only boast about what God has given me as a ministry. My only hope is that as your faith grows, the sphere of our influence might increase and that we might preach to those who haven't heard the gospel. We won't take credit for others' work; we will only boast about what God has done.

I hope you put up with my foolishness because I have godly jealousy for you. I promised that I would present you to Christ pure, but I'm afraid that just as Satan deceived Eve, the Devil might lead you away from your devotion to Christ. You do well enough with those who preach a different gospel. I am not inferior to so-called super-apostles, and even though I'm not a very good speaker, I do have knowledge.

I wasn't wrong to take from other churches so that I could preach to you for free. When I was in need while I was with you, I didn't take anything from you because the Macedonians were generous. I have never wanted to be a burden to you and I will continue in this manner.

I will not stop boasting and I will keep doing what I do so that I can cut the legs out from under those who want to take credit for our work. These people are false workers who pose as apostles, just like Satan poses as an angel of light. In the end, they will get what they deserve. I repeat, don't think I'm a fool; I only picked up this habit of boasting from others. In your wisdom, you put up with fools who enslave and rip you off, but I'm not strong enough to do that.

I am just as much a Jew and a servant of Christ as they are, even more so. I've done more and suffered far more imprisonments, beatings, and almost died. I received 39 lashes from Jews five times, was beaten with rods three times, I was stoned, and shipwrecked three times. I've been in danger from rivers, robbers, my own people, Gentiles, and false brothers; in the city, wilderness, and at sea; I've faced every possible hardship. On top of that, I bear the weight of all the churches; if anyone is weak or falls, I feel it. If I'm going to boast, I will only boast about my weaknesses.

God knows I'm not lying. When I was in Damascus, I escaped the governor by being lowered over the wall in a basket. Fourteen years ago, God took me to heaven, and I saw incredible things that I can't even describe. I can't boast about things like this so that no one thinks too highly of me.

To keep me from pride, God gave me a thorn in my side, harassment from Satan to keep me humble. I begged God three times to take this away, but he denied me because he perfects his power in my weakness. So, I will boast of my weaknesses so that Christ's power may rest on me. I'm okay with my weakness, insults, hardships, persecutions, and troubles because when I'm weak, that's when I'm strong in Christ.

You have made me act like a fool because I'm not inferior to these super-apostles even though I'm nothing. I showed you the authentic marks of an apostle with signs, wonders, and miracles. I'm coming to visit you for the third time, but I won't be a burden because I'm after your hearts, not your money. Parents should save up for their children, not the other way around; so, I will gladly spend everything I have on your behalf, even my life. But in all of this, I have not taken advantage of you; everything I do is for your benefit. When I come, I'm afraid I will find arguments, jealousy, anger, hostility, gossip, conceit, and chaos. I'm worried that those who sinned through impurity, sexual immorality, and sensuality will not have truly repented.

This is the third time I'm visiting you; two or three witnesses should confirm every fact. I warned you the last time I was there and I won't go easy on anyone who keeps sinning. You are demanding proof that Christ speaks through me and he will not be weak when dealing with you. He was crucified in weakness, but he lives in God's power; in the same way, we are weak in him, yet we live in his power.

Test yourselves to see if you truly have faith; know that Jesus is in you unless you fail the test. We have not failed the test and we pray that you will not do anything wrong. Not so that we look good, but so that you do the right thing even if people think we failed. We can only act for the truth.

> **Testing our faith**
> The admonition to test our faith is a reference to the practice of soldiers testing their weapons before taking them into battle. Before entering a fight, soldiers wanted to ensure their equipment wouldn't fail when the stakes were highest. We can test our faith by continually checking our belief and behavior to make sure they align with the Bible.

We pray for your restoration and are glad when we are weak, but you are strong. I don't want to be severe when I visit you, but I want to use my authority to build you up rather than tear you down.

Finally, rejoice! Aim for restoration, comfort one another, and agree with each other; live in peace, and the God of love and peace will be with you. Greet each other with a holy kiss. May Jesus' grace, God's love, and the Holy Spirit's fellowship be with you all.

CHAPTER TWENTY

THE PROBLEM OF SIN

Romans 1:1-3:20

> **Paul's letter to Rome**
>
> We are unsure how this church started, although it is likely a result of either people converted at Pentecost or people who heard the gospel during one of Paul's missionary journeys and then moved to Rome. It appears that the church consisted of several congregations that met in home groups. The Roman church was a mix of Jews and Gentiles, though it seems that Gentiles were the majority. Tertius probably wrote Paul's words down and Phoebe likely carried the letter to the believers.
>
> The Book of Romans is the longest letter in the New Testament. Paul wrote it from Corinth during his third missionary journey around 57 A.D. He was in his mid-40's at the time and had been a Christian for about 20 years. This letter is unique because it does not deal with a specific issue that the church had reported to Paul. It is essentially a theological treatise that Paul wrote to prepare them for his arrival (he had been unable to visit them before this). The central theme is that God saves us through his righteousness and grace. These are available to those who trust in Jesus Christ.

I thank God for all of you because news of your faith has spread around the world. God is my witness of how often I pray for you and that I might join you. I long to see you so that I can strengthen your faith and that we might encourage each other. I have wanted to come to you for quite some time to preach the gospel as I have to others. I have many obligations; that is why I am so eager to preach to those in Rome.

I am not ashamed of the gospel because it is God's power to save everyone who believes. First for the Jew, then for the Gentile. It reveals God's righteousness through our faith.

God is revealing his wrath against the ungodly and wicked who suppress the truth. God has plainly shown himself to them through his creation. Through nature, he has shown us his invisible qualities, eternal power, and divinity, so we have no excuse not to believe in him. Even though they knew God, they did not worship him; instead, they chose to worship created things. Although they claimed to be wise, they chose foolishness.

> **Natural revelation**
>
> Paul tells the Romans that God has revealed himself through his creation. His fingerprints are all over creation, from the number pi's infinite precision to the

> exclusive design of fingerprints. As we see the beauty of the universe and the intricacies of design, it shows God's existence beyond question. The world's current scientific interpretation favors a universe without God, but that is a far greater leap of faith than accepting his existence. His existence means that we must answer to our Maker.

Therefore, God let them follow their sinful desires into sexual impurity and degrading their bodies. They traded the truth about God for a lie and worshiped creation rather than the Creator. He gave them over to shameful lusts and they exchanged natural passions for unnatural ones. Women had sex with women, and men committed shameful sexual acts with each other. God gave them over to depravity and they committed great sins. They were full of evil: envy, murder, strife, lies, malice, gossip, slander, hating God, insolence, arrogance, disobedience to parents, foolishness, faithlessness, ruthlessness; they even invented new ways of sinning. They knew God's commands, and not only did they disobey, but they also encouraged others to disobey.

Therefore, those of you who judge condemn yourselves because you do the same things. We know God judges those who do such things. Do you think you can escape God's judgment? Do you have contempt for his kindness and patience? Don't you realize his kindness is meant to lead you to repentance? Because of your stubborn and unrepentant hearts, you are saving up his wrath for Judgment Day. God will repay everyone for their deeds. He will give eternal life to those who patiently do good, seeking glory, honor, and immortality. But there will be anger and wrath for those who are self-seeking, disobedient, and unrighteous.

There will be trouble and distress for those who do evil; glory, honor, and peace for those who do good, first for the Jew, then for the Gentile. God does not show favoritism.

All who have sinned without the Law will die without it and all who have sinned under the Law will be judged by it. It is not the hearers of the Law who are righteous but those who are obedient. When those who don't have God's commands do it by nature, they show that God wrote his Law on their hearts. Their conscience will alternately accuse and defend them on the day God judges everything through Jesus.

If you claim to be a Jew, rely on the Law and boast in God, if you approve what is right and claim to be a light to those in darkness, if you claim to teach others, don't you teach yourself? Do you preach that people shouldn't steal, commit adultery, or worship idols and then do the same? If you preach the Law and then do the same, then you dishonor God. The Gentiles blaspheme God's name because of you.

Circumcision is valuable if you obey the Law, but you may as well not be circumcised if you break it. Those who are not physically circumcised but obey the Law will condemn you. People are truly Jews if they are Jews on the inside because circumcision is of the heart, by the Holy Spirit, not by written Law. Their praise is from God and not people.

If this is true, then is there any advantage to being a Jew or circumcision? Of course, there is! First, God entrusted the Jews with his Word; if some were unfaithful, that doesn't nullify God's faithfulness. Even if we are all liars, God is true. If our unrighteousness causes God's righteousness to be more evident, that doesn't make him a liar or prove him unjust. If it did, he could not judge humanity. Some would argue that if my sin increases God's glory, then why am I condemned? Why not do evil if the result is good? They deserve their condemnation.

So, Jews are not better off since we are all sinners. None of us are righteous; none of us seek God. We have all turned away and become worthless; none of us do good. We lie, curse, and are swift to shed blood; we do not truly fear God. We know that the Law speaks to those under it so that every mouth may be silenced, and the world would be held accountable. Therefore, the Law will not justify us; instead, it reveals our sin.

CHAPTER TWENTY-ONE

SALVATION THROUGH FAITH

Romans 3:21-5:21

God reveals his righteousness both in the Law and apart from it. This righteousness comes through faith in Jesus to all who believe. We have all sinned and fallen short of God's glory. God only justifies us by his grace through the redemption we have in Jesus Christ. God gave Christ as an atoning sacrifice that we receive by faith through the shedding of his blood. He did this to show God's righteousness and because he had not punished our sins yet. He did this so that he can justify those who have faith in Jesus.

So, we cannot boast in the Law because we follow a law of faith and not works. Our faith justifies us, not the works of the Law. He is the God of all, and he justifies us all through faith, regardless of circumcision. This does not mean we overthrow the Law by faith; on the contrary, we uphold it.

> **Faith and the Law**
>
> The change from justification through the Law to justification by faith was a massive shift in thinking for people in the First Century. The Law gave commands for the people to follow, and if they did, they were righteous. However, none of the people could obey all the rules, so God gave the sacrificial system as a temporary remedy for sin. But after Jesus' death, righteousness could now be based on faith as opposed to our actions. It is about what Jesus has done as opposed to what we do.

If works justified our ancestor Abraham, then he could boast, but not before God. Scripture tells us that Abraham believed God, and the Lord counted it as righteousness. Those who work receive their wages as an obligation, not a gift. For those who believe in God, their faith counts as righteousness rather than work. David says the same thing when he writes that God blesses those whom he forgives.

This blessing has nothing to do with circumcision; Abraham had faith before he was circumcised. He was circumcised as a sign of righteousness so that he could be the father of all who believe without circumcision. Then God will count them as righteous if they walk in the same footsteps of the faith that Abraham walked in.

> **Circumcision**
>
> Circumcision was the sign of the covenant God made with Abraham in the Old Testament. Every Jewish male was to have the foreskin of his penis cut off at eight days old to show that the Israelites were set apart from the people around them. Nearly 2,000 years later, it seems foolish to argue about circumcision, but this was a big deal in the First Century. Circumcision was a requirement for Jews and

> one of the things that helped them remain distinct from the nations around them. However, since Jesus brought a New Covenant, circumcision is no longer a requirement for Christians. This was a massive change in thinking for Jewish converts to Christianity.

The promise to Abraham and his offspring was that he would become the heir of the world, not through the Law but through the righteousness that comes with faith. If it is through the Law, then faith is null, and the promise is void. For the Law brings wrath, but without it, there is no sin. That is why justification is by faith so that the promise is by grace and not through the Law.

That's why he is the father of many nations. He is our father in God's eyes, the God who gives life to the dead and creates something out of nothing. Abraham believed in the hope that he would be the father of many nations even when he was 100 years old and his wife was barren. His faith did not waver; he worshiped, convinced that God would fulfill his promises. That's why Abraham's faith counted as righteousness, not just for his sake alone, but for ours as well. It will count as righteousness for all who believe in Jesus' Resurrection from the dead. He died for our sins and rose to make us right with God.

Therefore, since we are right with God by faith, we have peace with God through Jesus Christ. This faith allows us to stand in his grace, and now we boast in the hope of God's glory. Beyond this, we also rejoice in our suffering because it leads to endurance, character, and then hope. Our hope does not shame us because God pours his love into our hearts through the Holy Spirit.

At the right time, while we were helpless, Jesus died for the ungodly. Rarely will anyone die for a righteous person and only occasionally for a truly good person. But God demonstrates his love for us in that Jesus died for us while we were still sinners.

Since Jesus' blood justifies us, it will also save us from God's wrath. If God reconciled us to him by his Son's death, his life will save us. Now we will rejoice in God through Jesus because he has given us reconciliation and made us his friends.

Just as sin entered the world through Adam and his sin led to death, we all face death because we have all sinned. Sin was in the world before the Law, but without the Law, no one was guilty. Yet death reigned from Adam to Moses, even over those who didn't break any commands. Adam was an example of Jesus, who was to come.

> ### Adam's sin
>
> In the Garden of Eden, Adam sinned on our behalf, and we all suffer from his decision. Some argue that this is unfair because God punishes us for Adam's sin, but we would make the same choices if we were in his place. Regardless of Adam's sin, we rebel against God every day whenever we sin.

But the gift is not like the sin. The punishment for one sin brought death, but the gift, even after many transgressions, makes us right with God. If death ruled because of one man's sin, even more so will the gift of righteousness rule through one man's life, Jesus Christ. As one person's sin led to everyone's death, his righteous life made us right with God. Just like Adam's sin made us all sinners, Jesus' obedience will make many righteous.

The Law came to identify sin, but where sin increased, grace increased even more. Sin reigned in death, now grace reigns through righteousness to bring eternal life through Jesus Christ our Lord.

> ### Salvation by faith
>
> In this passage, Paul tells us that we cannot justify ourselves with our actions alone because we have all sinned. The only way that we can be right with God is through our faith in Jesus' perfect life and death on the cross. Abraham's faith is an example for us to follow. Just as he believed God's promises and trusted that the Lord would follow through, we should trust God's promises and know that he will fulfill them.

CHAPTER TWENTY-TWO

RESULTS OF SALVATION

Romans 6-8

So, should we keep sinning so that there is even more grace? Of course not! If we have died to sin, we can't live in it any longer. If we are baptized into Christ, then we are baptized into his death. We were buried with him through baptism into death, and just as he was raised from death, we too can live a new life. Just as we join with him in his death, we unite with him in his Resurrection. Our old selves were crucified with him so that our sins would die and we would no longer be slaves to sin. If anyone has died, they have been set free from sin.

> **Baptism into Christ's death**
>
> Our baptism doesn't save us, but it is symbolic of our faith. The act of immersing ourselves in water is symbolic of dying to our old selves and as Christ died on the cross.

If we died with Christ, we know we will also live with him. If Christ rose from the dead, he cannot die again; death has no power over him. He died to sin once for all and now he lives to God. So, we are also dead to sin but alive to God. Don't let sin rule in your body so that you obey its evil desires. Don't offer any part of yourselves to wickedness, but offer every part of yourselves to God as an instrument of righteousness. Sin is no longer your master because you are under grace and not the Law.

Should we sin because we are under grace and not the Law? Of course not! You serve whomever you obey, either sin, which leads to death, or God, which leads to life. Thank God that though you used to be slaves to sin, now your heart obeys his teaching. You have been set free from sin and serve righteousness. When you were slaves of sin, you were free regarding righteousness. But that life only leads to death and destruction. Now that you are free from sin, you bear fruit that leads to sanctification and eternal life. The wage of sin is death, but the gift of God is eternal life in Jesus Christ.

The Law only has authority over people if they are alive. For example, a married woman is bound to her husband while he is alive, but she is free from the Law if he dies. If she sleeps with another man while her husband is alive, she commits adultery; but she can marry another man if her husband dies.

In the same way, you have died to the Law through Christ so that you may belong to God and bear fruit for him. While we lived under the Law, our sinful desires led us towards death. But now that we are free, we serve the Holy Spirit and not the letter of the Law.

That does not mean that the Law is sinful. The Law is perfect, and I would not have known what sin was if it didn't exist. But sin took the opportunity from the commandments and produced all kinds of evil in our lives. The Law that was meant to bring life revealed our sin and brought death. The Law is holy, righteous, and good; it did not cause our sin or death, but it revealed our sin and that sin leads us to death.

We know that the Law is spiritual, but I am unspiritual, a slave to sin. I don't understand my actions because I don't do what I want; I end up doing what I'm trying to avoid. Now, I am no longer the one doing it, but it is the sin that lives within me. Nothing good lives in my flesh because I have the desire to do the right thing, but I don't do it.

My soul delights in God's Law, but my flesh keeps waging war against my mind making me a prisoner to sin. I am wretched! Who will deliver me from this body of death? I thank God that he delivers me through our Lord Jesus Christ! Even though I serve God with my mind, my sinful nature serves sin.

Now, there is no condemnation for those who are in Christ because the Holy Spirit who gives life sets us free from the law of sin and death. The Law was powerless to free us, but God has freed us by sending his Son as a man to be a sin offering. He condemned sin in the flesh to fulfill the Law's righteous requirements for those of us who live by the Spirit. Those who live according to the flesh set their minds on the flesh, and death rules over them; they are hostile to God and cannot please him. But those who live by the Spirit set their mind on the Spirit's desires and life and peace rule over them. If anyone is in Christ, even though your body is subject to sin and death, the Spirit gives life because of righteousness. If the Spirit who lives in you raised Jesus from the dead, he will give you life as well.

Therefore, we must not live according to the flesh and sin. If you live according to the flesh, you will die, but if you live by the Spirit, you will put to death the deeds of the body and live. Those who are led by the Spirit of God are his children.

You did not receive a spirit of slavery to fall back into fear. God has adopted us as sons and we can cry out, "Daddy! Father!" The Spirit witnesses with our spirit that we are children of God and fellow heirs with Christ. If we suffer with him, then we will also have glory with him.

Our current suffering is not worth comparing to the glory God will reveal. Creation did not choose to be subjected to frustration, but the Creator subjected it in the hope that it would one day be freed from bondage to decay and brought into the freedom and glory of God's children. All of creation groans as in childbirth until now. We hope for this even though we have yet to see it. If it had already happened, we would not have to hope, but we patiently wait until it happens.

Sin's impact on the earth

Sin has had a tremendous impact on the world. When God created the universe, it was perfect; there were no natural disasters, no disease, or death. But Adam and Eve sinned and ruined everything. Since then, we see sin take its slow, gradual effect

> on the world around us. While we may not be able to blame a hurricane or COVID-19 on a specific sin, these were not a part of God's original design and only exist because of sin's impact on the universe.

In the same way, the Holy Spirit helps us in our weaknesses. When we do not know how to pray, the Spirit intercedes for us through groans deeper than words. God, who searches our hearts, also knows the Spirit's mind because the Spirit intercedes on our behalf by God's will.

We know that God works all things for good for those who love him, and he has called according to his purpose. Those God foreknew, he also predestined to be conformed to the image of his Son so he could be the firstborn among many brothers and sisters. Those he predestined, he called; those he called, he justified; and those he justified, he also glorified.

> **Predestination**
>
> Predestination is a doctrine that can be difficult to understand, and there is no single interpretation. It is the concept that God ordains all events and chooses whom to save. Some struggle with this because it seems to remove human choice from the equation. However, the Bible makes it clear that we make choices about our actions. These two ideas create a seeming paradox about whether we choose God or he chooses us.
>
> God is far beyond our understanding and we cannot comprehend how an infinite God can manage both with our finite minds. The reality is that both are true, and we may never fully get it before his return. This is a complicated doctrine, and I recommend further study.

If God is for us, then who can be against us? If he sacrificed his Son for us, he will also graciously give us everything. No one can bring a charge against God's chosen people because he is the one who declared us innocent. No one can condemn us because Jesus died and rose from the dead for us and now intercedes for us at the right hand of God.

Nothing can separate us from the love of Christ, not hardship, persecution, famine, nakedness, danger, or sword. We face death all day and are like sheep to be slaughtered. But in all these things, we are more than conquerors through him who loves us. I am convinced that nothing can separate us from God's love in Jesus Christ, our Lord; not death, life, angels, demons, things present or to come, powers, height nor depth, or anything else in creation.

God's promise to us

Even though we have faith, we still struggle with sin. Jesus lived as a human and he understands our weakness. He has even given us the Holy Spirit to live inside us and help us overcome our sin. No matter what, God promises us that we are still his and that nothing can separate us from him.

CHAPTER TWENTY-THREE

JEWS AND GENTILES
Romans 9-11

I have great sorrow over my fellow Israelites. I wish I could trade places with them and be cut off from Christ for their sake. God adopted them as children; they received the divine glory, the covenants, Law, temple, and God's promises. They have the Patriarchs and the Messiah, who is God over all. Amen!

But that doesn't mean God's Word failed because not all Israel's descendants truly belong to Israel, and not all of them are Abraham's children just because they share his blood. It is not the children of the flesh who are God's, but the children of the Promise who are Abraham's offspring.

Isaac was evidence of the Promise, as were his sons through Rebekah. But before Jacob and Esau (his sons) were born or had done anything good or bad, God chose Jacob to prove God's election. That doesn't make God unjust; just as he said to Moses, "I will have mercy and compassion on those I chose to." It doesn't depend on our effort or desire but God's mercy. Therefore, God raised Pharaoh so the Lord could display his power and that his name would be great in all the earth.

If he has mercy on who he wants and hardens who he wants, why does he still find fault because no one can resist his will? But who are we to question God? The created cannot ask the Creator why he made it this way. The potter uses the same clay to make some vessels for special purposes and some for everyday uses. What if God wants to show his wrath and power by making some vessels of wrath prepared for destruction? What if the Lord did this to reveal the riches of his glory to his objects of mercy that he prepared in advance for glory?

God has called us his people even though we were not his family, and he loves us even though we don't deserve it. Isaiah also told us that even though the Israelites will be as numerous as the sand on the shore, God will save only the remnant because the Lord will judge the earth. If he had not left us as his descendants, we would have become like Sodom and Gomorrah.

> **Sodom and Gomorrah**
>
> Sodom and Gomorrah were two wicked cities in the Old Testament. They became so evil that God destroyed them with fire and sulfur from heaven.

Those who did not pursue righteousness have obtained it by faith, but the Israelites who sought the Law have not reached their goal. Jesus has become a rock that people stumble over, but those who believe in him will not be ashamed.

I pray to God that he would save the Israelites; they are zealous for him but lack knowledge. Being ignorant of God's righteousness, they tried to do it on their own but have not submitted to him. Christ is the fulfillment of the Law for righteousness to everyone who believes.

Those who seek righteousness through the Law seek to obey the commandments. But righteousness through faith tells us that God will save you if you confess that Jesus is Lord and believe that God raised him from the dead. No one who trusts him will ever be ashamed.

There is no distinction between Jews and Gentiles because God is the Lord of both, and he gives his riches to all who believe. But they cannot call upon the Lord unless they believe, they cannot believe unless they hear, they cannot hear unless someone preaches, and no one will preach unless someone sends them. Those who preach bring good news, but not all Israelites believe. Faith comes from hearing the gospel of Christ.

Moses told us that God would make Israel envious and angry by a people who don't understand; Isaiah told us that those who didn't seek him would find God, and he would reveal himself to people who did not ask for him. God has held out his hands to Israel though they were a disobedient and rebellious nation.

God has not rejected his people that he knew beforehand. Elijah protested that Israel had killed the prophets, demolished God's altars, and sought his life. But God told Elijah that there were still 7,000 who had not bowed to false gods. In the same way, there is a remnant chosen by grace and not because of works.

Israel did not find what it was seeking; God's chosen found it, but the rest were hardened. God gave them a spirit of stupor, eyes that don't see, and ears that don't hear. He gave them an obstacle; now, their backs will be bent forever.

But they did not stumble so they would fall; their transgression led to salvation for the Gentiles to make Israel jealous. If their sin leads to riches for the world, how much more their faith! If their rejection brought reconciliation to the world, then their acceptance brings life from the dead. If the root is holy, so are the branches; God broke off some of the branches and grafted you into the tree. Now you share the nourishing sap with the root, but don't consider yourself better than the other branches.

Consider this; God grafted you in because he broke off other branches due to unbelief. You stand in faith, but don't be arrogant; tremble. If God didn't spare the natural branches, he won't spare you either. Consider God's severity to those who fall and his kindness to you if you remain in him; otherwise, he will cut you off. If they do not persist in unbelief, God will graft them back in because he can do that.

Understand that God has partially hardened Israel until the full number of Gentiles has come in. God will save all Israel because the Savior will come from Zion and turn godlessness away from Israel. That is his covenant with them when he takes away their sins. As far as the gospel is concerned, they are enemies of God for your sake, but he still loves them for the sake of Abraham, Isaac, and Jacob; his gifts and call are irrevocable. Just as you were once disobedient and have received mercy, now they are rebellious and will receive mercy so he can fulfill his plan.

Oh, the depth of the riches of the wisdom and knowledge of God! His judgments and paths are beyond understanding! We cannot possibly know his mind or give him counsel. Everything that exists is from him and through him. All glory to him forever! Amen.

CHAPTER TWENTY-FOUR

A TRANSFORMED LIFE

Romans 12-16

Present your bodies to God as a living sacrifice, which is your spiritual act of worship. Don't conform to this world, but transform your mind in Christ; then, you will know God's will and what is right, acceptable, and perfect.

> **Worship**
>
> Worship is defined as making much of something or someone. Often, we think of this as singing praises to God in private or as part of a group. Worship includes this, but it is also the way we live our lives. Serving God and loving others is an essential part of our worship. As humans, we worship whether we want to or not; it is a part of our design. As Christians, we should worship with our words and actions.

Don't think more highly of yourself than you should, but judge with sober judgment according to the faith God has given you. We have many members in the body of Christ, but not all of them have the same function; we are one body in Christ and members of each other. By grace, we have different gifts, and we should use them accordingly. Whether in prophecy, faith, service, encouragement, giving, leadership, or mercy; use them well.

Love must be sincere; hate what is evil and cling to what is right. Devote yourselves to each other in love and honor each other. Serve the Lord with zeal; rejoice in hope, be patient in trouble, and persistent in prayer. Give generously and practice hospitality. Bless those who persecute you, and do not curse them. Rejoice with those who rejoice and mourn with those who mourn. Live in harmony and do not be proud, instead be willing to associate with the lowly. Do not repay evil with evil, but always do the right thing. Don't take revenge, but leave room for God's vengeance. Give your enemies food and drink, and you will heap burning coals on their heads; overcome evil with good.

Everyone should be subject to the governing authorities because God established them. If you resist authority, you are resisting God because he appointed them, and he will judge. The government wields God's power for good; they do not bear the sword for no reason. Therefore, submit to the authorities to avoid punishment and for the sake of conscience. This is also why you pay taxes.

> **Christians and authority**
>
> Paul tells his readers to be subject to their government and this is the same for us today. During the First Century, the government was not perfect. The Roman Empire persecuted Christians and put them to death. When dealing with an

> oppressive government, we should engage, protest, and do everything we can to make a difference. We can engage in civil disobedience but understand that consequences may follow. We should not go against the Bible to be at peace with them because we answer to God. But at the end of the day, we must still live in subjection to their authority.

Pay to everyone what you owe, whether it be taxes, wages, respect, or honor. The only thing you should owe others is love; that is the fulfillment of the Law. All the commandments are summed up in the command: love your neighbor as yourself. Love does not harm and thus is the fulfillment of the Law.

Understand the present time; wake up because salvation is closer now than when we first believed. Put aside the deeds of darkness and put on the armor of light. Behave decently, not in drunkenness, sexual immorality, dissension, or jealousy. But put on the Lord Jesus Christ and don't think about how to gratify the flesh's desires.

Accept those who are weak in faith without arguing over secondary matters. Some have the faith to eat anything, but some only have the faith to eat vegetables. Neither should treat the other with either contempt or judgment because God accepts them both. Regardless of the issue in question, do whatever you do for the Lord. We don't just live for ourselves; we live for him; we don't die for ourselves; we die for him. No matter what, we are his because he is the Lord of both the living and the dead.

So, don't treat other believers with contempt or judgment because we will all bow before the Lord, and each of us will give him an account for our lives. Stop judging each other; instead, make up your mind not to cause anyone to stumble.

Nothing in and of itself is unclean, but if you think something is, then it is a sin for you. If what you eat or drink offends your brother or sister is, you no longer act in love. Don't destroy someone else that Christ died for, and don't let what you know is good be called evil.

The kingdom of God isn't about eating or drinking; it is about righteousness, peace, and joy in the Holy Spirit. Anyone who serves Christ pleases God and gains human approval; so, do whatever leads to peace and edification. Don't destroy God's work for food or drink because it's all clean unless it causes someone else to stumble. It is much better to abstain if it keeps someone else from falling. Be fully convinced of what you believe about questionable things. If someone does something that they are not convinced is right, it is a sin.

Those who are strong should accept the weak and not just please ourselves; we should do what's best for others and build them up. Not even Jesus lived to please himself but for us. The Scriptures exist to teach and encourage us so that through endurance, we might have hope. May we have the same attitude that Jesus had so that we may be unified in worshiping the Lord.

Accept one another as Christ accepted you so that you may praise God. Christ served the Jews on behalf of God's truth to fulfill the promises to the Patriarchs and so that the Gentiles would glorify the Lord. May the God of hope fill you with all joy and peace so that you may overflow with hope through the Holy Spirit's power.

I am convinced that you are full of goodness and knowledge and able to teach each other. I have written strong words to remind you about some issues so that you may minister to the Gentiles. He gave me the duty of preaching to them so that they might be an offering acceptable to God, sanctified by the Holy Spirit. I give glory to God because of what he has accomplished through me with them. I have faithfully preached and aim to continue to preach to those who have not yet heard.

I have wanted to come to you for some time, but now I'm on my way to Jerusalem to serve God's people. Once I'm done there, I want to go to Spain and visit you on my way. Please pray that I would be safe from the Jews there and that I would receive favor with those in Jerusalem so I can come to you and be refreshed. May the God of peace be with you all. Amen.

I urge you, brothers and sisters, to watch out for those who cause divisions and put obstacles in your way, contrary to what you've learned. People like these are not serving Christ but themselves with their smooth talk and flattery; they want to deceive whomever they can. I rejoice because of your obedience; be wise about what is good and innocent of evil. The God of peace will soon crush Satan underneath your feet.

To the only wise and powerful God who has revealed himself and can establish you in faith, be the glory forever through Jesus Christ! Amen.

CHAPTER TWENTY-FIVE

PAUL'S ARREST

Acts 21:1-23:11

> **Resumption of the historical narrative**
>
> We don't know the exact timeline of what Paul was doing while he wrote his letters, but the historical record of the church's spread picks up again with him leaving Ephesus.

Paul and his companions sailed from Ephesus on a course to Phoenicia and stopped at Tyre to load cargo and Paul decided to spend time with the church there. Through the Spirit, the church tried to convince them not to go to Jerusalem. After seven days, they prepared to leave, and the church came out to pray for Paul.

Eventually, they made their way to Caesarea, where they stayed with Philip, one of the original deacons. While staying there, a prophet named Agabus came from Judea. He took Paul's belt, bound his own hands and feet with it and said, "Thus says the Holy Spirit, 'the Jews will bind the man who owns this belt like this and turn him over to the Gentiles.'"

When the people heard this, the people tried to convince Paul not to go to Jerusalem. But Paul replied, "Why are you weeping and breaking my heart? I'm ready to not only be tied up but also die in Jerusalem for the name of Jesus." When the people saw that he wouldn't change his mind, they let it go.

Paul and his companions left for Jerusalem, and the people warmly received them. The next day, Paul met with James and the other elders to tell them everything God had been doing amongst the Gentiles. The church glorified God when they heard Paul's stories.

They told Paul, "There are thousands of Jews here who believe, and they are all zealous for the Law, but they've heard that you teach Jews to forsake Moses and our customs. They will certainly hear that you've come, so please do what we ask. We have four men under a vow; go with them to purify yourselves and pay for their expenses to shave their heads. Then they will know that the rumors they heard are false and that you do obey the Law. As for the Gentiles who have believed, we sent a letter stating that they should stay away from food sacrificed to idols, blood, meat from strangled animals, and sexual sin." The next day, Paul purified himself and the men then took them to the temple and provided the offering for them.

Near the end of the purification process, some Jews from Asia saw Paul in the temple and stirred up the crowd, crying out, "Men of Israel, help us! This is the man who preaches against Moses and the Law. He has even brought Gentiles into the temple to defile it."

The city was in an uproar, and a mob grabbed Paul and dragged him out of the temple; immediately, they shut the city gates. As the crowd was trying to kill Paul, word reached a city official that the city was in chaos. The official took troops to the temple and the mob stopped beating Paul. He took Paul into custody and bound him with two chains while trying to determine what Paul had done.

There were too many competing voices, so the official had Paul carried to the barracks to find out what was happening. As they were about to enter, Paul asked the official if he could speak to him. The man was surprised that Paul spoke Greek and answered, "Aren't you the Egyptian who started a revolt and led 4,000 terrorists into the wilderness?"

Paul replied, "I'm a Jewish citizen from Tarsus; please let me speak to the crowd." With the official's permission, Paul stood on the barracks' steps and motioned for the crowd to be quiet.

Once they were calm, Paul spoke to them in Hebrew, "I am a Jew, born in Tarsus, raised in Jerusalem, and educated by Gamaliel according to our laws' strictest interpretation. I have zealously lived my life for God, just like you. As the high priest and council can testify, I persecuted Christians, arresting them, and even putting some to death. I took some of them to Damascus in chains for punishment when suddenly a great light shone from heaven and I fell to the ground. Then Jesus told me that I had been persecuting him and that I should go into the city where he would tell me what to do. The people with me saw the light but did not understand the voice.

"They led me by the hand into Damascus, where Ananias came to me and restored my sight. He told me that the God of our fathers had appointed me to know his will, to see and hear from Jesus, and then tell the world his message. Then, I was baptized in the name of Jesus.

"When I returned to Jerusalem, I was praying in the temple when the Lord told me to leave the city because the people would not believe me. I tried to argue that my changed life would convince them of his power, but the Lord told me that he would send me to the Gentiles."

Once Paul mentioned Gentiles, the crowd cried out that Paul should die and threw off their cloaks and tossed dust in the air. The official pulled Paul into the barracks and commanded the soldiers to question him by flogging to determine why the mob was so angry.

Once the soldiers had stretched Paul out to whip him, Paul protested that he was a natural-born Roman citizen and that they had not convicted him of a crime. The official was afraid because he had put a citizen in chains, so they released him.

The next day, the official brought Paul back before the chief priests and court to figure out why the Jews were so angry. Paul looked at the council and said, "Brothers, I have always lived my life with a good conscience."

But Ananias, the high priest, cut him off and commanded that someone hit him in the mouth. Paul was furious and retorted, "God is going to strike you, you whitewashed wall! How will you judge me when you break the Law by ordering me to be hit?"

> **Who was this Ananias?**
>
> This was a fairly common name during the First Century. There were three different men named Ananias in the New Testament. The first was a man who deceived the church along with his wife, Sapphira. The second was a believer that helped Saul after the Lord met the apostle on the road to Damascus. The third Ananias was the high priest, who also presided over Jesus' trial.

Those nearby said, "Are you going to stand there and insult God's high priest?"

Paul apologized, "I'm sorry, I didn't know he was the high priest because we are commanded not to speak evil of our rulers." Paul looked around the room and realized that half the room was Pharisees, and the other half were Sadducees. So, he cried out, "Brothers! I am a Pharisee and I am on trial for the hope of the resurrection of the dead!"

When Paul said this, the crowd began to argue because the Pharisees believe in angels, the spirit, and resurrection, while the Sadducees deny them all. The two groups stopped listening to Paul and began arguing with each other. It became so heated that the official was afraid the two sides would rip Paul apart, so the man ordered the soldiers to take him back to the barracks. That night the Lord came to him and said, "Take courage, because you must testify about me in Rome after you are done here."

CHAPTER TWENTY-SIX

PAUL TRANSFERRED TO CAESAREA

Acts 23:12-26:32

The next day, more than 40 Jews planned to kill Paul, and they swore to neither eat nor drink until he was dead. They went to the chief priests and elders and told them of their plan and asked the officials to notify the conspirators when Paul was being moved so they could attack.

Paul's nephew heard of the plot, so he went to the barracks and told his uncle. Paul called for one of the soldiers to take his nephew to the official and shared the plot with him. After hearing the conspiracy, the official dismissed the boy and told him not to tell anyone else about the situation.

The official called for two commanders of a hundred soldiers and told them to take Paul with a squad of nearly 500 men in the middle of the night to Felix, the governor. He also sent a letter: "The Jews seized this man and were about to kill him when I learned he was a Roman citizen. I wanted to find out why they wanted to kill him, and I found out that there was a disagreement over their Law, but nothing requiring death or imprisonment. When I discovered a secret plot to kill him, I sent him to you so that we could find out what they have against him."

The soldiers brought Paul to Caesarea and delivered the letter. Felix received Paul and decided to keep him there until his accusers arrived.

PAUL'S DEFENSE BEFORE FELIX

After five days, Ananias and Tertullus came to Caesarea with some of the elders to make their case against Paul. When everyone had assembled, Tertullus began, "Felix, we have prospered so much under your rule, and we are so grateful for this audience, so I will get to the point. This man is a plague; he stirs up Jews around the world and is a ringleader of the Christians. He was trying to profane our temple when we stopped him. When you examine him, you will see everything we are accusing him of is true." The other Jews there joined in the accusations against Paul.

Felix nodded to Paul and he began his defense, "I am happy to make my case to you because you have judged our nation for many years. You can verify that it was only twelve days ago that I went to worship in Jerusalem and didn't argue with anyone or start a riot. Neither can you prove their accusations. But I confess this to you, this Christianity that they call a sect, I worship the God of our fathers and everything written in the Scriptures. We hope in God that there will be a resurrection of both the just and the unjust. I have always tried to live my life with a clear conscience towards both God and men.

"After several years, I went to Jerusalem to present my alms and offerings. They found me purified in the temple without any riot or disturbance. But then some Jews from

Asia, who should be here to accuse me, came and stirred up a mob. Let them, or these men, present evidence against me for anything except that I cried out that I was on trial for the resurrection of the dead."

Felix knew a bit about Christianity, so he dismissed the case until Lysias, an official from Jerusalem, arrived. He gave orders to keep Paul in custody but not restrict his movement and allow him to have visitors.

Felix was married to a Jew named Drusilla, and they sent for Paul because they wanted to hear about faith in Jesus. As Paul reasoned with them about righteousness, self-control, and the coming judgment, Felix became alarmed and sent Paul away. Felix secretly hoped that Paul would bribe him for his freedom, so he sent for him often. After two years, Porcius Festus succeeded Felix, and he wanted to do the Jews a favor and left Paul in prison.

PAUL'S DEFENSE BEFORE FESTUS

Three days after taking power, Festus went to Jerusalem, and the Jews asked him to transfer Paul to Jerusalem because they wanted to ambush him along the way and kill him. Festus replied that he was heading back to Caesarea and that Paul's accusers should come with him. He stayed for a little while longer and then headed back to Caesarea.

When he arrived, he took his seat and summoned Paul. Many Jews came before him and accused Paul of many heinous crimes, but they could not prove any of them. Paul stood to make his defense and appealed that he had not committed any crime against Rome or Jewish Law. Festus asked if Paul was willing to go to Jerusalem to stand trial.

Paul answered, "I'm standing before Caesar's court, where I ought to be tried. You know very well that I haven't committed any crime. If I committed some capital crime, I'm not afraid to die, but if they can't prove anything, I appeal to Caesar." Festus conferred with his counselors and then ruled that Paul would go to Caesar.

PAUL'S DEFENSE BEFORE AGRIPPA

Many days later, Agrippa (the ruler over the Syrian region) came to Caesarea with his sister, Bernice, on an unrelated matter. Festus laid Paul's case before the king, and Agrippa was intrigued, so he asked to see Paul the next day.

The next day, Agrippa and Bernice made a very showy entrance, and they brought Paul before them. Festus said, "King Agrippa and everyone present, you see this man before you that the Jews wish to kill, but I can't find any reason he should die. Now that he's petitioned to go before the emperor, I intend to send him. But I have no idea what to write, so I was hoping that all of you could help me figure out what to say. It seems foolish to send a prisoner with no charges."

Agrippa permitted Paul to speak and he said, "King Agrippa, I am fortunate to have this opportunity to make my case before you because you know a lot about Jewish customs. Everyone knows how I have lived from birth and how I have lived my life according to our religion's strictest party. Now I stand here on trial because of the hope I have in the promises made to our ancestors, the same promises that they hope for as they worship both day and night. It is for this hope that I am on trial! Why is it so unbelievable that God can raise the dead?!

"I used to be convinced that I should oppose Jesus of Nazareth; I locked up believers in prison and even agreed to put them to death. I punished them in the synagogues, tried to make them blaspheme, and even chased them to foreign nations.

"In my fury, I was on my way to Damascus when I saw a light brighter than the sun surrounding my companions and me. I fell to my knees and I heard Jesus' voice tell me that I was persecuting him. He told me to stand because he had appointed me to testify about everything that had happened and everything he was going to tell me. He told me that he would deliver me from the Jews and send me to the Gentiles to open their eyes and that they would turn from darkness to light and from the power of Satan. All of this so he could forgive their sins and save them.

"King Agrippa, I obeyed Jesus, and I preached everywhere that people should repent, turn to God, and live holy lives. Therefore, the Jews seized me in the temple and tried to kill me. Even to this day, God has helped me so that I can stand here before you to testify that God has fulfilled the promises. That the Messiah must suffer and that by being the first to resurrect, he would proclaim light to both Jews and Gentiles."

Festus cut Paul off and said, "Paul, you are out of your mind; all your learning is driving you crazy!"

Paul replied, "I am not crazy; I am speaking truthfully and rationally. I know King Agrippa knows all these things because none of this happened in secret. King Agrippa, I know you believe the Prophets."

Agrippa answered, "Paul, are you trying to make me a Christian?"

Paul said, "I wish that everyone would become like me other than these chains."

Agrippa, Bernice, and Festus stood up and left. As they conferred with each other, they agreed that he wasn't guilty of any crime. Then Agrippa said, "We could set him free except he appealed to Caesar."

CHAPTER TWENTY-SEVEN
PAUL'S JOURNEY TO ROME
Acts 27-28

Festus delivered Paul to an Augustinian centurion named Julius and they began the journey to Rome. They changed ships and continued their journey along the coast. Summer was over, so they began to face rough weather. Paul warned them that if they continued, they could lose the cargo and people's lives. But Julius listened to the captain rather than Paul, and they kept going.

Not wanting to spend the winter where they were, they thought they had good enough weather to proceed, so they launched again. But a vicious storm overtook them and they were adrift at sea. They did everything they could to save the ship, throwing anything they could overboard.

After several days, Paul stood before them and said, "You should have listened to me. But God appeared to me last night and told me that I must stand before Caesar and that we would all survive, but we will lose the ship. Take heart, because I believe that God will keep his promise to me. But we must run aground on an island."

After two weeks adrift, it seemed like they were finally approaching land. They feared hitting rocks, so they set anchor and prayed for morning to come. The sailors tried to escape, but Paul warned Julius that they would die if they left the ship. The centurion cut the ropes to the lifeboat and let it go.

Paul encouraged everyone on board to eat something because it had been two weeks, and they would need their strength. Paul took bread in the sight of all of them, thanked God, and ate. The 276 people on board ate their fill and threw the rest of the food overboard to lighten the load.

When morning came, the sailors did not recognize the land, but they saw a bay with a beach, and they made their way to run the ship aground. But they hit a reef and the boat began to break apart. The soldiers planned to kill the prisoners, but Julius believed Paul and told everyone to jump overboard and make their way to land. Those who could swim, did, and the others made their way to shore on planks from the ship; everyone made it to land safely.

Once safely on shore, they found out that they were on the island of Malta. The people on the island were very kind and they built a fire for the survivors. Paul gathered a bundle of sticks and threw it on the fire. As he did, a poisonous snake came out of the blaze and bit his hand. When the local people saw this, they assumed that Paul was getting his just reward; since the sea didn't kill him, the snake would. But when nothing happened to him, they believed that he was a god.

Publius was the head of the island and he welcomed them for three days. His father was very sick with fever and dysentery, and Paul prayed for him and healed the man.

When word of this miracle spread, all those who were sick on the island came to Paul, and he healed them. The grateful islanders allowed the survivors to stay with them for three months.

When it was finally time to depart, the local people provided everything that they needed. Eventually, the group made it to Rome, and they allowed Paul to stay on his own with the guard assigned to him.

Once Paul had been in Rome for three days, Paul called together the local leaders so he could lay out his case before them. He described his arrest and appealed to Caesar when the Jews could not prove any charges against him. The Roman Jews told him that they had not heard anything about him or the charges against him. But they set up an appointment for him to speak to them because they wanted to learn more about Christianity.

On the appointed day, many of the Jews came to Paul, and he spent all day reasoning with them from the Scriptures, explaining the kingdom of God, and trying to convince them about Jesus. Some believed, and others did not, but they decided to leave when Paul said, "Isaiah was right when he said, 'these people would see and hear, but never understand. These people have closed their eyes, shut their ears, and let their hearts become dull.' Now, God is sending his salvation to the Gentiles because they will listen."

Paul lived in Rome for two years under house arrest at his own expense and welcomed everyone who came to visit him, preaching the kingdom of God to anyone who would listen.

> **End of the historical record**
>
> The end of the historical narrative of the church's spread ends here, indicating that Luke wrote up to the point of Paul's transfer to Rome. While imprisoned under Nero's reign, he shared the gospel with anyone who would listen and continued writing letters to local congregations.

CHAPTER TWENTY-EIGHT

OUR RICHES IN CHRIST

Ephesians 1-6

> **Paul's letter to Ephesus**
>
> This was the first letter Paul wrote from prison in Rome. He established the church in Ephesus during his second missionary journey and this letter was to strengthen multiple churches that he had helped plant. He did not write it in response to any specific circumstance, and the main message is that Christ is in his church and the unity of the church in Christ.
>
> There is some debate over when Paul wrote this letter as well. The most likely scenario is that he wrote it while in prison in Rome around 62 A.D. It is likely a circular letter meant for the churches in and around Ephesus to read.

Praise the God and Father of our Lord Jesus Christ because he has given us every spiritual blessing. He chose us before the creation of the world to be in Christ, holy and blameless in his sight. His love has predestined us to adoption as children through Christ, according to his pleasure and will. Our adoption brings praise to his glorious grace, which he freely gives us through his beloved Son, Jesus. Through Christ's blood, he redeems us and forgives our sins through the grace he has poured out upon us.

In all wisdom and understanding, God shows us his will so that he may bring everything on heaven and earth under Christ's headship. He has chosen and predestined us through Jesus, who works everything out according to his plan. Then, those of us who hope in Christ can praise our glorious God. He sealed you in Christ with the Holy Spirit the moment you trusted in him. The Holy Spirit is the guarantee of our inheritance and redemption as God's people for his glory.

I have heard of your faith in the Lord Jesus and your love for other Christians, so I have not stopped thanking God for you. I continuously pray that God would give you a spirit of wisdom and revelation so that you will know him better. I also pray that he will open the eyes of your heart so that you may know the hope of his calling, the riches and glory of his inheritance for the saints, and the exceedingly great power for those who trust him. God used the same power and strength to raise Christ from the dead and seated him at his right hand in heaven. He is far above all other rulers, authority, power, and everything else that ever has been or will be. God has put all things under Christ's authority and has made him the head of the Church, which is his body.

You were dead in the sin you lived in when you followed the ways of the world and Satan, the spirit that is at work in the hearts of the disobedient. We all lived that way and gratified the desires of our sinful flesh and minds; we were children of wrath by nature, just like everyone else. But God loves us and showed us great mercy by making us alive even when we were dead in our sins.

God saved us by grace, and he has raised us up with Jesus and seated us with him in heaven so that he could show the incredible riches of his grace through Christ. God saves us by grace through faith, and this is not from ourselves; it is the gift of God. It is not the result of works, so that no one can boast about their salvation. We are God's masterpiece, created in Christ to do the good works that God prepared for us to do.

> ### Salvation by grace
>
> Salvation through grace is one of Christianity's fundamental teachings and it separates us from every other religion. Grace is favor that we have not done anything to earn. That is a perfect definition of our salvation because it has nothing to do with our actions. God saves us based on Jesus' death and Resurrection and not what we do. We cannot do anything to make us good enough for God, so he did it for us. This is grace. All other major religions require adherents to do certain things to earn salvation, but Christianity focuses on what God has done for us instead of our actions.

Therefore, remember that you Gentiles used to be called "uncircumcised" by those who are physically circumcised. Remember that you were separate from Christ, excluded from citizenship in Israel. You were unfamiliar with the covenants of promise and lived a hopeless and godless life. But now you belong to Jesus, and although you used to be far away, his blood has brought you near.

Jesus is our peace and he united Jews and Gentiles into one people by breaking down the wall of hostility. He has abolished the Law with its commandments and regulations to make the two groups into one. Christ has established peace through his death on the cross and reconciled the two into one body to God by putting their hostility to death. So, he preached peace to those who were far off and those who were near; now, we both have access to the Father through Christ in one Spirit.

Therefore, you are no longer strangers and aliens, but citizens and members of God's household. Our faith builds upon the foundation of the apostles and prophets, with Jesus as the chief cornerstone. Christ joins the whole building together and raises it to become a holy temple for the Lord. He is also building you into a spiritual dwelling place for God.

This is why I am a prisoner for Christ, for the sake of you Gentiles. Surely you have already heard about God's grace that he gave me; this is what I wrote about before.

I am a prisoner of Christ for the sake of the Gentiles and I know that you've heard about my ministry. So, you should understand my insight into God's revelation that we are all a part of Christ's body and share in his inheritance. I am a servant of God's grace, even though I'm the least deserving of all believers. He gave me this ministry to make the gospel clear to everyone, even though it was once hidden. God intended that the church would teach all God's wisdom and eternal purpose that he accomplished in Jesus Christ, our Lord. He gives us our faith so that we can approach God with freedom and confidence. Therefore, don't let my suffering discourage you because it's for your glory.

I bow my knees before the Father, who gives every family its name. I pray that from his glorious riches, he might strengthen you with the power of his Spirit so that Christ can live in your hearts through faith. As he grounds you in his love, I pray that you would have the power with all believers to understand the boundless depths of Christ's love. I pray that you would know this love that goes beyond knowledge and that God would fill you with his fullness. To him, who can do more than we can ask or imagine through his power within us, be glory in the church and in Jesus Christ forever! Amen.

EXHORTATIONS TO HOLY LIVING

I urge you to live a life worthy of your calling; be gentle and humble, patiently bearing with one another in love. Keep the Spirit's unity through peace because there is one body, one Spirit, one hope, one Lord, one faith, one baptism, and one God and Father who rules over everything.

He has given us all his grace as he desired; that's why it says, "When he ascended on high, he led forth many captives and gave his people gifts." When it says that he ascended, that means Jesus descended to the earth and that he has ascended to the highest heavens to fill the whole universe.

He gave his people the gifts of apostleship, prophecy, evangelism, pastoral care, and teaching to equip his people for ministry and building up the church until we reach the full unity of the faith, the knowledge of Christ, and maturity. Then every new teaching, human cunning, craftiness, and deceit will not toss us around. Instead, we should speak the truth in love so that we might grow in every respect to the maturity of Christ. From him, the whole body is joined together, and every part works together to grow and build itself up in love.

You should no longer live like the Gentiles in the futility of their thinking. They don't understand God and are separated from God's life through their ignorance and hard hearts. They have lost sensitivity and given themselves to sensuality, impurity, and greed. But that's not the life you learned when you heard the truth of the gospel in Christ. You were taught to put away your old self and its deceitful desires, to have a new attitude and put on the new self, created to be like God in true righteousness and holiness. Put off falsehood and speak the truth to each other because we are all members of one body.

If you are angry, don't sin; don't let the sun go down on your anger because you will give the Devil a foothold. Stop stealing and do something useful with your life so that you can help the needy. Don't speak unwholesome words, but only what can build others up and benefit them. Don't grieve the Holy Spirit, who sealed you for the day of redemption. Get rid of bitterness, rage, brawling, slander, and every form of malice. Be kind and compassionate to each other, forgiving each other, just as Christ forgave you.

Therefore, imitate God like children imitate their parents. Walk in love like Jesus loved us and gave himself as a sacrifice to God. There should not even be a hint of sexual immorality, impurity, or greed in you because people like that are idolaters and will not inherit the kingdom of God. Don't even let there be obscenity, foolish talk, or coarse joking in your speech; instead, give thanks.

Don't be deceived by empty words because these things bring God's wrath on the sons of disobedience. Do not become partners with them because you are children of light and no longer in the dark. Walk as children of light because the fruit of light brings all that is good, right, and true. Find out what is pleasing to God and avoid the unfruitful works of darkness. Their actions are shameful and the light will expose them when it comes and illuminates everything. Watch how you live, be wise, and make the most of every opportunity because the days are evil. Don't be foolish, but understand what the Lord's will is.

Don't get drunk because that leads to debauchery; instead, be filled with the Spirit speaking to one another with psalms, hymns, and songs. Make music for the Lord, giving thanks to God the Father for everything, in the name of our Lord Jesus Christ.

Submit to one another out of reverence for Christ. Wives, submit to your husbands as you do the Lord, for the husband is the head of the wife as Christ is the head of his body, the church. As the church submits to Christ, wives should submit to their husbands in everything. Husbands, love your wives like Christ loved the church and gave up his life to make her holy, cleansing her with the Word so he could present her as a perfect bride. Husbands should love their wives as they love their own bodies; loving your wife is the same as loving yourself. We all take care of our bodies, just like Christ does the church; we are all members of his body. This is why a man will leave his parents and be united with his wife, and the two shall become one flesh. This is just like Christ and the church; husbands must love their wives, and wives must respect their husbands.

> **Mutual submission**
>
> Many have used this passage to demand that women submit to men, but this command is in the context of mutual submission. As believers, we are to submit to each other and look out for other believers' best interests. Christianity is not about gender; it is about following Christ and putting others before ourselves. It is also interesting to note that men are to love their wives as Christ loved the church. He loved it by laying down his life for us; we should do the same.

Children, obey your parents in the Lord. Honor your father and mother is the first command with a promise so that life will go well and you will live a long time. Fathers, don't provoke your children to anger; instead, teach them the Lord's discipline and instruction. Servants, obey your earthly masters with sincerity like you serve Christ, not so that you gain their favor but because you are also serving the Lord, and he will repay you. Masters, treat your servants the same way because you both have the same Master, and he does not show favoritism.

Finally, be strong in the Lord's power and put on the full armor of God so that you might stand against the Devil's schemes. We do not wrestle with flesh and blood but against the rulers, authorities, and spiritual forces of this present world and the heavenly realms. Therefore, put on the full armor of God so that you can resist evil and stand strong. Put on the belt of truth, the breastplate of righteousness, the shoes of the preparation of the gospel, the shield of faith, the helmet of salvation, and the sword of the Spirit, which is God's Word. Always pray in the Spirit for the other believers and me so that we might boldly proclaim the gospel.

> **Spiritual armor and warfare**
>
> This passage advises us to arm ourselves with spiritual armor for battle. The reality is that the most important battles we fight are spiritual ones. While it is wise to prepare ourselves for what we face in life, our spiritual preparation is far more critical. Satan wants to destroy us and God's work and will use any means possible to drag us down with him. He will throw difficulties at us at every turn and the best way to fight them is through our spiritual armor.

So that you can know how I'm doing, I'm sending Tychicus to you, and he will fill you in. May the God and Father of our Lord Jesus Christ grant you grace, peace, and undying love.

CHAPTER TWENTY-NINE

REJOICE IN THE LORD
Philippians 1-4

> **Paul's letter to Philippi**
>
> The Philippian church was the first congregation in Europe and one that Paul planted himself. He had planted the church about ten years before he wrote to them, and they continued to have a positive relationship. The church had collected a gift for Paul and sent it with Epaphroditus to bless Paul. While in Rome with Paul, Epaphroditus became deathly ill. Paul sent him back with this letter to thank the church for their generosity, to warn them against divisions, and prepare them for Timothy's visit. This letter was written around 62 A.D. when Paul was in his late 40's. He wrote this letter from prison in Rome.

I thank my God for everything we have been through, and I always pray for you with joy because you have helped me spread the gospel from the first day you heard it until now. I am confident that God will perfect the good work he started in you until the day Jesus returns. It's only natural that I should feel this way about you because you love me, and you have shared in God's grace with me whether I was in prison or out defending and confirming the gospel. God is my witness to how I long for all of you with Christ's affection.

I pray that you would love each other more and keep growing in real knowledge and discernment. Then you can determine what is excellent so that you can be pure and blameless until Jesus returns. He will fill you with the fruit of righteousness through Jesus Christ, to God's glory and praise.

I want you to know, brothers, that my situation has helped spread the gospel. Now everyone here, including the palace guard, knows that I'm in prison because I'm a Christian. Because of my imprisonment, many believers trust in the Lord and are boldly sharing the gospel. It is true that some of them have impure motives and preach the gospel out of selfish ambition, envy, and strife so they can make my imprisonment even more painful. However, some of them preach Christ out of love and goodwill because they know that I am here to defend the gospel. It doesn't matter to me if their motives are pure, just that they proclaim Christ; therefore, I will rejoice.

I will continue to rejoice because I know that your prayers and the Spirit of Jesus Christ's help will deliver me. I eagerly expect and hope that I will never be ashamed but will continue to be bold and exalt Christ in my body, whether I live or die. In my opinion, to live is Christ and to die is gain. Living means fruitful labor for me, and I don't know which I prefer. I want to depart and be with Christ because that is much better for me, but it is better for you that I live. Therefore, I know that I will remain with you to share in your growth and joy in the faith so that after I arrive, your boasting in Christ can increase because of my presence.

Live a life worthy of the gospel, so that whether I see you or not, I will hear that you are united in spirit and mind as you walk together in faith. Don't let opponents of the gospel alarm you because God will save you and destroy them. God has given you the honor of believing in Christ and suffering for his glory as you experience the same problems I have.

If being in Christ encourages you, if his love comforts you, if we share the Holy Spirit, or if you have affection and compassion, then make me happy by being united in mind, love, and spirit. Don't act out of selfishness or pride, but be humble and think of others as more important than yourselves; don't just look out for yourselves, but look out for others as well.

You should have the same attitude that Jesus had: even though he was God, he didn't demand his rights, but made himself nothing, and came to earth as a servant. As a man, he humbled himself by being obedient to the point of death, even death on a cross. Therefore, God exalted him to the highest place and gave him the name above all names so that at the name of Jesus, every person who ever lived will bow down and confess that Jesus Christ is Lord, to the glory of God the Father.

> ### God's sacrifice
>
> When Jesus came to earth, he did not stop being God. However, in his earthly body, he did not access all his power as God. He loves us so much that he was willing to suffer in our place so that we can have a relationship with him.

Therefore, my dear friends, work out your salvation with fear and trembling by continuing to obey, just like you did when I was there. God is the one that gives you the desire and power to please him. Do everything without complaining or arguing so that you may become pure, innocent children of God that shine like lights in a crooked and perverse generation. Hold onto the Word of Life so that I will be able to rejoice when Christ returns because I did not run or work for nothing. But even if I die in service to your faith, I still rejoice and share my joy with you. In the same way, I urge you to rejoice and share your joy with me.

Lord willing, I want to send Timothy so that his report about you might encourage me. He's the only one I know that shares my mentality and will be genuinely concerned about your welfare. All the others focus on their interests rather than Jesus, but he has proven himself and has helped me spread the gospel like a child serving his father. Therefore, I want to send him to you as soon as I find out how things turn out for me. I trust in the Lord that I will be coming shortly after him.

I sent this letter with my brother and fellow worker Epaphroditus, whom you sent to minister to my needs. He missed you and was distressed because you had heard that he was sick. He was so sick that he almost died, but God showed him (and me) mercy because I would have been despondent if he had passed away. Therefore, I am eagerly sending him back to you so that you can see him again and so that I won't be as worried. Welcome him back in the Lord, with joy, and honor men like him because he almost died for Christ by helping me with what you could not.

Finally, rejoice in the Lord. It's not a problem for me to write the same things again, and it helps protect you. Beware of the dogs, evil workers, and the false circumcision. We are the true circumcision, and we worship in the Holy Spirit, boast in Jesus Christ, and put no confidence in the flesh.

If anyone could have confidence in the flesh, it's me. I was circumcised on the eighth day, a pureblooded Jew from the tribe of Benjamin. I was a Pharisee, I zealously persecuted the church, and was blameless according to the righteousness found in the Law.

But I have counted those things as nothing compared to Christ. In fact, everything is worthless compared to knowing my Lord Jesus, and I have given up everything for him and count it as crap. Now I can gain Christ and be found in him, having a righteousness that comes from God through faith in Christ rather than the works of the Law. Now I can know him, the power of his Resurrection, and share in his sufferings as he conforms me to his death so that he might raise me from the dead. I haven't obtained it yet, and I'm not perfect, but I keep going so that I may become what Jesus wants me to be. I am not there yet, but I forget the past and reach for what lies ahead as I press on towards the prize of God's heavenward calling in Jesus.

Paul's use of "crap."

In the original Greek, Paul uses the vulgar term for fecal matter. I opted for this translation, although some translations have opted for a stronger English word.

Those of us who are mature should have this attitude, and if you disagree, then God will make that clear to you as well. However, let us keep living by the same standard that we have been. Imitate my life and learn from those that follow our example. As I have told you before, I tell you now with tears, that many are enemies of the cross. Their end is destruction, their god is their appetite, they take pride in what should cause them shame, and they set their minds on earthly things. But we are citizens of heaven and we eagerly await the Lord Jesus Christ's return as our Savior. He will transform our humble bodies and make them like his glorious body by his power that brings everything under his control.

Brothers and sisters, stay true to the Lord. I love you and want to see you because you bring me joy, and you are the reward for my labor; therefore, stay faithful to the Lord. I urge Euodia and Syntyche to agree in the Lord. My true companions, I ask that you help these women get along because they have struggled with me to spread the gospel along with Clement and the others who have their names in the Book of Life.

Always rejoice in the Lord, and at the risk of repeating myself, rejoice! Let everyone see that you are gentle and kind; the Lord is near. Don't be anxious about anything; instead, take everything to God in prayer. Thank him for what he has done as you make your requests, and God's unfathomable peace will guard your hearts and minds in Jesus.

Finally, let your mind dwell on things that are true, honorable, right, pure, lovely, and of good repute. Spend your time thinking about things that are excellent and worthy of praise. Practice the things that I taught you and that you saw in my life, and the God of peace will be with you.

I'm happy, and I thank God that you are concerned about me again; I know you were worried before, but you couldn't do anything about it. I'm not saying this because I'm in need; I've learned to be content in whatever circumstances I'm in. I know how to live in prosperity and poverty because I have learned how to be happy, whether I have food or go hungry. I can do all things through Christ who strengthens me. But it was good of you to share with me in my current affliction.

When I first preached the gospel after leaving Macedonia, you were the only church that gave financially; you even sent multiple gifts to me when I was in Thessalonica. I'm not just looking for the gift itself, but I'm excited that God will reward you for your generosity. I've received your gift from Epaphroditus and I'm doing well; I have plenty because you sent a gift that greatly pleases God. My God will supply all your needs according to his glorious riches in Christ.

May our God and Father receive glory forever! Amen. Greet all the Christians there in my name, and all the believers that are with me greet you. All the Christians send their greetings, especially those in Caesar's household. May the grace of the Lord Jesus Christ be with you.

CHAPTER THIRTY

CHRIST'S SUPREMACY

Colossians 1-4

> **Paul's letter to Colossae**
>
> Paul wrote the letter to the Colossian church during his Roman imprisonment around 62 A.D. in conjunction with Timothy. He wrote it at the same time as he wrote the letter to Philemon, and it is to a primarily Gentile audience. Paul had never been to Colossae, and the church there was likely founded by Epaphras, one of the men Paul had introduced to Christ. The book's central message is that Christ is sufficient, and we do not need to add anything to his gospel.

We thank God for you when we pray because we have heard of your faith in Christ and the love you have for his people because of the hope laid up for you in heaven. You heard of this in the gospel, which has spread everywhere and is now bearing fruit and growing worldwide. Our brother Epaphras preached to you and he has told us of your love in the Spirit.

Since the day we heard of you, we have not stopped praying that you would know God's will with all spiritual wisdom and understanding so that you would live a life that pleases him and bears fruit in every good work. Then you will grow in the knowledge of God, strengthened with his power and might so that you might patiently endure and give thanks to the Father. He rescued you from darkness and made you qualified to inherit the kingdom of light through his Son, who gives us redemption and the forgiveness of sins.

Jesus is the image of the invisible God, the firstborn of all creation. He created all things on heaven and earth, whether visible or invisible, for his glory; he is before everything and holds everything together. He is the head of the church, the beginning, and firstborn from the dead so that he might be supreme. God was pleased to have his fullness dwell in Christ so that he can reconcile everything to himself, making peace by shedding his blood on the cross.

> **The Trinity**
>
> In this passage, Paul tells us that the fullness of God's deity dwells in Jesus. This is an explicit declaration that Jesus is God and the second person of the Trinity.
>
> The Trinity is an essential doctrine to the Christian faith; however, it is tough to understand. A careful examination of Scripture shows us how we derive the doctrine of the Trinity. The Bible clearly shows that God the Father, Jesus the Son, and the

> Holy Spirit are all divine, and each possesses the full essence of God. However, the Bible also clearly shows us that there is an indivisible unity of God and that he is one in nature (Christians do not believe in three gods). We also see that all three exist simultaneously in Jesus' baptism. With these things in mind, we can conclude that God is an undivided being who exists simultaneously as three persons, and all three are fully God.
>
> The word trinity is not in the Bible, but both the Old and New Testaments imply the doctrine. Some people agree that the Father, Son, and Holy Spirit are equally divine, but they argue that each is a different manifestation of God at different times. However, this passage shows that all three exist simultaneously.
>
> Others agree that the Father, Son, and Holy Spirit are all divine, and all three exist simultaneously, but they argue that God the Father is greater than Jesus, who, in turn, is greater than the Holy Spirit. However, while there may be a subordination of position, there is no subordination of nature. Another way of looking at this is a boss and an employee. The boss may have a greater status than the employee, but the boss is not fundamentally better than the employee. In the same way, God the Father has a superior role to Jesus, but they are equally divine. Each member is fully divine and cannot be subordinate to any being.
>
> Some people have problems with the doctrine of the Trinity and argue that a being cannot be three and one simultaneously. Part of the reason we have this problem is that we do not have the words to express God adequately. The Trinity is one of the great mysteries of the Christian faith and we must remember that God created the universe and our logic. God completely transcends natural laws. Our finite minds cannot grasp what is beyond these laws, and we must recognize that we will never fully comprehend God. Because if we could fully comprehend him, he would cease to be God, or we would become God. Even though it is difficult to understand this concept, the Bible teaches us that God is an undivided being who exists simultaneously as three persons, and all three are fully God.

Your evil behavior alienated you from God, but now he has reconciled you through Christ's physical death, so you could be blameless if you continue in your faith. This is the same message that I've been preaching since day one.

I rejoice in my suffering and finish whatever is lacking in Christ's afflictions for the church's sake. God has commissioned me to preach the full Word of God to you that he hid for many generations. But now, he has chosen to reveal his glorious riches to you in Christ. He gives me energy and power to proclaim him, warning and teaching everyone with all wisdom so we can be mature in Christ.

I want you to know how hard I'm working for you and those I have not yet met in Laodicea. I want to encourage their hearts to be united in love and know the riches of understanding, knowledge, and wisdom of God in Christ. Don't let anyone deceive you with fancy arguments because although I'm not there with you, my spirit is with you, and I rejoice to see your faith in Christ.

Keep living your lives in Christ, grounded, and built up in the faith we taught you. Don't let anyone capture your minds with philosophy and lies according to the world rather than Christ. All of God's deity lives in Jesus and gives him authority; now, he fills you.

He metaphorically circumcised your hearts; now, you have been buried with him in baptism and raised with him through faith by God's power. You were dead in your sin and uncircumcision, but God has brought you to life and forgiven all our sins. He has canceled our debts and taken away our condemnation by nailing it to the cross. He has disarmed this world's powers and authorities and made a spectacle of them in his triumph through the cross.

Therefore, don't let anyone judge you regarding food, drink, Sabbath, or festivals because these are only the shadow of what is to come, but the reality is in Christ. Don't let anyone who insists on severe discipline, angel worship, or who goes on and on about visions lead you astray. They are proud for no reason, and they have separated themselves from Christ, who is the head of the church.

If you died with Christ to this world's spiritual forces, why do you still behave as if you are subject to its legalism and rules about eating and drinking? While these seem like wisdom, they are only self-made religion and asceticism, neither of which help you truly control the flesh.

Since you have been raised with Christ, set your hearts on heavenly rather than earthly things. You died, and now your life is in Christ, who sits at God's right hand. When Jesus appears in glory, you will appear with him as well. Therefore, put your earthly nature to death: sexual immorality, impurity, lust, evil desires, greed, and idolatry. Put away anger, wrath, malice, slander, obscene talk, and lies because you used to practice these things, and God's wrath is coming for those who do them. Take off your old self along with its practices and put on the new self, which is being renewed in knowledge after the image of its Creator.

There is no more hierarchy or division because Christ is all and is in all. As his holy, chosen people, clothe yourselves with compassion, kindness, humility, gentleness, and patience. Put up with each other and forgive each other if you have any grievances, just as the Lord forgave you. Above all, love one another because this will bind you together in perfect unity. Let Christ's peace rule in your hearts, and be thankful. Let the gospel live in you as you teach and admonish each other with wisdom, psalms, and songs from the Spirit. Sing to God with gratitude, and no matter what you say or do, do it all in the name of the Lord Jesus.

Wives, submit to your husbands, as is fitting in the Lord; husbands, love your wives and do not be harsh with them. Children, obey your parents in everything because this pleases the Lord. Fathers, do not antagonize your children so you won't discourage them. Servants, do what your earthly masters tell you to do; give your best and not just the bare minimum because you are working for Jesus. One day, he will repay your labor with either his inheritance or punishment. God does not show favorites. Masters, treat your servants justly and fairly because your Master lives in heaven.

Devote yourselves to prayer, being watchful and thankful. Pray for us as well that God may give us opportunities to preach the gospel wherever possible and that I would know how to proclaim his name. Walk wisely with outsiders, making the most out of your opportunities. Let your conversation always be full of grace so that you may know how you should answer everyone.

I am sending Tychicus and Onesimus to fill you in about what's been happening with me. My companions send you greetings, share them with everyone who is there in Colossae.

CHAPTER THIRTY-ONE

RECONCILIATION WITH ONESIMUS

Philemon 1

> **Paul's letter to Philemon**
>
> Paul wrote this letter to Philemon, urging his reconciliation with Onesimus. Philemon was a wealthy Christian who was likely a bishop in the Colossian church. Paul likely wrote it at the same time as the Book of Colossians. Onesimus had been a slave to Philemon, and he escaped, possibly even stealing from his master at the same time. He made his way to Rome, where Paul led him to faith. Now, Paul was sending him back, seeking reconciliation between the two.

When I pray for you, I always thank God for what I hear about your faith in Jesus and love for all the other believers. I pray that you would be effective in sharing your faith so you may share our knowledge of every good thing for Christ's sake. The ministry and love that you provide to others brings me so much joy and comfort.

Even though I have the authority in Christ to command you to obey, I would rather appeal to you in love as an older man who is a prisoner for Jesus. I am sending Onesimus back to you even though previously, he was worthless to you. During my imprisonment, I led him to faith, and now he is useful to both of us. I am sending him back to you as if sending my heart.

I would have been happy to keep him serving me on your behalf while I'm in prison. But I didn't want to do anything without your consent so that your goodness would be voluntary, not compelled. Maybe he was away from you for a time that he could be back with you as more than a servant, but now as a brother to both of us in flesh and the Lord.

So, if you consider me your partner, receive him as you would me. If he has wronged you or owes you anything, charge it to my account; I will repay it (even though you owe me yourself). Brother, please redeem this situation, refresh my heart in Christ.

I know you will take him back and do even more than what I ask. Please prepare a guest room for me because I hope that God will answer your prayers, and I will be able to join you soon. Finally, all my fellow workers send their greetings. May the Lord Jesus' grace be with you.

CHAPTER THIRTY-TWO

TRUE AND PRACTICAL RELIGION

James 1-5

> **James' letter**
>
> This is a general letter without a specific audience that Jesus' half-brother James wrote to Jewish believers. At first, he did not believe Jesus was the Messiah, but he converted after the Resurrection. He wrote this letter as the leader of the church in Jerusalem. These believers were likely poor and oppressed and looked down on by Jews and Gentiles alike. James likely wrote this letter around 62 A.D.

Brothers, consider it pure joy when you experience various trials because tests of your faith produce patient endurance. Let endurance finish its work so that you may be mature and complete, not lacking anything.

> **Trials**
>
> Trials in life are inevitable; we will face difficult times regardless of our status. We can use these as an opportunity to draw closer to God or harden our hearts. God intends our trials to bring us to maturity and produce greater faith. He also uses them so we can share the comfort God gives us with others in similar circumstances.

If you need wisdom, ask God because he will generously give it to you without reproach. But if you ask, believe that he will answer and don't doubt because the one who doubts is like a wave of the sea, driven and tossed by the wind. People like that are double-minded and unstable; they should not expect to receive anything from the Lord.

Let the poor brother glory in his exaltation and the rich glory in their humiliation because they will disappear like a flower of the field. The sun rises with its scorching heat and withers the flowers and grass and destroys their beauty; in the same way, the rich man will fade away amid his pursuits.

Blessed are those who endure trials; after they have proved their faith, God will give them the crown of life that he promised to those who love him. During temptation, no one should say, "God is tempting me," because evil cannot tempt God, and he does not tempt anyone. Our evil desires tempt us, entice us, and then drag us away. These evil desires lead to sin, and sin leads to death. Don't be deceived.

Every good and perfect gift comes from the Father of Lights above; he does not change like shifting shadows. He chose to give us new birth through the Word of Truth so that we might be the first fruits of creation.

Be quick to listen, slow to speak, and slow to get angry because your anger does not produce God's righteousness. Therefore, get rid of all moral filth and evil and humbly accept the Word planted in your hearts that can save your souls.

Don't deceive yourselves by merely listening to God's Word; do what it says. Those who hear God's teaching and don't do anything about it are like people who look in a mirror and then forget what they look like as soon as they walk away. But God will bless those who look intently at the perfect Law of freedom and stick with it and obey rather than forgetting what it says.

If you think you are religious yet fail to control your tongue, you have deceived yourself, and your religion is worthless. True religion that God accepts is to look after widows and orphans in their troubles and to keep yourself unstained by the world.

My brothers, as believers in our glorious Lord Jesus Christ, don't show favoritism. If you save the best seats in church for rich people who come in with beautiful clothes and jewelry and the worst seats for the poor people wearing dirty rags, you have discriminated and become judges with evil thoughts.

Listen, my beloved brethren, hasn't God chosen the poor of this world to be rich in faith and receive the kingdom he promised to those who love him? You dishonor the poor even though it is the rich that oppress you, drag you into court, and slander the good name of Christ by which he called you. You will be doing the right thing if you obey the royal Law found in Scripture: "Love your neighbor as yourself." But if you show favoritism, then you are sinning and breaking the Law.

Whoever obeys the entire Law, but stumbles in one area, is guilty of breaking it all. The same God who commanded not to commit adultery also commanded not to commit murder; if you don't commit adultery, but do commit murder, then you are a Law-breaker. Speak and act as those about to be judged by the Law of freedom because those who do not show mercy will be judged without mercy; however, mercy triumphs over judgment.

What good is it if a man claims to have faith and does not have works? Can that kind of faith save him? If someone lacks clothing and food, what's the use of saying, "Be warm and well fed," if you don't do anything about the physical needs? In the same way, faith without works is dead. Some will argue that they have faith and others have works. Show me your faith without works and I will show you my faith by what I do. Do you believe in God? Good! Even demons believe that and tremble in fear.

You fool, don't you see that faith without works is dead? Our father Abraham's works justified him when he offered his son Isaac on the altar. His faith and actions were working together and his actions completed his faith. That's why Scripture says, "Abraham believed God and it was credited to him as righteousness," and he is God's friend. Our actions justify us, not just our faith. Similarly, Rahab's works justified her when she welcomed the spies and sent them out a different way. Just as the body without the spirit is dead, faith without works is dead.

> ### Faith and works
> Some people have struggled with this passage in conjunction with the many passages on salvation by faith alone. Our faith alone saves us and we do not need any additional action for salvation. But our works are evidence that we have a faith that has saved us. If we claim to have faith, but it doesn't motivate any change in our

> behavior, our faith may not be real. If we have authentic faith, then our actions will change as well.

Few of you should become teachers because they will face stricter judgment. We all stumble in many ways, and if anyone can keep from sinning with his mouth, then he is a perfect man and can control his whole body as well. We put a bit into a horse's mouth so that they will obey us and go wherever we want. Or look at ships: even though strong winds drive them, the pilot controls where he wants to go with a tiny rudder. In the same way, the tongue is a small body part, but it makes great boasts.

Small sparks set great fires! The tongue is set on fire by hell and is a world of evil that corrupts the whole person and sets his life course on fire. Humanity has tamed all kinds of animals, birds, reptiles, and sea creatures, but no one can tame the tongue because it is a restless evil that is full of deadly poison. We use our mouths to praise our Lord and Father and the same mouths to curse men that he made in his likeness. Out of the same mouth come both blessing and cursing; my brothers, this should not be! Can saltwater and freshwater flow in the same spring? Fig trees cannot grow olives, grapevines cannot grow figs, and salty water cannot produce fresh water.

If you are wise and understand God's ways, then live a good life and do deeds that come from the humility of wisdom. But if you have bitter envy and selfishness in your heart, then do not boast and lie about the truth. That kind of wisdom is not from heaven but is earthly, natural, and demonic. Wherever you have envy and selfishness, you also have disorder and everything evil. But God's wisdom is pure; then it is peaceful, gentle, reasonable, full of mercy and good fruits, impartial, and free from hypocrisy. Peacemakers who sow in peace reap a harvest of righteousness.

What causes fights and quarrels among you? Isn't it the desire for pleasures that war within you? You want and don't have; you kill and covet, but you cannot have what you want, so you bicker and fight. You don't have because you don't ask. Even when you ask, you don't receive because you ask with wrong motives to please yourselves.

You adulterous people, don't you know that friendship with the world is hostility towards God? Whoever wants to befriend the world becomes an enemy of God. Or do you think that Scripture says, "God longs jealously for the spirit that he has caused to live in us" for no reason? But God gives more grace; that's why Scripture says, "God opposes the proud, but he gives grace to the humble."

Therefore, submit yourselves to God; resist the Devil and he will run from you. Draw close to God and he will draw near to you. Wash your hands, you sinners, and purify your hearts, you double-minded. Be miserable, mourn, and cry; let your laughter turn into mourning and joy into gloom. Humble yourselves before the Lord and he will lift you up.

Brothers, do not slander one another because he who speaks against and judges a brother speaks against and judges the Law. When you judge the Law, you are no longer obedient but are now a judge. There is only one Lawgiver and Judge, the One who can give life and destroy it. So, who are you to judge your neighbor?

Some of you say, "Someday we will go to this place or that, spend a year there, do business, and make money." But you don't even know what will happen tomorrow; your life is just a vapor that is here and then gone. Instead, you should say, "If the Lord wills, we will live and do this or that." But now you arrogantly boast, and all such boasting is evil. Therefore, whoever knows what to do and doesn't do it is sinning.

> **Our plans and God's plans**
>
> As humans, we love to plan the future; it is one of the things that sets us apart from other animals. It is wise to prepare for what's to come, but we must remember that God's plan is more important in the overall scheme of the universe. There are times when he will establish our plans, but others when he has something else in mind. We should make plans but make sure that we submit them to the Lord.

Pay attention rich people, weep and wail because of the misery that is coming. Your wealth has rotted, and moths have eaten your clothes. The gold and silver you hoarded for the last days have rusted, and their rust will testify against you and eat your flesh like fire. Listen, the wages you didn't pay the workers who worked your fields are crying out against you, and the Lord Almighty has heard their cries. You have lived in luxury and self-indulgence and fattened your hearts in a day of slaughter. You have condemned and murdered righteous men, and they did not resist you.

Be patient until the Lord returns. See how the farmer waits for the earth to yield its valuable crop and how he is patient for the spring and autumn rains. In the same way, be patient and strengthen your hearts because he will return soon. Don't grumble against each other, or else you will be judged; behold, the Judge is standing at the door. As an example of suffering and patience, look at the prophets who spoke in the name of the Lord. We consider those that have suffered blessed. You have heard of Job's endurance and have seen God's compassion and mercy through what he has brought about.

Above all, don't swear by heaven, earth, or anything else; let your yes be yes, and your no be no; otherwise, you will be condemned. Are some of you suffering? Pray. Are any of you rejoicing? Sing songs of praise. Are any of you sick? Call the elders of the church and have them pray over him and anoint him with oil in the name of the Lord. The prayer of faith will heal the sick, and the Lord will raise them up and forgive the sins they have committed. Therefore, confess your sins to each other and pray for each other so that you may have healing; the prayer of the righteous is powerful and effective.

The prophet Elijah was a man just like us; he prayed that it would not rain, and it was dry for three-and-a-half years. Then he prayed again, and the heavens produced rain, and the earth produced its crops. You should know that if one of you wanders away from the truth and someone brings him back, the one that turns a sinner away from his error will save him from death and cover many sins.

CHAPTER THIRTY-THREE

PROPER LIVING DURING SUFFERING
I Peter 1-5

> **Peter's first letter**
>
> The church began to face persecution as it spread because those in power didn't like Christians acknowledging a different king. Christians were killed and blamed for many of the problems during the First Century. As a result, many of them scattered from where they had first known Jesus and took the gospel with them.
>
> Peter wrote this letter to Christians who were scattered during Nero's persecution of the early church. Nero was an emperor of Rome who had allowed much of the capital to burn and then blamed Christians for the inferno. Peter wrote this letter during the mid-60's A.D. The message went to both Jewish and Gentile believers and talked about how they were to live during their suffering.

Praise be to the God and Father of our Lord Jesus Christ! In his great mercy, he has given us new birth into a living hope through Jesus' Resurrection from the dead. He is giving us an inheritance that can never die, spoil, or fade, and it is waiting for us in heaven. He will reveal it to us at the last time and he is guarding us until then. We rejoice in this, even though we currently suffer various trials so that our faith may prove to be more genuine than gold and jewels refined by fire. This results in praise, glory, and honor at Jesus Christ's revelation.

Even though we don't see him, we love and believe in him with an inexpressible joy, filled with glory and faith that saves our souls. The prophets, who spoke of the grace to come, carefully searched for this salvation, trying to figure out how and when it would happen. They were serving you and not just themselves when they spoke of the gospel that you have heard through the Holy Spirit. Even angels wish they could understand these things.

Therefore, prepare your minds for action, be sober-minded, and set your hope on the grace that Jesus will bring when he is revealed. Don't conform to the passions of your former ignorance, but be holy as God is holy. You call on a Father who will judge everyone's work impartially. Therefore, live in fear during your exile, knowing that Christ's perfect blood has ransomed you from the ways of your ancestors, rather than perishable things like silver or gold. God chose Christ before creation but has revealed him in these last times for your sake. God raised him from the dead and glorified him, so your faith and hope are in God.

Now that you have purified yourselves by obeying the truth, love one another from a pure heart because you have been born again through God's living and abiding Word.

All flesh will wither and fall, just like the glory of grass and flowers, but the Lord's Word remains forever. This is the good news that we preached to you.

Get rid of all malice, deceit, hypocrisy, envy, and slander and crave spiritual milk like newborn babies so that you may grow up in your salvation now that you have tasted that the Lord is good.

You are living stones that God is building into a spiritual house to be a holy priesthood that offers spiritual sacrifices acceptable to God through Jesus Christ. He is the Living Stone that humans rejected. God has made him the chosen cornerstone, and whoever trusts in him will never be ashamed. To those who believe, the stone is precious, but it is an obstacle to those who do not believe, and it makes them fall. Their disobedience causes them to stumble, which is their destiny. But you are a chosen people, a royal priesthood, a holy nation, God's special possession, so that you may praise the One who called you out of darkness into his wonderful light.

Once, you were not a people and had not received mercy, but you are now God's people who have received his mercy. I urge you as foreigners and exiles to abstain from sinful desires which wage war against your soul. Keep your behavior among the Gentiles honorable, so that when they slander you, they may see your good deeds and glorify God.

For the Lord's sake, submit yourselves to every human authority because God sent them to punish wrongdoers and commend those who do what is right. God wants you to silence the ignorant talk of foolish people by doing good.

Live as free people, but don't use your freedom as a cover-up for evil; live as God's servants. Honor everyone, love the brotherhood, fear God, honor the emperor. Servants, be subject to your masters with all respect, regardless if they are righteous or not. It is commendable if someone endures sorrow because they are suffering unjustly for God. But if you are punished for sinning, your endurance doesn't matter.

Christ set an example for you and you should suffer as he did. Jesus was sinless, and when they insulted him, he did not retaliate; when he suffered, he did not threaten in return. Instead, he entrusted himself to God, who judges justly. Jesus bore our sins in his body on the cross so that we might die to our sins and live for righteousness because his wounds heal us. We were like sheep going astray, but now we have returned to the Shepherd and Overseer of our souls.

Wives should submit to their husbands so that if they are unbelievers, their wives' behavior might win them over. Your beauty should not only come from outward adornment but should come from the inner self, the unfading beauty of a gentle and quiet spirit, which is valuable in God's sight.

The holy women of the past adorned themselves this way by submitting to their husbands. For example, Sarah obeyed Abraham, and you are her children if you do good and do not fear. Also, husbands should live with their wives, showing understanding and treating them as a more delicate vessel since they are fellow heirs of the gracious gift of life. Then nothing will hinder your prayers.

> **More delicate vessels**
>
> Peter describes women as more delicate vessels, but this does not mean they are weak. This is a generalization that means they are different than men, and we should treat them as such. God created men and women differently to help fulfill his plan. Neither is better than the other, and we should not expect them to be the same.

Finally, you should all be like-minded, sympathetic, love one another, be compassionate, and humble. Do not repay evil with evil or insult with insult. On the contrary, repay evil with blessing because this is your calling. Those who want to love life and see good days should keep their tongues from evil and lips from lies; they should turn away from sin and do good, always seeking peace. The Lord watches over the righteous and listens to their prayers, but his face is against those who do evil.

No one will harm you if you are zealous for good, but God will bless you even if you suffer. Don't be afraid of threats, but revere Christ as Lord in your hearts. Always be ready to make a defense to anyone who asks you about why you have the hope that is in you. Answer with gentleness, respect, and a clear conscience so that those who slander your good behavior would be ashamed.

If it is God's will to suffer, it should be for good rather than evil. For Christ also suffered for sins, the righteous suffering for the unrighteous to bring you to God. He died in the body but is alive in the Spirit. Then he proclaimed the gospel to the spirits in prison who had not obeyed. God waited patiently in the days of Noah and he only saved eight people. Baptism corresponds to this; it saves you, not because it cleans you from dirt, but because it presents you to God through Jesus' Resurrection with a clear conscience. He is now at the right hand of God and everything is in submission to him.

Therefore, since Christ suffered in the body, arm yourselves with this same attitude. Whoever suffers in the body is finished with sin. Now, they live their earthly lives for the will of God rather than evil human desires. You have spent enough time acting like pagans, living in sensuality, passions, drunkenness, orgies, drinking parties, and lawless idolatry. Some of your former companions are surprised that you don't still partake, and they make fun of you, but they will give account to God, who judges the living and the dead. Therefore, the gospel was preached even to those who are now dead, so that they might be judged according to human standards regarding the body but alive according to God regarding the Spirit.

The end of all things is near; therefore, be self-controlled and sober-minded so that you may pray. Above all, love each other deeply because love covers many sins. Be hospitable without grumbling and each of you should use your gifts to serve others as faithful stewards of God's grace. Whatever you do, do it as if you are doing it for God so that he may be praised. To him be the glory and the power forever! Amen.

PROPER SUFFERING

Dear friends, do not be surprised at the fiery ordeal you face as if something strange were happening to you. But rejoice when you participate in the sufferings of Christ so that you may be overjoyed when he returns. God blesses you if others insult you for Christ's name because the Spirit of glory and God rests on you. Don't suffer as a murderer, thief, criminal, or meddler, but if you suffer as a Christian, praise God that you bear that name.

It is time for judgment to begin with God's household, and if it starts with us, it will be much worse for those who do not obey the gospel. If it is hard for the righteous to find salvation, what will become of the ungodly and the sinner? Those who suffer according to God's will should commit themselves to their faithful Creator and continue to do good.

I urge the elders to be shepherds of God's flock that is under your care. Watch over them willingly; not pursuing dishonest gain, but eager to serve; not domineering but as an example. When the Chief Shepherd appears, you will receive the crown of glory that will never fade away.

In the same way, young people should be subject to their elders. Clothe yourselves with humility because God opposes the proud and gives grace to the humble. Humble yourselves under the mighty hand of God so that he may exalt you at the proper time. Cast all your anxieties on him because he cares for you.

Be alert and sober-minded because your enemy, the Devil, prowls around like a roaring lion looking for someone to devour. Resist him and stand firm in your faith because you know that the family of believers worldwide is undergoing the same kind of suffering. After you have suffered for a little while, the God of all grace, who has called you to his eternal glory in Christ, will restore, confirm, strengthen, and establish you. To him, be the power forever! Amen.

Peace to all of you who are in Christ.

CHAPTER THIRTY-FOUR

SUPERIORITY OF CHRIST

Hebrews 1:1-8:6

> **The letter to the Hebrews**
>
> This is a unique letter in the New Testament because we do not know the author or the original audience. There is evidence that Paul wrote this letter just before his death, but we cannot be sure. The author wrote this letter to people who knew about Judaism. They may have faced the temptation to return to their previous belief system or been lazy Christians who had faced resistance. Regardless, this was a letter showing that Jesus is superior to all else.

In the past, God spoke through the prophets at different times in various ways, but now he has spoken to us by his Son, who created the universe and will inherit everything. The Son is the radiance of God's glory, the exact representation of his being. He holds the universe together with the power of his Word. After making purification for sin, he sat down at God's right hand, becoming superior to the angels because his name is more excellent than theirs.

To which of the angels did God ever call his Son or command us to worship? The angels are Jesus' servants, and God says about him, "Oh God, your throne will last forever and you shall rule with a scepter of justice. You love righteousness and hate wickedness; therefore, I have set you above your companions by anointing you with the oil of joy."

In the beginning, he laid the earth's foundations, and the heavens are the work of his hands. They will all wear out and perish, but he will remain forever. He will roll them up like a robe and change them like a shirt. But he remains the same forever. He sits at God's right hand until God makes his enemies a footstool for his feet. Angels are only ministering spirits sent to serve those who will inherit salvation.

We must pay close attention to what we've heard so we don't drift away. If we ignore the message of salvation that angels sent us, we will not escape punishment. God announced this salvation to us and testified to it with signs, wonders, miracles, and gifts of the Holy Spirit.

But God did not subject the coming world through angels. He has made humanity a little lower than the angels, crowned us with glory, and given us rule over everything. In subjecting everything to Christ, there is nothing outside his control.

> **Angels**
>
> The Bible tells us about non-human, created beings, known as angels. We don't know how or when God created them, but we can assume he did it before making humans. Popular culture has given us the picture of angels wearing white robes, having halos, flying around, and playing harps. The truth is that angels are eternal, spirit beings without physical bodies. Although the Bible records instances of them taking visible forms as human beings or unusual winged creatures, they are usually unseen. Scripture names the rankings and different types of angels, although it does not say much about their differences. The types of angels found in Scripture are archangel, angel, seraphim, cherubim, principalities, authorities, powers, thrones, might, and dominion.
>
> We do not know much about angels, and God likely left angels a relatively unknown area for a reason. We do know that we should not place undue focus on angels or their role; all these beings are lower than God, and we should never worship them or listen to them if they contradict the Bible. The Bible tells us that they worship God, war with demons, and minister to those who believe in God. This can happen through giving a message, protecting, providing care, etc.

Right now, we don't see everything subjected to him, but one day we will. Jesus was made a little lower than the angels for a time, but now he is crowned with glory because he suffered and died for everyone.

It's only right that the one who created everything should be the source of salvation for us, the sons of glory, through his suffering. The one who makes people holy and the holy people are of the same family, so he calls us brothers and sisters. Jesus shared our humanity with us to break Satan's power of death and free those enslaved by their fear of death. But he helps Abraham's descendants and not the angels. Therefore, Jesus became fully human to serve God as a merciful and faithful high priest and atone for people's sins. Since he suffered when tempted, he can help us when we face temptation.

Therefore, fix your thoughts on Jesus, our apostle and high priest. Jesus was faithful to the one who appointed him, just like Moses was faithful to God. But he is worthy of greater honor than Moses, just as the builder of the house is greater than the building. Moses bore witness to what would come, but Jesus is the faithful Son over God's house; we are his house if we continue to hold our confidence and the hope in which we glory.

Therefore, the Holy Spirit tells us not to harden our hearts as our ancestors did when they tested him in the wilderness. God was angry with them and he swore that they would not enter his rest. Make sure that none of you have a sinful, unbelieving heart that turns away from the living God. Instead, encourage each other while it is still today so that sin's deceitfulness won't harden any of you. Otherwise, you will be like our ancestors who came out of Egypt and died in the wilderness because of their unbelief.

Since the promise of entering his rest still stands, be careful that none of you fall short of it. They heard good news just like we have, but it didn't help them because they did not have faith. Those of us who believe shall enter his rest.

On the seventh day of creation, God rested from his works. Our ancestors did not enter his rest because of their disobedience. The promise is still true today if we listen and do not harden our hearts. If Joshua had given them rest, God would not have spoken of another day later on.

There is a Sabbath rest for God's people because those who enter it also rest from their works, just as God did from his. Let us do everything we can to enter that rest so that no one will die from following their disobedience.

The Word of God is alive and active, sharper than any two-edged sword. It penetrates the division of soul and spirit, joints, and marrow, and it judges the thoughts and attitudes of the heart. God sees every creature; nothing can hide from his eyes.

Therefore, since Jesus is our great high priest, and he ascended into heaven, let us hold firmly to our faith. We have a high priest who understands our weaknesses because he was tempted in every way like we are, but he did not sin. So, let us approach God's throne of grace with confidence so that we may receive grace and mercy in our time of need.

Every high priest selected from among the people is appointed to represent the people in everything relating to God. He can deal gently with them because he also knows weakness. Therefore, he must offer sacrifices for his sins as well as the people's sins. No one chooses this position; God calls him to it just as he called Aaron. In the same way, God exalted Jesus to the position of high priest forever, in the order of Melchizedek.

During Jesus' life on earth, he prayed with loud cries and tears to the one who could save him from death, and God heard him. Although he was the Son, he learned obedience through his suffering. Being perfect, he became the source of salvation to all who obey him as a high priest like Melchizedek.

> ### Melchizedek
>
> Melchizedek is a mysterious character from the Old Testament, and we don't know much about him. When Abraham rescued his nephew, Lot, from kidnappers, Abraham blessed him and paid him a tenth of everything. This passage goes on to tell us much more about this man.

We have much to teach you, but it is hard because you aren't trying to understand. By now, some of you should be teachers, but you still haven't grasped the basic teachings of God's Word. You need milk, not solid food! Those who live on milk are infants and they don't understand true righteousness. But solid food is for the mature who have trained themselves to discern good from evil.

Therefore, let's move beyond the basic teachings of Christ about repentance from sin, faith in God, ceremonial rituals, the Resurrection, and judgment. God willing, we will move past this to maturity.

It is impossible for those who have been enlightened, tasted the heavenly gift, shared in the Holy Spirit, and known God's goodness to fall away and then return to faith. They crucify the Son of God all over again and hold him in contempt.

Land that drinks in the rain and produces a useful crop receives God's blessing. But the land that produces thorns and thistles is in danger of being cursed and burned. We are convinced of better things about you and your salvation.

God is just; he will remember your work and love as you continue to help his people. We want you to show the same diligence to the end so that you may realize your hope. We don't want you to become lazy but to imitate those who inherit the promise through patience and faith.

When God made his promise to bless and multiply Abraham, he swore by himself because there was no one greater to swear by. God wanted to make the unchanging nature of his purpose very clear to the heirs and he confirmed it with an oath. Since God cannot lie, we can hold onto his promise and the hope that he will come through. Abraham waited patiently and obtained the promise because Jesus is a forerunner on our behalf, a high priest forever after the order of Melchizedek.

Melchizedek was the king of Salem and God's high priest when he met Abraham returning from rescuing Lot. Melchizedek blessed Abraham, and in return, Abraham gave him a tenth of everything. He was a king of righteousness and peace, without mother or father, having neither beginning nor end. But like the Son of God, he continues as a priest forever. He was so great that even our father Abraham gave him a tenth of everything. The Law requires the Levites to collect a tenth from the people even though they are Abraham's descendants. However, this man wasn't Abraham's descendant, yet he collected a tenth from him and blessed the one with the promises.

Typically, the greater blesses the lesser. For Israelites, those who die collect the tenth, but in Abraham's case it was collected by one declared to be living. We can even go so far as to say that Levi paid a tenth through Abraham because when Abraham met Melchizedek, Levi was still in his loins.

If the Levitical priesthood could have brought perfection, why would there need to be a priest in the order of Melchizedek and not Aaron? When the priesthood changes, the Law changes as well. We cannot make sense of this in the framework of the Levitical priesthood because Jesus descended from Judah, and the Law doesn't speak of priests in that family line.

This becomes clearer when another priest arises, like Melchizedek, who is a priest through an indestructible life and not through his bloodline. The previous commandment was set aside because it was weak and useless. A better hope was introduced that allows us to draw near to God.

Priests assume their position with an oath, and our perfect priest took that role when God swore that he would be a priest forever. God's promise makes Jesus the guarantee of a better covenant. There have been many Levitical priests because they die, but since Jesus is eternal, he is a permanent priest. Therefore, he can truly save those who draw near to God through him since he is always there to intercede for them. We need a priest like this, holy, innocent, unstained, separated from sinners, and exalted above the heavens.

He does not need to offer daily sacrifices for his sin and the people's sin like the Levitical priests because he gave a perfect sacrifice when he died on the cross. The Law appoints weak men as high priests, but the word of the oath, which came after the Law, appoints Jesus, who is perfect forever.

We have a high priest who sat down at the right hand of God in heaven and serves in the sanctuary, the tent of worship built by God and not man. Every high priest offers gifts and sacrifices, so Jesus had to have something to offer as well. These men are only a shadow of the heavenly things because God told Moses to set up everything as a pattern of what God established.

CHAPTER THIRTY-FIVE

SUPERIORITY OF THE NEW COVENANT
Hebrews 8:7-10:18

The ministry Jesus has received is better than the old one since the New Covenant is based on better promises. If nothing were wrong with the first covenant, then a new one wouldn't have been necessary. But God found fault with the people, and he promised a New Covenant that would be better than the old one because the people were unfaithful. He promised to put the New Covenant in their minds, write it on their hearts, be their God, and they would be his people. Then they will all know the Lord and he will forgive their sins by making the Old Covenant obsolete.

The first covenant had regulations for worship and an earthly sanctuary. When everything was properly set up, the priests regularly entered the outer rooms to perform ministry. But only the high priest could enter the innermost room, the Holy of Holies, and this was only once a year when he brought a blood offering for sin. The Holy Spirit was showing up there even though he had not yet been revealed. The gifts and sacrifices offered could not clear the worshiper's conscience because they were only external food and drink.

When Jesus came as the high priest, he brought the greater and more perfect tabernacle that is not made with human hands. He did not enter through the blood of goats and calves; he entered the Holy of Holies by his blood, bringing eternal redemption. Our offerings made us clean externally, but Christ's blood made us clean internally from our sin so that we may serve the living God. So, Christ is the mediator of a New Covenant. Those who are called may receive the promised eternal inheritance through his death that redeems the sins committed under the first covenant.

> **The sacrificial system**
>
> God established the Old Testament's sacrificial system to delay punishment for the people's sins until Christ came to be the ultimate sacrifice. There were different sacrifices for various transgressions and all of them foreshadowed Jesus' eventual death for the people.

A will only is in effect if there is a death since it is not valid for the living. Therefore, not even the first covenant was inaugurated without blood. Moses instituted the Law by sprinkling the people with the blood of goats and calves. In the same way, he sprinkled the Tabernacle and all the utensils of worship. In fact, the Law requires nearly everything to be cleansed with blood, and there is no forgiveness without the shedding of blood. If the copies of the heavenly things needed purification with blood, then Jesus' blood purifies the true sanctuary.

> **Why is blood necessary for forgiveness?**
>
> God requires blood for forgiveness to show the seriousness of sin. In the Garden of Eden, God promised Adam and Eve that their sin would lead to death, and Paul repeats this in his letter to the Romans. God cannot accept us with our sin because he would no longer be holy (a central aspect of his character). To forgive our sins, God required blood because it is the source of our life. Animal sacrifices were a temporary solution, but Jesus' perfect sacrifice was enough to forgive all our sins.

Jesus does not need to enter the Holy of Holies each year to offer animal sacrifices. He has offered his own blood once for all people because he is the culmination of the sacrificial system. Just as people die once and then face judgment, Christ was sacrificed once to take away the sins of many. He will appear a second time, not to bear sin, but to bring salvation to those waiting for him.

The Law is not the reality but a shadow of the good things coming because it can never make people perfect through repeated sacrifices. But now, we do not need to keep offering sacrifices because Christ's death cleansed us, and we don't need to feel guilt for our sin. The sacrifices were a reminder of our sins, even though they cannot take them away.

Therefore, when Christ came into the world, he did not desire our sacrifices, nor did they please him. The Scriptures were about him and he came to do God's will so that he could make us holy through his death for the last time.

Every day, priests serve by repeatedly offering sacrifices that cannot take away sins. But after Jesus died for our sins, he sat down at God's right hand, waiting for his enemies to be made a footstool for his feet. In a single offering, he perfected us for all time. The Holy Spirit gives further testimony that he will write his Law in our hearts and minds and no longer remember our sins. Where sin has been forgiven, there is no need for a sacrifice.

CHAPTER THIRTY-SIX

EXHORTATIONS

Hebrews 10:19-13:25

Therefore, we can enter the holiest place through Christ's blood because he has made a way for us through his death. Since we have a great high priest over God's house, we should draw near to God with a sincere heart and the full assurance that faith brings because he has washed us with his blood and pure water. Let us hold to the hope we profess without wavering because he is faithful.

Let us consider how we can stir each other up to love and good works, not neglecting to meet together as some do, but encouraging each other more and more as we see his return drawing near. If we keep deliberately sinning after learning the truth, the sacrifice is no longer valid. We can expect the fiery fury of judgment that will consume God's enemies.

Those who broke Moses' Law died based on the testimony of a handful of witnesses. The punishment will be much worse for those who have rejected the Son of God, profaned his blood, and outraged the Holy Spirit. We know that God will judge his people and have vengeance; it is a fearful thing to fall into the hands of the living God.

Remember how you suffered after you first believed, sometimes being publicly insulted and persecuted and sometimes being with those who suffered. You joyfully suffered with those in prison, and when your property was confiscated, you knew that you had better and lasting possessions. Don't throw away your confidence now because God will reward you. Persevere so that after doing God's will, you will receive his promise. He will come again soon and he wants you to live by faith. We do not wither and die; our faith saves us.

Faith is the confidence in what we hope for and the assurance of what we don't see. By faith, the people of old were commended, and by faith, we understand that God spoke the universe into existence, making the visible out of the invisible. By faith, Abel offered a more acceptable sacrifice than Cain, and God commended him as righteous. Even though he has died, he still speaks through his faith. By faith, Enoch did not die but was taken up into heaven because he pleased God. Without faith, it is impossible to please God because to draw near him, we must believe that he exists and rewards those who seek him.

By faith, Noah built an ark to save his household because God warned him of what was to come. By faith, Abraham obeyed when God called him to leave his homeland even though he didn't know where he was going. He went to a foreign land that God promised to him and lived in tents with Isaac and Jacob. He was looking forward to the city with foundations that God laid. By faith, Sarah had children even though she had gone through menopause because she believed God's promise. God gave descendants as numerous as the stars in the sky and grains of sand on the seashore to a man who was as good as dead.

All these people died in faith before receiving the promise, only seeing it far off because they were strangers and exiles on the earth. They sought a better homeland than the one they left, a heavenly one and not one where they could return. The Lord is not ashamed to be their God because he has prepared a city for them.

By faith, Abraham offered up his only son, Isaac, even though God had promised that his descendants would come through him. He believed that God would raise him from the dead if necessary. By faith, Isaac blessed Jacob and Esau. By faith, Jacob blessed his sons from his deathbed. By faith, Joseph spoke of the exodus and gave instructions concerning his bones before he died.

By faith, Moses' parents hid the child for three months after his birth because they were not afraid of the king's command. By faith, Moses refused to be the son of Pharaoh's daughter, instead choosing mistreatment with God's people rather than enjoying sin. He believed the insult of Christ was better than Egypt's wealth, and he waited for the reward.

By faith, Moses left Egypt without fearing the king because he was looking to God. By faith, he kept the Passover and put blood on the doorposts so that the firstborn of Israel would not die. By faith, the people crossed the Red Sea on dry land, but when the Egyptians followed, they drowned. By faith, the walls of Jericho fell after the army had marched around them for seven days. By faith, Rahab did not die because she welcomed the spies.

I don't have time to write about Gideon, Barak, Samson, Jephthah, David, Samuel, and the prophets who conquered kingdoms, administered justice, and gained the promise through faith. Through their faith, they shut the mouths of lions, quenched the fury of flames, and escaped the sword. Through their faith, weakness became strength, and they powerfully routed their enemies in battle. Women had their dead raised, and some were tortured, refusing release so that they might have a better resurrection. Some have faced insults, flogging, imprisonment, stoning, being sawed in two, and death by the sword. They were poorly clothed, broke, persecuted, and mistreated even though the world was not worthy. They lived on the fringes of society, and all of them were commended for their faith. However, none of them received the promise because God planned something better so that we might become perfect with them.

Therefore, since such a great cloud of witnesses surrounds us, let us throw off everything that hinders and the sin that entangles us. Run with endurance the race set before us, keeping our eyes on Jesus, the founder and perfecter of our faith. He endured the cross, despising its shame because he knew the joy that was to come, and now he is sitting at the right hand of God's throne. Think about his example so that you don't lose heart; in your struggle against sin, you have not resisted to the point of shedding blood.

You are enduring the Lord's discipline because he loves you like a father loves a son; if he doesn't discipline you, you are not truly his children. Our earthly fathers disciplined us, and we respected them; we should submit to God even more so! They disciplined us for a little while as they thought best, but God disciplines us for our good so that we may share in his holiness.

At the time, discipline seems painful, but later, it produces a harvest of righteousness and peace for those trained by it. Therefore, strengthen your feeble arms and weak knees, making level paths for your feet so the lame may not be disabled but rather healed.

Strive to live at peace with everyone and be holy so that you can see God. Make sure that no one falls short of God's grace and that no bitter root grows up to cause trouble and defile many. Make sure that people are not sexually immoral or godless like Esau, who sold his birthright for a single meal. Later, when he wanted to inherit his blessing, he was rejected even though he sought it with tears.

You have not come to a mountain burning with fire, shrouded in darkness, gloom, and storm, to a mountain that cannot be touched and inspires terror and trembling. You have come to Mount Zion, the city of the living God, the heavenly Jerusalem. You have come to the church of the firstborn, whose names are written in heaven with countless angels in joyful assembly. You are in God's presence, the judge of all; the spirits of the righteous; Jesus, the mediator of a New Covenant; and the sprinkled blood that speaks a better word than the blood of Abel.

Don't refuse God because if they didn't escape when they refused, we will not survive if we reject him either. He has promised that his voice will one day shake both the earth and the heavens. The shaken things will not remain, for they are created; the things that cannot be shaken will stand. Therefore, let us gratefully receive a kingdom that cannot be shaken and offer God acceptable worship with reverence and awe because he is a consuming fire.

Keep loving each other as brothers and sisters, and do not forget to show hospitality to strangers because some have entertained angels without knowing it. Remember the prisoners and mistreated as if you suffered with them. Everyone should honor marriage, and the marriage bed should be pure, for God will judge the sexually immoral and adulterous. Stay away from the love of money and be content with what you have because God will never leave or forsake you.

We can confidently claim that the Lord is our helper, and we have no need to fear mere mortals. Remember your leaders who preached God's Word to you, consider their lives, and imitate their faith. Jesus Christ is the same yesterday, today, and forever. Don't let various strange teachings carry you away, but let grace strengthen your hearts.

Don't worry about ceremonial foods because they don't benefit us; we have access to a better altar and tabernacle than the Israelite priests. The high priest brings animals' blood into the Holy of Holies as a sin offering and burns their bodies outside the camp. Jesus also suffered outside the city gate to make his people holy through his blood; let us go outside the camp with him and bear the disgrace he bore. We do not currently live in an enduring city; we are looking for a city to come.

Therefore, let us continually offer a sacrifice of praise to God, the fruit of lips that openly profess his name. Don't forget to do good and be generous because such sacrifices please God. Obey your leaders and submit to them because they watch over your souls, and they will have to give an account for you. Make their work joyful and not painful because it doesn't benefit you to be a burden. Pray for us because we have a clear conscience and want to live honorable lives. Also, pray that I can come to see you soon.

May the God of peace equip you with what you need to do his will so that he may accomplish what is pleasing in his sight through Jesus. He raised Jesus from the dead and is our great Shepherd. May Christ receive all glory forever and ever! Amen. Grace be with you.

CHAPTER THIRTY-SEVEN

LEADING A CHURCH
I Timothy 1-6

> **Paul's first letter to Timothy**
>
> This letter was in a group that Paul wrote not long before his death, known as the Pastoral Epistles. They are grouped like this because they were written to young men leading churches instead of the members of a congregation. He wrote this letter to a developed church in Ephesus led by Timothy. Paul's ministry partner had a Jewish mother and a Greek father and had worked extensively with Paul throughout his journeys. Paul gives his young friend instructions for leading a church.

I urge you to stay in Ephesus to instruct people not to teach false doctrine or devote themselves to myths and conspiracies. These things promote controversy rather than advancing God's work. Our goal is love from a pure heart, good conscience, and sincere faith. Some have left these and turned to meaningless talk; they want to be teachers, but they are clueless.

We know that the Law is good if one uses it correctly. We know that the Law did not come for the just, but for the lawless, disobedient, ungodly, sinners, unholy, profane, killers of parents, murderers, sexually immoral, homosexuals, enslavers, liars, perjurers, and those who do whatever is contrary to sound doctrine.

I thank our Lord Jesus Christ, who gives me strength that he has appointed me to preach the gospel of his glory. Even though I was once a blasphemer, persecutor, and violent, he showed me mercy because I was ignorant in my unbelief. He poured out his grace and love upon me. Jesus came into the world to save sinners, among whom I am the worst.

> **Paul's growing humility**
>
> As Paul continued in his Christian journey, he grew in his humility. In his first letter to the Corinthians, he calls himself the least of the apostles. In his later letter to the Ephesians, he calls himself the least of all believers. Finally, in this letter (written near the end of his life), he calls himself the worst of all sinners. The closer he got to God, the more in touch he was with his need for grace and God's salvation.

But he showed me mercy so that Jesus might display his perfect patience as an example to those who trust in him for eternal life. To the King eternal, immortal, invisible, the only God, be honor and glory forever! Amen.

My son, I am giving you this command so that you remember the prophecies about you, so that you would stand firm in faith and fight the battle well. Some have rejected this and have shipwrecked their faith; I have turned them over to Satan so they can learn not to blaspheme.

I urge people to pray and thank God for everyone, especially for people in high positions, so that we may lead a peaceful, quiet life that is godly and dignified. This pleases God, our Savior, who wants everyone to be saved and come to know the truth. Jesus Christ is the one God and mediator who gave himself as a ransom for all.

He has appointed me as a preacher and apostle of this truth to the Gentiles. I desire that men everywhere should lift holy hands in prayer without quarreling; women should likewise dress modestly with self-control and not in flashy clothing. They should clothe themselves with godliness and good works, focusing more on the spiritual than the physical.

Women should learn quietly without contention; they should not exercise authority over men but should remain quiet. God made Adam first and then Eve and she was deceived before Adam. Yet, women are saved through childbearing if they continue in faith, love, holiness, and self-control.

> **Women in the church**
>
> This is one of the most controversial passages in the New Testament and we must take it in the context of all Scripture. In other places, Paul argues for the equality of all believers and mutual submission. There is also evidence that points to this teaching being for the church in Ephesus and not for all believers. In this section, Paul uses singular nouns; in the rest, he uses the plural. This indicates that this message may be to an individual woman in Ephesus. This is too large of a topic for this book and I recommend further study.
>
> The statement that women will be saved through childbearing references the curse in Genesis 3 and does not mean that women must have children to be saved. As sin has continued to wreak havoc on the world around us, not all women can or want to have children. The only thing that saves or condemns us is what we do with the person of Jesus.

Those who want to be elders desire a noble task. An elder should be above reproach, faithful to their wife, sober-minded, self-controlled, respectable, hospitable, able to teach, gentle, not drunkards, not quarrelsome, and not in love with money. They must manage their households well and have obedient children because if they can't manage their own families, they can't take care of God's church. They should not be recent converts, so that they don't become conceited and fall under the same judgment as the Devil. They must also have a good reputation with outsiders so that they don't fall into disgrace.

Deacons must also be dignified, not double-tongued, drunkards, or greedy for dishonest gain; they must have faith with a clear conscience. Test them and let them serve as deacons if they prove to be blameless. Their wives must also be dignified, not slanderers, but sober-minded and faithful in all things. They must be the husbands of one wife and manage their children and households well. Those who serve well as deacons gain good standing and great confidence in their faith in Jesus Christ.

I hope to come to you soon, but if I can't make it, I want you to know how the church of the living God should operate. The mystery of godliness is great: he came in the flesh, vindicated by the Spirit, seen by angels, preached to the world, believed in, and taken up in glory.

The Spirit tells us that some will abandon the faith and follow deceiving spirits and demons in later times. This comes through hypocritical liars with burned consciences who forbid marriage and require abstinence from foods that God created for us to enjoy with thanksgiving and faith. God created everything good and makes it holy through his Word and prayer, so we should not reject it if we receive it with thanksgiving.

You serve Christ well if you teach these things to the church. Have nothing to do with irreverent, silly myths, but train yourself for godliness. Training the body has some value, but godliness is valuable in every way as it has promises for this life and the life to come. We work for these things because we set our hope on the living God who saves all people who believe.

Don't let anyone look down on your youth. Set an example for all believers in your speech, actions, love, faith, and purity. Devote yourself to the public reading of Scripture, exhortation, and teaching. Don't neglect your gift that was confirmed through prophecy and the elders' laying on of hands. Immerse yourself in these things so that everyone might see your growth; watch yourself and your teaching, and you will save yourself and your hearers.

Don't rebuke older men, but treat them like you would your father; treat older women as mothers, young men as brothers, and young women as sisters with absolute purity. Honor women who are truly widows, but if they have family who can take care of them, they should because this pleases God. Women are truly widows if they are alone and have set their hope on the Lord with constant prayers, but if they are self-indulgent, they are already dead while they live.

If people do not provide for their own families, they have denied their faith and are worse than unbelievers. Women should only be on the list of widows if they are older and have a reputation for good works, having raised children, shown hospitality, served the church, and cared for the afflicted. But don't enroll younger widows because many eventually will want to remarry. Besides, some get in the habit of idleness, gossip, and speaking out of turn. These women should remarry and manage their new households so they don't allow the enemy to slander us. Some have already turned away to follow Satan. If anyone is already taking care of widows, they should continue so that they don't burden the church.

Elders who lead the church well are worthy of extra honor, especially if they preach or teach; they are worthy of their wages. Don't listen to accusations brought against them unless there are multiple witnesses. But you should rebuke those elders who persist in sin in front of the congregation so that the others might take warning. Listen to this teaching without partiality and don't play favorites. Don't commission others by laying hands on them in haste so that you don't share in their sin.

Drink a little wine and not just water because of your frequent stomach problems. Some sins are obvious, while others take longer to become known. In the same way, some good deeds are obvious, but even hidden ones eventually become known.

> **Drink a little wine**
>
> The instruction to drink a little wine is an example of teaching for the original recipient, Timothy, and not for us today (see the box in chapter 2). It is okay for us to consume wine, but this is not something that everyone must do.

Servants should respect their masters so that they won't slander God's name and our teaching. Those with believing masters should not disrespect them just because they are fellow believers, but they should serve them all the more. If anyone teaches anything different, they are conceited and don't understand anything. They have an unhealthy fascination with controversies and teachings that lead to envy, strife, malicious talk, evil suspicions, and constant friction.

They believe that godliness is a means to financial gain, but godliness with contentment brings great profit. We came into the world with nothing, and we will leave with nothing, so we should be content with enough food and clothing. Those who want to be rich fall into temptation and the many senseless and harmful desires that lead to destruction. The love of money is the root of all kinds of evil, and it has led many away from the faith and into great pain.

> **Money**
>
> In our world, money has become one of the most common things for people to worship. People kill for money and prestige, and this is what Paul writes about when he says that "the love of money is the root of all kinds of evil." Money is neither evil nor good, but it becomes problematic when we elevate its purpose.
>
> Some have pitted the rich against the poor, but this is the wrong battle. God is not interested in the wealth we have but how we obtain it and use it. God wants us to love people and use money, not the other way around.

Flee these things and pursue righteousness, godliness, faith, love, endurance, and gentleness. Fight the good fight of the faith and take hold of the eternal life that God called to when you confessed your faith in the presence of many witnesses. I charge you in God's presence, who gives life, to keep the commandment free from reproach until Jesus comes back at the proper time.

Command those who are rich not to be arrogant or put their hope in their wealth; instead, they should put their hope in God, who gives us everything for our enjoyment. Command them to do good, be rich in good deeds, and generous, willing to share.

Then they will lay up treasure for themselves in the coming age and take hold of true life.

Guard what God entrusted to you and turn away from godless chatter and the opposing ideas of what is falsely called knowledge. Some have professed this and, in doing so, have left the faith. Grace be with you all.

He is the blessed and only Ruler, King of kings, and Lord of lords; he is the only Immortal who lives in unapproachable light that no one has seen or can see. To him be honor and might forever. Amen.

CHAPTER THIRTY-EIGHT

STAY STRONG

Titus 1-3

> **Paul's letter to Titus**
>
> Paul wrote this letter to Titus, who led the church in Crete. Titus was a Greek convert and had the difficult job of leading an immature church. Paul had worked with Titus in Macedonia and he sent Timothy to Crete to help bring them to maturity.

I left you in Crete so you could finish our work of appointing elders in every church. Elders must be blameless, faithful to their wives, and have obedient children. Since they will manage God's household, they should not be overbearing, quick-tempered, drunkards, violent, or after dishonest gain. Instead, they should be hospitable, lovers of good, self-controlled, upright, holy, and disciplined. They must hold on to the gospel so they may encourage others with sound doctrine and rebuke those who contradict it.

Many rebellious people are full of empty talk and lies, especially the circumcision group. Silence them because they are disrupting entire households with their false teaching for dishonest gain. They are evil brutes and lazy gluttons, so rebuke them sharply so they might have a solid faith and ignore myths and false commands. Everything is pure to the pure, but nothing is pure to the unbelieving and defiled because their minds and consciences are corrupted. They claim to know God, but they deny him with their lives; they are detestable, disobedient, and unfit for any good work.

But you must teach sound doctrine. Teach the older men to be sober-minded, dignified, self-controlled, strong in faith, love, and endurance. Likewise, teach older women to live reverent lives and teach what is good and not to be slanderers or drunkards. Then they can teach younger women to love their families, be self-controlled and pure, busy at home, kind, and submissive to their husbands so that no one would speak ill of the gospel. Teach young men to be self-controlled.

In everything, set an example by doing good, showing integrity, dignity, and sound speech so that our opponents are ashamed. Teach servants to be subject to their masters, please them, not talk back, and show that they are trustworthy so that the teaching about God, our Savior, is attractive.

For God's grace has appeared and offers salvation to all people. It teaches us to reject ungodliness and worldly passions and live self-controlled, upright, and godly lives while waiting for Jesus to come again. He gave himself to redeem us from wickedness and purify a people of his own who are eager to do good. Teach these things, encourage, rebuke with all authority, and do not let anyone despise you.

Remind people to be subject to authority, obedient, ready to do good, to not slander, to be peaceful, considerate, and gentle towards everyone. At one time, we were also foolish, disobedient, deceived, and enslaved by passions and pleasures. We were full of malice, envy, and hate. But when God's kindness and love appeared, he saved us, not because of our righteousness, but his mercy. He saved us through baptism and renewal by the Holy Spirit, whom he generously poured out on us through Jesus. He has justified us through grace so that we might inherit eternal life.

Those who believe in God must be careful to do good because this is excellent and profitable for everyone. Avoid foolish controversies, genealogies, and arguments about the Law because they are unprofitable. Warn divisive people twice and then have nothing to do with them because they are sinful and self-condemned.

Do your best to meet me at Nicopolis this winter. Our people must devote themselves to doing good, provide for urgent needs, and live productive lives. Greet those who love us in the faith; grace be with you all.

CHAPTER THIRTY-NINE

FINISH YOUR MINISTRY
II Timothy 1-4

> **Paul's second letter to Timothy**
>
> This is the last letter that Paul wrote and he penned it a year before his death in 67 A.D. He wrote to encourage his disciple to finish his ministry in leading the church in Ephesus.

I have a clear conscience as I thank God in my daily prayers for you. I long to see you so that I might be filled with joy. Your grandmother Lois and your mother Eunice had a sincere faith, and I'm convinced that you have it as well.

Fan the flame of God's gift that you received when I laid hands on you, for God did not give us a spirit of fear but of power, love, and self-control. Therefore, don't be ashamed of the gospel or me, his prisoner, instead share in suffering for the gospel. He saved us and called us to a holy life, not because of anything we did but because of his purpose and grace.

Christ gave us this gift before the beginning of time and now he has given it to us by appearing on earth. He abolished death and brought life and immortality to light through the gospel that God appointed me to preach and is the reason I suffer. But I am not ashamed because I know whom I believed, and I am convinced that he can guard what I entrusted to him until he returns. Follow my pattern of sound teaching with faith and love in Christ. Guard the gift that God gave to you with the help of the Holy Spirit, who lives in us.

You know that everyone in Asia has left me, including Phygelus and Hermogenes. May God show the household of Onesiphorus mercy because he often refreshed me and was not ashamed of my chains. When he came to Rome, he searched for me, and you know how much he helped me in Ephesus.

Be strong in Christ's grace and teach what I've taught you to reliable people who will also be able to teach others. Suffer with me like a good soldier of Christ because soldiers do not entangle themselves in civilian affairs; instead, they try to please their commanding officer. Similarly, athletes don't win unless they follow the rules, and hardworking farmers should have the first share of the crops. Reflect on my words because the Lord will give you insight into all of this.

> **Discipleship**
>
> God is the ultimate author of his glory and he works all things together for his plan. However, he allows us to be a part of it and share in his splendor. The most effective way that he allows us to do this is through discipleship. God wants us to share the

> gospel with others and train them to do the same so that others may also share in his work. Jesus himself showed us this model by teaching his disciples to train others who would then train others.

Remember Jesus, who descended from David and rose from the dead. This is the gospel that has imprisoned me, but God's Word is not chained. Therefore, I endure everything for the sake of the chosen so that they might have faith and eternal glory in Jesus Christ. If we died with him, we will live with him; if we endure, we will reign with him; if we disown him, he will disown us; but if we are faithless, he remains faithful because he cannot disown himself.

Remind God's people of these things and warn them about arguments because they only ruin those who listen to them. Present yourself to God as an approved worker who handles God's Word well and does not need to be ashamed. Avoid godless chatter because it only leads to further ungodliness, and it spreads like gangrene. Hymenaeus and Philetus are like this and have departed from the truth. They say that the resurrection has already happened, and they have destroyed some people's faith. But God's foundation stands firm because he knows his people, and they should turn away from sin.

In a big house, there are items with special purposes and some for everyday use. Those who cleanse themselves from dishonorable things will be vessels for honorable use, set apart as holy, useful, and ready for every good work. Flee the evil desires of youth and pursue righteousness, faith, love, and peace along with those who call on the Lord from a pure heart. Don't have anything to do with foolish arguments because they only produce trouble.

The Lord's servants must not be quarrelsome but kind to everyone, able to teach, and not resentful. Gently instruct your opponents in the hope that God will lead them into repentance and a knowledge of the truth. Then they will come to their senses and escape the Devil's snares, who has captured them to do his will.

In the last days, there will be much trouble; people will be lovers of self and money, proud, arrogant, abusive, disobedient, ungrateful, unholy, heartless, unforgiving, slanderous, uncontrolled, brutal, haters of good, treacherous, rash, conceited, lovers of pleasure rather than God. These people have a form of godliness but deny its power. Avoid these people because they worm their way into homes and gain control of gullible people weighed down by evil desires, always learning but never finding the truth. These teachers oppose the truth, just like Jannes and Jambres opposed Moses; they have depraved minds and have rejected the faith. They will not get very far because their folly will become evident to everyone.

> ### Faith will not be easy
> We like God's promises for our lives. It is comforting to know that he will always be with us, that he loves us, and that he came to offer the perfect sacrifice to reunite

> us with him. One of the uncomfortable promises that he gives is that we will face persecution and suffering. The world that is perishing doesn't want to hear God's good news and will battle against us to drag us down. But we can take heart because we know that he wins in the end.

But you have followed my teaching, actions, way of life, faith, patience, love, endurance, persecutions, and sufferings. Everyone who wants to live a godly life will face persecution. Simultaneously, evil people will go from bad to worse, deceiving others and being deceived. But you should continue with what you've learned and believed. You have learned these things from the Scriptures since childhood and how they can lead to salvation in Jesus. All Scripture is from God and is profitable for teaching, reproof, correction, and training in righteousness so that his servants may be competent, equipped for every good work.

I charge you in the presence of God and Christ, who will judge the living and the dead, to preach the Word, to always be ready to reprove, rebuke, and exhort with patience. For a time will come when people will not listen to sound teaching but will look for instruction that satisfies their own passions; they will turn away from the truth and wander off into myths.

But you should be sober-minded, endure suffering, share the gospel, and fulfill your ministry. I am being poured out as a drink offering and my death is at hand. I have fought the good fight, finished the race, and kept the faith. A crown of righteousness is waiting for me that God will give to everyone who believes when he returns.

Try to come to me with Mark as soon as possible because only Luke is with me and everyone else has deserted me. But the Lord has stood by me and strengthened me so that I might fully preach the gospel to all the Gentiles. The Lord will rescue me from every evil deed and bring me safely into his heavenly kingdom. May the Lord's grace be with your spirit. To him, be the glory forever! Amen.

CHAPTER FORTY

STEADFAST IN CHRIST

II Peter 1-3

> **Peter's second letter**
>
> Peter wrote his second letter to the believers scattered across Asia Minor around 66 A.D. before Nero's suicide. Peter wrote just before his death and wanted to make sure that his readers remained strong in their faith.

God's divine power has given us everything we need for a godly life through our knowledge of him. who called us by his glory and goodness. Through these, he has given us his precious and very great promises so that we may participate in the divine nature, having escaped the corruption of evil desires.

Therefore, make every effort to build upon your faith with goodness, knowledge, self-control, endurance, godliness, brotherly affection, and love. If you keep increasing in these qualities, they will keep you from being ineffective or unfruitful in the knowledge of our Lord Jesus Christ. Those who lack these qualities are so nearsighted that they are blind, having forgotten their cleansing from sin. Be diligent to make sure of your calling and election, for if you practice these qualities, you will never fall. You will receive a rich welcome into the eternal kingdom of our Lord and Savior, Jesus Christ.

Even though you already know this, I will keep reminding you of these truths. It's good to have reminders while we live in this body because we will put it aside before long. I will try to see you soon so that you will always remember these things after my death.

We did not follow clever stories when we told you about the power and coming of our Lord Jesus Christ; we were eyewitnesses of his majesty. He received honor and glory from God the Father when he called him his beloved son, who pleased him. We heard this same voice from heaven when we saw Jesus transfigured. We also have the prophetic message that you should obey. It will shine like a lamp in a dark place until a new dawn rises in your hearts. Prophecy has never been the matter of one's own interpretation; it comes from people who spoke God's Word as the Holy Spirit carried them along.

But false prophets arose among the people just like there will be false teachers among you. They will secretly introduce destructive heresies and even deny the Lord, bringing swift destruction on themselves. Many will follow their depravity and bring the faith into disrepute. In their greed, they will exploit you with made-up stories; their condemnation hangs over their heads.

God did not spare angels when they sinned but sent them to hell in chains of darkness for judgment. He did not spare the ancient world when he flooded it but only saved

Noah, a preacher of righteousness, and his family. He condemned the cities of Sodom and Gomorrah by burning them to ashes as an example of what will happen to the ungodly. But he rescued righteous Lot, who was tortured by the lawless deeds he saw and heard.

If these things are true, then the Lord knows how to rescue the godly from trials and hold the unrighteous for punishment on Judgment Day. Especially those who indulge in the lust of defiling passion and despise authority. They are bold and arrogant and not afraid to heap abuse on angels and beings who are greater than themselves.

These people blaspheme in matters they don't understand; they are unreasoning animals born to be caught and destroyed. The Lord will repay them for the harm they've done; they are blemishes who carouse in broad daylight. They are full of adultery and sin; they seduce the unstable and are experts in greed. They have left the straight path and follow the way of Balaam, looking for wicked wages. But his donkey rebuked him for his sin to restrain his madness.

These people are springs without water and God reserves the blackest darkness for them. They speak empty, boastful words and appeal to the lustful desires of the flesh; they entice people who are barely escaping error. They promise freedom, but they are slaves of corruption because whatever enslaves us overcomes us.

After they have escaped the world's defilements through knowledge of our Lord and Savior Jesus Christ, they are entangled in it again and worse off at the end than at the beginning. It would have been better for them not to be ignorant of righteousness than to have known it and then turned their backs on it. They are like dogs that return to their vomit or washed pigs that return to wallowing in the mud.

This is the second time I'm writing to you to remind you of the holy prophets and the Lord and Savior's commands through the apostles. In the last days, scoffers will come following their evil desires. They will claim that Jesus is not coming since everything continues as it always has. But they overlook the fact that it was the same way when God destroyed the world with the flood. Now, God reserves the present heavens and earth for fire on Judgment Day. Don't forget that a day is like 1,000 years and 1,000 years like a day with the Lord. He is not slow in keeping his promises; instead, he is patient with you, wanting everyone to repent.

The Day of the Lord will come like a thief, the heavens will pass away with a roar, the stars and heavens will burn, and God will expose the earth and its works. Since all of this will pass away, you should live holy and godly lives, waiting for the Day of the Lord. But according to his promise, we are waiting for new heavens and earth where righteousness will dwell.

Since we are waiting for these things, be diligent to live at peace without spot or blemish. Count the Lord's patience as salvation, just as Paul has written to you. His letters can be challenging to understand and the ignorant and unstable try to twist them just as they do other Scriptures. Therefore, be careful that lawless people's error doesn't carry you away, and you lose your stability, but grow in the grace and knowledge of our Lord and Savior Jesus Christ. To him, be the glory now and forever! Amen.

> **Paul's death**
>
> Paul never made it out of his Roman imprisonment. Around the time of Peter's martyrdom, Nero also had Paul beheaded. Paul's death likely happened sometime around 67 A.D.

CHAPTER FORTY-ONE

WARNING AGAINST FALSE TEACHING

Jude 1

> **Jude's letter**
>
> Jude, Jesus' half-brother, wrote this letter around the same time as Peter's two letters as a warning to Jewish Christians. This is a general letter and Jude warns his audience against false teaching.

Beloved, I had been preparing to write to you about our salvation, but I found it necessary to urge you to fight for the faith given to the saints. Some people have slipped in among you, saying that God's grace provides us with a license to sin. These godless people were condemned long ago, and they have turned their backs on our only Master and Lord, Jesus Christ.

Even though you already know, I want to remind you that the Lord delivered his people out of Egypt and destroyed those who did not believe. God has even kept the angels that did not keep their positions in eternal chains for judgment when he returns. Similarly, Sodom, Gomorrah, and the surrounding cities became sexually depraved and serve as an example of those that suffer the punishment of eternal fire.

These dreamers pollute their flesh, reject authority, and slander angelic majesties. Even when the archangel Michael was disputing with Satan about Moses' body, he did not dare slander him but said, "The Lord rebuke you!" But these men speak evil about things that they do not understand. What they do know, they know by instinct, just like unreasoning animals; destroy them. Woe to them! They have followed the way of Cain, rushed into Balaam's error, and destroyed themselves in Korah's rebellion. These men are blemishes at your love feasts; they fearlessly eat with you, serving only themselves. They are clouds without rain, carried along by the wind, autumn trees without fruit, uprooted, and doubly dead. They are like the wild waves of the sea, foaming up their own shame; they are like wandering stars, reserved for blackest darkness.

> **What are these errors Jude warns against?**
>
> Jude writes about three errors here, and without context, this passage can be confusing. Cain was Adam and Eve's second child, and he tried to pass off inferior sacrifices to God and then killed his brother out of jealousy. He attempted to worship God with impure motives. Balaam's error was to be an unfaithful prophet. God gave him a message, but he wanted to use his position to profit rather than proclaim what God had told him. Korah's rebellion was false teaching.

> While the Israelites were in the wilderness, he revolted against Moses and Aaron and tried to get the people to follow him. All these errors may look good on the surface but amount to nothing.

Enoch, the seventh from Adam, prophesied about these men, saying: "See, the Lord is coming with innumerable of his holy ones to judge everyone and convict the ungodly of their evil deeds and all the harsh things that ungodly sinners have said against him." These men are grumblers and complainers that follow their lusts, speak arrogantly, and flatter others for their own advantage.

Beloved, remember that the apostles of our Lord Jesus Christ told you beforehand that, "In the last time there will be mockers that follow after their own desires." It is these worldly people that do not have the Spirit that divide you. But you, beloved, build yourselves up on your most holy faith and pray in the Holy Spirit. Keep yourselves in God's love as you wait for our Lord Jesus Christ's mercy to bring you to eternal life. Have mercy on those that doubt; save others by snatching them out of the fire. Show mercy to others, mixed with fear, hating even the clothing that the flesh has stained. God can keep you from falling and make you stand in the presence of his glory without fault and with great joy.

To the only God our Savior, through the Lord Jesus Christ, be glory, majesty, power, and authority in the past, present, and forever! Amen.

CHAPTER FORTY-TWO

JESUS CAME IN THE FLESH AND GIVES ETERNAL LIFE
I John 1-5

> **John's first letter**
>
> The apostle John wrote this letter around the end of the First Century. He was likely writing to the churches in Ephesus and the surrounding area. His purpose is to assure Christians of their salvation and to counter teaching that denied Jesus had come in the flesh.

We proclaim to you what we have seen and heard concerning the Word of Life and how it appeared to give us eternal life. Now you may have fellowship with us, the Father, and his Son, Jesus Christ, to make our joy complete.

God is light and there is not even a shadow of darkness in him. If we claim to have fellowship with him while we walk in darkness, we lie and do not practice the truth. But if we walk in the light, we have fellowship with one another, and Jesus' blood cleanses us from our sin.

If we say we have no sin, we lie to ourselves, and the truth is not in us. But if we confess our sins, he is faithful and just to forgive and cleanse us from all unrighteousness. If we claim to have not sinned, we make him a liar, and his Word is not in us.

My dear children, I write so that you will not sin, but if anybody does, Jesus is our advocate with the Father. He is the atoning sacrifice for our sins and the sins of the whole world. We know him if we keep his commands, those who claim to know him but disobey, lie; the truth is not in them. But God's love is perfected in those who obey. We know that we are in him if we walk in the same way he walked.

Dear friends, I am not writing a new command, but an old one that you already know. However, it is also a new commandment because the darkness is passing away, and the true light already shines. Those who claim to be in the light but still hate their brothers and sisters are in the dark and do not know where they are going. Those who love their brothers and sisters walk in the light and there is no cause for suffering.

Dear children, I write to you because Jesus has forgiven your sin, and you know the Father. Fathers, I am writing to you because you know him, who is from the beginning. Young men, I write to you because you are strong, the Word of God lives in you, and you have overcome the evil one.

Do not love the world or worldly things because those who love the world do not have the Father's love. All the desires of the flesh and pride in possessions are from the world and not the Father. The world is passing away along with its desires, but those who do God's will abide forever.

Dear children, it is the last hour, and the Antichrist is coming, and many antichrists have already come. They went out from us because they do not belong to us; if they had been, they would have stayed. But the Holy One has anointed you and you all know the truth. I write to you because you know the truth and there is no lie in it. Those who deny that Jesus is the Christ are antichrist; no one who denies the Son has the Father, and those who acknowledge the Son have the Father.

> **Who is the Antichrist?**
>
> The Bible talks about the antichrist in two ways. The first is the Antichrist, the one John writes about in the Book of Revelation. He is the one who revolts against Jesus at the end of history. It also talks about those who are antichrist, who is anyone who claims that Jesus is not God. Many people in the world are antichrist, but not all who deny him are the Antichrist.

Make sure that what you've heard from the beginning remains in you, and then you will remain in the Son and the Father. He has promised us eternal life. Some want to lead you astray, but the anointing you received remains in you. We know it is real because it teaches us about all things, so stay in him.

Dear children, continue in him so that when he appears, we may be confident and unashamed when he comes. If he is righteous, then all who do right are born of him.

How great is the Father's love for us that he should call us his children? The reason the world does not know us is that it did not know him. We are God's children now, and what we will be has not yet appeared, but we will be like him when he appears. Those who hope in him purify themselves as he is pure. Everyone who makes a habit of sinning practices lawlessness because sin is lawlessness. He appeared to take away sin and he is sinless. Those who live in him don't keep on sinning; those who keep sinning have neither seen nor known him.

Dear children, don't let anyone lead you astray; those who do right are righteous just as God is righteous. Those who do what is sinful are from the Devil, who has sinned from the beginning. The Son of God appeared to destroy the Devil's work. None of those born of God continue to sin because God's seed lives in them, and they cannot keep sinning. They are born of God. It is evident who are children of God and who are children of the Devil: those who don't practice righteousness are not from God, nor are those who don't love their brothers or sisters.

The message you have heard from the beginning is to love each other. We should not be like Cain, who was from the Devil and murdered his brother. He murdered his brother because his deeds were evil and his brother's were righteous. Don't be surprised that the world hates you; we have passed out of death into life because we love, but those who don't love remain in death. Those who hate their brother are as guilty as murderers and no murderer has eternal life.

We know love because Jesus laid down his life for us, and we should lay down our lives for our brothers and sisters. If we have the world's goods, see someone in need, and close our hearts, God's love is not in us. We should not love in words alone but with our actions. This proves we are of the truth and reassures our hearts before him. Whenever our hearts condemn us, God is greater than our hearts, and he knows everything. If our hearts don't condemn us, we have confidence before God, and he will give us what we ask for because we do what pleases him.

His commandment is that we believe in the name of his Son, Jesus Christ, and love each other just as he commanded us. Those who obey his commandments remain in God and God in them; we know we are in him because of his Spirit.

Dear friends, don't believe every spirit but test them to see if they are from God because there are many false prophets in the world. You will recognize the Spirit of God because every spirit that acknowledges that Jesus Christ has come in the flesh is from God. Every spirit that does not acknowledge Jesus is not from God. This is the antichrist spirit, which you have heard is coming and is already in the world.

Dear children, you are from God and have overcome them because the Spirit in you is greater than the one in the world. They are worldly and speak from the world's perspective, so the world listens to them. We are from God and whoever knows God listens to us; that is how we know the Spirit of truth from the spirit of lies.

Dear friends, let us love one another because love comes from God, and those who love have been born from and know God. Those who do not love do not know God because God is love. God showed us his love by sending his only Son into the world so we might live. We know love because God sent his Son as an atoning sacrifice for our sins. Since God loved us, we should love one another. No one has ever seen God, but God lives in us if we love one another, and he completes his love in us.

We know that we are in God, and he is in us because he has given us his Spirit. We have seen and testified that the Father has sent his Son to save the world, and God is in those who confess Jesus is the Son of God, and he is in them. We know and believe the Lord loves us; God is love, and those who love stay connected to him.

Love is perfected in us so that we may have confidence for Judgment Day because we live like Jesus is in this world. There is no fear in love because perfect love casts out fear; fear has to do with punishment, and those who fear have not been perfected in love. We can only love because he first loved us. If people claim to love God but hate their brothers or sisters, they are liars because those who do not love those whom they have seen cannot love God whom they have not seen. Anyone who loves God must love their brothers and sisters.

Those who believe that Jesus is the Christ are born of God, and those who love the Father love his Son as well. We love the children of God when we love God and obey his commandments. Loving God is obedience and his commands are not a burden. Those who are born of God overcome the world because of our faith that Jesus is the Son of God.

The Spirit testifies that Jesus Christ has come in both the flesh and the spirit. God's testimony is greater than human testimony and he testifies about his Son. Those who believe in the Son of God have the testimony; those who do not believe call God a liar. God has given us eternal life, and this life is in his Son. Those who have the Son have life; those who do not have the Son of God do not have life.

These things are for you who believe in the Son of God so that you can know you have eternal life. The confidence we have is that he listens to us and gives us anything we ask for according to his will.

If you see a brother committing a sin that does not lead to death, you should pray for him; some sins lead to eternal death, don't pray for those. All wrongdoing is sin, but some sins don't lead to death. Those who are born of God do not keep sinning, Jesus protects them, and the Devil cannot harm them. We are children of God and the whole world is under the Devil's control. We also know that the Son of God has come and gives us understanding so that we may know the truth. We are in God by being in his Son, Jesus Christ, the true God and eternal life.

> ### Levels of sin
>
> On a forensic level, all sins are the same. All sin separates us from God, from white lies to murder, and even if we only sin once, we are guilty and worthy of death. But there also levels to the impacts of our sin. Some sins are minor in comparison to others. A lifestyle of denying Christ and his work is far more destructive and leads to eternal damnation.

Dear children, keep yourselves from idols.

> ### Idols
>
> An idol is anything that we put in a higher position than God. Our world is full of them and many tempt us to place them above Jesus. If we find anything competing with our devotion to Christ, then we need to avoid it.

CHAPTER FORTY-THREE

JOHN'S SECOND AND THIRD LETTERS
II John - III John

> **John's second and third letters**
>
> The apostle John wrote these letters around 90 A.D. to believers who were living as they should. A common practice in the First Century was for believers to welcome traveling missionaries into their homes. John writes his letters to two such believers. John's purpose was to remind his readers that they should love others and support those who spread the gospel, a common theme in the New Testament.

II JOHN

It gives me great joy to find some of your children walking in the truth, just as the Father commanded us. I am giving you the same commandment we have always known, to love one another. Love is to obey his commands. Many deceivers who deny that Jesus Christ came in the flesh are in the world; they are antichrist.

Do not lose what you've worked for; keep your reward. Those who run ahead and do not remain in Christ's teaching do not have God, but those who stay in his teachings remain in the Father and the Son. Reject anyone who brings you a different teaching and do not share in their wicked work.

I hope to visit you soon so that our joy may be complete.

III JOHN

Dear friend, I pray that you might have good health and that everything goes well with you. I greatly rejoiced when the brothers told me that you were walking in the truth because that is my greatest joy.

Beloved, you are faithful in what you do for the brothers and sisters, even though you don't know them. Please send them on their way in a manner that honors God. It was for Jesus' name that they went out, receiving no help from the pagans. Therefore, we should support them so that we may be fellow workers for the truth.

I already wrote to the church, but Diotrephes does not acknowledge our authority. If I can come, I will expose his wickedness because he refuses to welcome the brothers and stops those who want to help. Do not imitate evil but imitate good. Those who do good are from God; those who do evil have not seen him.

I have much more to say but prefer to do it face to face. I hope to see you soon.

CHAPTER FORTY-FOUR

JOHN'S VISION AND LETTERS TO THE CHURCHES
Revelation 1-3

> **John's Revelation**
>
> The apostle John wrote this letter from exile on Patmos during the Domitian persecution near the end of the First Century. Jesus gave him a vision one Sunday showing him what was to happen during the End Times. This is an apocalyptic letter, a writing style we are unfamiliar with, making it the source of much confusion in the modern church. It is full of symbolism, and we must understand it to interpret this letter. This was a popular writing style at the time and the early church likely had no problem understanding what John meant.

The revelation of Jesus Christ that God, through his angel, gave to John to show his servants the things that must happen. John bears witness to the Word of God and the testimony of Jesus Christ that he saw. Blessed are those who read these words, as are those who obey them for the time is near.

Grace and peace to the seven churches from God, the one who was, is, and is to come, the seven spirits who are before his throne, and Jesus Christ, the faithful witness, the firstborn of the dead, and the ruler of the earth. May all glory and power be to him who has made us a kingdom and priests forever! Amen.

> **What does "was, is, and is to come" mean?**
>
> The title "who was, is, and is to come" refers to God's eternal nature. He sees everything in an eternal instant because he was at creation, is now, and will be for all eternity.

He is coming with the clouds, everyone will see him, and the world will wail on his account. Even so, let it be. The Lord God is the Beginning and the End, the one who was, is, and is to come, the Almighty.

LETTERS TO THE CHURCHES

I was exiled on the island of Patmos because I kept preaching the gospel. One Sunday, I was praying. I heard a loud voice behind me like a trumpet telling me to write what I saw in a book to the seven churches in Ephesus, Smyrna, Pergamum, Thyatira, Sardis, Philadelphia, and Laodicea.

I turned to see the voice, and I saw seven golden lampstands. Amid them, I saw Jesus, clothed in a long robe with a golden sash across his chest. His hair was white like wool or snow, his eyes like a flame, his feet like bronze glowing in a furnace, and his voice was like the roar of rushing waters. He held seven stars in his right hand, and from his mouth came a sharp, double-edged sword, and his face shone like the noonday sun.

> **John's use of "like."**
>
> John's vision was far beyond what he could understand. If we look through this book, John uses the word "like" frequently. He had to do this because his vision was so far beyond his comprehension. The things he wrote about may not be exactly what he saw, but that's because we lack the human language to describe God and his works.

When I saw him, I fell at his feet like a dead man. But he laid his right hand on me and said, "Don't be afraid, I am the First and Last, the Living One. I died, and now I live forevermore, and I hold the keys of Death and Hades. Write what you see, things that are, and those that will take place. The seven stars you saw in my right hand are the angels of the seven churches, and the seven golden lampstands are the seven churches."

> **Letters to the churches**
>
> John wrote these letters to real churches that existed in the First Century. But we can also find ourselves in his messages.

To the angel of the church in Ephesus, these are Jesus' words:

I know your deeds, hard work, endurance, and how you cannot tolerate the wicked and false apostles. I know that you have not grown weary and patiently endure for my name's sake, but you have abandoned your early love. Remember where you were before you fell; repent, and do the deeds you did at first, or I will remove your lampstand from its place. But you hate the evil of the Nicolaitans, which I also hate. They forget me and try to fit in with the world around them. Listen to what the Spirit says to the churches; I will give the victorious the right to eat from the tree of life in God's paradise.

To the angel of the church in Smyrna, these are Jesus' words:

I know your afflictions and your poverty, though you are rich. I know how the false Jews who are of Satan's synagogue slander you. Don't be afraid of what you are about to suffer; the Devil is about to test you by throwing some of you into prison and persecute you for a time. Be faithful, even to the point of death, and I will give you the crown of life. Listen to what the Spirit says to the churches; the second death will not hurt those who conquer.

To the angel of the church in Pergamum, these are Jesus' words:

I know that you live near Satan's throne, yet you remain true to my name. You did not even renounce your faith when your enemies killed Antipas. Nevertheless, I have a few things against you. Some of you follow Balaam's teaching, who taught Balak to put obstacles before the Israelites so that they would eat food sacrificed to idols and practice sexual immorality. Also, some of you follow the teaching of the Nicolaitans and practice their debauchery. Repent, or I will come to you and wage war against you with the sword of my mouth. Listen to what the Spirit says to the churches; to those who conquer, I will give some of the hidden manna and a white stone with a name written on it that no one knows except those who receive it.

To the angel of the church in Thyatira, these are Jesus' words:

I know your deeds, service, perseverance, and that you are now doing more than you did at first. Nevertheless, you tolerate the woman Jezebel who calls herself a prophet and misleads my servants into sexual immorality and eating food sacrificed to idols. I gave her time to repent of her sin, but she has not. So, I will cast her on a bed of suffering along with those who commit adultery with her unless they repent. I will kill her children, then all the churches will know that I search hearts and minds, and I will repay you according to your deeds.

To the rest of you in Thyatira who do not follow her teachings and have not learned Satan's so-called deep secrets, I give you no other burden except to hold onto what you have until I come. To those who conquer and do my will to the end, I will give authority over the nations to rule with a rod of iron that shatters pottery; I will give them the morning star. Listen to what the Spirit says to the churches.

To the angel of the church in Sardis, these are Jesus' words:

I know your deeds and your reputation for being alive even though you're dead. Wake up and strengthen what is about to die because your work is not finished yet. Remember what you have learned and repent! If you do not wake up, I will come like a thief when you aren't ready. However, you have a few people who have not soiled their clothes; they will walk with me wearing white because they are worthy. God will also clothe the ones who conquer in white, their names will be in the Book of Life, and I will confess them before my Father and his angels. Listen to what the Spirit says to the churches.

To the angel of the church in Philadelphia, these are Jesus' words:

I know your deeds and I have set an open door before you that no one can shut. You don't have much power, but you have kept my word and not denied my name. I will make the fake Jews of Satan's synagogue come to bow down at your feet and learn that I love you. I will protect you from the trial coming to the earth because you have patiently endured. I am coming soon; hold on to what you have so that no one can take your crown. I will make those who conquer pillars in my God's temple and they will not leave it. I will write God's name, the name of the new Jerusalem, and my name on them. Listen to what the Spirit says to the churches.

To the angel of the church in Laodicea, these are Jesus' words:

I know your deeds, and that you are neither hot nor cold, I wish you were one or the other! Since you are lukewarm, I'm going to spit you out of my mouth. You think you don't need anything because you're rich, but you don't realize that you are wretched, pitiful, poor, blind, and naked. You should buy gold refined in fire from me so that you can become rich, white clothes to cover your nakedness, and salve to put on your eyes so you can see. I rebuke and discipline those whom I love, so be earnest and repent. I stand at the door and knock; if you hear my voice and open the door, I will come in and eat with you. I will give those who conquer the right to sit with me on my throne, just as I sat with my Father when I was victorious. Listen to what the Spirit says to the churches.

CHAPTER FORTY-FIVE

THE SEVEN SEALS AND FIRST FIVE TRUMPETS
Revelation 4:1-9:12

> **Numbers in apocalyptic literature**
>
> One of the key features in apocalyptic writing is the use of numbers. Sometimes, the numbers represent actual quantities, but they often hold a deeper meaning. In the Book of Revelation, most of the numbers that John uses have meaning beyond just amounts. Some of the primary meanings are:
>
> Three: God's number, fulfillment, or unity.
>
> Four: The world or all of creation.
>
> Six: The number of man or imperfection.
>
> Seven: The number of God or perfection.
>
> Ten: Earthly government.
>
> Twelve: Divine government, the tribes of Israel, or the apostles.
>
> Twenty-four: A witness to God's divine government represented by the twelve tribes of Israel and the twelve apostles.
>
> One-third or one-quarter: Not an exact calculation, but a significant portion.
>
> Three-and-a-half: Half of seven, a relatively short time that is precarious and dangerous.
>
> One thousand: A vast amount, often paired with other numbers.

After this, I saw a door in front of me open in heaven, and the voice said to me, "Come here and I will show you what must take place." Immediately, I was in the Spirit, and I saw someone seated on a throne in heaven. The one on the throne looked like jasper and ruby, and a rainbow shone around the throne like an emerald. Surrounding the throne were 24 other thrones with 24 elders seated on them, dressed in white with golden crowns.

There were flashes of lightning and peals of thunder coming from the throne and seven torches of fire before it, representing the perfection of God's Spirit. Before the throne was a sea of glass like crystal, and there were four living creatures around the throne, full of eyes all around them. The first was like a lion, the second like an ox, the third had a man's face, and the fourth looked like an eagle in flight. All four of them had six wings and were covered with eyes. They never stopped saying, "Holy, holy, holy, is the Lord God Almighty, who was, is, and is to come!"

Whenever the living creatures gave glory, honor, and thanks to the Eternal One on the throne, the 24 elders fell down before him to worship. They cast their crowns before the throne, saying, "Worthy are you, our Lord and God, to receive glory, honor, and power, for you created everything, and it exists because of your will."

Then I saw a scroll with writing on front and back, with seven seals, in the right hand of the one seated on the throne. I saw a strong angel cry out, "Who is worthy to break the seals and open the scroll?" There was no one in heaven, on earth, or under the earth who was worthy to open the scroll or read it, so I began to weep.

Then one of the elders said to me, "Do not weep, the Lion of the tribe of Judah, the Root of David, has conquered; he is worthy to break the seals and open the scroll." Between the throne and the four living creatures, I saw a Lamb standing amid the elders, looking as though it had been killed. The Lamb had seven horns with seven eyes, which are the seven spirits of God, and it took the scroll from the one sitting on the throne.

When he took the scroll, the four living creatures and the 24 elders fell down before the Lamb, each holding a harp and golden bowls of incense with the believers' prayers. They sang a new song, "Worthy are you to break the seals and open the scroll because you died and your blood ransomed people for God from everywhere on earth. You have made them a kingdom of priests to our God; they shall rule on earth."

Then I looked, and I heard around the throne, the living creatures, and the elders, the voices of countless angels declaring, "Worthy is the Lamb who was slain, to receive power, wealth, wisdom, might, honor, glory, and blessing!"

Every creature in heaven, on earth, and under the earth and sea cried out, "To God the Father and the Lamb be blessing, honor, glory, and might forever!"

The four living creatures said, "Amen!" and the elders fell down and worshiped.

I watched as the Lamb opened the first four of the seven seals, and as he opened each, one of the four living creatures said in a voice like thunder, "Come!" After the first seal, a rider came out on a white horse holding a bow; he was given a crown, and he rode out to conquer. After the second seal, a rider came out on a fiery red horse, and he was given a sword and the power to remove peace and cause people to kill each other. After the third seal, a rider came out on a black horse, and a voice told him a day's wages for a handful of grain but not to hurt the oil and wine. After the fourth seal, a rider came out on a pale horse, and its name was Death, and Hades followed him. These four were given authority over a fourth of the earth to kill with sword, famine, pestilence, and the earth's wild beasts.

> ### Color in Revelation
>
> Much like numbers have symbolic meaning in this letter, colors have implications as well. Some of the primary meanings are:
>
> White: Purity or victory.

> Red: Blood or violence.
>
> Black: Death.
>
> Purple: Royalty.
>
> Gold: God's splendor.

When he opened the fifth seal, I saw the souls of those martyred for God's Word underneath the altar. They cried out with a loud voice, "O Sovereign Lord, holy and true, how long before you judge and avenge our blood on those who dwell on the earth?" They were each given a white robe and told to rest a little longer until the number of other martyrs was complete.

When he opened the sixth seal, there was a great earthquake; the sun became black as sackcloth, and the moon like blood. The sky's stars fell to the earth like a fig tree sheds its winter fruit in a strong wind. The heavens vanished like a scroll rolled up, and every mountain and island moved from its place. Then everyone on earth hid in caves and among the rocks of the hills. They called to the rocks, "Fall on us to hide us from the face of the one on the throne and the wrath of the Lamb because no one can stand before him."

After this, I saw four angels standing at the ends of the earth, holding back the wind so that there would be no wind on earth, sea, or against any tree. Another angel came from the east, holding the seal of the living God, and he called out, "Do not harm the earth, sea, or trees until we have sealed the servants of our God on their foreheads." The angel sealed 12,000 from every tribe of Israel for a total of 144,000 (not an exact number, but representing a vast number of God's people).

Then I saw an innumerable multitude from every nation, tribe, people group, and language standing before the Lamb's throne. They wore white robes and waved palm branches, crying out, "Salvation belongs to our God who sits on the throne and to the Lamb!"

All the angels standing around the throne, the elders, and the four living creatures fell on their faces before the throne and worshiped God, saying, "Amen! Blessing, glory, wisdom, thanksgiving, honor, power, and might be to our God forever! Amen!"

One of the elders came to me and said, "These in the white robes are the ones who have come out of the Great Tribulation; they have washed their robes and made them white in the Lamb's blood. Now, they serve before God's throne day and night in his temple, and he shelters them with his presence. They will never hunger or thirst again and the sun will not scorch them anymore. The Lamb will be their shepherd, and he will guide them to springs of living water, then God will wipe away every tear from their eyes."

When the Lamb opened the seventh seal, there was silence in heaven for about half an hour; then, the seven angels who stand before God were each given trumpets. Another angel who held a golden container for burning incense came and stood at the altar. He was given incense to offer along with the believers' prayers on the golden altar before the throne. The smoke from his offering rose before God. Then, the angel filled the golden container with fire and threw it on the earth; then, there was lightning, thunder, and another earthquake.

The seven angels with the trumpets prepared to blow them. When the first angel blew his trumpet, hail and fire mixed with blood were thrown on the earth, and a third of the trees and all the green grass burned up.

The second angel blew his trumpet, and something like a vast mountain, burning with fire, was thrown into the sea, and a third of the sea became blood. A third of the sea creatures died and a third of all ships were destroyed.

The third angel blew his trumpet, and a great star fell from heaven like a blazing torch, and it fell on a third of the rivers and springs of water. The star made the water bitter and many people died who drank from those rivers and springs.

The fourth angel blew his trumpet, and a third of the sun, moon, and stars were struck so that their light might be darkened. Then I saw an eagle flying directly overhead; it cried out with a loud voice, "Woe to those who live on the earth because of the other trumpets that the three angels are about to blow!"

The fifth angel blew his trumpet, and I saw a star fall from heaven to earth, and he was given the key to the shaft of a bottomless pit. His name is Destroyer, and when he opened the shaft, smoke rose from it as if from a great furnace, and the sun and air were darkened. Then, locusts came from the smoke, and they were given power like scorpions. God told them not to harm any plant, but only those who did not have God's seal on their foreheads.

The locusts looked like horses prepared for battle; it seemed like they wore golden crowns, with long hair, human faces, and lions' teeth. They seemed to have iron breastplates and they sounded like horses and chariots rushing into battle. They had stinging tails and they tormented the people for five months. They could not kill, but people were so miserable that they wanted to die.

The first woe is past, but there are two more to come.

Signs of the Times

As we read about these signs in the Book of Revelation, it is difficult to know what exactly John describes. It is essential to remember that much of this book is figurative. Our job is not to figure out where we are in history and the End Times. When we see things that may be God's judgment, we should repent from our sin and make sure we are ready for his return. We should look for ways we can spread the gospel and tell people about Jesus.

CHAPTER FORTY-SIX

THE SIXTH AND SEVENTH TRUMPETS
Revelation 9:13-11:19

The sixth angel blew his trumpet, and I heard a voice coming from the four horns of the golden altar before God saying, "Release the four angels bound at the Euphrates." The angels, who had been prepared for this time, were released, and they led a seemingly infinite number of troops to kill a third of humanity. They wore fiery red, dark blue, and yellow breastplates, their horses' heads resembled lions, and their tails were like serpents that wound. They breathed out fire, smoke, and sulfur, and they killed a third of the earth's population. Yet, the rest of humanity did not repent of their murders, sorcery, sexual immorality, or theft. They did not stop worshiping demons or blind, lame, and mute idols.

Then another mighty angel came down from heaven, wrapped in a cloud, with a rainbow over his head; his face was like the sun, and his legs like pillars of fire. He held a little scroll in his hand, and he set his right foot on the sea, and his left on the land and then cried out like a roaring lion, and the seven thunders sounded. The angel forbade me to write what the thunder said. Then, the angel raised his right hand to heaven and swore by God that when the seventh trumpet sounded, God's mystery would be fulfilled as the prophets had promised.

The voice from heaven told me to take the scroll from the angel standing on the sea and the land. When I took the scroll from the angel, he said, "Eat this scroll; it will be sweet in your mouth, but bitter in your stomach. Then you must prophesy about many peoples, nations, languages, and kings." I obeyed, and the scroll made my stomach bitter.

I was given a measuring rod and told, "Measure God's temple and the altar with its worshipers but exclude the outer courts because they have been given to the Gentiles. They will trample the holy city for three-and-a-half years; during this time, I will appoint my two witnesses who will prophesy while mourning." They are the two olive trees and the two lampstands that stand before the Lord; if anyone tries to harm them, fire comes from their mouths to consume their foes.

These two witnesses will have the power to shut the sky so that it will not rain while they are prophesying. They will also have the ability to turn water into blood and strike the earth with every plague.

When they have finished their testimony, the beast that comes from the Abyss will attack and kill them. Their bodies will lie in Jerusalem's public square (figuratively Sodom and Egypt) for three-and-a-half days while they are denied a burial. The people of the earth will rejoice over their deaths and give each other gifts because these prophets had been a torment to the whole world. But then God will breathe life into them, and they will stand up, causing those who see to be afraid. Then they will be called into heaven in a cloud while their enemies look on. At that time, an earthquake will destroy a tenth of the city and kill thousands. The people will be terrified and glorify God.

The second woe has passed; the third is coming soon.

Then the seventh angel blew his trumpet and loud voices in heaven said, "The kingdom of the world has become the kingdom of our Lord and his Christ; he shall rule forever!"

The 24 elders on the thrones before God fell on their faces and worshiped, "We give thanks to you, Lord God Almighty, who was and is because you have used your great power and begun to rule. The nations were angry, but your wrath came, and now it's time to judge the dead, reward your servants, and destroy those who destroy the earth." Then God's temple in heaven opened, the ark of the covenant became visible, and there were flashes of lightning, thunder, an earthquake, and heavy hail.

CHAPTER FORTY-SEVEN
THE GREAT DRAGON AND THE BOWLS OF WRATH
Revelation 12-17

A great sign appeared in heaven: a woman clothed with the sun, the moon under her feet, and a crown of twelve stars on her head. She was crying out in pain as she gave birth. Suddenly, there was another sign: a great, red dragon with seven heads and ten horns wearing a crown on each head. It swept a third of the stars from the sky with its tail and flung them to the earth.

The dragon stood before the woman, waiting for her to give birth so that it could eat the child. She gave birth to a son who would rule the nations with an iron scepter, and God snatched the child up to his throne. The woman fled into the wilderness to a place God had prepared and he took care of her for three-and-a-half years.

Then war broke out in heaven, and Michael and his angels fought against the dragon and his angels. The great dragon, Satan, was not strong enough, and he and his angels were thrown to the earth.

Then I heard a loud voice in heaven say, "The salvation, the power, the kingdom of our God, and Christ's authority have come. For the one who accuses our brothers and sisters day and night has been thrown down. They have defeated him by the Lamb's blood and by the word of their testimony because they did not love their lives even to death. Therefore, heavens and you who dwell in them, rejoice! But woe to you earth and sea, for the Devil is angry because he knows his time is short!"

When the dragon saw his defeat, he chased the woman who gave birth to the child. But God gave the woman an eagle's wings so that she could fly to the wilderness where she would be out of the serpent's reach for three-and-a-half years. Then the serpent spewed water from its mouth like a river to overtake the woman and sweep her away. But the earth helped the woman by swallowing the dragon's river. The dragon was angry at the woman and went out to wage war against the rest of her offspring, those who obey God's commands and keep their testimony about Jesus.

The dragon stood on the seashore, and I saw a beast come out of the sea with seven heads, ten horns, and a crown on each horn; each head had a blasphemous name on it. The beast looked like a leopard, with feet like a bear and a mouth like a lion. The dragon gave the beast his power, throne, and great authority. One of the beast's heads seemed to have a fatal wound that had been healed, and the world marveled at the beast and followed him.

People worshiped the dragon. He had given the beast authority and they worshiped him because he was mighty. The beast was given a mouth to speak proud and blasphemous words, and it was given power for three-and-a-half years. It blasphemed God, slandered his name, his dwelling place, and those who live in heaven. It was allowed to make war on the believers and defeat them; it was given authority over all people on earth whose names were not written in the Lamb who was slain's Book of Life before the world's foundation.

Those marked for capture must be captured, and those who marked for death must be killed. This is a call for the endurance and faith of the believers.

Then another beast rose from the earth, it had two horns like a lamb, and it spoke like a dragon. It had the first beast's authority and it made the world worship the first beast with the healed mortal wound. It performed great signs and even made fire fall from heaven, commanding the world to create an image of the first beast. It was allowed to bring the image to life and it killed everyone who would not worship the image of the beast. It also caused everyone on earth to be marked on the right hand or forehead so that no one can buy or sell unless they have the mark of the beast. The number of the beast is the number of a man, 666.

> **Mark of the beast**
>
> There are many theories on what the mark of the beast is, but we don't know what the beast's mark will be. It will be something that will make it difficult to participate in the world if you don't have it. The fact that it is the number six three times means that it will represent humanity's power. As believers, we need to make sure we are more worried about what God thinks rather than what makes our lives on earth more comfortable.

I looked and saw the Lamb standing on Mount Zion with the 144,000 who had his name and his Father's name written on their foreheads. I heard a voice from heaven like rushing water, thunder, and harpists playing. The four living creatures and the 24 elders sang a new song before the throne, and no one could learn the song except the people the Lord redeemed from the earth. These are virgins who follow the Lamb wherever he goes; they have been redeemed from humanity, are the first fruits of God and the Lamb, and there was no lie in their mouths, for they are blameless.

Then I saw another angel flying directly overhead with an eternal gospel to proclaim to everyone who lives on earth. He said with a loud voice, "Fear God and give him glory because the hour of his judgment has come; worship him because he created all things."

A second angel followed him, saying, "Babylon the Great has fallen who made the nations drink the wine of her sexual immorality."

> **Babylon the Great**
>
> Babylon the Great is a symbol of the wicked people of earth. It is Satan's kingdom that God will overthrow when he returns. The wine of her sexual immorality is a symbol of the sin she leads her followers to commit.

A third angel followed them, saying, "Those who worship the beast or receive its mark will drink the wine of God's wrath, the full strength of his anger, and be tormented with fire and sulfur in the presence of the holy angels and the Lamb. The smoke of their torment goes up forever and they have no rest." This is a call for the believers' endurance, who obey God's commands and keep their faith in Jesus.

Then a voice from heaven said, "Blessed are those who die in the Lord from now on because they will have rest from their labor."

Then I saw Jesus seated on a cloud with a golden crown on his head and a sharp sickle in his hand. Another angel came out of the temple and cried out to Jesus, "Use the sickle and reap, for the earth's harvest is fully ripe, and it's time to reap." The one sitting on the cloud swung his sickle across the earth and it was reaped.

Then another angel came out of the temple with a sharp sickle. The angel with authority over the fire followed and told him, "Use your sickle and gather the grapes from the earth's vine because they are ripe." The angel swung its sickle, gathered the earth's grape harvest, and threw it into the winepress of God's wrath. The winepress was trampled outside the city, and blood flowed from it four feet deep for about 180 miles.

Then I saw seven angels with the seven last plagues, which complete God's wrath. I saw those who had conquered the beast, its image, and its number standing next to what looked like a sea of glass and fire. They held harps and sang the song of Moses and the Lamb, "Your deeds are great and marvelous, Lord God Almighty. King of the nations, your ways are just and true. All will fear you and glorify your name because you alone are holy. Every nation will worship you, for you have revealed your righteous acts."

Then I saw that the sanctuary of the tent of witness in heaven was open, and seven angels with the seven plagues came out wearing pure, bright linen with golden sashes across their chests. One of the four living creatures gave each of the seven angels golden bowls full of the eternal God's wrath and the sanctuary filled with the smoke of God's glory and power. No one could enter the sanctuary until the seven plagues of the seven angels were over.

Then I heard a loud voice from the temple tell the seven angels to pour out their bowls of God's wrath on the earth. The first angel poured out his bowl on the land, and painful, festering sores broke out on the people who had the mark of the beast and worshiped his image.

The second angel poured out his bowl on the sea, it became like a dead person's blood, and every living thing in the sea died.

The third angel poured out his bowl on the rivers and springs of water and they became like blood. Then the angel in charge of the waters said, "Holy One, who was and is, your judgments are just because they have killed your saints and prophets, and now you have given them blood to drink." The altar called in return, "Yes, Lord God Almighty, your judgments are true and just!"

The fourth angel poured out his bowl on the sun, and it began to scorch the people with fierce heat and fire. The people did not repent and give God glory but instead cursed his name.

The fifth angel poured out his bowl on the beast's throne and its kingdom was plunged into darkness. People gnawed their tongues in anguish and cursed God for their pain and sores, yet they did not repent.

The sixth angel poured out his bowl on the river Euphrates and the water dried up to prepare the way for the kings from the East. Then I saw three impure spirits that looked like frogs coming out of the dragon's mouths, the beast, and the false prophet. They are demonic spirits that perform signs and gather the earth together for the battle on the Great Day of God Almighty at Armageddon. He is coming like a thief! Blessed are those who stay awake and dressed so that they aren't naked and ashamed.

The seventh angel poured out his bowl into the air, and a loud voice came from the throne, saying, "It is done!" There was lightning, thunder, and the biggest earthquake to happen since creation. Jerusalem split into three parts, the cities of the nations fell, and God remembered Babylon the Great to make her drink the cup of his furious wrath. Every island fled away and the mountains were leveled. Hundred-pound hailstones fell from heaven and the people cursed God for the severity of the plague.

Then one of the angels who had the seven bowls said to me, "I will show you the judgment of the great prostitute seated on many waters and the kings of the earth who committed sexual immorality with her."

He carried me away in the Spirit into the wilderness. I saw a woman sitting on a scarlet beast with seven heads and ten horns covered with blasphemous names. The woman was wearing purple, scarlet, golden jewelry, and pearls. She held a golden cup full of the abominations and impurities of her sexual immorality. On her forehead was written, "Babylon the Great, mother of prostitutes and earth's abominations." She was drunk with the blood of the believers who had died for the name of Christ.

I marveled at her, but the angel asked me, "Why do you marvel? The beast you saw was, is not, and is about to rise from the bottomless pit and be destroyed. The earth's people whose names are not written in the Book of Life from the foundation of the world will marvel at the beast because it was, is not, and is to come.

> **Was, is not, and is to come**
>
> This is a reference to the mortal wound that the beast suffers. It refers to the beast's political rise, fall, and return to life.

"The beast's seven heads are seven mountains that the woman sits upon; they represent seven kings, five have fallen, one is, and the last is yet to come; his rule will only last a little while. The beast that was and is not is an eighth ruler, but it belongs to the seven and will be destroyed.

"The ten horns are ten rulers who have not come to power yet; they will rule for a short time with the beast. These kings share one mind, and they give their power and authority to the beast. They will make war with the Lamb, but the Lamb will defeat them because he is Lord of lords and King of kings, those who are with him are the chosen and faithful.

"The waters you saw are the people of the world. The ten horns you saw, they and the beast will hate the prostitute. They will bring her to ruin, leave her naked, eat her flesh, and burn her with fire. God has put it in their hearts to accomplish his purpose by agreeing to give the beast their royal authority until God's Word is fulfilled. The woman you saw is the great city that rules over the kings of the earth."

CHAPTER FORTY-EIGHT

JUDGMENT OF BABYLON

Revelation 18:1-19:10

After this, I saw another angel coming down from heaven with great authority, and the earth was bright with his glory. With a mighty voice, he shouted, "Babylon the Great is fallen! She has become a dwelling place for demons, every unclean spirit, and every unclean bird and detestable beast. All the nations have drunk the maddening wine of her sexual immorality, and the earth's powerful have made themselves rich from her luxurious living."

Then I heard another voice from heaven, "My people, come out of her so that you will not share in her sins or suffer her plagues because her sins are piled up to heaven, and God knows her crimes. Pay her back double for what she has done. Give her as much torment and grief as the glory and luxury she gave herself. She boasts that she is a queen, not a widow, and that she will never mourn. But her plagues will overtake her in a single day, death, mourning, and famine. She will be consumed by fire because the Lord God, who judges her, is mighty.

"When the rulers of earth who committed adultery with her and shared her luxury see the smoke of her burning, they will weep and mourn. They will be terrified of her torment and stand far away, crying out because they see that her doom has come. Then everyone she made rich will weep and mourn because no one buys the costly goods that she sold. Her delicacies and splendor are lost and will never be found. But heaven and God's people will rejoice because of God's judgment against her."

Then a mighty angel picked up a giant stone and threw it into the sea, saying, "Babylon will be thrown down with violence and never be found again, just like this stone. No one will make music in the city and no one will produce goods in her any longer. It will have no light and no one will rejoice because its sorcery deceived the whole earth. She is full of the blood of the prophets, believers, and everyone killed on the earth."

Then I heard the roar of a great multitude in heaven, "Hallelujah! Salvation, glory, and power belong to our God because his judgments are true and just. He has condemned the great prostitute who corrupted the earth and he has avenged his servants' blood on her. Hallelujah, her smoke goes up forever and ever!"

The 24 elders and the four living creatures fell down and worshiped God, who was seated on the throne. Then a voice came from the throne, "All God's servants give him praise, both small and great."

Then I heard the multitude shouting, "Hallelujah, the Lord God Almighty reigns! Let us rejoice, be glad, and give him glory! The Lamb's wedding is here, and his bride has made herself ready with fine linen that is bright and clean."

Then an angel told me to write, "Blessed are those invited to the Lamb's marriage supper! These are the true Words of God."

I fell at his feet to worship him, but he said, "Don't do that; I am a servant like you and your brothers who believe the testimony about Jesus. You should only worship God. It is the Spirit of prophecy who testifies about Jesus."

CHAPTER FORTY-NINE

THE FINAL BATTLE
Revelation 19:11-21:8

I saw heaven standing open, and a rider called Faithful and True (Jesus) seated on a white horse; he judges and wages war with justice. His eyes are like a blazing fire, wore many crowns, and has a name that only he knows. His robe is dipped in blood and his name is the Word of God. He led the armies of heaven on white horses, dressed in clean, white linen. A sharp sword came out of his mouth to strike down the nations that he will rule with an iron scepter. He treads the winepress of God's furious wrath, and he had his name written on his robe and thigh, King of kings and Lord of lords.

> **Jesus the Conquering King**
>
> When Jesus came the first time, he was a suffering servant. Finally, we see him come as a conquering king. This is the fulfillment of the Jews' messianic expectations at Jesus' first coming. He shows up to fight in white, something unheard of in battle. He knows he will defeat his enemies and has no fear of them even coming close enough to get his clothes dirty. He has a sword coming out of his mouth, ready to strike, and tattoos on his legs. This is a true warrior.

Then I saw an angel standing in the sun who cried out with a loud voice to all the birds of the air, "Come, gather for God's great supper to eat the mighty of earth's flesh."

The beast, the rulers of the earth, and their armies gathered to wage war against Jesus and his army. The beast and the false prophet were captured, and they were thrown alive into the lake of fire that burns with sulfur. Jesus killed the rest with the sword from his mouth and the birds gorged themselves on their flesh.

I saw an angel come down from heaven with the key to the bottomless pit in his hand on a great chain. He seized Satan, the great dragon, and locked him up in the pit for 1,000 years so that he could not deceive the earth until the time was up, and he would be released for a short time.

Then I saw those with authority to judge seated on thrones, the martyrs' souls, and those who had not worshiped the beast or taken its mark. They came to life and ruled with Christ for 1,000 years, but the rest of the dead did not rise until the end of the 1,000 years; this is the first resurrection. Those who share in this resurrection are blessed and holy, the second death has no power over them, and they will be priests of God and Christ.

When the 1,000 years are over, Satan will be released from his prison and will go out to deceive the world and gather them for battle. Their number will be like the sand of the seashore, and they will march up over the broad plain of the earth and surround the believers and the beloved city. But fire will come down from heaven and consume them and the Devil who leads them. Then they will be thrown into the lake of fire and sulfur where the beast and false prophet are, and they will be tormented day and night forever.

> ### Hell
>
> Hell is the unpopular concept of a place of eternal punishment and suffering for those who reject Jesus' life and ministry. Jesus talked about hell more than any other figure in the Bible. Scripture describes it as a fiery furnace where there will be weeping and gnashing of teeth, sorrow, torment, unquenchable fire, darkness, and destruction. Popular culture often depicts hell as a mildly warm place where all the "bad kids" hang out and do whatever they want, but this is not the picture the Bible paints.
>
> Some believe that a loving God would never condemn people to an eternal punishment like this, but God's wrath is a part of his nature that we cannot ignore. If God allows sin to go unpunished, then he is no longer holy. If we put our trust in Jesus, then his death pays the debt of our sin. We cannot pick and choose which of God's attributes we like and ignore the others.
>
> Many people wonder what will happen to those who never hear the gospel and never have an opportunity to come to faith. The Bible does not explicitly address what happens in these cases, but we know that God will do the right thing because he is good, righteous, and just. Ultimately, God gives us the choice to say, "your will be done." If we refuse, then he says to us, "your will be done."

Then I saw Jesus on a great white throne, and the earth and sky fled from his presence, and there was no place for them. Then the dead stood before the throne, and the books, including the Book of Life, were opened. Everyone who had died was judged by everything recorded in the books, and then Death and Hades were thrown into the lake of fire, which is the second death. Anyone whose name was not found in the Book of Life was thrown into the lake of fire.

Then I saw a new heaven and earth because the first had passed away, and there was no longer any sea. I saw the new Jerusalem coming down from heaven, a beautiful bride dressed for her husband. I heard a loud voice from the throne say, "Behold the dwelling place of God is with man; he will live with them, they will be his people, and he will be their God. He will wipe away every tear from their eyes; there will be no more death, mourning, crying, or pain, for the former things have passed away. I am making all things new. Write these words down, for this is trustworthy and true."

Then he said, "It is finished! I am the Alpha and the Omega, the Beginning and the End. I will give free water from the spring of life to the thirsty. Those who conquer will inherit all this, I will be their God, and they will be my children. But the cowardly, unbelieving, vile, murderers, sexually immoral, sorcerers, idolaters, and liars will burn in the fiery lake of sulfur; this is the second death."

> **What do we do with the Book of Revelation?**
>
> The Book of Revelation can be very confusing, and it has led to much debate about how we should interpret it. This book aims not to tell us when we get to leave this world but is to reassure us that God wins in the end. Even when we see the world falling apart around us, we should take comfort and use the signs of the times as motivation to draw closer to God and tell people about him.

CHAPTER FIFTY

THE NEW JERUSALEM
Revelation 21:9-22:21

One of the angels who had one of the seven bowls of God's plagues came to me and said, "Come, I will show you the Bride of the Lamb."

He carried me away in the Spirit to a great mountain. He showed me the holy city, Jerusalem, coming down from heaven. It shone with God's glory, and it was as brilliant as the rarest jewel, like a jasper, clear as crystal. It had a great, high wall, with twelve gates; there were angels at each of the gates, and they had the names of the twelve tribes of the sons of Israel written on them, three in each direction. The wall had twelve foundations, each with one of the apostles' names.

The angel had a gold measuring rod to measure the city. It was nearly 1,200 miles long, wide, and high, and the walls were more than 200 feet tall. The wall was of jasper and the city of gold as pure as glass. The foundation of the city walls was decorated with every kind of precious stone: jasper, sapphire, agate, emerald, onyx, ruby, chrysolite, beryl, topaz, turquoise, jacinth, and amethyst. Each gate was a single pearl, and the streets were made of gold, as clear as glass. There was no temple in the city because the Lord God Almighty and the Lamb were its temple.

> **Heaven**
>
> Heaven is the place that God is preparing for those who place faith in Jesus and follow him. There are many misconceptions about heaven. We will not become angels and float around on clouds playing harps. We will have a physical body and live for eternity with God. We will not struggle with sin, and everything broken will be made right as God had intended from creation. Our minds cannot comprehend how amazing this place will be, and we lack the language to describe it accurately. John saw a vision of heaven and he had to use descriptive language to express how tremendous it will be. For example, he writes that the streets will be paved with gold. This is one of the most valuable substances on earth, and in heaven, it is a common construction material.

There is no need for the sun or moon because God and the Lamb give the city light, and all the nations will walk in its glory. The rulers of the earth will bring their glory into it and the city gates will never shut because there will be no night there. Nothing unclean will ever enter, but only those written in the Lamb's Book of Life.

Then the angel showed me the river of the water of life, clear as crystal flowing from the throne of God and the Lamb. It flowed through the middle of the city's street; on either side of the river was the tree of life, bearing twelve kinds of fruit, one each month. The leaves of the tree were for healing the nations. There was no longer anything flawed, the throne of God and the Lamb was in it, and his servants would worship him. They will see his face, and his name will be on their foreheads. They will rule forever.

The angel said to me, "These words are trustworthy and true; the Lord God of the spirits of the prophets has sent his angel to show his servants what will happen. I am coming soon; blessed are those who keep the words of the prophecy of this book." Then I was back in Patmos, and the vision ended.

CLOSING WORDS

I am John, the one who heard and saw these things. When I did, I fell down at the angel's feet to worship him, but he said to me, "Don't do that; I am a servant like you and the other believers who obey this book's words. Worship God alone. Don't seal up the words of this prophecy because the time is near. Those who do wrong should keep doing wrong, the vile should keep being vile, those who do right should keep doing what's right, and the holy should keep being holy."

Jesus is coming soon and he will reward everyone for what they've done. He is the Alpha and the Omega, the First and the Last, the Beginning and the End. Blessed are those who wash their robes so that they may have the right to the tree of life so they may enter the city through the gates. The dogs, sorcerers, sexually immoral, murderers, idolaters, and everyone who loves and practices falsehood are left outside.

Jesus has sent his angel to testify to us about these things for the churches. He is the Root and Descendant of David, the bright Morning Star. The Spirit and the Bride beckon us to come, and whoever is thirsty should drink from the free water of life. Whoever adds to this book of prophecy, God will give him all the plagues in this book. Anyone who takes away from the words of this book of prophecy, God will take away his share in the tree of life and the holy city described in this book.

Jesus is coming soon. Amen. Come, Lord Jesus! May the grace of the Lord Jesus be with us all. Amen.

EPILOGUE

WHAT'S THE POINT?

In the beginning, God created the heavens and the earth. He made it for his glory and gave it to people as a perfect gift. There were no flaws, no bad things, and nothing ever went wrong. God put Adam and Eve in the Garden of Eden and gave them the task of tending the garden. He intended them to stay there and gave them one rule to protect them, not to eat from the tree of the knowledge of good and evil. God promised that if they disobeyed, they would die.

But this perfection didn't last long. Before long, Satan tempted our ancestors, and they failed. But God was gracious and didn't kill them immediately. Instead, he cursed them, Satan, and the earth. Since then, we have all sinned as our ancestors did. Sin is anytime we fall short of God's perfect standard, disobey his commands, or do what we know we should not do.

Sin is the cause of every bad thing in this world (creation was perfect beforehand). Sometimes, bad things happen because of our sin; sometimes, they happen because of someone else's sin; sometimes, they happen just because earth is suffering the consequences of sin (things like disease and natural disasters).

It is easy to dismiss this because we all sin, and we don't see God's immediate judgment. But our sin separates us from God; since he is perfect, he cannot accept us in our fallen state. But he does not kill us the moment we sin, even though we deserve it.

We all have this problem and we try different methods to deal with it. Some ignore it, but that doesn't fix anything. Others believe that doing more good than bad will solve the problem, but it doesn't. We cannot argue our way out of a speeding ticket because of all the times we didn't speed. Another option is to earn our way into God's favor, but that falls short as well. God tells us that our best deeds are like filthy rags in his sight. It seems like we have no hope.

But once again, God is gracious. Even though he didn't have to, God laid aside his glory and came to the earth in the person of Jesus. He was born in poverty, grew up, lived the perfect life we could not, and died in our place. He took our place on the cross and died. But he didn't stay dead; he rose again on the third day, defeating Satan, sin, and death.

After reading about Jesus' life, the astonishing things he did, his death, and resurrection, it can be tempting to walk away thinking that he was an amazing teacher and not much else. But he fits into the larger story of what God is doing in history.

We must deal with the same question that Pilate faced at Jesus' trial, what do we do with Jesus? C.S. Lewis put it best when he summed up the choice we have with this statement:

> "You must make your choice. Either this man was, and is, the Son of God; or else a madman or something worse. You can shut him up for a fool; you can spit at him and kill him for a demon; or you can fall at his feet and call him Lord and God. But let us not come with any patronizing nonsense about his being a great human teacher. He has not left that open to us. He did not intend to."

The options are these: Jesus was crazy, and he may as well have said he was a staple remover; he was a liar, knew he was not God, and formed the most elaborately constructed lie ever; or Jesus was God in the flesh. Jesus obviously was not a lunatic, nor was he a liar, so the only option we have left is that he is Lord.

Some people say he was merely a good teacher, but this is not a possibility either. If he was just a good teacher, then he could not make the claims he made, have them be false, and still be a good person. We cannot put him in the category of "only a good teacher."

A final possibility is that Jesus' later followers made up his claims to deity. However, the apostles wrote the New Testament within a couple of generations of the events they recorded, which is not nearly enough time to distort a true story into a legend. Today, this would be like someone claiming that John F. Kennedy performed many miracles, claimed to be God, and rose from the dead. People would dismiss anyone who made claims like that as a fraud. But people living at the time of the New Testament were not able to refute Christianity's claims.

Jesus is unique in history in that he was fully God and man. He needed to be human to identify with us and live the life we are incapable of living. He needed to be God to pay for our sins.

We must recognize that we are incapable of fixing our sin on our own. The only way we can truly deal with our sin problem is to place our faith in Christ and trust Jesus to fix it for us. We must believe the facts of the gospel, acknowledge our sins, turn away from them, and then live a life following his teachings.

Trusting Jesus is more than just intellectual assent. This is like how we interact with a chair. We can know everything about a chair, describe it, and say that we believe it will hold us up. But we do not have faith that the chair will support us until we act and sit in it. Saving faith is a gift, but it requires us to trust and act.

If you want to know more about faith in Jesus, you should read the Bible and find a church that can guide you in your journey to know him. Look for a church that preaches from the Bible that Jesus is God and that he lived a perfect life, died for our sins, and rose again. You can also go to www.rcpbible.com for more information.

OTHER BOOKS FROM RCP BIBLE

Each of the five books of the RCP Bible is available through Amazon. If you are interested in bulk orders of this or any other book in our library, email me at rcpbible@gmail.com.

I pray that this book has been useful in your spiritual journey. Please consider telling a friend or leaving a positive review on Amazon or through Goodreads. May God bless you and draw you closer to him.

In Christ, Obadiah Paulus

Made in the USA
Monee, IL
08 August 2021